Contents

Introduction

Welcome to the latest edition of BETTY CROCKER'S COOKBOOK! We asked you what you wanted, listened to your requests, and created this cookbook to answer your cooking needs. In fact, we made so many changes, we even changed the name to BETTY CROCKER'S NEW COOKBOOK! We're delighted that you've invited Betty Crocker into your kitchen to help you find everything you need to know to cook!

We've looked at every recipe and made sure they are completely up to date, easy to use and just about foolproof. In addition, you told us today's cook still wants to make favorite recipes, and they also want them to be lower in fat and calories. So, we added lighter variations to well-loved original recipes—the choice is yours. You told us how busy you are, so we added timesaving tips to reduce your time in the kitchen.

Blueberry Muffins (page 40)

And we included preparation and cook times with each recipe, to help plan your day.

Next we asked you to look at how the recipes are written, and you gave us good advice: number each step; place nutrition information—including number of calories from fat—right with the recipe; and, make them simple to understand and easy to read. We did it all!

You asked for a cookbook that reflects the foods you want to cook, and the techniques you need to know. You'll find the best new food trends here, not flash-in-the-pan fads. Learn how to make salsa or *Tira Mi Su*, enjoy an entire chapter on pasta, find delicious ways to eat more grains, or learn how to plan menus.

Our new design is fresh and colorful with bold blue accents that make it easier than ever to find and use the information you want. Look for lighter variations and timesaving tips in easy-to-read boxes; meat cooking timetables and other charts that are a breeze to follow; useful glossaries and identification photographs that take the mystery out of all kinds of foods—whether it's mushrooms or legumes.

Helpful line drawings and step-by-step photographs make new techniques easy to follow, and cooking basics in every section start you off on the right foot. You'll also find explanations of cooking terms, information on grilling, microwaving, entertaining, emergency substitutions—and so much more!

We're proud to bring you this new cookbook —we couldn't have done it without you!

Betty Crocker

Cook's Techniques & Ingredients

Measuring Ingredients

Graduated Nested Measuring Cups

Cups range in size from 1/4 cup to 1 cup; some sets have 1/8 cup (2 tablespoons), 2/3 cup and 3/4 cup measures as well. Use to measure dry ingredients and solid fats, such as shortening.

For flour, baking mix and sugar, spoon ingredient lightly into cup, then level with a straight-edged spatula or knife. Sift powdered sugar only if lumpy.

Graduated Measuring Spoons

Spoons range from 1/4 teaspoon to 1 tablespoon; some sets contain a 1/8 teaspoon and a 3/4 teaspoon. Use spoons to measure liquids and dry ingredients. *For thin liquids,* pour into spoon until full. *For thick liquids and dry ingredients,* pour or scoop into spoon until full, then level with a straight-edged spatula or knife.

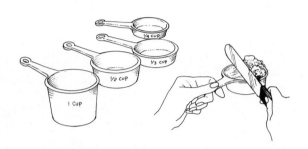

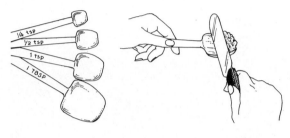

For cereal and dry bread crumbs, pour into cup. Level with a straight-edged spatula or knife.

For shredded cheese, chopped nuts, coconut and soft bread crumbs, spoon into cup and pack down lightly.

Glass Measuring Cups

Glass cups can be purchased in 1-, 2-, 4- and 8-cup sizes. Use to measure liquids. For an accurate amount, always read the measurement at eye level while the cup is on a flat surface. To measure sticky liquids, such as honey, molasses and corn syrup, first spread the cup lightly with oil so the liquid will be easier to remove.

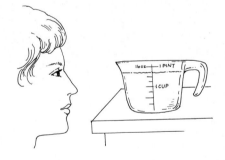

For solid fats and brown sugar, spoon into cup and pack down firmly with spatula or spoon.

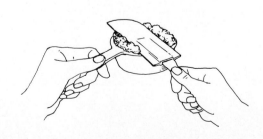

Mixing Ingredients

There's more than one way to combine ingredients and more than one tool to make it easy. If you've ever found the following terms confusing or aren't sure which tools to use, refer to this guide for help. The tools you choose for combining ingredients are determined by the job.

Mixing Terms

Beat: Combine ingredients vigorously with spoon, fork, wire whisk, hand beater or electric mixer until smooth and uniform.

Blend: Combine ingredients with spoon, wire whisk or rubber scraper until very smooth and uniform. A blender, hand blender or food processor may also be used.

Cut in: Distribute solid fat in dry ingredients until particles are desired size by crisscrossing two knives, using the side of a table fork, a wire whisk or by cutting with a pastry blender using a rolling motion.

Fold: Combine ingredients lightly while preventing loss of air by using two motions: Use a rubber spatula and first cut down vertically through mixture with rubber spatula. Next, slide spatula across bottom of bowl and up the side, turning the mixture over. Continue down-across-up-over motion while rotating bowl one-fourth turn with each series of strokes. For example, to fold dry ingredients into beaten egg whites for angel food cake or to fold liqueur into whipped cream.

Mix: Combine ingredients in any way that distributes them evenly.

Process: Use either food processor or mini chopper to liquefy, blend, chop, grind or knead food.

Stir: Combine ingredients with circular or figure-eight motion until uniform consistency. Stir once in a while for "stirring occasionally," stir often for "stirring frequently" and stir continuously for "stirring constantly."

Whip: Beat ingredients to add air and increase volume until ingredients are light and fluffy (cream, egg whites).

Mixing Tools

Fork or Hand Beater: For lightly beating eggs, sauces and salad dressings and for small amount of mixing of moist and dry ingredients for quick breads.

Hands: For doughs, streusel toppings and very thick mixtures such as meat loaf. Wash hands thoroughly before handling food. Wear plastic or rubber gloves, if desired.

Pastry Blender: For cutting solid fat into flour to make desired particle size for pie crust and biscuit doughs. Lift up and down with rolling motion.

Rubber Spatula: For folding, mixing and stirring batters or sauces (use heatproof rubber spatula for mixing hot foods in saucepans and skillets).

Spoon: For general all-purpose mixing and stirring, sturdy wooden or plastic cooking spoons are most commonly used.

Wire Whisk: For beating eggs, egg whites and thin batters; stirring puddings, sauces and gravies to remove lumps.

Electric Mixing Appliances

Handheld Mixer: For all but the thickest batters, as well as for eggs. Use for recipes in this book that specify "electric mixer," as a handheld mixer was used for testing.

Stand Mixer: More powerful motor than handheld mixer. Allows more freedom of hands. May have added attachments, including dough hook.

Blender: For liquefying or blending mixtures or chopping small amounts of nuts, herbs or bread crumbs. Not for most batters or doughs.

Handheld Blender: For liquefying or blending mixtures. May not perform as well as a regular blender for some mixtures.

Food Processor: For blending, pureeing, chopping, slicing, dicing, grinding, pulverizing and shredding many foods. Some will knead dough.

Mini Chopper: For mixing small amounts of sauces and dips or chopping small amounts of vegetables, nuts and herbs.

Helpful How-To's

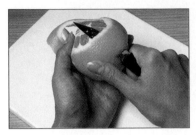

Peel: Cut off outer covering with a knife or vegetable peeler, or strip off outer covering with fingers.

Slice: Cut food into flat pieces of same size.

Diagonally slice: Place knife at 45° angle and cut into slices of equal width.

Julienne: Stack thin slices; cut into matchlike sticks.

Cube: Cut into 1/2-inch or wider strips; cut across into cubes.

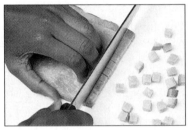

Dice: Cut into 1/2-inch or narrower strips; cut across into cubes.

Chop: Cut food into pieces of irregular sizes.

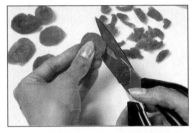

Cut up: Cut into small irregular pieces with kitchen scissors or knife.

Snip: Cut into very small pieces with kitchen scissors.

Shred: Cut into long thin pieces by rubbing food across the large holes of a shredder or by using a knife to slice very thinly.

Grate: Cut into tiny particles by rubbing food across the small rough holes of a grater.

Crush: Press with side of knife, mallet or rolling pin to break into small pieces.

Technique How-To's

Roasting Peppers: Broil whole peppers with tops 5 inches from heat, turning occasionally, until skin is blistered and evenly browned but not burned. Place peppers in plastic bag and let stand 20 minutes. Peel skin from peppers.

Toasting Coconut or Nuts: Sprinkle 1/2 cup coconut or nuts in ungreased heavy skillet. Cook over medium-low heat 6 to 14 minutes for coconut or 5 to 7 minutes for nuts, stirring frequently, until browning begins, then stirring constantly. (Watch carefully; time varies greatly between gas and electric ranges.)

Croutons: Cut bread into 1/2-inch slices; spread one side with softened margarine or butter. Cut into 1/2-inch cubes. Sprinkle with chopped herbs, grated Parmesan cheese or spices if desired. Cook in ungreased heavy skillet over medium heat 4 to 7 minutes, stirring frequently, until golden brown.

Cutting up Pineapple: Twist top from pineapple. Cut pineapple into fourths. Holding pineapple securely, cut fruit from rind. Cut off pineapple core and remove "eyes." Cut crosswise or lengthwise into chunks or spears.

Hulling Strawberries (removing the caps): Use the tip of a table knife or an inexpensive strawberry huller (a very short, fat tweezers), or push one end of a plastic drinking straw into the point of the berry and push it through to pop off the cap.

Seeding an Avocado: Hit the seed with the sharp edge of a knife. Grasp the fruit, then twist the knife to loosen and remove the seed.

Separating Eggs: Eggs are easiest to separate when cold. Purchase an inexpensive egg separator and place over a small bowl. Crack egg; open shell, allowing yolk to fall into center of separator. The white will slip through the slots of the separator into the bowl. Do not pass the yolk back and forth from shell half to shell half. Bacteria may be present in the pores of the shell, which could contaminate the yolk or white.

Bread Crumbs (dry): Place bread in 200° oven until dry; cool. Place in heavy plastic bag, and crush with rolling pin or mallet into very small pieces. Or blend in blender or food processor to make fine bread crumbs.

Bread Crumbs (soft): Tear soft bread with fingers into small pieces.

Coating Chicken or Fish: Place seasonings and bread crumbs or flour in a paper or plastic bag. Add a few pieces of chicken or fish at a time; shake until each piece is evenly coated. If dipped into milk or egg mixture before coating with crumbs, use one hand for handling the wet food and the other for handling the dry food.

Cooking Terms Glossary

Cooking has its own vocabulary just as any other activity. Although not all-inclusive, this glossary is a handy reference for both beginning and experienced cooks. We've included examples of foods, in most cases, to help you quickly familiarize yourself with the terms. For other food or cooking definitions, see Ingredients Glossary, page 12, Microwave Techniques, page 429, and Grilling Know-How, page 428.

Bake: Cook in oven surrounded by dry heat. Bake uncovered for dry, crisp surfaces (breads, cakes, cookies, chicken) or covered for moistness (vegetables, casseroles, stews).

Baste: Spoon liquid over food (pan juices over turkey) during cooking to keep it moist.

Batter: An uncooked mixture of flour, eggs and liquid with other ingredients; thin enough to be spooned or poured (muffins, pancakes).

Blanch: Plunge food into boiling water for a brief time to preserve color, texture and nutritional value or to remove skin (vegetables, fruits, nuts).

Boil: Heat liquid until bubbles rise continuously and break on the surface and steam is given off. For rolling boil, the bubbles form rapidly.

Broil: Cook directly under or above a red-hot heating unit.

Caramelize: Melt sugar slowly over low heat until it becomes a golden brown, caramel-flavored syrup. Or sprinkle granulated, powdered or brown sugar on top of a food, then place under a broiler until the sugar is melted and caramelized.

Chop: Cut into coarse or fine irregular pieces, using knife, food chopper, blender or food processor.

Coat: Cover food evenly with crumbs or sauce.

Cool: Allow hot food to stand at room temperature for a specified amount of time. Placing hot food on a wire rack will help it cool more quickly. Stirring mixtures occasionally also will help them cool more quickly and evenly.

Core: Remove the center of a fruit (apple, pear, pineapple). Cores contain small seeds (apple, pear) or are woody in texture (pineapple).

Crisp-tender: Doneness description of vegetables cooked until they retain some of the crisp texture of the raw food.

Crush: Press into very fine particles (crushing a clove of garlic, using chef's knife or garlic press).

Cube: Cut food into squares 1/2 inch or larger, using knife.

Cut up: Cut into small irregular pieces with kitchen scissors or knife. Or cut into smaller pieces (broiler-fryer chicken).

Dash: Less than 1/8 teaspoon of an ingredient.

Deep-fry or French-fry: Cook in hot fat that's deep enough to float the food.

Dice: Cut food into squares smaller than 1/2 inch, using knife.

Dissolve: Stir a dry ingredient (flavored gelatin) into a liquid ingredient (boiling water) until the dry ingredient disappears.

Dot: Drop small pieces of an ingredient (margarine or butter) randomly over food (sliced apples in an apple pie).

Dough: Mixture of flour and liquid with other ingredients (often including a leavening); it is stiff but pliable. Dough can be dropped from a spoon (cookies), rolled (pie crust) or kneaded (bread).

Drain: Pour off liquid by putting the food into a strainer or colander that has been set in the sink. If draining fat from meat, place strainer in disposable container. If liquid is to be saved, place the strainer in a bowl or other container.

Drizzle: Pour topping in thin lines from a spoon or liquid measuring cup in an uneven pattern over food (glaze on a cake, cookies).

Dust: Sprinkle lightly with flour, cornmeal, powdered sugar or cocoa; for example, dust coffee cake with powdered sugar.

Flake: Break lightly into small pieces, using fork; for example, flaking cooked fish.

Flute: Squeeze pastry edge with fingers to make a finished, ornamental edge. Also see page 96.

Fry: Cook in hot fat over moderate or high heat. Also see Panfry and Sauté.

Glaze: Brush, spread or drizzle an ingredient or mixture of ingredients (jam, melted chocolate) on hot or cold foods to give a glossy appearance or hard finish.

Grate: Rub a hard-textured food against the small, rough, sharp-edged holes of a grater, reducing them to tiny particles (citrus peel, chocolate, Parmesan cheese).

For citrus peel, grate only the skin, not the bitter white membrane.

Grease: Rub the inside surface of a pan with shortening, using pastry brush, waxed paper or paper towel, to prevent food from sticking during baking (muffins, some casseroles). Nonstick cooking spray may also be used. Margarine and butter usually contain salt that may cause hot foods to stick.

Grease and Flour: Rub the inside surface of a pan with shortening before dusting it with flour, to prevent food from sticking during baking, such as cakes. After flouring the pan, turn the pan upside down, and tap the bottom to remove excess flour.

Grill: See Grilling Know-How, page 428.

Heat Oven: Turn the oven controls to the desired temperature, allowing the oven to heat thoroughly before adding food. Heating takes about 10 minutes for most ovens. Also called preheating.

Julienne: Cut into thin, matchlike strips, using knife or food processor; for example, fruits, vegetables, meats.

Knead: Work dough on a floured surface into a smooth, elastic mass, using hands or an electric mixer with dough hooks. Kneading develops the gluten in flour and results in an even texture and a smooth, rounded top. It can take up to about 15 minutes by hand. Also see How to Mix Yeast Dough, page 54.

Marinate: Let food stand in a savory, usually acidic liquid in a glass or plastic container for several hours to add flavor or to tenderize. Marinade is the savory liquid in which the food is marinated.

Microwave: See Microwave Know-How, page 429.

Mince: Cut food into very fine pieces, smaller than chopped food.

Panfry: Fry meat or other food, starting with a cold skillet, using little or no fat and usually pouring off fat from meat as it accumulates during cooking.

Peel: Cut off outer covering, using knife or vegetable peeler (apples, potatoes). Also, to strip off outer covering, using fingers (bananas, oranges).

Poach: Cook in simmering liquid just below the boiling point (eggs, fish).

Reduce: Boil liquid uncovered to evaporate liquid and intensify flavor.

Roast: Cook meat uncovered on rack in shallow pan in oven without adding liquid.

Sauté: Cook over medium-high heat in hot fat with frequent tossing or turning motion.

Scald: Heat liquid to just below the boiling point. Tiny bubbles will form at the edge. A thin skin will form on the top of milk.

Score: Cut surface of food about 1/4 inch deep, using knife, to facilitate cooking, flavoring, tenderizing or for appearance (meat, yeast bread).

Shred: Cut into long, thin pieces, using round, smooth holes of shredder, a knife or food processor (cabbage, carrots, cheese).

Simmer: Cook in liquid on range top, just below the boiling point. Usually done after reducing heat from a boil. Bubbles will rise slowly and break just below the surface.

Slice: Cut into uniform-size flat pieces (bread, meat).

Soft Peaks: Egg whites beaten until peaks are rounded or curl when beaters are lifted from bowl, while still moist and glossy. Also see Stiff Peaks.

Soften: Let cold food stand at room temperature, or microwave at low power setting, until no longer hard (margarine, butter, cream cheese).

Steam: Cook food by placing on a rack or special steamer basket over a small amount of boiling or simmering water in a covered pan (see Cooking Fresh Vegetables, page 393). Steaming helps retain flavor, shape, color, texture and nutritional value.

Stew: Cook slowly in a small amount of liquid for a long time (stewed fruit, beef stew).

Stiff Peaks: Egg whites beaten until peaks stand up straight when beaters are lifted from bowl, while still moist and glossy. Also see Soft Peaks.

Stir-fry: A Chinese method of cooking uniform pieces of food in small amount of hot oil over high heat, stirring constantly.

Strain: Pour mixture or liquid through a fine sieve or strainer to remove larger particles.

Tear: Break into pieces, using fingers (lettuce for salads; bread slices for soft bread crumbs).

Toss: Tumble ingredients lightly with a lifting motion, such as a salad with greens.

Ingredients Glossary

Baking Powder: Leavening mixture made from baking soda, an acid and a moisture absorber. Double-acting baking powder forms carbon dioxide twice: once when mixed with moist ingredients and once during baking. Do not substitute for baking soda because acid proportions may be unbalanced in recipe.

Baking Soda: Leavening known as bicarbonate of soda. Must be mixed with an acid ingredient (lemon juice, buttermilk or molasses) to release carbon dioxide gas bubbles.

Chilies: A family of more than 200 varieties, chilies are used in cooking around the world. Available fresh and dried in red, green, yellow and purple. Length ranges from 1/4 inch to 12 inches. Seeds are hotter than flesh. Wash hands thoroughly after seeding or wear rubber gloves when handling to avoid transferring the irritating oils to your eyes or skin.

- **Jalapeño chilies:** Very hot, jade green or red chili, 2 to 3 inches long; smallest ones are the hottest. The favorite choice for nachos, salsas and other sauces. Available fresh and pickled.
- **Green chilies:** Mildly spicy, pale green chili. Often used in Mexican foods and salsas and to give a distinctive flavor to other foods. Available fresh and canned.

Chocolate: Made from ground, liquified roasted shelled cocoa beans, processed in various ways:

- **Baking cocoa:** Dried chocolate liquor (cocoa butter removed) is ground into unsweetened cocoa. Does not substitute directly for cocoa drink mixes that contain added milk powder and sugar.
- **Semisweet, bittersweet, sweet and milk chocolates:** Contain from 10 to 35 percent chocolate liquor, varying amounts of cocoa butter, sugar and for some, milk and flavorings. Available in bars and chips, use for baking or eating. Quality varies, so follow package directions for melting.
- **"White" chocolate:** Not a true chocolate. Contains some cocoa butter but no cocoa or chocolate liquor. Often called vanilla milk chips or vanilla baking bar.

Cheese: See About Cheese, page 171.

Corn Syrup: Clear, thick liquid (dark or light are interchangeable in recipes) made from corn sugar mixed with acid. It's one sweetener that doesn't crystallize and is especially good for pecan pie, frostings, fruit sauces and jams.

Cornstarch: A thickener for soups, sauces and desserts that comes from a portion of the corn kernel. This finely ground flour keeps sauces clear, not opaque as sauces thickened with wheat flour are. To substitute for all-purpose flour, use half as much cornstarch.

Cream: Smooth, rich product made from separating butterfat from the liquid in whole milk. Pasteurized and processed into several forms:

- **Half-and-half:** Milk and cream are mixed, containing 10 to 12 percent butterfat. It won't whip, but it can be used in place of whipping (heavy) cream in many recipes.
- **Sour cream:** Commercially cultured with lactic acid to give a tangy flavor. Regular sour cream is 18 to 20 percent butterfat. Reduced-fat sour cream is made from half-and-half and can be substituted for regular sour cream in most recipes. Nonfat sour cream has all fat removed and may not be successful in all recipes that call for regular sour cream.
- **Whipping (heavy) cream:** The richest cream available in the United States, it has 36 to 40 percent butterfat. It doubles in volume when whipped.

Cream of Tartar: After wine is made, the acid left in wine barrels is processed into cream of tartar. Egg whites are more stable and have more volume when cream of tartar is added in beginning beating stages. Also contributes to creamier frostings and candy.

Eggs: See About Eggs, page 162.

Fats and Oils: In cooking, they add richness and flavor to food, aid browning, help bind ingredients together, tenderize baked goods and are used for frying. But all fats are not created equal in texture and flavor. In our recipes, ingredient listings for fats vary because of their cooking and baking characteristics. See specific examples that follow.

- **Butter:** A saturated fat made from cream that must be at least 80 percent butterfat by USDA standards. It is high in flavor and has a melt-in-your-mouth texture. Butter is sold in sticks, whipped in tubs and as butter-flavored granules. Use only sticks for baking; whipped butter will give a different texture due to the air beaten into it.

- **Butter-margarine blends:** Available in sticks and tubs, blends usually are a combination of 60 percent margarine and 40 percent butter and are interchangeable with butter or margarine. Use only sticks for baking.
- **Lard:** A saturated fat made from rendered and refined pork fat, lard is not used as much now as in the past. Lard is softer and richer than butter or margarine and makes very tender, flaky biscuits and pastry.
- **Margarine:** An unsaturated butter substitute made with no less than 80 percent fat (most use vegetable oils made from soybeans, cottonseeds and corn) by weight and flavoring from dairy products. Textures and flavors vary. Use as a table spread and for cooking and baking. Sold in sticks and as soft spreads in tubs. Use only sticks for baking.
- **Reduced-calorie or low-fat butter or margarine:** These products have water and air added and contain at least 20 percent less fat than regular butter or margarine. Do not use for baking.
- **Vegetable Spreads:** Margarine products with less than 80 percent fat (vegetable oil) by weight usually are labeled as vegetable oil spreads. These products, like margarine, can be used for a variety of purposes, from spreading to cooking to baking.

  Because the percentage of fat is lower than for margarine, the amount of water is increased, which can affect the texture and quality of baked items, some candies and other foods that need to be crisp. *We do not recommend vegetable oil spreads with less than 65 percent fat be used for baking. And in some instances, we do not recommend spreads be used for baking at all.*

  Products with less than 60 percent fat are made to be used as table spreads, although they can be used for some cooking.

  Some spreads may have unusual odors when heated and can spatter at higher temperatures.

  Vegetable oil spreads are sold in sticks (for all-purpose use, including some baking if more than 65 percent fat), in tubs (to use as a table spread—*do not use for baking*) and as liquid squeeze spreads (to use for topping vegetables and popcorn or for basting—do not use for baking).

  Manufacturers of vegetable oil spreads may recommend their product for baking and provide recipes. Keep in mind those recipes are developed specifically for a particular vegetable oil spread.
- **Oils for cooking:** Low in saturated fats and containing no cholesterol, these liquid fats are delicate to bland in flavor and are treated to withstand high-temperature cooking and long storage. In our recipes, they are listed as follows:

  Nonstick cooking spray: Used to spray cookware and bakeware before using, to prevent food from sticking during cooking and baking. Sometimes used directly on foods in low-fat cooking.

Butter, Margarine & Vegetable Oil Spread Fat Comparison

Butter (80% fat) — 11 g fat per tablespoon

Margarine (80% fat) — 11 g fat per tablespoon

Vegetable Oil Spread (70% fat) — 10 g fat per tablespoon

Vegetable Oil Spread (60% fat) — 9 g fat per tablespoon

Vegetable Oil Spread (40% fat) — 6 g fat per tablespoon

Olive oil: Pressed from fully pitted ripe (black) olives. Olive oil is graded based on its acidity. The lower the acidity, the stronger the "olive" flavor. Cold-pressed (processed without heat) oil is called extra virgin. For the second olive pressing, solvents are used, and this yields virgin olive oil. Successive pressings yield less delicate oil. Use olive oil in marinades, salad dressings and cooking.

Vegetable oil: An economical blend of oils from various vegetables, such as corn, cottonseed, peanut, safflower and soybean. Use in all cooking and baking.

Shortening: Vegetable oils are hydrogenated to change them from liquid to solid at room temperature. Shortening is used especially for flaky, tender pastry and greasing baking pans. Butter-flavored shortening and regular shortening can be used interchangeably. Sold in cans and in stick form.

Flour: The primary ingredient in breads, cakes, cookies and quick breads.

- **All-purpose flour:** Selected wheats blended to be used for all kinds of baking. Available both bleached and unbleached.
- **Bread flour:** Wheats higher in gluten-forming protein than all-purpose flour, which gives more structure to bread. Bread flour absorbs more liquid and produces a more elastic dough, resulting in greater volume. Best choice for bread machine breads and yeast breads. For other bakings, bread flour can make some recipes too tough.
- **Cake flour:** Milled from soft wheats. It's lower in protein than all-purpose flour and not recommended to substitute for either all-purpose flour or bread flour. Cake flour results in tender, fine-textured cakes.
- **Quick-mixing flour:** Enriched, all-purpose flour that's granular and processed to blend easily with liquid to make gravies or sauces or to thicken main dishes.
- **Rye flour:** Milled from rye grain and low in gluten-forming protein, it is usually combined with wheat flour to increase the dough's gluten-forming capabilities.
- **Self-rising flour:** A convenience flour made from a blend of hard and soft wheats that includes leavening and salt. It's a favorite for light and fluffy biscuits and tender cakes. For best results, don't substitute self-rising flour for other kinds of flour unless directed in the recipe, as leavening and salt proportions won't be accurate.

- **Whole wheat flour:** Ground from the complete wheat kernel, whole wheat flour gives a nutty flavor and dense texture to breads and other baked goods. Stone-ground whole wheat flour is coarser than roller-milled whole wheat flour. Baked goods made with whole wheat flour rise less than those made with all-purpose flour.

Gingerroot: Plump tubers with knobby branches. Side branches have a milder tangy ginger flavor than the main root. Grate unpeeled gingerroot, or peel and chop or slice, to add flavor to foods such as stir-fries, sauces and baked goods. Look for gingerroot in the produce section of your supermarket.

Herbs: See Herbs Chart, page 350.

Legumes: See About Legumes, page 211.

Leavening: Ingredients that cause baked goods to rise and develop lighter textures. (Also see Baking Powder, Baking Soda, Yeast.)

Mayonnaise: Smooth, rich mixture made from egg yolks, vinegar and seasonings and available in jars. Beaten to make a permanent emulsion that retains its creamy texture through storage. The prepared product, salad dressing, is similarly prepared but is lower in fat because it's made with a starch thickener, vinegar, eggs and sweetener. Salad dressing can be substituted for mayonnaise in salads or spreads, but in hot or cooked dishes, use only mayonnaise, unless the recipe was developed for salad dressing, as salad dressing may separate when heated.

Milk: Refers to cow's milk throughout this cookbook.

- **Buttermilk:** Thick, smooth liquid that results when skim or part-skim milk is cultured with lactic acid bacteria. Used in baking for tangy flavor.
- **Evaporated milk:** Whole milk with more than half of the water removed before mixture is homogenized. Mixture is slightly thicker than whole milk. Use in recipes calling for evaporated milk, or mix with equal volume of water to substitute for whole milk.
- **Low-fat milk:** Contains 0.5 to 2% butterfat.
- **Skim milk:** Contains less than 0.5% butter fat.
- **Sweetened condensed milk:** Made when about half of the water is removed from whole milk and sweetener is added. Use for such desserts as Key Lime Pie (page 107).
- **Whole milk:** Contains at least 3.25% butterfat.

Mustard: From plants grown for sharp-tasting seeds and calcium-rich leaves (mustard greens). Use to add pungent flavor to foods.

- **Ground mustard:** Dried finely ground mustard seed.
- **Mustard seed:** Whole seeds used for pickling and seasoning savory dishes.
- **Mustard:** *Yellow mustard* (also called American mustard) is prepared from mild white mustard seeds and mixed with sugar, vinegar and seasonings. *Dijon mustard*, originating in Dijon, France, is prepared from brown mustard seeds mixed with wine, unfermented grape juice and seasonings. Many other flavors of mustards are also available.

Pasta: See About Pasta, page 272.

Phyllo (filo): Paper-thin pastry sheets whose name comes from the Greek word for "leaf" is the basis of many Greek and Middle Eastern main dishes and sweets. Available frozen or refrigerated. Sheets dry out quickly; cover unused sheets with waxed paper and a damp kitchen towel while working with phyllo.

Puff Pastry: Dozens of layers of chilled butter rolled between sheets of pastry dough. The basis of croissants, puff pastry shells for creamed poultry or seafood and such desserts as napoleons and fruit pastries.

Red Pepper Sauce: Condiment made from hot chili peppers and cured in either salt or vinegar brine. Many varieties and levels of hotness are available.

Roasted Bell Peppers: Sweet red or other color bell peppers to use for appetizers, soups and main dishes. See Roasting Peppers, page 9.

Salad Dressing: See Mayonnaise. Not to be confused with bottled dressings.

Soy Sauce: Chinese and Japanese specialty. A brown sauce made from soybeans, wheat, yeast and salt used to season main dishes and vegetables, and also as a condiment.

Sugar: Sweetener that may come from sugar beets or cane sugar. Available in several forms:

- **Granulated:** Standard white sugar available from 1-pound boxes to 100-pound bags, as well as in cubes and 1-teaspoon packets.
- **Brown:** Either produced after refined white sugar is removed from beets or cane or is the result of mixing refined molasses syrup with white sugar crystals. Dark brown sugar has a more intense flavor. If brown sugar hardens, store in closed container with a slice of apple or a moist slice of bread. When measuring, firmly pack it into the measuring cup.
- **Powdered:** Crushed granulated sugar used for frostings and for dusting pastries and cakes.

Sun-Dried Tomatoes: Tomatoes dried for use in appetizers, sauces, main dishes and other foods. Available packed in oil or dried; rehydrate the dried form in hot water before using as directed on the package.

Worcestershire Sauce: Common condiment made from exotic blend of ingredients: garlic, soy sauce, tamarind, onions, molasses, lime, anchovies, vinegar and other seasonings. Named for Worcester, England, where it was first bottled, but was actually developed in India by the English.

Yeast: Leavening whose fermentation is the essence of yeast bread. The combination of warmth, food (sugar) and liquid causes yeast to release carbon dioxide bubbles that cause dough to rise. Always use yeast before its expiration date.

- **Bread machine yeast:** Special strain of fine-grained, dehydrated yeast, designed to be thoroughly dissolved during mixing and kneading in bread machines.
- **Compressed cake yeast:** Moist yeast whose individual 0.6-ounce square can be substituted directly for each package of active dry yeast. Store in refrigerator up to two weeks, or freeze up to two months and use immediately after defrosting.
- **Quick active dry yeast:** Special strain of dehydrated yeast that allows bread to rise in less time than regular yeast. It is often mixed with part of the flour to withstand higher water temperatures (120° to 130°).
- **Regular active dry yeast:** Dehydrated yeast that can be substituted directly for quick active dry yeast

Helpful Nutrition and Cooking Information

Nutrition Guidelines:

We provide nutrition information for each recipe that includes calories, fat, cholesterol, sodium, carbohydrate, fiber and protein. Individual food choices can be based on this information.

Recommended intake for a daily diet of 2,000 calories (as set by the Food and Drug Administration)

Total Fat	Less than 65g
Saturated Fat	Less than 20g
Cholesterol	Less than 300mg
Sodium	Less than 2,400mg
Total Carbohydrate	300g
Dietary Fiber	25g

Criteria Used for Calculating Nutrition:

- The first ingredient was used wherever a choice is given (such as 1/3 cup sour cream or plain yogurt).
- The first ingredient amount was used wherever a range is given (such as 3 to 3 1/2 pound cut-up broiler-fryer chicken).
- The first serving number was used wherever a range is given (such as 4 to 6 servings).
- "If desired" ingredients are not included, whether mentioned in the ingredient list or in the recipe directions as a suggestion (such as, "Sprinkle with brown sugar if desired").
- Only the amount of a marinade or frying oil that is estimated to be absorbed by the food during preparation or cooking was calculated.

Ingredients Used in Recipe Testing and Nutrition Calculations:

- Ingredients used for testing represent those that the majority of consumers use in their homes: large eggs, 2% milk, 80%-lean ground beef, canned ready-to-use chicken broth, and vegetable oil spread with no less than 65% fat.
- Regular long-grain white rice was used wherever cooked rice is listed unless otherwise indicated.
- Fat-free, low-fat or low-sodium products were not used, unless otherwise indicated.
- Solid vegetable shortening (not margarine, butter, nonstick cooking sprays or vegetable oil spread as they can cause sticking problems) was used to grease pans, unless otherwise indicated.

- Preparation time at the top of each recipe is approximate and will vary based on experience, skill and kitchen equipment used. This time does not include assembling ingredients and equipment, heating the oven or preparing either precooked ingredients such as "hot cooked rice" or ingredients that are "if desired."

Equipment Used in Recipe Testing:

We use equipment for testing that the majority of consumers use in their homes. If a specific piece of equipment (such as a wire whisk) is necessary for recipe success, it will be listed in the recipe.

- Cookware and bakeware without nonstick coatings were used, unless indicated.
- No dark colored, black or insulated bakeware was used.
- When a baking *pan* is specified in a recipe, a *metal* pan was used; a baking *dish* or pie *plate* means *oven-proof glass* was used.
- An electric hand mixer was used for mixing *only when mixer speeds are specified* in the recipe directions. When a mixer speed is not given, a spoon or fork was used.

Equivalent Measures

3 teaspoons = 1 tablespoon
4 tablespoons = 1/4 cup
5 tablespoons + 1 teaspoon = 1/3 cup
8 tablespoons = 1/2 cup
12 tablespoons = 3/4 cup
16 tablespoons = 1 cup (8 ounces)
2 cups = 1 pint (16 ounces)
4 cups (2 pints) = 1 quart (32 ounces)
8 cups (4 pints) = 1/2 gallon (64 ounces)
4 quarts = 1 gallon (128 ounces)

Common Abbreviations

degree	° (or dg)	**package**	pkg
dozen	doz	**pint**	pt
gallon	gal	**pound**	lb (or #)
hour	hr	**quart**	qt
inch	″ (or in.)	**second**	sec
minute	min	**tablespoon**	Tbsp (or T)
ounce	oz	**teaspoon**	tsp (or t)

Appetizers & Beverages

About Appetizers

Appetizers are small savory tidbits hot or cold, originally meant to stimulate the appetite and make the meal to follow more appealing. This basic definition has expanded to include a variety of food types, called by a number of names, such as:

Canapé: Small toasted or untoasted pieces of bread, crackers or pastry topped with a savory topping such as cheese, anchovy or some type of spread. They can be hot or cold, simple or elaborate.

Crudité: Raw seasonal vegetables in slices, sticks or pieces, often accompanied by a dip.

Dips and dunks: Flavorful thin to slightly thick mixtures, often sour cream based, into which other foods such as tortilla chips, crudités or meatballs are dipped before eating.

Finger food: Term that describes those foods that can be picked up and eaten with the fingers, without the use of flatware or toothpicks.

First course: One or two appetizers served as one course during sit-down meal. Flatware is usually needed. It could also be a small serving of a main dish such as Fettucine Alfredo (page 280) or a soup.

Hors d'oeuvre: The French term for savory one- or two-bite-sized tidbits served before a meal, customarily with cocktails. Translated, hors d'oeuvre means "outside the work," or foods eaten apart from the regular meal.

Spreads: Thick mixtures, often cream cheese based, which need to be spread on a base such as crackers or vegetable slices, with a spreader or knife.

One or several appetizers may be served at a time. You'll find any of the appetizer recipes that follow delicious. Or, to save time, stop at the supermarket and pick up cheese and crackers, prepared dips or spreads, cut-up vegetables, cooked meatballs or chicken wings and other delicious fare. And with entertaining less formal, it is quite popular to serve a selection of appetizers to replace a meal. See Menu Planning Know-How, page 416.

Lemon-Thyme Dip

PREP: 10 min; CHILL: 1 hr
Makes about 1 3/4 cups dip

> 1 1/2 cups sour cream
> 1 tablespoon chopped fresh or 1 teaspoon dried thyme leaves
> 1 tablespoon grated lemon peel
> 2 tablespoons lemon juice
> 1/2 teaspoon salt
> Raw vegetables for dipping, if desired

1. Mix all ingredients except vegetables in glass or plastic bowl. Cover and refrigerate 1 hour to blend flavors.

2. Serve dip with vegetables.

1 TABLESPOON: Calories 20 (Calories from Fat 20); Fat 2g (Saturated 2g); Cholesterol 10mg; Sodium 45mg; Carbohydrate 1g (Dietary Fiber 0g); Protein 0g

---
LIGHTER LEMON-THYME DIP
For 1 gram of fat per serving, use fat-free sour cream (calories remain the same).

Guacamole

PREP: 20 min; CHILL: 1 hr
Makes about 2 3/4 cups dip

> 2 jalapeño chilies*
> 2 large ripe avocados, mashed
> 2 medium tomatoes, finely chopped (1 1/2 cups)
> 1 medium onion, chopped (1/2 cup)
> 1 clove garlic, finely chopped
> 2 tablespoons finely chopped cilantro
> 2 tablespoons lime or lemon juice
> 1/2 teaspoon salt
> Dash of pepper
> Tortilla chips, if desired

1. Remove stems, seeds and membranes from chilies; chop chilies. Mix chilies and remaining ingredients except tortilla chips in glass or plastic bowl.

2. Cover and refrigerate 1 hour to blend flavors. Serve with tortilla chips.

2 tablespoons canned chopped green chilies can be substituted for the jalapeño chilies.

1 TABLESPOON: Calories 30 (Calories from Fat 25); Fat 3g (Saturated 0g); Cholesterol 0mg; Sodium 35mg; Carbohydrate 1g (Dietary Fiber 0g); Protein 0g

Preceding page: Crostini (page 27), Sparkling Raspberry Tea (page 35), Italian Stuffed Mushrooms (page 25), Mahogany Chicken Wings (page 24)

Spinach Dip

LIGHTER GUACAMOLE

For 0 grams of fat and 5 calories per serving, substitute 1 can (15 ounces) asparagus cuts, drained then blended or processed until smooth, for the avocados. Stir in 1/4 cup fat-free mayonnaise.

Spinach Dip

PREP: 15 min; CHILL: 1 hr
Makes about 4 1/2 cups dip

For an attractive look, serve dip in the hollowed-out shell of a one-pound round bread loaf. Cut or tear the soft inside bread into pieces and use for dipping. When the dip is gone, you can enjoy eating the shell!

2 packages (10 ounces each) frozen chopped
    spinach, thawed
1 can (8 ounces) water chestnuts, drained
    and finely chopped
1 cup sour cream
1 cup plain yogurt
1 cup finely chopped green onions
    (9 medium)

2 teaspoons chopped fresh or 1/2 teaspoon
    dried tarragon leaves
1/2 teaspoon salt
1/2 teaspoon ground mustard (dry)
1/4 teaspoon pepper
1 clove garlic, crushed
Rye crackers, rice crackers or raw vegetables
    for dipping, if desired

1. Squeeze excess moisture from spinach until it is dry. Mix spinach with remaining ingredients except crackers in glass or plastic bowl.

2. Cover and refrigerate 1 hour to blend flavors. Serve with crackers.

1 TABLESPOON: Calories 15 (Calories from Fat 10); Fat 1g (Saturated 0g); Cholesterol 5mg; Sodium 25mg; Carbohydrate 1g (Dietary Fiber 0g); Protein 0g

---

LIGHTER SPINACH DIP

For 0 grams of fat and 10 calories per serving, substitute 1/2 cup light sour cream for the 1 cup sour cream and 1 1/2 cups plain fat-free yogurt for the 1 cup yogurt

Fantastic Fruit Dip

PREP: 5 min
Makes about 2 1/2 cups dip

Delicious dippers include apple, pear or peach slices and fresh plump strawberries. For an extraspecial treat, serve leftover fruit dip over pancakes, french toast or angel food cake.

> 1 package (16 ounces) frozen sliced peaches, thawed
> 1 package (10 ounces) frozen sweetened strawberries, thawed
> 1 tablespoon lemon juice
> 1/4 teaspoon almond extract
> Fruit for dipping, if desired

1. Place all ingredients except fruit for dipping in blender or food processor. Cover and blend on medium speed until smooth.

2. Serve dip with fruit.

1 TABLESPOON: Calories 15 (Calories from Fat 0); Fat 0g (Saturated 0g); Cholesterol 0mg; Sodium 0mg; Carbohydrate 4g (Dietary Fiber 0g); Protein 0g

Pimiento-Cheese Dip

PREP: 10 min; CHILL: 1 hr
Makes about 1 3/4 cups dip

> 1 cup large or small curd creamed cottage cheese
> 1 cup plain yogurt
> 1 tablespoon finely chopped onion or 1 teaspoon onion powder
> 1 jar (4 ounces) pimientos, well drained
> 1/2 cup shredded sharp Cheddar cheese (2 ounces)
> Raw vegetables or pretzels for dipping, if desired

1. Place cottage cheese, yogurt, onion and pimientos in blender or food processor. Cover and blend on high speed about 1 minute, stopping blender occasionally to scrape sides, until smooth.

2. Add Cheddar cheese. Cover and blend 15 seconds longer.

3. Spoon dip into serving dish. Cover and refrigerate 1 hour to blend flavors. Serve with vegetables.

1 TABLESPOON: Calories 20 (Calories from Fat 10); Fat 1g (Saturated 1g); Cholesterol 5mg; Sodium 20mg; Carbohydrate 1g (Dietary Fiber 0g); Protein 2g

---

LIGHTER PIMIENTO-CHEESE DIP

For 0 grams of fat and 10 calories per serving, use large curd dry cottage cheese, plain fat-free yogurt and reduced-fat Cheddar cheese.

Hummus

PREP: 10 min
Makes about 2 cups dip

This is the most famous of all Middle Eastern appetizers! Serve as a dip, a spread, a sandwich filling or as a salad.

> 1 can (15 to 16 ounces) garbanzo beans, drained and liquid reserved
> 1/2 cup sesame seeds
> 1 clove garlic, cut in half
> 3 tablespoons lemon juice
> 1 teaspoon salt
> Chopped fresh parsley
> Pita bread wedges, crackers or raw vegetables for dipping, if desired

1. Place reserved bean liquid, the sesame seeds and garlic in blender or food processor. Cover and blend on high speed until mixed.

2. Add beans, lemon juice and salt. Cover and blend on high speed, stopping blender occasionally to scrape sides if necessary, until uniform consistency.

3. Spoon dip into serving dish. Garnish with parsley. Serve with pita bread wedges.

1 TABLESPOON: Calories 25 (Calories from Fat 10); Fat 1g (Saturated 0g); Cholesterol 0mg; Sodium 90mg; Carbohydrate 3g (Dietary Fiber 0g); Protein 1g

Layered Asian Dip

PREP: 10 min
Makes about 3 1/2 cups dip

> 1 package (8 ounces) cream cheese, softened
> 1 tablespoon soy sauce
> 1 can (8 ounces) water chestnuts, drained and chopped
> 1/2 cup chopped bok choy
> 1 cup canned bean sprouts, drained
> 1/4 cup chopped green onions (3 medium)
> Rice crackers or raw vegetables for dipping, if desired

1. Mix cream cheese, soy sauce and water chestnuts; spread in 9-inch circle on 12-inch serving plate. Layer bok choy, bean sprouts and onions on cream cheese mixture.

2. Serve dip with rice crackers.

1 TABLESPOON: Calories 15 (Calories from Fat 10); Fat 1g (Saturated 1g); Cholesterol 5mg; Sodium 35mg; Carbohydrate 1g (Dietary Fiber 0g); Protein 0g

---

LIGHTER LAYERED ASIAN DIP

For 0 grams of fat and 5 calories per serving, use fat-free cream cheese.

Mexican Dip

PREP: 15 min
Makes about 3 1/2 cups dip

1/2 pound ground beef
1/2 teaspoon ground mustard (dry)
1/4 to 1/2 teaspoon chili powder
1 small onion, finely chopped (1/4 cup)
1/4 cup finely chopped green bell pepper
1 can (16 ounces) refried beans*
1 can (8 ounces) tomato sauce
1 envelope (1 1/4 ounces) taco seasoning
    mix
Sour Cream Topping (below)
Finely shredded lettuce
Shredded Cheddar cheese
Tortilla chips, if desired

1. Cook beef in 10-inch skillet, stirring occasionally, until brown; drain.

2. Stir in mustard, chili powder, onion, bell pepper,
beans, tomato sauce and seasoning mix (dry). Heat to
boiling, stirring constantly.

3. Spread beef mixture in ungreased pie plate,
9 × 1 1/4 inches. Spread Sour Cream Topping over
beef mixture. Sprinkle with lettuce and cheese. Serve
with tortilla chips.

*1 can (15 ounces) black beans, rinsed and drained, can be substi-
tuted for the refried beans.*

Sour Cream Topping

1 cup sour cream
2 tablespoons shredded Cheddar cheese
1/4 teaspoon chili powder

Mix all ingredients.

1 TABLESPOON: Calories 35 (Calories from Fat 20); Fat 2g
(Saturated 1g); Cholesterol 5mg; Sodium 95mg;
Carbohydrate 3g (Dietary Fiber 0g); Protein 1g

LIGHTER MEXICAN DIP

For 1 gram of fat and 30 calories per serving, substitute
ground turkey for the ground beef and plain fat-free
yogurt for the sour cream. Use black beans and
reduced-fat Cheddar cheese. Serve with Baked Tortilla
Chips (page 29) instead of tortilla chips.

Savory Shrimp Dip

PREP: 20 min; COOK: 5 min
Makes about 3 cups dip

2 tablespoons margarine or butter
1 medium stalk celery, chopped (1/2 cup)
1 small green bell pepper, chopped (1/2 cup)
1/4 cup chopped green onions (3 medium)
1 cup chopped cooked shrimp*
2 tablespoons chopped fresh parsley
1 teaspoon chopped fresh or 1/4 teaspoon
    dried thyme leaves
1/2 teaspoon paprika
1/4 to 1/2 teaspoon ground red pepper
    (cayenne)
1/4 teaspoon pepper
1 medium tomato, peeled and chopped
    (3/4 cup)
1 package (3 ounces) cream cheese, softened
2 containers (6 ounces each) plain yogurt
Assorted crackers or sliced raw vegetables for
    dipping, if desired

1. Melt margarine in 10-inch skillet over medium
heat. Cook celery, bell pepper and onions in margarine, stirring occasionally, until celery is crisp-tender.

2. Stir in remaining ingredients except yogurt and
crackers; heat through.

3. Remove shrimp mixture from heat. Stir in
yogurt. Serve dip warm, or refrigerate and serve cold.
Serve with crackers.

*1 can (4 to 4 1/2 ounces) small shrimp, rinsed and drained, can be
substituted for the cooked shrimp.*

1 TABLESPOON: Calories 15 (Calories from Fat 10); Fat 1g
(Saturated 1g); Cholesterol 10mg; Sodium 25mg;
Carbohydrate 1g (Dietary Fiber 0g); Protein 1g

TIMESAVING TIP

Stir 1 cup chopped cooked shrimp and 1 medium
tomato, peeled and chopped, into 2 cups purchased
herb sour cream dip. Serve cold or heat over low heat,
stirring occasionally until warm.

Hot Crab Dip

PREP: 15 min; BAKE: 20 min
Makes about 2 1/2 cups dip

1 package (8 ounces) cream cheese, softened
1/4 cup grated Parmesan cheese
1/4 cup thinly sliced green onions (3 medium)
1/4 cup mayonnaise or salad dressing
1/4 cup dry white wine or apple juice
2 teaspoons sugar
1 teaspoon ground mustard (dry)
1 clove garlic, finely chopped
1 can (6 ounces) crabmeat, drained, cartilage removed, and flaked*
1/3 cup sliced almonds, toasted (page 9)
Assorted crackers or sliced raw vegetables for dipping, if desired

1. Heat oven to 375°.

2. Mix all ingredients except crabmeat, almonds and crackers in medium bowl until well blended. Stir in crabmeat.

3. Spread crabmeat mixture in ungreased pie plate, 9 × 1 1/4 inches, or shallow 1-quart casserole. Sprinkle with almonds.

4. Bake uncovered 15 to 20 minutes or until hot and bubbly. Serve with crackers.

6 ounces imitation crabmeat, coarsely chopped, can be substituted for the canned crabmeat.

1 TABLESPOON: Calories 50 (Calories from Fat 35); Fat 4g (Saturated 2g); Cholesterol 10mg; Sodium 50mg; Carbohydrate 1g (Dietary Fiber 0g); Protein 2g

---

LIGHTER HOT CRAB DIP
For 1 gram of fat and 20 calories per serving, use fat-free cream cheese and fat-free mayonnaise. Omit almonds.

Cream Cheese Fiesta Spread

PREP: 10 min
Makes 8 servings

For a change, try serving these easy spreads with sliced raw vegetables such as bell pepper, jicama or zucchini instead of crackers.

1 package (8 ounces) cream cheese
1/4 cup salsa
1/4 cup apricot preserves or orange marmalade
1 tablespoon chopped fresh cilantro
1 tablespoon finely shredded Cheddar or Monterey Jack cheese
1 tablespoon chopped avocado
1 tablespoon chopped ripe olives
Assorted crackers, if desired

1. Place block of cream cheese on serving plate with shallow rim.

2. Mix salsa and preserves; spread over cream cheese. Sprinkle with remaining ingredients except crackers. Serve with crackers.

1 SERVING: Calories 130 (Calories from Fat 90); Fat 10g (Saturated 6g); Cholesterol 30mg; Sodium 140mg; Carbohydrate 8g (Dietary Fiber 0g); Protein 2g

---

LIGHTER CREAM CHEESE FIESTA SPREAD
For 0 grams of fat and 50 calories per serving, use fat-free cream cheese.

CRUNCHY CREAM CHEESE-RASPBERRY SPREAD: Omit salsa, preserves, cilantro, cheese, avocado and olives. Spread 1/3 cup raspberry spreadable fruit over cream cheese. Sprinkle with 2 tablespoons each of finely chopped toasted almonds, miniature semisweet chocolate chips and flaked coconut.

CURRIED CREAM CHEESE-CHUTNEY SPREAD: Omit salsa, preserves, cilantro, cheese, avocado and olives. Spread 1/3 cup chopped chutney over cream cheese. Sprinkle generously with curry powder. Sprinkle with 1 tablespoon each of chopped peanuts, chopped green onion, raisins and chopped cooked egg yolk.

Three-Cheese Ball

PREP: 10 min; CHILL: 10 hr
Makes about 3 1/2 cups spread

This tasty cheese ball can be made ahead and stored in the refrigerator for up to two weeks or in the freezer for up to two months. For a just-made look and taste, roll in the parsley shortly before serving.

2 packages (8 ounces each) cream cheese, softened
1 cup shredded sharp Cheddar cheese (4 ounces)
3/4 cup crumbled blue cheese (4 ounces), softened
1 small onion, finely chopped (1/4 cup)
1 tablespoon Worcestershire sauce
1/4 cup finely chopped fresh parsley or sunflower nuts
Assorted crackers, if desired

Roasted Garlic

1. Beat cheeses, onion and Worcestershire sauce with electric mixer on low speed until blended. Beat on medium speed, scraping bowl frequently, until fluffy. Cover and refrigerate at least 8 hours but no longer than 24 hours.

2. Shape cheese mixture into 1 large or 2 small balls or logs. Roll in parsley. Place on serving plate. Cover and refrigerate about 2 hours or until firm. Serve with crackers.

1 TABLESPOON: Calories 45 (Calories from Fat 35); Fat 4g (Saturated 3g); Cholesterol 15mg; Sodium 65mg; Carbohydrate 1g (Dietary Fiber 0g); Protein 1g

> **LIGHTER THREE-CHEESE BALL**
> For 2 grams of fat and 30 calories per serving, use reduced-fat cream cheese (Neufchâtel) and reduced-fat Cheddar cheese.

Roasted Garlic

PREP: 10 min; BAKE: 50 min
Makes 2 to 8 servings

Garlic becomes rich and mellow when roasted. Look for fresh garlic bulbs in the produce section.

> 1 to 4 bulbs garlic
> 2 teaspoons olive or vegetable oil for each bulb garlic
> Salt and pepper to taste
> Sliced French bread, if desired

1. Heat oven to 350°.

2. Carefully peel paperlike skin from around each bulb of garlic, leaving just enough to hold garlic cloves together. Cut 1/4 to 1/2 inch from top of each bulb to expose cloves. Place cut side up on 12-inch square of aluminum foil.

3. Drizzle each bulb with 2 teaspoons oil. Sprinkle with salt and pepper. Wrap securely in foil. Place in pie plate or shallow baking pan.

4. Bake 45 to 50 minutes or until garlic is tender when pierced with toothpick or fork. Cool slightly. To serve, gently squeeze soft garlic out of cloves. Spread on bread.

1 SERVING: Calories 75 (Calories from Fat 45); Fat 5g (Saturated 1g); Cholesterol 0mg; Sodium 270mg; Carbohydrate 8g (Dietary Fiber 1g); Protein 1g

Mahogany Chicken Wings

PREP: 15 min; CHILL: 1 hr; BAKE: 50 min
Makes 2 1/2 dozen appetizers

These zesty wings are also good served with a hot mustard sauce for dipping. (photograph on page 17)

 15 chicken wings (3 pounds)
 1/2 cup soy sauce
 1/2 cup honey
 1/4 cup molasses
 2 tablespoons chili sauce
 1 teaspoon ground ginger
 2 cloves garlic, finely chopped

1. Cut each chicken wing at joints to make 3 pieces; discard tip. Cut off excess skin; discard. Place chicken in shallow glass or plastic bowl. Mix remaining ingredients; pour over chicken. Cover and refrigerate 1 hour, turning occasionally.

2. Heat oven to 375°. Line broiler pan with aluminum foil.

3. Remove chicken from marinade; reserve marinade. Place chicken in single layer on rack in foil-lined broiler pan; brush with marinade.

4. Bake 30 minutes; turn. Bake about 20 minutes longer, brushing occasionally with marinade, until deep brown and juice of chicken is no longer pink when centers of thickest pieces are cut. Discard any remaining marinade.

1 APPETIZER: Calories 80 (Calories from Fat 35); Fat 4g (Saturated 1g); Cholesterol 15mg; Sodium 300mg; Carbohydrate 7g (Dietary Fiber 0g); Protein 4g

Oriental Barbecued Ribs

PREP: 15 min; MARINATE: 2 hr; BAKE 1 3/4 hr
Makes about 30 appetizers

You can make these ribs distinctively Chinese, or create a milder version using chili sauce and white wine. No matter how you make them, be sure to have plenty of napkins handy!

 2-pound rack pork back ribs, cut across bones
   in half
 1/4 cup soy sauce
 1/4 cup hoisin sauce or chili sauce
 2 tablespoons honey
 2 tablespoons sake, dry white wine or apple
   juice
 2 cloves garlic, crushed

1. Cut pork between ribs into 1 1/2-inch pieces. Place pork in shallow glass or plastic bowl. Mix remaining ingredients; spoon over pork. Cover and refrigerate at least 2 hours but no longer than 24 hours.

2. Heat oven to 325°. Line broiler pan with aluminum foil.

3. Remove pork from soy sauce mixture; reserve mixture. Arrange pork, meaty sides up, in single layer on rack in foil-lined broiler pan; brush with soy sauce mixture.

4. Cover and bake 1 hour; brush with marinade. Bake uncovered about 45 minutes longer, brushing occasionally with marinade, until tender. Discard any remaining marinade.

1 APPETIZER: Calories 70 (Calories from Fat 45); Fat 5g (Saturated 2g); Cholesterol 20mg; Sodium 150mg; Carbohydrate 2g (Dietary Fiber 0g); Protein 4g

Greek Broiled Shrimp

PREP: 10 min; BROIL: 5 min
Makes 12 servings

 1 1/2 pounds uncooked peeled deveined
   medium shrimp, thawed if frozen
 1 cup Winter Tomato Sauce (page 343)
 1/4 cup dry white wine or apple juice
 2 tablespoons lemon juice
 1 1/2 teaspoons chopped fresh or 1/2
   teaspoon dried oregano leaves
 1/4 cup crumbled feta cheese (about
   2 ounces)

1. Set oven control to broil. Grease bottom and sides of rectangular pan, 13 × 9 × 2 inches, with shortening.

2. Mix all ingredients except cheese. Arrange mixture in pan with shrimp in single layer. Sprinkle with cheese.

3. Broil with tops 4 inches from heat about 5 minutes or until shrimp are pink and firm. Serve hot.

1 SERVING: Calories 70 (Calories from Fat 20); Fat 2g (Saturated 1g); Cholesterol 85mg; Sodium 210mg; Carbohydrate 4g (Dietary Fiber 0g); Protein 9g

---

TIMESAVING TIP
The shrimp mixture can be prepared, covered and refrigerated up to 8 hours before serving. Broil 6 to 8 minutes or until shrimp are pink.

Buffalo Chicken Wings

PREP: 20 min; BAKE: 45 min
Makes 2 dozen appetizers

Blue Cheese Dressing (page 339)
12 chicken wings (2 1/2 pounds)
2 tablespoons margarine or butter
1/4 cup all-purpose flour
1 tablespoon margarine or butter, melted
1 tablespoon white vinegar
2 to 3 teaspoons red pepper sauce
1/4 teaspoon salt
Celery, carrot and zucchini sticks

1. Prepare Blue Cheese Dressing.

2. Heat oven to 425°.

3. Cut each chicken wing at joints to make 3 pieces; discard tip. Cut off excess skin; discard.

4. Melt 2 tablespoons margarine in rectangular pan, 13 × 9 × 2 inches, in oven. Coat chicken with flour; shake off extra flour. Place chicken in pan.

5. Bake uncovered 20 minutes; turn. Bake uncovered 20 to 25 minutes longer or until light golden brown and juice of chicken is no longer pink when centers of thickest pieces are cut; drain on paper towels.

6. Mix 1 tablespoon margarine, the vinegar, pepper sauce and salt in large bowl until well blended. Add chicken; toss until evenly coated with pepper sauce mixture. Serve with Blue Cheese Dressing and celery sticks.

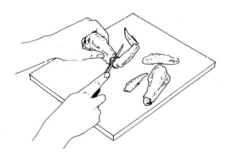

Cut chicken wings at joints to make 3 pieces; discard tips.

1 APPETIZER: Calories 125 (Calories from Fat 100); Fat 11g (Saturated 5g); Cholesterol 25mg; Sodium 150mg; Carbohydrate 2g (Dietary Fiber 0g); Protein 5g

DEEP-FRIED BUFFALO CHICKEN WINGS: Omit 2 tablespoons margarine and 1/4 cup flour. Heat vegetable oil (2 to 3 inches) in deep fryer or Dutch oven to 375°. Fry 4 to 6 chicken pieces at a time in oil 8 to 10 minutes, turning occasionally, until golden brown and juice of chicken is no longer pink when centers of thickest pieces are cut; drain on paper towels. Keep warm in 275° oven while frying remaining chicken wings. Increase melted margarine in pepper sauce mixture to 2 tablespoons.

TIMESAVING TIP
Prepare purchased frozen fried chicken wings as directed on package. Toss hot wings in pepper sauce mixture. Serve with bottled blue cheese dressing and celery sticks.

Italian Stuffed Mushrooms

PREP: 20 min; BAKE: 15 min; BROIL: 2 min
Makes 3 dozen appetizers

(photograph on page 17)

36 medium mushrooms (about 1 pound)
2 tablespoons margarine or butter
1/4 cup chopped green onions (3 medium)
1/4 cup chopped red bell pepper
1 1/2 cups soft bread crumbs
2 teaspoons chopped fresh or 1/2 teaspoon dried oregano leaves*
1/4 teaspoon salt
1/4 teaspoon pepper
1 tablespoon margarine or butter
Grated Parmesan cheese, if desired

1. Heat oven to 350°.

2. Twist mushroom stems to remove from mushroom caps. Finely chop enough stems to measure 1/3 cup. Reserve mushroom caps.

3. Melt 2 tablespoons margarine in 10-inch skillet over medium-high heat. Cook chopped mushroom stems, onions and bell pepper in margarine about 3 minutes, stirring frequently, until onions are softened; remove from heat. Stir in bread crumbs, oregano, salt and pepper. Fill mushroom caps with bread crumb mixture.

4. Melt 1 tablespoon margarine in rectangular pan, 13 × 9 × 2 inches, in oven. Place mushrooms, filled sides up, in pan. Sprinkle with cheese. Bake 15 minutes.

5. Set oven control to broil. Broil mushrooms with tops 3 to 4 inches from heat about 2 minutes or until tops are light brown. Serve hot.

2 teaspoons Italian seasoning can be substituted for the oregano.

1 APPETIZER: Calories 30 (Calories from Fat 10); Fat 1g (Saturated 0g); Cholesterol 0mg; Sodium 65mg; Carbohydrate 4g (Dietary Fiber 0g); Protein 1g

---

TIMESAVING TIP
Mushrooms can be stuffed, covered and refrigerated up to 24 hours before baking. Heat oven to 350°. Continue as directed in step 4.

Cheesy Potato Skins

Cheesy Potato Skins

PREP: 15 min; BAKE: 1 1/4 hr; BROIL: 11 min
Makes 8 servings

> 4 large potatoes (about 2 pounds)
> 2 tablespoons margarine or butter, melted
> 1 cup shredded Colby–Monterey Jack cheese
>   (4 ounces)
> 1/2 cup sour cream
> 1/2 cup sliced green onions (5 medium)

1. Bake potatoes as directed on page 400. Let stand until cool enough to handle. Cut potatoes lengthwise into fourths; carefully scoop out pulp, leaving 1/4-inch shells. Save potato pulp for another use.

2. Set oven control to Broil.

3. Place potato shells, skin sides down, on rack in broiler pan. Brush with margarine.

4. Broil with tops 4 to 5 inches from heat 8 to 10 minutes or until crisp and brown.

5. Sprinkle cheese over potato shells. Broil about 30 seconds or until cheese is melted. Serve hot with sour cream and green onions.

1 SERVING: Calories 205 (Calories from Fat 90); Fat 10g (Saturated 6g); Cholesterol 25mg; Sodium 140mg; Carbohydrate 25g (Dietary Fiber 2g); Protein 6g

---

LIGHTER CHEESY POTATO SKINS

For 5 grams of fat and 145 calories per serving, decrease cheese to 1/2 cup and use fat-free sour cream.

Cajun Oven-Fried Vegetables

PREP: 20 min; BAKE: 25 min
Makes about 3 dozen appetizers

Cajun or Creole seasoning usually contains hot peppers, garlic and paprika. If you'd like a milder flavor, leave out the Cajun seasoning and use 1/4 teaspoon salt and 1/8 teaspoon pepper instead.

> 2 large eggs
> 1 cup unseasoned dry bread crumbs
> 1/2 teaspoon Cajun seasoning
> 8 ounces whole mushrooms
> 1 medium zucchini, diagonally cut into
>   1/2-inch slices
> 1 medium bell pepper, cut into 1/2-inch
>   strips

1. Heat oven to 375°. Grease cookie sheet with shortening.

2. Beat eggs in small bowl with fork. Mix bread crumbs and Cajun seasoning in small bowl.

3. Dip mushrooms, zucchini and bell pepper into egg mixture, then coat with bread crumb mixture. Arrange vegetables in single layer, pieces not touching, on cookie sheet.

4. Bake 20 to 25 minutes, turning after 10 minutes, until coating is golden brown. Serve hot.

1 APPETIZER: Calories 25 (Calories from Fat 10); Fat 1g (Saturated 0g); Cholesterol 10mg; Sodium 30mg; Carbohydrate 3g (Dietary Fiber 0g); Protein 1g

Crostini

PREP: 15 min; BAKE: 8 min
Makes 12 appetizers

Crostini—an Italian appetizer—is crusty bread with different delicious toppings. Here we've highlighted fresh tomatoes, basil and mozzarella. (photograph on page 17)

> 12 slices Italian bread, each 1/2 inch thick
> 1/4 cup olive or vegetable oil
> 1 large tomato, chopped (1 cup)
> 3 tablespoons chopped fresh basil leaves
> 1 tablespoon large capers or chopped ripe olives
> 1/2 teaspoon salt
> 1/2 teaspoon pepper
> 12 slices (1 ounce each) mozzarella cheese

1. Heat oven to 375°.

2. Place bread slices on ungreased cookie sheets. Drizzle 1 teaspoon oil over each slice bread.

3. Mix tomato, basil, capers, salt and pepper. Spread half of the tomato mixture over bread slices; top each with cheese slice. Spread remaining tomato mixture over cheese.

4. Bake about 8 minutes or until bread is hot and cheese is melted. Serve hot.

1 APPETIZER: Calories 140 (Calories from Fat 70); Fat 8g (Saturated 3g); Cholesterol 10mg; Sodium 280mg; Carbohydrate 11g (Dietary Fiber 0g); Protein 6g

---

TIMESAVING TIP

Prepare and refrigerate tomato topping up to 24 hours ahead. Assemble for baking no longer than 1 hour ahead or the bread will get soggy.

Basil-Cheese Triangles

PREP: 25 min; BAKE: 20 min
Makes 3 dozen appetizers

> 1 pound feta or shredded Monterey Jack cheese
> 2 large eggs, slightly beaten
> 1/4 cup finely chopped fresh or 1 tablespoon dried basil leaves
> 1/4 teaspoon white pepper
> 1 package (16 ounces) frozen phyllo sheets (18 × 14 inches), thawed
> 1/4 cup *stick* margarine or butter, melted*

1. Heat oven to 350°. Grease cookie sheet with shortening.

2. Crumble feta cheese into small bowl; mash with fork. Stir in eggs, basil and white pepper until well mixed.

3. Cut stack of phyllo sheets lengthwise into thirds. Cover with waxed paper, then with damp towel to prevent them from drying out.

4. For each triangle, use 2 strips of phyllo. Place 1 heaping teaspoon cheese mixture on end of strip; fold phyllo strip end over end, in triangular shape, to opposite end. Place on cookie sheet. Brush margarine over triangles.

5. Bake about 20 minutes or until puffed and golden. Serve warm.

We do not recommend using vegetable oil spreads (see page 13).

a. Place 1 heaping teaspoon filling on end of strip.

b. Place phyllo end over end, in triangular shape, to opposite end.

1 APPETIZER: Calories 85 (Calories from Fat 35); Fat 4g (Saturated 2g); Cholesterol 25mg; Sodium 200mg; Carbohydrate 9g (Dietary Fiber 0g); Protein 3g

---

TIMESAVING TIP

Triangles can be covered and refrigerated up to 24 hours before baking. Bake as directed. Or freeze up to 2 months tightly covered. Increase bake time by 5 minutes.

Marinated Mushrooms and Cheese

PREP: 20 min; CHILL: 4 hr
Makes about 3 cups

If you have sun-dried tomatoes in oil on hand, you can use them (drained) in place of the dried tomatoes and skip the first step.

  1/2 cup sun-dried tomatoes (not oil-packed),
    cut into bite-size pieces
  1 cup boiling water
  1/4 cup olive or vegetable oil
  1/4 cup white vinegar
  1 tablespoon chopped fresh or 1 teaspoon
    dried marjoram leaves
  1 1/2 teaspoons chopped fresh or 1/2 tea-
    spoon dried rosemary leaves
  1/4 teaspoon garlic powder
  8 ounces tiny whole mushrooms
  8 ounces brick cheese, cut into 1/2-inch
    cubes

1. Mix tomatoes and boiling water. Let stand 5 minutes; drain.

2. Mix oil, vinegar, marjoram, rosemary and garlic powder in half-gallon heavy-duty plastic food-storage bag. Add tomatoes, mushrooms and cheese to bag; seal tightly.

3. Refrigerate at least 4 hours but no longer than 4 days, turning occasionally. Drain before serving.

1/4 CUP: Calories 90 (Calories from Fat 65); Fat 7g (Saturated 4g); Cholesterol 20mg; Sodium 170mg; Carbohydrate 2g (Dietary Fiber 0g); Protein 5g

Popcorn

PREP: 5 min; COOK: 5 min
Makes about 12 cups popcorn

  1/2 cup unpopped popcorn (not microwave
    popcorn)
  1/4 cup vegetable oil
  Salt, if desired

1. Pour popcorn and oil into Dutch oven. Tilt Dutch oven to spread popcorn evenly. Cover and cook over medium-high heat until 1 kernel pops; remove from heat. Let stand 1 minute, then return to heat.

2. Cook, shaking pan occasionally, until popcorn stops popping. *Immediately* pour into serving bowl. Salt and toss until evenly coated. Serve warm.

1 CUP: Calories 70 (Calories from Fat 45); Fat 5g (Saturated 1g); Cholesterol 0mg; Sodium 5mg; Carbohydrate 6g (Dietary Fiber 1g); Protein 1g

NACHO POPCORN: Prepare popcorn as directed above. Heat 1/4 cup margarine or butter (do not use spreads or tub products), 1 teaspoon chili powder, 1/2 teaspoon ground cumin and 1/2 teaspoon garlic powder until margarine is melted. Drizzle over hot popcorn; toss. *Immediately* sprinkle with 1/4 cup grated American or Parmesan cheese; toss. Serve warm.

Caramel-Nut Corn

PREP: 20 min; BAKE: 1 hr
Makes about 15 cups snack

While it's delicious any time of the year, homemade caramel corn is very welcome as a special gift or treat during the holidays.

  12 cups unsalted Popcorn (left)
  3 cups walnut halves, pecan halves or
    unblanched whole almonds
  1 cup packed brown sugar
  1/2 cup *stick* margarine or butter*
  1/4 cup light corn syrup
  1/2 teaspoon salt
  1/2 teaspoon baking soda

1. Heat oven to 200°.

2. Divide popcorn and walnut halves between 2 ungreased rectangular pans, 13 × 9 × 2 inches.

3. Cook brown sugar, margarine, corn syrup and salt in 2-quart saucepan over medium heat, stirring occasionally, until bubbly around edges. Continue cooking 5 minutes; remove from heat. Stir in baking soda until foamy.

4. Pour sugar mixture over popcorn mixture; toss until evenly coated.

5. Bake 1 hour, stirring every 15 minutes. Cool completely. Store tightly covered.

*We do not recommend using vegetable oil spreads (see page 13).

1 CUP: Calories 310 (Calories from Fat 200); Fat 22g (Saturated 3g); Cholesterol 0mg; Sodium 200mg; Carbohydrate 27g (Dietary Fiber 2g); Protein 3g

CARAMEL CORN: Increase popcorn to 15 cups and omit nuts.

TIMESAVING TIP
Use a high-quality purchased unsalted popped popcorn rather than popping corn.

Nachos

Baked Tortilla Chips

PREP: 10 min; BAKE: 8 min
Makes 4 dozen chips

> 4 corn or flour tortillas (8 inches in diameter)
> *Stick* margarine or butter, melted*
> Chili powder, if desired

1. Heat oven to 375°.

2. Brush tortillas lightly with margarine. Sprinkle with chili powder. Cut each into 12 wedges or pieces, using kitchen scissors. Place in single layer in 2 ungreased jelly roll pans, 15 1/2 × 10 1/2 × 1 inch, or on 2 cookie sheets.

3. Bake uncovered 6 to 8 minutes or until light brown and crisp. Cool slightly (chips will continue to crisp as they cool). Serve warm or cool. Store in tightly covered container up to 3 weeks at room temperature.

We do not recommend using vegetable oil spreads (see page 13).

1 CHIP: Calories 15 (Calories from Fat 10); Fat 1g (Saturated 0g); Cholesterol 0mg; Sodium 25mg; Carbohydrate 1g (Dietary Fiber 0g); Protein 0g

BAKED PITA CHIPS: Cut around outside edge of 6 pita breads (6 inches in diameter), using kitchen scissors, to separate layers. Brush with margarine. Sprinkle with dried basil leaves and grated Parmesan cheese if desired. Cut each layer into 8 wedges. Bake as directed.

Nachos

PREP: 5 min; BAKE: 4 min
Makes 4 servings

> 28 tortilla chips
> 1 cup shredded Monterey Jack or Cheddar cheese (4 ounces)
> 1/4 cup canned chopped mild green chilies, if desired
> 1/4 cup salsa

1. Heat oven to 400°. Line cookie sheet with aluminum foil.

2. Place tortilla chips on cookie sheet. Sprinkle with cheese and green chilies.

3. Bake about 4 minutes or until cheese is melted. Top with salsa. Serve hot.

1 SERVING: Calories 160 (Calories from Fat 100); Fat 11g (Saturated 6g); Cholesterol 25mg; Sodium 380mg; Carbohydrate 9g (Dietary Fiber 1g); Protein 7g

---

TIMESAVING TIP

To microwave each serving, arrange 7 tortilla chips in a circle on a microwavable paper plate. Sprinkle 1/4 cup of the cheese over chips. Sprinkle with 1 tablespoon green chilies. Microwave uncovered on High 20 to 30 seconds or until cheese is melted. Top with 1 tablespoon salsa.

Cinnamon-Sugared Nuts, Hot and Spicy Peanuts

Cinnamon-Sugared Nuts

PREP: 10 min; BAKE: 30 min
Makes 2 cups nuts

Served warm and made with almonds, these crusty nuts are similar to those sold by street vendors in both Europe and America.

> 1 tablespoon slightly beaten egg white
> 2 cups pecan halves, unblanched almonds or walnut halves
> 1/4 cup sugar
> 2 teaspoons ground cinnamon
> 1/4 teaspoon ground nutmeg
> 1/4 teaspoon ground cloves

1. Heat oven to 300°.

2. Mix egg white and pecan halves in medium bowl until pecans are coated and sticky.

3. Mix remaining ingredients; sprinkle over pecans. Stir until pecans are completely coated. Spread pecans in single layer in ungreased jelly roll pan, 15 1/2 × 10 1/2 × 1 inch.

4. Bake about 30 minutes or until toasted. Cool completely, or serve slightly warm.

1/4 CUP: Calories 210 (Calories from Fat 160); Fat 18g (Saturated 2g); Cholesterol 0mg; Sodium 5mg; Carbohydrate 12g (Dietary Fiber 2g); Protein 2g

Hot and Spicy Peanuts

PREP: 5 min; COOK: 5 min
Makes 2 cups peanuts

Serve these spicy snacking nuts with plenty of ice-cold beverages. For a milder flavor, substitute chili powder for the ground red pepper.

> 2 teaspoons vegetable oil
> 1 to 1 1/2 teaspoons ground red pepper (cayenne)
> 2 cups dry-roasted peanuts

1. Heat oil in 10-inch skillet over medium heat. Stir in red pepper.

2. Stir in peanuts. Cook about 2 minutes, stirring constantly, until evenly coated and hot. Cool slightly. Serve warm or cool.

1/4 CUP: Calories 215 (Calories from Fat 160); Fat 18g (Saturated 3g); Cholesterol 0mg; Sodium 145mg; Carbohydrate 6g (Dietary Fiber 2g); Protein 9g

About Beverages

Whether you prefer beverages that are cool and refreshing or warm and soothing, there are many from which to choose, and most beverages can be prepared quickly and conveniently with little advance preparation. Select beverages to suit the occasion, complement the food and fit the weather.

The selection of ready-to-drink beverages at your supermarket continues to grow. Punch, fruit juice, soda pop (regular or sugar free), bottled sparkling water (flavored and unflavored), nonalcoholic beer and wine or sparkling grape juice as well as interesting coffees (caffeinated or decaffeinated) and teas in different flavors are all good choices.

Coffee

The perfect cup of coffee is determined not only by the preference of the coffee drinker but also by the coffee bean, the roast and the equipment used to make the coffee. The best coffee is made from freshly roasted coffee beans, preferably ground just before brewing. Actually, they are not beans but the twin seeds of the cherry-red fruit produced by the tropical coffee plant. These seeds are cleaned, dried and graded, then exported. Roasting, blending and grinding are done once the beans arrive at their destination.

The two main species of coffee plants are robusta, an easy-to-grow hearty bean, and arabica, the more desirable bean, which is grown at higher elevations and has more flavor and aroma.

Coffee beans vary by country and region, year and age. They also differ by how they are roasted. Different types of beans are roasted to different levels to optimize their flavor and aroma. Roasting brings out the flavor inherent in the bean and determines the richness, mellowness and smoothness of the coffee; the longer the bean is roasted, the darker and stronger-flavored the coffee. Beans can also be roasted with or without added flavorings such as vanilla or hazelnut.

Most coffees are blends, combinations of different coffees, that result in a pleasant balance of body, flavor, sweetness and acidity. The strength of the coffee depends directly on the ratio of coffee to water when brewing. For best results, use the grind of coffee that is recommended by the manufacturer of your coffeemaker:

- **Regular grind** is an intermediate grind size used in automatic percolator-type coffeemakers and range-top percolators.
- **Drip or fine grind** is used in drip coffeemakers and espresso machines in which the water passes through the grounds only once.
- **Special grinds**, such as automatic drip, electric perk and flaked, are designed especially for specific electric coffeemakers.

Store whole beans and ground coffee in airtight containers in the freezer (up to three months) or refrigerator (up to two weeks) to slow oxidation and loss of flavor. For optimum flavor, grind coffee beans just before using.

Some popular coffee roasts and blends are:
- **American,** medium-roasted with a moderate brew
- **French,** heavy-roasted with deep brown color and strong brew
- **Italian,** brown-black, strongly flavored and used for espresso
- **European,** blend of two-thirds heavy-roasted beans and one-third medium-roasted
- **Viennese,** blend of two-thirds medium-roasted beans and one-third heavy-roasted

Decaffeinated Coffee

Coffee, as well as tea and chocolate, contains caffeine, a stimulant that can affect many parts of the body, including the nervous system. Many people prefer to drink coffees that have been decaffeinated, even though some of the aroma and flavor of pure ground coffee can be lost in this process.

Caffeine is removed from coffee by either the water process or the solvent process. The solvent process is quicker, less expensive and disturbs fewer of the flavor components. Coffee drinkers concerned about solvent residues, however, prefer water-processed decaffeinated coffee.

Instant Coffee

Quickly dissolved in either hot or cold water, instant coffee powders are made by brewing pure ground coffee and evaporating the water. Freeze-dried coffee crystals are made from brewed coffee frozen into a slush before the water is evaporated. Because of this process, freeze-dried coffee is slightly more expensive than other instant coffees.

Specialty Coffees

Coffee is the essential ingredient in a variety of popular beverages served in both classic and unique combinations. Restaurants, coffeehouses and coffee and tea shops serve their own special creations that may or may not include flavorings and liquor.
- **Espresso** is made using a special coffeemaker with a pressurized brewing chamber that uses steaming-hot water for brewing and a steam valve for steaming and foaming or frothing milk.

- **Cappuccino** is espresso plus hot steamed milk topped with a cap of foamed milk.
- **Café Latté** is espresso plus hot steamed milk with or without foam.
- **Café Mocha** is espresso plus chocolate syrup and steamed milk. It is topped with whipped cream and a sprinkle of sweetened cocoa.
- **Café au lait**, originally popular in France as a breakfast beverage, is a combination (usually equal parts) of hot coffee and hot milk.

After-dinner coffees, such as Irish coffee and Spanish coffee, can be enjoyed any time or even replace dessert. Often they are a mixture of hot coffee, liquor or liqueur(s), and sugar or cream and are topped with whipped cream.

A variety of flavored instant coffee mixes are available, including combinations such as chocolate-mint and raspberry-cream, easy and convenient to prepare any time.

How to Make Coffee

Many different types of electric and nonelectric coffeemakers are available, so follow the manufacturer's directions for selecting the grind of coffee and the amount to use. The general guidelines below will help you prepare a great cup of coffee!

1. Start with a thoroughly clean coffeemaker. Wash after each use with hot, soapy water, and rinse well with hot water. Never scour with an abrasive pad. Follow the manufacturer's directions for water temperatures, use of filters and cleaning.

2. Serve hot coffee as soon as possible after brewing. If coffee must stand any length of time, remove the grounds and hold coffee at serving temperature in an insulated container, or place over very low heat. Coffee can also be covered and refrigerated for heating later in the microwave or pouring over ice.

Coffee Brewing Strength*
(For each serving)

Strength of Brew	Ground Coffee (level tablespoon)	Water
Weak	1	3/4 cup (6 ounces)
Medium	2	3/4 cup (6 ounces)
Strong	3	3/4 cup (6 ounces)

Best general recommendation.

Iced Coffee

Iced coffee is refreshing anytime and can be freshly brewed or made from leftover brewed coffee. When preparing iced coffee from fresh coffee, a strong brew is usually preferred because it will be served over ice that will dilute the coffee; adjust the brew to suit your taste. Allow coffee to cool after brewing. Cover and refrigerate if it is not to be used within 2 hours. Pour over ice cubes in tall glasses.

- For a special treat, use dark-roasted or flavored coffee.
- Try a slightly finer grind to extract more flavor.
- Add half-and-half or whole milk for a richer taste and creamy color (add about 2 ounces to 3/4 cup brewed coffee).
- Sugar or sweetener can be added.
- Make ice cubes from brewed coffee so the ice doesn't dilute the flavor.

Tea

Tea is native to China but enjoyed around the world. From the afternoon high tea of the English to the tea ceremony of the Japanese, the Russian glass of tea to the minted tea of the Middle East, a cup of tea can be a cultural rite with meaning far beyond the American cup of coffee. The tea you buy is a delicate blend of some twenty to thirty varieties of leaves that come from a magnolia-related evergreen shrub. Quality varies according to the soil, climate and altitude in which the shrub is grown and the age and size of the leaves when they are picked.

There are seven basic types of tea:

- **Black tea** derives its amber color and aromatic flavor from a special processing treatment in which the leaves are allowed to ferment. The leaves are then processed to preserve the oils in the tea.
- **Blended tea** is a combination of many grades of teas from many countries and tea estates. Some of the best known are Earl Grey, English breakfast, Russian-style and spiced blends.
- **Green tea**, the favorite of the eastern countries of the world, is pale green in color. The flavor is slightly bitter, and the lightest-color leaves produce the best brew.
- **Herb tea** is not a true tea made with tea-shrub leaves but is a tealike drink (also called tisane) made by steeping a mixture of dried herbs, flowers and spices in different combinations in boiling water. Such brews, such as lemon balm, chamomile and tansy, have long been used for medicinal purposes. Although herb teas are sometimes found in supermarkets, health-food stores usually offer the largest variety.
- **Instant tea** is quickly dissolved in either hot or cold water and is made by brewing tea and evaporating the water. It can be purchased unsweetened, sweetened (with sugar or sweetener) and flavored (with flavorings such as

lemon, peach and cinnamon). Prepare instant tea as directed on the jar.

- **Oolong tea** is partially fermented and is a cross between green and black teas. It is amber in color.
- **Specialty tea** is flavored with additions of spices or flowers, such as jasmine, chrysanthemum blossoms and orange or lemon peel.

How to Make Tea

Whether you use loose tea or tea bags, the preparation method is the same:

1. Start with a spotlessly clean teapot made of glass, china or earthenware. Add rapidly boiling water, and allow to stand a few minutes to "hot the pot." Pour out just before brewing the tea.

2. Heat cold water to a full rolling boil. (Use water from the cold-water tap; water from the hot-water tap may contain mineral deposits from water pipes that can affect the flavor of the tea.)

3. Add tea to the warm pot, allowing 1 teaspoon of loose tea or 1 tea bag for each cup of tea. Pour boiling water over the tea (3/4 cup for each cup of tea); let stand 3 to 5 minutes to bring out the full flavor. Stir the tea once to ensure uniform strength. Do not judge the strength of tea by its color; you must taste it. Strain the tea or remove tea bags. Serve with sugar and milk or lemon if desired.

Iced Tea

Iced tea has been enjoyed by many people over the years. It is a refreshing summer beverage to prepare ahead and have available in the refrigerator. To prevent cloudy iced tea, cool the hot, brewed tea to room temperature before refrigerating it.

- To serve iced tea immediately, prepare tea as directed above except double the amount of tea. Strain tea while pouring over ice in pitcher or into ice-filled glasses.
- Iced tea can be prepared by steeping in the refrigerator. Use 2 teaspoons loose tea or 2 tea bags for each cup of cold water. Place tea in glass container; add water. Cover and refrigerator at least 24 hours. Serve over crushed ice.
- Herb and specialty teas can be used to make a flavorful glass of iced tea.
- Add crushed fresh mint leaves to iced tea for a refreshing drink.
- Sugar, sweetener or honey can be added.
- Make ice cubes from brewed tea so the ice doesn't dilute the flavor.
- Tea that has been steeped too long or refrigerated hot will become cloudy. Pour a small amount of boiling water into tea to make it clear.

Punches

Just about any beverage can be served as a punch. Small amounts (about 1/2 cup) make an average serving. Punches are usually served in a punch bowl, crystal, crockery, or whatever you have on hand.

- Chill all ingredients for cold punches before mixing. Fruit juices and spices may be mixed ahead and refrigerated, but soft drinks and alcohol should be added just before serving. An ice ring in a punch bowl will last longer than ice cubes—be sure the size of the ice ring will fit the punch bowl. To keep a rich flavor and not dilute the punch, make the ice ring from the same juices that are in the punch, adding colorful fruits if desired.
- For hot punches, be sure the punch bowl is heat-resistant, and warm it by rinsing with hot water before adding the punch. Hot punches also can be served in an attractive saucepan right from the stove or in a fondue pot, chafing dish or slow cooker.

Hot Spiced Cider

PREP: 5 min; COOK: 20 min
Makes 6 servings, about 1 cup each

Invite guests into the kitchen and let them ladle their own cider right from the stovetop. Keep cider warm over a low heat until you are ready to serve.

> 6 cups apple cider
> 1/2 teaspoon whole cloves
> 1/4 teaspoon ground nutmeg
> 3 sticks cinnamon

1. Heat all ingredients to boiling in 3-quart saucepan over medium-high heat; reduce heat to low. Simmer uncovered 10 minutes.

2. Strain cider mixture to remove cloves and cinnamon if desired. Serve hot.

1 CUP: Calories 115 (Calories from Fat 0); Fat 0g (Saturated 0g); Cholesterol 0mg; Sodium 10mg; Carbohydrate 29g (Dietary Fiber 0g); Protein 0g

HOT BUTTERED RUM-SPICED CIDER: Prepare cider as directed above. For each serving, place 1 tablespoon butter (we do not recommend using margarine or spreads), 1 tablespoon packed brown sugar and 2 tablespoons rum in mug. Fill with hot cider.

Hot Chocolate

PREP: 5 min; COOK: 15 min
Makes 6 servings, about 1 cup each

3 ounces unsweetened baking chocolate
1 1/2 cups water
1/3 cup sugar
Dash of salt
4 1/2 cups milk

1. Heat chocolate and water in 1 1/2-quart saucepan over medium heat, stirring constantly, until chocolate is melted and mixture is smooth.

2. Stir in sugar and salt. Heat to boiling; reduce heat to low. Simmer uncovered 4 minutes, stirring constantly. Stir in milk. Heat just until hot (do not boil because skin will form on top).

3. Beat with hand beater until foamy, or stir until smooth. Serve immediately.

1 CUP: Calories 215 (Calories from Fat 100); Fat 11g (Saturated 7g); Cholesterol 15mg; Sodium 140mg; Carbohydrate 24g (Dietary Fiber 2g); Protein 7g

> **LIGHTER HOT CHOCOLATE**
> For 1 gram of fat and 125 calories, substitute 1/3 cup baking cocoa for the chocolate and use skim milk. Mix cocoa, sugar and salt in saucepan; stir in water. Continue as directed in step 2.

Chocolate Milk Shakes

PREP: 10 min
Makes 2 servings, about 1 cup each

Like to make a malt? Just add about 1 tablespoon natural or flavored instant malt before blending.

3/4 cup milk
1/4 cup chocolate-flavored syrup
3 scoops (1/2 cup each) vanilla ice cream

1. Place milk and syrup in blender. Cover and blend on high speed 2 seconds.

2. Add ice cream. Cover and blend on low speed about 5 seconds or until smooth. Pour into glasses. Serve immediately.

1 CUP: Calories 345 (Calories from Fat 115); Fat 13g (Saturated 8g); Cholesterol 50mg; Sodium 160mg; Carbohydrate 51g (Dietary Fiber 1g); Protein 7g

BERRY MILK SHAKES: Substitute strawberry or cherry ice-cream topping or frozen strawberries or raspberries in syrup, thawed, for the chocolate-flavored syrup.

> **LIGHTER CHOCOLATE MILK SHAKES**
> For 1 gram of fat and 275 calories, use skim milk and substitute fat-free frozen yogurt for the ice cream.

Berry Milk Shake, Cranberry-Apple Spritzer

Sparkling Raspberry Tea

PREP: 5 min
Makes 6 servings, about 1 cup each

(photograph on page 17)

> 2 cups cold brewed tea (page 33)
> 2 cups raspberry or cranberry-raspberry
> juice, chilled
> 2 cups sparkling water, chilled

Mix all ingredients. Serve over ice. Garnish with raspberries, lime or lemon slices and fresh mint if desired.

1 CUP: Calories 45 (Calories from Fat 0); Fat 0g (Saturated 0g); Cholesterol 0mg; Sodium 20mg; Carbohydrate 12g (Dietary Fiber 1g); Protein 0g

> **TIMESAVING TIP**
> Substitute instant tea dissolved in cold water for the cold brewed tea.

Cranberry-Apple Spritzer

PREP: 5 min
Makes 6 servings, about 3/4 cup each

Try your favorite juice flavors or investigate a more unusual blend such as guava-pineapple in this refreshing mixture of wine and sparkling water.

> 2 cups chilled dry white wine (or
> nonalcoholic) or apple juice
> 1 cup chilled cranberry-apple juice drink
> 1 cup chilled sparkling water

Mix all ingredients. Serve over ice. Garnish with apple slices and fresh mint if desired.

3/4 CUP: Calories 110 (Calories from Fat 0); Fat 0g (Saturated 0g); Cholesterol 0mg; Sodium 10mg; Carbohydrate 9g (Dietary Fiber 1g); Protein 0g

Sangria

PREP: 10 min
Makes 8 servings, about 1/2 cup each

> 2/3 cup lemon juice
> 1/3 cup orange juice
> 1/4 cup sugar
> 1 bottle (750 milliliters) dry red wine (or
> nonalcoholic)

1. Strain juices into half-gallon glass pitcher. Stir sugar into juices until sugar is dissolved.

2. Stir wine into juice mixture. Add ice if desired. Garnish with lemon and orange slices if desired.

1/2 CUP: Calories 95 (Calories from Fat 0); Fat 0g (Saturated 0g); Cholesterol 0mg; Sodium 10mg; Carbohydrate 10g (Dietary Fiber 0g); Protein 0g

Eggnog

PREP: 35 min; CHILL: 2 hr
Makes 10 servings, about 1/2 cup each

When serving eggnog in a buffet or when it will be sitting out for a while, keep it chilled by nesting the punch bowl of eggnog in a larger bowl of ice.

> Soft Custard (below)
> 1 cup whipping (heavy) cream
> 2 tablespoons powdered sugar
> 1/2 teaspoon vanilla
> 1/2 cup rum
> 1 or 2 drops yellow food color, if desired
> Ground nutmeg

1. Prepare Soft Custard.

2. Just before serving, beat whipping cream, powdered sugar and vanilla in chilled medium bowl with electric mixer on high speed until stiff. Gently stir 1 cup of the whipped cream, the rum and food color into custard.

3. Pour custard mixture into small punch bowl. Drop remaining whipped cream in mounds onto custard mixture. Sprinkle with nutmeg. Serve immediately. Refrigerate any remaining eggnog.

Soft Custard

> 3 large eggs, slightly beaten
> 1/3 cup sugar
> Dash of salt
> 2 1/2 cups milk
> 1 teaspoon vanilla

Mix eggs, sugar and salt in heavy 2-quart saucepan. Gradually stir in milk. Cook over medium heat 10 to 15 minutes, stirring constantly, until mixture just coats a metal spoon; remove from heat. Stir in vanilla. Place saucepan in cold water until custard is cool. (If custard curdles, beat vigorously with hand beater until smooth.) Cover and refrigerate at least 2 hours but no longer than 24 hours.

1/2 CUP: Calories 180 (Calories from Fat 90); Fat 10g (Saturated 6g); Cholesterol 95mg; Sodium 85mg; Carbohydrate 12g (Dietary Fiber 0g); Protein 4g

> **LIGHTER EGGNOG**
> For 3 grams of fat and 120 calories, substitute 2 eggs plus 2 egg whites for the 3 eggs and 2 1/4 cups skim milk for the milk in the Soft Custard. Substitute 2 cups frozen (thawed) reduced-fat whipped topping for the beaten whipping cream, powdered sugar and vanilla.

Sparkling Citrus Punch

Lemonade

PREP: 10 min
Makes 6 servings, about 3/4 cup each

Fresh lemons are the best for lemonade, but if none are handy, try frozen lemon juice. However, don't use lemon juice concentrate unless you dilute it first.

> 3 cups water
> 1 cup lemon juice (about 4 lemons)
> 1/2 cup sugar

Mix all ingredients until sugar is dissolved. Serve over ice. Garnish with lemon or orange slices and fresh mint if desired.

3/4 CUP: Calories 75 (Calories from Fat 0); Fat 0g (Saturated 0g); Cholesterol 0mg; Sodium 10mg; Carbohydrate 19g (Dietary Fiber 0g); Protein 0g

LIMEADE: Substitute lime juice (about 10 limes) for the lemon juice and increase sugar to 3/4 cup. Garnish with lime slices and strawberries if desired.

> **TIMESAVING TIP**
> Squeeze juice from lemons when you have time (or when lemons are on sale) and freeze the juice so it's ready to use when you need it.

Sparkling Citrus Punch

PREP: 5 min
Makes 12 servings, about 1/2 cup each

Make an easy ice ring using a ring mold or bundt pan that fits inside your punch bowl. Arrange sliced fruit or berries and mint leaves for color in ring mold. Add water to fill three-fourths full; freeze until solid; unmold. Or with the same technique, use muffin cups to make floating ice disks, which take less time to freeze solid.

> 2 cups cold water
> 1 can (6 ounces) frozen tangerine or orange
>   juice concentrate, thawed
> 1 can (6 ounces) frozen grapefruit juice
>   concentrate, thawed
> 1 bottle (1 liter) sparkling water, chilled

Mix all ingredients in half-gallon glass pitcher. Serve over ice. Garnish with fresh mint and strawberries if desired.

1/2 CUP: Calories 10 (Calories from Fat 0); Fat 0g (Saturated 0g); Cholesterol 0mg; Sodium 15mg; Carbohydrate 3g (Dietary Fiber 0g); Protein 0g

About Quick Breads

Quick breads are fast and easy to make. They range from light and fluffy pancakes to tender, flaky biscuits and moist, rich nut breads. Some quick breads are made from batters while others are made from doughs. The proportions of liquid to flour, fat and eggs create the different quick bread categories, such as muffins, biscuits or pancakes.

Double-acting baking powder, rather than slower-acting yeast, is most often the leavening used in quick breads. It consists of an acid, such as cream of tartar, and an alkali, such as baking soda, which react with one another when liquid is added, and gives off a harmless gas (carbon dioxide). In batter or dough, this gas forms tiny bubbles that expand quickly, creating the structure of the quick bread. This happens twice, once when mixed with wet ingredients and again during baking. To be sure baking powder is always fresh, purchase only a small quantity at a time, and stir it before using.

Pans and Pan Preparation

- Use shiny pans and cookie sheets, which reflect heat, for golden, delicate and tender crusts on muffins, coffee cakes and nut breads.
- Dark pans or pans with dark nonstick coating absorb heat more readily than shiny pans, so watch carefully to be sure foods don't over-brown. Follow manufacturer's directions for both baking and greasing. Many suggest reducing the oven temperature by 25°, and some do not recommend greasing or using nonstick cooking spray at all.
- If using insulated pans, you may need to increase baking times slightly.
- Only the bottoms of pans are usually greased with shortening for muffins and nut breads. This prevents a lip from forming around the edge of the bread.

Mixing Quick Breads

- Follow individual recipes for mixing instructions. Some batters are mixed until smooth, others only until moistened. Overmixing can result in less tender breads.
- We recommend that *stick* margarine or butter be used for quick breads when margarine or butter is specified. Vegetable oil spreads (also in stick form) with *at least* 65% fat can be substituted and the baked result will be satisfactory, although the batter or dough may have a slightly softer consistency.

- We do not recommend using vegetable oil spreads with less than 65% fat, tub margarines or whipped products whether butter, margarine or spreads. Because these products contain more water and less fat, using them can result in poor quality overall (thinner or softer consistency when mixing; less tender or wet and gummy after baking).
- Doughs and batters for the "Lighter" variations usually contain reduced-fat or fat-free ingredients, which result in a different consistency or texture during mixing than you may be used to. Because fat is a flavor carrier, when it is reduced, the amount of flavorings is sometimes increased.

Baking Quick Breads

- For the best circulation of heat, place the oven rack in the center of the oven, unless otherwise directed.
- Ovens vary, so check for doneness at the minimum baking time, and add one- or two-minute intervals before checking again.
- Quick breads are usually removed from their pans to a wire rack to cool immediately or shortly after baking. This gives the bread a drier, crisper surface; if left in the pan, the bread would be steamed and soft.
- To reheat quick breads in the microwave, see Microwave How-To's, page 430.

Preceding page: Blueberry Streusel Muffins (page 40), Cranberry-Orange Streusel Muffins (page 40), Bran-Date Muffins (page 41)

Tips for Muffins

- Grease only the bottoms of muffin cups with shortening for nicely shaped muffins that have no rim around the edge. The ungreased sides give the batter a surface to cling to as it rises during baking, resulting in muffins with nicely rounded tops. Some recipes, however, require greasing the entire cup to prevent sticking. You can eliminate the greasing and make cleanup easier by using paper baking cups.
- Stir in the dry ingredients just until the flour is moistened. The batter should be lumpy. Overmixing can result in a less tender muffin with an uneven texture and a pointed top, instead of a slightly rounded, pebbly top.
- For evenly shaped muffins, use a spring-handled ice-cream scoop when distributing batter among cups. These are sold in different sizes referred to by number (the number of level scoops per quart of ice cream); we recommend number 20 or 24. Wipe off any batter that spills onto the edge of the pan to avoid burning.
- When muffins are done, immediately remove them from the muffin pan. Muffins left to cool in the pan will become soggy from trapped steam. If paper baking cups are used, muffins should lift out easily. Otherwise, loosen the muffins with a knife or metal spatula, then lift them out. Occasionally, a recipe will specify that muffins be left in the pan for a few minutes before removing. This is to allow fragile muffins to set up or to steam the sides a bit so they're easier to release from the pan.

Specialty Muffins

Convert your favorite 12-muffin regular muffin recipe to mini, bakery-style (very large regular muffins), or jumbo muffins, or to regular or jumbo muffin tops, using the guidelines below. When you determine the bake times for your favorite muffin recipes, be sure to write them down for future use.

- There is a wide range in bake times, so check for doneness at the minimum time, then every minute or two until done.
- When making bakery-style muffins with softer, more fluid batters, make ten muffins. Stiffer, thicker batters can be used to make eight bakery-style muffins.
- Muffin batters with large pieces of nuts, fruit or chocolate work better as bakery-style or jumbo muffins because the stir-ins are too large for mini muffins.
- Muffin batters that are very rich work better as mini muffins because a larger muffin may be too much for one serving.
- Muffin top pans often have a dark nonstick surface. Be sure to check the manufacturer's directions to see if reducing the oven temperature by 25° is recommended.

Specialty Muffin Baking Chart

Muffin Size	Muffin Cup Size	Oven Temperature	Bake Time	Yield
Muffins				
Mini	1 3/4 × 1 inch (small)	400°	10 to 17 minutes	24
Bakery-style	2 1/2 × 1 1/4 inches (medium)	400°	20 to 26 minutes	8 to 10
Jumbo	3 1/2 × 1 3/4 inches (large)	375°	25 to 35 minutes	4
Muffin Tops				
Regular	2 3/4 × 3/8 inch	400°	8 to 10 minutes	18
Jumbo	4 × 1/2 inch	400°	15 to 20 minutes	6

Baking with Confidence

Perfect Muffins Are

Golden brown
Slightly rounded
    with bumpy tops
Tender and light
Even-textured with
    medium, round holes
Moist inside
Easy to remove from the pan

Problem	Possible Cause
Pale muffins	• oven too cool
Peaked and smooth tops	• too much mixing
Tough and heavy	• too much flour • too much mixing
Uneven texture with long holes or tunnels	• too much mixing
Dry	• too much flour • oven too hot • baked too long
Sticks to pan or paper liners	• not enough fat
Dark crust but center not done	• muffin pan was dull or dark • oven too hot

Blueberry Streusel Muffins

PREP: 10 min; BAKE: 25 min
Makes 12 muffins

You can make these muffins without the streusel topping if you like—the baking time will be the same. (photograph on page 37)

Streusel Topping (right)
1 cup milk
1/4 cup vegetable oil
1/2 teaspoon vanilla
1 large egg
2 cups all-purpose* or whole wheat flour
1/3 cup sugar
3 teaspoons baking powder
1/2 teaspoon salt
1 cup fresh or canned (drained) blueberries**

1. Heat oven to 400°. Grease bottoms only of 12 medium muffin cups, 2 1/2 × 1 1/4 inches, with shortening, or line with paper baking cups.

2. Prepare Streusel Topping; set aside.

3. Beat milk, oil, vanilla and egg in large bowl. Stir in flour, sugar, baking powder and salt all at once just until flour is moistened (batter will be lumpy). Fold in blueberries. Divide batter evenly among muffin cups. Sprinkle each with about 2 teaspoons topping.

4. Bake 20 to 25 minutes or until golden brown. Immediately remove from pan to wire rack. Serve warm if desired.

Streusel Topping

2 tablespoons firm *stick* margarine or butter***
1/4 cup all-purpose flour
2 tablespoons packed brown sugar
1/4 teaspoon ground cinnamon

Cut margarine into flour, brown sugar and cinnamon in medium bowl, using pastry blender or crisscrossing 2 knives, until crumbly.

If using self-rising flour, omit baking powder and salt.

**3/4 cup frozen (thawed and well drained) blueberries can be substituted for the fresh or canned blueberries.*

***Spreads with at least 65% vegetable oil can be substituted (see page 13).*

1 MUFFIN: Calories 195 (Calories from Fat 70); Fat 8g (Saturated 1g); Cholesterol 20mg; Sodium 250mg; Carbohydrate 29g (Dietary Fiber 1g); Protein 3g

---

LIGHTER BLUEBERRY STREUSEL MUFFINS
For 5 grams of fat and 180 calories per serving, use skim milk and decrease the vegetable oil to 2 tablespoons and add 1/4 cup unsweetened applesauce.

APPLE-CINNAMON STREUSEL MUFFINS: Omit blueberries. Stir in 1 cup shredded apple with the milk. Stir in 1/2 teaspoon ground cinnamon with the flour. Bake 25 to 30 minutes.

CRANBERRY-ORANGE STREUSEL MUFFINS: Omit blueberries. Stir in 1 tablespoon grated orange peel with the milk. Fold 1 cup cranberry halves into batter. Top with Streusel Topping if desired.

Bran-Date Muffins

PREP: 10 min; BAKE: 22 min; COOL: 5 min
Makes 12 muffins

(photograph on page 37)

> 1/2 cup hot water
> 1/4 cup chopped dates
> 1 1/2 cups wheat bran
> 1 cup whole wheat flour
> 1 teaspoon baking powder
> 1/2 teaspoon baking soda
> 1/2 teaspoon salt
> 1/3 cup vegetable oil
> 1 egg
> 1 cup buttermilk
> 1/2 cup chopped dates

1. Pour water over 1/4 cup dates; set aside.

2. Heat oven to 400°. Grease bottoms only of 12 medium muffin cups, 2 1/2 × 1 1/4 inches, with shortening, or line with paper baking cups.

3. Mix wheat bran, flour, baking powder, baking soda and salt in large bowl.

4. Place date-water mixture, the oil and egg in blender or food processor. Cover and blend on medium speed about 1 minute or until smooth. Stir date mixture and buttermilk into flour mixture just until flour is moistened (batter will be lumpy). Gently stir in 1/2 cup dates. Divide batter evenly among muffin cups.

5. Bake 20 to 22 minutes or until toothpick inserted in center comes out clean. Cool muffins in pan 5 minutes; remove from pan to wire rack. Serve warm if desired.

1 MUFFIN: Calories 180 (Calories from Fat 90); Fat 10g (Saturated 2g); Cholesterol 20mg; Sodium 320mg; Carbohydrate 21g (Dietary Fiber 1g); Protein 3g

LIGHTER BRAN-DATE MUFFINS

For 6 grams of fat and 155 calories per serving, substitute fat-free buttermilk for the milk, 1/4 cup fat-free cholesterol-free egg product for the egg and 1/4 cup Prune Sauce (page 344) or prune baby food for 1/4 cup of the oil.

Banana Muffins

PREP: 10 min; BAKE: 15 min; COOL: 5 min
Makes 12 muffins

Ripe bananas freeze well. Mash, adding 1 tablespoon lemon juice for each cup of banana to prevent darkening. For this recipe, freeze in 1 1/4-cup quantities.

> 1 1/4 cups mashed ripe bananas (3 medium)
> 3 tablespoons vegetable oil
> 1 large egg
> 1/3 cup sugar
> 2 cups Bisquick® Original baking mix
> 1/2 cup raisins or chopped nuts, if desired

1. Heat oven to 400°. Grease bottoms only of 12 medium muffin cups, 2 1/2 × 1 1/4 inches, with shortening, or line with paper baking cups.

2. Beat bananas, oil, egg and sugar in large bowl until well blended. Stir in baking mix and raisins just until baking mix is moistened (batter will be lumpy). Divide batter evenly among muffin cups.

3. Bake about 15 minutes or until golden brown. Cool muffins in pan 5 minutes; remove from pan to wire rack. Serve warm if desired.

1 MUFFIN: Calories 165 (Calories from Fat 65); Fat 7g (Saturated 1g); Cholesterol 20mg; Sodium 290mg; Carbohydrate 23g (Dietary Fiber 0g); Protein 2g

LIGHTER BANANA MUFFINS

For 4 grams of fat and 145 calories per serving, increase mashed bananas to 1 1/2 cups, decrease oil to 2 tablespoons, substitute 2 egg whites for the egg and use Bisquick Reduced Fat baking mix.

Tips for Nut Breads

- Grease only the bottoms of loaf pans for fruit or nut breads. The ungreased sides allow the batter to cling while rising during baking, which helps form a gently rounded top. If sides of pan are greased, edges of the loaf may have ridges.
- Chop or shred fruits, vegetables or nuts before you start making the batter. If you prepare the batter and then stop to chop or shred ingredients, the batter may become too stiff.
- To avoid overmixing, mix by hand instead of using an electric mixer.
- A large, lengthwise crack in the thin, tender top crust is typical.
- Cool nut breads completely before slicing to prevent crumbling (preferably, store tightly covered twenty-four hours after cooling). Cut with a sharp, thin-bladed knife, using a light sawing motion.
- After cooling, loaves can be wrapped tightly and refrigerated for one week.

Mini Nut Bread Loaves

Miniloaves or those in unusual shapes make wonderful treats and gifts. Try using miniature loaf pans, muffin pans or small cake molds. Grease the pans as directed, and use the chart at right as a guide for baking.

- Measure the volume of pans by filling them to the top with water, then pouring the water into a measuring cup.
- Let the breads cool for a few minutes, then loosen the edges and carefully remove the breads from the pans. Cool completely on a wire rack.

Mini Nut Bread Loaves Baking Chart

Approximate Pan Size	Amount of Batter	Approximate Bake Time at 350°
1/3 cup	1/4 cup	15 to 20 minutes
1/2 cup	1/3 cup	15 to 20 minutes
2/3 to 3/4 cup	1/2 cup	25 to 35 minutes
1 cup	3/4 cup	35 to 40 minutes

Zucchini Bread, Pumpkin Bread

Zucchini Bread

PREP: 15 min; BAKE: 1 hr
Makes 2 loaves, 24 slices each

3 cups shredded zucchini (3 medium)
1 2/3 cups sugar
2/3 cup vegetable oil
2 teaspoons vanilla
4 large eggs
3 cups all-purpose* or whole wheat flour
2 teaspoons baking soda
1 teaspoon salt
1 teaspoon ground cinnamon
1/2 teaspoon ground cloves
1/2 teaspoon baking powder
1/2 cup coarsely chopped nuts
1/2 cup raisins, if desired

1. Move oven rack to low position so that tops of pans will be in center of oven. Heat oven to 350°. Grease bottoms only of 2 loaf pans, 8 1/2 × 4 1/2 × 2 1/2 inches, or 1 loaf pan, 9 × 5 × 3 inches, with shortening.

2. Mix zucchini, sugar, oil, vanilla and eggs in large bowl. Stir in remaining ingredients. Pour into pans.

3. Bake 8-inch loaves 50 to 60 minutes, 9-inch loaf 1 hour 10 minutes to 1 hour 20 minutes, until toothpick inserted in center comes out clean. Cool 10 minutes in pans on wire rack. Loosen sides of loaves from pans; remove from pans and place top side up on wire rack. Cool completely before slicing. Wrap tightly and store at room temperature up to 4 days, or refrigerate up to 10 days.

If using self-rising flour, omit baking soda, salt and baking powder.

1 SLICE: Calories 95 (Calories from Fat 35); Fat 4g (Saturated 1g); Cholesterol 20mg; Sodium 110mg; Carbohydrate 14g (Dietary Fiber 0g); Protein 1g

---

LIGHTER ZUCCHINI BREAD
For 0 grams of fat and 70 calories per serving, substitute Prune Sauce (page 344) for the oil and 2 eggs plus 4 egg whites for the 4 eggs. Omit nuts.

CRANBERRY BREAD: Substitute fresh or frozen (thawed and drained) cranberries for the zucchini. Add 1/2 cup milk with the oil. Add 2 teaspoons grated lemon or orange peel with the vanilla. Omit cinnamon, cloves and raisins. Bake 60 to 70 minutes.

PUMPKIN BREAD: Substitute 1 can (16 ounces) pumpkin for the zucchini.

Banana Bread

PREP: 15 min; BAKE: 1 hr
Makes 2 loaves, 24 slices each

1 1/4 cups sugar
1/2 cup *stick* margarine or butter, softened*
2 large eggs
1 1/2 cups mashed ripe bananas (3 to 4 medium)
1/2 cup buttermilk
1 teaspoon vanilla
2 1/2 cups all-purpose flour**
1 teaspoon baking soda
1 teaspoon salt
1 cup chopped nuts, if desired

1. Move oven rack to low position so that tops of pans will be in center of oven. Heat oven to 350°. Grease bottoms only of 2 loaf pans, 8 1/2 × 4 1/2 × 2 1/2 inches, or 1 loaf pan, 9 × 5 × 3 inches, with shortening.

2. Mix sugar and margarine in large bowl. Stir in eggs until well blended. Add bananas, buttermilk and vanilla. Beat until smooth. Stir in flour, baking soda and salt just until moistened. Stir in the nuts. Pour into pans.

3. Bake 8-inch loaves about 1 hour, 9-inch loaf about 1 1/4 hours, or until toothpick inserted in center comes out clean. Cool 5 minutes in pans on wire rack. Loosen sides of loaves from pans; remove from pans and place top side up on wire rack. Cool completely before slicing. Wrap tightly and store at room temperature up to 4 days, or refrigerate up to 10 days.

Spreads with at least 65% vegetable oil can be substituted (see page 13).

**If using self-rising flour, omit baking soda and salt.*

1 SLICE: Calories 70 (Calories from Fat 20); Fat 2g (Saturated 1g); Cholesterol 10mg; Sodium 100mg; Carbohydrate 12g (Dietary Fiber 0g); Protein 1g

---

LIGHTER BANANA BREAD
For 1 gram of fat and 65 calories per serving, substitute 1/4 cup unsweetened applesauce for 1/4 cup of the margarine and 1/2 cup fat-free cholesterol-free egg product for the eggs.

DATE-BANANA BREAD: Stir in 1/2 cup chopped dates with the nuts.

Baking with Confidence

Perfect Nut Bread Is

Golden brown,
   rounded top
Lengthwise crack (or
   split) along the top
Thin, tender crust
Moist texture with
   small even holes
Fruits and/or nuts are
   evenly distributed

Problem	Possible Cause
Didn't rise	• too much mixing • check expiration date on leavening
Tough	• too much mixing • not enough fat
Tunnels	• too much mixing
Rims around the edges	• sides of pan were greased
Compact texture	• too much flour • too little leavening

Crumbly	• not cooled com-
	   pletely, cut too
	   soon after baking

Sour Cream Coffee Cake

**PREP: 30 min; BAKE: 1 hr; COOL: 10 min
Makes 16 servings**

   Brown Sugar Filling (right)
   1 1/2 cups sugar
   3/4 cup *stick* margarine or butter, softened*
   1 1/2 teaspoons vanilla
   3 large eggs
   3 cups all-purpose** or whole wheat flour
   1 1/2 teaspoons baking powder
   1 1/2 teaspoons baking soda
   3/4 teaspoon salt
   1 1/2 cups sour cream
   Vanilla Glaze (right)

1. Heat oven to 350°. Grease bottom and side of angel food cake pan (tube pan), 10 × 4 inches, 12-cup bundt cake pan or 2 loaf pans, 9 × 5 × 3 inches, with shortening.

2. Prepare Brown Sugar Filling; set aside.

3. Beat sugar, margarine, vanilla and eggs in large bowl with electric mixer on medium speed 2 minutes, scraping bowl occasionally. Mix flour, baking powder, baking soda and salt. Beat flour mixture and sour cream alternately into sugar mixture on low speed until blended.

4. For angel food or bundt cake pan, spread one-third of the batter (about 2 cups) in pan, then sprinkle with one-third of the filling; repeat twice. For loaf pans, spread one-fourth of the batter (about 1 1/2 cups) in each pan, then sprinkle each with one-fourth of the filling; repeat once.

5. Bake angel food or bundt cake pan about 1 hour, loaf pans about 45 minutes, or until toothpick inserted near center comes out clean. Cool slightly; remove from pan(s) and place top side up on wire rack. Cool 10 minutes. Drizzle with Vanilla Glaze. Serve warm or cool.

Brown Sugar Filling

   1/2 cup packed brown sugar
   1/2 cup finely chopped nuts
   1 1/2 teaspoons ground cinnamon

Mix all ingredients.

Vanilla Glaze

   1/2 cup powdered sugar
   1/4 teaspoon vanilla
   2 to 3 teaspoons milk

Mix all ingredients until smooth and drizzling consistency.

Spreads with at least 65% vegetable oil can be substituted (see page 13).

**If using self-rising flour, omit baking powder, baking soda and salt.*

1 SERVING: Calories 355 (Calories from Fat 145); Fat 16g (Saturated 5g); Cholesterol 55mg; Sodium 390mg; Carbohydrate 49g (Dietary Fiber 1g); Protein 5g

---

LIGHTER SOUR CREAM COFFEE CAKE

For 8 grams of fat and 305 calories per serving, substitute unsweetened applesauce for 1/4 cup of the margarine, increase vanilla in the cake to 2 teaspoons and use fat-free sour cream. This batter may look curdled.

Apple-Oatmeal Coffee Cake

PREP: 25 min; BAKE: 55 min
Makes 9 servings

Oat-Streusel Topping (below)
1 3/4 cups all-purpose flour*
1 cup packed brown sugar
3/4 cup quick-cooking or old-fashioned oats
1/2 cup *stick* margarine or butter, softened**
1 cup buttermilk
3 teaspoons baking powder
1 teaspoon ground cinnamon
1/2 teaspoon baking soda
1/4 teaspoon salt
1/4 teaspoon ground nutmeg
1 large egg
1 1/2 cups chopped apples (2 small)

1. Heat oven to 350°. Grease bottom and sides of square pan, 9 × 9 × 2 inches, with shortening.

2. Prepare Oat-Streusel Topping; set aside.

3. Beat remaining ingredients except apples in large bowl with electric mixer on low speed 30 seconds. Beat on medium speed 2 minutes, scraping bowl occasionally. Stir in apples. Spread batter in pan. Sprinkle with topping.

4. Bake 50 to 55 minutes or until golden brown and toothpick inserted in center comes out clean. Cool on wire rack, or serve warm.

Oat-Streusel Topping

2 tablespoons firm *stick* margarine or butter**
1/4 cup all-purpose flour
2 tablespoons packed brown sugar
1/2 teaspoon ground cinnamon
1/4 cup quick-cooking or old-fashioned oats

Cut margarine into flour, brown sugar and cinnamon in medium bowl, using pastry blender or crisscrossing 2 knives, until crumbly. Stir in oats.

If using self-rising flour, omit baking powder, baking soda and salt.

**Spreads with at least 65% vegetable oil can be substituted (see page 13).*

1 SERVING: Calories 380 (Calories from Fat 125); Fat 14g (Saturated 3g); Cholesterol 25mg; Sodium 490mg; Carbohydrate 59g (Dietary Fiber 2g); Protein 6g

---

LIGHTER APPLE-OATMEAL COFFEE CAKE

For 9 grams of fat and 335 calories per serving, decrease margarine to 1/4 cup; add 1/4 cup unsweetened applesauce and 1/4 cup fat-free cholesterol-free egg product for the egg. Use fat-free buttermilk..

Raspberry-Marzipan Coffee Cake

PREP: 20 min; BAKE: 50 min
Makes 12 servings

Almond Streusel (below)
2 cups all-purpose flour*
3/4 cup sugar
1/4 cup *stick* margarine or butter, softened**
1 cup milk
2 teaspoons baking powder
1 teaspoon vanilla
1/2 teaspoon salt
1 large egg
1/2 package (about 8-ounce size) almond paste, finely chopped
1 cup fresh or unsweetened frozen (thawed and drained) raspberries

1. Heat oven to 350°. Grease bottom and sides of square pan, 9 × 9 × 2 inches, with shortening.

2. Prepare Almond Streusel; set aside.

3. Beat remaining ingredients except almond paste and raspberries in medium bowl with electric mixer on low speed 30 seconds. Beat on medium speed 2 minutes, scraping bowl occasionally.

4. Spread half of the batter in pan. Sprinkle with half each of the almond paste, raspberries and Streusel. Repeat with remaining batter, almond paste, raspberries and Streusel.

5. Bake about 50 minutes or until toothpick inserted in center comes out clean.

Almond Streusel

1/4 cup firm *stick* margarine or butter**
1/3 cup all-purpose flour
1/4 cup sugar
1/3 cup slivered almonds

Cut margarine into flour and sugar in medium bowl, using pastry blender or crisscrossing 2 knives, until crumbly. Stir in almonds.

If using self-rising flour, omit baking powder and salt.

**Spreads with at least 65% vegetable oil can be substituted (see page 13).*

1 SERVING: Calories 290 (Calories from Fat 110); Fat 12g (Saturated 2g); Cholesterol 20mg; Sodium 280mg; Carbohydrate 43g (Dietary Fiber 2g); Protein 5g

RASPBERRY-CHOCOLATE COFFEE CAKE: Substitute 1 package (6 ounces) semisweet chocolate chips for the almond paste.

Tips for Biscuits

- When making biscuits, cut in shortening or other fat by using a pastry blender, crisscrossing 2 table knives, using the side of a fork or cutting with a wire whisk. "Cutting in" results in cutting the shortening into tiny lumps that will produce a flaky texture throughout the biscuits as the shortening melts during baking.
- Roll or pat biscuit dough to an even thickness for attractive biscuits and even baking. A clever way to roll dough evenly is between two wooden sticks that are 1/2 inch high and 14 inches long. Anyone who works with wood can make a pair. See photo 3, How to Make Biscuits, below.
- Cut the dough with a biscuit cutter dipped into flour. Cut the biscuits out of the dough as close together as possible. Push the cutter straight down into the dough—twisting as you cut will result in uneven biscuits.
- If a biscuit cutter is not available, cut biscuits with an opened 6-ounce juice can or other narrow can or glass dipped into flour. Or use cookie cutters to make fun shapes.
- After cutting as many biscuits as possible, press the scraps of dough together lightly, but do not knead. Roll or pat the remaining dough to 1/2-inch thickness and cut. These biscuits will have a slightly uneven appearance.

How to Make Biscuits

1. Cut shortening into flour mixture until the mixture resembles fine crumbs.

2. Stir in enough milk until dough leaves side of bowl (dough will be soft).

3. Roll or pat the dough 1/2-inch thick. Cut with floured 2 1/2-inch round cutter.

Baking Powder Biscuits

PREP: 10 min; BAKE: 12 min
Makes 12 biscuits

Add a bit of extra flavor to your biscuits by stirring in 2 teaspoons chopped fresh or 3/4 teaspoon dried dill weed or basil with the flour.

> 1/2 cup shortening
> 2 cups all-purpose flour*
> 1 tablespoon sugar
> 3 teaspoons baking powder
> 1 teaspoon salt
> 3/4 cup milk

1. Heat oven to 450°.

2. Cut shortening into flour, sugar, baking powder and salt in medium bowl, using pastry blender or crisscrossing 2 knives, until mixture looks like fine crumbs.

Stir in milk until dough leaves side of bowl (dough will be soft and sticky).

3. Turn dough onto lightly floured surface. Knead lightly 10 times. Roll or pat 1/2 inch thick. Cut with floured 2 1/2-inch round cutter. Place on ungreased cookie sheet about 1 inch apart for crusty sides, touching for soft sides.

4. Bake 10 to 12 minutes or until golden brown. *Immediately* remove from cookie sheet. Serve warm.

If using self-rising flour, omit baking powder and salt.

1 BISCUIT: Calories 160 (Calories from Fat 80); Fat 9g (Saturated 2g); Cholesterol 5mg; Sodium 310mg; Carbohydrate 18g (Dietary Fiber 0g); Protein 2g

BUTTERMILK BISCUITS: Decrease baking powder to 2 teaspoons and add 1/4 teaspoon baking soda with the sugar. Substitute buttermilk for the milk. (If buttermilk is thick, it may be necessary to add slightly more than 3/4 cup.)

DROP BISCUITS: Increase milk to 1 cup. Drop dough by 12 spoonfuls onto cookie sheet greased with shortening.

Baking with Confidence

Perfect Baking Powder Biscuits Are

Light golden brown
  outside
High with fairly
  smooth, level tops
Tender and light
Flaky and slightly
  moist inside

Problem	Possible Cause
Not high	• too little baking powder • too much mixing • too hot oven
Dark bottom crust	• baking sheet was dull dull or dark, not shiny • oven rack placed too low in oven
Tough	• too little baking powder • too much mixing • too hot oven
Not flaky	• too little shortening • too much mixing • too little kneading

Easy Garlic-Cheese Biscuits

PREP: 10 min; BAKE: 10 min
Makes 10 to 12 biscuits

These melt-in-your-mouth biscuits are especially good with a crisp tossed salad or bowl of soup. The next time you make them, experiment with a different cheese, such as smoky Cheddar or pizza mozzarella. (photograph on page 366)

> 2 cups Bisquick Original baking mix
> 2/3 cup milk
> 1/2 cup shredded Cheddar cheese (2 ounces)
> 1/4 cup *stick* margarine or butter, melted*
> 1/4 teaspoon garlic powder

1. Heat oven to 450°.

2. Mix baking mix, milk and cheese to make a soft dough. Beat vigorously 30 seconds. Drop dough by 10 to 12 spoonfuls onto ungreased cookie sheet.

3. Bake 8 to 10 minutes or until golden brown. Mix margarine and garlic powder; brush on warm biscuits before removing from cookie sheet. Serve warm.

Spreads with at least 65% vegetable oil can be substituted (see page 13).

1 BISCUIT: Calories 160 (Calories from Fat 90); Fat 10g (Saturated 3g); Cholesterol 10mg; Sodium 440mg; Carbohydrate 15g (Dietary Fiber 0g); Protein 3g

EASY HERBED-CHEESE BISCUITS: Mix 3/4 teaspoon dried dill weed, crushed rosemary leaves or Italian seasoning with the baking mix.

Spicy Fruit-Oat Scones, Overnight Danish Twists (page 64)

Lemon-Oat Scones

PREP: 15 min; BAKE: 12 min
Makes about 15 scones

Dried blueberries, cherries or cranberries used in place of the raisins give these scones seasonal appeal.

   1/3 cup firm *stick* margarine or butter*
   1 1/4 cups all-purpose** or whole wheat flour
   1/2 cup quick-cooking oats
   3 tablespoons sugar
   2 1/2 teaspoons baking powder
   2 teaspoons grated lemon peel
   1/4 teaspoon salt
   1 large egg, beaten
   1/2 cup raisins or currants
   4 to 6 tablespoons half-and-half
   1 large egg, beaten

1. Heat oven to 400°.

2. Cut margarine into flour, oats, sugar, baking powder, lemon peel and salt in medium bowl, using pastry blender or crisscrossing 2 knives, until mixture looks like fine crumbs. Stir in 1 egg, the raisins and just enough half-and-half so dough leaves side of bowl.

3. Turn dough onto lightly floured surface. Knead lightly 10 times. Roll or pat 1/2 inch thick and cut with floured biscuit cutter, or pat into 1/2-inch-thick rectangle and cut into diamond shapes with sharp knife. Place on ungreased cookie sheet. Brush dough with beaten egg.

4. Bake 10 to 12 minutes or until golden brown. *Immediately* remove from cookie sheet to wire rack. Serve warm if desired.

*Spreads with at least 65% vegetable oil can be substituted (see page 13).

**If using self-rising flour, omit baking powder and salt.

1 SCONE: Calories 115 (Calories from Fat 45); Fat 5g (Saturated 1g); Cholesterol 30mg; Sodium 170mg; Carbohydrate 17g (Dietary Fiber 1g); Protein 2g

SPICY FRUIT-OAT SCONES: Omit lemon peel. Add 3/4 teaspoon ground cinnamon and 1/8 teaspoon ground cloves with the sugar. Substitute 1/2 cup diced dried fruit and raisin mixture for the raisins.

Tips for Pancakes and French Toast

- Heat the griddle or skillet on medium heat or set at 375° about 10 minutes before cooking pancakes or French toast. The griddle will be evenly heated, ensuring more evenly browned foods.
- Because pan materials and thicknesses vary, as do cooktops, adjust heat as necessary.
- Mix pancake batter right in a 4- or 8-cup glass measure with a handle and spout, which makes for easy pouring onto the griddle.
- Turn pancakes as soon as they are puffed and just as the bubbles begin to break. The second side never browns as evenly as the first.
- Serve pancakes and French toast immediately, or keep them warm in a single layer on a wire rack or towel-lined cookie sheet in a 200° oven. Stacking while keeping them warm will produce steam that can make pancakes and French toast soggy.

Pancakes

PREP: 5 min; COOK: 10 min
Makes nine 4-inch pancakes

1 large egg
1 cup all-purpose* or whole wheat flour
3/4 cup milk
1 tablespoon granulated or packed brown sugar
2 tablespoons vegetable oil
3 teaspoons baking powder
1/4 teaspoon salt
Margarine or shortening

1. Beat egg in medium bowl with hand beater until fluffy. Beat in remaining ingredients except margarine just until smooth. For thinner pancakes, stir in additional 1 to 2 tablespoons milk.

2. Heat griddle or skillet over medium heat or to 375°. Grease griddle with margarine if necessary. (To test griddle, sprinkle with a few drops of water. If bubbles jump around, heat is just right.)

3. For each pancake, pour slightly less than 1/4 cup batter from cup or pitcher onto hot griddle. Cook pancake until puffed and dry around edges. Turn and cook other side until golden brown.

If using self-rising flour, omit baking powder and salt.

1 PANCAKE: Calories 100 (Calories from Fat 35); Fat 4g (Saturated 1g); Cholesterol 25mg; Sodium 240mg; Carbohydrate 13g (Dietary Fiber 0g); Protein 3g

BERRY PANCAKES: Stir 1/2 cup fresh or frozen (thawed and well drained) blackberries, blueberries or raspberries into batter.

BUTTERMILK PANCAKES: Substitute 1 cup buttermilk for the 3/4 cup milk. Decrease baking powder to 1 teaspoon and beat in 1/2 teaspoon baking soda.

CRUNCHY PANCAKES: Stir 1/2 cup coarsely chopped trail mix or chopped nuts into batter.

French Toast

PREP: 5 min; COOK: 16 min
Makes 8 slices

To make ahead, arrange dipped bread in rectangular baking dish, 13 × 9 × 2 inches, overlapping edges slightly. Drizzle any remaining egg mixture over bread. Cover and refrigerate overnight. Cook in skillet or bake on cookie sheet.

3 eggs
3/4 cup milk
1 tablespoon sugar
1/4 teaspoon vanilla
1/8 teaspoon salt
8 slices sandwich bread or 1-inch-thick slices French bread

1. Beat eggs, milk, sugar, vanilla and salt with hand beater until smooth.

2. Heat griddle or skillet over medium-low heat or to 375°. Grease griddle with margarine if necessary. (To test griddle, sprinkle with a few drops water. If bubbles jump around, heat is just right.)

3. Dip bread into egg mixture. Place on griddle. Cook about 4 minutes on each side or until golden brown.

1 SLICE: Calories 105 (Calories from Fat 25); Fat 3g (Saturated 1g); Cholesterol 80mg; Sodium 200mg; Carbohydrate 15g (Dietary Fiber 0g); Protein 5g

---

LIGHTER FRENCH TOAST

For 2 grams of fat and 95 calories per serving, substitute 1 egg and 2 egg whites for the 3 eggs and use 2/3 cup skim milk. Increase vanilla to 1/2 teaspoon.

OVEN FRENCH TOAST: Heat oven to 500°. Generously butter jelly roll pan, 15 1/2 × 10 1/2 × 1 inch. Heat pan in oven 1 minute; remove from oven. Arrange dipped bread in hot pan. Drizzle any remaining egg mixture over bread. Bake 5 to 8 minutes or until bottoms are golden brown; turn bread. Bake 2 to 4 minutes longer or until golden brown.

Apple Oven Pancake

Puffy Oven Pancake

PREP: 10 min; BAKE: 30 min
Makes 2 to 4 servings

This fun pancake is German in origin. When it's baked it puffs into an incredible shell shape. The Triple Berry Filling (page 90) is another delicious way to top this special treat.

> 2 tablespoons *stick* margarine or butter*
> 2 large eggs
> 1/2 cup all-purpose flour**
> 1/2 cup milk
> 1/4 teaspoon salt
> Lemon juice and powdered sugar or cut-up
>   fruit, if desired

1. Heat oven to 400°. Melt margarine in pie plate, 9 × 1 1/4 inches, in oven; brush margarine on side of pie plate.

2. Beat eggs slightly in medium bowl with wire whisk or hand beater. Beat in remaining ingredients except lemon juice just until mixed (do not overbeat). Pour into pie plate.

3. Bake 25 to 30 minutes or until puffy and deep golden brown. Serve immediately sprinkled with lemon juice and powdered sugar.

*Spreads with at least 65% vegetable oil can be substituted (see page 13).

**Do not use self-rising flour in this recipe.

1 SERVING: Calories 315 (Calories from Fat 160); Fat 18g (Saturated 5g); Cholesterol 215mg; Sodium 490mg; Carbohydrate 28g (Dietary Fiber 1g); Protein 11g

APPLE OVEN PANCAKE: Prepare Puffy Oven Pancake as directed—except sprinkle 2 tablespoons packed brown sugar and 1/4 teaspoon ground cinnamon evenly over melted margarine in pie plate. Arrange 1 cup thinly sliced peeled baking apple (1 medium) over sugar. Pour batter over apple. Bake 30 to 35 minutes. *Immediately* loosen edge of pancake and turn upside down onto heatproof serving plate.

Dumplings

PREP: 10 min; COOK: 20 min
Makes 10 dumplings

Dumplings added to stews are especially welcome in cold and dreary weather. See Beef Stew, page 366, or use this recipe for the dumplings in Chicken and Dumplings, page 367, if you don't have baking mix on hand.

    3 tablespoons shortening
    1 1/2 cups all-purpose flour*
    1 tablespoon dried parsley flakes, if desired
    2 teaspoons baking powder
    1/2 teaspoon salt
    3/4 cup milk

1. Cut shortening into flour, parsley, baking powder and salt in medium bowl, using pastry blender or crisscrossing 2 knives, until mixture looks like fine crumbs. Stir in milk.

2. Drop dough by 10 spoonfuls onto hot meat or vegetables in boiling stew (do not drop directly into liquid). Cook uncovered 10 minutes. Cover and cook 10 minutes longer.

If using self-rising flour, omit baking powder and salt.

1 DUMPLING: Calories 105 (Calories from Fat 35); Fat 4g (Saturated 1g); Cholesterol 5mg; Sodium 210mg; Carbohydrate 15g (Dietary Fiber 0g); Protein 2g

HERB DUMPLINGS: Substitute 2 teaspoons chopped fresh or 1 teaspoon dried herbs (such as basil, sage or thyme leaves or celery seed) for the parsley.

Popovers

PREP: 10 min; BAKE: 40 min
Makes 6 popovers

To freeze up to three months, pierce each baked popover with the point of a knife to let the steam out, and cool completely on wire rack. Freeze on a cookie sheet, then seal airtight in a freezer bag. When ready to serve, heat popovers on cookie sheet in 350° oven about 10 minutes or until piping hot.

    2 eggs
    1 cup all-purpose flour*
    1 cup milk
    1/2 teaspoon salt

1. Heat oven to 450°. Generously grease 6-cup popover pan or six 6-ounce custard cups with shortening. Set aside.

2. Beat eggs slightly in medium bowl. Beat in remaining ingredients just until smooth (do not overbeat). Fill cups about 1/2 full.

3. Bake 20 minutes.

4. Reduce oven temperature to 350°. Bake about 20 minutes longer or until deep golden brown. *Immediately* remove from cups. Serve hot.

Do not use self-rising flour in this recipe.

1 POPOVER: Calories 120 (Calories from Fat 25); Fat 3g (Saturated 1g); Cholesterol 75mg; Sodium 220mg; Carbohydrate 18g (Dietary Fiber 0g); Protein 5g

---

LIGHTER POPOVERS
For 1 gram of fat and 100 calories per serving, substitute 1 egg plus 2 egg whites for the 2 eggs and use skim milk.

Waffles

PREP: 5 min; BAKE: 15 min
Makes six 7-inch round waffles

Also called waffle bakers or waffle makers, waffle irons are available in quite a variety of shapes and sizes, which will determine how much batter is needed for each waffle. (photograph on page 361)

    2 large eggs
    2 cups all-purpose* or whole wheat flour
    1 3/4 cups milk
    1/2 cup vegetable oil**
    1 tablespoon granulated or brown sugar
    4 teaspoons baking powder
    1/4 teaspoon salt

1. Heat waffle iron.

2. Beat eggs in large bowl with hand beater until fluffy. Beat in remaining ingredients just until smooth.

3. Pour a scant 2/3 cup batter from cup or pitcher onto center of hot waffle iron. (Check manufacturer's directions for recommended amount of batter.) Close lid of waffle iron.

4. Bake about 5 minutes or until steaming stops. Carefully remove waffle. Serve immediately. Repeat with remaining batter.

If using self-rising flour, omit baking powder and salt.

****1/2 cup margarine or butter, melted, can be substituted for the oil.*

1 WAFFLE SQUARE: Calories 380 (Calories from Fat 200); Fat 22g (Saturated 4g); Cholesterol 80mg; Sodium 480mg; Carbohydrate 38g (Dietary Fiber 0g); Protein 8g

---

LIGHTER WAFFLES
For 2 grams of fat and 210 calories per serving, substitute 1 egg plus 2 egg whites for the 2 eggs and 1/4 cup unsweetened applesauce for 1/4 cup of the oil.

NUT WAFFLES: For each waffle, pour batter onto center of hot waffle iron. *Immediately* sprinkle with about 2 tablespoons coarsely chopped or broken nuts for each 7-inch waffle.

Corn Bread

PREP: 10 min; BAKE: 25 min
Makes 12 servings

This corn bread is sweeter and lighter in texture than the Southern Buttermilk Corn Bread recipe that follows. Choose the one that best suits your taste.

    1 cup milk
    1/4 cup *stick* margarine or butter, melted*
    1 large egg
    1 1/4 cups yellow, white or blue cornmeal
    1 cup all-purpose flour**
    1/2 cup sugar
    1 tablespoon baking powder
    1/2 teaspoon salt

1. Heat oven to 400°. Grease bottom and side of round pan, 9 × 1 1/2 inches, or square pan, 8 × 8 × 2 inches, with shortening.

2. Beat milk, margarine and egg in large bowl. Stir in remaining ingredients all at once just until flour is moistened (batter will be lumpy). Pour batter into pan.

3. Bake 20 to 25 minutes or until golden brown and toothpick inserted in center comes out clean.

*Spreads with at least 65% vegetable oil can be substituted (see page 13).

**If using self-rising flour, omit baking powder and salt.

1 SERVING: Calories 170 (Calories from Fat 45); Fat 5g (Saturated 1g); Cholesterol 20mg; Sodium 270mg; Carbohydrate 29g (Dietary Fiber 1g); Protein 3g

CORN MUFFINS: Grease bottoms only of 12 medium muffin cups, 2 1/2 × 1 1/4 inches, with shortening, or line with paper baking cups. Fill about 3/4 full.

TIMESAVING TIP
To get a head start, measure the dry ingredients into a plastic bag or a bowl, then seal or cover, so they're ready when needed.

Southern Buttermilk Corn Bread

PREP: 10 min; BAKE: 30 min
Makes 12 servings

(photograph on page 190)

    1 1/2 cups yellow, white or blue cornmeal
    1/2 cup all-purpose flour*
    1 1/2 cups buttermilk
    1/4 cup vegetable oil or shortening
    2 teaspoons baking powder
    1 teaspoon sugar
    1 teaspoon salt
    1/2 teaspoon baking soda
    2 large eggs

1. Heat oven to 450°. Grease bottom and side of round pan, 9 × 1 1/2 inches, square pan, 8 × 8 × 2 inches, or 10-inch ovenproof skillet with shortening.

2. Mix all ingredients. Beat vigorously 30 seconds. Pour batter into pan.

3. Bake round or square pan 25 to 30 minutes, skillet about 20 minutes, or until golden brown. Serve warm.

*If using self-rising flour, decrease baking powder to 1 teaspoon and omit salt.

1 SERVING: Calories 145 (Calories from Fat 55); Fat 6g (Saturated 1g); Cholesterol 35mg; Sodium 350mg; Carbohydrate 20g (Dietary Fiber 1g); Protein 4g

---

LIGHTER SOUTHERN BUTTERMILK CORN BREAD
For 3 grams of fat and 120 calories per serving, use fat-free buttermilk, decrease oil to 2 tablespoons and substitute 1/2 cup fat-free cholesterol-free egg product for the eggs.

CHEESY MEXICAN CORN BREAD: Decrease buttermilk to 1 cup. Stir in 1 can (about 8 ounces) cream-style corn, 1 can (4 ounces) chopped green chiles, well drained, 1/2 cup shredded Monterey Jack or Cheddar cheese (2 ounces) and 1 teaspoon chili powder.

CORN STICKS: Grease 18 corn stick pans with shortening. Fill about 7/8 full. Bake 12 to 15 minutes. Makes 18 corn sticks.

About Yeast Breads

Almost nothing smells as wonderful or is more tempting than bread fresh and warm from the oven! Yeast breads require some rising time, but the final results are definitely worth the wait. Sample delicious kneaded breads, biscuits, coffee cakes, sweet rolls and more—these breads rise to any occasion!

Pans and Pan Preparation

- Use loaf pans of anodized aluminum, darkened metal or glass for bread with well-browned crusts. If using pans with dark nonstick coating, watch carefully so bread doesn't overbrown. Follow manufacturer's directions, because reducing the oven temperature by 25° is often recommended.
- Use shiny cookie sheets and muffin cups, which reflect heat, for tender, golden brown crusts on rolls and sweet rolls.

Ingredients

When mixed together, kneaded and baked, these basic ingredients provide a variety of breads.

Flour: All-purpose flour is the most widely used flour. The amount of protein in flour varies with the wheat crop, as does the moisture within the flour itself. This is why most kneaded dough recipes give a range of amount of flour. Also see Flour, page 14.

Yeast: Yeast is a live plant that gives off a gas that makes dough rise. It is very sensitive—too much heat will kill it, but cold will stunt its growth. Always check the expiration date on the yeast before using.

Most of the recipes follow the "quick-mix" method of mixing the yeast with part of the flour, then beating in very warm liquid (120° to 130°). Some recipes, however, yield better results by the traditional method of dissolving the yeast in warm water (105° to 115°). The water temperature is higher for the quick-mix method as the flour and other ingredients dilute the yeast.

If using quick active dry yeast, you can omit the first rising, if desired. After kneading, cover the dough and let it rest 10 minutes before continuing with the next step.

Be sure you correctly follow the temperatures for liquids stated in each recipe, because using the wrong temperature for either method will give poor results. Also see Yeast, page 15.

Liquids: Water and milk are the most commonly used liquids. Water gives bread a crispier crust; milk, a velvety texture and added nutrients.

Sweeteners: Sugar, honey and molasses provide "food" for the yeast to help it grow, enhance flavor and help brown the crust. Do not use artificial sweeteners because they do not properly "feed" the yeast.

Salt: Salt is a flavoring needed to control yeast growth and prevent overrising, which can cause bread to collapse. If salt is reduced, decrease both rising times.

Fat: Margarine, butter, shortening or vegetable oil is added to contribute tenderness and flavor.

Eggs: Eggs are sometimes added for flavor, richness and color.

Baking Yeast Breads

- Stagger loaf pans on a lower oven rack so they do not touch the sides of the oven or each other. The top of each pan should be level with, or slightly above, the middle of the oven.
- If baking round loaves on a cookie sheet, place the sheet on a rack in the center of the oven.
- Determine the doneness by tapping the crust. The loaf will have a hollow sound when done.
- Remove loaves from pans immediately so the sides remain crusty, and place on wire racks away from drafts to cool.
- For a shiny, soft crust, brush just-baked bread with margarine, butter or shortening.

Cutting Bread

- Cut into slices with a serrated bread knife or an electric knife on a cutting board or other surface designed for cutting.
- If bread is very fresh or warm, turn the loaf on its side to avoid squashing the top.
- Bread can be cut into fun shapes such as wedges (round loaves) or from slices, cut into fingers. Use cookie cutters for special shapes— leftover pieces can be used in Croutons (page 9) or Bread Pudding with Whiskey Sauce (page 152).

Storing Bread

- Breads and rolls can be stored in airtight containers in a cool, dry place up to five days. Refrigerate only in hot, humid weather.
- Breads can be stored tightly wrapped in moistureproof or vaporproof material, labeled and dated, in the freezer for up to three months. To thaw, let stand wrapped at room temperature for two to three hours.

How to Mix Yeast Dough

1. After the first addition of flour has been beaten in, the dough will be very soft and fall in "sheets" off rubber spatula.

2. The second addition of flour makes the dough stiff enough to knead. Mix in only enough flour so dough leaves side of the bowl.

3. To knead, fold dough toward you. With heels of your hands, push the dough away from you with short rocking motions. Give dough a quarter turn; repeat.

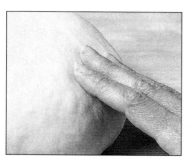

4. When the dough is properly kneaded, it will feel elastic and the top will be smooth with some blisters appearing on the surface.

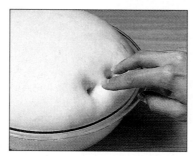

5. Dough should rise until double. Test by pressing fingertips 1/2 inch into dough. If the impression remains, the dough has risen enough.

6. Punch down center of dough with your fist. Fold dough over and form into a ball. This releases large air bubbles to produce a finer texture.

Types of Yeast Doughs

There are two kinds of yeast doughs: batter and kneaded. Batter breads are shortcut, no-knead yeast breads. Kneaded breads require more time to prepare, as well as energy for kneading the dough. Both kinds need to rise before shaping and baking to allow the yeast to activate. To let dough rise, cover and keep in a warm, draft-free place. If necessary, place the covered bowl of dough on a wire rack over a bowl of warm water.

Batter dough: Because less flour is used than for kneaded dough, batter dough is stickier and instead of being kneaded, is beaten with an electric mixer with the first addition of flour. The batter is generally not shaped but is spread in the pan. There is usually only one rising time. Batter bread has a coarser texture than kneaded bread and has a pebbled surface.

Kneaded dough: Kneading develops the gluten and results in even texture and a smooth, rounded top. If dough is not sufficiently kneaded, the bread will be coarse, heavy, crumbly and dry. To knead, follow the directions in How to Mix Yeast Dough (above).

A standard countertop electric mixer with a dough-hook attachment mixes dough enough for satisfactory loaves of bread, although the loaves may have slightly less volume than those kneaded by hand. A heavy-duty mixer yields loaves of higher volumes. Be sure to follow manufacturer's directions for the size of recipe the mixer can handle, as well as mixing time.

Shaping Dough

Shaping the perfect loaf of bread can be achieved by several methods. We find the method in How to Shape Yeast Bread Loaves (below) one of the best. This method is used in Traditional White Bread (page 56) and Honey-Whole Wheat Bread (page 59).

As an alternate shaping method, you may wish to try the following: Flatten each half of the dough with your hands or a rolling pin into a rectangle, 18 × 9 inches. Fold rectangle crosswise into thirds, overlapping the two sides. Flatten or roll into a 9-inch square. Roll dough up tightly, beginning at one of the open (unfolded) ends, to form a loaf; press with thumbs to seal after each turn. Pinch edge of dough firmly into roll to seal. Press each end of the roll with side of hand to seal; fold ends under loaf. This shaping method is not recommended for Cinnamon-Raisin Bread (page 56) because when cut, the bread would not have an even, spiral appearance.

How to Shape Yeast Bread Loaves

1. Flatten dough with hands or rolling pin into rectangle, 18 × 9 inches.

2. Roll dough up tightly toward you, beginning at one of the open ends.

3. Press with thumbs to seal after each turn; pinch edge of dough into roll to seal.

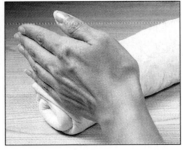

4. Press each end with side of hand to seal; fold ends under loaf.

How to Cut Special Doughs

French Bread: Make 1/4-inch deep slashes across loaf at 2-inch intervals.

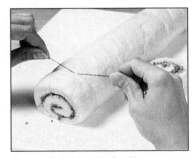

Caramel Sticky Rolls: To cut even slices, place a piece of dental floss or heavy thread under roll. Bring ends of floss up and crisscross at top of roll. Pull strings in opposite directions.

Traditional White Bread

PREP: 35 min; PROOF: 1 hr 50 min; BAKE: 30 min
Makes 2 loaves, 16 slices each

Do you have a need to use less salt in your diet? If so, decrease sugar to 2 tablespoons and salt to 1 teaspoon. Substitute vegetable oil for the shortening. Each rising time will be 10 to 15 minutes shorter.

> 6 to 7 cups all-purpose* or bread flour
> 3 tablespoons sugar
> 1 tablespoon salt
> 2 tablespoons shortening
> 2 packages regular or quick active dry yeast
> 2 1/4 cups very warm water (120° to 130°)
> Margarine or butter, melted

1. Mix 3 1/2 cups of the flour, the sugar, salt, shortening and yeast in large bowl. Add warm water. Beat with electric mixer on low speed 1 minute, scraping bowl frequently. Beat on medium speed 1 minute, scraping bowl frequently. Stir in enough remaining flour, 1 cup at a time, to make dough easy to handle.

2. Turn dough onto lightly floured surface. Knead about 10 minutes or until smooth and elastic. Place in greased bowl and turn greased side up. Cover and let rise in warm place 40 to 60 minutes or until double. Dough is ready if indentation remains when touched.

3. Grease bottoms and sides of 2 loaf pans, 8 1/2 × 4 1/2 × 2 1/2 or 9 × 5 × 3 inches, with shortening.

4. Punch down dough and divide in half. Flatten each half with hands or rolling pin into rectangle, 18 × 9 inches, on lightly floured surface. Roll dough up tightly, beginning at 9-inch side, to form a loaf. Press with thumbs to seal after each turn. Pinch edge of dough into roll to seal. Press each end with side of hand to seal. Fold ends under loaf. (See How to Shape Yeast Bread Loaves, page 55.) Place seam side down in pan. Brush loaves lightly with margarine. Cover and let rise in warm place 35 to 50 minutes or until double.

5. Move oven rack to low position so that tops of pans will be in center of oven. Heat oven to 425°.

6. Bake 25 to 30 minutes or until loaves are deep golden brown and sound hollow when tapped. Remove from pans to wire rack. Brush loaves with margarine; cool.

If using self-rising flour, omit salt.

1 SLICE: Calories 90 (Calories from Fat 10); Fat 1g (Saturated 0g); Cholesterol 0mg; Sodium 200mg; Carbohydrate 19g (Dietary Fiber 1g); Protein 2g

CINNAMON-RAISIN BREAD: Stir in 1 cup raisins with the second addition of flour. Mix 1/4 cup sugar and 2 teaspoons ground cinnamon. After rolling dough into rectangles, sprinkle each with 1 tablespoon water and half of the sugar mixture.

FRESH HERB BREAD: Stir in 2 tablespoons chopped fresh chives, 2 tablespoons chopped fresh sage leaves and 2 tablespoons chopped fresh thyme leaves just before the second addition of flour.

Baking with Confidence

Perfect Yeast Bread and Rolls Are

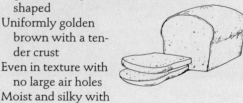

High and evenly
  shaped
Uniformly golden
  brown with a tender crust
Even in texture with
  no large air holes
Moist and silky with
  an elastic quality

Problem	Possible Cause
Not high	• water too hot for yeast • too little flour • too little kneading • too short rising period • pan too large
Coarse texture	• rising time too long • too little flour • too little kneading • oven too cool
Harsh, dry and not silky	• too much flour • not kneaded enough
Yeasty taste	• rising time too long • temperature too high during rising time

Cinnamon-Raisin Bread

Focaccia

PREP: 30 min; PROOF: 1 hr 50 min; BAKE: 15 min
Makes 2 focaccia, 12 slices each

For best results, we recommend using canned grated Parmesan cheese in this recipe. We found in our testing that freshly grated cheese overbrowns during baking. (photograph on page 333)

2 1/2 to 3 cups all-purpose* or bread flour
2 teaspoons sugar
1/4 teaspoon salt
1 package regular or quick active dry yeast
1/4 cup olive or vegetable oil
1 cup very warm water (120° to 130°)
Olive or vegetable oil
2 tablespoons grated canned Parmesan
   cheese
2 tablespoons chopped fresh or 2 teaspoons
   dried herb leaves (such as basil, oregano
   or rosemary)

1. Mix 1 cup of the flour, the sugar, salt and yeast in large bowl. Add 1/4 cup oil and the water. Beat with electric mixer on medium speed 3 minutes, scraping bowl occasionally. Stir in enough remaining flour until dough is soft and leaves side of bowl.

2. Turn dough onto lightly floured surface. Knead 5 to 10 minutes or until dough is smooth and elastic. Place in greased bowl and turn greased side up. Cover and let rise in warm place 1 to 1 1/2 hours or until double. Dough is ready if indentation remains when touched.

3. Heat oven to 425°. Grease 2 cookie sheets with shortening.

4. Punch down dough and divide in half. Shape each half into a flattened 12-inch round on cookie sheet. Cover and let rise in warm place 20 minutes.

5. Prick centers of rounds and 1 inch in from edge of rounds thoroughly with fork. Brush with oil. Sprinkle with cheese and herbs.

6. Bake 12 to 15 minutes or until golden brown. Remove from cookie sheets to wire rack. Serve warm or cool.

*Do not use self-rising flour in this recipe.

1 SLICE: Calories 70 (Calories from Fat 25); Fat 3g (Saturated 0g); Cholesterol 0mg; Sodium 30mg; Carbohydrate 10g (Dietary Fiber 0g); Protein 1g

FOCACCIA WITH PEPPERS AND ONIONS: Do not brush rounds with oil. Heat 1 tablespoon olive or vegetable oil in 10-inch skillet over medium heat. Cook 2 medium bell peppers, cut into 1/4-inch rings, and 1 small onion, sliced and separated into rings, in oil about 5 minutes, stirring occasionally, until softened. Arrange half of mixture over each focaccia, pressing lightly into dough, before sprinkling with cheese and herbs.

French Bread

PREP: 25 min; PROOF: 3 hr; BAKE: 30 min
Makes 2 loaves, 12 slices each

This crusty bread is just right with soups—or use it to make Crostini (page 27). (Herbed Breadsticks photographed on page 209.)

3 to 3 1/2 cups all-purpose* or bread flour
1 tablespoon sugar
1 teaspoon salt
1 package regular or quick active dry yeast
1 cup very warm water (120° to 130°)
2 tablespoons vegetable oil
Cornmeal
1 large egg white
1 tablespoon cold water
Poppy seed or sesame seed

1. Mix 2 cups of the flour, the sugar, salt and yeast in large bowl. Add warm water and oil. Beat with electric mixer on low speed 1 minute, scraping bowl frequently. Beat on medium speed 1 minute, scraping bowl frequently. Stir in enough remaining flour, 1/2 cup at a time, to make dough easy to handle (dough will be soft). Turn dough onto lightly floured surface. Knead about 5 minutes or until smooth and elastic.

2. Place dough in greased bowl and turn greased side up. Cover and let rise in warm place 1 1/2 to 2 hours or until double. Rising time is longer than times for traditional breads, which gives the typical French bread texture. Dough is ready if indentation remains when touched.

3. Grease large cookie sheet with shortening; sprinkle with cornmeal.

4. Punch down dough and divide in half. Roll each half into rectangle, 15 × 8 inches, on lightly floured surface. Roll up tightly, beginning at 15-inch side, to form a loaf. Pinch edge of dough into roll to seal. Roll gently back and forth to taper ends. Place both loaves on cookie sheet.

5. Cut 1/4-inch-deep slashes across loaves at 2-inch intervals with sharp knife. (See How to Cut Special Doughs, page 55.) Brush loaves with cold water. Let rise uncovered in warm place about 1 hour or until double.

6. Heat oven to 375°. Mix egg white and 1 tablespoon cold water; brush over loaves. Sprinkle with poppy or sesame seed.

7. Bake 25 to 30 minutes or until loaves are golden brown and sound hollow when tapped.

Do not use self-rising flour in this recipe.

1 SLICE: Calories 70 (Calories from Fat 10); Fat 1g (Saturated 0g); Cholesterol 0mg; Sodium 90mg; Carbohydrate 14g (Dietary Fiber 1g); Protein 2g

CRUSTY HARD ROLLS: Grease large cookie sheet with shortening; sprinkle with cornmeal. Prepare dough as directed—except after punching down dough, divide into 12 equal parts. Shape each part into ball and place on cookie sheet. Brush rolls with cold water. Let rise uncovered about 1 hour or until double. Heat oven to 425°. Mix egg white and 1 tablespoon cold water; brush over rolls. Sprinkle with poppy or sesame seed. Bake 15 to 20 minutes or until brown. Makes 12 rolls.

HERBED BREADSTICKS: Grease 2 cookie sheets with shortening; sprinkle with cornmeal if desired. Prepare dough as directed—except add 2 teaspoons dried rosemary leaves, crushed, and 1 teaspoon dried oregano leaves with the salt. After punching down dough, divide into 24 equal parts. Roll and shape each part into rope, about 9 inches long, sprinkling with flour if dough is too sticky. Place on cookie sheet. Mix egg white and 2 tablespoons cold water; brush over breadsticks. Sprinkle with poppy seed or coarse salt. Heat oven to 400°. Bake about 20 minutes or until crust is deep golden brown and crisp. *Immediately* remove from cookie sheet to wire rack. Store loosely covered. Makes 24 breadsticks.

> **TIMESAVING TIP**
> Place warm water (heat only to 110° to 115°) and yeast in food processor. Cover and process, using quick on-and-off motions, until yeast is dissolved. Add flour, sugar and salt. Cover and process about 30 seconds or until dough forms a ball. (If dough is too sticky, add flour, 1 tablespoon at a time.) Do not knead dough. Continue as directed in step 2.

Challah Braid

PREP: 30 min; PROOF: 2 hr 50 min; BAKE: 30 min
Makes 1 braid, 16 slices

Brushing the dough with egg yolk results in a lustrous shiny top after baking. (photograph on page 376)

> 2 1/2 to 2 3/4 cups all-purpose* or bread
> flour
> 1 package regular or quick active dry yeast
> 2 tablespoons sugar
> 1 teaspoon salt
> 3/4 cup water
> 1 tablespoon vegetable oil
> 1 large egg
> Vegetable oil
> 1 egg yolk
> 2 tablespoons cold water
> Poppy seed

1. Mix 1 1/4 cups of the flour, the yeast, sugar and salt in large bowl. Heat water and 1 tablespoon oil until very warm (120° to 130°). Add water mixture to flour mixture. Beat with electric mixer on low speed 1 minute, scraping bowl frequently. Beat on medium speed 1 minute, scraping bowl frequently. Beat in 1 egg until smooth. Stir in enough remaining flour to make dough easy to handle.

2. Turn dough onto lightly floured surface. Knead about 5 minutes or until smooth and elastic. Place in greased bowl and turn greased side up. Cover and let rise in warm place 1 1/2 to 2 hours or until double. Dough is ready if indentation remains when touched.

3. Lightly grease cookie sheet with shortening.

4. Punch down dough and divide into 3 equal parts. Roll each part into a rope, 14 inches long. Place ropes close together on cookie sheet. Braid ropes gently and loosely; do not stretch. Fasten ends; tuck ends under braid securely. Brush with oil. Cover and let rise in warm place 40 to 50 minutes or until double.

5. Heat oven to 375°. Mix egg yolk and 2 tablespoons water; brush over braid. Sprinkle with poppy seed.

6. Bake 25 to 30 minutes or until golden brown. Check bread at 15 minutes and tent with aluminum foil if it seems to be browning too quickly. Remove from cookie sheet to wire rack; cool.

If using self-rising flour, omit salt.

1 SLICE: Calories 95 (Calories from Fat 20); Fat 2g (Saturated 0g); Cholesterol 25mg; Sodium 140mg; Carbohydrate 17g (Dietary Fiber 1g); Protein 3g

Honey-Whole Wheat Bread

PREP: 35 min; PROOF: 1 hr 50 min; BAKE: 45 min
Makes 2 loaves, 16 slices each

> 3 cups stone-ground whole wheat or graham
> flour
> 1/3 cup honey
> 1/4 cup shortening
> 1 tablespoon salt
> 2 packages regular or quick active dry yeast
> 2 1/4 cups very warm water (120° to 130°)
> 3 to 4 cups all-purpose* or bread flour
> Margarine or butter, melted, if desired

1. Mix whole wheat flour, honey, shortening, salt and yeast in large bowl. Add warm water. Beat with electric mixer on low speed 1 minute, scraping bowl frequently. Beat on medium speed 1 minute, scraping bowl frequently. Stir in enough all-purpose flour, 1 cup at a time, to make dough easy to handle.

2. Turn dough onto lightly floured surface. Knead about 10 minutes or until smooth and elastic. Place in greased bowl and turn greased side up. Cover and let rise in warm place 40 to 60 minutes or until double. Dough is ready if indentation remains when touched.

3. Grease bottoms and sides of 2 loaf pans, 8 1/2 × 4 1/2 × 2 1/2 or 9 × 5 × 3 inches, with shortening.

4. Punch down dough and divide in half. Flatten each half with hands or rolling pin into rectangle, 18 × 9 inches, on lightly floured surface. Roll dough up tightly, beginning at 9-inch side, to form a loaf. Press with thumbs to seal after each turn. Pinch edge of dough into roll to seal. Press each end with side of hand to seal. Fold ends under loaf. (See How to Shape Yeast Bread Loaves, page 55.) Place seam side down in pan. Brush loaves lightly with margarine. Cover and let rise in warm place 35 to 50 minutes or until double.

5. Move oven rack to low position so that tops of pans will be in center of oven. Heat oven to 375°.

6. Bake 40 to 45 minutes or until loaves are deep golden brown and sound hollow when tapped. Remove from pans to wire rack. Brush loaves with margarine; cool.

If using self-rising flour, decrease salt to 1 teaspoon.

1 SLICE: Calories 105 (Calories from Fat 20); Fat 2g (Saturated 1g); Cholesterol 0mg; Sodium 210mg; Carbohydrate 21g (Dietary Fiber 2g); Protein 3g

APRICOT-CASHEW LOAVES: Grease cookie sheet. Stir in 1/2 cup finely chopped dried apricots and 1 cup finely chopped cashews with the all-purpose flour. After punching down dough, divide into fourths; shape each into round flat loaf. Place on cookie sheet. Cover and let rise in warm place 35 to 50 minutes. Before baking, cut 1/4-inch-deep crosscut slashes across center of each loaf. Bake 35 to 40 minutes. 4 loaves.

Sunflower Seven-Grain Bread

PREP: 25 min; PROOF: 2 hr; BAKE: 30 min
Makes 1 loaf, 16 slices

Using ready-to-eat seven-grain cereal eliminates the need to buy seven different grains to make this wholesome bread. (photograph on page 313)

> 1 1/2 cups all-purpose* or bread flour
> 3 tablespoons packed brown sugar
> 2 tablespoons vegetable oil
> 1 1/2 teaspoons salt
> 1 package regular or quick active dry yeast
> 1 cup very warm water (120° to 130°)
> 1 1/2 cups 7-grain ready-to-eat cereal
> 1/2 cup raw sunflower nuts
> 1 to 1 1/2 cups whole wheat flour
> Vegetable oil

1. Mix all-purpose flour, brown sugar, 2 tablespoons oil, the salt and yeast in large bowl. Add warm water. Beat with electric mixer on low speed 1 minute, scraping bowl frequently. Beat on medium speed 1 minute, scraping bowl frequently.

2. Stir in cereal and nuts. Stir in enough whole wheat flour, 1/2 cup at a time, to make dough easy to handle.

3. Turn dough onto lightly floured surface. Knead about 10 minutes or until smooth and elastic. Place in greased bowl and turn greased side up. Cover and let rise in warm place about 1 hour or until double. Dough is ready if indentation remains when touched.

4. Grease bottom and sides of loaf pan, 8 1/2 × 4 1/2 × 2 1/2 or 9 × 5 × 3 inches, with shortening.

5. Punch down dough. Flatten with hands or rolling pin into rectangle, 18 × 9 inches, on lightly floured surface. Roll up tightly, beginning at 9-inch side, to form a loaf. Press with thumbs to seal after each turn. Pinch edge of dough into roll to seal. Press each end with side of hand to seal. Fold ends under loaf. (See How to Shape Yeast Bread Loaves, page 55.) Place seam side down in pan. Brush loaves lightly with oil. Cover and let rise in warm place 45 minutes to 1 hour or until double.

6. Move oven rack to low position so that top of pan will be in center of oven. Heat oven to 400°.

7. Bake 25 to 30 minutes or until loaf is deep golden brown and sounds hollow when tapped. Remove from pan to wire rack; cool.

*If using self-rising flour, omit salt.

1 SLICE: Calories 140 (Calories from Fat 35); Fat 4g (Saturated 1g); Cholesterol 0mg; Sodium 200mg; Carbohydrate 25g (Dietary Fiber 3g); Protein 4g

Dark Pumpernickel Bread

PREP: 40 min; PROOF: 1 hr 40 min; BAKE: 30 min
Makes 2 loaves, 12 slices each

This bread has a wonderful texture. The result of extra yeast and additional rising time to offset the heavier rye flour. (photograph on page 349)

> 2 1/2 cups all-purpose* or bread flour
> 1/4 cup baking cocoa
> 2 tablespoons caraway seed
> 1 tablespoon plus 1 teaspoon salt
> 3 packages regular or quick active dry yeast
> 1 1/2 cups water
> 1/2 cup dark molasses
> 2 tablespoons shortening
> 2 3/4 to 3 cups rye flour
> Cornmeal
> Margarine or butter, melted, if desired

1. Mix bread flour, cocoa, caraway seed, salt and yeast in large bowl. Heat water, molasses and shortening in 1-quart saucepan over medium heat until very warm (120° to 130°). Add molasses mixture to flour mixture. Beat with electric mixer on low speed 1 minute, scraping bowl frequently. Beat on medium speed 1 minute, scraping bowl frequently. Stir in enough rye flour, 1 cup at a time, to make dough easy to handle.

2. Turn dough onto lightly floured surface. Cover and let rest 15 minutes. Knead 5 to 10 minutes or until smooth. Place in greased bowl and turn greased side up. Cover and let rise in warm place about 2 hours or until double. Dough is ready if indentation remains when touched.

3. Punch down dough. Cover and let rise about 40 minutes or until double.

4. Grease cookie sheet with shortening; sprinkle with cornmeal.

5. Punch down dough and divide in half. Shape each half into a round, slightly flat loaf. Place loaves in opposite corners of cookie sheet. Cover and let rise in warm place 1 hour.

6. Heat oven to 375°.

7. Bake 25 to 30 minutes or until loaves sound hollow when tapped. Remove from cookie sheet to wire rack. Brush with margarine; cool.

*If using self-rising flour, omit salt.

1 SLICE: Calories 125 (Calories from Fat 20); Fat 2g (Saturated 1g); Cholesterol 0mg; Sodium 360mg; Carbohydrate 26g (Dietary Fiber 2g); Protein 3g

Honey-Mustard Oatmeal Bread

Honey-Mustard Oatmeal Bread

PREP: 25 min; PROOF: 2 hr; BAKE: 35 min
Makes 1 loaf, 16 slices

> 3 to 3 1/2 cups all-purpose* or bread flour
> 1/2 cup quick-cooking oats
> 1 teaspoon salt
> 1/4 cup honey
> 2 tablespoons Dijon mustard
> 2 tablespoons margarine or butter,
>   softened**
> 1 package regular or quick active dry yeast
> 1 cup very warm water (120° to 130°)
> 1 large egg
> 1 egg white, slightly beaten
> 1 tablespoon water
> Quick-cooking oats

1. Mix 1 1/2 cups of the flour, 1/2 cup oats, the salt, honey, mustard, margarine and yeast in large bowl. Add 1 cup warm water. Beat with electric mixer on low speed 1 minute, scraping bowl frequently. Beat on medium speed 1 minute, scraping bowl frequently. Beat in egg. Stir in enough remaining flour, 1/2 cup at a time, to make dough easy to handle.

2. Turn dough onto lightly floured surface. Knead about 10 minutes or until smooth and elastic. Place in greased bowl and turn greased side up. Cover and let rise in warm place about 1 hour or until double. Dough is ready if indentation remains when touched.

3. Grease bottom and side of pie plate, 9 × 1 1/4 inches, with shortening.

4. Punch down dough. Shape dough into a ball. Place in pie plate; flatten slightly. Mix egg white and 1 tablespoon water; brush on loaf. Sprinkle with oats. Cover and let rise in warm place 45 to 60 minutes or until double.

5. Heat oven to 375°.

6. Bake about 35 minutes or until loaf sounds hollow when tapped and is deep golden brown. Remove from pan to wire rack; cool.

*If using self-rising flour, omit salt.

**Spreads with at least 65% vegetable oil can be substituted (see page 13).

1 SLICE: Calories 120 (Calories from Fat 20); Fat 2g (Saturated 0g); Cholesterol 0mg; Sodium 180mg; Carbohydrate 24g (Dietary Fiber 1g); Protein 3g

Swedish Rye Bread

PREP: 25 min; PROOF: 2 hr; BAKE: 50 min
Makes 2 loaves, 12 slices each

2 1/2 cups all-purpose* or bread flour
1/3 cup packed brown sugar
1 tablespoon salt
1 tablespoon anise seed or fennel seed, crushed
1 tablespoon finely shredded orange peel
2 packages regular or quick active dry yeast
1 1/2 cups water
1/3 cup molasses
2 tablespoons vegetable oil
2 1/4 to 2 3/4 cups medium rye flour
Margarine or butter, melted, if desired

1. Mix all-purpose flour, brown sugar, salt, anise seed, orange peel and yeast in large bowl. Heat water, molasses and oil in 1-quart saucepan until very warm (120° to 130°). Add molasses mixture to flour mixture. Beat with electric mixer on low speed 1 minute, scraping bowl frequently. Beat on medium speed 1 minute, scraping bowl frequently. Stir in enough rye flour, 1 cup at a time, to make dough easy to handle.

2. Turn dough onto lightly floured surface. Cover and let rest 10 to 15 minutes. Knead about 5 minutes or until smooth and elastic. Place in greased bowl and turn greased side up. Cover and let rise in warm place about 1 hour or until double. Dough is ready if indentation remains when touched.

3. Grease cookie sheet with shortening.

4. Punch down dough and divide in half. Shape each half into a round, slightly flat loaf. Place loaves in opposite corners of cookie sheet. Cover and let rise in warm place about 1 hour or until double.

5. Heat oven to 375°.

6. Bake 40 to 50 minutes or until loaves sound hollow when tapped. Remove from cookie sheet to wire rack. Brush loaves with margarine; cool.

*If using self-rising flour, omit salt.

1 SLICE: Calories 115 (Calories from Fat 20); Fat 2g (Saturated 0g); Cholesterol 0mg; Sodium 270mg; Carbohydrate 24g (Dietary Fiber 2g); Protein 2g

CARAWAY-RYE BREAD: Omit anise seed and orange peel. Stir in 1 tablespoon caraway seed with the brown sugar.

SWISS-RYE BREAD: Omit anise seed and orange peel. Stir in 1 cup 1/4-inch cubes Swiss cheese (8 ounces) before adding rye flour.

Pan Rolls

PREP: 30 min; PROOF: 1 hr 30 min; BAKE: 18 min
Makes 48 rolls

3 1/2 to 3 3/4 cups all-purpose flour*
1/4 cup sugar
1/4 cup shortening
1 teaspoon salt
1 package regular or quick active dry yeast
1/2 cup very warm water (120° to 130°)
1/2 cup very warm milk (120° to 130°)
1 large egg
Margarine or butter, melted

1. Mix 2 cups of the flour, the sugar, shortening, salt and yeast in medium bowl. Add warm water, warm milk and egg. Beat with electric mixer on low speed 1 minute, scraping bowl frequently. Beat on medium speed 1 minute, scraping bowl frequently. Stir in enough remaining flour to make dough easy to handle.

2. Turn dough onto lightly floured surface. Knead about 5 minutes or until smooth and elastic. Place in greased bowl and turn greased side up. Cover and let rise in warm place about 1 hour or until double. Dough is ready if indentation remains when touched.

3. Grease bottoms and sides of 2 round pans, 9 × 1 1/2 inches, with shortening.

4. Punch down dough. Cut dough in half; cut each half into 24 pieces. Shape into balls. Place close together in pans. Brush with margarine. Cover and let rise in warm place about 30 minutes or until double.

5. Heat oven to 400°.

6. Bake 12 to 18 minutes or until golden brown.

*If using self-rising flour, omit salt.

1 ROLL: Calories 55 (Calories from Fat 20); Fat 2g (Saturated 1g); Cholesterol 5mg; Sodium 50mg; Carbohydrate 8g (Dietary Fiber 0g); Protein 1g

CLOVERLEAF ROLLS: Grease bottoms and sides of 24 medium muffin cups, 2 1/2 × 1 1/4 inches, with shortening. After punching down dough, cut dough in half; cut each half into 36 pieces. Shape into balls. Place 3 balls in each muffin cup. Brush with margarine. Cover and let rise in warm place about 30 minutes or until double. Bake as directed in steps 5 and 6. Makes 24 rolls.

CRESCENT ROLLS: Grease cookie sheet with shortening. After punching down dough, cut dough in half; roll each half into 12-inch circle on floured surface. Spread with margarine. Cut each circle into 16 wedges. Roll up each wedge, beginning at rounded edge. Place rolls, with points underneath, on cookie sheet and curve slightly. Brush with margarine. Cover and let rise in warm place about 30 minutes or until double. Bake as directed in steps 5 and 6. Makes 32 rolls.

Caramel-Pecan Sticky Rolls

PREP: 40 min; PROOF: 2 hr; BAKE: 35 min
Makes 15 rolls

You can make these rolls the day before baking. Prepare dough as directed—except do not let dough rise after placing rolls in pan. Wrap pan tightly with heavy-duty aluminum foil. Refrigerate at least 12 hours but no longer than 24 hours. Bake as directed.

3 1/2 to 4 cups all-purpose* or bread flour
1/3 cup granulated sugar
1 teaspoon salt
2 packages regular or quick active dry yeast
1 cup very warm milk (120° to 130°)
1/3 cup *stick* margarine or butter, softened**
1 large egg
1 cup packed brown sugar
1/2 cup *stick* margarine or butter, softened**
1/4 cup dark corn syrup
1 cup pecan halves (4 ounces)
2 tablespoons *stick* margarine or butter, softened**
1/2 cup chopped pecans or raisins, if desired
1/4 cup granulated or packed brown sugar
1 teaspoon ground cinnamon

1. Mix 2 cups of the flour, 1/3 cup granulated sugar, the salt and yeast in large bowl. Add warm milk, 1/3 cup margarine and the egg. Beat with electric mixer on low speed 1 minute, scraping bowl frequently. Beat on medium speed 1 minute, scraping bowl frequently. Stir in enough remaining flour to make dough easy to handle.

2. Turn dough onto lightly floured surface. Knead about 5 minutes or until smooth and elastic. Place in greased bowl and turn greased side up. Cover and let rise in warm place about 1 hour 30 minutes or until double. Dough is ready if indentation remains when touched.

3. Heat 1 cup brown sugar and 1/2 cup margarine to boiling in 2-quart saucepan, stirring constantly; remove from heat. Stir in corn syrup. Pour into ungreased rectangular pan, 13 × 9 × 2 inches. Sprinkle with pecan halves.

4. Punch down dough. Flatten with hands or rolling pin into rectangle, 15 × 10 inches, on lightly floured surface. Spread with 2 tablespoons margarine. Mix chopped pecans, 1/4 cup granulated sugar and the cinnamon; sprinkle evenly over margarine. Roll rectangle up tightly, beginning at 15-inch side. Pinch edge of dough into roll to seal. Stretch and shape until even. Cut roll into fifteen 1-inch slices. Place slightly apart in pan. Cover and let rise in warm place about 30 minutes or until double.

5. Heat oven to 350°.

6. Bake 30 to 35 minutes or until golden brown. *Immediately* turn upside down onto heatproof tray or serving plate. Let stand 1 minute so caramel will drizzle over rolls; remove pan. Serve warm.

*If using self-rising flour, omit salt.

**Spreads with at least 65% vegetable oil can be substituted (see page 13).

1 ROLL: Calories 370 (Calories from Fat 155); Fat 17g (Saturated 3g); Cholesterol 15mg; Sodium 300mg; Carbohydrate 51g (Dietary Fiber 2g); Protein 5g

---

LIGHTER CARAMEL-PECAN STICKY ROLLS

For 7 grams of fat and 245 calories per serving, omit 1 cup brown sugar, 1/2 cup margarine, the corn syrup, pecan halves and step 3.

Line pan with aluminum foil; spray with nonstick cooking spray. Drizzle 3/4 cup light caramel ice-cream topping over foil. Sprinkle with 2/3 cup chopped pecans. Continue as directed in steps 4, 5 and 6—except omit the chopped pecans from the filling.

CINNAMON ROLLS: Omit 1 cup brown sugar, 1/2 cup margarine, the corn syrup, pecan halves, chopped pecans and step 3. Grease bottom and sides of rectangular pan, 13 × 9 × 2 inches, with shortening. Place dough slices in pan. Let rise and bake as directed in steps 4, 5 and 6—except do not turn pan upside down. Remove from the pan to wire rack. Cool 10 minutes. Drizzle rolls with Vanilla Glaze (page 44) if desired.

Overnight Danish Twists

PREP: 55 min; CHILL: 8 hr; BAKE: 15 min
Makes 27 twists

(photograph on page 48)

    2 packages regular or quick active dry yeast
    1/2 cup warm water (105° to 115°)
    4 cups all-purpose flour*
    1/3 cup sugar
    2 teaspoons salt
    1 cup cold *stick* butter, cut into small pieces**
    4 large eggs
    1 cup milk
    Jam or preserves
    Powdered Sugar Glaze (below)

1. Dissolve yeast in warm water in large bowl. Mix in flour, sugar and salt. Cut in butter, using pastry blender or crisscrossing 2 knives, until mixture looks like fine crumbs.

2. Separate egg yolks from egg whites; refrigerate egg whites for use in steps 5 and 7. Stir egg yolks and milk into flour mixture until soft dough forms. Cover bowl with plastic wrap and refrigerate at least 8 hours but no longer than 24 hours.

3. Lightly grease 2 large cookie sheets with shortening.

4. Punch down dough. Divide dough into 3 equal parts. Roll 1 part dough at a time into rectangle, 9 × 7 inches, on lightly floured surface. (If dough becomes too sticky while shaping, refrigerate 5 to 10 minutes.) Cut rectangle crosswise into nine 1-inch strips.

5. For each twist, pinch ends of each strip together to form ring, stretching strip slightly, then twist to form figure 8. Place at least 2 inches apart on cookie sheet. Brush with egg white. Let rise uncovered at room temperature about 25 minutes or until dough is puffy and loops fill in.

6. Heat oven to 350°.

7. Make an indentation in center of each loop. Fill with 1/2 to 1 teaspoon jam. Brush dough with egg white. Bake about 15 minutes or until light golden brown. *Immediately* remove to wire rack; cool slightly. Drizzle Powdered Sugar Glaze over warm twists.

Powdered Sugar Glaze

    1 1/2 cups powdered sugar
    3/4 teaspoon vanilla
    2 to 3 tablespoons water or milk

Mix all ingredients until smooth. If necessary, stir in additional water, 1/2 teaspoon at a time, until drizzling consistency.

*Do not use self-rising flour in this recipe.

**We do not recommend using margarine or vegetable oil spreads.

1 TWIST: Calories 190 (Calories from Fat 70); Fat 8g (Saturated 5g); Cholesterol 50mg; Sodium 220mg; Carbohydrate 28g (Dietary Fiber 1g); Protein 3g

Four-Grain Batter Bread

PREP: 15 min; PROOF: 30 min; BAKE: 25 min
Makes 2 loaves, 16 slices each

There's only one rising time for this easy batter bread, which has extra yeast to help the heavier batter rise. (photograph on page 382)

    Cornmeal
    4 1/2 to 4 3/4 cups all-purpose* or bread
      flour
    2 tablespoons sugar
    1 teaspoon salt
    1/4 teaspoon baking soda
    2 packages regular or quick active dry yeast
    2 cups milk
    1/2 cup water
    1/2 cup whole wheat flour
    1/2 cup wheat germ
    1/2 cup quick-cooking oats

1. Grease bottoms and sides of 2 loaf pans, 8 1/2 × 4 1/2 × 2 1/2 inches, with shortening; sprinkle with cornmeal.

2. Mix 3 1/2 cups bread flour, the sugar, salt, baking soda and yeast in large bowl. Heat milk and water in 1-quart saucepan over medium heat, stirring occasionally, until very warm (120° to 130°). Add milk mixture to flour mixture. Beat with electric mixer on low speed until moistened. Beat on medium speed 3 minutes, scraping bowl occasionally.

3. Stir in whole wheat flour, wheat germ, oats and enough remaining bread flour to make a stiff batter. Divide batter evenly between pans. Round tops of loaves by patting with floured hands. Sprinkle with cornmeal. Cover and let rise in warm place about 30 minutes or until batter is about 1 inch below tops of pans.

4. Heat oven to 400°.

5. Bake about 25 minutes or until tops of loaves are light brown. Remove from pans to wire rack; cool.

*If using self-rising flour, omit salt and baking soda.

1 SLICE: Calories 95 (Calories from Fat 10); Fat 1g (Saturated 0g); Cholesterol 5mg; Sodium 85mg; Carbohydrate 19g (Dietary Fiber 1g); Protein 3g

WHOLE WHEAT BATTER BREAD: Increase whole wheat flour to 2 cups. Omit wheat germ and oats. Stir in 1 cup raisins with second addition of bread flour.

Tomato-Pesto Batter Bread

Tomato-Pesto Batter Bread

PREP: 25 min; PROOF: 1 hr 10 min; BAKE: 45 min
Makes 1 loaf, 16 slices

You can serve this bread in slices or wedges. Or, for a different look, cut into slices, then cut them diagonally into 1- to 1 1/2-inch fingers—they are great for serving with salads or soups.

3 cups all-purpose* or bread flour
2 tablespoons sugar
1 1/2 teaspoons salt
1/3 cup Pesto (page 345) or prepared pesto
1 package regular or quick active dry yeast
1 cup very warm water (120° to 130°)
1/2 cup coarsely chopped sun-dried
    tomatoes (not oil-packed)
Margarine or butter, softened

1. Mix 1 1/2 cups of the flour, the sugar, salt, pesto and yeast in large bowl. Add warm water. Beat with electric mixer on low speed 1 minute, scraping bowl frequently. Beat on medium speed 2 minutes, scraping bowl occasionally.

2. Stir in tomatoes. Stir in remaining flour until smooth. (Batter will be very stiff.) Scrape batter from side of bowl. Cover and let rise in warm place about 30 minutes or until double. (Batter is ready if indentation remains when touched with floured finger.)

3. Grease bottom and side of 2-quart casserole with shortening.

4. Stir down batter by beating about 25 strokes. Spread evenly in casserole. Round top of loaf by patting with floured hands. Cover and let rise in warm place about 40 minutes or until double.

5. Move oven rack to low position so that top of casserole will be in center of oven. Heat oven to 375°.

6. Bake 40 to 45 minutes or until loaf is brown and sounds hollow when tapped. *Immediately* remove loaf from casserole to wire rack. Brush top of loaf with margarine; cool.

*If using self-rising flour, omit salt.

1 SLICE: Calories 120 (Calories from Fat 25); Fat 3g (Saturated 1g); Cholesterol 0mg; Sodium 250mg; Carbohydrate 21g (Dietary Fiber 1g); Protein 3g

Garlic Bread

PREP: 5 min; BAKE: 20 min
Makes 1 loaf, 18 slices

(photogaph on page 271)

> 1/3 cup stick margarine or butter, softened*
> 1 clove garlic, finely chopped, or 1/4 teaspoon garlic powder
> 1 loaf (1 pound) French bread, cut into 1-inch slices

1. Heat oven to 400°.

2. Mix margarine and garlic; spread over 1 side of each bread slice. Reassemble loaf and wrap securely in heavy-duty aluminum foil.

3. Bake 15 to 20 minutes or until hot.

*Spreads with at least 65% vegetable oil can be substituted (see page 13).

1 SLICE: Calories 110 (Calories from Fat 55); Fat 6g (Saturated 1g); Cholesterol 0mg; Sodium 210mg; Carbohydrate 13g (Dietary Fiber 1g); Protein 2g

---

TIMESAVING TIP

To microwave, do not wrap loaf in aluminum foil. Divide loaf in half and place side by side in napkin-lined microwavable basket or dinner plate. Cover with napkin and microwave on Medium (50%) 1 1/2 to 3 minutes, rotating basket 1/2 turn after 1 minute, until bread is warm.

Southwest Cheese Bread

PREP: 10 min; BAKE: 20 min
Makes 1 loaf, 16 slices

You'll find this zesty bread is easier to cut before you heat it.

> 1 loaf (1 pound) French bread
> 1 cup shredded mozzarella or Cheddar cheese (4 ounces)
> 1/2 cup mayonnaise or salad dressing
> 1/4 cup finely chopped bell pepper
> 1 tablespoon chopped fresh cilantro
> 1/2 teaspoon ground cumin
> 1 small onion, finely chopped (1/4 cup)

1. Heat oven to 400°.

2. Cut bread loaf horizontally to make 3 layers.

3. Mix remaining ingredients. Spread half of the cheese mixture over bottom bread layer. Top with middle bread layer. Spread remaining cheese mixture over middle bread layer. Cover with top bread layer; press firmly. Cut loaf into 16 slices. Wrap loaf securely in heavy-duty aluminum foil.

4. Bake 15 to 20 minutes or until hot.

1 SLICE: Calories 145 (Calories from Fat 70); Fat 8g (Saturated 2g); Cholesterol 10mg; Sodium 240mg; Carbohydrate 15g (Dietary Fiber 1g); Protein 4g

---

LIGHTER SOUTHWEST CHEESE BREAD

For 2 grams of fat and 100 calories per serving, use reduced-fat mozzarella cheese and fat-free mayonnaise.

Pepper-Cheese Twists

PREP: 15 min; BAKE: 12 min
Makes 18 twists

> 1/2 package (17 1/4-ounce size) frozen puff pastry, thawed
> 1 large egg, beaten
> 1 cup shredded Cheddar cheese (4 ounces)
> 2 teaspoons cracked black pepper

1. Heat oven to 425°. Line cookie sheet with aluminum foil or cooking parchment paper.

2. Roll sheet of pastry into rectangle, 18 × 12 inches, on lightly floured surface.

3. Brush pastry with egg. Sprinkle cheese crosswise over half of rectangle. Fold remaining half of rectangle over cheese; press edges to seal. Brush pastry with egg. Sprinkle with pepper.

4. Cut pastry lengthwise into eighteen 1/2-inch strips. Grasp each end of a strip and roll ends in opposite directions to twist. Place twists on cookie sheet.

5. Bake 10 to 12 minutes or until puffed and golden brown. Serve warm or cool.

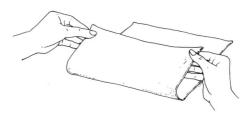

a. Fold remaining half of rectangle over cheese; press edges to seal.

b. Grasp ends of each strip and roll in opposite directions to twist.

1 TWIST: Calories 185 (Calories from Fat 135); Fat 15g (Saturated 6g); Cholesterol 25mg; Sodium 100mg; Carbohydrate 10g (Dietary Fiber 0g); Protein 3g

Tips for Bread Machine Breads

- Read your bread machine manual carefully, especially the tips and hints. Add ingredients in the order specified by the bread machine manufacturer.
- Ingredients should be at room temperature, except for those normally stored in the refrigerator.
- Using bread flour will result in breads with the highest volume. Also see Flour, page 14.
- *Carefully* measure ingredients because over- or undermeasuring can dramatically affect the results. Use standard household measuring cups and spoons for all ingredients.
- Although you can check the dough during mixing and kneading, never open the machine during the rising or baking stages because the loaf could collapse.
- When using a delay cycle, be sure the yeast does not come in contact with liquid or wet ingredients. Do not use the delay cycle for recipes that contain eggs, fresh milk, meats or vegetables because bacteria could grow while these ingredients remain in the bread machine for several hours.
- Each bread machine works a little differently, and your bread machine may produce a loaf that might not meet your expectations. When trying slight adjustments to ingredients to improve results, change only one thing at a time.

Almond-Chocolate Chip Bread

PREP: 5 min; BAKE: About 3 1/2 hr
Makes 1 1/2-Pound Loaf, 12 slices

(photograph on page 68)

    1 cup plus 2 tablespoons water
    2 tablespoons *stick* margarine or butter,
        softened*
    1/2 teaspoon vanilla
    3 cups bread flour
    3/4 cup semisweet chocolate chips
    3 tablespoons sugar
    1 tablespoon nonfat dry milk
    3/4 teaspoon salt
    1 1/2 teaspoons bread machine yeast
    1/3 cup sliced almonds

1. Measure carefully, placing all ingredients except almonds in bread machine pan in the order recommended by the manufacturer. Add almonds at the raisin/nut signal or 5 to 10 minutes before last kneading cycle ends.

2. Select Sweet or Basic/White cycle. Use Medium or Light crust color. Do not use delay cycles. Remove baked bread from pan and cool on wire rack.

*Spreads with at least 65% vegetable oil can be substituted (see page 13).

1 SLICE: Calories 225 (Calories from Fat 65); Fat 7g (Saturated 3g); Cholesterol 2mg; Sodium 170mg; Carbohydrate 37g (Dietary Fiber 2g); Protein 5g

Jalapeño Corn Bread

PREP: 10 min; BAKE: About 3 1/2 hr
Makes 1 1/2-Pound Loaf, 12 slices

This bread adds zip to an everyday ham and cheese sandwich! (photograph on page 68)

    3/4 cup plus 2 tablespoons water
    2/3 cup frozen whole kernel corn, thawed
    2 tablespoons *stick* margarine or butter,
        softened*
    1 tablespoon chopped jalapeño chili
    3 1/4 cups bread flour
    1/3 cup cornmeal
    2 tablespoons sugar
    1 1/2 teaspoons salt
    2 1/2 teaspoons bread machine yeast

1. Measure carefully, placing all ingredients in bread machine pan in the order recommended by the manufacturer.

2. Select Basic/White cycle. Use Medium or Light crust color. Do not use delay cycles. Remove baked bread from pan and cool on wire rack.

*Spreads with at least 65% vegetable oil can be substituted (see page 13).

1 SLICE: Calories 170 (Calories from Fat 20); Fat 2g (Saturated 1g); Cholesterol 0mg; Sodium 290mg; Carbohydrate 36g (Dietary Fiber 2g); Protein 4g

Note: *This recipe is not recommended for bread machines with glass-domed lids.*

Almond-Chocolate Chip Bread (page 67), Jalapeño Corn Bread (page 67)

Classic White Bread

PREP: 5 min; BAKE: About 3 1/2 hr
Makes 1 1/2-Pound Loaf, 12 slices

> 1 cup plus 2 tablespoons water
> 2 tablespoons *stick* margarine or butter, softened*
> 3 cups bread flour
> 3 tablespoons nonfat dry milk
> 2 tablespoons sugar
> 1 1/2 teaspoons salt
> 2 teaspoons bread machine yeast

1. Measure carefully, placing all ingredients in bread machine pan in the order recommended by the manufacturer.

2. Select Basic/White cycle. Use Medium or Light crust color. Remove baked bread from pan and cool on wire rack.

*Spreads with at least 65% vegetable oil can be substituted (see page 13).

1 SLICE: Calories 145 (Calories from Fat 20); Fat 2g (Saturated 1g); Cholesterol 0mg; Sodium 300mg; Carbohydrate 29g (Dietary Fiber 1g); Protein 4g

Crunchy Whole Wheat Bread

PREP: 15 min; BAKE: About 4 1/2 hr
Makes 1 1/2-Pound Loaf, 12 slices

> 1 cup plus 2 tablespoons water
> 3 tablespoons honey
> 2 tablespoons *stick* margarine or butter, softened*
> 1 1/2 cups bread flour
> 1 1/2 cups whole wheat flour
> 1/4 cup chopped toasted walnuts
> 1 teaspoon salt
> 1 1/2 teaspoons bread machine yeast

1. Measure carefully, placing all ingredients in bread machine pan in the order recommended by the manufacturer.

2. Select Whole Wheat or Basic/White cycle. Use Medium or Light crust color. Remove baked bread from pan and cool on wire rack.

*Spreads with at least 65% vegetable oil can be substituted (see page 13).

1 SLICE: Calories 160 (Calories from Fat 35); Fat 4g (Saturated 1g); Cholesterol 0mg; Sodium 200mg; Carbohydrate 29g (Dietary Fiber 2g); Protein 4g

Cakes & Pies

About Cakes

Cakes play many roles—all of them delicious! There are cakes for celebrations, cakes for busy days, and for folks looking for fat-free desserts, there's exceptional homemade Angel Food Cake. Frostings and glazes add the finishing touch and also give you a wonderful variety of combinations—from Starlight Yellow Cake with Chocolate Buttercream Frosting to Applesauce Cake with Maple-Nut Frosting. So have some fun, and bake a cake!

Pans and Pan Preparation

- Use pans of the size called for in the recipe. To check the width of the pan, measure across the top from *inside* edge to *inside* edge. Baking a cake in too large of a pan will result in a pale, flat and shrunken cake. Too small or too shallow a pan will result in a bulge and a loss of shape.
- Shiny metal pans are preferred for baking cakes. They reflect heat away from the cake and produce a tender, light brown crust.
- Dark nonstick or glass baking pans should be used following the manufacturer's directions. These pans readily absorb heat, and a better result may be achieved if the baking temperature is reduced by 25°.
- Fill cake pans no more than half full. If using an unusually shaped pan (heart, star, bell), measure the capacity by filling the pan with water, then measure the water and use half that amount of batter. Cupcakes can be made from any remaining batter.

Mixing Cakes

- The cake recipes in this cookbook have been tested with electric handheld mixers. Because mixers vary in power, you may need to adjust the speed, particularly during the initial step of combining ingredients. If using a powerful stand mixer, be careful not to overmix. Overmixing can result in tunnels (large air holes) or cause the cake to sink in the center.
- The one-bowl cake-mixing method was developed using the electric mixer, but mixing also can be done by hand. Stir the ingredients to moisten, and combine them well. Beat 150 strokes for each minute of beating time (3 minutes equals 450 strokes). If a cake is not beaten enough, the volume will be lower.
- We recommend that *stick* margarine or butter be used for cakes when margarine or butter is specified. Vegetable oil spreads (also in stick form) with at least 65% fat can be substituted and the baked result will be satisfactory, although the batter may have a slightly softer consistency.
- We do not recommend using vegetable oil spreads with less than 65% fat (either in stick form or tubs), tub margarines or whipped products (whether butter, margarine or spreads). Because these products contain more water and less fat, using them can result in poor quality overall (thinner or softer consistency when mixing; less tender or wet and gummy texture after baking).
- Cake batters for lighter variations usually contain reduced-fat or fat-free ingredients. These batters are generally thinner than regular batters or may have a slightly different texture during mixing. Because fat is a flavor carrier, when it is reduced, the amount of flavorings is sometimes increased.

Baking Cakes

- Except where noted, bake cakes on the oven rack placed in the center of the oven.
- Cakes are done when a toothpick stuck in the center comes out clean.

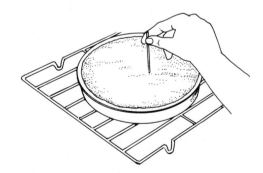

- Do not place cakes directly from the oven in a drafty place to cool.

Preceding page: Fresh Strawberry Pie (page 100)

Storing Cakes

- Cool unfrosted cakes completely before storing. They will become sticky if covered while warm.
- Store cakes with creamy-type frosting under a cake safe (or large inverted bowl). Or cover *loosely* with aluminum foil, plastic wrap or waxed paper.
- Serve cakes with fluffy-type frosting the same day they are made. If it is necessary to store this type of cake, use a cake safe or inverted bowl with a knife slipped under the edge so the container is not airtight.
- Refrigerate cakes with whipped cream toppings, cream fillings or cream cheese frostings.
- Cakes containing very moist ingredients such as chopped apples, applesauce, shredded carrots or zucchini, mashed bananas or pumpkin should be refrigerated in humid weather or climates. They tend to mold quickly when covered and stored at room temperature.

Cutting Cakes

- For layer cakes, use a sharp, long, thin knife.
- For angel food, chiffon and pound cakes, use a long serrated knife or an electric knife.
- If the frosting sticks to the knife, dip the knife into hot water and wipe with a damp towel after cutting each slice.
- For fruitcake, use a thin, nonserrated or electric knife. For easiest slicing and a mellow flavor, make fruitcake three to four weeks ahead of time, then wrap and store in the refrigerator. It can be occasionally brushed with rum, brandy or bourbon for a rich mellow flavor.

Cake Yields

Size and Kind	Number of Servings
8- or 9-inch one-layer round cake	8
8- or 9-inch two-layer round cake	16
8- or 9-inch square cake	9
13 × 9 × 2-inch rectangular cake	16
10 × 4-inch angel food or pound cake	16 to 24
12-cup bundt cake	16 to 24

Baking Cupcakes

Cupcakes are great to make for easy individual servings, especially at parties or picnics. They can be made from any of the cake batters, and will yield 24 to 36 cupcakes.

- Line medium muffin cups, 2 1/2 × 1 1/4 inches, with paper baking cups.
- Fill each cup about 1/2 full. Bake 20 to 25 minutes or until toothpick inserted in center comes out clean.
- If you have only one 12-cup muffin pan, cover and refrigerate the remaining batter while the first cupcakes are baking. Then bake the remaining batter, adding 1 or 2 minutes to the baking time.

Shortening Cakes

Shortening cakes are all similar as the ingredients they contain are the same: shortening, margarine or butter; flour; eggs; a liquid; and a leavening agent such as baking powder or soda. Only the flavorings are different.

Pans and Pan Preparation

- Place oven racks in the middle of the oven and pans in the center of the rack. Arrange 8- or 9-inch round pans so they do not touch and so there is at least 1 inch of space between the pans and the oven sides.
- Generously grease bottoms and sides of pans with shortening. (Do not use margarine, butter or oil because they will not coat as evenly.) Use about 1 tablespoon shortening for each round pan. Dust each greased pan with flour (or cocoa for a chocolate cake), shaking pan until bottom and sides are well coated. Shake out excess flour. For nonstick pans, follow manufacturer's directions for pan preparation.
- For cupcakes, line medium muffin cups, 2 1/2 × 1 1/4 inches, with paper baking cups. They help keep cupcakes moist and make them easier to transport, plus cleanup is easy.
- For fruitcakes, line pans with aluminum foil, then grease with shortening. Or line with cooking parchment paper. Leave short "ears" on two opposite sides so the baked cake can be easily lifted out of the pan. Extend the foil up over the pan if you intend to store the cake before serving. When the cake has cooled, bring the foil up and over the top of the cake, then seal.
- Do not substitute oil for shortening, margarine or butter, even when those ingredients are to be melted. Recipes formulated with shortening need the solids for proper structure and texture.
- Cool round cakes in their pans on wire racks 5 to 10 minutes, then loosen edge and remove cakes from pans. Cool completely on wire racks.

How to Split Cake Layers

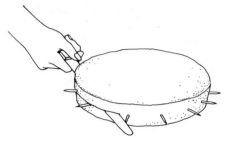

1. Mark middle points on sides of layer with toothpicks. Using picks as a guide, cut through the layer with long, thin sharp knife.

2. Split the layer by pulling a piece of heavy sewing thread horizontally, back and forth, through the layer.

Baking with Confidence

Perfect Shortening Cakes Are

High, golden brown
Slightly rounded, smooth top
Fine-grained, even
    texture, not crumbly
Soft, velvety, slightly moist,
    light, tender

Problem	Possible Cause
Pale	• too little sugar • too short baking time
Does not rise properly	• too much liquid • too much fat • too large pan • oven too cool
Peaked or cracked on top	• too much flour • too hot oven
Coarse grained	• too much shortenin • underbeaten
Crumbly	• too much shortening • too much sugar • underbeaten
Dry	• too much baking powder • too long baking time
Heavy	• too much liquid • too much shortening • too much flour
Batter overflows	• too much batter in pan • pan too small • too much leavening

Devil's Food Cake

PREP: 20 min; BAKE: 45 min; COOL: 10 min
Makes 16 servings

Why is this called Devil's Food? Because this dense, luscious and very chocolaty cake is the total opposite of the white and feathery Angel Food Cake (page 83).

> 2 1/4 cups all-purpose* or 2 1/2 cups cake flour
> 1 2/3 cups sugar
> 3/4 cup shortening
> 2/3 cup baking cocoa
> 1 1/2 cups water
> 1 1/4 teaspoons baking soda
> 1 teaspoon salt
> 1 teaspoon vanilla
> 1/4 teaspoon baking powder
> 2 large eggs
> Browned Butter Buttercream Frosting (page 86) or White Mountain Frosting (page 88), if desired

1. Heat oven to 350°. Grease bottom and sides of rectangular pan, 13 × 9 × 2 inches, 2 round pans, 9 × 1 1/2 inches, or 3 round pans, 8 × 1 1/2 inches, with shortening; lightly flour.

2. Beat all ingredients except Browned Butter Frosting with electric mixer on low speed 30 seconds, scraping bowl constantly. Beat on high speed 3 minutes, scraping bowl occasionally. Pour into pan(s).

3. Bake rectangle 40 to 45 minutes, rounds 30 to 35 minutes, or until toothpick inserted in center comes out clean. Cool rectangle in pan on wire rack. Cool rounds 10 minutes; remove from pans to wire rack. Cool completely.

4. Frost rectangle or fill and frost layers with Browned Butter Frosting.

*Do not use self-rising flour in this recipe.

1 SERVING: Calories 250 (Calories from Fat 100); Fat 11g (Saturated 3g); Cholesterol 25mg; Sodium 250mg; Carbohydrate 36g (Dietary Fiber 1g); Protein 3g

> ### LIGHTER DEVIL'S FOOD CAKE
> For 5 grams of fat and 210 calories per serving, substitute 1/2 cup Prune Sauce (page 344) for 1/2 cup of the shortening.

RED VELVET DEVIL'S FOOD CAKE: Add 1 teaspoon red food color with the vanilla.

Best Chocolate Cake

PREP: 20 min; BAKE: 45 min; COOL: 10 min
Makes 16 servings

> 2 cups all-purpose* or 2 1/4 cups cake flour
> 2 cups sugar
> 1/2 cup shortening
> 3/4 cup water
> 3/4 cup buttermilk
> 1 teaspoon baking soda
> 1 teaspoon salt
> 1 teaspoon vanilla
> 1/2 teaspoon baking powder
> 2 large eggs
> 4 ounces unsweetened baking chocolate, melted and cooled
> Chocolate Buttercream Frosting (page 86) or Caramel Frosting (page 88), if desired

1. Heat oven to 350°. Grease bottom and sides of rectangular pan, 13 × 9 × 2 inches, 2 round pans, 9 × 1 1/2 inches, 3 round pans, 8 × 1 1/2 inches, or 12-cup bundt cake pan, with shortening; lightly flour.

2. Beat all ingredients except Chocolate Buttercream Frosting with electric mixer on low speed 30 seconds, scraping bowl constantly. Beat on high speed 3 minutes, scraping bowl occasionally. Pour into pan(s).

3. Bake rectangle 40 to 45 minutes, rounds 30 to 35 minutes, bundt pan 50 to 55 minutes, or until toothpick inserted in center comes out clean. Cool rectangle in pan on wire rack. Cool rounds or bundt pan 10 minutes; remove from pan(s) to wire rack. Cool completely.

4. Frost rectangle or fill and frost layers with Chocolate Buttercream Frosting.

*If using self-rising flour, omit baking soda, salt and baking powder.

1 SERVING: Calories 265 (Calories from Fat 100); Fat 11g (Saturated 4g); Cholesterol 25mg; Sodium 250mg; Carbohydrate 40g (Dietary Fiber 1g); Protein 3g

> ### LIGHTER BEST CHOCOLATE CAKE
> For 5 grams of fat and 225 calories per serving, substitute Prune Sauce (page 344) for the shortening.

BLACK FOREST TORTE: Prepare cake as directed using 2 round pans, 9 × 1 1/2 inches. Place 1 cake layer upside down on serving plate. Spread with half of 2 1/3 cups Sweetened Whipped Cream (page 89). Drain 1 can (21 ounces) cherry pie filling; spread half of the cherries over whipped cream. Place other cake layer, top side up, on whipped cream. Spread with remaining cherry filling and whipped cream. Sprinkle top with chocolate curls or shaved chocolate if desired.

Chocolate Truffle Torte

Chocolate Truffle Torte

PREP: 35 min; BAKE: 25 min; COOL: 2 hr
Makes 12 servings

We find it easier to bake two thin layers for this torte, rather than to bake one cake and split in two layers. The torte makes an elegant company dessert or chocolate-lover's birthday cake.

> 1 package (6 ounces) semisweet chocolate
>   chips (1 cup)
> 1/2 cup *stick* margarine or butter*
> 1/2 cup all-purpose flour**
> 4 eggs, separated
> 1/2 cup sugar
> 1 package (2 1/2 ounces) hazelnuts, finely
>   chopped and toasted (2/3 cup)
> Chocolate Truffle Filling (page 90)
> Whole or chopped hazelnuts, if desired

1. Heat oven to 325°. Grease bottoms and sides of 2 round pans, 9 × 1 1/2 inches, with shortening. Line bottoms of pans with waxed paper or cooking parchment paper.

2. Melt chocolate chips and margarine in heavy 2-quart saucepan over medium heat, stirring constantly; cool 5 minutes. Stir in flour until smooth. Stir in egg yolks until well blended.

3. Beat egg whites in large bowl with electric mixer on high speed until foamy. Beat in sugar, 1 tablespoon at a time, until soft peaks form. Fold chocolate mixture into egg whites. Fold in toasted hazelnuts. Spread in pans.

4. Bake about 25 minutes or until tops of cakes appear dry and toothpick inserted in center comes out clean. Cool 5 minutes. Run knife along side of each cake to loosen; remove from pan to wire rack. Remove waxed paper. Cool completely.

5. Prepare Chocolate Truffle Filling. Spread 2/3 cup of the filling on bottom layer. Top with other layer. Frost top and sides of cake with remaining filling. Drizzle with any remaining filling and garnish with hazelnuts.

*Spreads with at least 65% vegetable oil can be substituted (see page 13).

**Do not use self-rising flour in this recipe.

1 SERVING: Calories 465 (Calories from Fat 295); Fat 33g (Saturated 13g); Cholesterol 80mg; Sodium 165mg; Carbohydrate 41g (Dietary Fiber 4g); Protein 5g

German Chocolate Cake

PREP: 30 min; BAKE: 40 min; COOL: 2 hr
Makes 16 servings

The pan is greased only—not floured—and the bottom of the pan lined for this cake, so the unfrosted sides of the finished cake will be more attractive.

> 4 ounces sweet cooking chocolate
> 1/2 cup water
> 2 cups sugar
> 1 cup *stick* margarine or butter, softened*
> 4 large eggs
> 2 1/4 cups all-purpose flour** or 2 1/2 cups
>   cake flour
> 1 teaspoon baking soda
> 1 teaspoon salt
> 1 teaspoon vanilla
> 1 cup buttermilk
> Coconut-Pecan Frosting (page 88)

1. Heat oven to 350°. Grease bottom and sides of 3 round pans, 8 × 1 1/2 or 9 × 1 1/2 inches. Line bottoms of pans with waxed paper or cooking parchment paper.

2. Heat chocolate and water in 1-quart saucepan over low heat, stirring until chocolate is melted; cool.

3. Beat sugar and margarine in medium bowl with electric mixer on high speed until light and fluffy. Beat in eggs, one at a time. Beat in chocolate and vanilla on low speed. Add remaining ingredients except frosting. Beat on low speed just until blended. Pour into pans.

4. Bake 8-inch rounds 35 to 40 minutes, 9-inch rounds 30 to 35 minutes, or until toothpick inserted in center comes out clean. Cool 10 minutes; remove from pans to wire rack. Remove waxed paper. Cool completely.

5. Fill layers and frost top of cake with Coconut-Pecan Frosting, leaving side of cake unfrosted.

*Spreads with at least 65% vegetable oil can be substituted (see page 13).

**Do not use self-rising flour in this recipe.

1 SERVING: Calories 540 (Calories from Fat 270); Fat 30g (Saturated 9g); Cholesterol 100mg; Sodium 480mg; Carbohydrate 63g (Dietary Fiber 2g); Protein 7g

Double Chocolate Snack Cake

PREP: 10 min; BAKE: 40 min
Makes 9 servings

This quick cake is mixed with a fork right in the baking pan—it's great for a busy day.

> 1 2/3 cups all-purpose flour*
> 1 cup packed brown sugar or granulated
>   sugar
> 1/4 cup baking cocoa
> 1 teaspoon baking soda
> 1/2 teaspoon salt
> 1 cup water
> 1/3 cup vegetable oil
> 1 teaspoon white vinegar
> 1/2 teaspoon vanilla
> 1/2 cup semisweet chocolate chips
> Powdered sugar, if desired

1. Heat oven to 350°.

2. Mix flour, brown sugar, cocoa, baking soda and salt with fork in ungreased square pan, 8 × 8 × 2 inches. Stir in remaining ingredients except chocolate chips and powdered sugar. Sprinkle chocolate chips over batter.

3. Bake 35 to 40 minutes or until toothpick inserted in center comes out clean. Cool in pan on wire rack. Sprinkle with powdered sugar.

*Do not use self-rising flour in this recipe.

1 SERVING: Calories 300 (Calories from Fat 100); Fat 11g (Saturated 3g); Cholesterol 0mg; Sodium 270mg; Carbohydrate 49g (Dietary Fiber 2g); Protein 3g

FRUITY CHOCOLATE SNACK CAKE: Omit chocolate chips. Stir 1/2 cup diced dried fruit and raisins mixture into flour mixture.

OATMEAL-MOLASSES SNACK CAKE: Omit cocoa, vanilla and chocolate chips. Stir 3/4 cup quick-cooking oats, 1/2 cup raisins and 1 teaspoon ground allspice into flour mixture. Stir in 2 tablespoons dark molasses with the remaining ingredients.

Silver White Cake

PREP: 10 min; BAKE: 45; COOL: 10 min
Makes 16 servings

This cake will become a Fourth of July dessert when filled and topped with Triple Berry Filling (page 90). Frost sides with 1 1/2 cups Sweetened Whipped Cream (page 89) for a red, white and blue punch.

> 2 1/4 cups all-purpose* or 2 1/2 cups cake
>   flour
> 1 2/3 cups sugar
> 2/3 cup shortening
> 1 1/4 cups milk
> 3 1/2 teaspoons baking powder
> 1 teaspoon salt
> 1 teaspoon vanilla or almond extract
> 5 large egg whites
> Mocha Frosting (page 86) or Chocolate Sour
>   Cream Frosting (page 85), if desired

1. Heat oven to 350°. Grease bottom and sides of rectangular pan, 13 × 9 × 2 inches, 2 round pans, 9 × 1 1/2 inches, or 3 round pans, 8 × 1 1/2 inches, with shortening; lightly flour.

2. Beat all ingredients except egg whites and Mocha Frosting in large bowl with electric mixer on low speed 30 seconds, scraping bowl constantly. Beat on high speed 2 minutes, scraping bowl occasionally.

3. Beat in egg whites on high speed 2 minutes, scraping bowl occasionally. Pour into pan(s).

4. Bake rectangle 40 to 45 minutes, 9-inch rounds 30 to 35 minutes, 8-inch rounds 23 to 28 minutes, or until toothpick inserted in center comes out clean or until cake springs back when touched lightly in center. Cool rectangle in pan on wire rack. Cool rounds 10 minutes; remove from pans to wire rack. Cool completely.

5. Frost rectangle or fill and frost layers with Mocha Frosting.

*Do not use self-rising flour in this recipe.

1 SERVING: Calories 235 (Calories from Fat 80); Fat 9g (Saturated 3g); Cholesterol 2mg; Sodium 270mg; Carbohydrate 36g (Dietary Fiber 0g); Protein 3g

---

LIGHTER SILVER WHITE CAKE

For 4 grams of fat and 195 calories per serving, substitute 1/3 cup unsweetened applesauce for 1/3 cup of the shortening, use skim milk and increase vanilla to 2 teaspoons.

CHOCOLATE CHIP CAKE: Fold 1/2 cup miniature or finely chopped regular semisweet chocolate chips into batter. Frost with Chocolate Buttercream Frosting (page 86) if desired.

COCONUT-LEMON CAKE: Spread rectangle or fill layers with Lemon Filling (page 90). Frost with White Mountain Frosting (page 88). Sprinkle cake with about 1 cup flaked or shredded coconut.

Pound Cake

PREP: 20 min; BAKE: 1 hr 20 min; COOL: 20 min
Makes 24 servings

Rich, moist and firm-textured, this cake freezes exceptionally well. It's also easy to dress up with sorbet, or for a more decadent treat, ice cream and Hot Fudge Sauce (page 159).

> 2 1/2 cups sugar
> 1 cup *stick* margarine or butter, softened*
> 1 teaspoon vanilla or almond extract
> 5 large eggs
> 3 cups all-purpose flour**
> 1 teaspoon baking powder
> 1/4 teaspoon salt
> 1 cup milk or evaporated milk

1. Heat oven to 350°. Grease bottom and side of angel food cake pan (tube pan), 10 × 4 inches, 12-cup bundt cake pan or 2 loaf pans, 9 × 5 × 3 inches, with shortening; lightly flour.

2. Beat sugar, margarine, vanilla and eggs in large bowl with electric mixer on low speed 30 seconds, scraping bowl constantly. Beat on high speed 5 minutes, scraping bowl occasionally. Mix flour, baking powder and salt. Beat flour mixture into sugar mixture alternately with milk on low speed. Spread in pan.

3. Bake angel food or bundt pan 1 hour 10 minutes to 1 hour 20 minutes, loaf pans 55 to 60 minutes, or until toothpick inserted in center comes out clean. Cool 20 minutes; remove from pan(s) and place top side up on wire rack. Cool completely.

*Spreads with at least 65% vegetable oil can be substituted (see page 13).

**Do not use self-rising flour in this recipe.

1 SERVING: Calories 230 (Calories from Fat 80); Fat 9g (Saturated 2g); Cholesterol 45mg; Sodium 150mg; Carbohydrate 34g (Dietary Fiber 0g); Protein 3g

LEMON POUND CAKE: Substitute 1 teaspoon lemon extract for the vanilla. Fold 1 tablespoon grated lemon peel into batter.

Peanut Butter Marble Cake

Starlight Yellow Cake

PREP: 10 min; BAKE: 45 min
Makes 16 servings

Jazz up this favorite cake by stirring in 1/2 cup chopped nuts, dried cherries or flaked coconut before pouring into pans.

  2 1/4 cups all-purpose flour*
  1 1/2 cups sugar
  1/2 cup shortening
  1 1/4 cups milk
  3 1/2 teaspoons baking powder
  1 teaspoon salt
  1 teaspoon vanilla
  3 large eggs
  Chocolate Buttercream Frosting (page 86) or
    Peanut Butter Buttercream Frosting (page
    86), if desired

1. Heat oven to 350°. Grease bottom and sides of rectangular pan, 13 × 9 × 2 inches, 2 round pans, 9 × 1 1/2 inches, or 3 round pans, 8 × 1 1/2 inches, with shortening; lightly flour.

2. Beat all ingredients except Chocolate Buttercream Frosting with electric mixer on low speed 30 seconds, scraping bowl constantly. Beat on high speed 3 minutes, scraping bowl occasionally. Pour into pan(s).

3. Bake rectangle 40 to 45 minutes, 9-inch rounds 30 to 35 minutes, 8-inch rounds 20 to 25 minutes, or until toothpick inserted in center comes out clean or until cake springs back when touched lightly in center. Cool rectangle in pan on wire rack. Cool rounds 10 minutes; remove from pans to wire rack. Cool completely.

4. Frost rectangle or fill and frost layers with Chocolate Buttercream Frosting.

*If using self-rising flour, omit baking powder and salt.

1 SERVING: Calories 220 (Calories from Fat 70); Fat 8g (Saturated 2g); Cholesterol 40mg; Sodium 260mg; Carbohydrate 34g (Dietary Fiber 0g); Protein 3g

PEANUT BUTTER MARBLE CAKE: Substitute peanut butter for the shortening. Pour two-thirds of the batter (about 3 cups) into pan(s). Stir 3 tablespoons baking cocoa and 1/8 teaspoon baking soda into remaining batter. Drop chocolate batter by generous tablespoonfuls randomly in mounds onto peanut butter batter. Pull knife through batters in S-shaped curves in one continuous motion for marbled design. Turn pan one-fourth turn; repeat marbling. Bake and cool as directed in step 3. Frost with Peanut Butter Buttercream Frosting (page 86). If desired, drop about 1/4 cup prepared fudge topping by teaspoonfuls randomly over the top and marble as directed for the batter.

POPPY SEED CAKE: Stir in 1/4 cup poppy seed with the sugar.

Cookie-Sour Cream Cake

PREP: 20 min; BAKE: 35 min
Makes 8 servings

Make this cake extra-easy by placing all ingredients except the cookies in your food processor. Cover and process about thirty seconds or until smooth. Add the cookies (leave them whole), then process, using quick on-and-off motions, until the cookies are coarsely chopped.

> 1 cup all-purpose flour*
> 3/4 cup sugar
> 1/2 cup sour cream
> 1/4 cup *stick* margarine or butter, softened**
> 1/4 cup water
> 1/2 teaspoon baking powder
> 1/2 teaspoon baking soda
> 1 large egg
> 8 creme-filled sandwich cookies, coarsely chopped
> 1 cup Sweetened Whipped Cream (page 89), if desired

1. Heat oven to 350°. Grease bottom and side of round pan, 8 × 1 1/2 or 9 × 1 1/2 inches, with shortening; lightly flour.

2. Beat all ingredients except cookies and Sweetened Whipped Cream in large bowl with electric mixer on low speed 30 seconds, scraping bowl constantly. Beat on high speed 2 minutes, scraping bowl occasionally. Stir in cookies. Pour into pan.

3. Bake 30 to 35 minutes or until cake springs back when touched lightly in center. Cool 10 minutes; remove from pan to wire rack. Cool completely.

4. Frost top of cake with Sweetened Whipped Cream. Garnish with additional cookies if desired.

If using self-rising flour, omit baking powder and decrease baking soda to 1/4 teaspoon.

**Spreads with at least 65% vegetable oil can be substituted (see page 13).*

1 SERVING: Calories 260 (Calories from Fat 100); Fat 11g (Saturated 4g); Cholesterol 35mg; Sodium 240mg; Carbohydrate 38g (Dietary Fiber 1g); Protein 3g

---

LIGHTER COOKIE-SOUR CREAM CAKE

For 7 grams of fat and 235 calories per serving, use fat-free sour cream and reduced-fat creme-filled sandwich cookies.

COOKIE-SOUR CREAM LAYER CAKE: Use 2 round pans or rectangular pan, 13 × 9 × 2 inches. Double all ingredients (do not use a food processor). Bake rounds as directed in step 3, or rectangle, 40 to 45 minutes. Makes 16 servings.

Pineapple Upside-Down Cake

PREP: 15 min; BAKE: 50 min
Makes 9 servings

Explore your artistic talents when arranging the pineapple—try cutting the slices in half or quarters and arrange them in any way you wish. For a more conventional presentation, place the pieces in circles or arrange them like spokes of a wheel.

> 1/4 cup *stick* margarine or butter*
> 2/3 cup packed brown sugar
> 1 can (20 ounces) sliced pineapple in juice, drained
> Maraschino cherries, if desired
> 1 1/3 cups all-purpose flour**
> 1 cup granulated sugar
> 1/3 cup shortening
> 3/4 cup milk
> 1 1/2 teaspoons baking powder
> 1/2 teaspoon salt
> 1 large egg
> Sweetened Whipped Cream (page 89), if desired

1. Heat oven to 350°.

2. Melt margarine in 10-inch ovenproof skillet or square pan, 9 × 9 × 2 inches, in oven. Sprinkle brown sugar over margarine. Arrange pineapple slices on brown sugar. Place cherry in center of each pineapple slice (cherries with stems can be added *after* baking).

3. Beat remaining ingredients except Sweetened Whipped Cream with electric mixer on low speed 30 seconds, scraping bowl constantly. Beat on high speed 3 minutes, scraping bowl occasionally. Pour over pineapple.

4. Bake skillet 45 to 50 minutes, square pan 50 to 55 minutes, or until toothpick inserted in center comes out clean. *Immediately* turn upside down onto heatproof plate. Let skillet or pan remain over cake a few minutes. Serve warm with Sweetened Whipped Cream.

Spreads with at least 65% vegetable oil can be substituted (see page 13).

**If using self-rising flour, omit baking powder and salt.*

1 SERVING: Calories 370 (Calories from Fat 125); Fat 14g (Saturated 4g); Cholesterol 25mg; Sodium 280mg; Carbohydrate 59g (Dietary Fiber 1g); Protein 3g

Sour Cream Spice Cake

PREP: 15 min; BAKE: 45 min
Makes 16 servings

Chocolate frosting complements this moist spice cake nicely. You could also use Cream Cheese Frosting (page 86) or Caramel Frosting (page 88) to create other pleasing combinations.

2 cups all-purpose flour*
1 1/2 cups packed brown sugar
1 cup raisins, chopped
1 cup sour cream
1/2 cup chopped walnuts
1/4 cup *stick* margarine or butter, softened**
1/4 cup shortening
1/2 cup water
2 teaspoons ground cinnamon
1 1/4 teaspoons baking soda
1 teaspoon baking powder
3/4 teaspoon ground cloves
1/2 teaspoon salt
1/2 teaspoon ground nutmeg
2 large eggs
Chocolate Buttercream Frosting (page 86) or
    Browned Butter Buttercream Frosting
    (page 86), if desired

1. Heat oven to 350°. Grease bottom and sides of rectangular pan, 13 × 9 × 2 inches, or 2 round pans, 8 × 1 1/2 or 9 × 1 1/2 inches, with shortening; lightly flour.

2. Beat all ingredients except Chocolate Buttercream Frosting with electric mixer on low speed 30 seconds, scraping bowl constantly. Beat on high speed 3 minutes, scraping bowl occasionally. Pour into pan(s).

3. Bake rectangle 40 to 45 minutes, rounds 30 to 35 minutes, or until toothpick inserted in center comes out clean. Cool rectangle in pan on wire rack. Cool rounds 10 minutes; remove from pans to wire rack. Cool completely.

4. Frost rectangle or fill and frost layers with Chocolate Buttercream Frosting.

If using self-rising flour, decrease baking soda to 3/4 teaspoon and omit baking powder and salt.

**Spreads with at least 65% vegetable oil can be substituted (see page 13).*

1 SERVING: Calories 280 (Calories from Fat 110); Fat 12g (Saturated 4g); Cholesterol 35mg; Sodium 250mg; Carbohydrate 41g (Dietary Fiber 1g); Protein 3g

> **TIMESAVING TIP**
> Carefully wipe the knife blade with vegetable oil before chopping the raisins, to prevent sticking.

Gingerbread

PREP: 10 min; BAKE: 55 min
Makes 9 servings

For a smooth and creamy treat, add a spoonful of whipped cream cheese before topping with sauce, or serve with whipped cream and a sprinkle of cinnamon.

2 1/3 cups all-purpose flour*
1/2 cup shortening
1/3 cup sugar
1 cup molasses
3/4 cup hot water
1 teaspoon baking soda
1 teaspoon ground ginger
1 teaspoon ground cinnamon
3/4 teaspoon salt
1 large egg
Divine Caramel Sauce (page 159) or Lemon
    Sauce (page 160), if desired

1. Heat oven to 325°. Grease bottom and sides of square pan, 9 × 9 × 2 inches, with shortening; lightly flour.

2. Beat all ingredients except Divine Caramel Sauce with electric mixer on low speed 30 seconds, scraping bowl constantly. Beat on medium speed 3 minutes, scraping bowl occasionally. Pour into pan.

3. Bake 50 to 55 minutes or until toothpick inserted in center comes out clean. Serve warm with Divine Caramel Sauce.

Do not use self-rising flour in this recipe.

1 SERVING: Calories 350 (Calories from Fat 110); Fat 12g (Saturated 3g); Cholesterol 25mg; Sodium 340mg; Carbohydrate 58g (Dietary Fiber 1g); Protein 4g

Banana Cake with Chocolate Sour Cream Frosting (page 85)

Applesauce Cake

PREP: 15 min; BAKE: 50 min
Makes 16 servings

The applesauce in this one-bowl cake makes for a moist and delicious cake.

> 2 1/2 cups all-purpose flour*
> 1 1/2 cups unsweetened applesauce
> 1 1/4 cups sugar
> 1/2 cup stick margarine or butter, softened**
> 1/2 cup water
> 1 1/2 teaspoons baking soda
> 1 1/2 teaspoons pumpkin pie spice
> 1 teaspoon salt
> 3/4 teaspoon baking powder
> 2 large eggs
> 1 cup raisins
> 2/3 cup chopped nuts
> Maple-Nut Buttercream Frosting
>   (page 86) or Cream Cheese Frosting
>   (page 86), if desired

1. Heat oven to 350°. Grease bottom and sides of rectangular pan, 13 × 9 × 2 inches, or 2 round pans, 8 × 1 1/2 or 9 × 1 1/2 inches, with shortening; lightly flour.

2. Beat all ingredients except raisins, nuts and Maple-Nut Frosting in large bowl with electric mixer on low speed 30 seconds, scraping bowl constantly. Beat on high speed 3 minutes, scraping bowl occasionally. Stir in raisins and nuts. Pour into pan(s).

3. Bake rectangle 45 to 50 minutes, rounds 40 to 45 minutes, or until toothpick inserted in center comes out clean. Cool rectangle in pan on wire rack. Cool rounds 10 minutes; remove from pans to wire rack. Cool completely.

4. Frost rectangle or fill and frost layers with Maple-Nut Frosting.

*Do not use self-rising flour in this recipe.

**Spreads with at least 65% vegetable oil can be substituted (see page 13).

1 SERVING: Calories 265 (Calories from Fat 90); Fat 10g (Saturated 2g); Cholesterol 25mg; Sodium 350mg; Carbohydrate 42g (Dietary Fiber 1g); Protein 3g

BANANA CAKE: Substitute 1 1/2 cups mashed ripe bananas (3 medium) for the applesauce and buttermilk for the water. Omit pumpkin pie spice and raisins. Increase baking powder to 1 teaspoon. Frost with Browned Butter Buttercream Frosting (page 86), Peanut Buttercream Frosting (page 86), or Chocolate Sour Cream Frosting (page 85), if desired.

Carrot Cake

PREP: 20 min; BAKE: 45 min
Makes 16 servings

This cake is mixed without an electric mixer. Use a food processor to shred the carrots and put the cake together even faster.

> 1 1/2 cups sugar
> 1 cup vegetable oil
> 3 large eggs
> 2 cups all-purpose flour*
> 1 1/2 teaspoons ground cinnamon
> 1 teaspoon baking soda
> 1 teaspoon vanilla
> 1/2 teaspoon salt
> 1/4 teaspoon ground nutmeg
> 3 cups shredded carrots (5 medium)
> 1 cup coarsely chopped nuts
> Cream Cheese Frosting (page 86), if desired

1. Heat oven to 350°. Grease bottom and sides of rectangular pan, 13 × 9 × 2 inches, or 2 round pans, 8 × 1 1/2 or 9 × 1 1/2 inches, with shortening; lightly flour.

2. Mix sugar, oil and eggs in large bowl until blended; beat 1 minute. Stir in remaining ingredients except carrots, nuts and Cream Cheese Frosting; beat 1 minute. Stir in carrots and nuts. Pour into pan.

3. Bake rectangle 40 to 45 minutes, rounds 30 to 35 minutes, or until toothpick inserted in center comes out clean. Cool in pan on wire rack.

4. Frost rectangle or fill and frost layers with Cream Cheese Frosting.

If using self rising flour, omit baking soda and salt.

1 SERVING: Calories 325 (Calories from Fat 180); Fat 20g (Saturated 3g); Cholesterol 40mg; Sodium 160mg; Carbohydrate 35g (Dietary Fiber 2g); Protein 3g

---

LIGHTER CARROT CAKE

For 12 grams of fat and 255 calories per serving, substitute 1/2 cup unsweetened applesauce for 1/2 cup of the oil and 1 egg plus 4 egg whites for the eggs. Decrease the chopped nuts to 1/2 cup.

ZUCCHINI CAKE: Substitute zucchini for the carrots.

Jeweled Fruitcake

PREP: 15 min; BAKE: 1 3/4 hr
Makes 32 servings

These cakes are good make-ahead holiday treats—use them as gifts, or to serve whenever you want a sweet treat. If you'd like, brush any of these cakes occasionally with brandy, rum or bourbon during storage. It adds a rich mellow flavor to fruitcake.

> 2 cups dried apricots (11 ounces)
> 2 cups pitted dates (12 ounces)
> 1 1/2 cups Brazil nuts (8 ounces)
> 1 cup red and green candied pineapple, chopped (7 ounces)
> 1 cup red and green maraschino cherries, drained (12 ounces)
> 3/4 cup all-purpose flour*
> 3/4 cup sugar
> 1/2 teaspoon baking powder
> 1/2 teaspoon salt
> 1 1/2 teaspoons vanilla
> 3 large eggs

1. Heat oven to 300°. Line loaf pan, 9 × 5 × 3 or 8 1/2 × 4 1/2 × 2 1/2 inches, with aluminum foil; grease foil with shortening.

2. Mix all ingredients. Spread in pan.

3. Bake about 1 hour 45 minutes or until toothpick inserted in center comes out clean. If necessary, cover with aluminum foil during last 30 minutes of baking to prevent excessive browning.

4. Remove fruitcake from pan (with foil) to wire rack. For a glossy top, *immediately* brush with light corn syrup. Cool completely. Wrap tightly and store in refrigerator no longer than 2 months.

If using self-rising flour, omit baking powder and salt.

1 SERVING: Calories 165 (Calories from Fat 45); Fat 5g (Saturated 1g); Cholesterol 20mg; Sodium 65mg; Carbohydrate 30g (Dietary Fiber 2g); Protein 2g

PETITE JEWELED FRUITCAKES: Line 24 medium muffin cups, 2 1/2 × 1 1/4 inches, with foil liners. Divide batter evenly among cups (about 1/3 cup each). Bake 35 to 40 minutes or until toothpick inserted in center comes out clean. Remove from pans to wire rack. Cool completely. Makes 24 servings.

MINI JEWELED FRUITCAKES: Generously grease bottoms and sides of 7 or 8 miniature loaf pans, 4 1/2 × 2 3/4 × 1 1/4 inches, with shortening, or line with aluminum foil and grease with shortening. Divide batter evenly among pans (about 1 cup each). Bake about 1 hour or until toothpick inserted in center comes out clean. Remove from pans to wire rack. Cool completely. Makes 7 or 8 mini loaves.

Foam Cakes

Although angel food, sponge and chiffon cakes all depend on beaten egg whites for lightness, not chemical leavening, each one differs slightly.

Angel food cakes have no added leavening (such as baking powder), shortening or egg yolks. They contain a high proportion of beaten egg whites to flour. Because there are no egg yolks, this type of cake is an excellent treat for those concerned with cholesterol or calories. See Angel Food Cake, page 83.

Sponge cakes use both the egg whites and the yolks. Sometimes additional leavening is called for, but fat never is used as it would break down the foam created by beating. See Jelly Roll, page 84.

Chiffon cakes combine the qualities of both foam and shortening cakes because they use egg yolks, leavening and vegetable oil or shortening. See Lemon Chiffon Cake, page 83.

Pans and Pan Preparation

- Do not grease and flour the pans for foam cakes unless directed in the recipe. To rise properly, the batter must cling to the side and tube of the pan.
- For foam cakes that will be baked in angel food cake pans (tube pans), move the oven rack to the lowest position before heating. With the rack in this position, the cake will bake completely without overbrowning the top.

Mixing Foam Cakes

- Beat egg whites until stiff, straight peaks form. Underbeating or underfolding the egg whites can cause coarse, low-volume cakes. Overbeating or overfolding can break down the egg whites and result in a compact cake. Be sure the bowl and beaters are clean and dry. Even a speck of grease or egg yolk will prevent egg whites from beating properly.
- Always fold another mixture into beaten egg whites by pouring the mixture over the egg whites. Cut down through the mixture, then slide the spatula across the bottom and up the side of the bowl. Rotate the bowl one-fourth turn and continue folding just until no streaks remain.

Baking Foam Cakes

- Foam cakes baked in rectangular, round or jelly roll pans are done when a toothpick inserted in the center comes out clean.
- Angel food cakes are done when the cracks feel dry and the top springs back when touched lightly. A cake that pulls away and/or falls out of the pan is underbaked.
- Foam cakes baked in angel food cake pans can be removed after cooling completely by sliding a stiff knife or metal spatula firmly against the side of pan and moving it in up-and-down strokes, being careful not to damage cake. Invert the pan, and hit one side against the counter. The cake will slip out.
- Foam cakes will stay fresh overnight when stored in the baking pan covered with waxed paper. Remove the cake from the pan and frost it the day it's served.

Baking with Confidence

Perfect Foam Cakes Are

High, golden brown with rounded top and cracks in surface
Soft, moist and delicate
Angel Food—feathery and fine-textured
Chiffon—springy and medium-textured
Sponge—springy and fine-textured

Problem	Possible Cause
Low and compact	• underbeaten or extremely overbeaten egg whites (use medium speeds on powerful stand mixers) • overfolded batter • incorrect cooling (not cooled upside down)
Coarse	• underfolded batter
Tough	• underbeaten egg whites • overfolded batter • incorrect storing after cooling

Angel Food Cake

PREP: 20 min; BAKE: 35 min; COOL: 2 hr
Makes 16 servings

1 1/2 cups powdered sugar
1 cup cake flour
1 1/2 cups large egg whites (about 12)
1 1/2 teaspoons cream of tartar
1 cup granulated sugar
1 1/2 teaspoons vanilla
1/2 teaspoon almond extract
1/4 teaspoon salt
Vanilla Glaze (page 89) or Chocolate Glaze
    (page 89), if desired

1. Move oven rack to lowest position. Heat oven to 375°.

2. Mix powdered sugar and flour; set aside. Beat egg whites and cream of tartar in large bowl with electric mixer on medium speed until foamy. Beat in granulated sugar, 2 tablespoons at a time, on high speed, adding vanilla, almond extract and salt with the last addition of sugar. Continue beating until stiff and glossy meringue forms. Do not underbeat.

3. Sprinkle sugar-flour mixture, 1/4 cup at a time, over meringue, folding in just until sugar-flour mixture disappears. Push batter into ungreased angel food cake pan (tube pan), 10 × 4 inches. Cut gently through batter with metal spatula.

4. Bake 30 to 35 minutes or until cracks feel dry and top springs back when touched lightly. *Immediately* turn pan upside down onto heatproof funnel or bottle. Let hang about 2 hours or until cake is completely cool. Loosen side of cake with knife or long, metal spatula; remove from pan.

5. Spread or drizzle top of cake with Vanilla Glaze.

1 SERVING: Calories 130 (Calories from Fat 0); Fat 0g (Saturated 0g); Cholesterol 0mg; Sodium 70mg; Carbohydrate 30g (Dietary Fiber 0g); Protein 3g

Lemon Chiffon Cake

PREP: 20 min; BAKE: 1 1/4 hr; COOL: 2 hr
Makes 16 servings

2 cups all-purpose flour* or 2 1/4 cups cake
    flour
1 1/2 cups sugar
3 teaspoons baking powder
1 teaspoon salt
3/4 cup cold water
1/2 cup vegetable oil
2 teaspoons vanilla
2 teaspoons grated lemon peel
7 large egg yolks (with all-purpose flour) or 5
    large egg yolks (with cake flour)
1 cup large egg whites (about 8)
1/2 teaspoon cream of tartar
Citrus Glaze (page 89), if desired

1. Move oven rack to lowest position. Heat oven to 325°.

2. Mix flour, sugar, baking powder and salt in large bowl. Beat in cold water, oil, vanilla, lemon peel and egg yolks until smooth.

3. Beat egg whites and cream of tartar in large bowl with electric mixer on high speed until stiff peaks form. Gradually pour egg yolk mixture over beaten egg whites, folding with rubber spatula just until blended. Pour into ungreased angel food cake pan (tube pan), 10 × 4 inches.

4. Bake about 1 hour 15 minutes or until top springs back when touched lightly. *Immediately* turn pan upside down onto heatproof funnel or bottle. Let hang about 2 hours or until cake is completely cool. Loosen side of cake with knife or long, metal spatula; remove from pan.

5. Spread or drizzle top of cake with Citrus Glaze.

If using self-rising flour, omit baking powder and salt.

1 SERVING: Calories 220 (Calories from Fat 80); Fat 9g (Saturated 2g); Cholesterol 95mg; Sodium 250mg; Carbohydrate 31g (Dietary Fiber 0g); Protein 4g

How to Make Angel Food Cakes

1. To fold, cut down through center of egg whites, along bottom and up side of bowl; rotate bowl a quarter turn. Repeat.

2. Use a knife to cut through batter and break large air pockets and to seal batter against side of pan and tube.

3. Cool cake upside down in pan by placing tube on heatproof funnel or bottle so cake does not touch counter.

Icy Chocolate Roll

Jelly Roll

PREP: 20 min; BAKE: 15 min; COOL: 30 min
Makes 10 servings

Use your favorite jelly or jam for the jelly roll filling. Or use two flavors, such as raspberry and apricot, spreading cross-wise in alternating strips so there are two colors in each spiral when you slice the roll.

3 large eggs
1 cup granulated sugar
1/3 cup water
1 teaspoon vanilla
3/4 cup all-purpose flour* or 1 cup cake flour
1 teaspoon baking powder
1/4 teaspoon salt
Powdered sugar
About 2/3 cup jelly or jam

1. Heat oven to 375°. Line jelly roll pan, 15 1/2 × 10 1/2 × 1 inch, with waxed paper, aluminum foil or cooking parchment paper; generously grease foil or waxed paper with shortening.

2. Beat eggs in small bowl with electric mixer on high speed about 5 minutes or until very thick and lemon colored. Pour eggs into medium bowl. Gradu-ally beat in granulated sugar. Beat in water and vanilla on low speed. Gradually add flour, baking powder and salt, beating just until batter is smooth. Pour into pan, spreading to corners.

3. Bake 12 to 15 minutes or until toothpick inserted in center comes out clean. Immediately loosen cake from edges of pan and turn upside down onto towel generously sprinkled with powdered sugar. Carefully remove paper. Trim off stiff edges of cake if necessary. While hot, carefully roll cake and towel from narrow end. Cool on wire rack at least 30 minutes.

4. Unroll cake and remove towel. Beat jelly slightly with fork to soften; spread over cake. Roll up cake. Sprinkle with powdered sugar.

*If using self-rising flour, omit baking powder and salt.

1 SERVING: Calories 200 (Calories from Fat 20); Fat 2g (Saturated 1g); Cholesterol 65mg; Sodium 130mg; Carbohydrate 42g (Dietary Fiber 0g); Protein 3g

ICY CHOCOLATE ROLL: Do not use self-rising flour. Increase eggs to 4. Beat in 1/4 cup baking cocoa with the flour. Spread 1 to 1 1/2 pints ice cream, slightly softened, over cooled cake. Roll up cake and wrap in plastic wrap. Freeze about 4 hours or until firm. Serve with Hot Fudge Sauce (page 159) if desired.

Tips for Frosting

- A good frosting has a smooth consistency that holds swirls and has a soft, lustrous appearance. It is soft enough to spread on the cake without running down the sides.
- The amount of frosting people like on their cake varies considerably. Frost cakes to your preference.
- For step-by-step directions for How to Frost a Cake, see page 87.
- Creamy frostings that are too thick can pull and tear the cake surface being frosted. Thin frosting with a few drops of water or milk, then coat the side of the cake with a thin layer as shown.
- When a range of ingredients is listed, be sure to use the smaller amount first, adding the rest only if necessary. That way you have better control over the consistency of the frosting.
- Fluffy frostings, such as White Mountain Frosting (page 88), are not as stable as creamy frostings made with powdered sugar, and in humid or rainy weather they should be prepared with caution. Because of moisture in the air, beating time will be longer, or the amount of water may need to be reduced slightly. It's difficult to predict exactly by how much water will need to be decreased due to varying humidity levels, so you'll have to experiment. Serve a cake with fluffy frosting on the same day it is frosted.
- Use a flexible metal or plastic spatula and a light touch when frosting cakes.
- Our testing gave us the best results when *stick* margarine or butter was used as the amount of fat was the same for both at 80%. For the best and most consistent results, we do not recommend using vegetable oil spreads or tub margarines or butters when making frostings as the fat content is lower and they contain more water and/or air, resulting in softer frostings. Also, ingredients such as chocolates do not always melt or mix well with these fats either.
- To drizzle glazes easily, pour glaze into corner of a heavy food storage bag. Use a scissors to snip off a tiny corner and squeeze gently while moving it over the top of the food. Snip off a little more of the bag if needed to make the size of drizzle you want.

Fudge Frosting

PREP: 5 min; COOK: 10 min
Makes 8 servings, about 1 1/4 cups

1/2 cup granulated sugar
1/4 cup baking cocoa
1/4 cup milk
2 tablespoons *stick* margarine or butter*
1 tablespoon light corn syrup
Dash of salt
1/2 to 3/4 cup powdered sugar
1/2 teaspoon vanilla

1. Mix granulated sugar and cocoa in 2-quart saucepan. Stir in milk, margarine, corn syrup and salt. Heat to boiling, stirring frequently. Boil 3 minutes, stirring occasionally; cool.

2. Beat in powdered sugar and vanilla until smooth. Frosts one 8- or 9-inch cake or 13 × 9-inch cake.

Note: *To fill and frost one 8- or 9-inch two-layer cake, use a 3-quart saucepan and double the ingredients.*

We do not recommend using vegetable oil spreads (see page 13).

1 SERVING: Calories 65 (Calories from Fat 20); Fat 2g (Saturated 0g); Cholesterol 0mg; Sodium 55mg; Carbohydrate 12g (Dietary Fiber 0g); Protein 0g

Sour Cream Frosting

PREP: 5 min
Makes 16 servings, about 2 cups

(Chocolate Sour Cream Frosting photographed on page 80.)

1/3 cup *stick* margarine or butter, softened*
3 cups powdered sugar
1/2 cup sour cream
2 teaspoons vanilla

1. Mix margarine and powdered sugar until blended.

2. Stir in sour cream and vanilla. Beat until smooth and spreadable. Frosts one 13 × 9-inch cake or fills and frosts one 8- or 9-inch two-layer cake.

We do not recommend using vegetable oil spreads (see page 13).

1 SERVING: Calories 135 (Calories from Fat 45); Fat 5g (Saturated 2g); Cholesterol 5mg; Sodium 45mg; Carbohydrate 23g (Dietary Fiber 0g); Protein 0g

CHOCOLATE SOUR CREAM FROSTING: Mix 3 ounces unsweetened baking chocolate, melted and cooled, with the margarine before adding powdered sugar.

Chocolate Buttercream Frosting

PREP: 15 min
Makes 16 servings, about 2 1/4 cups

3 cups powdered sugar
1/3 cup *stick* margarine or butter, softened*
2 teaspoons vanilla
3 ounces unsweetened baking chocolate,
    melted and cooled
2 to 3 tablespoons milk

1. Mix all ingredients except milk in medium bowl.

2. Stir in milk until smooth and spreadable. Frosts one 13 × 9-inch cake generously or fills and frosts one 8- or 9-inch two-layer cake.

Note: *To fill and frost one 8-inch three-layer cake, use 4 1/2 cups powdered sugar, 1/2 cup stick margarine or butter, softened, 3 teaspoons vanilla and about 1/4 cup milk.*

We do not recommend using vegetable oil spreads (see page 13).

1 SERVING: Calories 110 (Calories from Fat 45); Fat 5g (Saturated 2g); Cholesterol 0mg; Sodium 35mg; Carbohydrate 16g (Dietary Fiber 0g); Protein 0g

CREAMY COCOA FROSTING: Substitute 1/3 cup baking cocoa for the chocolate.

MOCHA FROSTING: Stir in 2 1/2 teaspoons powdered instant coffee with the powdered sugar.

WHITE CHOCOLATE FROSTING: Substitute 3/4 cup (3 ounces) white baking chips, melted and cooled, for the chocolate.

TIMESAVING TIP
Place all ingredients in food processor. Cover and process, stopping occasionally to scrape sides, until smooth and spreadable.

Vanilla Buttercream Frosting

PREP: 5 min
Makes 16 servings, about 2 cups

3 cups powdered sugar
1/3 cup *stick* margarine or butter, softened*
1 1/2 teaspoons vanilla
1 to 2 tablespoons milk

1. Mix powdered sugar and margarine in medium bowl. Stir in vanilla and milk.

2. Beat until smooth and spreadable. Frosts one 13 × 9-inch cake or fills and frosts one 8- or 9-inch two-layer cake.

Note: *To fill and frost one 8-inch three-layer cake, use 4 1/2 cups powdered sugar, 1/2 cup stick margarine or butter, softened, 2 teaspoons vanilla and about 3 tablespoons milk.*

We do not recommend using vegetable oil spreads (see page 13).

1 SERVING: Calories 130 (Calories from Fat 35); Fat 4g (Saturated 1g); Cholesterol 0mg; Sodium 45mg; Carbohydrate 23g (Dietary Fiber 0g); Protein 0g

BROWNED BUTTER BUTTERCREAM FROSTING: Heat 1/3 cup butter (do not use margarine or spreads) over medium heat until light brown. Watch carefully because butter can brown and burn quickly. Cool. Substitute melted butter for softened margarine.

LEMON BUTTERCREAM FROSTING: Omit vanilla. Substitute lemon juice for the milk. Stir in 1/2 teaspoon grated lemon peel.

MAPLE-NUT BUTTERCREAM FROSTING: Substitute 1/2 cup maple-flavored syrup for the vanilla and milk. Stir in 1/4 cup finely chopped nuts.

ORANGE BUTTERCREAM FROSTING: Omit vanilla. Substitute orange juice for the milk. Stir in 2 teaspoons grated orange peel.

PEANUT BUTTER BUTTERCREAM FROSTING: Substitute peanut butter for the margarine. Increase milk to 1/4 cup, adding more if necessary.

Cream Cheese Frosting

PREP: 10 min
Makes 16 servings, about 2 1/2 cups

If you don't use all the frosting when topping a rectangular cake, spread the extra leftovers on cookies, or slices of pound cake or graham crackers.

1 package (8 ounces) cream cheese, softened
1/4 cup *stick* margarine or butter, softened*
2 teaspoons milk
1 teaspoon vanilla
4 cups powdered sugar

1. Beat cream cheese, margarine, milk and vanilla in medium bowl with electric mixer on low speed until smooth.

2. Gradually beat in powdered sugar on low speed, 1 cup at a time, until smooth and spreadable. Frosts one 13 × 9-inch cake generously, or fills and frosts one 8- or 9-inch two-layer cake. Refrigerate any remaining frosting.

We do not recommend using vegetable oil spreads (see page 13).

1 SERVING: Calories 195 (Calories from Fat 70); Fat 8g (Saturated 4g); Cholesterol 15mg; Sodium 75mg; Carbohydrate 30g (Dietary Fiber 0g); Protein 1g

CHOCOLATE CREAM CHEESE FROSTING: Add 2 ounces unsweetened baking chocolate, melted and cooled, with the margarine.

How to Frost a Cake

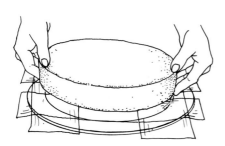

1. Brush away any loose crumbs from the cooled cake layer. Place 4 strips of waxed paper around the edge of cake plate. Place the layer on the plate, rounded side down. (The waxed paper will protect the plate as you frost and can be removed later.)

3. Place the second layer, rounded side up, on the first layer so that the 2 flat sides of the layers are together with frosting in between. Coat the side of the cake with a very thin layer of frosting to seal in the crumbs.

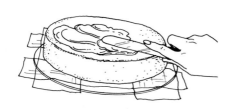

2. Spread about 1/3 cup creamy frosting (1/2 cup if fluffy frosting) over the top of the first layer to within about 1/4 inch of the edge.

4. Frost the side of the cake in swirls, making a rim about 1/4 inch high above the top of the cake to prevent the top from appearing sloped. Spread the remaining frosting on top, just to the built-up rim.

How to Coat Cake Sides

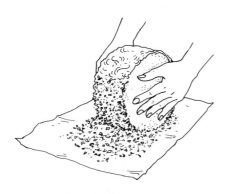

Two filled cake layers with frosted sides (not top) can be rolled in chopped nuts or candies to evenly coat the sides. Place nuts on waxed paper or cutting board. Hold cake as shown. Roll side carefully in nuts to coat.

How to Glaze a Cake

Glaze an angel food, chiffon, pound, bundt or single cake layer by pouring or drizzling a small amount of glaze on top of cake. Spread glaze with back of spoon or spatula if desired, allowing some to drizzle down side. Repeat until the desired look is reached or all glaze is used.

Caramel Frosting

PREP: 10 min; COOK: 10 min; COOL: 30 min
Makes 16 servings, about 2 cups

1/2 cup *stick* margarine or butter*
1 cup packed brown sugar
1/4 cup milk
2 cups powdered sugar

1. Melt margarine in 2-quart saucepan over medium heat. Stir in brown sugar. Heat to boiling, stirring constantly; reduce heat to low. Boil and stir 2 minutes. Stir in milk. Heat to boiling; remove from heat. Cool to lukewarm.

2. Gradually stir in powdered sugar. Place saucepan of frosting in bowl of cold water. Beat until smooth and spreadable. If frosting becomes too stiff, stir in additional milk, 1 teaspoon at a time, or heat over low heat, stirring constantly. Frosts one 13 × 9-inch cake or fills and frosts one 8- or 9-inch two-layer cake.

*We do not recommend using vegetable oil spreads (see page 13).

1 SERVING: Calories 170 (Calories from Fat 55); Fat 6g (Saturated 1g); Cholesterol 0mg; Sodium 75mg; Carbohydrate 29g (Dietary Fiber 0g); Protein 0g

Coconut-Pecan Frosting

PREP: 10 min; COOK: 12 min; COOL: 30 min
Makes 16 servings, about 3 cups

This is the filling used for German Chocolate Cake (page 75). Traditionally the cake is frosted only on top and between the layers—the sides are unfrosted.

1 cup sugar
1/2 cup *stick* margarine or butter*
1 cup evaporated milk
1 teaspoon vanilla
3 large egg yolks
1 1/3 cups flaked coconut
1 cup chopped pecans

1. Mix sugar, margarine, milk, vanilla and egg yolks in 2-quart saucepan. Cook over medium heat about 12 minutes, stirring occasionally, until thick.

2. Stir in coconut and pecans. Cool about 30 minutes, beating occasionally, until spreadable. Fills one 8- or 9-inch two- or three-layer cake.

*We do not recommend using vegetable oil spreads (see page 13).

1 SERVING: Calories 215 (Calories from Fat 135); Fat 15g (Saturated 5g); Cholesterol 45mg; Sodium 100mg; Carbohydrate 19g (Dietary Fiber 1g); Protein 2g

White Mountain Frosting

PREP: 20 min; COOK: 10 min
Makes 16 servings, about 3 cups

If you prepare this frosting on a humid day, it may require a longer beating time.

1/2 cup sugar
1/4 cup light corn syrup
2 tablespoons water
2 large egg whites
1 teaspoon vanilla

1. Mix sugar, corn syrup and water in 1-quart saucepan. Cover and heat to rolling boil over medium heat. Uncover and boil 4 to 8 minutes without stirring to 242° on candy thermometer or until small amount of mixture dropped into very cold water forms a ball that flattens when removed from water. To get an accurate temperature reading on the thermometer, it may be necessary to tilt the saucepan slightly.

2. While mixture boils, beat egg whites in medium bowl with electric mixer on high speed just until stiff peaks form.

3. Pour hot syrup very slowly in thin stream into egg whites, beating constantly on medium speed. Add vanilla. Beat on high speed about 10 minutes or until stiff peaks form. Frosts one 13 × 9-inch cake or fills and frosts one 8- or 9-inch two-layer cake.

1 SERVING: Calories 40 (Calories from Fat 0); Fat 0g (Saturated 0g); Cholesterol 0mg; Sodium 15mg; Carbohydrate 10g (Dietary Fiber 0g); Protein 0g

CHERRY-NUT FROSTING: Stir in 1/4 cup cut-up candied cherries, 1/4 cup chopped nuts and, if desired, 6 to 8 drops red food color.

COFFEE FROSTING: Beat 1 teaspoon powdered instant coffee into Satiny Beige Frosting (below).

PEPPERMINT FROSTING: Stir in 1/3 cup coarsely crushed peppermint candy or 1/2 teaspoon peppermint extract.

SATINY BEIGE FROSTING: Substitute packed brown sugar for the granulated sugar. Decrease vanilla to 1/2 teaspoon.

Sweetened Whipped Cream

PREP: 5 min

Tailor this favorite topping to suit the dessert on which it's mounded, and have fun choosing a compatible flavor variation to make it even more special.

For 1 cup whipped cream: Beat 1/2 cup whipping (heavy) cream and 1 tablespoon granulated or powdered sugar in chilled small bowl with electric mixer on high speed until stiff.

For 1 1/2 cups whipped cream: Beat 3/4 cup whipping (heavy) cream and 2 tablespoons granulated or powdered sugar in chilled small bowl with electric mixer on high speed until stiff.

For 2 1/3 cups whipped cream: Beat 1 cup whipping (heavy) cream and 3 tablespoons granulated or powdered sugar in chilled medium bowl with electric mixer on high speed until stiff.

1 SERVING: Calories 55 (Calories from Fat 45); Fat 5g (Saturated 3g); Cholesterol 15mg; Sodium 5mg; Carbohydrate 2g (Dietary Fiber 0g); Protein 0g

FLAVORED SWEETENED WHIPPED CREAM: Beat 1 cup whipping (heavy) cream, 3 tablespoons granulated or powdered sugar and one of the following ingredients in chilled medium bowl with electric mixer on high speed until stiff.

> 1 teaspoon grated lemon or orange peel
> 1 teaspoon vanilla
> 1/2 teaspoon ground cinnamon
> 1/2 teaspoon ground ginger
> 1/2 teaspoon ground nutmeg
> 1/2 teaspoon almond extract
> 1/2 teaspoon peppermint extract
> 1/2 teaspoon rum flavoring
> 1/4 teaspoon maple flavoring

Chocolate Glaze

PREP: 5 min; COOK: 5 min; COOL: 10 min
Makes 16 servings, about 1/2 cup

For a dazzling presentation, drizzle this easy glaze on plates before adding the dessert.

> 1/2 cup semisweet chocolate chips
> 2 tablespoons *stick* margarine or butter*
> 2 tablespoons corn syrup
> 1 to 2 teaspoons hot water

1. Heat chocolate chips, margarine and corn syrup in 1-quart saucepan over low heat, stirring constantly, until chocolate chips are melted; cool slightly.

2. Stir in hot water, 1 teaspoon at a time, until consistency of thick syrup. Glazes one 12-cup bundt cake or 10-inch angel food or chiffon cake.

We do not recommend using vegetable oil spreads (see page 13).

1 SERVING: Calories 45 (Calories from Fat 25); Fat 3g (Saturated 1g); Cholesterol 0mg; Sodium 20mg; Carbohydrate 5g (Dietary Fiber 0g); Protein 0g

WHITE CHOCOLATE GLAZE: Substitute vanilla milk chips for the chocolate chips.

TIMESAVING TIP

To microwave, place chocolate chips, margarine and corn syrup in 2-cup microwavable measure. Microwave uncovered on Medium (50%) 1 to 2 minutes or until chocolate can be stirred smooth. Omit water.

Vanilla Glaze

PREP: 5 min
Makes 16 servings, about 1 cup

> 1/3 cup *stick* margarine or butter*
> 2 cups powdered sugar
> 1 1/2 teaspoons vanilla or clear vanilla
> 2 to 4 tablespoons hot water

1. Melt margarine in 1 1/2-quart saucepan.

2. Stir in powdered sugar and vanilla. Stir in hot water, 1 tablespoon at a time, until smooth and consistency of thick syrup. Glazes one 12-cup bundt cake or 10-inch angel food or chiffon cake.

We do not recommend using vegetable oil spreads (see page 13).

1 SERVING: Calories 95 (Calories from Fat 35); Fat 4g (Saturated 1g); Cholesterol 0mg; Sodium 45mg; Carbohydrate 15g (Dietary Fiber 0g); Protein 0g

CITRUS GLAZE: Stir 1/2 teaspoon grated lemon, orange, lime or grapefruit peel into melted margarine. Substitute lemon, orange, lime or grapefruit juice for the vanilla and hot water.

TIMESAVING TIP

Use vanilla ready-to-spread frosting sold in tubs. Place 1/2 cup frosting in microwavable bowl. Microwave uncovered on High about 15 seconds or until frosting can be stirred smooth and is thin enough to drizzle.

Chocolate Ganache

PREP: 5 min; COOK: 5 min; COOL: 10 min
Makes 16 servings, about 1 1/4 cups

A rich mixture of chocolate and heavy cream, a ganache is usually poured over a cake or torte. For the smoothest appearance, don't spread with a knife or spatula.

> 2/3 cup whipping (heavy) cream
> 6 ounces semisweet baking chocolate, chopped

1. Heat whipping cream in 1-quart saucepan until hot but not boiling; remove from heat.

2. Stir in chocolate until melted. Let stand 5 minutes. Ganache is ready to use when mixture mounds slightly when dropped from spoon. Mixture becomes firmer the longer it cools. Frosts one 13 × 9-inch cake or covers one 8- or 9-inch cake layer.

3. To frost, place cake layer on wire rack over waxed paper. Pour ganache in center of cake; tilt wire rack so it flows evenly over the top and down to cover the side.

1 SERVING: Calories 80 (Calories from Fat 55); Fat 6g (Saturated 4g); Cholesterol 10mg; Sodium 5mg; Carbohydrate 7g (Dietary Fiber 1g); Protein 1g

Lemon Filling

PREP: 5 min; COOK: 10 min; CHILL: 2 hr
Makes 16 servings, about 1 1/4 cups

This lemony filling in wonderful used in the Coconut-Lemon Cake (page 76), as a filling for cream puffs (page 145) or as a filling instead of jelly in Jelly Roll (page 84).

> 3/4 cup sugar
> 3 tablespoons cornstarch
> 1/4 teaspoon salt
> 2/3 cup water
> 1 tablespoon *stick* margarine or butter*
> 1 teaspoon grated lemon peel
> 1/4 cup lemon juice
> 2 drops yellow food color, if desired

1. Mix sugar, cornstarch and salt in 1 1/2-quart saucepan. Gradually stir in water. Cook over medium heat, stirring constantly, until mixture thickens and boils. Boil and stir 1 minute; remove from heat.

2. Stir in margarine and lemon peel until margarine is melted. Gradually stir in lemon juice and food color. Press plastic wrap onto filling. Refrigerate about 2 hours or until set. Refrigerate cakes or pastries filled with Lemon Filling.

*We do not recommend using vegetable oil spreads (see page 13).

1 SERVING: Calories 55 (Calories from Fat 10); Fat 1g (Saturated 0g); Cholesterol 0mg; Sodium 45mg; Carbohydrate 11g (Dietary Fiber 0g); Protein 0g

Triple Berry Filling

PREP: 5 min; COOK: 10 min
Makes 16 servings, about 1 1/4 cups

> 1 package (10 ounces) frozen raspberries in light syrup, thawed
> 2 tablespoons sugar
> 1 tablespoon cornstarch
> 1/2 cup blueberries
> 1/2 cup cut-up strawberries

1. Drain raspberries, reserving 1/3 cup liquid. Mix sugar and cornstarch in 1-quart saucepan. Stir in reserved raspberry liquid.

2. Heat sugar mixture over medium heat, stirring constantly, until mixture thickens and boils. Boil and stir 1 minute.

3. Stir raspberries, blueberries and strawberries into sugar mixture. Cool completely.

1 SERVING: Calories 30 (Calories from Fat 0); Fat 0g (Saturated 0g); Cholesterol 0mg; Sodium 0mg; Carbohydrate 8g (Dietary Fiber 0g); Protein 0g

---

TIMESAVING TIP

To microwave, use microwavable 4-cup glass measure. Microwave sugar mixture uncovered on high (100%) 2 to 3 minutes, stirring every minute, until thickened.

Chocolate Truffle Filling

PREP: 5 min; COOK: 5 min; CHILL: 40 min
Makes 12 servings, about 1 2/3 cups

For an extra flavor punch, substitute hazelnut or other flavors of nondairy liquid creamer for the whipping cream.

> 1 package (12 ounces) semisweet chocolate chips (2 cups)
> 1/4 cup *stick* margarine or butter*
> 1/2 cup whipping (heavy) cream or hazelnut-flavored nondairy liquid creamer

1. Heat chocolate chips and margarine in heavy 2-quart saucepan over low heat, stirring constantly, until chocolate is melted; remove from heat.

2. Stir in whipping cream. Refrigerate 30 to 40 minutes, stirring frequently, just until thick enough to mound and hold its shape when dropped from a spoon. If filling becomes too thick, microwave on High (100%) 10 to 15 seconds to soften.) Fills and frosts one 8- or 9-inch cake layer, split.

*We do not recommend using vegetable oil spreads (see page 13).

1 SERVING: Calories 205 (Calories from Fat 135); Fat 15g (Saturated 8g); Cholesterol 10mg; Sodium 50mg; Carbohydrate 18g (Dietary Fiber 2g); Protein 1g

About Pies and Pastry

Enjoy the collection of pies and pastries here, from luscious fruit pies to airy meringue-topped pies and creamy custard-based favorites such as Pumpkin Pie. Have fun experimenting with pretty crusts—everything you need to know is right here!

Pans and Preparation

- Choose heat-resistant glass pie plates or dull-finish (anodized) aluminum pie pans. Never use a shiny pan because the pan reflects heat and the pie will have a soggy bottom crust.
- The most common pie size is 9 inches. Even though pie plates and pans on the market may be labeled 9 inches, they can vary in capacity. Our pie recipes were developed with pie plates that hold about 5 cups. However, we often use 8 cups of fruit for 2-crust pies for a full baked pie, as the fruit does cook down during baking.
- Because of the amount of fat in pastry and crusts, pie plates and pans usually are not greased.
- Nonstick pie pans can cause pastry to shrink excessively when baking one-crust pie shells. Be sure pastry is securely hooked over the edge of the pan.

Mixing and Rolling Pastry

- A pastry blender is a great help to cut the shortening evenly into the flour. If you don't own one, use two knives; with the knife blades almost touching each other, move the knives back and forth in opposite directions in a parallel cutting motion. The side of a fork or a wire whisk also can be used. The shortening melts during baking, producing a flaky texture throughout.
- Don't overwork pastry or it will become tough.
- If using self-rising flour, omit the salt. Pastry made with self-rising flour will be slightly different—mealy and tender instead of flaky and tender.
- Unbleached flour works especially well for pastry, as shrinkage is diminished and the baked pastry color is more golden.
- To roll out pastry, choose the method that works best for you. (See How to Shape Pastry, page 94.) We like the following method best because the pastry does not stick to the flat surface or the rolling pin. Anchor a pastry cloth or kitchen towel (not terry-cloth) around a large cutting board (at least 12 × 12 inches) with masking tape, and use a cloth cover (stockinet) for your rolling pin to keep the dough from sticking. Rub flour into both cloths; this will prevent sticking, yet the flour won't be absorbed by the dough.

If a pastry cloth or rolling pin cover is not available, rub flour into a large cutting board (at least 12 × 12 inches) and into the rolling pin.

Begin rolling from the center out, lifting and turning the pastry occasionally. This will help prevent sticking. If the dough begins to stick, rub more flour into the flat surface and rolling pin a little at a time.

- To make rolling and shaping even easier, wrap flattened round of pastry tightly and refrigerate at least 15 minutes. This allows the moisture to be evenly absorbed, the shortening to solidify and the gluten to relax for easier rolling.

Baking Pies and Pastry

- Bake pies and pie crusts on the oven shelf located in the center of the oven. In some electric ovens, placing the oven shelf on the lowest rack puts the pie closer to the heating element, resulting in a drier, flakier bottom crust. You may also find the top of the pie may not have to be shielded with aluminum foil to prevent over-browning.
- To give a special, more finished look to the top crust of two-crust pies, try one of the following *before* baking:
    Shiny crust—brush with milk.
    Sugary crust—moisten with water, then sprinkle with granulated sugar.
    Glazed crust—brush the crust lightly with a beaten egg or an egg yolk mixed with a little water.
- To glaze a two-crust pie *after* baking, brush with a mixture of 1/2 cup powdered sugar, 2 teaspoons finely shredded orange or lemon peel and 1 tablespoon orange or lemon juice. (Do not allow glaze to run over edge of pie.)
- Pies are baked at higher temperatures (375° to 425°) than cakes so the rich pastry dries and becomes flaky and golden brown while the filling cooks throughout.
- To prevent excessive browning, add aluminum foil. (See How to Prevent Excessive Browning of Pastry Edges, page 92.) Bake as directed, removing foil 15 minutes before end of baking time to allow edge to brown.

- Prevent an unbaked unfilled one-crust pie shell from puffing up as it bakes by pricking the pastry thoroughly with a fork just before baking to allow steam to escape. For one-crust pies such as pumpkin or pecan pie where the filling is baked in the shell, do not prick the crust because the filling would seep under the crust during baking.
- Shape crumb crusts evenly and make them firm and smooth by pressing another pie plate of the same diameter firmly into the crust. Do this after pressing crumbs by hand.

How to Prevent Excessive Browning of Pastry Edges

Cover edge of a two-crust pie with a 2- to 3-inch strip of aluminum foil and gently mold to edge of pie.

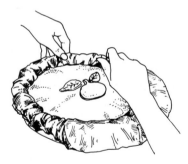

Fold a 12-inch square of aluminum foil into fourths; trim the open corner to make a 12-inch circle. Cut a 3-inch strip from the curved edge. Unfold and gently mold to edge of pie.

Pie Yields and Storage

- Most of the pies in this cookbook make 8 servings. Serving sizes for very rich pies are listed at 10 to 12 servings.
- Refrigerate pies that contain eggs, such as pumpkin and cream pies.
- Pie shells can be frozen either unbaked or baked. Frozen unbaked shells will keep two months and baked shells four months. To thaw baked pie shells, unwrap and let stand at room temper-

ature, or heat in 350° oven about 6 minutes. Do not thaw unbaked shells; immediately bake after removing from freezer.
- Do not freeze custard or cream pies with meringue topping.
- Baked fruit pies can be frozen. They are easiest to wrap if frozen uncovered first, then wrapped tightly or placed in plastic freezer bags. Baking before freezing prevents soggy crusts or the possible texture breakdown of raw fruit. Frozen baked pies will keep up to four months.
- To serve frozen two-crust pies, unwrap and thaw at room temperature 1 hour. Heat in 375° oven on lowest rack 35 to 40 minutes or until warm.

Baking with Confidence

Perfect Pastry Is

Golden brown and blistered on top
Crisp, brown undercrust
Tender, cuts easily and holds its shape when served
Flaky and crisp

Problem	Possible Cause
Pale color	• baked in shiny, not dull pan • underbaked
Pastry looks smooth	• dough was handled too much
Bottom crust is soggy	• baked in shiny, not dull pan • baking temperature too low
Tough	• too much water • too much flour • too much mixing
Too tender; falls apart	• too little water • too much shortening
Dry and mealy, not flaky	• shortening was cut in too fine • too little water

Pastry for Pies and Tarts

PREP: 15 min; BAKE: 10 min
Makes 8 servings

Mastering the art of shaping pastry is easy when you follow our step-by-step directions, page 94.

One-Crust Pie

> 1/3 cup plus 1 tablespoon shortening or
> 1/3 cup lard
> 1 cup all-purpose* or unbleached flour
> 1/4 teaspoon salt
> 2 to 3 tablespoons cold water

Two-Crust Pie

> 2/3 cup plus 2 tablespoons shortening or
> 2/3 cup lard
> 2 cups all-purpose* or unbleached flour
> 1 teaspoon salt
> 4 to 5 tablespoons cold water

1. Cut shortening into flour and salt, using pastry blender or crisscrossing 2 knives, until particles are size of coarse crumbs. Sprinkle with cold water, 1 tablespoon at a time, tossing with fork until all flour is moistened and pastry almost cleans side of bowl (1 to 2 teaspoons more water can be added if necessary).

2. Gather pastry into a ball. Shape into flattened round on lightly floured cloth-covered board. (For Two-Crust Pie, divide pastry in half and shape into 2 rounds.)

3. Roll pastry into circle 2 inches larger than upside-down pie plate, 9 × 1 1/4 inches, or 3 inches larger than 10- or 11-inch tart pan, with floured cloth-covered rolling pin. Fold pastry into fourths; place in pie plate. Unfold and ease into plate, pressing firmly against bottom and side.

One-Crust Pie

Filled Crust: *For pie,* trim overhanging edge of pastry 1 inch from rim of pie plate. Fold and roll pastry under, even with plate; flute (see Pastry Edges, page 96). *For tart,* trim overhanging edge of pastry even with top of tart pan. Fill and bake as directed in pie or tart recipe.

Baked Crust (unfilled): Heat oven to 475°. *For pie,* trim overhanging edge of pastry 1 inch from rim of pie plate. Fold and roll pastry under, even with plate; flute (page 96). *For tart,* trim overhanging edge of pastry even with top of tart pan. Prick bottom and side of pastry thoroughly with fork. Bake 8 to 10 minutes or until light brown; cool on wire rack.

Two-Crust Pie

Turn desired filling into pastry-lined pie plate, 9 × 11/4 inches. Trim overhanging edge of pastry 1/2 inch from rim of plate. Roll other round of pastry. Fold into fourths and cut slits so steam can escape.

Place pastry over filling and unfold. Trim overhanging edge of top pastry 1 inch from rim of plate. Fold and roll top edge under lower edge, pressing on rim to seal; flute (see Pastry Edges, page 96). Or prepare Lattice Top (page 95) if desired.

Baked Tart Shells

Prepare pastry as directed for One-Crust Pie (left)— except roll pastry into 13-inch circle. Cut into eight 4 1/2-inch circles.

Heat oven to 475°. Fit circles over backs of medium muffin cups, 2 1/2 × 1 1/4 inches, or 6-ounce custard cups, making pleats so pastry will fit closely. (If using individual pie pans or tart pans, cut pastry circles 1 inch larger than upside-down pans; fit into pans.) Prick pastry thoroughly with fork to prevent puffing. Place on cookie sheet.

Bake 8 to 10 minutes or until light brown. Cool before removing from cups. Fill each shell with 1/3 to 1/2 cup of your favorite filling pudding, fresh fruit, or ice cream.

If using self-rising flour, omit salt. Pie crusts made with self-rising flour differ in flavor and texture from those made with all-purpose flour.

1 SERVING (one crust): Calories 140 (Calories from Fat 90); Fat 10g (Saturated 3g); Cholesterol 0mg; Sodium 65mg; Carbohydrate 12g (Dietary Fiber 0g); Protein 1g

---

TIMESAVING TIP

Use a food processor—measure 2 tablespoons water (for One-Crust Pie) or 4 tablespoons water (for Two-Crust Pie) into small bowl. Place shortening, flour and salt in food processor. Cover and process, using quick on-and-off motions, until mixture is crumbly. With food processor running, pour water all at once through feed tube just until dough leaves side of bowl (dough should not form a ball). Continue as directed in step 2.

How to Shape Pastry

1. Roll pastry from center to outside edge in all directions, occasionally giving it a quarter turn. For even thickness, lift the rolling pin as it approaches the edge.

2. Push edge of pastry in gently with sides of hands to keep it circular when rolling it out. Lift pastry occasionally to prevent it from sticking to cloth.

3. Fold pastry into quarters; place in pie plate with point in center. Unfold and gently ease into plate, being careful not to stretch pastry. Trim as directed (page 96).

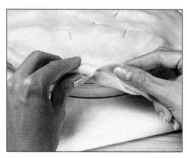

4. For two-crust pie, cut slits or special design in top pastry before folding. Carefully place folded pastry over filling and unfold. Let top pastry overhang 1 inch beyond edge of pie plate. Fold and roll overhanging pastry under edge of bottom pastry, pressing to seal.

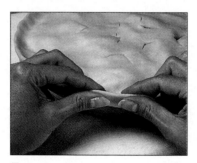

5. Form a stand-up rim on the edge of the pie plate while pinching the top and bottom edges together. This seals the pastry and makes fluting easier.

For pastry top with lots of cut-outs, be sure bottom of pastry is floured well. Roll onto rolling pin and unroll over filling. Or slide flat end of cookie sheet under pastry and gently slide over filling, shaking pan if needed.

Lattice Pie Top

Prepare pastry as directed for Two-Crust Pie (page 93)—except leave 1-inch overhang on lower crust. After rolling pastry circle for top crust, cut into strips about 1/2 inch wide. (Use a pastry wheel for decorative strips.)

Place 5 to 7 strips (depending on size of pie) across filling in pie plate. Weave a cross-strip through center by first folding back every other strip going the other way. Continue weaving until lattice is complete, folding back alternate strips each time cross-strip is added. (To save time, do not weave strips. Simply lay second half of strips across first strips.) Trim ends of strips.

Fold trimmed edge of lower crust over ends of strips, building up a high edge. Seal and flute (page 96). (A juicy fruit pie with a lattice top is more likely to bubble over than a two-crust pie, so be sure to build up a high pastry edge.)

Two-Crust Pie Tops

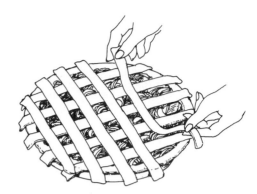

Classic Lattice Top: Place 5 to 7 strips on filling; fold back alternate strips as each cross-strip is added. Strips can be twisted if desired.

Easy Lattice Top: Place 5 to 7 strips on filling. Rotate the pie plate 1/4 turn and place 5 to 7 strips crosswise over top at right angles. Do not weave strips.

Diamond Lattice Top: Weave or lay second half of pastry strips diagonally across first strips on filling.

Mock Lattice Top: Use a small cookie cutter or canapé cutter to make a cutout in the center. Repeat the cutouts in a regular pattern, working from the center to 1 inch from the edge.

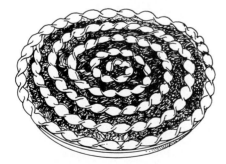

Spiral Top: Begin from center of pie. Twist one strip and coil it outward on pie, adding length by moistening ends of other strips and pinching. Moisten trimmed edge of bottom crust; place tightly twisted pastry strip around edge, pressing to seal.

Cutout Top: Cut top crust in wedges or into large designs with cookie cutter. Arrange over filling.

Pastry Edges

Fork Edge: Flatten pastry evenly on rim of pie plate. Press firmly around edge with tines of fork. Press diagonally for herringbone effect. To prevent sticking, dip fork into flour.

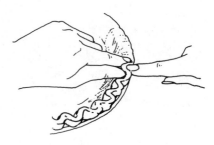

Pinch Edge: Place index finger on inside of pastry rim and knuckles (or thumb and index finger) on outside. Pinch pastry into V shape along entire edge. Pinch again to sharpen.

Rope Edge: Place side of thumb on pastry rim at an angle. Pinch pastry by pressing the knuckle of your index finger down into pastry toward thumb.

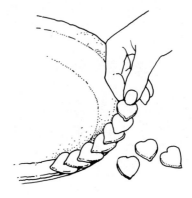

Cutout Edge: Trim overhang even or flatten pastry on rim. Use tiny cookie cutter, thimble or bottlecap to cut 3/4-inch circles, leaves, hearts, etc., from pastry scraps. Moisten rim and slightly overlap cutouts around rim. Press into place.

Pointed Edge: Flatten pastry evenly on rim of pie plate. Cut edge 1/2-inch deep every 1/2 inch. Moisten rim. Fold each piece diagonally in half to form a triangle, pressing lightly to seal.

Braided Edge: Braid three 1/4-inch strips of pastry loosely, making the braid long enough to fit the edge of the pie. Moisten rim and lay braid on top, pressing lightly to seal.

Pat-in-the-Pan Oil Pastry

PREP: 15 min; BAKE: 12 min
Makes 8 servings

This pastry is quick and easy because it doesn't have to be rolled out. The texture of pastry made with vegetable oil is less flaky than pastry made with shortening, but it is also free of cholesterol.

> 1 1/3 cups all-purpose* or unbleached flour
> 1/3 cup vegetable oil
> 1/2 teaspoon salt
> 2 tablespoons cold water

1. Mix flour, oil and salt until all flour is moistened. Sprinkle with cold water, 1 tablespoon at a time, tossing with fork until all water is absorbed.

2. Gather pastry into a ball. Press in bottom and up side of pie plate, 9 × 1 1/4 inches; flute edge (page 96).

- Filled Crust: Fill and bake as directed in recipe.
- Baked Pie Crust (unfilled): Heat oven to 475°. Prick bottom and side of pastry thoroughly with fork. Bake 10 to 12 minutes or until light brown; cool on wire rack.

If using self-rising flour, omit salt.

1 SERVING: Calories 150 (Calories from Fat 80); Fat 9g (Saturated 2g); Cholesterol 0mg; Sodium 135mg; Carbohydrate 16g (Dietary Fiber 1g); Protein 2g

Cookie Tart Pastry

PREP: 10 min; BAKE: 12 min
Makes 8 servings

> 1 1/4 cups all-purpose* or unbleached flour
> 1/2 cup *stick* margarine or butter, softened**
> 2 tablespoons packed brown sugar
> 1 large egg

1. Heat oven to 400°.

2. Mix all ingredients until dough forms. Press firmly and evenly against bottom and side of ungreased 11-inch tart pan.

3. Bake 10 to 12 minutes or until light brown; cool.

Do not use self-rising flour in this recipe.

**We do not recommend using vegetable oil spreads (see page 13).*

1 SERVING: Calories 255 (Calories from Fat 145); Fat 16g (Saturated 4g); Cholesterol 25mg; Sodium 190mg; Carbohydrate 25g (Dietary Fiber 1g); Protein 3g

---

> **TIMESAVING TIP**
> Place all ingredients in food processor. Cover and process, using quick on-and-off motions, until dough forms a ball. Continue as directed in step 2, pressing into tart pan.

Graham Cracker Crust

PREP: 10 min; BAKE: 10 min
Makes 8 servings

Graham cracker and cookie crumb crusts are easy to make and can hold just about any type of filling—we used it for a delicious Grasshopper Pie (page 108) and the Caramel-Chocolate Pie Supreme (page 108). Baking the crust will help it hold together better when cut.

> 1 1/2 cups (about 20 squares) regular or
>   cinnamon graham crackers, finely crushed
> 1/3 cup *stick* margarine or butter, melted*
> 3 tablespoons sugar

1. Heat oven to 350°.

2. Mix crumbs, margarine and sugar. Reserve 3 tablespoons mixture for topping if desired. Press remaining mixture firmly against bottom and side of pie plate, 9 × 1 1/4 inches.

3. Bake about 10 minutes or until light brown; cool.

Spreads with at least 65% vegetable oil can be substituted (see page 13).

1 SERVING: Calories 155 (Calories from Fat 80); Fat 9g (Saturated 2g); Cholesterol 0mg; Sodium 180mg; Carbohydrate 17g (Dietary Fiber 0g); Protein 1g

COCONUT CRUST: Heat oven to 325°. Substitute flaked coconut for the graham cracker crumbs. Decrease margarine to 3 tablespoons and omit the sugar. Bake about 15 minutes or until light brown.

COOKIE CRUMB CRUST: Substitute chocolate or vanilla wafer cookies or gingersnaps for the graham crackers. Decrease the margarine to 1/4 cup and omit the sugar.

> **TIMESAVING TIP**
> To microwave, prepare as directed—except use microwavable pie plate. Microwave uncovered on High 2 to 3 minutes, rotating pie plate 1/2 turn every minute, until set; cool.

Blueberry Pie (page 100), Cranberry-Apple Pie

Apple Pie

PREP: 45 min; BAKE: 50 min
Makes 8 servings

For a creamy Dutch Apple Pie, make extra-large slits in the top crust. Five minutes before the end of baking, pour 1/2 cup whipping (heavy) cream through the slits in the crust.

> Pastry for Two-Crust Pie (page 93)
> 1/3 to 2/3 cup sugar
> 1/4 cup all-purpose flour*
> 1/2 teaspoon ground cinnamon
> 1/2 teaspoon ground nutmeg
> Dash of salt
> 8 cups thinly sliced peeled tart apples
>   (8 medium)
> 2 tablespoons *stick* margarine or butter**

1. Heat oven to 425°. Prepare pastry.

2. Mix sugar, flour, cinnamon, nutmeg and salt in large bowl. Stir in apples. Turn into pastry-lined pie plate. Dot with margarine. Cover with top pastry that has slits cut in it; seal and flute. Cover edge with 3-inch strip of aluminum foil to prevent excessive browning. Remove foil during last 15 minutes of baking.

3. Bake 40 to 50 minutes or until crust is brown and juice begins to bubble through slits in crust. Cool in pie plate on wire rack. Serve warm if desired.

*If using self-rising flour, omit salt.

**Spreads with at least 65% vegetable oil can be substituted (see page 13).

1 SERVING: Calories 430 (Calories from Fat 215); Fat 24g (Saturated 6g); Cholesterol 0mg; Sodium 370mg; Carbohydrate 54g (Dietary Fiber 4g); Protein 4g

CRANBERRY-APPLE PIE: Substitute 2 cups fresh or frozen (thawed) cranberries for 3 cups apples. Increase sugar to 1 1/3 cups. Omit cinnamon and nutmeg.

FRENCH APPLE PIE: Prepare pastry for One-Crust Pie (page 92). Turn apple mixture into pastry-lined pie plate. Omit margarine. Sprinkle apple mixture with Crumb Topping: Mix 1 cup all-purpose flour, 1/2 cup packed brown sugar and 1/2 cup firm *stick* margarine or butter** until crumbly. Cover topping with aluminum foil during last 10 minutes of baking to prevent excessive browning. Bake 50 minutes. Serve warm.

**Spreads with at least 65% vegetable oil can be substituted (see page 13).

TIMESAVING TIP

Substitute 3 cans (20 ounces each) sliced apples, drained, for the 8 cups fresh apples. To bake in half the time, prepare pie as directed—except use microwavable pie plate. Microwave uncovered on High 12 to 14 minutes or until filling begins to bubble through slits in crust. Transfer pie to conventional oven (do not preheat). Bake at 450° 12 to 18 minutes or until crust is brown and flaky.

Deep-Dish Apple Pie

PREP: 45 min; BAKE: 1 hr
Makes 12 servings

Watching your fat intake? This fruity one-crust pie has significantly less fat than the more traditional two-crust apple pie.

> Pastry for One-Crust Pie (page 93)
> 1 1/4 cups sugar
> 1/2 cup all-purpose flour*
> 1 teaspoon ground cinnamon
> 1/2 teaspoon ground nutmeg
> 1/4 teaspoon salt
> 11 cups thinly sliced peeled tart apples
>   (10 medium)
> 1 tablespoon *stick* margarine or butter**

1. Heat oven to 425°. Prepare pastry as directed—except roll into 10-inch square. Cut slits near center so steam can escape; fold pastry in half.

2. Mix sugar, flour, cinnamon, nutmeg and salt in large bowl. Stir in apples. Turn into ungreased square pan, 9 × 9 × 2 inches. Dot with margarine. Place top pastry that has slits cut in it over filling and unfold. Fold edges under just inside edge of pan.

3. Bake 50 to 60 minutes or until juice begins to bubble through slits in crust. Cool in pan on wire rack. Serve warm if desired.

*If using self-rising flour, omit salt.

**Spreads with at least 65% vegetable oil can be substituted (see page 13).

1 SERVING: Calories 270 (Calories from Fat 70); Fat 8g (Saturated 2g); Cholesterol 0mg; Sodium 145mg; Carbohydrate 49g (Dietary Fiber 2g); Protein 2g

Cherry Pie

PREP: 40 min; BAKE: 45 min
Makes 8 servings

This is the perfect pie for any of the Lattice Tops (page 95). If you use fresh cherries often, consider purchasing a cherry pitter or stoner, available at kitchen specialty shops. You can also use the point of a knife, or try the tip of a vegetable peeler or a paper clip.

> Pastry for Two-Crust Pie (page 93)
> 1 1/3 cups sugar
> 1/2 cup all-purpose flour
> 6 cups red tart cherries, pitted
> 2 tablespoons *stick* margarine or butter*

1. Heat oven to 425°. Prepare pastry.

2. Mix sugar and flour in large bowl. Stir in cherries. Turn into pastry-lined pie plate. Dot with margarine. Cover with top pastry that has slits cut in it; seal and flute. Cover edge with 2- to 3-inch strip of

aluminum foil to prevent excessive browning. Remove foil during last 15 minutes of baking.

3. Bake 35 to 45 minutes or until crust is brown and juice begins to bubble through slits in crust. Cool in pie plate on wire rack. Serve warm if desired.

*Spreads with at least 65% vegetable oil can be substituted (see page 13).

1 SERVING: Calories 520 (Calories from Fat 190); Fat 21g (Saturated 5g); Cholesterol 0mg; Sodium 300mg; Carbohydrate 81g (Dietary Fiber 3g); Protein 5g

---

TIMESAVING TIP

Substitute 6 cups frozen unsweetened pitted red tart cherries, thawed and drained, or 3 cans (16 ounces each) pitted red tart cherries, drained, for the fresh cherries.

Peach Pie

PREP: 45 min; BAKE: 45 min
Makes 8 servings

> Pastry for Two-Crust Pie (page 93)
> 2/3 cup sugar
> 1/3 cup all-purpose flour
> 1/4 teaspoon ground cinnamon
> 6 cups sliced peaches (6 to 8 medium)
> 1 teaspoon lemon juice
> 1 tablespoon *stick* margarine or butter*

1. Heat oven to 425°. Prepare pastry.

2. Mix sugar, flour and cinnamon in large bowl. Stir in peaches and lemon juice. Turn into pastry-lined pie plate. Dot with margarine. Cover with top pastry that has slits cut in it; seal and flute. Cover edge with 2- to 3-inch strip of aluminum foil to prevent excessive browning. Remove foil during last 15 minutes of baking.

3. Bake about 45 minutes or until crust is brown and juice begins to bubble through slits in crust. Cool in pie plate on wire rack. Serve warm if desired.

*Spreads with at least 65% vegetable oil can be substituted (see page 13).

1 SERVING: Calories 410 (Calories from Fat 170); Fat 19g (Saturated 5g); Cholesterol 0mg; Sodium 280mg; Carbohydrate 59g (Dietary Fiber 3g); Protein 4g

APRICOT PIE: Substitute 6 cups fresh apricot halves for the peaches.

TIMESAVING TIP

Substitute 6 cups frozen sliced peaches, partially thawed and drained, for the fresh peaches.

Blueberry Pie

PREP: 30 min; BAKE: 45 min
Makes 8 servings

(photograph on page 98)

>   Pastry for Two-Crust Pie (page 93)
>   3/4 cup sugar
>   1/2 cup all-purpose flour
>   1/2 teaspoon ground cinnamon, if desired
>   6 cups blueberries
>   1 tablespoon lemon juice
>   1 tablespoon *stick* margarine or butter**

1. Heat oven to 425°. Prepare pastry.

2. Mix sugar, flour and cinnamon in large bowl. Stir in blueberries. Turn into pastry-lined pie plate. Sprinkle with lemon juice. Dot with margarine. Cover with top pastry that has slits cut in it; seal and flute. Cover edge with 2- to 3-inch strip of aluminum foil to prevent excessive browning. Remove foil during last 15 minutes of baking.

3. Bake 35 to 45 minutes or until crust is brown and juice begins to bubble through slits in crust. Cool in pie plate on wire rack. Serve warm if desired.

***Spreads with at least 65% vegetable oil can be substituted (see page 13).*

1 SERVING: Calories 435 (Calories from Fat 170); Fat 19g (Saturated 5g); Cholesterol 0mg; Sodium 290mg; Carbohydrate 64g (Dietary Fiber 3g); Protein 5g

BLACKBERRY, BOYSENBERRY, LOGANBERRY OR RASPBERRY PIE: Increase sugar to 1 cup. Substitute fresh berries for the blueberries. Omit lemon juice.

> **TIMESAVING TIP**
> Substitute 6 cups drained canned blueberries or unsweetened frozen (thawed) blueberries for the fresh blueberries.

Rhubarb Pie

PREP: 35 min; BAKE: 55 min
Makes 8 servings

Rhubarb is traditionally served as a fruit, although it's actually a vegetable! Due to its tartness, the amount of sugar used in rhubarb recipes is usually quite high.

>   Pastry for Two-Crust Pie (page 93)
>   2 to 2 1/3 cups sugar
>   2/3 cup all-purpose flour
>   1 teaspoon grated orange peel, if desired
>   6 cups cut-up rhubarb (1/2-inch pieces)*
>   1 tablespoon *stick* margarine or butter**

1. Heat oven to 425°. Prepare pastry.

2. Mix sugar, flour and orange peel in large bowl. Stir in rhubarb. Turn into pastry-lined pie plate. Dot with margarine. Cover with top pastry that has slits cut in it; seal and flute. Sprinkle with sugar if desired. Cover edge with 2- to 3-inch strip of aluminum foil to prevent excessive browning. Remove foil during last 15 minutes of baking.

3. Bake about 55 minutes or until crust is brown and juice begins to bubble through slits in crust. Cool in pie plate on wire rack. Serve warm if desired.

**2 packages (16 ounces each) unsweetened frozen rhubarb, completely thawed and drained, can be substituted for the cut-up rhubarb.*

***Spreads with at least 65% vegetable oil can be substituted (see page 13).*

1 SERVING: Calories 515 (Calories from Fat 170); Fat 19g (Saturated 5g); Cholesterol 0mg; Sodium 290mg; Carbohydrate 84g (Dietary Fiber 3g); Protein 5g

STRAWBERRY-RHUBARB PIE: Substitute 3 cups sliced strawberries for 3 cups of the rhubarb. Use 2 cups sugar.

Fresh Strawberry Pie

PREP: 30 min; COOK: 10 min; BAKE: 10 min; CHILL: 3 hr
Makes 8 servings

Enjoy this fresh fruit pie when the fruit is at its peak of ripeness. A mixture of berries and sliced fruits can also be used, but in step 2 mash only one type of fruit for the prettiest pie. (photograph on page 69)

>   Baked Pie Crust (page 93)
>   1 1/2 quarts strawberries
>   1 cup sugar
>   3 tablespoons cornstarch
>   1/2 cup water
>   1 package (3 ounces) cream cheese, softened

1. Prepare Baked Pie Crust.

2. Mash enough strawberries to measure 1 cup. Mix sugar and cornstarch in 2-quart saucepan. Gradually stir in water and mashed strawberries. Cook over medium heat, stirring constantly, until mixture thickens and boils. Boil and stir 1 minute; cool.

3. Beat cream cheese until smooth. Spread in pie shell. Fill shell with remaining strawberries. Pour cooked strawberry mixture over top. Refrigerate about 3 hours or until set. Refrigerate any remaining pie.

1 SERVING: Calories 320 (Calories from Fat 125); Fat 14g (Saturated 5g); Cholesterol 10mg; Sodium 165mg; Carbohydrate 48g (Dietary Fiber 2g); Protein 3g

FRESH PEACH PIE: Substitute 5 cups sliced peaches (5 medium) for the strawberries. To prevent peaches from discoloring, use fruit protector as directed on package.

FRESH RASPBERRY PIE: Substitute 6 cups raspberries for the strawberries.

Creamy Fruit Tarts

Creamy Fruit Tarts

PREP: 30 min; BAKE: 12 min; COOL: 30 min
Makes 6 servings

Pastry made with cream cheese has a softer texture than regular pastry. Use fresh fruits in season and create your own colorful combinations.

1 cup Bisquick Original baking mix
2 tablespoons sugar
1 tablespoon *stick* margarine or butter, softened*
2 packages (3 ounces each) cream cheese, softened
1/4 cup sugar
1/4 cup sour cream
1 1/2 cups assorted sliced fruit or berries
1/3 cup apple jelly, melted

1. Heat oven to 375°.

2. Mix baking mix, 2 tablespoons sugar, the margarine and 1 package cream cheese in small bowl until dough forms a ball.

3. Divide into 6 parts. Press each part dough on bottom and 3/4 inch up side in each of 6 tart pans, 4 1/4 × 1 inch, or 10-ounce custard cups. Place on cookie sheet.

4. Bake 10 to 12 minutes or until light brown; cool on wire rack. Remove tart shells from pans.

5. Beat remaining package cream cheese, 1/4 cup sugar and the sour cream until smooth. Spoon into tart shells, spreading over bottoms. Top each with about 1/4 cup fruit. Brush with jelly.

Spreads with at least 65% vegetable oil can be substituted (see page 13).

1 SERVING: Calories 300 (Calories from Fat 155); Fat 17g (Saturated 9g); Cholesterol 35mg; Sodium 400mg; Carbohydrate 40g (Dietary Fiber 1g); Protein 4g

> **TIMESAVING TIP**
> After preparing the pastry, measure the milk using an 8-cup glass measure, then carefully beat in the remaining ingredients.

Brown Sugar-Pear Tart

PREP: 25 min; BAKE: 28 min
Makes 8 servings

Serve this scrumptious tart warm with ice cream, then drizzle both with warm caramel sauce for an exceptional treat.

> Pecan Crust (below)
> 3 or 4 medium pears (about 2 pounds), peeled
> 1/2 cup packed brown sugar
> 2 tablespoons all-purpose flour*
> 1/2 teaspoon ground cinnamon

1. Prepare and bake Pecan Crust.

2. Heat oven to 375°.

3. Cut each pear lengthwise in half and remove core. Place each pear half, cut side down, on cutting surface. Cut crosswise into thin slices. Lift each pear half with spatula and arrange on crust, separating and overlapping slices (retain pear shape) to cover surface of crust.

4. Mix remaining ingredients; sprinkle over pears.

5. Bake 15 to 20 minutes or until crust is golden brown and pears are tender.

*Do not use self-rising flour in this recipe.

Pecan Crust

> 1 1/3 cups all-purpose flour*
> 1/3 cup packed brown sugar
> 1/3 cup finely chopped pecans
> 1/2 teaspoon ground nutmeg
> 1/2 teaspoon grated lemon peel
> 2/3 cup *stick* margarine or butter, softened**

Heat oven to 375°. Mix all ingredients except margarine in medium bowl. Cut in margarine, using pastry blender or crisscrossing 2 knives, until crumbly. Press firmly and evenly against bottom and side of ungreased 12-inch pizza pan. Bake 8 minutes; cool.

*Do not use self-rising flour in this recipe.

**We do not recommend using vegetable oil spreads (see page 13).

1 SERVING: Calories 370 (Calories from Fat 170); Fat 19g (Saturated 4g); Cholesterol 0mg; Sodium 185mg; Carbohydrate 50g (Dietary Fiber 3g); Protein 3g

BROWN SUGAR-PLUM TART: Bake the crust 10 to 12 minutes until the edges are light brown. Substitute 2 pounds plums, pitted and cut lengthwise into thin slices, for the pears. Bake tart about 30 minutes.

Fruit and Cream Phyllo Pie

PREP: 30 min; BAKE: 50 min; CHILL: 3 hr
8 servings

Phyllo is Greek in origin, and its translation is "leaf." It is used in both sweet and savory dishes. Here, it forms an easy, light crust.

> 10 sheets frozen (thawed) phyllo (14 × 18 inches)
> 1/3 cup *stick* margarine or butter, melted*
> 1 package (8 ounces) cream cheese, softened
> 1/4 cup sugar
> 1 large egg
> 1/2 teaspoon almond extract
> 1 can (21 ounces) pie filling (any fruit flavor)

1. Heat oven to 350°.

2. Beat cream cheese in small bowl with electric mixer on high speed about 2 minutes or until fluffy. Beat in sugar, egg and almond extract on medium speed until smooth.

3. Cut stack of phyllo sheets into 12-inch squares. Discard remaining strips. Cover squares with damp towel to prevent them from drying out.

4. Carefully separate 1 square; brush lightly with margarine. Place in ungreased pie plate, 9 × 1 1/4 inches, allowing corners of phyllo to hang over edge of pie plate. Repeat with 4 squares.

5. Spread cream cheese mixture in phyllo-lined pie plate. Spread pie filling over cream cheese mixture.

6. Fold overhanging phyllo corners over filling. Brush each remaining phyllo square lightly with margarine; arrange on filling to make top crust, allowing corners to hang over edge of plate. Fold overhanging corners of phyllo under, between bottom layers and rim of plate. Cut through top layers of phyllo with scissors to make 8 wedges.

7. Bake 45 to 50 minutes or until phyllo is golden brown and juice begins to bubble through cuts in phyllo. Cool 15 minutes on wire rack. Cover and refrigerate about 3 hours or until chilled. Refrigerate any remaining pie.

*We do not recommend using vegetable oil spreads (see page 13).

1 SERVING: Calories 355 (Calories from Fat 160); Fat 18g (Saturated 8g); Cholesterol 60mg; Sodium 270mg; Carbohydrate 45g (Dietary Fiber 2g); Protein 5g

---

TIMESAVING TIP

Omit phyllo sheets and margarine. Spread cream cheese mixture in purchased 9-inch crumb crust; top with pie filling. Bake as directed in step 7 until center is set and edge of pie is light brown.

Coconut Cream Pie

PREP: 30 min; COOK: 15 min; CHILL: 2 hr
Makes 8 servings

> Baked Pie Crust (page 93)
> 4 large egg yolks, slightly beaten
> 2/3 cup sugar
> 1/4 cup cornstarch
> 1/2 teaspoon salt
> 3 cups milk
> 2 tablespoons *stick* margarine or butter,
>   softened*
> 2 teaspoons vanilla
> 1 cup flaked coconut
> 1 cup Sweetened Whipped Cream (page 89)

1. Prepare Baked Pie Crust.

2. Beat egg yolks with fork in small bowl. Mix sugar, cornstarch and salt in 2-quart saucepan. Gradually stir in milk. Cook over medium heat, stirring constantly, until mixture thickens and boils. Boil and stir 1 minute.

3. *Immediately* stir at least half of the hot mixture gradually into egg yolks; stir back into hot mixture in saucepan. Boil and stir 1 minute; remove from heat. Stir in margarine, vanilla and 3/4 cup of the coconut. Pour into pie shell. Press plastic wrap onto filling. Refrigerate about 2 hours or until set.

4. Remove plastic wrap. Top pie with Sweetened Whipped Cream and remaining coconut. *Immediately* refrigerate any remaining pie after serving.

Spreads with at least 65% vegetable oil can be substituted (see page 13).

1 SERVING: Calories 415 (Calories from Fat 225); Fat 25g (Saturated 11g); Cholesterol 130mg; Sodium 380mg; Carbohydrate 43g (Dietary Fiber 1g); Protein 6g

BANANA CREAM PIE: Increase vanilla to 1 tablespoon plus 1 teaspoon. Omit coconut. Press plastic wrap onto filling in saucepan. Refrigerate until room temperature. Slice 2 large bananas into pie shell. Pour filling over bananas. Garnish with banana slices if desired.

CHOCOLATE CREAM PIE: Increase sugar to 1 1/2 cups and cornstarch to 1/3 cup. Omit margarine and coconut. Stir in 2 ounces unsweetened baking chocolate, cut up, after stirring in milk in step 2.

TIMESAVING TIP

Substitute Graham Cracker Crust (page 97) for the Baked Pie Crust and frozen (thawed) whipped topping for the Sweetened Whipped Cream.

Lemon Meringue Pie

PREP: 30 min; COOK: 10 min; BAKE: 22 min
Makes 8 servings

Carefully measure the water and lemon juice in the filling. That way you'll get the right consistency to hold a cut.

> Baked Pie Crust (page 93)
> 3 large egg yolks
> 1 1/2 cups sugar
> 1/3 cup plus 1 tablespoon cornstarch
> 1 1/2 cups water
> 3 tablespoons *stick* margarine or butter*
> 2 teaspoons grated lemon peel
> 1/2 cup lemon juice
> 2 drops yellow food color, if desired
> Meringue for 9-inch Pie (page 154)

1. Prepare Baked Pie Crust.

2. Heat oven to 400°.

3. Beat egg yolks with fork in small bowl. Mix sugar and cornstarch in 2-quart saucepan. Gradually stir in water. Cook over medium heat, stirring constantly, until mixture thickens and boils. Boil and stir 1 minute.

4. *Immediately* stir at least half of the hot mixture into egg yolks; stir back into hot mixture in saucepan. Boil and stir 1 minute; remove from heat. Stir in margarine, lemon peel, lemon juice and food color. Pour into pie crust.

5. Prepare Meringue for 9-inch Pie. Spoon onto hot pie filling. Spread over filling, carefully sealing meringue to edge of crust to prevent shrinking or weeping.

6. Bake 8 to 12 minutes or until meringue is light brown. Cool away from draft. Cover and refrigerate cooled pie until serving. *Immediately* refrigerate any remaining pie.

Spreads with at least 65% vegetable oil can be substituted (see page 13).

1 SERVING: Calories 425 (Calories from Fat 145); Fat 16g (Saturated 4g); Cholesterol 80mg; Sodium 210mg; Carbohydrate 66g (Dietary Fiber 0g); Protein 4g

Pumpkin Pie, Pecan Pie

Pumpkin Pie

PREP: 20 min; BAKE: 45 min; CHILL: 4 hr
Makes 8 servings

Be sure to use canned pumpkin, not pumpkin pie mix, in this recipe. Or, if you'd like, 1 1/2 cups cooked pumpkin (see page 401) can be used. For a special garnish, cut leftover pastry into special shapes and bake separately on a cookie sheet until light golden brown. Arrange cut outs over baked filling.

Pastry for 9-Inch One-Crust Pie (page 93)
2 large eggs
1/2 cup sugar
1 teaspoon ground cinnamon
1/2 teaspoon salt
1/2 teaspoon ground ginger
1/8 teaspoon ground cloves
1 can (16 ounces) pumpkin
1 can (12 ounces) evaporated milk
Sweetened Whipped Cream (page 89)

1. Heat oven to 425°. Prepare pastry.

2. Beat eggs slightly in medium bowl with wire whisk or hand beater. Beat in remaining ingredients except Sweetened Whipped Cream.

3. To prevent spilling, place pastry-lined pie plate on oven rack. Pour filling into pie plate. Bake 15 minutes.

4. Reduce oven temperature to 350°. Bake about 45 minutes longer or until knife inserted in center comes out clean. Refrigerate about 4 hours or until chilled. Serve with Sweetened Whipped Cream. *Immediately refrigerate any remaining pie after serving.*

1 SERVING: Calories 295 (Calories from Fat 135); Fat 15g (Saturated 5g); Cholesterol 65mg; Sodium 330mg; Carbohydrate 34g (Dietary Fiber 1g); Protein 7g

---

LIGHTER PUMPKIN PIE
For 2 grams of fat and 125 calories per serving, omit Pastry for 9-Inch One-Crust Pie. Heat oven to 350°. Spray pie plate, 9 × 1 1/4 inches, with nonstick cooking spray. Prepare filling as directed using evaporated skimmed milk; pour into pie plate. Bake about 45 minutes or until knife inserted in center comes out clean.

PRALINE PUMPKIN PIE: Prepare pie as directed—except decrease second bake time to 35 minutes. Mix 1/3 cup packed brown sugar, 1/3 cup chopped pecans and 1 tablespoon *stick* margarine or butter, softened. Sprinkle over pie. Bake about 10 minutes longer or until knife inserted in center comes out clean.

Custard Pie

PREP: 15 min; BAKE: 35 min; CHILL: 4 hr
Makes 8 servings

> Pastry for 9-Inch One-Crust Pie (page 93) or
>   Pat-in-the-Pan Oil Pastry (page 97)
> 4 large eggs
> 1/2 cup sugar
> 2 2/3 cups milk
> 1 teaspoon vanilla
> 1/2 teaspoon salt
> 1/4 teaspoon ground nutmeg

1. Move oven rack to lowest position. Heat oven to 450°. Prepare pastry.

2. Beat eggs slightly in medium bowl with wire whisk or hand beater. Beat in remaining ingredients. To prevent spilling, place pastry-lined pie plate on oven rack. Pour filling into pie plate.

3. Bake 20 minutes.

4. Reduce oven temperature to 350°. Bake 10 to 15 minutes longer or until knife inserted halfway between center and edge comes out clean. Refrigerate about 4 hours or until chilled. *Immediately* refrigerate any remaining pie after serving.

1 SERVING: Calories 270 (Calories from Fat 125); Fat 14g (Saturated 5g); Cholesterol 110mg; Sodium 340mg; Carbohydrate 29g (Dietary Fiber 0g); Protein 7g

Pecan Pie

PREP: 20 min; BAKE: 50 min
Makes 8 servings

> Pastry for 9-Inch One-Crust Pie (page 93)
> 2/3 cup sugar
> 1/3 cup stick margarine or butter, melted*
> 1 cup corn syrup
> 1/2 teaspoon salt
> 3 large eggs
> 1 cup pecan halves or broken pecans

1. Heat oven to 375°. Prepare pastry.

2. Beat sugar, margarine, corn syrup, salt and eggs in medium bowl with wire whisk or hand beater until well blended. Stir in pecans. Pour into pastry-lined pie plate.

3. Bake 40 to 50 minutes or until center is set.

Spreads with at least 65% vegetable oil can be substituted (see page 13).

1 SERVING: Calories 530 (Calories from Fat 260); Fat 29g (Saturated 6g); Cholesterol 80mg; Sodium 430mg; Carbohydrate 63g (Dietary Fiber 1g); Protein 5g

---

> **LIGHTER PECAN PIE**
> For 22 grams of fat and 475 calories per serving, decrease the margarine to 1/4 cup. Substitute 1 egg plus 4 egg whites for the 3 eggs. Add 1 teaspoon vanilla with the egg. Substitute 1/2 cup quick-cooking or old-fashioned oats and 1/2 cup chopped pecans for the 1 cup pecan halves.

KENTUCKY PECAN PIE: Add 2 tablespoons bourbon with the corn syrup. Stir in 1 package (6 ounces) semisweet chocolate chips (1 cup) with the pecans.

Mixed Nut Tart

PREP: 25 min; BAKE: 30 min
Makes 12 servings

The coffee-flavored liqueur adds even more depth to the toasted flavor of the nuts.

> Cookie Tart Pastry (page 97)
> 1 can (12 ounces) lightly salted mixed nuts,
>   coarsely chopped
> 1/2 cup sugar
> 1/3 cup margarine or butter, melted*
> 3/4 cup corn syrup
> 1/4 cup coffee-flavored liqueur, if desired
> 3 large eggs
> Whipped cream, if desired

1. Prepare Cookie Tart Pastry, but do not bake.

2. Heat oven to 375°.

3. Sprinkle nuts evenly over pastry. Beat remaining ingredients except whipped cream with wire whisk or hand beater until smooth; pour over nuts.

4. Bake about 30 minutes or until center is set. Serve warm or cool with whipped cream.

Spreads with at least 65% vegetable oil can be substituted (see page 13).

1 SERVING: Calories 475 (Calories from Fat 270); Fat 30g (Saturated 8g); Cholesterol 55mg; Sodium 240mg; Carbohydrate 46g (Dietary Fiber 3g); Protein 8g

Mud Pie

PREP: 20 min; CHILL: 30 min; FREEZE: 7 hr
Makes 10 servings

A favorite for both kids and adults! Have fun picking the ice cream flavor for this special treat.

  18 chocolate sandwich cookies,
    finely crushed
  3 tablespoons stick margarine or butter,
    melted*
  1 quart coffee, chocolate or other flavor
    ice cream, slightly softened
  1 cup Hot Fudge Sauce (page 159), cooled
  1/4 cup chopped almonds, toasted (page 9)
  Sweetened Whipped Cream (page 89),
    if desired

1. Mix crushed cookies and margarine until well blended. Press on bottom and up side of pie plate, 9 × 1 1/4 inches. Refrigerate 30 minutes.

2. Carefully spread ice cream evenly in crust. Freeze about 3 hours or until firm.

3. Spread Hot Fudge Sauce over top of pie. Sprinkle with almonds. Freeze about 4 hours or until firm. Remove from freezer about 10 minutes before serving. Top with Sweetened Whipped Cream. *Immediately freeze any remaining pie after serving.*

Spreads with at least 65% vegetable oil can be substituted (see page 13).

1 SERVING: Calories 435 (Calories from Fat 225); Fat 25g (Saturated 8g); Cholesterol 20mg; Sodium 220mg; Carbohydrate 49g (Dietary Fiber 3g); Protein 7g

---

TIMESAVING TIP

Use a purchased chocolate crumb crust, prepared fudge sauce and frozen (thawed) whipped topping. Quickly soften the ice cream by microwaving on High 15 to 30 seconds.

Mud Pie

Key Lime Pie

PREP: 30 min; BAKE: 35 min; COOL: 15 min; CHILL: 2 hr
Makes 8 servings

This flavorful pie is named after the delicious key limes, found in the Florida Keys. Commercially marketed key lime juice is available at your supermarket or in specialty stores.

Baked Pie Crust (page 93)
3 large eggs
1 can (14 ounces) sweetened condensed milk
1/2 cup Key lime juice or lime juice
1 teaspoon grated lime or lemon peel
1 1/2 cups Sweetened Whipped Cream
  (page 89)

1. Prepare Baked Pie Crust. Cool completely.

2. Heat oven to 350°.

3. Beat eggs, milk, lime juice and lime peel in medium bowl with electric mixer on medium speed about 1 minute or until well blended. Pour into pie crust.

4. Bake 30 to 35 minutes or until center is set. Cool in pan on wire rack 15 minutes. Cover and refrigerate at least 2 hours until chilled but no longer than 3 days. Spread with Sweetened Whipped Cream. *Immediately* refrigerate any remaining pie.

1 SERVING: Calories 410 (Calories from Fat 205); Fat 23g (Saturated 10g); Cholesterol 120mg; Sodium 230mg; Carbohydrate 43g (Dietary Fiber 0g); Protein 8g

French Silk Pie

PREP: 25 min; COOK: 10 min; FREEZE: 4 hr
Makes 10 servings

Have you ever had chocolate seize, tighten or get thick when you're trying to melt it with margarine? Just a few drops of water left in the pan or use of a spread or whipped margarine, containing more water than regular margarine, could be the cause.

Baked Pie Crust (page 93)
1/4 cup *stick* margarine or butter*
3 ounces unsweetened baking chocolate
1 cup sugar
3 tablespoons cornstarch
3 large eggs
1 teaspoon vanilla
1 cup whipping (heavy) cream
Whipped cream

1. Prepare Baked Pie Crust.

2. Melt margarine and chocolate in 2-quart saucepan over low heat, stirring occasionally; remove from heat. Mix sugar and cornstarch; stir into chocolate mixture.

3. Beat eggs in small bowl with electric mixer on medium speed until thick and lemon colored; stir into chocolate mixture. Cook chocolate mixture over medium heat 5 minutes, stirring constantly, until thick and glossy. Stir in vanilla. Cool 10 minutes, stirring occasionally.

4. Beat whipping cream in chilled medium bowl with electric mixer on high speed, until stiff. Fold chocolate mixture into whipped cream. Spread in pie shell. Cover and refrigerate about 4 hours or until set. Garnish with whipped cream. Immediately refrigerate any remaining pie.

*We do not recommend using vegetable oil spreads (see page 13).

1 SERVING: Calories 430 (Calories from Fat 270); Fat 30g (Saturated 14g); Cholesterol 105mg; Sodium 190mg; Carbohydrate 36g (Dietary Fiber 1g); Protein 5g

MOCHA FRENCH SILK PIE: Stir in 2 teaspoons instant coffee (dry) with the chocolate.

Caramel-Chocolate Pie Supreme

PREP: 35 min; COOK: 15 min; CHILL: 2 1/4 hr
Makes 12 servings

You'll get rave reviews when you make this pie—the extra effort is definitely worthwhile!

Cookie Crumb Crust (page 97)
30 vanilla caramels
2 tablespoons *stick* margarine or butter*
2 tablespoons water
1/2 cup chopped pecans, toasted (page 9)
2 packages (3 ounces each) cream cheese,
    softened
1/3 cup powdered sugar
4 ounces sweet cooking chocolate
3 tablespoons hot water
1 teaspoon vanilla
2 cups whipping (heavy) cream
2 tablespoons powdered sugar
Chocolate curls, if desired

1. Prepare and bake crust as directed—except use pecan shortbread cookies, decrease the margarine to 3 tablespoons and omit the sugar.

2. Heat caramels, margarine and 2 tablespoons water in 1 1/2-quart saucepan over medium heat, stirring frequently, until caramels are melted. Pour into crust. Sprinkle with pecans. Refrigerate about 1 hour or until chilled.

3. Beat cream cheese and 1/3 cup powdered sugar until smooth. Spread over caramel and pecans; refrigerate.

4. Heat chocolate and 3 tablespoons hot water over low heat, stirring constantly, until chocolate is melted. Cool to room temperature. Stir in vanilla.

5. Beat whipping cream and 2 tablespoons powdered sugar in chilled medium bowl with electric mixer on high speed until stiff; reserve 1 1/2 cups. Fold chocolate mixture into remaining whipped cream; spread over cream cheese mixture. Top with reserved whipped cream. Garnish with chocolate curls. Refrigerate at least 1 hour until firm. Refrigerate any remaining pie.

*Spreads with at least 65% vegetable oil can be substituted (see page 13).

1 SERVING: Calories 505 (Calories from Fat 315); Fat 35g (Saturated 19g); Cholesterol 60mg; Sodium 230mg; Carbohydrate 44g (Dietary Fiber 2g); Protein 5g

CARAMEL-PEANUT BUTTER PIE SUPREME: Prepare pie as directed—except use peanut butter cookies in the crust. Substitute dry-roasted peanuts (do not toast) for the pecans and 1/3 cup peanut butter for 1 package of the cream cheese. Omit sweet cooking chocolate, hot water, vanilla and step 4. Mix 1/3 cup peanut butter and 1/3 cup of the whipping cream until smooth. Beat remaining whipping cream and continue as directed in step 5, substituting the peanut butter-cream mixture for the chocolate mixture. Sprinkle pie with dry-roasted peanuts if desired

Grasshopper Pie

PREP: 20 min; COOK: 10 min; CHILL: 4 hr 20 min
Makes 8 servings

This pie freezes well and is especially refreshing when served after standing at room temperature about ten minutes.

Chocolate Cookie Crumb Crust for 9-inch Pie
    (page 97)
1/2 cup milk
32 large jet-puffed marshmallows
1/4 cup crème de menthe
3 tablespoons white crème de cacao
1 1/2 cups whipping (heavy) cream
Few drops green food color, if desired
Grated semisweet baking chocolate,
    if desired

1. Prepare and bake crust as directed, using chocolate wafer cookies.

2. Heat milk and marshmallows in 3-quart saucepan over low heat, stirring constantly, just until marshmallows are melted. Refrigerate about 20 minutes, stirring occasionally, until mixture mounds slightly when dropped from a spoon. (If mixture becomes too thick, place saucepan in bowl of warm water; stir mixture until proper consistency.)

3. *Gradually* stir in crème de menthe and crème de cacao.

4. Beat whipping cream in chilled medium bowl with electric mixer on high speed, until stiff. Fold marshmallow mixture into whipped cream. Fold in food color. Spread in crust. Sprinkle with chocolate. Refrigerate about 4 hours or until set. Refrigerate any remaining pie after serving.

1 SERVING: Calories 430 (Calories from Fat 215); Fat 24g (Saturated 11g); Cholesterol 50mg; Sodium 270mg; Carbohydrate 50g (Dietary Fiber 1g); Protein 4g

IRISH CREAM PIE: Substitute 1/3 cup Irish cream liqueur for the crème de menthe and white crème de cacao.

COFFEE CORDIAL PIE: Substitute water for the milk and add 1 tablespoon instant coffee (dry) with the water. Substitute coffee liqueur for the crème de menthe and Irish whiskey for the crème de cacao.

About Cookies

There's probably no dessert so well loved as cookies! Whether warm from the oven, packed in school lunches or enjoyed with cold milk or a good cup of coffee, the cookie recipes that follow will please anyone. To make the best cookies, read the helpful tips that follow and the ones throughout the chapter.

Pans and Pan Preparation

- Use a shiny cookie sheet at least two inches narrower and shorter than the oven. The sheet may be open on one to three sides. If the cookie sheet has four sides, cookies may not brown as evenly.
- If using a cookie sheet with a nonstick coating, watch carefully—cookies may brown quickly. Follow manufacturer's directions, as many suggest reducing the oven temperature by 25°.
- If cookie sheets are thin, consider using two cookie sheets (one on top of the other) for insulation.
- Insulated cookie sheets help prevent cookies from becoming too dark on the bottom. Cookies baked on insulated cookie sheets may take longer to bake.
- Grease the cookie sheet only if directed in the recipe, using solid shortening (not margarine or butter) or nonstick cooking spray. Do not use margarine, butter or vegetable oil for greasing; the area between the cookies will burn during baking and will be almost impossible to clean.

Ingredients

- *Flour* is presifted these days, so no sifting is needed. Use all-purpose flour (either bleached or unbleached) for most cookies; when using whole wheat flour, substitute it for half the amount of all-purpose flour to avoid dryness. Too much flour makes cookies dry and tough; too little flour causes them to spread and lose their shape.
- *Sugar* adds sweetness and color (by browning) and contributes to spreading. The higher the sugar-to-flour ratio in a recipe, the more tender and crisp the cookies will be.
- *Liquids* tend to make cookies crisper by making them spread more during baking
- *Fats* add tenderness and flavor to cookies. Pay special attention to the fat ingredients in cookies. The fat used will affect the final results. Also see Fats and Oils, page 12.

Margarine and *butter* both produce a crisper cookie than shortening and can be used interchangeably. Butter gives a more buttery flavor and a crisper cookie than margarine. Our testing showed that the very best results are achieved using *stick* margarine or butter rather than substituting vegetable oil spreads, tub products, or lower fat products containing less than 80% fat. The lower the amount of fat, the more water or air added, making the doughs very soft to work with and the baked cookies softer with a different texture. Spreads with at least 65% vegetable oil can be substituted for the margarine or butter in some softer cookies and bar recipes with acceptable results. But refrain from substituting in cookies or crusts that need to be dry and crisp. Each recipe will tell you whether we felt that change was acceptable.

Shortening gives cookies a softer texture than margarine or butter, and the cookies can be somewhat drier and crumbly. Shortening and butter-flavored shortening can be used interchangeably.

Vegetable oil gives cookies a soft, moist texture. It is often used for fruit bars and soft drop cookies. Never directly substitute vegetable oil for a solid fat.

- *Eggs* add richness, moisture and structure to cookies. Too many eggs can make cookies tough and crumbly.

Mixing Cookies

- Sugars, fats and liquids are usually mixed together first, either by electric mixer or by hand, until ingredients are well combined. Then the dry ingredients are stirred in by hand just until moistened.
- Use an electric mixer only when specified in the recipe.
- Cookies mixed by hand will be more compact and dense than cookies mixed with an electric mixer because less air is beaten into the fat.
- Do not overmix dough or cookies will be tough.
- Cookie doughs for lighter variations usually

Preceding page: Sugar Cookies (page 127), Chocolate Drop Cookies (page 117) contain reduced-fat or fat-free ingredients. Since fat helps intensify flavor but is reduced in these variations, spices and flavorings are sometimes increased to achieve the same flavor as the original recipe. The doughs are usually softer and may have a slightly different texture during mixing. If specified in the recipe, refrigerate dough before baking.

Baking Cookies

- Bake a "test" cookie. If it spreads more than desired, add 1 to 2 tablespoons flour or refrigerate the dough. If it is too dry, stir in 1 to 2 tablespoons milk.
- Make cookies the same size and thickness to ensure uniform baking.
- We recommend baking one sheet of cookies at a time in the center of the oven for most even baking. If you wish to bake two sheets at once, position the oven racks so they are evenly spaced from the oven top and bottom, and switch sheets halfway through baking each batch.
- Check cookies at the minimum baking time— just one minute can make a difference, especially for cookies high in sugar and fat.

- Cool the cookie sheets between batches, or the dough will spread if placed on hot sheets.
- Unless the recipe states otherwise, remove baked cookies immediately from the cookie sheet with a wide spatula, and place on a wire rack to cool. Cool completely.

Cookies Yields and Storage

- Store crisp, thin cookies in a container with a loose-fitting cover, which allows the flow of air to keep them crisp. If they soften, recrisp them by placing in a 300° oven for 3 to 5 minutes.
- Store unfrosted soft cookies in an airtight container to preserve their moistness. A piece of bread or apple (replaced frequently) in the container will help keep them soft.
- Store frosted soft cookies in a single layer in an airtight container so the frosting will maintain its shape and the cookies will retain their moistness.
- Do not mix crisp and soft cookies in the same container, or the crisp cookies will become soft.
- Store bar cookies in a tightly covered container, or leave them in the pan and cover tightly with aluminum foil.

Tips for Bar Cookies

- Use the size pan specified in the recipe. Cookies made in a larger pan will be dry and overbaked; those made in a smaller pan will be underbaked.
- Cut into bars, squares or triangles when completely cool unless recipe specifies cutting while warm. This helps prevent the bars from crumbling.
- For quicker cleanup and to ensure evenly cut bars and brownies, line the pan with aluminum foil (grease the foil if recommended in recipe). When the bars are cool, just lift them out of the pan onto a cutting board and peel back the foil from the sides before cutting.
- To easily cut bar cookies with a delicate crust, such as brownies, use a plastic knife.

Butterscotch Brownies

PREP: 15 min; BAKE: 25 min
Makes 16 brownies

1/4 cup shortening
1 cup packed brown sugar
1 teaspoon vanilla
1 large egg
3/4 cup all-purpose flour*
1/2 cup chopped nuts
1 teaspoon baking powder
1/2 teaspoon salt

1. Heat oven to 350°. Grease bottom and sides of square pan, 8 × 8 × 2 inches, with shortening.

2. Melt shortening in 1 1/2-quart saucepan over low heat; remove from heat. Stir in brown sugar, vanilla and egg. Stir in remaining ingredients. Spread in pan.

3. Bake 25 minutes. Cool slightly in pan on wire rack. Cut into about 2-inch squares while warm.

If using self-rising flour, omit baking powder and salt.

1 BROWNIE: Calories 135 (Calories from Fat 55); Fat 6g (Saturated 1g); Cholesterol 15mg; Sodium 105mg; Carbohydrate 19g (Dietary Fiber 0g); Protein 1g

Chocolate Brownies

PREP: 25 min; BAKE: 45 min
Makes 16 brownies

This is our all-time favorite brownie—rich and chocolaty!

2/3 cup *stick* margarine or butter*
5 ounces unsweetened baking chocolate, cut
    into pieces
1 3/4 cups sugar
2 teaspoons vanilla
3 large eggs
1 cup all-purpose flour**
1 cup chopped walnuts
Chocolate Buttercream Frosting (page 86),
    if desired

1. Heat oven to 350°. Grease bottom and sides of square pan, 9 × 9 × 2 inches, with shortening.

2. Melt margarine and chocolate in 1-quart saucepan over low heat, stirring constantly. Cool slightly.

3. Beat sugar, vanilla and eggs in medium bowl with electric mixer on high speed 5 minutes. Beat in chocolate mixture on low speed. Beat in flour just until blended. Stir in walnuts. Spread in pan.

4. Bake 40 to 45 minutes or just until brownies begin to pull away from sides of pan. Cool completely in pan on wire rack. Spread with Chocolate Buttercream Frosting. Cut into about 2-inch squares.

*Spreads with at least 65% vegetable oil can be substituted (see page 13).

**Do not use self-rising flour in this recipe.

1 BROWNIE: Calories 300 (Calories from Fat 160); Fat 18g (Saturated 5g); Cholesterol 40mg; Sodium 100mg; Carbohydrate 32g (Dietary Fiber 2g); Protein 4g

---

LIGHTER CHOCOLATE BROWNIES

For 3 grams of fat and 160 calories, substitute 1/3 cup unsweetened applesauce for 1/3 cup of the margarine, 1/2 cup baking cocoa for the unsweetened baking chocolate and 1 egg plus 4 egg whites for the 3 eggs. Decrease walnuts to 1/2 cup.

CHOCOLATE-PEANUT BUTTER BROWNIES: Substitute 1/3 cup crunchy peanut butter for 1/3 cup of the margarine. Omit walnuts. Before baking, arrange 16 miniature peanut butter cups over top; press into batter so tops of cups are even with top of batter.

CHOCOLATE BROWNIE PIE: Grease bottom and side of pie plate, 10 × 1 1/2 inches, with shortening. Spread batter in pie plate. Bake 35 to 40 minutes or until center is set. Cool completely in pan on wire rack. Cut into wedges. Serve with ice cream and Hot Fudge Sauce (page 159) if desired. Makes 12 servings.

Cream Cheese Brownies

PREP: 25 min; BAKE: 50 min
Makes 4 dozen brownies

4 ounces unsweetened baking chocolate
1 cup *stick* margarine or butter*
    Cream Cheese Filling (below)
2 cups sugar
2 teaspoons vanilla
4 large eggs
1 1/2 cups all-purpose flour**
1/2 teaspoon salt
1 cup coarsely chopped nuts

1. Heat oven to 350°. Grease bottom and sides of rectangular pan, 13 × 9 × 2 inches, with shortening.

2. Melt chocolate and margarine in 1-quart saucepan over low heat, stirring frequently; cool.

3. Prepare Cream Cheese Filling; set aside.

4. Beat chocolate mixture, sugar, vanilla and eggs in large bowl with electric mixer on medium speed 1 minute, scraping bowl occasionally. Beat in flour and salt on low speed 30 seconds, scraping bowl occasionally. Beat on medium speed 1 minute. Stir in nuts. Spread half of the batter (about 2 1/2 cups) in pan. Spread filling over batter. Carefully spread remaining batter over filling.

5. Bake 45 to 50 minutes or until toothpick inserted in center comes out clean. Cool in pan on wire rack. Cut into 2 × 1-inch bars. Refrigerate any remaining brownies.

Cream Cheese Filling

2 packages (8 ounces each) cream cheese,
    softened
1/2 cup sugar
2 teaspoons vanilla
1 egg

Beat all ingredients until smooth.

*Spreads with at least 65% vegetable oil can be substituted (see page 13).

**If using self-rising flour, omit salt.

1 BROWNIE: Calories 165 (Calories from Fat 100); Fat 11g (Saturated 4g); Cholesterol 35mg; Sodium 100mg; Carbohydrate 15g (Dietary Fiber 0g); Protein 2g

---

LIGHTER CREAM CHEESE BROWNIES

For 7 grams of fat and 130 calories per serving, substitute 1/2 cup unsweetened applesauce for 1/2 cup of the margarine and 2 eggs plus 4 egg whites for the 4 eggs. Decrease chopped nuts to 1/2 cup. Use reduced-fat cream cheese (Neufchâtel), softened, in the Cream Cheese Filling.

Toffee Bars

PREP: 20 min; BAKE: 30 min; COOL: 30 min
Makes 32 bars

> 1 cup *stick* margarine or butter, softened*
> 1 cup packed brown sugar
> 1 teaspoon vanilla
> 1 large egg yolk
> 2 cups all-purpose flour**
> 1/4 teaspoon salt
> 2/3 cup milk chocolate chips or 3 bars (1.55
>   ounces each) milk chocolate candy,
>   broken into small pieces
> 1/2 cup chopped nuts

1. Heat oven to 350°.

2. Mix margarine, brown sugar, vanilla and egg yolk in large bowl. Stir in flour and salt. Press dough in ungreased rectangular pan, 13 × 9 × 2 inches.

3. Bake 25 to 30 minutes or until very light brown (crust will be soft). *Immediately* sprinkle chocolate chips on hot crust. Let stand about 5 minutes or until soft; spread evenly. Sprinkle with nuts. Cool 30 minutes in pan on wire rack. Cut into 2 × 1 1/2-inch bars while warm.

*We do not recommend using vegetable oil spreads (see page 13).

**If using self-rising flour, omit salt.

1 BAR: Calories 135 (Calories from Fat 70); Fat 8g (Saturated 2g); Cholesterol 10mg; Sodium 90mg; Carbohydrate 15g (Dietary Fiber 0g); Protein 1g

---

LIGHTER TOFFEE BARS

For 6 grams of fat and 120 calories per serving, substitute 1/2 package (8-ounce size) reduced-fat cream cheese (Neufchâtel), softened, for 1/2 cup of the margarine and 1/4 cup finely chopped nuts for the 1/2 cup chopped nuts.

Lemon Squares

PREP: 10 min; BAKE: 50 min
Makes 25 squares

(photograph on page 114)

> 1 cup all-purpose flour*
> 1/2 cup *stick* margarine or butter, softened**
> 1/4 cup powdered sugar
> 1 cup granulated sugar
> 2 teaspoons grated lemon peel, if desired
> 2 tablespoons lemon juice
> 1/2 teaspoon baking powder
> 1/4 teaspoon salt
> 2 large eggs
> Powdered sugar

1. Heat oven to 350°.

2. Mix flour, margarine and powdered sugar. Press in ungreased square pan, 8 × 8 × 2 or 9 × 9 × 2 inches, building up 1/2-inch edges.

3. Bake crust 20 minutes.

4. Beat remaining ingredients with electric mixer on high speed about 3 minutes or until light and fluffy. Pour over hot crust.

5. Bake 25 to 30 minutes or until no indentation remains when touched lightly in center. Cool in pan on wire rack. Dust with powdered sugar. Cut into about 1 1/2-inch squares.

*Self-rising flour can be used in this recipe.

**We do not recommend using vegetable oil spreads (see page 13).

1 SQUARE: Calories 90 (Calories from Fat 35); Fat 4g (Saturated 1g); Cholesterol 20mg; Sodium 80mg; Carbohydrate 13g (Dietary Fiber 0g); Protein 1g

Apple Bars

PREP: 20 min; BAKE: 20 min; COOL: 30 min
Makes 3 dozen bars

> 1 cup packed brown sugar
> 1/4 cup vegetable oil
> 1/4 cup milk
> 1 large egg
> 2 cups all-purpose* or whole wheat flour
> 1 teaspoon baking soda
> 1 teaspoon ground cinnamon
> 1/2 teaspoon ground nutmeg
> 1/4 teaspoon ground cloves
> 1 1/2 cups chopped peeled cooking apples
>   (2 small)
> 1 cup chopped walnuts
> Spice Glaze (below)

1. Heat oven to 350°. Grease bottom and sides of rectangular pan, 13 × 9 × 2 inches, with shortening.

2. Mix brown sugar, oil, milk and egg in large bowl. Stir in flour, baking soda, cinnamon, nutmeg and cloves. Stir in apples and walnuts. Spread in pan.

3. Bake about 20 minutes or until toothpick inserted in center comes out clean. Cool 30 minutes in pan on wire rack. Drizzle with Spice Glaze. Cool completely. Cut into 2 × 1 1/2-inch bars.

Spice Glaze

> 3/4 cup powdered sugar
> 1/4 teaspoon ground cinnamon
> 1 to 2 tablespoons apple juice or milk

Mix all ingredients until smooth and spreadable.

*If using self-rising flour, omit baking soda.

1 BAR: Calories 95 (Calories from Fat 35); Fat 4g (Saturated 1g); Cholesterol 10mg; Sodium 40mg; Carbohydrate 15g (Dietary Fiber 1g); Protein 1g

Lemon Squares (page 113), Raspberry Cheesecake Bars

Raspberry Cheesecake Bars

PREP: 20 min; BAKE: 40 min; CHILL: 3 hr
Makes 3 dozen bars

  2 cups all-purpose flour*
  1/4 cup granulated sugar
  1/2 teaspoon salt
  3/4 cup *stick* margarine or butter, softened**
  1/3 cup light corn syrup
  2 packages (8 ounces each) cream cheese,
    softened
  3 large eggs
  1 cup light corn syrup
  2 teaspoons vanilla
  3/4 cup raspberry or strawberry jam
  Powdered sugar, if desired

1. Heat oven to 375°. Grease bottom and sides of rectangular pan, 13 × 9 × 2 inches, with shortening.

2. Beat flour, granulated sugar, salt, margarine and 1/3 cup corn syrup with electric mixer on medium speed until dough forms. Press evenly in pan.

3. Beat cream cheese in medium bowl until smooth. Beat in eggs until well blended. Beat in 1 cup corn syrup and the vanilla until smooth. Pour over dough.

4. Bake 35 to 40 minutes or until edges are light golden brown and filling is set (filling may appear puffy). Stir jam; spread over hot bars. Refrigerate at least 3 hours until chilled.

5. Cut into 2 × 1 1/2-inch bars. Sprinkle with powdered sugar just before serving. Refrigerate any remaining bars.

If using self-rising flour, omit the salt.

**We do not recommend using vegetable oil spreads (see page 13).*

1 BAR: Calories 175 (Calories from Fat 80); Fat 9g (Saturated 4g); Cholesterol 30mg; Sodium 135mg; Carbohydrate 22g (Dietary Fiber 0g); Protein 2g

---

**LIGHTER RASPBERRY
CHEESECAKE BARS**

For 5 grams of fat and 145 calories per serving, substitute 1/2 package (8-ounce size) reduced-fat cream cheese (Neufchâtel), softened, for 1/2 cup of the margarine. Also use reduced-fat cream cheese for the 2 packages of cream cheese. Substitute 2 eggs and 2 egg whites for the 3 eggs.

Pumpkin-Spice Bars

PREP: 15 min; BAKE: 30 min; COOL: 2 hr
Makes 49 bars

4 large eggs
2 cups sugar
1 cup vegetable oil
1 can (16 ounces) pumpkin
2 cups all-purpose flour*
2 teaspoons baking powder
2 teaspoons ground cinnamon
1 teaspoon baking soda
1/2 teaspoon salt
1/2 teaspoon ground ginger
1/4 teaspoon ground cloves
1 cup raisins
Cream Cheese Frosting (below)
1/2 cup chopped walnuts

1. Heat oven to 350°. Grease bottom and sides of jelly roll pan, 15 1/2 × 10 1/2 × 1 inch, lightly with shortening.

2. Beat eggs, sugar, oil and pumpkin in large bowl until smooth. Stir in flour, baking powder, cinnamon, baking soda, salt, ginger and cloves. Stir in raisins. Spread in pan.

3. Bake 25 to 30 minutes or until light brown. Cool completely in pan on wire rack. Frost with Cream Cheese Frosting. Sprinkle with walnuts. Cut into 2 × 1 1/2-inch bars. Refrigerate any remaining bars.

Cream Cheese Frosting

1 package (3 ounces) cream cheese, softened
1/3 cup *stick* margarine or butter, softened**
1 teaspoon vanilla
2 cups powdered sugar

Mix cream cheese, margarine and vanilla in medium bowl. Gradually beat in powdered sugar until smooth.

If using self-rising flour, omit baking powder, baking soda and salt.

**Spreads with at least 65% vegetable oil can be substituted (see page 13).*

1 BAR: Calories 160 (Calories from Fat 70); Fat 8g (Saturated 2g); Cholesterol 20mg; Sodium 95mg; Carbohydrate 21g (Dietary Fiber 0g); Protein 1g

---

LIGHTER PUMPKIN-SPICE BARS
For 4 grams of fat and 125 calories per serving, substitute 2 eggs plus 4 egg whites for the 4 eggs and 1/2 cup unsweetened applesauce for 1/2 cup of the oil. Omit the walnuts.

Date Bars

PREP: 30 min; BAKE: 30 min
Makes 3 dozen bars

Date Filling (below)
1 cup packed brown sugar
1 cup *stick* margarine or butter, softened*
1 3/4 cups all-purpose** or whole wheat flour
1 1/2 cups quick-cooking oats
1/2 teaspoon salt
1/2 teaspoon baking soda

1. Prepare Date Filling.

2. Heat oven to 400°. Grease bottom and sides of rectangular pan, 13 × 9 × 2 inches, with shortening.

3. Mix brown sugar and margarine in large bowl. Stir in remaining ingredients until crumbly. Press half of the crumb mixture evenly in bottom of pan. Spread with filling. Top with remaining crumb mixture; press lightly.

4. Bake 25 to 30 minutes or until light brown. Cool slightly in pan on wire rack. Cut into about 2 × 1 1/2-inch bars while warm.

Date Filling

3 cups cut-up pitted dates (1 pound)
1/4 cup sugar
1 1/2 cups water

Cook all ingredients in 2-quart saucepan over low heat about 10 minutes, stirring constantly, until thickened; cool.

We do not recommend using vegetable oil spreads (see page 13).

**If using self-rising flour, omit salt and baking soda.*

1 BAR: Calories 145 (Calories from Fat 45); Fat 5g (Saturated 1g); Cholesterol 0mg; Sodium 110mg; Carbohydrate 25g (Dietary Fiber 1g); Protein 1g

---

LIGHTER DATE BARS
For 4 grams of fat and 145 calories per serving, substitute 1/2 package (8-ounce size) reduced-fat cream cheese (Neufchâtel), softened, for 1/2 cup of the margarine.

Marshmallow Bars

PREP: 10 min; COOL: 1 hr
Makes 3 dozen bars

Make these crispy cereal bars more like a candy bar by dipping either the cut sides or the entire bar into melted chocolate or white chocolate candy coating. Place on waxed paper until chocolate is set.

32 large marshmallows or 3 cups miniature
marshmallows
1/4 cup *stick* margarine or butter*
1/2 teaspoon vanilla
5 cups crispy corn puff, toasted whole-grain
oat or corn flake cereal (Kix®, Cheerios®,
Country® Corn Flakes)

1. Grease bottom and sides of square pan, 9 × 9 × 2 inches, with margarine.

2. Heat marshmallows and margarine in 3-quart saucepan over low heat, stirring constantly, until marshmallows are melted and mixture is smooth; remove from heat. Stir in vanilla.

3. Stir half of the cereal at a time into marshmallow mixture until evenly coated. Press evenly in pan; cool. Cut into about 2 × 1-inch bars.

We do not recommend using vegetable oil spreads (see page 13).

1 BAR: Calories 45 (Calories from Fat 10); Fat 1g (Saturated 0g); Cholesterol 0mg; Sodium 60mg; Carbohydrate 9g (Dietary Fiber 0g); Protein 0g

---

TIMESAVING TIP

To microwave, place marshmallows in 3-quart microwavable bowl or casserole. Cut margarine into 4 pieces; place on marshmallows. Microwave uncovered on High 1 minute 30 seconds to 2 minutes 30 seconds, stirring every minute, until marshmallows can be stirred smooth. Stir in vanilla, then continue as directed in step 3.

Tips for Drop Cookies

- Spoon dough with a tableware spoon (not a measuring spoon, unless a level teaspoon or tablespoon is specified). Push dough onto cookie sheet with another spoon or rubber spatula.
- Use a spring-handle ice-cream scoop for making uniformly shaped cookies. These are sold in various sizes and are referred to by number. (The number corresponds to the number of level scoops per quart of ice cream.) For example, if your recipe says to drop dough by rounded teaspoonfuls, use a number 70 scoop.
- Drop dough about two inches apart (or as directed in the recipe) onto cookie sheet to prevent cookies from baking together as the dough spreads during baking.
- If edges are dark and crusty, cookies were overbaked, the cookie sheet was too large for oven or a dark cookie sheet was used. If center of cookie is doughy, it was underbaked.
- Excess spreading may be caused by dough being too warm, the cookie sheet being too hot or incorrect oven temperature. Chill soft doughs before dropping onto cookie sheet. Also, let cookie sheet cool between bakings.

Chocolate Chip Cookies

PREP: 10 min; BAKE: 40 min
Makes about 4 dozen cookies

"The ultimate" is how we describe this chocolate chip cookie recipe. Chocolate Chip Cookies are the reigning favorites—they are always welcome any time! We prefer mixing these with a spoon because the baked cookies are bumpier than if an electric mixer is used. (Candy Cookies photographed on page 121)

> 3/4 cup granulated sugar
> 3/4 cup packed brown sugar
> 1 cup *stick* margarine or butter, softened*
> 1 large egg
> 2 1/4 cups all-purpose flour**
> 1 teaspoon baking soda
> 1/2 teaspoon salt
> 1 cup coarsely chopped nuts
> 1 package (12 ounces) semisweet chocolate chips (2 cups)

1. Heat oven to 375°.

2. Mix sugars, margarine and egg in large bowl. Stir in flour, baking soda and salt (dough will be stiff). Stir in nuts and chocolate chips.

3. Drop dough by rounded tablespoonfuls about 2 inches apart onto ungreased cookie sheet.

4. Bake 8 to 10 minutes or until light brown (centers will be soft). Cool slightly; remove from cookie sheet. Cool on wire rack.

*Spread with at least 65% vegetable oil can be substituted (see page 13).

**If using self-rising flour, omit baking soda and salt.

1 COOKIE: Calories 135 (Calories from Fat 70); Fat 8g (Saturated 2g); Cholesterol 5mg; Sodium 100mg; Carbohydrate 16g (Dietary Fiber 1g); Protein 1g

---

LIGHTER CHOCOLATE CHIP COOKIES
For 4 grams of fat and 90 calories per serving, decrease margarine to 3/4 cup, add 1 teaspoon vanilla with the egg and omit nuts. Substitute 1 cup miniature chocolate chips for the 12-ounce package of chocolate chips.

CANDY COOKIES: Substitute 2 cups candy-coated chocolate candies for the chocolate chips.

CHOCOLATE CHIP BARS: Press dough in ungreased rectangular pan, 13 × 9 × 2 inches. Bake 15 to 20 minutes or until golden brown. Cool in pan on wire rack. Makes 4 dozen bars.

JUMBO CHOCOLATE CHIP COOKIES: Drop dough by 1/4 cupfuls about 3 inches apart onto ungreased cookie sheet. Bake 12 to 15 minutes or until edges are set. Cool completely on cookie sheet. Makes 1 1/2 dozen cookies.

Chocolate Drop Cookies

PREP: 25 min; BAKE: 33 min; COOL: 1 hr
Makes about 3 dozen cookies

(photograph on page 109)

> 1 cup sugar
> 1/2 cup *stick* margarine or butter, softened*
> 1/3 cup buttermilk
> 1 teaspoon vanilla
> 1 large egg
> 2 ounces unsweetened baking chocolate, melted and cooled
> 1 3/4 cups all-purpose flour**
> 1/2 teaspoon baking soda
> 1/2 teaspoon salt
> 1 cup chopped nuts
> Chocolate Frosting (below)

1. Heat oven to 400°. Grease cookie sheet with shortening.

2. Mix sugar, margarine, buttermilk, vanilla, egg and chocolate in large bowl. Stir in flour, baking soda, salt and nuts.

3. Drop dough by rounded tablespoonfuls about 2 inches apart onto cookie sheet.

4. Bake 9 to 11 minutes or until almost no indentation remains when touched in center. *Immediately* remove from cookie sheet. Cool completely on wire rack. Frost with Chocolate Frosting.

Chocolate Frosting

> 2 ounces unsweetened baking chocolate
> 2 tablespoons *stick* margarine or butter*
> 2 cups powdered sugar
> 3 tablespoons hot water

Melt chocolate and margarine in 2-quart saucepan over low heat, stirring occasionally; remove from heat.

Stir in powdered sugar and hot water until smooth. (If frosting is too thick, add more water, 1 teaspoon at a time. If frosting is too thin, add more powdered sugar, 1 tablespoon at a time.)

*Spreads with at least 65% vegetable oil can be substituted (see page 13).

**If using self-rising flour, omit baking soda and salt.

1 COOKIE: Calories 140 (Calories from Fat 65); Fat 7g (Saturated 2g); Cholesterol 5mg; Sodium 90mg; Carbohydrate 19g (Dietary Fiber 1g); Protein 1g

---

TIMESAVING TIP
Use your microwave to melt the chocolate for the cookie dough (see page 430) and melt the chocolate and margarine for the frosting.

Chocolate Muddies

Chocolate Muddies

PREP: 30 min; BAKE: 1 hr 15 min
Makes about 5 dozen cookies

These enticing cookies just ooze with rich chocolate flavor! If you like, use three cups of the same kind of chips, rather than a mixture. If you're a peanut butter fan, substitute peanut butter chips for the vanilla milk chips.

1 package (3 ounces) cream cheese, softened
3/4 cup *stick* margarine or butter, softened*
1 cup granulated sugar
1 cup packed brown sugar
2 teaspoons vanilla
1/8 teaspoon almond extract
2 large eggs
2/3 cup chocolate fudge ice-cream topping
2 cups all-purpose flour**
1/2 cup baking cocoa
1 teaspoon baking soda
1 teaspoon salt
1 cup vanilla milk chips
1/2 package (11 1/2-ounce size) milk
    chocolate chips (1 cup)
2 packages (3 ounces each) bittersweet
    chocolate, coarsely chopped (1 cup)

1. Heat oven to 350°. Line cookie sheet with aluminum foil or cooking parchment paper; if using foil, grease with shortening.

2. Beat cream cheese and margarine in large bowl with electric mixer on medium speed about 2 minutes or until fluffy. Add sugars, vanilla, almond extract, eggs and ice-cream topping. Beat about 3 minutes or until fluffy.

3. Mix flour, cocoa, baking soda and salt. Stir into margarine mixture until evenly mixed. Stir in remaining ingredients.

4. Drop dough by heaping teaspoonfuls about 2 inches apart onto cookie sheet.

5. Bake 13 to 15 minutes or until edges are set (centers will be very soft). Cool 5 minutes; remove from cookie sheet. Cool on wire rack.

*We do not recommend using vegetable oil spreads (see page 13).

**If using self-rising flour, omit baking soda and salt.

1 COOKIE: Calories 130 (Calories from Fat 65); Fat 7g (Saturated 3g); Cholesterol 10mg; Sodium 100mg; Carbohydrate 17g (Dietary Fiber 1g); Protein 1g

---

TIMESAVING TIP

This is a perfect recipe to double. Make a double batch and bake half, freezing the other half. To freeze, refrigerate dough until firm. Shape dough into a roll about 2 inches in diameter; wrap tightly in aluminum foil and freeze. To bake, thaw dough in refrigerator 1 hour. Cut dough into 1/2-inch slices. Place on cookie sheet lined with cooking parchment paper. Baking time may need to be increased to 15 to 17 minutes.

Oatmeal-Raisin Cookies

PREP: 15 min; BAKE: 33 min
Makes about 3 dozen cookies

Tired of raisins? Try dried cherries or dried cranberries for a refreshing change of flavor and color.

2/3 cup granulated sugar
2/3 cup packed brown sugar
1/2 cup *stick* margarine or butter, softened*
1/2 cup shortening
1 teaspoon baking soda
1 teaspoon ground cinnamon
1 teaspoon vanilla
1/2 teaspoon baking powder
1/2 teaspoon salt
2 large eggs
3 cups quick-cooking or old-fashioned oats
1 cup all-purpose flour**
1 cup raisins, chopped nuts or semisweet
    chocolate chips, if desired

1. Heat oven to 375°.

2. Mix all ingredients except oats, flour and raisins in large bowl. Stir in oats, flour and raisins.

3. Drop dough by rounded tablespoonfuls about 2 inches apart onto ungreased cookie sheet.

4. Bake 9 to 11 minutes or until light brown. *Immediately* remove from cookie sheet. Cool on wire rack.

*Spreads with at least 65% vegetable oil can be substituted (see page 13).

**If using self-rising flour, omit baking soda, baking powder and salt.

1 COOKIE: Calories 120 (Calories from Fat 55); Fat 6g (Saturated 1g); Cholesterol 10mg; Sodium 110mg; Carbohydrate 15g (Dietary Fiber 1g); Protein 2g

OATMEAL-RAISIN SQUARES: Press dough in ungreased square pan, 8 × 8 × 2 inches. Bake about 25 minutes or until light brown. Cool in pan on wire rack. Cut into about 2-inch squares. Makes 16 squares.

LIGHTER OATMEAL-RAISIN COOKIES
For 3 grams of fat and 90 calories per serving, substitute unsweetened applesauce for the shortening and 1/2 cup fat-free cholesterol-free egg product for the eggs. Increase cinnamon and vanilla to 1 1/2 teaspoons each.

Coconut Cream Macaroons

PREP: 15 min; BAKE: 42 min
Makes about 3 1/2 dozen cookies

The addition of toasted coconut to the batter adds a delightful crunch and golden color to these rich and chewy macaroons.

3 packages (7 ounces each) flaked coconut
    (7 2/3 cups)
1 cup all-purpose flour*
1/2 teaspoon salt
1 can (14 ounces) sweetened condensed milk
2/3 cup canned cream of coconut
3 teaspoons vanilla
1/4 teaspoon almond extract
1 large egg
1 package (6 ounces) semisweet chocolate
    chips (1 cup), if desired
1 tablespoon vegetable oil, if desired

1. Heat oven to 350°. Line cookie sheet with aluminum foil or cooking parchment paper.

2. Sprinkle 1 cup of the coconut over aluminum foil. Bake 5 to 7 minutes, stirring occasionally, or until golden brown; cool. Reserve aluminum foil for baking cookies.

3. Mix toasted coconut, remaining coconut, the flour and salt in large bowl. Beat milk, cream of coconut, vanilla, almond extract and egg in medium bowl until well mixed. Pour milk mixture over coconut mixture; stir until well mixed.

4. Drop mixture by heaping tablespoonfuls onto cookie sheet.

5. Bake 12 to 14 minutes or until golden brown (cookies will be soft in center and set at edges). *Immediately* slide aluminum foil with cookies from cookie sheet to wire rack. Cool completely.

6. Heat chocolate chips and oil in 1-quart saucepan over low heat, stirring constantly, until chips are melted. Drizzle over cookies. Let stand about 30 minutes or until chocolate is set.

*If using self-rising flour, omit salt.

1 COOKIE: Calories 125 (Calories from Fat 65); Fat 7g (Saturated 6g); Cholesterol 10mg; Sodium 80mg; Carbohydrate 15g (Dietary Fiber 1g); Protein 1g

---

TIMESAVING TIP
Omit toasting coconut in step 2 and drizzling with chocolate in step 6.

Pumpkin-Date Cookies

PREP: 20 min; BAKE: 40 min; COOL: 1 hr
Makes about 4 dozen cookies

Browned Butter Buttercream Frosting is the perfect topping for this fruit-and-spice bar.

1 cup sugar
1/2 cup *stick* margarine or butter, softened*
1 cup canned pumpkin
2 large eggs
2 cups all-purpose flour**
1 cup chopped dates
1/2 cup chopped walnuts
2 teaspoons baking powder
2 teaspoons ground cinnamon
1/2 teaspoon ground nutmeg
1/2 teaspoon ground ginger
1/4 teaspoon ground cloves
Browned Butter Buttercream Frosting
   (page 86)

1. Heat oven to 375°.

2. Beat sugar and margarine in large bowl with electric mixer on medium speed about 3 minutes or until light and fluffy. Beat in pumpkin and eggs. Stir in remaining ingredients except Browned Butter Frosting.

3. Drop dough by rounded teaspoonfuls about 2 inches apart onto ungreased cookie sheet.

4. Bake 8 to 10 minutes or until edges are set. *Immediately* remove from cookie sheet. Cool completely on wire rack. Frost with Browned Butter Frosting.

*Spreads with at least 65% vegetable oil can be substituted (see page 13).

**If using self-rising flour, omit baking powder.

1 COOKIE: Calories 115 (Calories from Fat 35); Fat 4g (Saturated 1g); Cholesterol 15mg; Sodium 55mg; Carbohydrate 19g (Dietary Fiber 0g); Protein 1g

BANANA-DATE COOKIES: Substitute 1 cup mashed ripe bananas (2 medium) for the pumpkin and add 1/4 teaspoon baking soda with the baking powder.

Soft Molasses Cookies

PREP: 10 min; 44 min
Makes about 4 dozen cookies

1 cup sugar
3/4 cup sour cream
1/2 cup *stick* margarine or butter, softened*
1/2 cup shortening
1/2 cup molasses
1 large egg
3 cups all-purpose flour**
1 1/2 teaspoons baking soda
1 teaspoon ground cinnamon
1 teaspoon ground ginger
1/2 teaspoon salt

1. Heat oven to 375°.

2. Mix sugar, sour cream, margarine, shortening, molasses and egg in large bowl with until smooth. Stir in remaining ingredients.

3. Drop dough by rounded tablespoonfuls about 2 inches apart onto ungreased cookie sheet.

4. Bake 9 to 11 minutes or until almost no indentation remains when touched in center. Cool slightly; remove from cookie sheet. Sprinkle with sugar while warm if desired. Cool on wire rack.

*Spreads with at least 65% vegetable oil can be substituted (see page 13).

**If using self-rising flour, omit baking soda and salt.

1 COOKIE: Calories 100 (Calories from Fat 45); Fat 5g (Saturated 1g); Cholesterol 10mg; Sodium 90mg; Carbohydrate 13g (Dietary Fiber 0g); Protein 1g

---

LIGHTER SOFT MOLASSES COOKIES
For 3 grams of fat and 85 calories per serving, use dark molasses and substitute 1/2 package (8-ounce size) reduced-fat cream cheese (Neufchâtel), softened, for the shortening and unsweetened applesauce for the sour cream. Increase cinnamon and ginger to 1 1/4 teaspoons each.

Tips for Shaped Cookies

- Rich, soft dough must be chilled before shaping. Work with small amounts, keeping remaining dough refrigerated.
- If dough is too soft after chilling, mix in 1 to 2 tablespoons flour. If dough is too dry and crumbly, work in 1 to 2 tablespoons milk, water or softened *stick* margarine or butter.
- Take the time to mold fancy shapes (such as crescents, candy canes, wreaths, bells) so that cookies are uniform in shape and size. This helps them bake evenly.
- Shape refrigerator cookie dough firmly into a smooth roll of the length or diameter specified in the recipe. Wrap rolled dough in waxed paper, plastic wrap or aluminum foil, twisting ends.
- Refrigerate rolled dough until firm enough to slice easily. Use a thin, sharp knife to slice dough.
- Rolls of dough can be refrigerated up to twenty-four hours or wrapped airtight and frozen up to twelve months.

Chocolate Crinkles (page 122), Candy Cookies (page 117), Peanut Butter Cookies

Peanut Butter Cookies

PREP: 15 min; CHILL: 2 hr; BAKE: 30 min
Makes about 2 1/2 dozen cookies

Want something different than the crisscross marks a fork makes? Try using the bottom of a cut crystal glass, a potato masher or cookie stamp for a new look.

> 1/2 cup granulated sugar
> 1/2 cup packed brown sugar
> 1/2 cup peanut butter
> 1/4 cup shortening
> 1/4 cup *stick* margarine or butter, softened*
> 1 large egg
> 1 1/4 cups all-purpose flour**
> 3/4 teaspoon baking soda
> 1/2 teaspoon baking powder
> 1/4 teaspoon salt
> Granulated sugar

1. Mix 1/2 cup granulated sugar, the brown sugar, peanut butter, shortening, margarine and egg in large bowl. Stir in flour, baking soda, baking powder and salt. Cover and refrigerate about 2 hours or until firm.

2. Heat oven to 375°.

3. Shape dough into 1 1/4-inch balls. Place about 3 inches apart on ungreased cookie sheet. Flatten in crisscross pattern with fork dipped in granulated sugar.

4. Bake 9 to 10 minutes or until light brown. Cool 5 minutes; remove from cookie sheet. Cool on wire rack.

*Spreads with at least 65% vegetable oil can be substituted (see page 13).

**If using self-rising flour, omit baking soda, baking powder and salt.

1 COOKIE: Calories 115 (Calories from Fat 55); Fat 6g (Saturated 1g); Cholesterol 10mg; Sodium 100mg; Carbohydrate 13g (Dietary Fiber 0g); Protein 2g

---

LIGHTER PEANUT BUTTER COOKIES

For 1 gram of fat and 95 calories per serving, use reduced-fat peanut butter. Substitute 1/4 package (8-ounce size) reduced-fat cream cheese (Neufchâtel), softened, for the shortening. Add 1/2 teaspoon vanilla with the egg.

Chocolate Crinkles

PREP: 20 min; CHILL: 3 hr; BAKE: 1 hr 12 min
Makes about 6 dozen cookies

These cookies with their attractive light and dark contrast make an interesting addition to a cookie tray any time of year. They are also great served by themselves! (photograph on page 121)

2 cups granulated sugar
1/2 cup vegetable oil
2 teaspoons vanilla
4 ounces unsweetened baking chocolate, melted and cooled
4 large eggs
2 cups all-purpose flour*
2 teaspoons baking powder
1/2 teaspoon salt
1 cup powdered sugar

1. Mix granulated sugar, oil, vanilla and chocolate in large bowl. Mix in eggs, one at a time. Stir in flour, baking powder and salt. Cover and refrigerate at least 3 hours.

2. Heat oven to 350°. Grease cookie sheet with shortening.

3. Drop dough by teaspoonfuls into powdered sugar; roll around to coat. Shape into balls. Place about 2 inches apart on cookie sheet.

4. Bake 10 to 12 minutes or until almost no indentation remains when touched. Remove from cookie sheet. Cool on wire rack.

*If using self-rising flour, omit baking powder and salt.

1 COOKIE: Calories 70 (Calories from Fat 25); Fat 3g (Saturated 1g); Cholesterol 10mg; Sodium 35mg; Carbohydrate 10g (Dietary Fiber 0g); Protein 1g

Gingersnaps

PREP: 15 min; CHILL: 2 hr; BAKE: 48 min
Makes about 4 dozen cookies

After baking, these spicy cookies have a crackly top, and are very nice served with ice cream, fresh fruit, sorbet or coffee.

1 cup packed brown sugar
3/4 cup shortening
1/4 cup molasses
1 large egg
2 1/4 cups all-purpose flour*
2 teaspoons baking soda
1 teaspoon ground cinnamon
1 teaspoon ground ginger
1/2 teaspoon ground cloves
1/4 teaspoon salt
Granulated sugar

1. Mix brown sugar, shortening, molasses and egg in large bowl. Stir in remaining ingredients except granulated sugar. Cover and refrigerate at least 1 hour.

2. Heat oven to 375°. Grease cookie sheet lightly with shortening.

3. Shape dough by rounded teaspoonfuls into balls. Dip tops into granulated sugar. Place balls, sugared sides up, about 3 inches apart on cookie sheet.

4. Bake 10 to 12 minutes or just until set. Remove from cookie sheet. Cool on wire rack.

*If using self-rising flour, decrease baking soda to 1 teaspoon and omit salt.

1 COOKIE: Calories 70 (Calories from Fat 25); Fat 3g (Saturated 1g); Cholesterol 5mg; Sodium 70mg; Carbohydrate 11g (Dietary Fiber 0g); Protein 0g

Snickerdoodles

PREP: 10 min; BAKE: 40 min
Makes about 4 dozen cookies

This favorite cookie is traditionally rolled in or sprinkled with cinnamon-sugar before baking. The cookie originated in New England in the 1800s and was named purely for fun!

1 1/2 cups sugar
1/2 cup *stick* margarine or butter, softened*
1/2 cup shortening
2 large eggs
2 3/4 cups all-purpose flour**
2 teaspoons cream of tartar
1 teaspoon baking soda
1/4 teaspoon salt
1/4 cup sugar
2 teaspoons ground cinnamon

1. Heat oven to 400°.

2. Mix 1 1/2 cups sugar, the margarine, shortening and eggs in large bowl. Stir in flour, cream of tartar, baking soda and salt.

3. Shape dough into 1 1/4-inch balls. Mix 1/4 cup sugar and the cinnamon. Roll balls in cinnamon-sugar mixture. Place 2 inches apart on ungreased cookie sheet.

4. Bake 8 to 10 minutes or until set. Remove from cookie sheet. Cool on wire rack.

*Spreads with at least 65% vegetable oil can be substituted (see page 13).

**If using self-rising flour, omit cream of tartar, baking soda and salt.

1 COOKIE: Calories 90 (Calories from Fat 35); Fat 4g (Saturated 1g); Cholesterol 10mg; Sodium 65mg; Carbohydrate 13g (Dietary Fiber 0g); Protein 1g

Bonbon Cookies

PREP: 25 min; BAKE: 30 min; COOL: 1 hr
Makes about 2 dozen cookies

Glazing these cookies is a breeze when glaze is placed in a shallow bowl. Just turn each cookie upside down and dip into the glaze, then place cookie back on the wire rack so the glaze can set.

3/4 cup powdered sugar
1/2 cup *stick* margarine or butter, softened*
1 tablespoon vanilla
Food color, if desired
1 1/2 cups all-purpose flour**
1/8 teaspoon salt
Dates, nuts, semisweet chocolate chips and candied or maraschino cherries
Vanilla Glaze or Chocolate Glaze (right)

1. Heat oven to 350°.

2. Mix powdered sugar, margarine, vanilla and a few drops food color in medium bowl. Stir in flour and salt until dough holds together. (If dough is dry, mix in 1 to 2 tablespoons milk.)

3. For each cookie, shape dough by tablespoonful around date, nut, chocolate chips or cherry to form a ball. Place about 1 inch apart on ungreased cookie sheet.

4. Bake 12 to 15 minutes or until set but not brown. Remove from cookie sheet. Cool completely on wire rack. Dip tops of cookies into Vanilla Glaze. Decorate with coconut, nuts, colored sugar, chocolate chips or chocolate shot if desired.

Vanilla Glaze

1 cup powdered sugar
1 tablespoon plus 1 1/2 teaspoons milk
1 teaspoon vanilla
Food color, if desired

Mix powdered sugar, milk and vanilla until smooth. Tint with a few drops food color.

Chocolate Glaze

1 cup powdered sugar
2 tablespoons milk
1 teaspoon vanilla
1 ounce unsweetened baking chocolate, melted and cooled

Mix powdered sugar, milk and vanilla until smooth. Stir in chocolate.

We do not recommend using vegetable oil spreads (see page 13).

**Do not use self-rising flour in this recipe.*

1 COOKIE: Calories 155 (Calories from Fat 45); Fat 5g (Saturated 1g); Cholesterol 0mg; Sodium 60mg; Carbohydrate 27g (Dietary Fiber 1g); Protein 1g

CHOCOLATE BONBON COOKIES: Omit food color. Stir in 1 ounce unsweetened baking chocolate, melted and cooled, with the vanilla.

Russian Tea Cakes

PREP: 20 min; BAKE: 48 min
Makes about 4 dozen cookies

1 cup *stick* margarine or butter, softened*
1/2 cup powdered sugar
1 teaspoon vanilla
2 1/4 cups all-purpose flour**
3/4 cup finely chopped nuts
1/4 teaspoon salt
Powdered sugar

1. Heat oven to 400°.

2. Mix margarine, 1/2 cup powdered sugar and the vanilla in large bowl. Stir in flour, nuts and salt until dough holds together.

3. Shape dough into 1-inch balls. Place about 1 inch apart on ungreased cookie sheet.

4. Bake 10 to 12 minutes or until set but not brown. Remove from cookie sheet. Cool slightly on wire rack.

5. Roll warm cookies in powdered sugar; cool on wire rack. Roll in powdered sugar again.

We do not recommend using vegetable oil spreads (see page 13).

**Do not use self-rising flour in this recipe.*

1 COOKIE: Calories 75 (Calories from Fat 45); Fat 5g (Saturated 1g); Cholesterol 0mg; Sodium 55mg; Carbohydrate 7g (Dietary Fiber 0g); Protein 1g

TIMESAVING TIP
Use the food processor to chop the nuts and mix the dough. Do not overmix, or cookies will be tough.

Orange-Almond Biscotti

Thumbprint Cookies

PREP: 30 min; BAKE: 30 min; COOL: 1 hr
Makes about 3 dozen cookies

> 1/4 cup packed brown sugar
> 1/4 cup shortening
> 1/4 cup *stick* margarine or butter, softened*
> 1/2 teaspoon vanilla
> 1 large egg, separated
> 1 cup all-purpose flour**
> 1/4 teaspoon salt
> 1 cup finely chopped nuts
> Jelly

1. Heat oven to 350°.

2. Mix brown sugar, shortening, margarine, vanilla and egg yolk in medium bowl. Stir in flour and salt until dough holds together.

3. Shape dough into 1-inch balls. Beat egg white slightly. Dip each ball into egg white. Roll in nuts. Place about 1 inch apart on ungreased cookie sheet. Press thumb deeply in center of each.

4. Bake about 10 minutes or until light brown. Remove from cookie sheet. Cool completely on wire rack. Fill thumbprints with jelly.

*We do not recommend using vegetable oil spreads (see page 13).

**If using self-rising flour, omit salt.

1 COOKIE: Calories 85 (Calories from Fat 45); Fat 5g (Saturated 1g); Cholesterol 6mg; Sodium 35mg; Carbohydrate 9g (Dietary Fiber 0g); Protein 1g

Shortbread Cookies

PREP: 20 min; BAKE: 40 min
Makes about 2 dozen 1 1/2-inch cookies

Serve these buttery cookies plain, or for a more festive look, dip the edges in melted chocolate and then in chopped pistachios.

> 3/4 cup *stick* margarine or butter, softened*
> 1/4 cup sugar
> 2 cups all-purpose flour**

1. Heat oven to 350°.

2. Mix margarine and sugar in large bowl. Stir in flour. (If dough is crumbly, mix in 1 to 2 tablespoons margarine, butter or spread, softened.)

3. Roll dough 1/2 inch thick on lightly floured surface. Cut into small shapes by hand or use cookie cutters. Place 1/2 inch apart on ungreased cookie sheet.

4. Bake about 20 minutes or until set. Remove from cookie sheet. Cool on wire rack.

*We do not recommend using vegetable oil spreads (see page 13).

**Do not use self-rising flour in this recipe.

1 COOKIE: Calories 100 (Calories from Fat 55); Fat 6g (Saturated 1g); Cholesterol 0mg; Sodium 70mg; Carbohydrate 10g (Dietary Fiber 0g); Protein 1g

PECAN SHORTBREAD COOKIES: Mix in 1/2 cup chopped pecans, toasted if desired, with the flour.

Orange-Almond Biscotti

PREP: 25 min; BAKE: 1 hr 20 min; COOL: 15 min
Makes about 3 1/2 dozen cookies

Biscotti is an Italian cookie that's baked twice, first in a loaf, then sliced and baked again. Its crunchy texture makes it perfect for dipping into all sorts of beverages such as coffee, milk or dessert wine. Make them even more special—melt 1/2 cup semisweet chocolate chips with 1 teaspoon shortening and drizzle over tops.

> 1 cup sugar
> 1/2 cup *stick* margarine or butter, softened*
> 1 tablespoon grated orange peel
> 2 large eggs
> 3 1/2 cups all-purpose flour**
> 1 teaspoon baking powder
> 1/2 teaspoon salt
> 1/3 cup slivered almonds, toasted and
>   chopped (see page 9)

1. Heat oven to 350°.

2. Beat sugar, margarine, orange peel and eggs in large bowl. Stir in flour, baking powder, salt and almonds.

3. Shape half of dough at a time into rectangle, 10 × 3 inches, on ungreased cookie sheet.

4. Bake about 20 minutes or until toothpick inserted in center comes out clean. Cool on cookie sheet 15 minutes.

5. Cut crosswise into 1/2-inch slices. Place slices cut sides down on cookie sheet.

6. Bake about 15 minutes or until crisp and light brown. Remove from cookie sheet. Cool on wire rack.

We do not recommend using vegetable oil spreads (see page 13).

**If using self-rising flour, omit baking powder and salt.*

1 COOKIE: Calories 85 (Calories from Fat 25); Fat 3g (Saturated 1g); Cholesterol 10mg; Sodium 65mg; Carbohydrate 13g (Dietary Fiber 0g); Protein 1g

Brown Sugar Refrigerator Cookies

PREP: 20 min; CHILL: 2 hr; BAKE: 48 min
Makes about 6 dozen cookies

Slice and bake these cookies any time you please. Just freeze the cookie dough tightly wrapped for up to two months, and add one or two additional minutes to the baking time when they come straight from the freezer.

> 1 cup packed brown sugar
> 1 cup *stick* margarine or butter, softened*
> 1 teaspoon vanilla
> 1 large egg
> 3 cups all-purpose flour**
> 1 1/2 teaspoons ground cinnamon
> 1/2 teaspoon baking soda
> 1/2 teaspoon salt
> 1/3 cup chopped nuts

1. Mix brown sugar, margarine, vanilla and egg in large bowl. Stir in remaining ingredients.

2. Shape dough into rectangle, 10 × 3 inches, on plastic wrap. Wrap and refrigerate about 2 hours or until firm but no longer than 24 hours.

3. Heat oven to 375°.

4. Cut rectangle into 1/8-inch slices. Place 2 inches apart on ungreased cookie sheet.

5. Bake 6 to 8 minutes or until light brown. Cool slightly; remove from cookie sheet. Cool on wire rack.

We do not recommend using vegetable oil spreads (see page 13).

**If using self-rising flour, omit baking soda and salt.*

1 COOKIE: Calories 55 (Calories from Fat 30); Fat 3g (Saturated 1g); Cholesterol 5mg; Sodium 55mg; Carbohydrate 7g (Dietary Fiber 0g); Protein 0g

Tips for Pressed Cookies

- Use room-temperature margarine, butter or shortening.
- Test dough for consistency before adding all of the flour. Put a small amount of dough in cookie press; squeeze out. Dough should be soft and pliable but not crumbly. If dough is too stiff, add 1 egg yolk; if dough is too soft, add 1 to 2 tablespoons flour.
- Chill dough only if specified in the recipe.
- Be sure cookie sheet is cool. A hot cookie sheet causes dough to soften and spread before baking.
- Hold cookie press so that it rests on the cookie sheet. Raise press straight up from the cookie sheet after enough dough has been released to form a cookie.

Buttery Spritz

PREP: 25 min; BAKE: 45 min
Makes about 5 dozen cookies

> 1 cup stick butter, softened*
> 1/2 cup sugar
> 2 1/4 cups all-purpose flour**
> 1 teaspoon almond extract or vanilla
> 1/2 teaspoon salt
> 1 large egg
> Few drops red or green food color, if desired

1. Heat oven to 400°.

2. Mix butter and sugar in large bowl. Stir in remaining ingredients.

3. Place dough in cookie press. Form desired shapes on ungreased cookie sheet.

4. Bake 6 to 9 minutes or until set but not brown. *Immediately* remove from cookie sheet. Cool on wire rack.

* We do not recommend using margarine or vegetable oil spreads.

**Do not use self-rising flour in this recipe.

1 COOKIE: Calories 45 (Calories from Fat 25); Fat 3g (Saturated 2g); Cholesterol 10mg; Sodium 40mg; Carbohydrate 5g (Dietary Fiber 0g); Protein 0g

CHOCOLATE BUTTERY SPRITZ: Stir 2 ounces unsweetened baking chocolate, melted and cooled, into butter-sugar mixture.

Bourbon Balls

PREP: 20 min; CHILL: 3 Days
Makes about 5 dozen cookies

> 3 cups finely crushed chocolate wafers
>   (about 60 cookies)
> 2 cups powdered sugar
> 1 cup finely chopped almonds, pecans or
>   walnuts
> 1/2 cup bourbon
> 1/4 cup light corn syrup
> Granulated sugar, powdered sugar or baking
>   cocoa

1. Mix crushed wafers, powdered sugar and pecans in large bowl. Stir in bourbon and corn syrup.

2. Shape mixture into 1-inch balls. Roll in granulated sugar. Cover tightly and refrigerate at least 3 days before serving to blend flavors.

1 COOKIE: Calories 60 (Calories from Fat 20); Fat 2g (Saturated 0g); Cholesterol 0mg; Sodium 30mg; Carbohydrate 10g (Dietary Fiber 0g); Protein 0g

BRANDY BALLS: Substitute 1/2 cup brandy for the bourbon. Cut Brandy Balls if needed.

RUM BALLS: Substitute 1/2 cup light rum for the bourbon

TIMESAVING TIP
Use your food processor to crush the cookies and finely chop the nuts. If your processor is large enough, omit the bowl and use it for mixing all the ingredients, pulsing on and off until the mixture is evenly blended.

Date Balls

PREP: 25 min; COOK: 10 min
Makes about 6 dozen cookies

These cookies are great to have on hand during the holidays —or any time you're entertaining.

> 3/4 cup sugar
> 1/2 cup *stick* margarine or butter*
> 1 pound pitted dates, chopped
> 1 tablespoon milk
> 1 teaspoon vanilla
> 1/2 teaspoon salt
> 1 large egg, well beaten
> 1/2 cup chopped nuts
> 4 cups whole-grain multivitamin supplement
>   cereal, crushed (Total®)
> Finely chopped nuts or shredded coconut

1. Mix sugar, margarine and dates in 2-quart saucepan. Cook over low heat, stirring constantly, until margarine is melted; remove from heat.

2. Stir in milk, vanilla, salt and egg. Cook over very low heat 4 minutes, stirring constantly; remove from heat.

3. Stir in 1/2 cup nuts. Cool 5 minutes. Stir in cereal.

4. Shape mixture by teaspoonfuls into balls. Roll balls in finely chopped nuts. Cover tightly and refrigerate up to 2 weeks or freeze up to 2 months.

*We do not recommend using vegetable oil spreads (see page 13).

1 COOKIE: Calories 50 (Calories from Fat 20); Fat 2g (Saturated 0g); Cholesterol 5mg; Sodium 40mg; Carbohydrate 8g (Dietary Fiber 0g); Protein 0g

Tips for Rolled Cookies

- Roll only part of the chilled dough at a time, and keep the remainder refrigerated.
- To prevent dough from sticking, sprinkle rolling surface with flour and rub flour onto rolling pin. Use only enough flour to prevent dough from sticking during rolling. Too much flour and rerolling the dough results in dry, tough cookies.
- To ensure even baking, roll dough evenly to maintain uniform thickness. Rolling dough between two 15- or 18-inch rulers or wooden dowels or sticks of the correct height helps keep dough even.
- Dip cookie cutter into flour or powdered sugar and shake off excess before each cut.
- Cut cookies close together to avoid rerolling leftover dough (rerolled dough will be a little tougher).
- Use a wide metal spatula to lift cut dough to the cookie sheet to avoid stretching the dough.

Sugar Cookies

PREP: 25 min; CHILL: 2 hr; BAKE: 40 min
Makes about 5 dozen 2-inch cookies

(photograph on page 109)

1 1/2 cups powdered sugar
1 cup margarine or butter, softened*
1 teaspoon vanilla
1/2 teaspoon almond extract
1 large egg
2 1/2 cups all-purpose flour**
1 teaspoon baking soda
1 teaspoon cream of tartar
Granulated sugar

1. Mix powdered sugar, margarine, vanilla, almond extract and egg in large bowl. Stir in remaining ingredients except granulated sugar. Cover and refrigerate at least 2 hours.

2. Heat oven to 375°. Grease cookie sheet lightly with shortening.

3. Divide dough in half. Roll each half 1/4 inch thick on lightly floured surface. Cut into desired shapes with 2- to 2 1/2-inch cookie cutters. Sprinkle with granulated sugar. Place on cookie sheet.

4. Bake 7 to 8 minutes or until edges are light brown. Remove from cookie sheet. Cool on wire rack.

We do not recommend using vegetable oil spreads (see page 13).

**If using self-rising flour, omit baking soda and cream of tartar.*

1 **COOKIE:** Calories 60 (Calories from Fat 25); Fat 3g (Saturated 1g); Cholesterol 5mg; Sodium 60mg; Carbohydrate 8g (Dietary Fiber 0g); Protein 0g

DECORATED SUGAR COOKIES: Omit granulated sugar. Frost and decorate cooled cookies with Vanilla Buttercream Frosting (page 86) tinted with food color if desired. Decorate with colored sugar, small candies, candied fruit or nuts if desired.

PAINTBRUSH SUGAR COOKIES: Omit granulated sugar. Cut rolled dough into desired shapes with cookie cutters. (Cut no more than 12 cookies at a time to keep them from drying out.) Mix 1 egg yolk and 1/4 teaspoon water. Divide mixture among several custard cups. Tint each with different food color to make bright colors. (If paint thickens while standing, stir in a few drops water.) Paint designs on cookies with small paintbrushes. Bake as directed.

Gingerbread Cookies

PREP: 25 min; CHILL: 2 hr; BAKE: 36 min
Makes about 2 1/2 dozen 2 1/2-inch cookies

1 cup packed brown sugar
1/3 cup shortening
1 1/2 cups dark molasses
2/3 cup cold water
7 cups all-purpose flour*
2 teaspoons baking soda
2 teaspoons ground ginger
1 teaspoon ground allspice
1 teaspoon ground cinnamon
1 teaspoon ground cloves
1/2 teaspoon salt

1. Mix brown sugar, shortening, molasses and water in large bowl. Stir in remaining ingredients. Cover and refrigerate at least 2 hours.

2. Heat oven to 350°. Grease cookie sheet lightly with shortening.

3. Roll dough 1/4 inch thick on floured surface. Cut with floured gingerbread cutter or other favorite shaped cutter. Place about 2 inches apart on cookie sheet.

4. Bake 10 to 12 minutes or until no indentation remains when touched. Remove from cookie sheet. Cool completely on wire rack. Decorate with colored frosting, colored sugar and candies if desired.

If using self-rising flour, omit baking soda and salt.

1 **COOKIE:** Calories 195 (Calories from Fat 25); Fat 3g (Saturated 1g); Cholesterol 0mg; Sodium 135mg; Carbohydrate 40g (Dietary Fiber 1g); Protein 3g

About Candies

If candy shops are a favorite of yours, why not create your own? Stir up some fudge, taffy, caramels or any of the other treats here—they taste so special when they come from your own kitchen.

Pans and Pan Preparation

- Always use the size saucepan given in the recipe. A smaller or larger pan could affect cooking time and quality. If a size is not stated, size is not important.
- Use the recommended size baking pan for shaping cooked candy. A pan too large can make candy too thin; a pan too small can make candy too thick. Using a square or rectangular pan with straight sides will give the most evenly shaped pieces when cut.
- Grease pans with margarine or butter, not shortening, as the flavor is better and the candy is not baked. Or line with aluminum foil for easy removal and cutting.

Mixing and Cooking Candies

- Don't double the recipe—make another batch. Increasing ingredients changes cooking time.
- A cool, dry day is best for making candy. Heat, humidity and altitude can affect quality. On a humid day, cook candy to a temperature one degree or so higher than the recipe indicates to drive off extra moisture.
- To help prevent crystallization or grainy candy, sugar must dissolve completely over low heat; stir down any grains from side of saucepan. Or, cover the pan for a few minutes at the beginning of cooking; the steam generated will wash down any sugar crystals.
- After candy has boiled, do not stir until it has cooled as the recipe indicates. To prevent crystals, do not scrape pan or stir candy during cooling.
- We recommend margarine or butter (not vegetable oil spreads or tub products) be used for all candies, since the use of lower fat products can cause candies not to set up or have as brittle or crisp texture as they should.

Determining Candy Doneness

- Use a reliable candy thermometer. Check your candy thermometer for accuracy by placing it in water and heating the water to boiling. The thermometer should read 212°. If the reading is higher or lower, take the difference into account when making candy.
- Consult an altitude table to determine the boiling point in your area, then adjust if necessary.
- To get an accurate reading, be sure the thermometer stands upright in the cooking mixture and the bulb does not rest on bottom of pan. Read the thermometer at eye level. Watch temperature closely—after 200°, it goes up very quickly.
- If you don't have a thermometer, use the cold water test. Using a clean spoon, drop a small amount of cooking mixture into a cupful of very cold water. Test hardness with fingers (see chart). If candy does not pass test, continue cooking.

Candy Cooking Tests

Hardness	Temperature	Cold Water Test
Soft ball	234° to 240°	Forms a ball that flattens when removed from water
Firm ball	242° to 248°	Forms a firm ball holds its shape until pressed
Hard ball	250° to 268°	Forms a ball that holds its shape but is pliable
Soft crack	270° to 290°	Separates into hard but not brittle threads
Hard crack	300° to 310°	Separates into hard, brittle threads
Caramel	320° to 350°	Do not use cold water test. Mixture coats metal spoon and forms light caramel-colored mass when poured on a plate.

Candy Yields and Storage

- Amounts may vary depending on the size of the pieces cut or shaped.
- Store candy tightly covered at room temperature for up to two weeks, unless otherwise directed in recipe. Or wrap tightly and freeze up to six months. Let stand covered at room temperature one to two hours before serving.

How to Test Candy

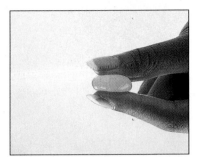

Soft ball: Forms a soft ball that flattens when removed from water.

Firm ball: Forms a firm ball that holds its shape until pressed.

Hard ball: Forms a hard ball that holds its shape but is pliable.

Soft crack: Separates into hard but not brittle threads.

Hard crack: Separates into hard, brittle threads.

Caramel: Do *not* use cold water test. Mixture coats metal spoon and forms light caramel-colored mass when poured on plate.

Luscious Chocolate Truffles

PREP: 20 min; CHILL: 25 min: FREEZE: 30 min
Makes about 15 candies

These truffles are as good as any you can buy! The shortening helps set the chocolate coating so it doesn't melt.

    1 package (12 ounces) semisweet chocolate
        chips (2 cups)*
    2 tablespoons *stick* margarine or butter**
    1/4 cup whipping (heavy) cream
    2 tablespoons liqueur (almond, cherry,
        coffee, hazelnut, Irish cream, orange,
        raspberry, etc.), if desired
    1 tablespoon shortening
    Finely chopped nuts, if desired
    1/4 cup powdered sugar, if desired
    1/2 teaspoon milk, if desired

1. Line cookie sheet with aluminum foil.

2. Melt 1 cup of the chocolate chips in heavy 2-quart saucepan over low heat, stirring constantly; remove from heat. Stir in margarine. Stir in whipping cream and liqueur. Refrigerate 10 to 15 minutes, stirring frequently, just until thick enough to hold a shape.

3. Drop mixture by teaspoonfuls onto cookie sheet.

Shape into balls. (If mixture is too sticky, refrigerate until firm enough to shape.) Freeze 30 minutes.

4. Heat shortening and remaining 1 cup chocolate chips over low heat, stirring constantly, until chocolate is melted and mixture is smooth; remove from heat. Dip truffles, one at a time, into chocolate. Return to aluminum foil-covered cookie sheet. *Immediately* sprinkle some of the truffles with finely chopped nuts. Refrigerate about 10 minutes or until coating is set.

5. Drizzle some of the truffles with a mixture of 1/4 cup powdered sugar and 1/2 teaspoon milk. Refrigerate just until set. Serve at room temperature. Store truffles in airtight container.

*1 cup milk chocolate chips can be substituted for the first cup of semisweet chocolate chips.

**We do not recommend using vegetable oil spreads (see page 13).

1 CANDY: Calories 155 (Calories from Fat 90); Fat 10g (Saturated 5g); Cholesterol 5mg; Sodium 20mg; Carbohydrate 15g (Dietary Fiber 0g); Protein 1g

APRICOT TRUFFLES: Soak 3 tablespoons chopped dried apricots in 1 tablespoon brandy 15 minutes. Stir into whipping cream mixture.

CASHEW TRUFFLES: Stir 3 tablespoons chopped cashews into whipping cream mixture.

Triple Chocolate Marble Fudge, Peanut Brittle (page 132)

Triple Chocolate Marble Fudge

PREP: 20 min; COOK: 23 min; CHILL: 3 hr
Makes 96 candies

This melt-in-your mouth fudge rivals any fudge shop! If you like, use only one variety of chocolate rather than mixing milk and bittersweet chocolate.

> 6 cups sugar
> 1 can (12 ounces) evaporated milk
> 1 cup *stick* margarine or butter*
> 1 tub (8 ounces) mascarpone cheese, softened, or 1 package (8 ounces) cream cheese, softened
> 1 jar (13 ounces) marshmallow creme or 1 package (10 1/2 ounces) miniature marshmallows
> 1 tablespoon vanilla
> 1 package (11 ounces) vanilla milk chips (2 cups)
> 1/2 package (11 1/2-ounce size) milk chocolate chips (1 cup)
> 2 packages (3 ounces each) bittersweet chocolate, chopped (1 cup)
> 2 tablespoons baking cocoa

1. Grease bottom and sides of rectangular pan, 13 × 9 × 2 inches, with butter, or line with aluminum foil.

2. Heat sugar, milk, butter and cheese to boiling in 6-quart Dutch oven over medium-high heat 6 to 8 minutes, stirring constantly.

3. Reduce heat to medium. Cook about 10 minutes, stirring occasionally, to 225° on candy thermometer; remove from heat.

4. *Quickly* stir in marshmallow creme and vanilla. Pour 4 cups hot marshmallow mixture over vanilla milk chips in large bowl; stir to mix. Stir chocolate chips, bittersweet chocolate and cocoa into remaining marshmallow mixture.

5. Pour one-third of the white mixture into pan, spreading evenly. *Quickly* pour one-third of the chocolate mixture over top, spreading evenly. Repeat twice. Pull and swirl knife greased with butter through mixtures for marbled design. Cool until set. Refrigerate uncovered about 3 hours or until set. Cut into 1 1/2-inch squares with knife greased with butter.

We do not recommend using vegetable oil spreads (see page 13).

1 CANDY: Calories 130 (Calories from Fat 45); Fat 5g (Saturated 3g); Cholesterol 10mg; Sodium 30mg; Carbohydrate 20g (Dietary Fiber 0g); Protein 1g

> **TIMESAVING TIP**
> Measure out vanilla milk chips and chocolate ingredients ahead of time and place in heatproof bowls, along with heatproof spoons.

Easy Fruit and Nut Fudge

PREP: 10 min; COOK: 5 min; CHILL: 2 hr
Makes 6 dozen candies

    1 1/2 packages (12 ounces each) semisweet
        chocolate chips (3 cups)
    2 cups miniature marshmallows or 16 large
        marshmallows, cut in half
    1 can (14 ounces) sweetened condensed milk
    1 teaspoon vanilla
    1 cup chopped nuts
    1/2 cup dried cherries, or chopped dried
        apricots

1. Grease bottom and sides of square pan, 9 × 9 × 2 inches, with margarine, or line with aluminum foil.

2. Heat chocolate chips, marshmallows and milk in 2-quart saucepan over medium heat, stirring constantly, until chips and marshmallows are melted and mixture can be stirred smooth.

3. Stir in vanilla, nuts and cherries. *Immediately* pour into pan. Cover and refrigerate about 2 hours or until firm. Cut into 1-inch squares.

1 CANDY: Calories 75 (Calories from Fat 35); Fat 4g (Saturated 2g); Cholesterol 5mg; Sodium 10mg; Carbohydrate 9g (Dietary Fiber 0g); Protein 1g

WHITE CHOCOLATE-TOASTED ALMOND FUDGE: Substitute vanilla milk chips for the chocolate chips, 1/2 teaspoon almond extract for the vanilla and whole almonds, toasted (page 9), for the nuts. Decrease sweetened condensed milk to 1 cup. Cover and refrigerate about 4 hours or until firm.

> ### TIMESAVING TIP
> To microwave, place chocolate chips, marshmallows and milk in 8-cup microwavable measure. Microwave uncovered on High 3 to 5 minutes, stirring every minute, until chips and marshmallows are melted and can be stirred smooth. Continue as directed in step 3.

Toffee

PREP: 10 min; COOK: 10 min; CHILL: 2 hr
Makes 36 candies

    1 cup pecans, chopped
    3/4 cup packed brown sugar
    1/2 cup *stick* margarine or butter*
    1/2 cup semisweet chocolate chips

1. Grease bottom and sides of square pan, 9 × 9 × 2 inches, with margarine.

2. Spread pecans in pan. Heat brown sugar and margarine to boiling in 1 1/2-quart saucepan over medium heat, stirring constantly. Boil 7 minutes, stirring constantly. *Immediately* spread evenly over pecans. Sprinkle with chocolate chips.

3. Cover pan with cookie sheet. Let stand about 1 minute or until chocolate chips soften. Spread softened chocolate over candy. Cut into 1 1/2-inch squares while hot. Refrigerate uncovered about 2 hours or until firm.

We do not recommend using vegetable oil spreads (see page 13).

1 CANDY: Calories 75 (Calories from Fat 45); Fat 5g (Saturated 1g); Cholesterol 0mg; Sodium 30mg; Carbohydrate 7g (Dietary Fiber 0g); Protein 0g

> ### TIMESAVING TIP
> To microwave, prepare pan with pecans as directed. Place brown sugar and margarine in 4-cup microwavable measure. Microwave uncovered on High 5 minutes, stirring every minute, until sugar is dissolved. Immediately spread evenly over pecans. Sprinkle with chocolate chips. Continue as directed in step 3.

Caramels

PREP: 5 min; COOK: 30 min
Makes 64 candies

Calling all caramel lovers—this is your ultimate recipe! (photograph on page 132)

    1/2 cup finely chopped pecans
    2 cups sugar
    1/2 cup *stick* margarine or butter*
    2 cups whipping (heavy) cream
    3/4 cup light corn syrup

1. Grease bottom and sides of square pan, 8 × 8 × 2 or 9 × 9 × 2 inches, with margarine.

2. Spread pecans in pan. Heat remaining ingredients to boiling in 3-quart heavy saucepan over medium heat, stirring constantly. Cook, stirring frequently, to 245° on candy thermometer or until small amount of mixture dropped into very cold water forms a firm ball that holds its shape until pressed. *Immediately* spread over pecans; cool.

3. Cut into 1-inch squares. Wrap individually in plastic wrap or waxed paper.

We do not recommend using vegetable oil spreads (see page 13).

1 CANDY: Calories 75 (Calories from Fat 35); Fat 4g (Saturated 2g); Cholesterol 10mg; Sodium 25mg; Carbohydrate 10g (Dietary Fiber 0g); Protein 0g

CHOCOLATE CARAMELS: Heat 2 ounces unsweetened baking chocolate with the sugar mixture.

Pralines, Caramels (page 131)

Pralines

**PREP: 15 min; COOK: 30 min; COOL: 1 1/2 hr;
STAND: 12 hr
Makes about 1 1/2 dozen candies**

This confection originated in Louisiana, where brown sugar and pecans are abundant. You'll agree they put the local foods to good use!

> 2 cups packed light brown sugar
> 1 cup granulated sugar
> 1 1/4 cups milk
> 1/4 cup light corn syrup
> 1/8 teaspoon salt
> 1 teaspoon vanilla
> 1 1/2 cups pecan halves (5 1/2 ounces)

1. Heat sugars, milk, corn syrup and salt to boiling in Dutch oven, stirring constantly. Reduce heat to medium. Cook, without stirring, to 236° on candy thermometer or until small amount of mixture dropped into very cold water forms a soft ball that flattens when removed from water. Cool, without stirring, about 1 hour or until saucepan is cool to touch.

2. Add vanilla and pecan halves. Beat about 1 minute or until mixture is slightly thickened and just coats pecans but does not lose its gloss. Drop mixture by spoonfuls onto waxed paper, trying to divide pecans equally. Let stand uncovered 12 to 18 hours or until candies are firm and no longer glossy.

3. Wrap individually in plastic wrap or waxed paper. Store slightly covered at room temperature.

1 CANDY: Calories 220 (Calories from Fat 55); Fat 6g (Saturated 1g); Cholesterol 5mg; Sodium 40mg; Carbohydrate 41g (Dietary Fiber 0g); Protein 1g

Peanut Brittle

**PREP: 15 min; COOK: 30 min; COOL: 1 hr
Makes about 6 dozen candies**

Just about everyone loves peanut brittle, and when it's home-made, it seems even better. (photograph on page 130)

> 1 1/2 teaspoons baking soda
> 1 teaspoon water
> 1 teaspoon vanilla
> 1 1/2 cups sugar
> 1 cup water
> 1 cup light corn syrup
> 3 tablespoons *stick* margarine or butter*
> 1 pound shelled unroasted peanuts

1. Heat oven to 200°. Grease 2 cookie sheets, 15 1/2 × 12 inches, with margarine, and keep warm in oven. (Keeping the cookie sheets warm allows the candy to be spread 1/4 inch thick without it setting up.) Grease long metal spatula with margarine; set aside.

2. Mix baking soda, 1 teaspoon water and the vanilla; set aside. Mix sugar, 1 cup water and the corn syrup in 3-quart saucepan. Cook over medium heat, stirring occasionally, to 240° on candy thermometer or until small amount of mixture dropped into very cold water forms a soft ball that flattens when removed from water.

3. Stir in margarine and peanuts. Cook, stirring constantly, to 300° or until small amount of mixture dropped into very cold water separates into hard, brittle threads. (Watch carefully so mixture does not burn.) *Immediately* remove from heat. *Quickly* stir in baking soda mixture until light and foamy.

4. Pour half of the candy mixture onto each cookie sheet and quickly spread with buttered spatula about 1/4 inch thick. Cool completely, at least 1 hour. Break into pieces. Store in covered container.

We do not recommend using vegetable oil spreads (see page 13).

1 CANDY: Calories 75 (Calories from Fat 35); Fat 4g (Saturated 1g); Cholesterol 0mg; Sodium 40mg; Carbohydrate 9g (Dietary Fiber 0g); Protein 1g

---

TIMESAVING TIP

To microwave, prepare cookie sheets as directed. Omit all water. Mix sugar, corn syrup and peanuts in 8-cup microwavable measure. Microwave uncovered on High 10 to 12 minutes, stirring every 5 minutes, until peanuts are light brown. Stir in vanilla and margarine thoroughly. Microwave uncovered on High 4 to 6 minutes to 300° on microwave candy thermometer or until small amount of mixture dropped into very cold water separates into hard, brittle threads. *Quickly* stir in baking soda until mixture is light and foamy. Continue as directed in step 4.

Peanut Clusters

PREP: 10 min; COOK: 10 min; STAND: 30 min
Makes 2 1/2 dozen candies

    1 cup sugar
    1/4 cup *stick* margarine or butter*
    1/3 cup evaporated milk
    1/4 cup crunchy peanut butter
    1/2 teaspoon vanilla
    1 cup quick-cooking or old-fashioned oats
    1/2 cup Spanish peanuts

1. Line cookie sheet with waxed paper.

2. Heat sugar, margarine and milk to rolling boil in 2-quart saucepan, stirring constantly. Boil 3 minutes, stirring frequently; remove from heat. Mix in peanut butter and vanilla. Stir in oats and peanuts.

3. Drop mixture by scant tablespoonfuls onto cookie sheet. (If mixture becomes too stiff, stir in 1 or 2 drops milk.) Let stand about 30 minutes or until firm.

We do not recommend using vegetable oil spreads (see page 13).

1 CANDY: Calories 85 (Calories from Fat 35); Fat 4g (Saturated 1g); Cholesterol 5mg; Sodium 35mg; Carbohydrate 10g (Dietary Fiber 0g); Protein 2g

CASHEW-CARAMEL CLUSTERS: Substitute caramel-fudge ice-cream topping for the peanut butter and coarsely chopped cashews for the peanuts.

Popcorn Balls

PREP: 10 min; COOK: 10 min; COOL: 45 min
Makes 8 popcorn balls

The popcorn mixture can also be pressed into a buttered rectangular pan, 13 × 9 × 2 inches, and cut into bars or squares.

    1/2 cup sugar
    1/4 cup *stick* margarine or butter*
    1/2 cup light corn syrup
    1/4 teaspoon salt
    Few drops food color, if desired
    8 cups popped popcorn

1. Heat all ingredients except popcorn to boiling in Dutch oven over medium-high heat, stirring constantly. Boil and stir 2 minutes; remove from heat. Stir in popcorn until well coated; cool slightly.

2. Dip hands into cold water. Shape mixture into 8 balls, each about 2 1/2 inches in diameter. Place on waxed paper; cool. Wrap individually in plastic wrap, or place in plastic bags and tie with ribbon or raffia.

We do not recommend using vegetable oil spreads (see page 13).

1 BALL: Calories 235 (Calories from Fat 100); Fat 11g (Saturated 2g); Cholesterol 0mg; Sodium 160mg; Carbohydrate 34g (Dietary Fiber 1g); Protein 1g

---

TIMESAVING TIP
Use microwave popcorn and omit the salt.

Divinity

Divinity

PREP: 20 min; COOK: 35 min; STAND: 12 hr
Makes about 4 dozen candies

Making this candy on humid days will require a longer beating time.

- 2 2/3 cups sugar
- 2/3 cup light corn syrup
- 1/2 cup water
- 2 large egg whites
- 1 teaspoon vanilla
- 2/3 cup coarsely chopped nuts

1. Cook sugar, corn syrup and water (use 1 tablespoon less water on humid days) in 2-quart saucepan over low heat, stirring constantly, until sugar is dissolved. Cook, without stirring, to 260° on candy thermometer or until small amount of mixture dropped into very cold water forms a hard ball that holds its shape but is pliable.

2. Beat egg whites in medium bowl with electric mixer on high speed until stiff peaks form. Continue beating while pouring hot syrup in a thin stream into egg whites, beating constantly on medium speed. (For best results, use electric stand mixer, not a portable handheld mixer since beating time is about 10 minutes and mixture is thick.) Add vanilla. Beat until mixture holds its shape and becomes slightly dull. (Mixture may become too stiff for mixer.) Fold in nuts.

3. Drop mixture from buttered spoon onto waxed paper. Let stand uncovered at room temperature at least 12 hours, turning candies over once, until candies feel firm. Store in airtight container.

1 CANDY: Calories 70 (Calories from Fat 10); Fat 1g (Saturated 0g); Cholesterol 0mg; Sodium 10mg; Carbohydrate 15g (Dietary Fiber 0g); Protein 0g

About Desserts

It is very satisfying to end a meal with dessert from a simple baked apple to a rich, elegant cheesecake. The desserts here go beyond cakes and pies or cookies and candies, and lead you into a sweet territory all their own. Why not make one tonight?

Tropical & Specialty Fruits

Tips for Fruit Desserts

- A great variety of fresh fruits are now available year-round. However, the seasonal peak will bring the fullest flavors and the most economical prices.
- Fruits may be served at any time or any meal of the day. Serve fruits whole and uncut, cut up and mixed, or baked in delicious cobblers or other dessert specialties.
- Orchard fruits, citrus fruits and even those that used to be considered exotic, such as kiwifruit, mangoes and papayas, are almost staples today. Even the unusual fruits such as carambolas, tamarinds and prickly pears are becoming easier to find.
- Canned and frozen fruits may be used in many recipes for fresh fruits not in season.
- See Apples and Their Uses, page 326, to learn about apple varieties that work well in desserts.

Preceding page: Lindy's Cheesecake (page 144)

Apple Crisp

PREP: 20 min; BAKE: 30 min
Makes 6 servings

> 4 medium, tart cooking apples (Rome Beauty,
> Golden Delicious, Greening), sliced
> (4 cups)
> 2/3 to 3/4 cup packed brown sugar
> 1/2 cup all-purpose flour*
> 1/2 cup quick-cooking or old-fashioned oats
> 1/3 cup *stick* margarine or butter, softened**
> 3/4 teaspoon ground cinnamon
> 3/4 teaspoon ground nutmeg

1. Heat oven to 375°. Grease bottom and sides of square pan, 8 × 8 × 2 inches, with shortening.

2. Arrange apples in pan. Mix remaining ingredients. Sprinkle over apples.

3. Bake about 30 minutes or until topping is golden brown and apples are tender. Serve warm and, if desired, with cream or ice cream.

Self-rising flour can be used in this recipe.

**Spreads with at least 65% vegetable oil can be substituted (see page 13).*

1 SERVING: Calories 285 (Calories from Fat 100); Fat 11g (Saturated 2g); Cholesterol 0mg; Sodium 130mg; Carbohydrate 47g (Dietary Fiber 2g); Protein 2g

BLUEBERRY CRISP: Substitute 4 cups fresh or frozen (thawed and drained) blueberries for the apples.

CHERRY CRISP: Substitute 1 can (21 ounces) cherry pie filling for the apples and use 2/3 cup brown sugar.

RHUBARB CRISP: Substitute 4 cups cut-up rhubarb for the apples.

TIMESAVING TIP

To microwave, use ungreased 2-quart microwavable casserole or square microwavable dish, 8 × 8 × 2 inches. Microwave uncovered on High 10 to 12 minutes, rotating dish 1/2 turn after 5 minutes, until apples are tender.

Apple Dumplings

PREP: 55 min; BAKE: 40 min
Makes 6 dumplings

For a pretty presentation, save the pastry scraps and cut them into favorite shapes. Place on top of dumpling before baking.

> Pastry for 9-Inch Two-Crust Pie (page 93)
> 6 eating apples (each about 3 inches in
> diameter), peeled and cored
> 3 tablespoons raisins
> 3 tablespoons chopped nuts
> 1/2 cup sugar
> 1/2 cup corn syrup
> 1 cup water
> 2 tablespoons *stick* margarine or butter*
> 1/4 teaspoon ground cinnamon

1. Heat oven to 425°. Prepare pastry as directed—except roll two-thirds of the pastry into 14-inch square; cut into 4 squares. Roll remaining pastry into rectangle, 14 × 7 inches; cut into 2 squares. Place apple on each square.

2. Mix raisins and nuts. Fill each apple with raisin mixture. Moisten corners of pastry squares. Bring 2 opposite corners up over apple and pinch together. Repeat with remaining corners and pinch edges of pastry to seal. Place dumplings in ungreased rectangular baking dish, 13 × 9 × 2 inches.

3. Heat remaining ingredients to boiling in 2-quart saucepan, stirring occasionally. Boil 3 minutes. Carefully pour around dumplings. Bake about 40 minutes, spooning syrup over dumplings 2 or 3 times, until crust is golden and apples are tender. Serve warm or cool with cream or Sweetened Whipped Cream (page 89) if desired.

**Spreads with at least 65% vegetable oil can be substituted (see page 13).*

1 DUMPLING: Calories 680 (Calories from Fat 305); Fat 34g (Saturated 8g); Cholesterol 0mg; Sodium 430mg; Carbohydrate 93g (Dietary Fiber 4g); Protein 5g

---

LIGHTER APPLE DUMPLINGS

For 4 grams of fat and 330 calories per serving, omit Pastry for 9-Inch Two-Crust Pie. Cut stack of 6 sheets frozen (thawed) phyllo (14 × 18 inches) into 14-inch square. Discard remaining strips. Cover squares with damp towel to prevent them from drying out. Make 3 stacks of 2 sheets, spraying each lightly with butter-flavored nonstick cooking spray. Fold each stack in half; spray top. Cut stacks in half. Place apple on each square. Omit chopped nuts. Continue as directed in step 2.

Caramel Apple Pizza

PREP: 40 min; COOK: 10 min; BAKE: 30 min
Makes two 10-inch pizzas, 6 servings each

Caramel Syrup (right)
2 medium cooking apples, thinly sliced
1 tablespoon lemon juice
1/2 cup sugar
2 teaspoons ground cinnamon
1 teaspoon ground nutmeg
1 package (3 ounces) cream cheese, softened
1 large egg
1 teaspoon vanilla
1 package (17 1/4 ounces) frozen puff pastry,
  thawed
1 cup chopped nuts, toasted (page 9)

1. Heat oven to 400°. Line 2 cookie sheets with aluminum foil or cooking parchment paper. Prepare Caramel Syrup.

2. Toss apples and lemon juice in medium bowl. Stir in sugar, the cinnamon and nutmeg.

3. Beat cream cheese in small bowl with electric mixer on medium speed until fluffy. Beat in egg and vanilla on medium speed until blended.

4. Roll each sheet of pastry into 10-inch square on foil-lined cookie sheet. Cut into 10-inch circle. Place scraps in center and roll into pastry.

5. Spread half of the cream cheese mixture over each pastry circle. Arrange apple slices on circles. Sprinkle with nuts. Drizzle about 1/4 cup syrup over each circle.

6. Bake 25 to 30 minutes or until puffy and golden brown. Pour remaining syrup over pizzas. Serve hot.

Caramel Syrup

1/2 cup plus 2 tablespoons packed brown
  sugar
1/3 cup corn syrup
2 tablespoons *stick* margarine or butter*
1/3 cup whipping (heavy) cream
1 teaspoon rum extract or vanilla

Heat brown sugar, corn syrup and margarine to boiling in 1-quart saucepan over medium heat, stirring occasionally. Cook 5 to 7 minutes, stirring constantly, until thickened; remove from heat. Cool slightly, about 30 minutes. Stir in whipping cream and rum extract.

We do not recommend using vegetable oil spreads (see page 13).

1 SERVING: Calories 520 (Calories from Fat 290); Fat 32g (Saturated 11g); Cholesterol 45mg; Sodium 160mg; Carbohydrate 55g (Dietary Fiber 1g); Protein 4g

Caramel Apple Pizza

Baked Apples

PREP: 10 min; BAKE: 40 min
Makes 4 servings

(photograph on page 417)

> 4 large unpeeled cooking apples (Rome Beauty, Golden Delicious, Greening)
> 2 to 4 tablespoons granulated or packed brown sugar
> 4 teaspoons margarine or butter
> 1/2 teaspoon ground cinnamon

1. Heat oven to 375°.

2. Core apples to within 1/2 inch of bottom. Peel 1-inch strip of skin around middle of each apple or peel upper half of each to prevent splitting. Place apples in ungreased baking dish.

3. Place 1 teaspoon to 1 tablespoon sugar, 1 teaspoon margarine and 1/8 teaspoon cinnamon in center of each apple. Sprinkle with cinnamon. Pour water into baking dish until 1/4 inch deep.

4. Bake 30 to 40 minutes or until tender when pierced with fork. (Time will vary with size and variety of apple.) Spoon syrup in dish over apples several times during baking if desired.

1 SERVING: Calories 185 (Calories from Fat 45); Fat 5g (Saturated 1g); Cholesterol 0mg; Sodium 45mg; Carbohydrate 39g (Dietary Fiber 4g); Protein 0g

Fresh Peach Cobbler

PREP: 25 min; COOK: 10 min; BAKE: 30 min
Makes 6 servings

Cobblers are a homey way to use fruit in season. Short on time? Try the blueberry variation—there's no peeling or pitting!

> 1/2 cup sugar
> 1 tablespoon cornstarch
> 1/4 teaspoon ground cinnamon
> 4 cups sliced peaches (6 medium)
> 1 teaspoon lemon juice
> 3 tablespoons shortening
> 1 cup all-purpose flour*
> 1 tablespoon sugar
> 1 1/2 teaspoons baking powder
> 1/2 teaspoon salt
> 1/2 cup milk

1. Heat oven to 400°.

2. Mix 1/2 cup sugar, the cornstarch and cinnamon in 2-quart saucepan. Stir in peaches and lemon juice. Cook, stirring constantly, until mixture thickens and boils. Boil and stir 1 minute. Pour into ungreased 2-quart casserole; keep peach mixture hot in oven.

3. Cut shortening into flour, 1 tablespoon sugar, the baking powder and salt in medium bowl, using pastry blender or crisscrossing 2 knives, until mixture looks like fine crumbs. Stir in milk. Drop dough by 6 spoonfuls onto hot peach mixture.

4. Bake 25 to 30 minutes or until topping is golden brown. Serve warm and, if desired, with Sweetened Whipped Cream (page 89).

If using self-rising flour, omit baking powder and salt.

1 SERVING: Calories 260 (Calories from Fat 65); Fat 7g (Saturated 2g); Cholesterol 5mg; Sodium 310mg; Carbohydrate 48g (Dietary Fiber 2g); Protein 3g

FRESH BLUEBERRY COBBLER: Substitute 4 cups blueberries for the peaches. Omit cinnamon.

FRESH CHERRY COBBLER: Substitute 4 cups pitted red tart cherries for the blueberries. Increase sugar in cherry mixture to 1 1/4 cups and cornstarch to 3 tablespoons. Substitute 1/4 teaspoon almond extract for the lemon juice.

Hot Chocolate Soufflé

PREP: 45 min; BAKE: 1 1/4 hr
Makes 6 servings

1/3 cup sugar
1/3 cup baking cocoa
1/4 cup all-purpose flour*
1 cup milk
3 large egg yolks
2 tablespoons *stick* margarine or butter,
   softened**
1 teaspoon vanilla
4 large egg whites
1/4 teaspoon cream of tartar
1/8 teaspoon salt
3 tablespoons sugar
Best Sauce (below) or Sweetened Whipped
   Cream (page 89)

1. Move oven rack to lowest position. Heat oven to 350°. Grease 6-cup soufflé dish with butter; lightly sugar. Make a 4-inch band of triple-thickness aluminum foil 2 inches longer than circumference of dish. Grease one side of band with butter; lightly sugar. Extend dish by securing band, buttered side in, around top outside edge.

2. Mix 1/3 cup sugar, the cocoa and flour in 1 1/2-quart saucepan. Gradually stir in milk. Heat to boiling, stirring constantly; remove from heat.

3. Beat egg yolks in small bowl with fork. Beat in about one-third of the cocoa mixture. Gradually stir in remaining cocoa mixture. Stir in margarine and vanilla; cool slightly.

4. Beat egg whites, cream of tartar and salt in medium bowl with electric mixer on high speed until foamy. Beat in 3 tablespoons sugar, 1 tablespoon at a time; continue beating until stiff and glossy. Do not underbeat.

5. Stir about one-fourth of the egg whites into cocoa mixture. Fold in remaining egg whites. Carefully pour into soufflé dish. Place dish in square pan, 9 × 9 × 2 inches, on oven rack. Pour very hot water into pan until 1 inch deep.

6. Bake 1 1/4 hours or until puffed in center and edges are set. While soufflé is baking, prepare Best Sauce. *Immediately* serve soufflé with warm sauce.

Best Sauce

1/2 cup powdered sugar
1/2 cup *stick* margarine or butter, softened**
1/2 cup whipping (heavy) cream

Beat powdered sugar and margarine in 1-quart saucepan until creamy. Beat whipping cream in chilled small bowl with electric mixer on high speed until stiff. Fold whipped cream into sugar mixture. Heat to boiling, stirring occasionally.

* Do not use self-rising flour in this recipe.

**Spreads with at least 65% vegetable oil can be substituted (see page 13).

1 SERVING: Calories 435 (Calories from Fat 260); Fat 29g (Saturated 9g); Cholesterol 130mg; Sodium 340mg; Carbohydrate 37g (Dietary Fiber 1g); Protein 7g

Hot Fudge Sundae Cake

PREP: 20 min; BAKE: 40 min
Makes 9 servings

1 cup all-purpose flour*
3/4 cup granulated sugar
2 tablespoons baking cocoa
2 teaspoons baking powder
1/4 teaspoon salt
1/2 cup milk
2 tablespoons vegetable oil
1 teaspoon vanilla
1 cup chopped nuts, if desired
1 cup packed brown sugar
1/4 cup baking cocoa
1 3/4 cups very hot water
Ice cream, if desired

1. Heat oven to 350°.

2. Mix flour, granulated sugar, 2 tablespoons cocoa, the baking powder and salt in ungreased square pan, 9 × 9 × 2 inches. Mix in milk, oil and vanilla with fork until smooth. Stir in nuts. Spread in pan.

3. Sprinkle brown sugar and 1/4 cup cocoa over batter. Pour water over batter.

4. Bake 40 minutes or until top is dry.

5. Spoon warm cake into dessert dishes. Top with ice cream. Spoon sauce from pan onto each serving.

* If using self-rising flour, omit baking powder and salt.

1 SERVING: Calories 400 (Calories from Fat 100); Fat 11g (Saturated 5g); Cholesterol 30mg; Sodium 240mg; Carbohydrate 71g (Dietary Fiber 1g); Protein 5g

> **TIMESAVING TIP**
> To microwave, mix flour, granulated sugar, 2 tablespoons cocoa, the baking powder and salt in 2-quart microwavable casserole. Mix in milk, oil and vanilla with fork until smooth. Stir in nuts. Sprinkle with brown sugar and 1/4 cup cocoa. Pour water over batter. Microwave uncovered on Medium (50%) 9 minutes; rotate casserole 1/4 turn. Microwave uncovered on High 5 to 7 minutes longer or until top is almost dry. Continue as directed in step 5.

Strawberry Shortcakes

Strawberry Shortcakes

PREP: 15 min; STAND: 1 hr; BAKE: 12 min
Makes 6 servings

> 1 quart strawberries, sliced
> 1/2 cup sugar
> 1/3 cup shortening
> 2 cups all-purpose flour*
> 2 tablespoons sugar
> 3 teaspoons baking powder
> 1 teaspoon salt
> 3/4 cup milk
> Margarine or butter, softened
> Sweetened Whipped Cream (page 89)

1. Mix strawberries and 1/2 cup sugar. Let stand 1 hour.

2. Heat oven to 450°.

3. Cut shortening into flour, 2 tablespoons sugar, the baking powder and salt in medium bowl, using pastry blender or crisscrossing 2 knives, until mixture looks like fine crumbs. Stir in milk just until blended.

4. Turn dough onto lightly floured surface. Gently smooth into a ball. Knead 20 to 25 times. Roll 1/2 inch thick. Cut with floured 3-inch cutter. Place about 1 inch apart on ungreased cookie sheet.

5. Bake 10 to 12 minutes or until golden brown.

6. Split shortcakes horizontally in half while hot. Spread margarine on split sides. Fill with strawberries; replace tops. Top with strawberries and Sweetened Whipped Cream.

If using self-rising flour, omit baking powder and salt.

1 SERVING: Calories 400 (Calories from Fat 135); Fat 15g (Saturated 5g); Cholesterol 10mg; Sodium 630mg; Carbohydrate 63g (Dietary Fiber 3g); Protein 6g

PAT-IN-THE-PAN SHORTCAKES: Grease bottom and side of round pan, 8 × 1 1/2 inches, with shortening. Omit step 4. Pat dough in pan. Bake 15 to 20 minutes. Cut into wedges. Continue as directed in step 6.

TIMESAVING TIP

Pat dough into rectangle about 1/2 inch thick on ungreased cookie sheet. Cut into 6 squares and spread squares about 1 inch apart before baking.

Boston Cream Pie

PREP: 20 min; BAKE: 35 min; COOL: 2 hr
Makes 8 servings

This really isn't a pie, but more a cakelike dessert, welcome in any town.

1 1/4 cups all-purpose flour* or 1 1/2 cups
  cake flour
1 cup sugar
1/3 cup shortening
3/4 cup milk
1 1/2 teaspoons baking powder
1 teaspoon vanilla
1/2 teaspoon salt
1 large egg
Cream Filling (below)
Chocolate Glaze (right)

1. Heat oven to 350°. Grease bottom and side of round pan, 9 × 1 1/2 inches, with shortening; lightly flour.

2. Beat all ingredients except Cream Filling and Chocolate Glaze in large bowl with electric mixer on low speed 30 seconds, scraping bowl constantly. Beat on high speed 3 minutes, scraping bowl occasionally. Pour into pan.

3. Bake about 35 minutes or until toothpick inserted in center comes out clean. Cool 10 minutes; remove from pan. Cool completely on wire rack.

4. Prepare Cream Filling and Chocolate Glaze. Split cake horizontally in half. Spread filling over bottom layer; top with top layer. Spread glaze over top of cake. Cover and refrigerate until serving. *Immediately refrigerate any remaining dessert.*

Cream Filling

1/3 cup sugar
2 tablespoons cornstarch
1/8 teaspoon salt
1 1/2 cups milk
2 large egg yolks, slightly beaten
2 teaspoons vanilla

Mix sugar, cornstarch and salt in 2-quart saucepan. Mix milk and egg yolks; gradually stir into sugar mixture. Cook over medium heat, stirring constantly, until mixture thickens and boils. Boil and stir 1 minute; remove from heat. Stir in vanilla; cool.

Chocolate Glaze

3 tablespoons *stick* margarine or butter**
3 ounces unsweetened baking chocolate
1 cup powdered sugar
3/4 teaspoon vanilla
About 2 tablespoons hot water

Melt margarine and chocolate in 1-quart saucepan over low heat, stirring occasionally; remove from heat. Stir in powdered sugar and vanilla. Stir in water, 1 teaspoon at a time, until smooth and spreadable.

*If using self-rising flour, omit baking powder and salt.

**Spreads with at least 65% vegetable oil can be substituted (see page 13).

1 SERVING: Calories 505 (Calories from Fat 200); Fat 22g (Saturated 8g); Cholesterol 85mg; Sodium 350mg; Carbohydrate 72g (Dietary Fiber 2g); Protein 7g

---

TIMESAVING TIP
Use a single-layer cake mix instead of the cake recipe and 1 package (4-serving size) vanilla instant pudding and pie filling instead of the Cream Filling. Prepare both following package directions.

Banana-Almond Flip

PREP: 35 min; CHILL: 3 hr
Makes 12 servings

45 vanilla wafer cookies, crushed (1 1/2 cups)
1/3 cup *stick* margarine or butter, melted*
1/4 cup finely ground almonds
3 cups powdered sugar
1 cup margarine or butter, softened*
1/4 cup whipping (heavy) cream
1/3 cup almond paste, softened
2 teaspoons vanilla
1 teaspoon almond extract
2 cups whipping (heavy) cream, divided
6 medium bananas, cut lengthwise into
  thirds

1. Grease bottom and sides of rectangular pan, 13 × 9 × 2 inches, with shortening.

2. Mix cookie crumbs, 1/3 cup margarine and the almonds. Press evenly in bottom of pan. Refrigerate.

3. Meanwhile, beat powdered sugar, 1 cup margarine and 1/4 cup whipping cream in large bowl with electric mixer on high speed until fluffy. Beat in almond paste, vanilla and almond extract.

4. Beat 2 cups whipping cream in chilled medium bowl with electric mixer on high speed until soft peaks form. Fold into powdered sugar mixture.

5. Arrange half of the bananas on crust. Pour half of the filling over bananas. Repeat with remaining bananas and filling. Cover and refrigerate about 3 hours or until chilled. Refrigerate any remaining dessert.

We do not recommend using vegetable oil spreads (see page 13).

1 SERVING: Calories 465 (Calories from Fat 280); Fat 31g (Saturated 12g); Cholesterol 240mg; Sodium 240mg; Carbohydrate 46g (Dietary Fiber 2g); Protein 3g

---

TIMESAVING TIP

Save time by using 1 container (16 ounces) frozen whipped topping, thawed, instead of the 2 cups whipping cream, whipped. Beat 4 tablespoons whipped topping into powdered sugar mixture, then fold in remaining whipped topping as directed in step 4. Use reduced-fat whipped topping to reduce calories as well.

Strawberry-Rum Cream Dessert

PREP: 45 min; BAKE: 1 hr 20 min; COOL: 2 hr; CHILL: 6 hr
Makes 24 servings

To really show off the layers of this pretty dessert, use an ice cream scoop to scoop dessert into parfait glasses and serve topped with a fresh strawberry.

1 recipe Pound Cake (page 76)
1 cup *stick* margarine or butter, softened*
3 cups powdered sugar
2 teaspoons rum extract
2 teaspoons vanilla
2 cups whipping (heavy) cream
2 tablespoons powdered sugar
1 package (16 ounces) frozen sweetened
    strawberries, thawed and drained
1/3 cup powdered sugar

1. Prepare Pound Cake.

2. Lightly grease bottom and sides of rectangular pan, 13 × 9 × 2 inches, with shortening.

3. Beat margarine and 3 cups powdered sugar in large bowl with electric mixer on high speed until fluffy. Beat in rum extract and vanilla. Beat in 1/4 cup of the whipping cream.

4. Beat remaining 1 3/4 cups whipping cream and 2 tablespoons powdered sugar in chilled medium bowl with electric mixer on high speed until soft peaks form. Fold into powdered sugar mixture.

5. Cut pound cake into 1/4-inch slices. Arrange one-third of the slices on bottom of pan. Spread one-third of the filling over cake slices. Repeat with one-third of the cake slices and filling. Arrange strawberries evenly on filling. Layer with remaining cake slices and filling. Sprinkle with 1/3 cup powdered sugar. Cover and refrigerate at least 6 hours but no longer than 48 hours. Refrigerate any remaining dessert.

Spreads with at least 65% vegetable oil can be substituted (see page 13).

1 SERVING: Calories 450 (Calories from Fat 205); Fat 34g (Saturated 11g); Cholesterol 100mg; Sodium 370mg; Carbohydrate 86g (Dietary Fiber 1g); Protein 6g

---

TIMESAVING TIP

Substitute purchased pound cake (about 1 1/2 pounds) for the Pound Cake recipe and 4 cups frozen (thawed) whipped topping for the whipping cream, whipped, and the 2 tablespoons powdered sugar. Use 1/2 cup whipped topping in step 3 and the remaining amount in step 4. Reduced-fat whipped topping can be used, but the filling will not be as thick.

Tips for Cheesecakes

- Cheesecakes are baked at low temperatures to prevent excess shrinkage. The center may look slightly soft but will set while chilling. Refrigerate cheesecakes for at least three hours (or as directed in recipe) before serving.
- To check for doneness, do not insert a knife in the center, because the hole could cause cheesecake to crack. Touch lightly or gently shake the pan. Center may jiggle slightly but will set while refrigerated.
- Let cheesecake stand at room temperature no longer than 15 minutes after baking and before refrigerating. Then refrigerate up to 3 hours uncovered. If covered immediately, moisture may condense and drip on cheesecake top. Cover cheesecake for remaining refrigeration to prevent drying out or picking up other food odors.
- Run metal spatula along side of cheesecakes with side crusts to loosen after baking and after refrigerating. Otherwise, cheesecake could pull away from crust as it cools if not loosened from side of pan.
- Cheesecakes cut easily when a wet knife is used, cleaning after each cut. Or, use a piece of dental floss.

Key Lime Cheesecake

**PREP: 30 min; BAKE: 1 hr 8 min; COOL: 15 min;
CHILL: 12 hr**
Makes 16 servings

*Key limes are grown in Florida and are smaller and rounder,
with a color that's more yellow than green. While they are not
as widely available as the common green or Persian limes we
are more familiar with, bottled key lime juice is generally
available. Either type of lime works well in this recipe.*

> 1 cup Key Lime Curd (page 362)
> Lime Crust (below)
> 4 packages (8 ounces each) cream cheese,
>   softened
> 3/4 cup powdered sugar
> 1/2 cup granulated sugar
> 2 large eggs
> 2 tablespoons grated lime peel
> 2 tablespoons lime juice
> 2 tablespoons cornstarch
> 1 cup sour cream

1. Prepare Key Lime Curd and Lime Crust.

2. Heat oven to 425°.

3. Beat cream cheese and sugars in large bowl with
electric mixer on medium speed until smooth. Beat in
eggs, one at a time, on low speed just until well
blended. Beat in lime peel, lime juice and cornstarch.
Fold in sour cream until blended. Pour over baked crust.

4. Bake 47 to 52 minutes or until center is set and
top is golden. Cool in pan on wire rack 15 minutes.

5. Run metal spatula along side of cheesecake to
loosen. Refrigerate uncovered about 3 hours or until
chilled; cover and continue refrigerating at least 9
hours, but no longer than 48 hours.

6. Run metal spatula along side of cheesecake to
loosen; remove side of pan. Spread Key Lime Curd
over top of cheesecake. Refrigerate any remaining
dessert.

Lime Crust

> 1/2 cup sugar
> 1/2 cup *stick* margarine or butter, softened*
> 1 cup all-purpose flour
> 1 tablespoon grated lime peel
> 1 teaspoon vanilla

Heat oven to 400°. Grease bottom and side of springform pan, 10 × 3 inches, with shortening. Beat sugar
and margarine in medium bowl with electric mixer on
medium speed until smooth. Beat in remaining ingredients on low speed just until crumbly. Press evenly in
bottom of pan. Bake 13 to 16 minutes or until light
golden brown; cool.

We do not recommend using vegetable oil spreads (see page 13).

1 SERVING: Calories 445 (Calories from Fat 290); Fat 31g
(Saturated 16g); Cholesterol 120mg; Sodium 270mg;
Carbohydrate 34g (Dietary Fiber 0g); Protein 7g

LIGHTER KEY LIME CHEESECAKE
For 18 grams of fat and 345 calories per serving, in
cheesecake, use reduced-fat cream cheese (Neufchâtel)
and substitute vanilla low-fat yogurt for the sour cream.

Lindy's Cheesecake

**PREP: 30 min; BAKE: 1 hr 20 min; COOL: 15 min;
CHILL: 12 hr**
Makes 16 servings

*Serve this wonderful classic plain, with fresh fruit or drizzled
with Hot Fudge Sauce (page 159). (photograph on page 135)*

> Crust (right)
> 5 packages (8 ounces each) cream cheese,
>   softened
> 1 3/4 cups sugar
> 3 tablespoons all-purpose flour
> 1 tablespoon grated orange peel
> 1 tablespoon grated lemon peel
> 1/4 teaspoon salt
> 5 large eggs
> 2 large egg yolks
> 1/4 cup whipping (heavy) cream
> 3/4 cup whipping (heavy) cream
> 1/3 cup slivered almonds, toasted, if desired

1. Prepare Crust.

2. Heat oven to 425°.

3. Beat cream cheese, sugar, flour, orange peel,
lemon peel and salt in large bowl with electric mixer on
medium speed about 1 minute or until smooth. Beat in
eggs, egg yolks and 1/4 cup whipping cream, beating
on low speed until well blended. Pour into baked crust.

4. Bake 20 minutes.

5. Reduce oven temperature to 300°. Bake about 45
minutes longer or until center is set. (Do not insert a
knife because the hole could cause cheesecake to
crack.) Turn off oven and leave cheesecake in oven 15
minutes. Cool in pan on wire rack 15 minutes.

6. Run metal spatula along side of cheesecake to
loosen. Refrigerate uncovered about 3 hours or until
chilled; cover and continue refrigerating at least 9
hours but no longer than 48 hours.

7. Run metal spatula along side of cheesecake to
loosen; remove side of pan. Beat 3/4 cup whipping
cream in chilled small bowl with electric mixer on
high speed until stiff. Spread whipped cream over top
of cheesecake. Decorate with almonds. Refrigerate
any remaining dessert.

Crust

1 cup all-purpose flour
1/2 cup *stick* margarine or butter, softened*
1/4 cup sugar
1 tablespoon grated lemon peel
1 large egg yolk

Move oven rack to lowest position. Heat oven to 425°. Lightly grease spring form pan 9 × 3 inches; remove bottom. Mix all ingredients with hands. Press one-third of the mixture evenly on bottom of pan. Place on cookie sheet. Bake 8 to 10 minutes or until light golden brown; cool. Assemble bottom and side of pan; secure side. Press remaining mixture all the way up side of pan.

*We do not recommend using vegetable oil spreads (see page 13).

1 SERVING: Calories 520 (Calories from Fat 340); Fat 38g (Saturated 20g); Cholesterol 200mg; Sodium 340mg; Carbohydrate 35g (Dietary Fiber 0g); Protein 9g

---

LIGHTER LINDY'S CHEESECAKE

For 19 grams of fat and 330 calories per serving, omit Crust. Move oven rack to lowest position. Heat oven to 425°. Lightly grease side only of springform pan, 9 × 3 inches, with shortening. Mix 3/4 cup graham cracker crumbs, 2 tablespoons margarine, melted, and 2 tablespoons sugar; press evenly in bottom of pan. Use reduced-fat cream cheese (Neufchâtel) and increase flour to 1/4 cup. Substitute 1 1/4 cups fat-free cholesterol-free egg product for the 5 eggs. Omit 1/4 cup whipping cream. Bake as directed in steps 4 through 6. Omit 3/4 cup whipping cream and almonds. Serve with fresh fruit if desired. Refrigerate any remaining dessert.

CHOCOLATE CHIP LINDY'S CHEESECAKE: Fold 1 cup miniature semi-sweet chocolate chips (3 ounces) into cheese mixture before pouring into crust.

Cream Puffs

**PREP: 30 min; COOK: 15 min; BAKE: 40 min;
COOL: 30 min
Makes 12 cream puffs**

1 cup water
1/2 cup *stick* margarine or butter*
1 cup all-purpose flour**
4 large eggs
Cream Filling (right) or Sweetened Whipped
    Cream (page 89)
Powdered sugar

1. Heat oven to 400°.

2. Heat water and margarine to rolling boil in 2 1/2-quart saucepan. Stir in flour; reduce heat to low. Stir vigorously over low heat about 1 minute or until mixture forms a ball; remove from heat.

3. Beat in eggs, all at once; continue beating until smooth. Drop dough by scant 1/4 cupfuls about 3 inches apart onto ungreased cookie sheet.

4. Bake 35 to 40 minutes or until puffed and golden. Cool away from draft. Cut off top third of each puff and pull out any strands of soft dough.

5. Fill puffs with Cream Filling; replace tops. Dust with powdered sugar. Cover and refrigerate until serving. Refrigerate any remaining dessert.

Cream Filling

1/3 cup sugar
2 tablespoons cornstarch
1/8 teaspoon salt
2 cups milk
2 large egg yolks, slightly beaten
2 tablespoons *stick* margarine or butter,
    softened*
2 teaspoons vanilla

Mix sugar, cornstarch and salt in 2-quart saucepan. Gradually stir in milk. Cook over medium heat, stirring constantly, until mixture thickens and boils. Boil and stir 1 minute. Gradually stir at least half of the hot mixture into egg yolks; stir back into hot mixture in saucepan. Boil and stir 1 minute; remove from heat. Stir in margarine and vanilla; cool.

CHOCOLATE ECLAIRS: Prepare as directed in steps 1, 2 and 3—except shape each scant 1/4 cupful of dough into finger 4 1/2 inches long and 1 1/2 inches wide, using spatula. Continue as directed in steps 4 and 5. Fill with Cream Filling (above). Omit powdered sugar. Frost with Chocolate Frosting (below).

Chocolate Frosting

1 ounce unsweetened baking chocolate
1 teaspoon *stick* margarine or butter*
1 cup powdered sugar
1 to 2 tablespoons hot water

Melt chocolate and margarine in 1-quart saucepan over low heat, stirring occasionally; remove from heat. Stir in powdered sugar and water. Beat until smooth and spreadable.

*Spreads with at least 65% vegetable oil can be substituted (see page 13).

**Self-rising flour can be used in this recipe.

1 CREAM PUFF: Calories 265 (Calories from Fat 135); Fat 15g (Saturated 4g); Cholesterol 110mg; Sodium 180mg; Carbohydrate 28g (Dietary Fiber 0g); Protein 5g

---

TIMESAVING TIP

Omit the filling and frosting and fill with ice cream, sherbet, sorbet, berries or whipped cream. Dust with powdered sugar or drizzle with purchased chocolate sauce.

Mixed Fruit and Nut Cheese Tart, Cheese Crowns

Mixed Fruit and Nut Cheese Tart

PREP: 25 min; CHILL: 2 1/2 hr
Makes 12 servings

This tart filling also makes a great appetizer spread. Omit the crust and prepare the fruit and nut mixture as directed. Spread in a decorative bowl, place on a large platter and surround with sliced fruits.

Tart Crust (right)
1 cup chopped pitted dates (4 ounces)
1 cup chopped dried figs (5 ounces)
1 package (6 ounces) dried apricots, chopped
  (1 1/4 cups)
1 cup chopped walnuts, toasted (4 ounces)
2 tablespoons powdered sugar
3 packages (8 ounces each) cream cheese,
  softened
2 cups powdered sugar
1/2 cup *stick* margarine or butter, softened*
2 teaspoons vanilla

1. Prepare Tart Crust.

2. Toss dates, figs, apricots, walnuts and 2 tablespoons powdered sugar.

3. Beat remaining ingredients in large bowl with electric mixer on high speed about 6 minutes until fluffy. Fold in fruit mixture. Spread over crust.

4. Cover and refrigerate at least 2 hours until firm. Run metal spatula along side of tart to loosen; remove side of pan. Refrigerate any remaining dessert.

Tart Crust

3/4 cup graham cracker crumbs (8 squares)
2 tablespoons sugar
3 tablespoons *stick* margarine or butter,
  melted*
1/2 teaspoon vanilla

Lightly grease springform pan, 9 × 3 inches, or round pan, 9 × 1 1/2 inches, with margarine. Mix all ingredients. Press evenly in bottom of pan. Refrigerate 30 minutes.

Spreads with at least 65% vegetable oil can be substituted (see page 13).

1 SERVING: Calories 535 (Calories from Fat 335); Fat 37g (Saturated 15g); Cholesterol 60mg; Sodium 330mg; Carbohydrate 62g (Dietary Fiber 3g); Protein 7g

---

**LIGHTER MIXED FRUIT AND NUT
CHEESE TART**

For 23 grams of fat and 470 calories per serving, substitute 1/2 cup roasted sunflower nuts for the walnuts and reduced-fat cream cheese (Neufchâtel) for the regular cream cheese. Decrease margarine to 1/4 cup.

Cheese Crowns

PREP: 40 min; BAKE: 22 min
Makes 12 servings

This recipe could easily become a breakfast tradition, as well as a favorite dessert, so it is well worth the purchase of jumbo muffin pans! Do not try to press pastry sheets into tiny muffin cups because the pastry rises so much you will have difficulty separating them after baking.

> 1 1/2 packages (17 1/4-ounce size) frozen
>   puff pastry (3 sheets), thawed
> 1/4 cup firm *stick* margarine or butter*
> 1/2 cup all-purpose flour
> 1/2 cup chopped pecans, toasted
> 1/4 cup packed brown sugar
> 1/2 teaspoon ground cinnamon
> 3 packages (8 ounces each) cream cheese,
>   softened
> 1 cup sugar
> 3 large eggs
> 2 tablespoons vanilla

1. Heat oven to 425°. Grease bottoms and sides of 12 jumbo muffin cups, 3 1/2 × 1 3/4 inches, or 6-ounce custard cups with shortening.

2. Place 1 sheet of cold puff pastry on lightly floured surface. Cut into 4 squares. Press each square gently into muffin cup, pulling the 4 corners up and out of cup. Press corners down on muffin pan. Repeat with remaining sheets of pastry.

3. Mix flour, pecans, brown sugar and cinnamon in small bowl. Cut margarine into flour, pecans, brown sugar and cinnamon. Sprinkle 1 heaping tablespoon of the pecan mixture over bottom of pastry in each cup.

4. Beat cream cheese and sugar in medium bowl with electric mixer on high speed about 2 minutes or until fluffy. Beat in eggs, one at a time. Beat in vanilla. Pour about 1/3 cup of the cheese mixture over pecan mixture in each cup.

5. Bake 15 minutes.

6. Reduce oven temperature to 375°. Bake 5 to 7 minutes longer or until pastry is golden brown. Cool 15 minutes in pan on wire rack. Gently remove from pan. Refrigerate uncovered about 1 hour or until chilled; cover and continue refrigerating no longer than 48 hours. Refrigerate any remaining crowns.

We do not recommend using vegetable oil spreads (see page 13).

1 SERVING: Calories 415 (Calories from Fat 270); Fat 30g (Saturated 15g); Cholesterol 115mg; Sodium 240mg; Carbohydrate 40g (Dietary Fiber 0g); Protein 7g

Crepes

PREP: 10 min; COOK: 25 min
Makes 12 crepes

Crepes can be eaten by themselves or used as part of a recipe.

> 1 1/2 cups all-purpose flour*
> 1 tablespoon sugar
> 1/2 teaspoon baking powder
> 1/2 teaspoon salt
> 2 cups milk
> 2 tablespoons *stick* margarine or butter,
>   melted**
> 1/2 teaspoon vanilla
> 2 large eggs

1. Mix flour, sugar, baking powder and salt in medium bowl. Stir in remaining ingredients. Beat with hand beater until smooth.

2. Lightly butter 6- to 8-inch skillet. Heat over medium heat until bubbly.

3. For each crepe, pour scant 1/4 cup batter into skillet. *Immediately* rotate skillet until thin film covers bottom. Cook until light brown. Run wide spatula around edge to loosen; turn and cook other side until light brown.

4. Stack crepes, placing waxed paper between each; keep covered. If desired, spread applesauce, sweetened strawberries, currant jelly or raspberry jam thinly over each warm crepe; roll up. (Be sure to fill crepes so the more attractive side is on the outside.) Sprinkle with powdered sugar if desired.

If using self-rising flour, omit baking powder and salt.

***Spreads with at least 65% vegetable oil can be substituted (see page 13).*

1 CREPE: Calories 110 (Calories from Fat 35); Fat 4g (Saturated 1g); Cholesterol 40mg; Sodium 160mg; Carbohydrate 151g (Dietary Fiber 0g); Protein 4g

---

TIMESAVING TIP

Prepare a double recipe of crepes, wrap airtight and freeze up to two months so they're ready when you want them.

Caramel Custard

Creamy Stirred Custard

**PREP: 10 min; COOK: 20 min; COOL: 30 min;
CHILL: 2 hr
Makes 5 servings**

This custard is terrific as a pudding, served as a sauce or for making plate designs (page 158).

> **3 large eggs
> 1/3 cup sugar
> Dash of salt
> 2 1/2 cups milk
> 1 teaspoon vanilla**

1. Beat eggs slightly in heavy 2-quart saucepan. Stir in sugar and salt. Gradually stir in milk. Cook over medium heat 15 to 20 minutes, stirring constantly, until mixture just coats a metal spoon; remove from heat. Stir in vanilla.

2. Place saucepan in cold water until custard is cool. (If custard curdles, beat vigorously with hand beater until smooth.) Cover and refrigerate at least 2 hours but no longer than 48 hours. Refrigerate any remaining dessert.

1 SERVING: Calories 155 (Calories from Fat 45); Fat 5g (Saturated 2g); Cholesterol 140mg; Sodium 125mg; Carbohydrate 20g (Dietary Fiber 0g); Protein 8g

Baked Custard

**PREP: 15 min; BAKE: 45 min
Makes 6 servings**

> **3 large eggs, slightly beaten
> 1/3 cup sugar
> 1 teaspoon vanilla
> Dash of salt
> 2 1/2 cups very warm milk
> Ground nutmeg**

1. Heat oven to 350°.

2. Mix eggs, sugar, vanilla and salt in medium bowl. Gradually stir in milk. Pour into six 6-ounce custard cups. Sprinkle with nutmeg.

3. Place cups in rectangular pan, 13 × 9 × 2 inches, on oven rack. Pour very hot water into pan to within 1/2 inch of tops of cups.

4. Bake about 45 minutes or until knife inserted halfway between center and edge comes out clean. Remove cups from water. Unmold and serve warm, or if desired, refrigerate and unmold at serving time. *Immediately* refrigerate any remaining dessert.

1 SERVING: Calories 135 (Calories from Fat 45); Fat 5g (Saturated 2g); Cholesterol 115mg; Sodium 105mg; Carbohydrate 17g (Dietary Fiber 0g); Protein 6g

CARAMEL CUSTARD: Before preparing custard, heat 1/2 cup sugar in heavy 1-quart saucepan over low heat, stirring constantly, until sugar is melted and golden brown. Divide syrup among custard cups; tilt cups to coat bottoms. Allow syrup to harden in cups about 10 minutes. Pour custard mixture over syrup. Bake as directed in steps 3 and 4. Caramel syrup will run down sides of custard, forming a sauce.

TIMESAVING TIP

Use a 4-cup glass measuring cup to measure the milk, then microwave it on High (100%) until very warm, about 5 minutes.

Tira Mi Su

PREP: 35 min; CHILL: 5 hr
Makes 8 to 12 servings

This popular Italian dessert is easy to make at home. Tira Mi Su literally means "pick me up," and this satisfying dessert should do just that!

6 large egg yolks
3/4 cup sugar
2/3 cup milk
1 pound mascarpone cheese or 2 packages
    (8 ounces each) cream cheese, softened
1 1/4 cups whipping (heavy) cream
1/2 teaspoon vanilla
2 packages (3 ounces each) ladyfingers
1/4 cup cold prepared espresso or very
    strong coffee
2 tablespoons rum*
1 tablespoon baking cocoa

1. Beat egg yolks and sugar in 2-quart saucepan with wire whisk until well blended. Beat in milk. Heat to boiling over medium heat, stirring constantly; reduce heat to low. Boil and stir 1 minute; remove from heat.

2. Place plastic wrap or waxed paper directly onto egg yolk mixture in saucepan. Refrigerate 1 hour.

3. Mix egg yolk mixture and cheese with wire whisk until smooth. Beat whipping cream and vanilla in chilled medium bowl with electric mixer on high speed until stiff.

4. Separate ladyfingers horizontally in half. Mix espresso and rum. Drizzle ladyfingers with espresso mixture.

5. Arrange half of the ladyfingers in single layer in ungreased rectangular baking dish, 11 × 7 × 1 1/2 inches. Spread half of the cheese mixture then half of the whipped cream over ladyfingers. Repeat layers.

Sprinkle with cocoa. Cover and refrigerate 4 to 6 hours or until set. Refrigerate any remaining dessert.

*1/8 teaspoon rum extract mixed with 2 tablespoons water can be substituted for the rum.

1 SERVING: Calories 510 (Calories from Fat 335); Fat 37g (Saturated 21g); Cholesterol 300mg; Sodium 210mg; Carbohydrate 35g (Dietary Fiber 0g); Protein 9g

---

LIGHTER TIRA MI SU

For 20 grams of fat and 375 calories per serving, substitute 2 eggs plus 2 egg yolks for the 6 egg yolks, 2 packages (8 ounces) reduced-fat cream cheese (Neufchâtel) for the mascarpone cheese and 2 1/2 cups frozen (thawed) reduced-fat whipped topping for the 1 1/4 cups whipping cream, whipped.

Crème Brûlée

PREP: 15 min; COOK: 15 min; CHILL: 2 hr
Makes 8 servings

This dessert can be served by itself or spooned over slices of angel food cake or pound cake.

4 large egg yolks
3 tablespoons granulated sugar
2 cups whipping (heavy) cream
1/3 cup packed brown sugar
4 cups cut-up fruit

1. Beat egg yolks in medium bowl with electric mixer on high speed about 5 minutes or until thick and lemon colored. Gradually beat in granulated sugar.

2. Heat whipping cream in 2-quart saucepan over medium heat just until hot.

3. Gradually stir at least half of the hot cream into egg yolk mixture; stir back into hot cream in saucepan. Cook over low heat 5 to 8 minutes, stirring constantly, until mixture thickens (do not boil).

4. Pour custard into ungreased pie plate, 9 × 1 1/4 inches. Cover and refrigerate at least 2 hours but no longer than 24 hours.

5. Set oven control to Broil. Sprinkle brown sugar over custard. Broil with top about 5 inches from heat about 3 minutes or until sugar is melted and forms a glaze. Spoon over fruit. Refrigerate any remaining dessert.

1 SERVING: Calories 305 (Calories from Fat 190); Fat 21g (Saturated 12g); Cholesterol 170mg; Sodium 30mg; Carbohydrate 27g (Dietary Fiber 1g); Protein 3g

Baked Fudge

PREP: 35 min; BAKE: 30 min; CHILL: 2 hr
Makes 8 servings, about 1/2 cup each

This very chocolaty, puddinglike dessert is a chocoholic's treasure! Enjoy as is, topped with a dollop of whipped cream or spooned over ice cream, pound cake or fresh berries.

1/2 package (11 1/2-ounce size) milk
  chocolate chips (1 cup)
2 packages (3 ounces each) bittersweet
  chocolate, coarsely chopped (1 cup)
1 ounce unsweetened baking chocolate,
  chopped
3/4 cup *stick* margarine or butter*
5 large eggs, separated
1/2 cup granulated sugar
1 tablespoon all-purpose flour
2 tablespoons brandy or 1 tablespoon
  brandy extract
1 teaspoon vanilla
3 tablespoons powdered sugar
Boiling water

1. Heat oven to 300°. Grease bottom and sides of square pan, 8 × 8 × 2 inches, with shortening.

2. Heat chocolates and margarine in 1-quart saucepan over low heat, stirring occasionally until melted and smooth.

3. Beat egg yolks and granulated sugar in small bowl with electric mixer on high speed 5 to 7 minutes or until thick and lemon colored. Sprinkle flour, brandy and vanilla over egg yolk mixture; stir in until well mixed.

4. Beat egg whites in medium bowl with electric mixer on high speed until soft peaks form. Fold in egg yolk mixture. Fold in chocolate mixture. Pour into square pan. Place rectangular pan, 13 × 9 × 2 inches, on bottom oven rack; pour boiling water into rectangular pan until 1 inch deep.

5. Bake 25 to 30 minutes or until edges are set (center will be soft). Refrigerate uncovered about 2 hours or until chilled. Serve warm or cold. Sprinkle with powdered sugar. Spoon into dessert bowls. Refrigerate any remaining dessert.

We do not recommend using vegetable oil spreads (see page 13).

1 SERVING: Calories 530 (Calories from Fat 370); Fat 41g (Saturated 24g); Cholesterol 180mg; Sodium 180mg; Carbohydrate 36g (Dietary Fiber 4g); Protein 8g

Chocolate Mousse and Cups

PREP: 25 min; CHILL: 2 hr
Makes 8 servings

4 large egg yolks
1/4 cup sugar
1 cup whipping (heavy) cream
1 package (6 ounces) semisweet chocolate
  chips (1 cup)
Chocolate Cups (below)
1 1/2 cups whipping (heavy) cream

1. Beat egg yolks in small bowl with electric mixer on high speed about 3 minutes or until thick and lemon colored. Gradually beat in sugar.

2. Heat 1 cup whipping cream in 2-quart saucepan over medium heat just until hot.

3. Gradually stir at least half of the cream into egg yolk mixture; stir back into hot cream in saucepan. Cook over low heat about 5 minutes, stirring constantly, until mixture thickens (do not boil).

4. Stir in chocolate chips until melted. Cover and refrigerate about 2 hours, stirring occasionally, just until chilled.

5. Meanwhile, prepare Chocolate Cups.

6. Beat 1 1/2 cups whipping cream in chilled medium bowl with electric mixer on high speed until stiff. Fold chocolate mixture into whipped cream. Pipe or spoon mixture into cups. Refrigerate any remaining dessert.

Chocolate Cups

Wrap the outsides of eight 6-ounce custard cups with aluminum foil. Melt 1 1/3 cups semisweet chocolate chips in heavy 1-quart saucepan over low heat, stirring constantly; remove from heat. Spread about 1 1/2 tablespoons melted chocolate over foil on bottom and about 1 1/2 inches up side of each cup. Refrigerate about 30 minutes or until chocolate is firm. Carefully remove foil from custard cups, then remove foil from chocolate cups. Refrigerate chocolate cups.

1 SERVING: Calories 525 (Calories from Fat 360); Fat 40g (Saturated 24g); Cholesterol 190mg; Sodium 35mg; Carbohydrate 40g (Dietary Fiber 4g); Protein 5g

---

LIGHTER CHOCOLATE MOUSSE

For 14 grams of fat and 240 calories per serving, substitute 2 eggs for the 4 egg yolks, half-and-half for the 1 cup whipping cream and 3 cups frozen (thawed) reduced-fat whipped topping for the 1 1/2 cups whipping cream, whipped. Omit Chocolate Cups.

WHITE CHOCOLATE MOUSSE AND CUPS: Substitute vanilla milk chips for the chocolate chips.

English Trifle

PREP: 30 min; COOK: 20 min; CHILL: 3 hr
Makes 10 servings

1/2 cup sugar
3 tablespoons cornstarch
1/4 teaspoon salt
3 cups milk
1/2 cup dry sherry or other dry white wine or
    white grape juice
3 large egg yolks, beaten
3 tablespoons *stick* margarine or butter*
1 tablespoon vanilla
2 packages (3 ounces each) ladyfingers
1/2 cup strawberry preserves
1 pint strawberries, sliced, or 1 package
    (10 ounces) frozen sliced strawberries,
    thawed
1 cup whipping (heavy) cream
2 tablespoons sugar
2 tablespoons slivered almonds, toasted

1. Mix 1/2 cup sugar, the cornstarch and salt in 3-quart saucepan. Gradually stir in milk and sherry. Heat to boiling over medium heat, stirring constantly. Boil and stir 1 minute.

2. Gradually stir at least half of the hot mixture into egg yolks; stir back into hot mixture in saucepan. Boil and stir 1 minute; remove from heat. Stir in margarine and vanilla. Cover and refrigerate about 3 hours or until chilled.

3. Separate ladyfingers horizontally in half. Spread cut sides with preserves. Layer one-fourth of the ladyfingers, cut sides up, half of the strawberries and half of the pudding in 2-quart serving bowl; repeat. Arrange remaining ladyfingers around edge of bowl in upright position and with cut sides toward center. (It may be necessary to gently ease ladyfingers down into pudding about 1 inch so they remain upright.) Cover and refrigerate.

4. Beat whipping cream and 2 tablespoons sugar in chilled medium bowl with electric mixer on high speed until stiff. Spread over dessert. Sprinkle with almonds. Refrigerate any remaining dessert.

Spreads with at least 65% vegetable oil can be substituted (see page 13).

1 SERVING: Calories 325 (Calories from Fat 135); Fat 15g (Saturated 7g); Cholesterol 125mg; Sodium 160mg; Carbohydrate 43g (Dietary Fiber 1g); Protein 5g

Rice Pudding

PREP: 30 min; BAKE: 45 min; STAND: 15 min
Makes 8 servings, about 2/3 cup each

Why not enjoy rice pudding for breakfast as well as dessert? This is comfort food with which you can be comfortable any time of day. (photograph on page 152)

1/2 cup uncooked regular long grain rice
1 cup water
2 large eggs or 4 large egg yolks
1/2 cup sugar
1/2 cup raisins or chopped dried apricots
2 1/2 cups milk
1 teaspoon vanilla
1/4 teaspoon salt
Ground cinnamon or nutmeg
Whipped cream, if desired

1. Heat rice and water to boiling in 1 1/2-quart saucepan, stirring once or twice; reduce heat to low. Cover and simmer 14 minutes (do not lift cover or stir). All water should be absorbed.

2. Heat oven to 325°.

3. Beat eggs in ungreased 1 1/2-quart casserole. Stir in sugar, raisins, milk, vanilla, salt and hot rice. Sprinkle with cinnamon.

4. Bake uncovered 45 minutes, stirring every 15 minutes. (Overbaking may cause pudding to curdle.) Top of pudding will be very wet and not set.

5. Stir well; let stand 15 minutes. Enough liquid will be absorbed while standing to make pudding creamy. Serve warm, or cover and refrigerate about 3 hours or until chilled. Serve with whipped cream. Refrigerate any remaining dessert.

1 SERVING: Calories 195 (Calories from Fat 25); Fat 3g (Saturated 1g); Cholesterol 60mg; Sodium 115mg; Carbohydrate 37g (Dietary Fiber 0g); Protein 5g

TIMESAVING TIP
Leftover cooked rice also can be used in this recipe. Use 2 cups rice and increase baking time by about 5 minutes.

Bread Pudding with Whiskey Sauce, Rice Pudding (page 151)

Bread Pudding with Whiskey Sauce

PREP: 15 min; COOK: 10 min; BAKE: 45 min
Makes 8 servings

In addition to white bread, try whole wheat, cinnamon-raisin, egg bread or other flavors of bread that appeal to you in combination with the rich Whiskey Sauce.

> **2 cups milk**
> **1/4 cup *stick* margarine or butter***
> **1/2 cup sugar**
> **1 teaspoon ground cinnamon or nutmeg**
> **1/4 teaspoon salt**
> **2 large eggs, slightly beaten**
> **6 cups dry bread cubes (8 slices bread)**
> **1/2 cup raisins, if desired**
> **Whiskey Sauce (right)**

1. Heat oven to 350°.

2. Heat milk and margarine in 2-quart saucepan over medium heat until margarine is melted and milk is hot.

3. Mix sugar, cinnamon, salt and eggs in large bowl with wire whisk until well blended. Stir in bread cubes and raisins. Stir in milk mixture. Pour into ungreased 1 1/2-quart casserole or square baking dish, 8 × 8 × 2 inches. Place casserole in rectangular pan, 13 × 9 × 2 inches; pour boiling water into rectangular pan until 1 inch deep.

4. Bake uncovered 40 to 45 minutes or until knife inserted 1 inch from edge of casserole comes out clean.

5. Prepare Whiskey Sauce. Serve sauce over warm bread pudding. Refrigerate any remaining dessert.

Whiskey Sauce

> **1 cup packed brown sugar**
> **1/2 cup *stick* margarine or butter***
> **3 to 4 tablespoons bourbon or 2 teaspoons**
> **brandy extract**

Heat all ingredients to boiling in heavy 1-quart saucepan over medium heat, stirring constantly, until sugar is dissolved. Serve warm or cool.

*Spreads with at least 65% vegetable oil can be substituted (see page 13).

1 SERVING: Calories 665 (Calories from Fat 215); Fat 24g (Saturated 6g); Cholesterol 60mg; Sodium 1020mg; Carbohydrate 101g (Dietary Fiber 3g); Protein 14g

---

LIGHTER BREAD PUDDING WITH WHISKEY SAUCE

For 8 grams of fat and 555 calories per serving, use skim milk and decrease margarine to 2 tablespoons. Substitute 1 egg plus 2 egg whites for the 2 eggs. Instead of Whiskey Sauce, stir 1 tablespoon bourbon into 1 cup fat-free caramel sauce; heat if desired.

Steamed Plum Pudding

PREP: 30 min; COOK: 3 hr; CHILL: 1 hr
Makes 8 servings

For a dramatic presentation, serve this pudding flaming. Place sugar cubes soaked in lemon extract around the pudding, then light one, and watch the flames circle the pudding.

> 1 cup milk
> 3 cups soft bread crumbs (about 5 slices bread)
> 1/2 cup shortening, melted
> 1/2 cup molasses
> 1 cup all-purpose flour*
> 1/2 cup chopped raisins
> 1/2 cup finely chopped citron
> 1 teaspoon baking soda
> 1/2 teaspoon salt
> 2 teaspoons ground cinnamon
> 1/4 teaspoon ground allspice
> 1/4 teaspoon ground cloves
> Sherried Hard Sauce (below) or Divine Caramel Sauce (page 159)

1. Generously grease bottom and side of 4-cup mold with shortening.

2. Pour milk over bread crumbs in large bowl. Mix in shortening and molasses. Stir in remaining ingredients except Sherried Hard Sauce. Pour into mold. Cover with aluminum foil.

3. Place mold on rack in Dutch oven. Pour in boiling water up to level of rack. Cover and heat to boiling. Keep water boiling over low heat about 3 hours or until toothpick inserted in center comes out clean. (If it is necessary to add water during steaming, uncover and quickly add boiling water.)

4. Meanwhile, prepare Sherried Hard Sauce. Unmold pudding; cut into slices. Serve warm with sauce.

Sherried Hard Sauce

> 1/2 cup margarine or butter, softened
> 1 cup powdered sugar
> 1 tablespoon sherry or brandy or 1 teaspoon sherry or brandy extract

Beat margarine in small bowl with electric mixer on high speed about 5 minutes or until fluffy and light in color. Gradually beat in powdered sugar until smooth. Stir in sherry. Cover and refrigerate about 1 hour or until chilled.

*If using self-rising flour, decrease baking soda to 1/2 teaspoon and omit salt.

1 SERVING: Calories 620 (Calories from Fat 245); Fat 27g (Saturated 6g); Cholesterol 5mg; Sodium 830mg; Carbo-hydrate 89g (Dietary Fiber 3g); Protein 8g

To steam without a steamer, use a Dutch oven or large saucepan with a tight-fitting cover. Place a wire rack or trivet inside to raise the mold about 1 inch above the bottom of the pan.

Vanilla Pudding

PREP: 10 min; COOK: 10 min; CHILL: 1 hr
Makes 4 servings

This rich pudding can also be used over cake or fruit as a sweet sauce—try it over unfrosted Devil's Food Cake (page 73).

> 1/3 cup sugar
> 2 tablespoons cornstarch
> 1/8 teaspoon salt
> 2 cups milk
> 2 large egg yolks, slightly beaten
> 2 tablespoons *stick* margarine or butter, softened*
> 2 teaspoons vanilla

1. Mix sugar, cornstarch and salt in 2-quart saucepan. Gradually stir in milk. Cook over medium heat, stirring constantly, until mixture thickens and boils. Boil and stir 1 minute.

2. Gradually stir at least half of the hot mixture into egg yolks; stir back into hot mixture in saucepan. Boil and stir 1 minute; remove from heat. Stir in margarine and vanilla.

3. Pour pudding into dessert dishes. Cover and refrigerate until serving. Refrigerate any remaining dessert.

*Spreads with at least 65% vegetable oil can be substituted (see page 13).

1 SERVING: Calories 225 (Calories from Fat 100); Fat 11g (Saturated 3g); Cholesterol 115mg; Sodium 200mg; Carbohydrate 27g (Dietary Fiber 0g); Protein 5g

BUTTERSCOTCH PUDDING: Substitute 2/3 cup packed brown sugar for the granulated sugar and decrease vanilla to 1 teaspoon.

CHOCOLATE PUDDING: Increase sugar to 1/2 cup and stir 1/3 cup baking cocoa into sugar mixture. Omit margarine.

Tips for Meringues

Meringue can be used to make high, melt-in-your-mouth soft-meringue toppings for pies and tarts such as Lemon Meringue Pie (page 103), or it can be used to make a hard, crisp meringue crust to hold your favorite creamy filling, fruit or ice cream. The basic difference between the two is the proportion of sugar to egg whites. Whichever you choose to make, these guidelines will help you make the best meringue:

- Separate eggs very carefully while cold, using an egg separator. To prevent contamination, do not move egg yolk back and forth between shell halves. Make certain no yolk gets into the whites, as even a speck of yolk or grease will prevent whites from beating properly.
- For greatest volume, let egg whites stand at room temperature 30 minutes before beating. Or place in a microwavable bowl and microwave uncovered on High about 10 seconds per egg white to bring to room temperature. (Do not overcook.)
- Gradually beat in sugar, about 1 tablespoon at a time. Continue beating until mixture stands in stiff peaks when beaters are lifted. (Meringue should feel smooth, not gritty, when rubbed between your fingers.)
- A meringue made on a humid or rainy day may cause the sugar to absorb moisture from the air, resulting in a sticky, spongy texture. Drops of sugar syrup formed on the surface of the meringue (beading) may result.

Soft Meringue

- Spread soft meringue over hot filling, sealing the meringue right up to the crust all the way around. This prevents shrinking and weeping (the liquid that oozes out of a meringue topping). Swirl or pull top of meringue up into points for a fluffier, lighter look.
- Cool baked meringue gradually and away from drafts to prevent shrinking.

Hard Meringue

- When properly baked, a hard-meringue pie shell should be thoroughly dry. Underbaking can result in a gummy, limp texture, which makes removing it from the pie plate difficult.
- Cool a meringue pie shell in the turned-off oven for the same amount of time as the bake time so the shell will become dry and crisp.

❖

Meringue for 9-inch Pie

PREP: 10 min
Makes 8 servings

Billows of meringue are the traditional toppings for Lemon Meringue Pie. Meringue can also be used as a topping for similar pies, desserts or even bar cookies.

    3 large egg whites
    1/4 teaspoon cream of tartar
    6 tablespoons sugar
    1/2 teaspoon vanilla

1. Beat egg whites and cream of tartar in medium bowl with electric mixer on high speed until foamy.

2. Beat in sugar, 1 tablespoon at a time; continue beating until stiff and glossy. Do not underbeat. Beat in vanilla.

1 SERVING: Calories 45 (Calories from Fat 0); Fat 0g (Saturated 0g); Cholesterol 0mg; Sodium 20mg; Carbohydrate 10g (Dietary Fiber 0g); Protein 1g

Meringue Shell

PREP: 15 min; BAKE: 2 1/2 hr; COOL: 2 hr
Makes 8 servings

This no-fat shell is tailor-made to hold light desserts such as sliced fruit and fresh berries dusted with powdered sugar, or a fruit sorbet. If you're feeling decadent, try filling it with Baked Fudge (page 150) or ice cream.

    3 large egg whites
    1/4 teaspoon cream of tartar
    3/4 cup sugar

1. Heat oven to 275°. Line cookie sheet with cooking parchment paper or heavy brown paper.

2. Beat egg whites and cream of tartar in medium bowl with electric mixer on high speed until foamy. Beat in sugar, 1 tablespoon at a time; continue beating until stiff and glossy. Do not underbeat. Shape meringue on cookie sheet into 9-inch circle with back of spoon, building up side.

3. Bake 1 1/2 hours. Turn off oven and leave meringue in oven with door closed 1 hour. Finish cooling at room temperature.

a. Beat egg whites until stiff peaks form and mixture is glossy.

b. Shape meringue with back of spoon into desired shape.

1 SERVING: Calories 80 (Calories from Fat 0); Fat 0g (Saturated 0g); Cholesterol 0mg; Sodium 20mg; Carbohydrate 19g (Dietary Fiber 0g); Protein 1g

CRÈME DE MENTHE MERINGUE: Fold 1 ounce unsweetened baking chocolate, coarsely grated, into meringue after beating. Fill cooled baked meringue with 1 quart French vanilla ice cream and drizzle with about 1/3 cup green crème de menthe.

INDIVIDUAL MERINGUES: Drop meringue by 1/3 cupfuls onto cookie sheet. Shape into circles, building up sides. Bake 1 hour. Turn off oven and leave meringues in oven with door closed 1 1/2 hours. Finish cooling at room temperature. Fill cooled baked meringues with 1 quart ice cream and drizzle with 1 cup Hot Fudge Sauce (page 159) or Butterscotch-Rum Sauce (page 159). Makes 8 to 10 meringues.

Berry Pirouette

PREP: 30 min; CHILL: 4 hr
Makes 10 to 12 servings

This is an easy and impressive dessert. Make it even more spectacular by drizzling it with Hot Fudge Sauce (page 159) in a design.

> 1 3/4 cups boiling water
> 2 packages (4-serving size each) raspberry-flavored gelatin
> 1 package (16 ounces) frozen raspberries or boysenberries, partially thawed
> 2 cups whipping (heavy) cream
> 1 package (5 1/2 ounces) tubular-shaped pirouette cookies (about 24)

1. Pour boiling water on gelatin in large bowl; stir until gelatin is dissolved.

2. Reserve 3 to 5 boysenberries for garnish. Place remaining berries in food processor or blender. Cover and process until smooth. Stir berries into gelatin. Cover and refrigerate about 1 hour or until very thick but not set.

3. Beat gelatin mixture with electric mixer on high speed about 4 minutes or until thick and fluffy. Beat 1 cup of the whipping cream in chilled medium bowl with electric mixer on high speed until stiff; fold into gelatin mixture. Pour into ungreased springform pan, 9 × 3 inches. Cover and refrigerate about 3 hours or until set.

4. Run knife around edge of dessert to loosen; remove side of pan. Place dessert on serving plate. Beat remaining 1 cup whipping cream in chilled medium bowl until stiff. Spread side of dessert with half of the whipped cream.

5. Carefully cut cookies crosswise in half. Arrange cookies, cut sides down, vertically around side of dessert; press lightly. Garnish with remaining whipped cream and berries. Refrigerate any remaining dessert.

1 SERVING: Calories 295 (Calories from Fat 155); Fat 17g (Saturated 10g); Cholesterol 55mg; Sodium 110mg; Carbohydrate 34g (Dietary Fiber 1g); Protein 3g

PEACH PIROUETTE: Substitute 1 package (16 ounces) frozen sliced peaches, partially thawed, for the boysenberries and orange-flavored gelatin for the raspberry-flavored gelatin. Reserve 3 peach slices for garnish.

Lemon Schaum Torte

Lemon Schaum Torte

**PREP: 35 min; BAKE: 2 1/2 hr; COOL: 2 hr;
CHILL: 12 hr
Makes 8 to 10 servings**

*Lemon desserts are especially popular in the spring, but this
favorite transcends the seasons. It's pretty garnished with
fresh strawberries or raspberries .*

> Meringue Shell (page 154)
> 3/4 cup sugar
> 3 tablespoons cornstarch
> 1/4 teaspoon salt
> 3/4 cup water
> 3 large egg yolks, slightly beaten
> 1 tablespoon *stick* margarine or butter*
> 1 teaspoon grated lemon peel
> 1/3 cup lemon juice
> 1 cup whipping (heavy) cream

1. Bake and cool Meringue Shell.

2. Mix sugar, cornstarch and salt in 2-quart
saucepan. Gradually stir in water. Cook over medium
heat, stirring constantly, until mixture thickens and
boils. Boil and stir 1 minute.

3. Gradually stir at least half of the hot mixture
into egg yolks; stir back into hot mixture in saucepan.
Boil and stir 1 minute; remove from heat.

4. Stir in margarine, lemon peel and lemon juice.
Cool to room temperature. Spoon into shell. Cover
and refrigerate at least 12 hours but no longer than 24
hours.

5. Beat whipping cream in chilled medium bowl
with electric mixer on high speed until stiff. Spread
over filling. Refrigerate any remaining dessert.

**Spreads with at least 65% vegetable oil can be substituted (see
page 13).*

1 SERVING: Calories 295 (Calories from Fat 115); Fat 13g
(Saturated 7g); Cholesterol 115mg; Sodium 120mg;
Carbohydrate 42g (Dietary Fiber 0g); Protein 3g

LIME SCHAUM TORTE: Substitute grated lime peel
and lime juice for the lemon peel and lemon juice. Stir
in 1 or 2 drops green food color with the lime juice.

Raspberry Bavarian Cream

PREP: 15 min
Makes 4 to 6 servings

Serve this creamy dessert in stemmed dessert dishes accompanied by a crisp cookie, over fresh raspberries or over a slice of Pound Cake (page 76).

> 2 containers (6 ounces each) raspberry yogurt
> 1 package (3 1/2 ounces) vanilla instant pudding and pie filling
> 1 cup whipping (heavy) cream
> 1 cup fresh or frozen (thawed) raspberries

1. Beat yogurt and pudding and pie filling (dry) in medium bowl with electric mixer on low speed 30 seconds.

2. Beat in whipping cream on medium speed 3 to 5 minutes, scraping bowl occasionally, until soft peaks form. Fold in raspberries. Refrigerate any remaining dessert.

1 SERVING: Calories 375 (Calories from Fat 180); Fat 20g (Saturated 12g); Cholesterol 70mg; Sodium 430mg; Carbohydrate 45g (Dietary Fiber 1g); Protein 5g

---

Tips for Ice Cream

- Ice cream is a universal favorite, and homemade ice cream is especially welcome! While we've become used to electric freezers and those that do not need to be cranked, there is still something to be said for the old-fashioned hand crank freezer. It makes for great family entertainment—pass it around, share the cranking and pass the time by telling stories and catching up. However, if your time is short, an electric freezer will still do the job.
- Before making homemade ice cream, frozen yogurt or sorbet, clear a space in the freezer. Ice cream freezers vary in type, capacity and operation. Be sure to follow the manufacturer's directions for freezing.
- Eggs must be cooked for ice creams, in which eggs are an ingredient, to make them safe to eat.

Vanilla Ice Cream

PREP: 10 min; COOK: 10 min; CHILL: 3 hr;
FREEZE: 35 min
Makes 1 quart ice cream, eight 1/2-cup servings

> 3 large egg yolks, slightly beaten
> 1/2 cup sugar
> 1 cup milk
> 1/4 teaspoon salt
> 2 cups whipping (heavy) cream
> 1 tablespoon vanilla

1. Mix egg yolks, sugar, milk and salt in 2-quart saucepan. Cook over medium heat, stirring constantly, just to boiling (do not boil). Refrigerate uncovered in chilled bowl 2 to 3 hours, stirring occasionally, until room temperature.

2. Stir whipping cream and vanilla into milk mixture. Pour into 1-quart ice-cream freezer and freeze according to manufacturer's directions.

1 SERVING: Calories 265 (Calories from Fat 190); Fat 21g (Saturated 13g); Cholesterol 150mg; Sodium 105mg; Carbohydrate 16g (Dietary Fiber 0g); Protein 3g

CHOCOLATE ICE CREAM: Increase sugar to 1 cup. Beat 2 ounces unsweetened baking chocolate, melted and cooled, into milk mixture before cooking. Decrease vanilla to 1 teaspoon.

PEPPERMINT ICE CREAM: Decrease vanilla to 1 teaspoon. Stir 1/2 cup crushed peppermint candy into milk mixture after adding vanilla. Stir in a few drops green or red food color.

> **TIMESAVING TIP**
> The egg mixture can be cooked up to 24 hours ahead if it's more convenient.

Fresh Lemon Sherbet

PREP: 10 min; FREEZE: 35 min
Makes 1 quart sherbet, eight 1/2-cup servings

Freshly grated lemon peel gives this sherbet extra-fresh flavor.

1 1/4 cups sugar
2 cups half-and-half
1/3 cup lemon juice
1 to 2 tablespoons grated lemon peel
1 or 2 drops yellow food color

1. Mix all ingredients until sugar is dissolved.

2. Pour into 1-quart ice-cream freezer and freeze according to manufacturer's directions.

1 SERVING: Calories 210 (Calories from Fat 65); Fat 7g (Saturated 4g); Cholesterol 25mg; Sodium 30mg; Carbohydrate 35g (Dietary Fiber 0g); Protein 2g

Frozen Berry Yogurt

PREP: 15 min; FREEZE: 35 min
Makes 22 servings, 1/2 cup each

Serve either of these fruit yogurts on wedges of Chocolate Brownie Pie (page 112) topped with Hot Fudge Sauce (page 159) for guaranteed raves.

2 pints strawberries or raspberries
1/2 cup sugar
8 cups vanilla yogurt

1. Mash strawberries with sugar in medium bowl. Stir in yogurt.

2. Pour into 2-quart ice-cream freezer and freeze according to manufacturer's directions.*

A 1-quart ice-cream freezer can be used. Divide ingredients in half.

1 SERVING: Calories 115 (Calories from Fat 10); Fat 1g (Saturated 1g); Cholesterol 5mg; Sodium 55mg; Carbohydrate 23g (Dietary Fiber 0g); Protein 4g

FROZEN BANANA YOGURT: Substitute 3 cups mashed ripe bananas (6 medium) for the strawberries.

> **TIMESAVING TIP**
> Substitute 1 package (16 ounces) frozen whole strawberries or raspberries, thawed and drained, for the fresh berries.

Tips for Dessert Sauces

- There are no hard and fast rules for how dessert sauces should be served—you can feel free to use your imagination! Most dessert sauces are delicious over ice cream, cake or fresh fruit. Try your hand at creating some delicious and unique combinations, such as Hot Fudge Sauce (page 159) over orange sherbet, Butterscotch-Rum Sauce (page 159) over pound cake or Lemon Sauce (page 160) over Rice Pudding.
- Use the sauces here under food by drizzling on the plate, then adding the dessert. This is surprisingly easy to do. You can use a spoon, a heavy plastic bag with a corner cut off or inexpensive plastic squeeze bottles (which might be red or yellow because they were originally intended for ketchup and mustard) available at grocery stores and drug stores.
- To make eye-catching designs on plates for desserts, use contrasting colors of sauces and/or glazes. (These designs can also be used with frostings and glazes for the tops of cakes and tortes.) Follow the directions below for the designs:

Wispy Heart Design—Spoon sauce onto plate. Pipe or drop dots of contrasting sauce in a circle 1-inch from edge of sauce and in smaller circle in center. Draw a knife or toothpick through dots to make heart shapes.

Sunburst Design—Spoon sauce onto plate. Pipe or drizzle semicircular lines of contrasting sauce across plate about 1-inch apart. Starting at smallest semicircle, draw knife or toothpick across lines toward edge of plate.

Chevron Design—Spoon sauce onto plate. Drizzle 3 lines of contrasting sauce across plate; immediately draw knife or toothpick back and forth across lines.

Hot Fudge Sauce

PREP: 5 min; COOK: 5 min
Makes 3 cups sauce

Everyone loves this rich, thick and chocolaty sauce, so make plenty!

> 1 can (12 ounces) evaporated milk
> 1 package (12 ounces) semisweet chocolate
>   chips (2 cups)
> 1/2 cup sugar
> 1 tablespoon *stick* margarine or butter*
> 1 teaspoon vanilla

1. Heat milk, chocolate chips and sugar to boiling in 2-quart saucepan over medium heat, stirring constantly; remove from heat.

2. Stir in margarine and vanilla until mixture is smooth and creamy. Serve warm over ice cream, cake or brownies. Store in refrigerator up to 4 weeks.

*Spreads with at least 65% vegetable oil can be substituted (see page 13).

1 TABLESPOON: Calories 60 (Calories from Fat 25); Fat 3g (Saturated 1g); Cholesterol 5mg; Sodium 10mg; Carbohydrate 7g (Dietary Fiber 0g); Protein 1g

ORANGE FUDGE SAUCE: Substitute 2 teaspoons orange-flavored liqueur for the 1 teaspoon vanilla.

TIMESAVING TIP

To microwave, mix milk, chocolate chips and sugar in 8-cup microwavable measure. Microwave uncovered on High 6 to 8 minutes, stirring every 2 minutes, until thickened and smooth. Stir in margarine and vanilla until mixture is smooth and creamy.

Divine Caramel Sauce

PREP: 5 min; COOK: 40 min
Makes 4 cups sauce

This recipe was created from a smooth and creamy caramel recipe. You need to use the large pan, as the sauce bubbles up when it cooks.

> 2 cups sugar
> 3/4 cup *stick* margarine or butter*
> 2 cups whipping (heavy) cream
> 1 cup light corn syrup
> Pinch of salt
> 1 teaspoon vanilla

1. Heat all ingredients except vanilla to boiling in heavy Dutch oven over medium heat, stirring constantly; reduce heat slightly. Boil about 30 minutes, stirring frequently, until sugar is dissolved and mixture is caramel colored.

2. Stir in vanilla. Serve hot or warm. Store in refrigerator up to 2 months.

*We do not recommend using vegetable oil spreads (see page 13).

1 TABLESPOON: Calories 75 (Calories from Fat 35); Fat 4g (Saturated 2g); Cholesterol 10mg; Sodium 35mg; Carbohydrate 10g (Dietary Fiber 0g); Protein 0g

Butterscotch-Rum Sauce

PREP: 10 min; COOK: 20 min
Makes 1 3/4 cups sauce

Serve this luscious sauce over ice cream, bread pudding or Baked Apples (page 139).

> 1 can (5 ounces) evaporated milk (2/3 cup)
> 1/4 cup light corn syrup
> 1 cup packed brown sugar
> 1 cup granulated sugar
> 1/8 teaspoon salt
> 2 tablespoons *stick* margarine or butter*
> 1 tablespoon rum or 2 teaspoons rum
>   flavoring
> 1 teaspoon lemon juice
> 1/2 cup golden raisins, if desired

1. Mix milk, corn syrup, sugars and salt in 2-quart saucepan. Cook over very low heat about 20 minutes, stirring frequently, until thickened; remove from heat.

2. Stir in remaining ingredients. Serve warm or cold. Cover and refrigerate any remaining sauce.

*Spreads with at least 65% vegetable oil can be substituted (see page 13).

1 TABLESPOON: Calories 80 (Calories from Fat 10); Fat 1g (Saturated 0g); Cholesterol 5mg; Sodium 30mg; Carbohydrate 18g (Dietary Fiber 0g); Protein 0g

Marshmallow Sauce

PREP: 5 min; COOK: 10 min
Makes 1 1/2 cups sauce

This is a favorite with kids for sundaes and banana splits—but adults will want their share as well!

    2/3 cup sugar
    1/4 cup water
    3 tablespoons light corn syrup
    2 cups miniature marshmallows*
    3/4 teaspoon vanilla
    Dash of salt

1. Heat sugar, water and corn syrup to boiling in 2-quart saucepan; reduce heat to low. Simmer uncovered 4 minutes, stirring occasionally; remove from heat.

2. Stir in remaining ingredients until marshmallows are melted and mixture is smooth. Serve warm or cold. Cover and refrigerate any remaining sauce.

*20 large marshmallows, cut into fourths, can be substituted for the miniature marshmallows.

1 TABLESPOON: Calories 50 (Calories from Fat 0); Fat 0g (Saturated 0g); Cholesterol 0mg; Sodium 10mg; Carbohydrate 12g (Dietary Fiber 0g); Protein 0g

---

TIMESAVING TIP

To microwave, mix sugar, water and corn syrup in 2-quart microwavable casserole. Microwave uncovered on High 2 minutes 30 seconds to 3 minutes or until boiling. Stir in remaining ingredients. Microwave uncovered about 1 minute longer or until marshmallows can be stirred smooth.

Lemon Sauce

PREP: 5 min; COOK: 10 min
Makes 1 1/4 cups sauce

    1/2 cup sugar
    2 tablespoons cornstarch
    3/4 cup water
    1 tablespoon grated lemon peel
    1/4 cup lemon juice
    2 tablespoons *stick* margarine or butter*

1. Mix sugar and cornstarch in 1-quart saucepan. Gradually stir in water. Cook over medium heat, stirring constantly, until mixture thickens and boils. Boil and stir 1 minute; remove from heat.

2. Stir in remaining ingredients. Serve warm or cool. Cover and refrigerate any remaining sauce.

*Spreads with at least 65% vegetable oil can be substituted (see page 13).

---

1 TABLESPOON: Calories 35 (Calories from Fat 10); Fat 1g (Saturated 0g); Cholesterol 0mg; Sodium 15mg; Carbohydrate 6g (Dietary Fiber 0g); Protein 0g

---

TIMESAVING TIP

To microwave, mix sugar and cornstarch in 4-cup microwavable measure. Gradually stir in water. Microwave uncovered on High 3 to 4 minutes, stirring every minute, until thickened and clear. Stir in remaining ingredients.

Orange Sauce

PREP: 10 min; COOK: 15 min
Makes about 2 1/3 cups sauce

Try serving this versatile sauce over Gingerbread (page 79), Bread Pudding (page 152), Angel Food Cake (page 83) or cut-up fresh fruit or berries.

    1 cup sugar
    2 tablespoons cornstarch
    1 tablespoon all-purpose flour
    1/4 teaspoon salt
    1 1/4 cups orange juice
    1/2 cup water
    1/4 cup lemon juice
    1 tablespoon *stick* margarine or butter*
    1 teaspoon grated orange peel
    1 teaspoon grated lemon peel

1. Mix sugar, cornstarch, flour and salt in 1 1/2-quart saucepan. Gradually stir in orange juice, water and lemon juice. Heat to boiling over low heat, stirring constantly. Boil and stir 3 minutes; remove from heat.

2. Stir in remaining ingredients. Serve warm. Cover and refrigerate any remaining sauce.

*Spreads with at least 65% vegetable oil can be substituted (see page 13).

1 TABLESPOON: Calories 30 (Calories from Fat 0); Fat 0g (Saturated 0g); Cholesterol 0mg; Sodium 20mg; Carbohydrate 7g (Dietary Fiber 0g); Protein 0g

---

TIMESAVING TIP

To microwave, decrease water to 1/4 cup. Mix sugar, cornstarch, flour and salt in 4-cup microwavable measure. Gradually stir in orange juice, water and lemon juice. Microwave uncovered on High 5 to 7 minutes, stirring every minute, until thickened and boiling. Stir in remaining ingredients.

Eggs & Cheese

About Eggs

Eggs are delicious eaten by themselves or as an ingredient in a variety of recipes from appetizers to desserts. As an ingredient, they add nutrients as well as richness, flavor, texture, thickening and/or leavening. Chicken eggs are most commonly used, although the eggs of ducks, geese, quail and other poultry are often used in other cuisines.

The egg white is mostly water with some protein, and the egg yolk contains much of the protein and all of the fat, cholesterol, vitamins and minerals. People with high cholesterol counts may need to limit their intake of egg yolks. As a general guide, two egg whites may be substituted for one whole egg, although the proportion varies as the quantity of eggs becomes larger.

Purchasing Eggs

Eggs are marketed according to size, grade and color. Standards for size and grade of eggs are established by the U.S. Department of Agriculture.

- **Size:** The most popular egg size is large; other sizes available include extra large, medium and small. Recipes in this cookbook were tested with large eggs.
- **Grade:** The grade is determined by the quality of both the egg and its shell at the time the egg was packed. There is little difference in quality between grades AA and A, and there is no difference in nutritive content. Gradings are based on thickness of the white, firmness of the yolk and size of interior air pocket. Thick whites, compact, rounded yolks and a small air pocket are characteristics of high-grade fresh eggs. As eggs get older, the white gradually thins and the yolk flattens. Grade B eggs are rarely seen in the retail market.
- **Color:** Egg shell color (white or brown) and yolk color (pale or deep yellow) vary with the breed and diet of the hen. White eggs are most in demand, but in some parts of the country brown are preferred. Flavor, nutritive value and cooking performance are the same for white and brown eggs.

Safe Handling and Storing of Eggs

Recently, raw eggs contaminated with salmonella have caused some outbreaks of food-borne illness. Although scientists suspect the bacteria can be transmitted from infected laying hens directly into the interior of the eggs before the shells are formed, the extent of the problem is not yet known. People in high-risk categories who are particularly vulnerable to salmonella infections include the very young, the elderly, pregnant women (because of risk to the fetus) and people already weakened by serious illness or whose immune systems are weakened.

As a perishable food, eggs require proper storage and cooking to prevent the growth of potentially harmful bacteria.

- Purchase eggs from a refrigerated case, and refrigerate immediately at a temperature no higher than 40° upon arriving home. Do not wash eggs before storing or using because washing is a routine part of commercial egg processing.
- Look for eggshells that are clean and not cracked. Open the carton and gently move each egg to be sure it has not cracked and stuck to the carton. If a shell cracks between the market and home, discard the egg.
- Store fresh eggs in the carton to help prevent absorption of refrigerator odors. Storing eggs point down helps center the yolk, resulting in more attractive hard- and soft-cooked eggs.
- Wash hands, utensils, equipment and work areas with hot, soapy water before and after they come in contact with raw eggs and egg-rich dishes where eggs are the main ingredient, such as quiches and baked custards.
- Avoid keeping eggs at room temperature for more than two hours, including time for preparing and serving (not including cooking). If hard-cooked eggs are hidden for an egg hunt, either follow the two-hour rule or don't eat the eggs!
- Separated egg whites may safely stand at room temperature up to 30 minutes. The closer the egg white is to room temperature before heating, the more volume it will have when used in foods like meringue.
- Refrigerate raw and cooked eggs. Use raw eggs in the shell within three weeks and hard-cooked eggs (in the shell or peeled) within one week. Use leftover raw yolks and whites within four days. Unbroken egg yolks store best when covered with a small amount of water.

Preceding page: Quiche Lorraine (page 172)

- For longer storage, freeze raw egg whites in a plastic ice-cube tray; remove to a plastic freezer bag for storage. Thaw frozen egg whites in the refrigerator. When measuring, note that 2 tablespoons thawed liquid egg white is equal to 1 fresh egg white.
- Egg yolks require special treatment for freezing. If the yolks are to be used in savory dishes such as scrambled eggs, add 1/8 teaspoon salt for each 1/4 cup of egg yolks. If the yolks are to be used in sweet dishes such as custards, add 1 1/2 teaspoons sugar or 1 1/2 teaspoons corn syrup for each 1/4 cup of egg yolks.
- Hard-cooked egg yolks can be frozen successfully, but hard-cooked egg whites become tough and watery.

For more information on handling eggs safely, call the USDA Meat and Poultry Hotline at 800-535-4555.

Cooking Eggs

- Avoid eating raw eggs and foods containing raw eggs. Favorite homemade foods such as ice cream, eggnog and mayonnaise should be avoided unless any eggs within the recipes are cooked. Purchased forms of these foods are safe to serve because they contain pasteurized eggs. Commercial pasteurization destroys salmonella bacteria.
- To measure 1 cup, you need 4 to 6 eggs, 8 to 10 whites or 12 to 14 yolks.
- Use medium to low cooking temperatures. High heat and overcooking cause egg whites to shrink and become tough and rubbery; yolks become tough and their surface may turn green. Omelets are the exception; prepare over medium-high heat.

- Cook eggs thoroughly until both the yolk and white are firm, not runny, to kill any bacteria present.
- Do not let food mixtures containing raw or cooked eggs, such as Cheese Strata or Quiche Lorraine, stand for any length of time at room temperature before baking.
- Serve cooked eggs and egg dishes immediately after cooking, or refrigerate as soon as possible after serving for later use. Use within two days.
- Leave just-baked hot cream or custard pie fillings, cheesecakes and other egg-rich dishes at room temperature no more than fifteen minutes to cool before refrigerating.
- "Do-ahead" instructions for recipes with eggs should not exceed twenty-four hours' refrigeration time before baking.
- Store cream or custard pie fillings, cheesecakes, egg salads, quiches and other dishes containing combinations of eggs and milk in the refrigerator as soon after serving as possible. Store no longer than two days.
- Divide large amounts of hot, cooked, egg-rich dishes into several shallow containers to cool quickly in the refrigerator.

Determining Egg Doneness

Cook eggs thoroughly until both the white and yolk are firm, not runny. An egg is cooked when it reaches a temperature of 160°. Cooking at low temperatures helps to achieve the desired internal temperature. Timings and doneness tests for our recipes achieve this temperature. For some recipes, eggs may be firmer than expected, but this doneness ensures that the eggs will be safe to eat.

Eggs Cooking Chart

Cook any number of large eggs, choosing the size of cooking utensil that will best hold the number of eggs being cooked.

Type	Other Ingredients	Directions	Success Tips
Soft-Cooked Eggs	Cold water at least 1 inch above egg(s)	Heat to boiling in saucepan; remove from heat. Cover and let stand 3 minutes. *Immediately* cool briefly in cold water to prevent further cooking. Cut lengthwise in half; scoop from shells.	Before cooking, pierce large end of eggs with a pushpin to help prevent them from cracking during cooking.
Hard-Cooked Eggs	Cold water at least 1 inch above egg(s)	Heat to boiling in saucepan; remove from heat. Cover and let stand 18 minutes. *Immediately* cool briefly in cold water to prevent further cooking. Tap egg to crack shell; roll egg between hands to loosen shell, then peel.	If shell is hard to peel, hold egg in cold water while peeling.
Poached Eggs	1 1/2 to 2 inches water	Heat water to boiling in skillet or saucepan; reduce to simmering. Break each egg into custard cup or saucer. *Carefully* slip egg into water. Cook about 5 minutes or until whites and yolks are firm, not runny. Remove with slotted spoon.	• Hold cup or saucer close to surface of water for best shape and to avoid splashing. • Use a large enough pan so eggs do not touch while cooking. • Substitute chicken or beef broth for the water if desired.
Fried Eggs	Margarine, butter or bacon fat	Heat 1/8 inch fat in heavy skillet over medium heat until hot. Break each egg into custard cup or saucer. *Carefully* slip egg into skillet. *Immediately* reduce heat to low. Cook 5 to 7 minutes, spooning fat over eggs, until whites are set, a film forms over top and whites and yolks are firm, not runny. For over-easy eggs, *gently* turn over after 3 minutes and cook 1 to 2 minutes longer.	Lighter Fried Eggs: Use a nonstick skillet and spray skillet with nonstick cooking spray. Cook eggs over low heat about 1 minute or until edges turn white. Add 2 teaspoons water for each egg. Cover and cook about 5 minutes longer or until a film forms over top and whites and yolks are firm, not runny.
Baked Eggs (Shirred)	Margarine or butter, softened	Heat oven to 325°. Grease custard cups with margarine. *Carefully* break 1 egg into each cup. Sprinkle with salt and pepper. Top each with 1 tablespoon milk or half-and-half. Dot with margarine. Bake 15 to 18 minutes or until whites and yolks are firm, not runny.	Instead of dotting with margarine, sprinkle each egg with 1 tablespoon shredded Cheddar or grated Parmesan cheese if desired.

Huevos Rancheros, Quesadillas (page 179)

Huevos Rancheros

PREP: 45 min
Makes 6 servings

This is a spunky weekend brunch favorite. Try serving it with frosty Sangria (page 35).

1 1/4 cups Tomato Salsa (page 359)
1/2 pound bulk chorizo or pork sausage
Vegetable oil
6 corn tortillas (6 to 7 inches in diameter)
6 Fried Eggs (page 164)
1 1/2 cups shredded Cheddar cheese
   (6 ounces)

1. Prepare Tomato Salsa.

2. Cook sausage in 8-inch skillet over medium heat, stirring occasionally, until no longer pink; drain. Cover and keep warm.

3. Heat 1/8 inch oil in 8-inch skillet over medium heat just until hot. Cook tortillas, one at a time, in oil about 1 minute , turning once, until crisp; drain.

4. Heat salsa in 1-quart saucepan, stirring occasionally, until hot.

5. Prepare Fried Eggs.

6. Spread each tortilla with 1 tablespoon salsa to soften. Place egg on each tortilla. Top each with salsa, sausage, additional salsa and cheese.

1 SERVING: Calories 505 (Calories from Fat 335); Fat 37g (Saturated 14g); Cholesterol 280mg; Sodium 1050mg; Carbohydrate 20g (Dietary Fiber 2g); Protein 25g

---

TIMESAVING TIP

Use prepared salsa for the Tomato Salsa. Microwave salsa in 4-cup glass microwavable measure about 2 minutes or until hot; stir. Omit oil and step 3; use purchased crisp tortilla shells and heat as directed on package.

Eggs Benedict

PREP: 30 min
Makes 6 servings

This favorite brunch dish was created years ago and named after Mr. and Mrs. LeGrand Benedict, patrons of Delmonico's Restaurant in New York, after they complained there was nothing new on the lunch menu.

> Hollandaise Sauce (page 347)
> 3 English muffins
> 3 tablespoons margarine or butter, softened
> 1 teaspoon margarine, butter or spread
> 6 thin slices Canadian-style bacon or fully
>   cooked smoked ham
> 6 Poached Eggs (page 164)

1. Prepare Hollandaise Sauce; keep warm.

2. Split English muffins; toast. Spread each muffin half with margarine; keep warm.

3. Melt 1 teaspoon margarine in 10-inch skillet over medium heat. Cook bacon in margarine until light brown on both sides; keep warm.

4. Prepare Poached Eggs.

5. Place 1 slice bacon on each muffin half. Top with poached egg. Spoon warm sauce over eggs.

1 SERVING: Calories 380 (Calories from Fat 270); Fat 30g (Saturated 14g); Cholesterol 370mg; Sodium 680mg; Carbohydrate 14g (Dietary Fiber 1g); Protein 15g

SEAFOOD BENEDICT: Substitute 1 1/2 cups chopped cooked crabmeat, scallops, shrimp or lobster or a mixture for the bacon. Heat in margarine just until hot.

Deviled Eggs

PREP: 15 min
Makes 12 deviled eggs

This versatile dish is welcome as an appetizer, snack, main dish and even for breakfast.

> 6 Hard-Cooked Eggs (page 164), peeled
> 3 tablespoons mayonnaise, salad dressing or
>   half-and-half
> 1/2 teaspoon ground mustard (dry)
> 1/8 teaspoon salt
> 1/4 teaspoon pepper

1. Cut eggs lengthwise in half. Slip out yolks and mash with fork.

2. Stir in mayonnaise, mustard, salt and pepper. Fill whites with egg yolk mixture, heaping it lightly. Cover and refrigerate up to 24 hours.

1 DEVILED EGG: Calories 55 (Calories from Fat 45); Fat 5g (Saturated 1g); Cholesterol 110mg; Sodium 75mg; Carbohydrate 0g (Dietary Fiber 0g); Protein 3g

---

LIGHTER DEVILED EGGS

For 1 gram of fat and 20 calories per serving, mash only 6 yolk halves in step 1 (reserve remaining yolks for another purpose or discard). Use fat-free mayonnaise and stir in 1/3 cup finely chopped zucchini.

DEVILED EGGS WITH OLIVES: Omit mustard. Mix 1/4 cup finely chopped ripe or pimiento-stuffed olives and 1/4 teaspoon curry powder into egg yolk mixture.

MEXICAN DEVILED EGGS: Omit mustard. Mix 2 tablespoons salsa, drained, 1 tablespoon chopped cilantro and 1 teaspoon ground cumin into egg yolk mixture.

ZESTY DEVILED EGGS: Mix 1/2 cup finely shredded cheese (2 ounces) and 2 tablespoons chopped fresh parsley or 1 teaspoon prepared horseradish into egg yolk mixture.

Puffy Omelet

PREP: 15 min; BAKE: 15 min
Makes 2 servings

Using an omelet pan with its slanted curved sides makes it easier to turn out this puffy concoction.

> 4 large eggs, separated
> 1/4 cup water
> 1/4 teaspoon salt
> 1/8 teaspoon pepper
> 1 tablespoon margarine or butter
> Italian Tomato Sauce (page 343), if desired

1. Heat oven to 325°.

2. Beat egg whites, water and salt in medium bowl with electric mixer on high speed until stiff but not dry. Beat egg yolks and pepper on high speed about 3 minutes or until very thick and lemon colored. Fold egg yolks into egg whites.

3. Melt margarine in 10-inch ovenproof skillet over medium heat. As margarine melts, tilt skillet to coat bottom. Pour egg mixture into skillet. *Gently* level surface; reduce heat to low. Cook about 5 minutes or until puffy and light brown on bottom. (*Carefully* lift omelet at edge to judge color.)

4. Bake uncovered 12 to 15 minutes or until knife inserted in center comes out clean.

5. Tilt skillet and slip pancake turner or spatula under omelet to loosen. Fold omelet in half, being careful not to break it. Slip onto warm plate. Serve with Italian Tomato Sauce.

1 SERVING: Calories 195 (Calories from Fat 145); Fat 16g (Saturated 4g); Cholesterol 425mg; Sodium 460mg; Carbohydrate 1g (Dietary Fiber 0g); Protein 12g

Brunch Oven Omelet

PREP: 10 min; BAKE: 25 min
Makes 6 servings

This omelet is great served with Canadian-style bacon or Italian sausage. When doubled, it can serve a crowd up to 12—just use a 13 × 9 × 2-inch baking dish, double the ingredients and increase the baking time to about 35 minutes.

2 tablespoons margarine or butter
9 large eggs
1/2 cup sour cream
1/2 cup milk
1 teaspoon salt
2 tablespoons chopped green onions

1. Heat oven to 325°.

2. Melt margarine in square baking dish, 8 × 8 × 2 inches, in oven. Tilt dish to coat bottom.

3. Beat eggs, sour cream, milk and salt until blended. Stir in onions. Pour into dish.

4. Bake about 25 minutes or until eggs are set in center but still moist.

1 SERVING: Calories 190 (Calories from Fat 135); Fat 15g (Saturated 6g); Cholesterol 335mg; Sodium 510mg; Carbohydrate 3g (Dietary Fiber 0g); Protein 10g

> ### LIGHTER BRUNCH OVEN OMELET
> For 5 grams of fat and 100 calories per serving, substitute 2 1/4 cups fat-free cholesterol-free egg product for the eggs. Use low-fat sour cream and skim milk.

Ham and Egg Bake

PREP: 20 min; BAKE: 50 min
Makes 8 servings

This is a perfect dish to make ahead. Just cover and refrigerate no longer than 24 hours; increase bake time to 55 to 60 minutes.

6 cups frozen (not thawed) hash brown
    potatoes
2 cups diced, fully cooked smoked ham
2 cups shredded Swiss cheese (8 ounces)
1 jar (7 ounces) roasted red bell peppers,
    drained and chopped
1 jar (4 1/2 ounces) sliced mushrooms,
    drained
6 large eggs
1/3 cup milk
1 cup small curd, creamed cottage cheese
1/4 teaspoon pepper

1. Heat oven to 350°. Grease rectangular baking dish, 13 × 9 × 2 inches, with shortening.

2. Sprinkle 3 cups of the potatoes evenly in baking dish. Layer with ham, Swiss cheese, bell peppers and mushrooms. Sprinkle remaining potatoes over mushrooms.

3. Beat eggs, milk, cottage cheese and pepper with fork or wire whisk until blended. Pour egg mixture over potatoes.

4. Bake uncovered 45 to 50 minutes or until light golden brown and set in center.

1 SERVING: Calories 350 (Calories from Fat 155); Fat 17g (Saturated 9g); Cholesterol 210mg; Sodium 920mg; Carbohydrate 24g (Dietary Fiber 2g); Protein 25g

> ### LIGHTER HAM AND EGG BAKE
> For 7 grams of fat and 255 calories per serving, use extra-lean ham and reduced-fat Swiss cheese. Substitute 1 1/2 cups fat-free cholesterol-free egg product for the eggs.

Denver Omelet, Hash Brown Potatoes (page 408)

Vegetable Frittata

PREP: 15 min; COOK: 15 min
Makes 4 servings

Frittatas are Italian omelets that have the ingredients stirred into the eggs before cooking rather than being folded inside after the eggs are set.

> 1 tablespoon vegetable oil
> 1 cup broccoli flowerets
> 1 medium carrot, shredded (1/2 cup)
> 1 medium onion, chopped (1/2 cup)
> 1/4 cup sliced ripe olives
> 4 large eggs
> 1/4 cup milk
> 1 tablespoon chopped fresh parsley
> 1/4 teaspoon salt
> 1/4 teaspoon red pepper sauce
> 1 cup shredded Cheddar cheese (4 ounces)
> 1 tablespoon grated Parmesan cheese

1. Heat oil in 10-inch skillet over medium-high heat. Cook broccoli, carrot, onion and olives in oil about 5 minutes, stirring frequently, until vegetables are crisp-tender.

2. Meanwhile beat eggs, milk, parsley, salt and pepper sauce thoroughly with fork or wire whisk until a uniform yellow color. Pour egg mixture over vegetables. Sprinkle with cheeses; reduce heat to low.

3. Cover and cook about 10 minutes or until set in center. Cut into 4 wedges. Serve immediately.

1 SERVING: Calories 260 (Calories from Fat 180); Fat 20g (Saturated 9g); Cholesterol 245mg; Sodium 490mg; Carbohydrate 7g (Dietary Fiber 2g); Protein 15g

> **TIMESAVING TIP**
> Substitute 2 cups broccoli slaw for the broccoli flowerets and carrot. Pick up chopped onion and sliced ripe olives at the salad bar of your supermarket.

French Omelet

PREP: 10 min
Makes 1 serving

> 2 teaspoons margarine or butter
> 2 large eggs, beaten

1. Heat margarine in 8-inch omelet pan or skillet over medium-high heat just until margarine begins to brown. As margarine melts, tilt pan to coat bottom.

2. *Quickly* pour eggs into pan. While sliding pan back and forth rapidly over heat, *quickly* stir with fork to spread eggs continuously over bottom of pan as they thicken. Let stand over heat a few seconds to lightly brown bottom of omelet. (Do not overcook—omelet will continue to cook after folding.)

3. Tilt pan and run fork under edge of omelet, then jerk pan sharply to loosen eggs from bottom of pan. Fold portion of omelet nearest you just to center. (Allow for portion of omelet to slide up side of pan.) Turn omelet onto warm plate, flipping folded portion of omelet over so far side is on bottom. Tuck sides of omelet under if necessary.

a. Tilt pan and run fork under edge of omelet, then jerk skillet sharply to loosen eggs from bottom of skillet. Fold portion of omelet just to center.

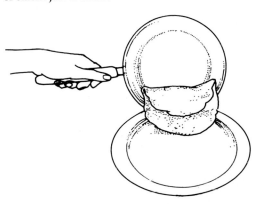

b. Turn omelet onto plate, flipping folded portion of omelet over so it rolls over the bottom.

1 SERVING: Calories 215 (Calories from Fat 160); Fat 18g (Saturated 5g); Cholesterol 425mg; Sodium 220mg; Carbohydrate 1g (Dietary Fiber 0g); Protein 12g

> **LIGHTER FRENCH OMELET**
> For 8 grams of fat and 115 calories per serving, substitute 1/2 cup fat-free cholesterol-free egg product for the eggs.

CHEESE OMELET: Sprinkle omelet with 1/4 cup shredded Cheddar, Monterey Jack or Swiss cheese (1 ounce) or 1/4 cup crumbled blue cheese before folding.

DENVER OMELET: Cook 2 tablespoons chopped fully cooked smoked ham, 1 tablespoon finely chopped bell pepper and 1 tablespoon finely chopped onion in margarine about 2 minutes, stirring frequently, before adding eggs.

Scrambled Eggs

PREP: 5 min; COOK: 10 min
Makes 4 servings

> 6 eggs
> 1/3 cup milk, half-and-half or water
> 1/4 teaspoon salt
> 1/8 teaspoon pepper
> 1 tablespoon margarine or butter

1. Beat eggs, milk, salt and pepper thoroughly with fork or wire whisk until a uniform yellow, or beat slightly for streaks of white and yellow.

2. Heat margarine in 10-inch skillet over medium heat just until hot enough to sizzle a drop of water. Pour egg mixture into skillet.

3. As mixture begins to set at bottom and side, *gently* lift cooked portions with spatula so that thin, uncooked portion can flow to bottom. Avoid constant stirring. Cook 3 to 4 minutes or until eggs are thickened throughout but still moist.

1 SERVING: Calories 145 (Calories from Fat 100); Fat 11g (Saturated 3g); Cholesterol 320mg; Sodium 270mg; Carbohydrate 2g (Dietary Fiber 0g); Protein 10g

MEXICAN SCRAMBLED EGGS: Cook 1/2 pound chorizo sausage links, cut lengthwise in half, then into slices, 1 small green or red bell pepper, chopped (1/2 cup), and 1 medium onion, chopped (1/2 cup), in 10-inch skillet over medium-high heat about 5 minutes, stirring frequently, until sausage is no longer pink; drain. Add sausage mixture to eggs before cooking the last 3 to 4 minutes in step 3. Serve egg mixture wrapped in flour tortillas and topped with salsa, shredded cheese and sour cream if desired.

ORIENTAL SCRAMBLED EGGS: Omit margarine and step 2. Prepare egg mixture as directed in step 1. Mix 2 teaspoons soy sauce, 1 teaspoon lemon juice and 6 ounces uncooked medium shrimp, peeled and deveined; set aside. Heat 1 tablespoon vegetable oil in 10-inch skillet over medium-high heat. Cook 1/2 cup diagonally sliced green onions and 1 cup Chinese pea pods, cut into 1/2-inch diagonal slices, in oil, stirring frequently until vegetables are crisp-tender. Stir in shrimp mixture. Cook 1 to 2 minutes, stirring frequently, just until shrimp are pink and firm. Add egg mixture to skillet; cook as directed in step 3.

SMOKED SALMON-DILL SCRAMBLED EGGS: Beat 1 package (3 ounces) cream cheese, softened, and 2 teaspoons chopped fresh or 1/2 teaspoon dried dill weed with the eggs, using wire whisk, before adding milk, salt and pepper in step 1. Stir in 3 ounces smoked salmon, chopped, and continue as directed in step 2.

Country Egg Scramble

PREP: 15 min; COOK: 10 min
Makes 4 servings

This satisfying dish makes a hearty breakfast or lunch. It's also good for brunch with English Muffins and a fruit salad.

1 pound new red potatoes, cubed (6 to 7)
6 large eggs
1/3 cup milk
1/4 teaspoon salt
1/8 teaspoon pepper
2 tablespoons margarine or butter
1/2 cup sliced green onions (5 medium)
8 slices bacon, crisply cooked and crumbled

1. Heat 1 inch water to boiling in 2-quart saucepan. Add potatoes. Cover and heat to boiling; reduce heat to medium-low. Cover and cook 6 to 8 minutes or until potatoes are tender; drain.

2. Beat eggs, milk, salt and pepper with fork or wire whisk until a uniform yellow color.

3. Melt margarine in 10-inch skillet over medium-high heat. Cook potatoes in margarine 3 to 5 minutes, turning potatoes occasionally, until light brown. Stir in onions. Cook 1 minute, stirring constantly.

4. Pour egg mixture into skillet. As mixture begins to set at bottom and side, *gently* lift cooked portions with spatula so that thin, uncooked portion can flow to bottom. Avoid constant stirring. Cook 3 to 4 minutes or until eggs are thickened throughout but still moist. Sprinkle with bacon.

1 SERVING: Calories 340 (Calories from Fat 180); Fat 20g (Saturated 6g); Cholesterol 330mg; Sodium 520mg; Carbohydrate 26g (Dietary Fiber 2g); Protein 16g

---

TIMESAVING TIP
Use 3 cups leftover cooked cubed potatoes and omit step 1. Substitute 1/3 cup canned, crumbled, cooked bacon or imitation bacon bits for the 8 slices bacon.

Eggs with Kielbasa

PREP: 10 min; COOK: 10 min
Makes 4 servings

Kielbasa is a smoked Polish sausage usually made from pork, although beef can be added. It comes in a horseshoe-shaped ring, about 1 1/2 inches in diameter.

2 teaspoons vegetable oil
1/2 pound kielbasa, cut lengthwise in half,
   then sliced
1 large onion, sliced
1 medium green bell pepper, thinly sliced
8 large eggs
1/2 cup milk
1/4 teaspoon salt
1/8 to 1/4 teaspoon pepper

1. Heat oil in 10-inch skillet over medium heat. Cook kielbasa, onion and bell pepper in oil about 5 minutes, stirring occasionally, until vegetables are tender.

2. Meanwhile, beat eggs, milk, salt and pepper thoroughly with fork or wire whisk until a uniform yellow, or beat slightly for streaks of white and yellow.

3. Pour egg mixture into skillet. As mixture begins to set at bottom and side, *gently* lift cooked portions with spatula so that thin, uncooked portion can flow to bottom. Avoid constant stirring. Cook 3 to 4 minutes or until eggs are thickened throughout but still moist.

1 SERVING: Calories 375 (Calories from Fat 260); Fat 29g (Saturated 10g); Cholesterol 460mg; Sodium 850mg; Carbohydrate 8g (Dietary Fiber 1g); Protein 21g

---

LIGHTER EGGS WITH KIELBASA
For 11 grams of fat and 205 calories per serving, use turkey kielbasa. Substitute 2 cups fat-free cholesterol-free egg product for the eggs and use skim milk.

About Cheese

New cheeses are introduced frequently, so exploring the world of domestic and imported cheeses can be a true adventure in taste and experimentation. The variety of flavors, textures and shapes can add excitement to both eating and cooking.

Cheeses vary in fat content, depending on the amount of milk fat used to make a particular type. Reduced-fat and low-fat cheeses are now seen more frequently and are becoming more similar in taste to traditional higher-fat cheeses. They do not melt as readily as the higher-fat cheeses, however, and the texture and flavor can be somewhat different.

There are four categories of identification for all cheeses: natural cheese, pasteurized process cheese, cheese food and pasteurized cheese spread.

Kinds of Cheese

- **Natural cheeses** are made from the milk (whole, skim and sometimes raw) or cream of cows, sheep or goats that has been solidified by the process of curdling and the liquid (whey) removed. There are enough differences in the process of each type of cheese to give distinctive characteristics such as holes in Swiss or the texture differences between mild and extra-sharp Cheddar. They may or may not be aged or ripened. Cheeses not aged (such as cottage cheese or cream cheese) are referred to as fresh or unripened cheeses.

  It is difficult to categorize natural cheeses into satisfactory groups due to the many types of cheeses and cheese-making methods, the kinds of milk from which they are made, as well as the way they are aged or ripened and their very mild to very sharp flavors. One cheese can easily fit into more than one category. The Varieties of Natural Cheese chart (page 175) is a guide to many favorite cheeses and their uses; the cheeses are grouped according to hardness.

- **Pasteurized process cheese** is a blend of one or more varieties of natural cheese that are ground, blended and heated. The process stops the aging or ripening, resulting in unchanging flavor and better keeping quality. The very popular American cheese is a good example of pasteurized process cheese.

- **Cheese food** is made of one or more varieties of natural cheese blended without the aid of heat (cold pack) or with heat (pasteurized process cheese). Dairy products such as cream, milk, skim milk or whey are added, and the food has a higher percentage of moisture than natural or pasteurized process cheese. Cheese food is usually sold in tubs or jars and is often flavored.

- **Pasteurized cheese spread** is similar to pasteurized process cheese except it is easily spreadable at room temperature. This cheese is higher in moisture and lower in fat than cheese food. Cheeses in aerosol cans are good examples of pasteurized cheese spread.

Handling and Storing of Cheese

- Serve natural cheeses, except fresh cheeses such as cottage cheese, at room temperature to bring out the fullest flavor when serving cheese as appetizers or snacks. Remove cheese from refrigerator and let stand covered about one hour before serving. You can also microwave firm cheese uncovered on Medium-low (30%) about 30 seconds for 8 ounces of cheese, rotating a half turn after half the time. Let stand a few minutes before serving. For cooking, cheeses can be used right from the refrigerator.

- Wrap all cheeses tightly to minimize moisture loss and retain texture, then store in the refrigerator. Ripened cheeses will continue to age during storage. Mold that forms on natural cheese is harmless but looks unappetizing. The mold may be removed by cutting off approximately one inch from each affected area; use the remaining cheese within one week. Changing the wrap each time cheese is used will reduce mold growth.

- Fresh, unripened cheeses, such as cottage cheese and cream cheese, are more perishable because they have a higher water content than hard cheeses. These cheeses do not improve with age and should be used within two weeks of purchase.

- Refrigerated cheese is firmer and therefore easier to shred than cheese at room temperature. Use a food processor to quickly shred or chop cheese.

- Very soft cheese shreds more easily if a shredder with large holes is used or if it is first placed in the freezer for fifteen minutes. Or it can be finely chopped instead of shredded.

- Mold-ripened or blue-veined cheeses can be cut easily and cleanly into slices at room temperature with dental floss or heavy thread. Crumbling or chopping works best when cheese is at refrigerator temperature. It won't stick at all if it's frozen.

Cooking with Cheese

- Four ounces of shredded, crumbled or grated cheese equals 1 cup.
- Keep cooking temperature low and the cooking time short. High heat and overcooking cause cheese to become stringy and tough.
- When adding cheese to other ingredients, cut it into small pieces so it melts evenly and quickly.
- Cheeses with similar flavors and textures can be used interchangeably.
- Cheese microwaves well, but lower power settings work best for the most even heating. Soften cream cheese by removing foil wrapper and microwaving uncovered on Medium (50%) until softened, a 3-ounce package for 30 to 45 seconds and an 8-ounce package for 60 to 90 seconds.

Quiche Lorraine

PREP: 25 min; BAKE: 45 min; STAND: 10 min
Makes 6 servings

(photograph on page 161)

> Pastry for 9-Inch One-Crust Pie (page 93)
> 8 slices bacon, crisply cooked and crumbled
> 1 cup shredded natural Swiss cheese
>   (4 ounces)
> 1/3 cup finely chopped onion
> 4 large eggs
> 2 cups whipping (heavy) cream
> 1/4 teaspoon salt
> 1/4 teaspoon pepper
> 1/8 teaspoon ground red pepper (cayenne)

1. Heat oven to 425°.

2. Prepare pastry. Ease into quiche dish, 9 × 1 1/2 inches, or pie plate, 9 × 1 1/4 inches.

3. Sprinkle bacon, cheese and onion in pastry-lined quiche dish. Beat eggs slightly; beat in remaining ingredients. Pour into quiche dish. Bake 15 minutes.

4. Reduce oven temperature to 300°. Bake about 30 minutes longer or until knife inserted in center comes out clean. Let stand 10 minutes before cutting.

1 SERVING: Calories 600 (Calories from Fat 460); Fat 51g (Saturated 25g); Cholesterol 255mg; Sodium 520mg; Carbohydrate 20g (Dietary Fiber 1g); Protein 16g

MUSHROOM QUICHE: Add 1 can (4 ounces) mushroom stems and pieces, drained, and 1 jar (2 ounces) diced pimientos, well drained, with the bacon.

SEAFOOD QUICHE: Substitute 1 cup chopped cooked crabmeat, shrimp, seafood sticks or salmon for the bacon and green onion for the onion. (Pat crabmeat dry.) Increase salt to 1/2 teaspoon.

Cheese Fondue Bake

PREP: 20 min; BAKE: 50 min
Makes 8 servings

This recipe can easily be prepared the night before, then covered, refrigerated and baked the next morning before serving. Increase the bake time to 55 to 60 minutes.

> 1/4 cup margarine or butter, softened
> 2 tablespoons Dijon mustard
> 10 to 12 slices French bread, 1-inch thick
> 8 large eggs
> 1 cup milk
> 1/4 teaspoon salt
> 1/8 teaspoon pepper
> Dash of ground nutmeg
> 1/3 cup dry white wine (or nonalcoholic) or
>   chicken broth
> 2 cups shredded Swiss or Gruyère cheese
>   (8 ounces)

1. Heat oven to 350°. Grease rectangular baking dish, 13 × 9 × 2 inches, with shortening.

2. Mix margarine and mustard. Spread evenly on one side of each slice bread. Cut bread into enough cubes to measure 8 cups.

3. Beat eggs, milk, salt, pepper and nutmeg in large bowl with wire whisk. Stir in wine and cheese. Stir in bread cubes. Let stand 5 minutes.

4. Spoon bread mixture evenly into baking dish. Bake uncovered 45 to 50 minutes or until golden brown and set in center.

1 SERVING: Calories 325 (Calories from Fat 180); Fat 20g (Saturated 8g); Cholesterol 240mg; Sodium 520mg; Carbohydrate 19g (Dietary Fiber 1g); Protein 18g

---

LIGHTER CHEESE FONDUE BAKE

For 8 grams of fat and 215 calories per serving, decrease margarine to 2 tablespoons. Substitute 2 cups fat-free cholesterol-free egg product for the eggs. Use skim milk and reduced-fat cheese.

Cheese Strata

PREP: 20 min; **CHILL:** 2 hr; **BAKE:** 1 1/4 hr;
STAND: 10 min
Makes 6 servings

1/3 cup margarine or butter, softened
1/2 teaspoon ground mustard (dry)
1 clove garlic, crushed
10 slices white bread, crusts removed
2 cups shredded sharp Cheddar cheese
    (8 ounces)
2 tablespoons chopped fresh parsley
2 tablespoons chopped onion
1 teaspoon salt
1/2 teaspoon Worcestershire sauce
1/8 teaspoon pepper
Dash of ground red pepper (cayenne)
4 eggs
2 1/2 cups milk

1. Mix margarine, mustard and garlic. Spread evenly over each slice bread. Cut each slice into thirds. Line bottom and sides of ungreased square baking dish, 8 × 8 × 2 inches, with half of the bread slices, buttered sides down, cutting to fit.

2. Mix cheese, parsley, onion, salt, Worcestershire sauce, pepper and red pepper. Spread evenly over bread slices in dish. Top with remaining bread slices, buttered sides up.

3. Beat eggs in medium bowl. Stir in milk. Pour over bread. Cover and refrigerate at least 2 hours but no longer than 24 hours.

4. Heat oven to 325°.

5. Bake uncovered about 1 1/4 hours or until knife inserted in center comes out clean. Let stand 10 minutes before cutting.

1 SERVING: Calories 445 (Calories from Fat 260); Fat 29g (Saturated 13g); Cholesterol 190mg; Sodium 1030mg; Carbohydrate 27g (Dietary Fiber 1g); Protein 20g

---

TIMESAVING TIP
Use finely chopped garlic from a jar, and don't remove the crusts from the bread. Purchase the cheese already shredded in an 8-ounce package.

Chilies Rellenos Bake

PREP: 10 min; **BAKE:** 45 min
Makes 8 servings

This simplified version of the Mexican dish chilies rellenos is just as tasty even without the extra work of stuffing and frying whole chilies.

8 large eggs
1 cup sour cream
1/4 teaspoon salt
2 drops red pepper sauce
2 cups shredded Monterey Jack cheese
    (8 ounces)
2 cups shredded Cheddar cheese (8 ounces)
2 cans (4 ounces each) chopped green
    chilies, undrained
Fresh Cilantro Salsa (below)
Black Bean and Corn Salsa (below)

1. Heat oven to 350°. Grease rectangular baking dish, 13 × 9 × 2 inches, with shortening.

2. Beat eggs, sour cream, salt and pepper sauce in large bowl with wire whisk. Stir in cheeses and chilies. Pour into baking dish.

3. Bake uncovered about 45 minutes or until golden brown and set in center.

4. While casserole is baking, prepare Fresh Cilantro Salsa and Black Bean and Corn Salsa. Serve salsas with casserole.

Fresh Cilantro Salsa

1 cup salsa
2 tablespoons chopped fresh cilantro

Mix salsa and cilantro.

Black Bean and Corn Salsa

1 cup salsa
1/2 cup canned black beans, rinsed and
    drained
1/2 cup frozen (thawed) or canned (drained)
    corn

Mix all ingredients.

1 SERVING: Calories 395 (Calories from Fat 260); Fat 29g (Saturated 17g); Cholesterol 290mg; Sodium 1180mg; Carbohydrate 13g (Dietary Fiber 3g); Protein 23g

---

LIGHTER CHILIES RELLENOS BAKE
For 8 grams of fat and 235 calories per serving, substitute 2 cups fat-free cholesterol-free egg product for the eggs. Use reduced-fat sour cream and Cheddar cheese. Substitute 2 cups cooked rice for the Monterey Jack cheese.

Jarlsberg
Gruyére
Swiss
Gouda
Cheddar
Parmesan
Romano
Asiago
Port du Salut
Muenster
String Mozzarella
Feta
Curds
Monterey Jack
Brick
Brie
Bel Paese
Farmer
Camembert
Colby
Provolone
Havarti
Boursin
Montrachet
Stilton
Gorgonzola
Fontina
Roquefort
Blue
Cottage
Marscapone
Ricotta
Cream

Varieties of Natural Cheese

Texture	Flavor	Use
Very Hard (grating)		
Asiago	pungent, sharp	cooking, seasoning
Parmesan	piquant, sharp	cooking, pasta, salad, seasoning
Romano	piquant, sharp	cooking, pasta, seasoning
Hard		
Cheddar	mild to very sharp	cooking, dessert, with fruit
Cheshire	rich, robust	cooking, with fruit
Edam, Gouda	milky, nutty	appetizer, dessert
Gjetost	caramel, sweet	sandwich, snack
Gruyère	nutty, slightly sharp	cooking, dessert
Jarlsberg	buttery, slightly sharp	appetizer, sandwich, cooking
Nökkelost	spicy, creamy	appetizer, sandwich, cooking
Swiss	mild, nutty, sweet	appetizer, cooking, dessert, sandwich
Semisoft		
Blue	tangy, sharp, robust	appetizer, dessert, salad
Brick	mild to sharp	appetizer, sandwich
Colby	mild	cooking, sandwich
Curds	mild, chewy	appetizer, snack
Feta	salty, sharp	cooking, salad
Fontina	buttery	appetizer, cooking
Gorgonzola	piquant, salty	dessert, salad
Havarti	mild, mellow	appetizer, cooking
Monterey Jack	creamy, mild	appetizer, cooking, sandwich
Mozzarella, string	mild, chewy	cooking, pizza, appetizer
Muenster	mild to sharp	appetizer, dessert, sandwich
Port du Salut	mild to robust	appetizer, dessert, sandwich
Provolone	mild to sharp, smoky	cooking, sandwich
Reblochon	mild	appetizer, dessert
Roquefort	salty, sharp	appetizer, dessert, salad
Stilton	piquant, rich	dessert, salad, snack
Taleggio	creamy, mild to strong	appetizer, cooking
Soft		
Bel Paese	creamy, mild	cooking, dessert
Boursin	sharp	appetizer
Brie	mild to pungent	appetizer, dessert
Bucheron	sharp	cooking, dessert
Camembert	mild to pungent	appetizer, dessert, sandwich
Cottage, dry or creamed	mild	cooking, salad
Cream	very mild	appetizer, dessert, salad
Farmer	mild	cooking
Liederkranz	pungent	appetizer, dessert
Limburger	very pungent	appetizer, snack
Mascarpone	very mild, sweet	dessert
Montrachet	creamy, mild	appetizer, cooking
Neufchâtel	mild	appetizer, dessert, salad, spread
Ricotta	mild	cooking, dessert, pasta

Spinach Phyllo Pie

Classic Cheese Soufflé

PREP: 25 min; BAKE: 1 hr
Makes 4 servings

Serve this fluffy soufflé with asparagus spears, sliced ham, whole-grain bread and fresh fruit for a delicious, meal.

1/4 cup margarine or butter
1/4 cup all-purpose flour
1/2 teaspoon salt
1/4 teaspoon ground mustard (dry)
Dash of ground red pepper (cayenne)
1 cup milk
1 cup shredded Cheddar cheese (4 ounces)
3 large eggs, separated
1/4 teaspoon cream of tartar

1. Heat oven to 350°. Butter 1-quart soufflé dish or casserole. Make a 4-inch band of triple-thickness aluminum foil 2 inches longer than circumference of dish. Butter one side of foil. Secure foil band, buttered side in, around top edge of dish.

2. Melt margarine in 2-quart saucepan over medium heat. Stir in flour, salt, mustard and red pepper. Cook over medium heat, stirring constantly, until smooth and bubbly; remove from heat. Stir in milk. Heat to boiling, stirring constantly. Boil and stir 1 minute. Stir in cheese until melted; remove from heat.

3. Beat egg whites and cream of tartar in medium bowl with electric mixer on high speed until stiff but not dry. Beat egg yolks on high speed about 3 minutes or until very thick and lemon colored; stir into cheese mixture. Stir about one-fourth of the egg whites into cheese mixture. Fold cheese mixture into remaining egg whites. *Carefully* pour into soufflé dish.

4. Bake 50 to 60 minutes or until knife inserted halfway between center and edge comes out clean. *Carefully* remove foil band and *quickly* divide soufflé into sections with 2 forks. Serve immediately.

1 SERVING: Calories 335 (Calories from Fat 235); Fat 26g (Saturated 10g); Cholesterol 195mg; Sodium 650mg; Carbohydrate 10g (Dietary Fiber 0g); Protein 15g

CLASSIC SHRIMP SOUFFLÉ: Omit mustard, red pepper and cheese. Add 1 can (4 to 4 1/2 ounces) shrimp, rinsed and drained, and 1 tablespoon chopped fresh or 1 teaspoon dried tarragon to sauce before adding the beaten egg yolks.

Spinach Phyllo Pie

PREP: 30 min; BAKE; 45 min
Makes 6 servings

For best results, it is important to have phyllo completely thawed and to work quickly with each layer.

1 tablespoon olive or vegetable oil
1 medium onion, chopped (1/2 cup)
1 medium red bell pepper, chopped (1 cup)
1 clove garlic, finely chopped
2 packages (9 ounces each) frozen chopped
    spinach, thawed and squeezed to drain
1 package (8 ounces) cream cheese, softened
1/2 cup crumbled feta or Gorgonzola cheese
    (2 ounces)
2 large eggs
1 tablespoon chopped fresh or 1 teaspoon
    dried dill weed
1/2 teaspoon salt
1/4 teaspoon pepper
8 sheets frozen phyllo (18 × 14 inches),
    thawed
2 tablespoons *stick* margarine or butter,
    melted*

1. Heat oven to 375°. Grease bottom and side of pie plate, 9 × 1 1/4 inches, with margarine.

2. Heat oil in 10-inch skillet over medium-high heat. Cook onion, bell pepper and garlic in oil, stirring frequently, until vegetables are crisp-tender; remove from heat.

3. Stir in spinach, cream cheese, feta cheese, eggs, dill weed, salt and pepper.

4. Cut stack of phyllo sheets into 12-inch square; discard extra phyllo. Cover with waxed paper, then with damp towel to prevent them from drying out. Brush each of 4 phyllo squares with margarine and layer in pie plate. *Gently* press into pie plate, allowing corners to drape over edge.

5. Spread spinach mixture evenly over phyllo. Fold ends of phyllo up and over filling so corners overlap on top. Brush with margarine and layer remaining 4 phyllo sheets over pie, allowing corners to drape over edge.

6. *Gently* tuck phyllo draping over top inside edge of pie plate. Cut through top phyllo layers into 6 wedges, using sharp knife or scissors.

7. Bake 35 to 45 minutes or until crust is golden brown and filling is hot. Let stand 10 minutes before serving.

We do not recommend using vegetable oil spreads (see page 13).

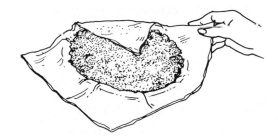

a. Fold ends of phyllo up and over filling so corners overlap on top. Brush with margarine and layer remaining 4 phyllo sheets over pie, allowing corners to drape over edge.

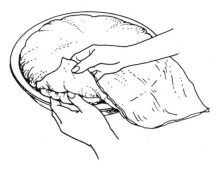

b. *Carefully* lift bottom layers of phyllo and tuck top corners between bottom layers and plate to seal.

1 SERVING: Calories 320 (Calories from Fat 190); Fat 21g (Saturated 11g); Cholesterol 120mg; Sodium 610mg; Carbohydrate 25g (Dietary Fiber 2g); Protein 10g

---

LIGHTER SPINACH PHYLLO PIE

For 7 grams of fat and 195 calories per serving, decrease oil to 1 teaspoon and use a nonstick skillet. Use reduced-fat cream cheese (Neufchatel). Substitute 1/2 cup fat-free cholesterol-free egg product for the 2 eggs. Omit the margarine and spray phyllo sheets with butter-flavored nonstick cooking spray.

Triple Cheese Pesto Pita Pizzas

Cheese Enchiladas

PREP: 1 hr; BAKE: 15 min
Makes 6 servings

2 tablespoons vegetable oil
1 large onion, chopped (1 cup)
2 large cloves garlic, crushed
1 tablespoon chili powder
1 can (28 ounces) whole tomatoes,
   undrained
1 teaspoon ground cumin
1 teaspoon dried oregano leaves
1/2 teaspoon salt
1/8 teaspoon pepper
1 1/2 cups shredded Cheddar cheese
   (6 ounces)
1 1/2 cups shredded Monterey Jack cheese
   (6 ounces)
1/4 cup vegetable oil
12 corn or flour tortillas (7 inches in
   diameter)
1 1/2 cups shredded lettuce, if desired
1/4 cup sliced ripe olives, if desired
Sour cream, if desired

1. Heat 2 tablespoons oil in Dutch oven over medium heat. Cook onion, garlic and chili powder in oil about 5 minutes, stirring occasionally, until onion is tender.

2. Stir in tomatoes, cumin, oregano, salt and pepper, breaking up tomatoes. Heat to boiling; reduce heat to low. Simmer uncovered about 30 minutes or until thickened.

3. Heat oven to 350°.

4. Mix cheeses. Heat 1/4 cup oil in 8-inch skillet until hot. Dip each tortilla lightly into hot oil to soften; drain. Dip each tortilla into sauce to coat both sides. Spoon about 2 tablespoons cheese mixture onto each tortilla; roll tortilla around cheese. Place tortillas, seam sides down, in ungreased rectangular baking dish, 13 × 9 × 2 inches. Pour remaining sauce over top. Sprinkle with remaining cheese mixture.

5. Bake uncovered about 15 minutes or until cheese is melted and enchiladas are hot. Top with lettuce and olives. Serve with sour cream.

1 SERVING: Calories 475 (Calories from Fat 305); Fat 34g (Saturated 14g); Cholesterol 55mg; Sodium 880mg; Carbohydrate 28g (Dietary Fiber 4g); Protein 18g

TURKEY ENCHILADAS: Substitute 1 1/2 cups finely chopped cooked turkey for the Cheddar cheese.

> **TIMESAVING TIP**
> Omit 2 tablespoons oil, the onion, garlic, chili powder, tomatoes, cumin, oregano, salt, pepper and 1/4 cup oil. Omit steps 1 and 2. Do not dip tortillas into hot oil or sauce. Fill tortillas with cheeses, roll and place in dish as directed in step 4. Pour 3 1/2 cups thick-and-chunky salsa over top. Bake about 25 minutes or until hot.

Triple Cheese Pesto Pita Pizzas

PREP: 15 min; BAKE: 12 min
Makes 6 servings

Shortcut preparation by using prepared pesto and mixing it with the cream cheese and milk. The final color will be a bit lighter, but it will have the same great taste. (photograph on page 176)

> 1 package (8 ounces) cream cheese, softened
> 2 tablespoons milk
> 6 whole wheat or white pita breads (6 inches in diameter)
> 6 tablespoons Pesto (page 345)
> 1 can (2 1/4 ounces) sliced ripe olives, drained
> 1 cup shredded mozzarella cheese (4 ounces)
> 2 tablespoons grated Parmesan cheese
> 2 tablespoons chopped fresh parsley

1. Heat oven to 425°.

2. Mix cream cheese and milk until smooth.

3. Place pita breads on ungreased large cookie sheet. Spread cream cheese mixture on pita breads to within 1/4 inch of edge. *Carefully* spread pesto over cream cheese. Top with olives. Sprinkle with cheeses and parsley.

4. Bake 7 to 12 minutes or until thoroughly heated and cheese is melted.

1 SERVING: Calories 410 (Calories from Fat 215); Fat 24g (Saturated 10g); Cholesterol 40mg; Sodium 800mg; Carbohydrate 36g (Dietary Fiber 5g); Protein 17g

---

LIGHTER TRIPLE CHEESE PESTO PITA PIZZAS

For 24 grams of fat and 410 calories per serving, substitute reduced-fat cream cheese (Neufchâtel) for the regular cream cheese and use part-skim mozzarella cheese.

Quesadillas

PREP: 10 min; BAKE: 5 min
Makes 6 servings

Quesadillas are perhaps served more often as an appetizer than as a main dish. For heartier fare, you can add shredded cooked beef or chicken or refried beans to the filling. (photograph on page 165)

> 2 cups shredded Colby or Cheddar cheese (8 ounces)
> 6 flour tortillas (8 to 10 inches in diameter)
> 1 small tomato, chopped (1/2 cup)
> 1/4 cup chopped green onions (3 medium)
> 2 tablespoons canned, chopped green chilies
> Chopped fresh cilantro or parsley

1. Heat oven to 350°.

2. Sprinkle 1/3 cup of the cheese evenly over half of each tortilla. Top cheese with remaining ingredients. Fold tortilla over filling. Place on ungreased cookie sheet.

3. Bake about 5 minutes or just until cheese is melted. Serve quesadillas whole, or cut each into wedges or strips, beginning cuts from center of folded side.

1 SERVING: Calories 290 (Calories from Fat 145); Fat 16g (Saturated 8g); Cholesterol 40mg; Sodium 470mg; Carbohydrate 25g (Dietary Fiber 1g); Protein 13g

---

LIGHTER QUESADILLAS

For / grams of fat and 220 calories per serving, use reduced-fat cheese and tortillas.

Cheese Pizza

PREP: 45 min; BAKE: 20 min
Makes 2 pizzas, 8 slices each

One pizza too many? Wrap the partially baked extra pizza, label and freeze no longer than 2 months. Heat oven to 375°. Bake a thin-crust pizza on a greased cookie sheet uncovered about 25 minutes or a thick-crust pizza about 55 minutes.

> Pizza Crust (below)
> 1 can (8 ounces) pizza sauce
> 1 can (4 ounces) sliced mushrooms or
>   chopped green chilies, drained
> 3 cups shredded mozzarella, Cheddar or
>   Monterey Jack cheese (12 ounces)
> 1/4 cup grated Parmesan or Romano cheese

1. Prepare Pizza Crust.

2. Spread pizza sauce over partially baked crusts. Sprinkle with mushrooms and cheeses.

3. Bake thin-crust pizzas at 425° about 10 minutes, or thick-crust pizzas at 375° about 20 minutes, until cheese is melted and pizzas are bubbly.

Pizza Crust

> 1 package regular or quick active dry yeast
> 1 cup warm water (105° to 115°)
> 2 1/2 cups all-purpose flour*
> 2 tablespoons olive or vegetable oil
> 1/2 teaspoon salt
> Olive or vegetable oil
> Cornmeal

Dissolve yeast in warm water in medium bowl. Stir in flour, 2 tablespoons oil and the salt. Beat vigorously 20 strokes. Cover and let rest 20 minutes. Follow directions below for thin or thick crusts.

FOR THIN CRUSTS: Move oven rack to lowest position. Heat oven to 425°. Grease 2 cookie sheets or 12-inch pizza pans with oil. Sprinkle with cornmeal. Divide dough in half; pat each half into 11-inch circle on cookie sheet with floured fingers. Prick dough thoroughly with fork. Bake about 10 minutes or until crust just begins to brown.

FOR THICK CRUSTS: Move oven rack to lowest position. Heat oven to 375°. Grease 2 square pans, $8 \times 8 \times 2$ inches, with oil. Sprinkle with cornmeal. Divide dough in half; pat each half onto bottom of pan. Cover and let rise in warm place 30 to 45 minutes or until almost double. Bake 20 to 22 minutes or until crust just begins to brown.

*If using self-rising flour, omit salt. One cup whole wheat flour can be substituted for 1 cup of the all-purpose flour if desired.

1 SLICE: Calories 190 (Calories from Fat 80); Fat 9g (Saturated 4g); Cholesterol 25mg; Sodium 260mg; Carbohydrate 17g (Dietary Fiber 2g); Protein 12g

MEAT PIZZA: Cook 1 pound ground beef, bulk Italian sausage or ground turkey, 1 teaspoon Italian seasoning and 2 cloves garlic, finely chopped, in 10-inch skillet over medium heat, stirring occasionally, until beef is brown; drain. Sprinkle beef mixture over pizza sauce. Decrease mozzarella cheese to 2 cups.

Chunky Vegetable Pizza with Cornmeal Crust

PREP: 25 min; BAKE: 20 min
Makes 1 pizza, 6 slices

> Cornmeal Crust (below)
> 2 tablespoons olive or vegetable oil
> 1 clove garlic, finely chopped
> 1 teaspoon dried basil leaves
> 1 package (16 ounces) frozen broccoli, red
>   peppers, onions and mushrooms, thawed
> 2 cups shredded mozzarella cheese
>   (8 ounces)

1. Heat oven to 425°. Prepare Cornmeal Crust.

2. Mix oil, garlic and basil. Sprinkle vegetables over partially baked crust. Sprinkle with cheese. Drizzle with oil mixture.

3. Bake 15 to 20 minutes or until cheese is melted and vegetables are hot.

Cornmeal Crust

> 2 1/3 cups water
> 1 cup yellow cornmeal
> 1 tablespoon margarine or butter
> 1/4 teaspoon salt
> 1/8 teaspoon ground red pepper (cayenne)

Heat oven to 425°. Grease 12-inch pizza pan with shortening. Heat water to boiling in 2-quart saucepan. Stir in remaining ingredients with wire whisk until mixture is smooth and thickens. Spoon onto pizza pan and spread evenly, mounding edge slightly. Bake 5 to 7 minutes or until set and light brown.

1 SLICE: Calories 255 (Calories from Fat 115); Fat 13g (Saturated 5g); Cholesterol 20mg; Sodium 340mg; Carbohydrate 24g (Dietary Fiber 3g); Protein 14g

> **TIMESAVING TIP**
> Use a purchased baked pizza crust and omit the Cornmeal Crust and step 1. Heat oven to 425°.

Fish & Shellfish

About Fish

Fish gets more popular every day, which isn't the least bit surprising. It's healthy, flavorful and available just about everywhere. All the basics for cooking fish are here, plus tempting recipe ideas. With so much choice, we think fish will soon be more popular at your house, too!

Selecting Fish

Fresh

- Eyes should be bright, clear and bulging.
- Gills should be reddish-pink.
- Scales should be bright with a sheen.
- Flesh should be firm and elastic; it will spring back when touched.
- There should be no odor.

Frozen

- Package should be tightly wrapped and frozen solid with little or no airspace between packaging and fish.
- There should be no discoloration. If the fish is discolored this could indicate freezer burn.
- There should be no odor.

How Much Fish To Buy

The amount of fish you buy depends on the form you select and the appetites of those you are serving. Below you'll find some general guidelines to use when purchasing different forms of fish.

- **Whole fish** is sold as it comes from the water. Allow about 1 pound per serving.

- **Drawn fish** is whole with only internal organs removed. Allow about 3/4 pound per serving.

- **Pan-dressed fish** is scaled with internal organs removed. The head, tail and fins have usually been removed. Allow about 1/2 pound per serving.

- **Fish steaks** are the cross-section slices of a large pan-dressed fish. Steaks are 3/4 to 1 1/2 inches thick. Allow 1/4 to 1/3 pound per serving.

- **Fish fillets** are the sides of the fish, cut lengthwise from the fish. They can be purchased with or without skin. You may also find butterfly fillets, which are two fillets held together by the uncut flesh and skin of the belly. Fillets are usually boneless; however, small bones called pins may be present. Allow 1/4 to 1/3 pound per serving.

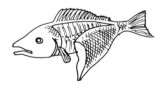

Determining Fish Doneness

Fish is delicate and tender, so avoid overcooking it, which makes it dry and tough. Cook until fish flakes easily with a fork. You can test this by inserting a fork at an angle into the thickest part of the fish and twisting gently. For food safety reasons we recommend cooking fish to an internal temperature of 160°.

To test fish for doneness, place a fork in the thickest part of the fish. Gently twist the fork. The fish will flake easily when done.

Preceding page: Mandarin Almond Shrimp (page 194)

How Fish is Classified by Fat Content

Fish is naturally rich in high-quality protein, yet low in fat, saturated fat, cholesterol and calories. Percentages of fat in individual fish vary with the season, stage of maturity, locale, species and diet. One type of fish can be substituted for another of the same classification when preparing recipes.

Lean Fish: Less than 2.5% fat. Mild flavored with tender, white or pale flesh. Best steamed, poached, microwaved or fried.

Medium-Fat Fish: Between 2.5 and 5% fat. Suitable for all cooking methods.

Fatty Fish: Over 5% fat. Firmer texture, more pronounced flavor and deeper color. Best broiled, grilled, poached, baked or microwaved.

Classification of Fish

Lean Fish	Medium-Fat Fish	Fatty Fish
Bass, sea striped	Anchovy	Amberjack
Burbot (freshwater cod)	Bluefish	Butterfish
Cod	Buffalofish	Carp
Cusk	Catfish	Eel
Flounder	Croaker	Herring, Sardine
Grouper	Mullet	Mackerel, Atlantic
Haddock	Porgy	Opah
Halibut	Redfish	Pacific
Lingcod	Salmon, pink chum	Spanish
Mackerel, king	Shark	Pompano
Mahimahi (dolphinfish)	Sturgeon	Sablefish
Monkfish	Swordfish	Salmon, Atlantic chinook
Orange roughy	Trout, rainbow sea	coho, King sockeye
Perch, ocean	Turbot	Sardines
Pike, northern	Whitefish	Shad
Pollock		Trout, lake
Red snapper		Tuna, albacore bluefin
Rockfish		
Scrod		
Smelt		
Sole		
Tilefish		
Tuna, skipjack yellowfin		
Whiting		

Microwaving Fish

1. Arrange fish fillets or steaks with thickest parts to outside edge in shallow microwavable dish, large enough to hold fish in a single layer. (Fold thin ends of fillets under for more even thickness.)
2. Cover with plastic wrap, folding back edge about 2 inches to vent.
3. Microwave on High (100%) as directed below or until fish flakes easily with fork.

Timetable for Microwaving Fish

Type	Approximate Weight	Microwave Time	Stand Time
Fillets (1/2 to 3/4 inch thick)	1 pound	5 to 7 minutes, rotating dish 1/2 turn after 3 minutes	2 minutes
	1 1/2 pounds	7 to 9 minutes, rotating dish 1/2 turn after 4 minutes	3 minutes
Steaks (1 inch thick)	1 pound	5 to 7 minutes, rotating dish 1/2 turn after 3 minutes	3 minutes
	2 pounds	8 to 10 minutes, rotating dish 1/2 turn after 4 minutes	3 minutes

Broiled Fish Steaks

PREP: 5 min; BROIL: 15 min
Makes 4 servings

A perfectly cooked piece of fish can be enjoyed with just a squeeze of fresh lemon or with your favorite sauces, such as tartar sauce, cocktail sauce or salsa.

> 4 small salmon or other medium-fat or fatty
>   fish steaks, about 3/4 inch thick
>   (1 1/2 pounds)
> Salt
> Pepper
> 2 tablespoons margarine or butter, melted

1. Set oven control to Broil.

2. Sprinkle both sides of fish steaks with salt and pepper. Brush with half of the margarine.

3. Place fish on rack in broiler pan. Broil fish with tops about 4 inches from heat 5 minutes. Brush with margarine. *Carefully* turn fish and brush with margarine. Broil 4 to 6 minutes longer or until fish flakes easily with fork.

1 SERVING: Calories 200 (Calories from Fat 70); Fat 8g (Saturated 2g); Cholesterol 90mg; Sodium 470mg; Carbohydrate 0g (Dietary Fiber 0g); Protein 32g

BROILED FISH FILLETS: Substitute 1 pound fish fillets, cut into 4 serving pieces, for the fish steaks. Broil with tops about 4 inches from heat 5 to 6 minutes or until fish flakes easily with fork (do not turn).

Panfried Fish

PREP: 10 min; COOK: 10 min
Makes 6 servings

> 1 1/2 pounds perch, sole or other lean fish
>   fillets, about 3/4 inch thick, or pan-
>   dressed fish
> 1/2 teaspoon salt
> 1/8 teaspoon pepper
> 1 large egg
> 1 tablespoon water
> 1/2 cup all-purpose flour, cornmeal or grated
>   Parmesan cheese
> Vegetable oil or shortening

1. Heat oil (1/8 inch) in 10-inch skillet over medium heat.

2. Cut fish fillets into 6 serving pieces. Sprinkle both sides of fish with salt and pepper. Beat egg and water until blended. Dip fish into egg, then coat with flour.

3. Fry fish in hot oil 6 to 10 minutes, turning fish once, until fish flakes easily with fork and is brown on both sides. Drain on paper towels.

1 SERVING: Calories 225 (Calories from Fat 100); Fat 11g (Saturated 2g); Cholesterol 95mg; Sodium 280mg; Carbohydrate 8g (Dietary Fiber 0g); Protein 23g

---

LIGHTER PANFRIED FISH

For 2 grams of fat and 140 calories per serving, omit vegetable oil. Spray 10-inch nonstick skillet with nonstick cooking spray and heat over medium heat.

Oven-Fried Fish

PREP: 15 min; BAKE: 10 min
Makes 4 servings

> 1 pound cod, haddock or other lean fish
>   fillets, about 3/4 inch thick
> 1/4 cup cornmeal
> 1/4 cup dry bread crumbs
> 3/4 teaspoon chopped fresh or
>   1/4 teaspoon dried dill weed
> 1/2 teaspoon paprika
> 1/4 teaspoon salt
> 1/8 teaspoon pepper
> 1/4 cup milk
> 3 tablespoons margarine or butter, melted

1. Move oven rack to position slightly above middle of oven. Heat oven to 500°.

2. Cut fish fillets into 2 × 1 1/2-inch pieces. Mix cornmeal, bread crumbs, dill weed, paprika, salt and pepper. Dip fish into milk, then coat with cornmeal mixture.

3. Place fish in ungreased rectangular pan, 13 × 9 × 2 inches. Drizzle margarine over fish. Bake uncovered about 10 minutes or until fish flakes easily with fork.

1 SERVING: Calories 240 (Calories from Fat 100); Fat 11g (Saturated 2g); Cholesterol 60mg; Sodium 390mg; Carbohydrate 13g (Dietary Fiber 1g); Protein 23g

---

TIMESAVING TIP

If you serve oven-fried fish often, keep extra batches of already-mixed cornmeal coating (use dried dill weed) on hand to make this fish dish extra easy to assemble. Mix two extra batches in sealable plastic bags and store in a cool dry place up to two months.

Cold Salmon with Cucumber Sauce

Cold Salmon with Cucumber Sauce

PREP: 25 min; COOK: 20 min; CHILL: 2 hr
Makes 6 servings

Cucumber Sauce (right)
2 cups water
1 cup dry white wine (or nonalcoholic) or
    apple juice
1 teaspoon salt
1/4 teaspoon dried thyme leaves
1/4 teaspoon dried oregano leaves
1/8 teaspoon ground red pepper (cayenne)
4 black peppercorns
4 sprigs cilantro
1 small onion, sliced
2 pounds salmon, whitefish or other
    medium-fat or fatty fish fillets
Lemon wedges, if desired

1. Prepare Cucumber Sauce.

2. Heat remaining ingredients except salmon fillets and lemon wedges to boiling in 12-inch skillet; reduce heat to low. Cover and simmer 5 minutes.

3. Cut salmon into 6 serving pieces. Place salmon in skillet; add water to cover if necessary. Heat to boiling; reduce heat to low. Simmer uncovered about 14 minutes or until salmon flakes easily with fork.

4. *Carefully* remove salmon with slotted spatula; drain on wire rack. Cover and refrigerate about 2 hours or until chilled.

5. Serve salmon with sauce and lemon wedges.

Cucumber Sauce

1 cup sour cream
1 cup plain yogurt
1/4 cup chopped fresh parsley
1/4 cup chopped fresh cilantro
1 teaspoon ground cumin
1/2 teaspoon salt
2 medium cucumbers, peeled, seeded and
    coarsely shredded

Mix all ingredients. Cover and refrigerate about 2 hours or until chilled.

1 SERVING: Calories 325 (Calories from Fat 155); Fat 17g (Saturated 7g); Cholesterol 125mg; Sodium 400mg; Carbohydrate 7g (Dietary Fiber 0g); Protein 36g

---

LIGHTER COLD SALMON WITH CUCUMBER SAUCE

For 12 grams of fat and 305 calories per serving, use reduced-fat sour cream and plain fat-free yogurt in the Cucumber Sauce.

Batter-Fried Fish

PREP: 15 min; COOK: 15 min
Makes 4 servings

Vegetable oil or shortening
1 pound sole, pike or other lean fish fillets,
   about 3/4 inch thick
1 1/2 cups Bisquick® Original baking mix
1/2 teaspoon cracked black pepper
1 large egg, beaten
1 cup beer or club soda

1. Heat oil (2 to 3 inches) in deep fryer or Dutch oven to 375°.

2. Cut fish fillets into 8 serving pieces. Mix baking mix and pepper in medium bowl. Stir in egg and beer to make thick batter. Dip fish into batter.

3. Fry a few pieces fish at a time in oil about 5 minutes or until fish flakes easily with fork and is deep golden brown. Drain on paper towels.

1 SERVING: Calories 450 (Calories from Fat 245); Fat 27g (Saturated 5g); Cholesterol 105mg; Sodium 740mg; Carbohydrate 30g (Dietary Fiber 1g); Protein 23g

---

LIGHTER BATTER-FRIED FISH

For 5 grams of fat and 280 calories per serving, substitute 1 cup flour for 1 cup of the baking mix. Omit vegetable oil. Heat oven to 500°. Spray cookie sheet with nonstick cooking spray. Bake fish on lightly oiled cookie sheet about 10 minutes or until fish flakes easily with fork.

Snapper en Papillote

PREP: 25 min; BAKE: 25 min
Makes 4 servings

En papillote is a French term describing food baked inside a wrapping of parchment paper. The packet puffs during baking as the food lets off steam. For a dramatic presentation, slit the packet at the table—be careful though to avoid the hot steam that is released when the packet is cut.

1 1/2 pounds red snapper, sea bass or other
   lean fish fillets, about 1/2 inch thick
1 teaspoon lemon pepper
1 large carrot, shredded (1 cup)
1 medium yellow summer squash, thinly
   sliced (2 cups)
1 medium red bell pepper, cut into
   2 × 1/2-inch strips
2 tablespoons grated lemon peel
1 tablespoon chopped fresh or 1 teaspoon
   dried chives
1 tablespoon chopped fresh or 1 teaspoon
   dried thyme leaves
1/2 teaspoon salt

1. Heat oven to 375°. Cut four 12-inch circles from cooking parchment paper or aluminum foil.

2. Cut fish fillets into 4 serving pieces. Place each piece fish on half of each parchment circle. Sprinkle with lemon pepper.

3. Mix remaining ingredients. Spoon about 1 cup vegetable mixture on top of each piece fish. Fold other half of parchment circle over fish and vegetables. Beginning at one end, seal edge by turning up and folding tightly 2 or 3 times. Twist each end several times to secure.

4. Place packets on ungreased cookie sheet. Bake 20 to 25 minutes or until vegetables are crisp-tender and fish flakes easily with fork. To serve, cut a large X in top of each packet; *carefully* fold back points.

a. Place fish and vegetables on half of each parchment circle; fold other half of parchment circle over top.

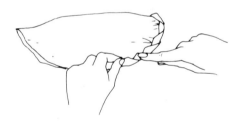

b. Beginning at one end, seal edge by turning up and folding tightly 2 or 3 times. Twist each end several times to secure.

1 SERVING: Calories 165 (Calories from Fat 20); Fat 2g (Saturated 1g); Cholesterol 90mg; Sodium 510mg; Carbohydrate 6g (Dietary Fiber 2g); Protein 33g

---

TIMESAVING TIP

Tear off 12-inch pieces (squares) of aluminum foil and place the food in the center. Bring the corners of each square up and twist together about 1 inch above the food to form a packet.

Spicy Cornmeal Cod, Tortellini Broccoli Salad (page 330)

Spicy Cornmeal Cod

PREP: 15 min; BAKE: 15 min
Makes 6 servings

Turning the fish over after halfway through the baking time helps keep it crispy on both sides.

1 1/2 pounds cod, perch or other lean fish
    fillets, about 1/2 inch thick
3/4 cup cornmeal
1/4 cup all-purpose flour
1/2 teaspoon salt
1/2 teaspoon garlic powder
1/2 teaspoon dried oregano leaves
1/2 teaspoon ground red pepper (cayenne)
1/2 teaspoon pepper
2 large eggs, beaten
3 tablespoons margarine or butter, melted

1. Heat oven to 500°.

2. Cut fish fillets into 4 × 2-inch pieces. Mix remaining ingredients except eggs and margarine. Dip fish into eggs, then coat with cornmeal mixture.

3. Place fish on ungreased cookie sheet. Drizzle margarine over fish. Bake 10 to 12 minutes, turning fish once, until golden brown.

1 SERVING: Calories 250 (Calories from Fat 80); Fat 9g (Saturated 2g); Cholesterol 130mg; Sodium 360mg; Carbohydrate 18g (Dietary Fiber 1g); Protein 25g

---

LIGHTER SPICY CORNMEAL COD

For 4 grams of fat and 205 calories per serving, substitute 1/2 cup fat-free cholesterol-free egg product for the eggs. Lightly grease cookie sheet with shortening. Decrease margarine to 1 tablespoon.

Sole Amandine

PREP: 15 min; BAKE: 20 min
Makes 6 servings

A French term, amandine means "garnished with almonds" and is often misspelled as "almondine." A shallow oval-shaped baking dish (au gratin dish) also can be used to bake this classic dish.

> 1 1/2 pounds sole, orange roughy or other
>   lean fish fillets, about 3/4 inch thick
> 1/2 cup sliced almonds
> 1/4 cup margarine or butter, softened
> 2 tablespoons grated lemon peel
> 1/2 teaspoon salt
> 1/2 teaspoon paprika
> 2 tablespoons lemon juice

1. Heat oven to 375°. Grease rectangular baking dish, 11 × 7 × 1 1/2 inches, with shortening.

2. Cut fish into 6 serving pieces if necessary; place skin side down in baking dish. Mix almonds, margarine, lemon peel, salt and paprika; spoon over fish. Sprinkle with lemon juice.

3. Bake uncovered 15 to 20 minutes or until fish flakes easily with fork.

1 SERVING: Calories 210 (Calories from Fat 115); Fat 13g (Saturated 2g); Cholesterol 55mg; Sodium 350mg; Carbohydrate 3g (Dietary Fiber 1g); Protein 21g

---

LIGHTER SOLE AMANDINE

For 6 grams of fat and 135 calories per serving, decrease almonds to 2 tablespoons and margarine to 2 tablespoons.

Orange Roughy with Tropical Salsa

PREP: 20 min; CHILL: 30 min; BROIL: 6 min
Makes 6 servings

Can't find fresh papayas for the salsa? Buy them canned or substitute fresh or frozen (thawed) peaches.

> Tropical Salsa (right)
> 1 1/2 pounds orange roughy, rockfish or
>   other lean fish fillets, about 1/2 inch thick
> 1/4 teaspoon cracked black pepper

1. Prepare Tropical Salsa.

2. Set oven control to Broil. Lightly grease broiler pan rack with shortening.

3. Cut fish into 6 serving pieces if necessary. Sprinkle with pepper.

4. Place fish on rack in broiler pan. Broil fish with tops about 4 inches from heat 5 to 6 minutes or until fish flakes easily with fork. Serve with salsa.

Tropical Salsa

> 2 medium papayas, peeled and chopped
>   (3 cups)
> 1 large tomato, chopped (1 cup)
> 1 medium red bell pepper, chopped (1 cup)
> 1/4 cup chopped fresh cilantro or parsley
> 3 tablespoons vegetable oil
> 2 tablespoons white wine vinegar
> 1/4 teaspoon salt

Mix all ingredients. Cover and refrigerate 30 minutes to blend flavors.

1 SERVING: Calories 205 (Calories from Fat 70); Fat 8g (Saturated 1g); Cholesterol 60mg; Sodium 190mg; Carbohydrate 13g (Dietary Fiber 3g); Protein 23g

Savory Fish Patties

PREP: 20 min; COOK: 10 min
Makes 4 servings

Serve these fish patties just as they are or embellished with Winter Tomato Sauce (page 343) or Sweet-and-Sour Sauce (page 344). They also make great sandwiches with lettuce, tomato and tartar sauce.

> 1 pound medium-fat or fatty fish, cooked and
>   flaked (about 3 cups)*
> 1 medium onion, finely chopped (1/2 cup)
> 2 slices bread, torn into crumbs (1 1/3 cups)
> 2 large eggs, beaten
> 2 tablespoons lemon juice
> 1 teaspoon chopped fresh or 1/2 teaspoon
>   dried marjoram leaves
> 1/2 teaspoon salt
> 1/2 teaspoon ground mustard (dry)
> 1 tablespoon vegetable oil

1. Mix all ingredients except oil. Shape mixture into 8 patties.

2. Heat oil in 10-inch skillet over medium heat. Cook patties in oil about 8 minutes, turning once, until golden brown.

3 cans (6 to 7 ounces each) salmon or tuna, drained and flaked, can be substituted for the cooked fish.

1 SERVING: Calories 235 (Calories from Fat 70); Fat 8g (Saturated 2g); Cholesterol 185mg; Sodium 490mg; Carbohydrate 9g (Dietary Fiber 0g); Protein 32g

---

LIGHTER SAVORY FISH PATTIES

For 2 grams of fat and 175 calories per serving, substitute 1/2 cup fat-free cholesterol-free egg product for the eggs. Omit oil. Spray 10-inch nonstick skillet with nonstick cooking spray and heat over medium heat.

How to Carve a Whole Fish

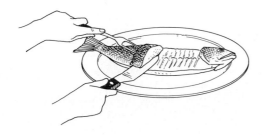

a. Using a sharp knife, cut the top side of fish into serving pieces, just down to the bone. Carefully remove pieces from the rib bones.

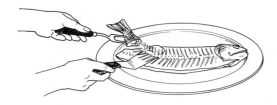

b. Carefully remove bones and discard. Cut the lower portion into serving pieces.

Seafood-Stuffed Whitefish

PREP: 30 min; BAKE: 1 hr
Makes 6 servings

Present this masterpiece on a long shallow platter, and garnish with salad greens and orange slices.

Seafood-Rice Stuffing (right)
2- to 2 1/2-pound pan-dressed whitefish,
　trout or other medium-fat fish
3 tablespoons margarine or butter, melted
1 tablespoon grated orange peel

1. Prepare Seafood-Rice Stuffing.

2. Heat oven to 350°.

3. Loosely stuff fish with stuffing. Close opening with skewers; lace with string.

4. Place fish in shallow roasting pan. Mix margarine and orange peel. Brush half of the margarine mixture over fish. Bake uncovered 50 to 60 minutes, brushing occasionally with margarine mixture, until fish flakes easily with fork. Remove skewers and string. See diagram above for carving.

Seafood-Rice Stuffing

1/2 cup uncooked parboiled (converted)
　white or brown rice
1/4 cup chopped green onions (3 medium)
1/4 cup chopped pecans
1 1/3 cups orange juice
1 medium stalk celery, thinly sliced (1/2 cup)
1 can (4 to 4 1/4 ounces) tiny shrimp, rinsed
　and drained

Cook rice as directed on package. Mix rice and remaining ingredients.

1 SERVING: Calories 395 (Calories from Fat 170); Fat 19g (Saturated 3g); Cholesterol 120mg; Sodium 180mg; Carbohydrate 21g (Dietary Fiber 1g); Protein 36g

Salmon Loaf

PREP: 15 min; BAKE: 45 min
Makes 8 servings

2 cans (14 3/4 ounces each) salmon, drained,
　flaked and liquid reserved
2 large eggs
About 1 cup milk
3 cups coarse cracker crumbs
1/4 cup chopped green onions (3 medium)
2 tablespoons lemon juice
1/4 teaspoon salt
1/4 teaspoon pepper
Lemon wedges, if desired

1. Heat oven to 350°. Grease loaf pan, 9 × 5 × 3 inches, with shortening.

2. Mix salmon and eggs in large bowl. Add enough milk to reserved salmon liquid to measure 1 1/2 cups. Stir liquid mixture and remaining ingredients except lemon wedges into salmon mixture. Spoon lightly into pan.

3. Bake about 45 minutes or until center is set. Garnish with lemon wedges.

1 SERVING: Calories 255 (Calories from Fat 100); Fat 11g (Saturated 3g); Cholesterol 105mg; Sodium 890mg; Carbohydrate 18g (Dietary Fiber 1g); Protein 22g

---

LIGHTER SALMON LOAF

For 9 grams of fat and 235 calories per serving, use salmon packed in water and skim milk. Substitute 1/2 cup fat-free cholesterol-free egg product for the eggs.

TUNA LOAF: Substitute 3 cans (9 1/4 ounces each) light tuna in water, drained, flaked and liquid reserved, for the salmon.

Southwest Tuna with Black Beans, Southern Buttermilk Corn Bread (page 52)

Southwest Tuna with Black Beans

PREP: 15 min; COOK: 10 min
Makes 4 servings

This dish can also be a fun filling for burritos—fill flour tortillas and fold as directed for Beef Burritos (page 386). Or try serving the fish with Corn Bread or Corn Muffins (page 52).

1 tablespoon vegetable oil
1 small onion, chopped (1/4 cup)
1 Anaheim chili, chopped, or 1/4 cup canned
   chopped green chilies
1 clove garlic, crushed
1 tablespoon grated lime peel
3 tablespoons lime juice
1 medium tomato, chopped (3/4 cup)
2 cans (15 ounces each) black beans, rinsed
   and drained
2 cans (6 1/8 ounces each) white tuna in
   water, rinsed and drained

1. Heat oil in 10-inch skillet over medium heat. Cook onion, chili and garlic in oil about 2 minutes, stirring constantly until onion is softened.

2. Stir in remaining ingredients. Cook about 5 minutes, stirring occasionally, until hot.

1 SERVING: Calories 355 (Calories from Fat 45); Fat 5g (Saturated 1g); Cholesterol 25mg; Sodium 480mg; Carbohydrate 54g (Dietary Fiber 14g); Protein 37g

---

TIMESAVING TIP
Pick up the chopped onion, green chilies and tomato from your supermarket's salad bar.

About Shellfish

Shellfish adds variety to any meal with the many types, flavors, shapes and colors available. These saltwater animals with shells of some kind are divided into two broad categories. There are different varieties of each type that come from various parts of the world and can be purchased fresh or frozen. The selection available at your supermarket or fish market will depend on demand, season and price.

Crustaceans have long bodies with soft, jointed shells and legs. Crabs, crayfish, lobster and shrimp fall into this category.

Mollusks have soft bodies with no spinal column and are covered by a shell in one or more pieces. Abalone, clams, mussels, oysters, scallops, snails, octopus and squid fall into this category.

Imitation seafood products such as imitation crab legs and lobster bites have become popular and are available at a lower price than shellfish. These are prepared from pollock, a mild white-fleshed fish. Real shellfish, a shellfish extract or artificial shellfish flavoring is added, along with stabilizers, to form a shellfishlike product. These products are tasty and can generally be substituted for shellfish.

Selecting Shellfish

- **Live clams, oysters, mussels and scallops** should have tightly closed shells. Shells should not be cracked, chipped or broken. To test if open shellfish are alive, tap the shell. Live shellfish will close when tapped. If shellfish are not alive, do not use. They should have a mild odor.
- **Shucked clams, oysters and mussels** (those with their shells removed) should be plump, surrounded by a clear, slightly opalescent liquid. Clams may range in color from pale to deep orange. Oysters are typically creamy white, but may also be tinted green, red, brown or pink. Mussels can be light tan to deep orange.
- **Shucked scallops** are available in two sizes: sea scallops, which are about 2 inches in diameter, or bay scallops, which average about 1/2 inch in diameter. They will have a mild, sweet odor and should be moist looking but not be in liquid or in direct contact with ice. Sea scallops are usually creamy white and may be tinted light orange or pink. Bay scallops are also creamy white and may be tinted light tan or pink.

Shellfish

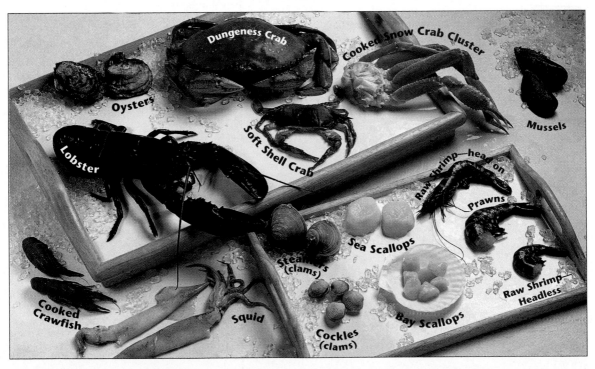

- **Live lobsters and crabs** should have hard shells and leg movement. A lobster will tightly curl its tail under when picked up. Discard crabs or lobsters that show no movement.
- **Shrimp** may be sold raw, also known as "green," with the heads on; raw in the shell without the heads; raw but peeled and deveined or cleaned; cooked in the shell; or cooked, peeled and deveined. They are usually sold by count or number per pound; however, neither by count nor by description is size universally defined and regulated. Ask the fish manager for help if necessary.

  The smaller the shrimp size, the higher the count per pound; the larger the shrimp, the higher the price. Following is an approximate guide to the number or count per pound of shrimp *with* shells:

  Jumbo—10 to 12   *Medium*—26 to 30
  Large—15 to 20   *Small*—40 to 50

  Squid, also known as calamari, should be cream colored with reddish brown spots. As the squid ages the skin will turn pinkish. Skin should be untorn. Meat should be firm, and the squid should be in juices. There should be a mild sealike odor.

How Much Shellfish to Buy

- **Live clams, oysters, mussels and scallops**—Allow about 6 oysters or small hard-shell clams or 3 large hard-shell clams or 18 mussels or soft-shell clams per serving.
- **Shucked oysters, scallops, clams or mussels**—Allow about 1/4 pound shucked oysters, scallops, clams or mussels per serving.

- **Squid** can be purchased whole or cleaned. Allow about 1/2 pound whole squid or 1/4 pound cleaned squid per serving.
- **Raw shrimp** can be purchased with or without shells. Fully cooked shrimp may be purchased frozen or in the deli or seafood section of the supermarket. Allow about 1 pound whole shrimp, 1/2 pound headless, unpeeled shrimp or 1/4 pound headless, peeled shrimp per serving.
- **Live crab and lobsters** can be purchased in the seafood section of the supermarket or at a seafood store. Cooked lobster or crabmeat can be purchased frozen or in the deli section of the supermarket. Allow about 1 1/4 pounds live or 1/4 pound cooked meat per serving.

Determining Shellfish Doneness

These are the clues to watch for when determining when cooked shellfish is done:

- **Raw shrimp** will turn pink and become firm. The cooking time will depend on the size of the shrimp.
- **Live oysters, clams and mussels** will open individually as they are done.
- **Shucked oysters, clams and mussels** will become plump and opaque. Oyster edges will start to curl.
- **Scallops** turn white or opaque and become firm. The cooking time will depend on the size of the scallops.
- **Crabs and lobsters** will turn bright red.

Microwaving Shellfish

1. Cut large scallops in half or rinse shrimp. Arrange shellfish in circle in shallow microwavable dish large enough to hold a single layer.
2. Cover with plastic wrap, folding back about 2 inch edge to vent.
3. Microwave on High (100%) as directed in chart or until shrimp is pink or until scallops are opaque.

Timetable for Microwaving Shellfish

Type	Approximate Weight	Microwave Time	Stand Time
Scallops, sea	1 1/2 pounds	6 to 9 minutes, stirring after 4 minutes	3 minutes
Shrimp, peeled and deveined	1 pound	6 to 8 minutes, stirring after 3 minutes	3 minutes
Shrimp in the shell	1 pound	5 to 7 minutes, stirring after 3 minutes	3 minutes

How to Devein Shrimp

Using a small, pointed knife or shrimp deveiner, make a shallow cut along the center back of each shrimp, and wash out vein.

Boiled Shrimp

PREP: 15 min; COOK: 15 min
Makes 4 servings, about 1/4 pound each

Shrimp can be cooked either fresh or frozen. They make great appetizers served with cocktail sauce, added to stir-fries, or made into refreshing salad.

> 4 cups water
> 1 1/2 pounds uncooked fresh or frozen
>   medium shrimp in shells
> Cocktail sauce, if desired

1. Heat water to boiling in 3-quart saucepan. Add shrimp. Cover and heat to boiling; reduce heat to low. Simmer 3 to 5 minutes or until shrimp are pink and firm; drain.

2. Peel shrimp, leaving tails on. Make a shallow cut lengthwise down back of each shrimp; wash out vein (see How to Devein Shrimp, above). Serve shrimp with cocktail sauce.

1 SERVING: Calories 75 (Calories from Fat 10); Fat 1g (Saturated 0g); Cholesterol 160mg; Sodium 180mg; Carbohydrate 0g (Dietary Fiber 0g); Protein 17g

Deep-Fried Shrimp

PREP: 20 min; COOK: 15 min
Makes 4 servings

> 1 1/2 pounds uncooked fresh or frozen
>   (thawed) medium shrimp in shells
> Vegetable oil
> 1/2 cup all-purpose flour
> 1 teaspoon salt
> 1/2 teaspoon pepper
> 2 large eggs, slightly beaten
> 3/4 cup dry bread crumbs

1. Peel shrimp, leaving tails on. Make a shallow cut lengthwise down back of each shrimp; wash out vein (see How to Devein Shrimp, left).

2. Heat oil (2 to 3 inches) in deep fryer or Dutch oven to 325°.

3. Mix flour, salt and pepper. Coat shrimp with flour mixture. Dip shrimp into eggs, then coat with bread crumbs.

4. Fry 3 or 4 shrimp at a time in oil about 2 minutes or until golden brown. Drain on paper towels.

1 SERVING: Calories 490 (Calories from Fat 290); Fat 32g (Saturated 5g); Cholesterol 270mg; Sodium 920mg; Carbohydrate 27g (Dietary Fiber 1g); Protein 24g

DEEP-FRIED SCALLOPS: Substitute 12 ounces shucked scallops, drained, for the shrimp. Fry 3 to 4 minutes or until golden brown.

DEEP-FRIED OYSTERS OR CLAMS: Substitute 12 ounces shucked oysters or clams, drained, for the shrimp.

Shrimp Scampi

PREP: 25 min; COOK: 5 min
Makes 6 servings

Scampi is a term often used in restaurants to describe a dish made with large shrimp (sometimes butterflied) that are prepared with garlic, oil or butter, then broiled in shallow ramekins. This easy version is cooked in a skillet.

> 1 1/2 pounds uncooked fresh or frozen
>   (thawed) medium shrimp in shells
> 2 tablespoons olive or vegetable oil
> 2 tablespoons thinly sliced green onions
> 1 tablespoon chopped fresh or
>   1 1/2 teaspoons dried basil leaves
> 1 tablespoon chopped fresh parsley
> 2 tablespoons lemon juice
> 1/4 teaspoon salt
> 2 cloves garlic, finely chopped
> Grated Parmesan cheese, if desired

1. Peel shrimp. Make a shallow cut lengthwise down back of each shrimp; wash out vein (see How to Devein Shrimp, left).

2. Heat oil in 10-inch skillet over medium heat. Cook shrimp and remaining ingredients except cheese in oil 2 to 3 minutes, stirring frequently, until shrimp are pink and firm; remove from heat. Sprinkle with cheese.

1 SERVING: Calories 145 (Calories from Fat 70); Fat 8g (Saturated 1g); Cholesterol 160mg; Sodium 320mg; Carbohydrate 1g (Dietary Fiber 0g); Protein 17g

SHRIMP SCAMPI WITH FETTUCCINE: Cook 8 ounces uncooked spinach fetuccine as directed on package. Toss fettuccine with shrimp mixture in skillet.

Shrimp Creole

PREP: 45 min; COOK: 5 min
Makes 6 servings

> 2 pounds uncooked fresh or frozen (thawed)
>   medium shrimp in shells
> 1/4 cup margarine or butter
> 3 medium onions, chopped (1 1/2 cups)
> 2 medium green bell peppers, finely chopped
>   (2 cups)
> 2 medium stalks celery, finely chopped
>   (1 cup)
> 2 cloves garlic, finely chopped
> 1 cup water
> 2 teaspoons chopped fresh parsley
> 1 teaspoon salt
> 1/8 teaspoon ground red pepper (cayenne)
> 2 bay leaves
> 1 can (15 ounces) tomato sauce
> 6 cups hot cooked rice (page 204)

1. Peel shrimp. Make a shallow cut lengthwise down back of each shrimp; wash out vein (see How to Devein Shrimp, page 193). Cover and refrigerate.

2. Melt margarine in 3-quart saucepan over medium heat. Cook onions, bell peppers, celery and garlic in margarine about 10 minutes, stirring occasionally, until onions are tender.

3. Stir in water, parsley, salt, red pepper, bay leaves and tomato sauce. Heat to boiling; reduce heat to low. Simmer uncovered 10 minutes.

4. Stir in shrimp. Heat to boiling; reduce heat to medium. Cover and cook 10 to 20 minutes, stirring occasionally, until shrimp are pink and firm. Remove bay leaves. Serve over rice.

1 SERVING: Calories 380 (Calories from Fat 80); Fat 9g (Saturated 2g); Cholesterol 140mg; Sodium 1050mg; Carbohydrate 57g (Dietary Fiber 3g); Protein 21g

---

LIGHTER SHRIMP CREOLE

For 3 grams of fat and 325 calories per serving, decrease margarine to 1 tablespoon and use a nonstick saucepan.

Mandarin Almond Shrimp

PREP: 30 min; BAKE: 40 min; STAND: 3 min
Makes 6 servings, about 1 1/2 cups each

This no-fuss dish is perfect for entertaining and works very well when served from a buffet. (photograph on page 181)

> 1 pound uncooked fresh or frozen (thawed)
>   medium shrimp in shells
> 2 cups sliced mushrooms (6 ounces)
> 1 cup uncooked regular long grain rice
> 2 cups boiling water
> 1 teaspoon salt
> 3/4 teaspoon ground ginger
> 1 small onion, thinly sliced
> 1 cup unblanched whole almonds, toasted
>   (page 9)
> 1 can (15 ounces) mandarin orange
>   segments, drained
> 1 package (6 ounces) frozen Chinese pea
>   pods, thawed and drained
> Soy sauce, if desired

1. Peel shrimp. Make a shallow cut lengthwise down back of each shrimp; wash out vein (see How to Devein Shrimp, page 193).

2. Heat oven to 350°.

3. Mix shrimp, mushrooms, rice, boiling water, salt, ginger and onion in ungreased rectangular baking dish, 13 × 9 × 2 inches.

4. Cover tightly with aluminum foil and bake about 40 minutes or until liquid is absorbed and shrimp are pink and firm.

5. Stir in almonds, orange segments and pea pods. Cover and let stand about 3 minutes or until pea pods are hot. Serve with soy sauce.

1 SERVING: Calories 355 (Calories from Fat 125); Fat 14g (Saturated 2g); Cholesterol 70mg; Sodium 440mg; Carbohydrate 44g (Dietary Fiber 4g); Protein 17g

How to Open Raw Clams

a. Hold a clam with the hinged side against a heavy cloth or oven mitt. Insert a blunt-tipped knife between shell halves. Be sure to work over a bowl or plate to catch juices.

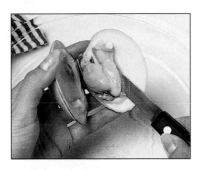

b. Hold the clam firmly and move knife around the clam, cutting the muscle at the hinge. Gently twist the knife to pry open the shell. Cut the clam meat free from the shell.

Steamed Clams

PREP: 5 min; STAND: 30 min; COOK: 8 min
Makes 4 servings

These are favorites on both coasts. If you don't live by the sea, check specialty fish shops for fresh clams.

> 4 pounds soft-shell clams in shells (steamers)
> 6 cups water
> 1/3 cup white vinegar
> 1/2 cup boiling water
> Margarine or butter, melted, if desired

1. Discard any broken-shell or open (dead) clams. Place remaining clams in large container. Cover with 6 cups water and the vinegar. Let stand 30 minutes; drain. Scrub clams in cold water.

2. Place clams in steamer* with boiling water. Steam 5 to 8 minutes or until clams open at least 1

inch, removing clams as they open. Discard any unopened clams.

3. Serve hot in shells with margarine.

If steamer is not available, place clams in 6-quart Dutch oven. Add 1 inch boiling water; cover tightly.

1 SERVING: Calories 75 (Calories from Fat 10); Fat 1g (Saturated 0g); Cholesterol 35mg; Sodium 60mg; Carbohydrate 3g (Dietary Fiber 0g); Protein 13g

Steamed Clams with Sausage

PREP: 25 min; COOK: 40 min
Makes 4 servings

> 2 pounds very small clams
> 1 large onion, thinly sliced
> 3 cloves garlic, chopped
> 1 small red or green pepper, cut into
>   1-inch pieces
> 1/2 teaspoon paprika
> 1/8 teaspoon crushed red pepper
> 2 tablespoons olive or vegetable oil
> 1/2 cup dry white wine
> 1/2 cup chopped fully cooked smoked ham
> 1 package (5 ounces) unsliced pepperoni,
>   chopped
> 1 can (16 ounces) whole tomatoes
>   (with liquid)
> 2 bay leaves
> French bread, if desired

1. Clean clams as directed in Steamed Clams, left, step 1.

2. Cook and stir onion, garlic, red pepper pieces, paprika and crushed red pepper in oil in Dutch oven over medium heat until onion is tender.

3. Stir in remaining ingredients; break up tomatoes with fork. Heat to boiling; reduce heat to low. Simmer uncovered 15 minutes.

4. Add clams to vegetable mixture. Cover and simmer 20 minutes. (Do not lift cover or stir.) Remove bay leaves and any unopened clams. Serve with French bread.

1 SERVING: Calories 335 (Calories from Fat 225); Fat 25g (Saturated 7g); Cholesterol 50mg; Sodium 1200mg; Carbohydrate 12g (Dietary Fiber 2g); Protein 17g

Steamed Mussels

PREP: 20 min; COOK: 10 min
Makes 4 servings

4 pounds mussels in shells
1/2 cup boiling water
Margarine or butter, melted, if desired

1. Discard any broken-shell or open (dead) mussels. Scrub remaining mussels in cold water, removing any barnacles with a dull paring knife. Remove beards (see How to Remove Beards from Mussels, below).

2. Place mussels in large container. Cover with cool water. Agitate water with hand, then drain and discard water. Repeat several times until water runs clear; drain.

3. Place half of the mussels in steamer* with boiling water. Cover and steam 3 to 5 minutes, removing mussels as they open. Discard any unopened mussels. Repeat with remaining mussels.

4. Serve hot in shells with margarine.

If steamer is not available, place mussels in 6-quart Dutch oven. Add 1 inch boiling water; cover tightly.

1 SERVING: Calories 140 (Calories from Fat 20); Fat 2g (Saturated 0g); Cholesterol 70mg; Sodium 115mg; Carbohydrate 5g (Dietary Fiber 0g); Protein 26g

STEAMED OYSTERS: Substitute oysters for the mussels. Do not cover with cool water. Continue as directed. Steam 5 to 8 minutes.

How to Remove Beards from Mussels

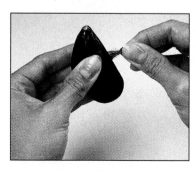

Pull beard by giving it a tug (using a kitchen towel may help). If you have trouble removing it, use a pliers to grip and pull gently.

Saucy Steamed Mussels

PREP: 30 min; COOK: 10 min
Makes 6 servings

6 pounds mussels in shells
3 medium roma (plum) tomatoes, finely chopped (1 1/2 cups)
2 tablespoons lemon juice
1 tablespoon chopped fresh or 1 teaspoon dried basil leaves
1 tablespoon chopped fresh chives
1 cup vegetable broth or chicken broth
1/4 teaspoon salt
1/4 teaspoon pepper
1 clove garlic, finely chopped

1. Prepare and clean mussels as directed in Steamed Mussels, left, steps 1 and 2.

2. Mix tomatoes, lemon juice, basil and chives.

3. Mix mussels and remaining ingredients in 6-quart Dutch oven or stockpot. Cover and heat to boiling. Boil 5 to 6 minutes, removing mussels as they open. Discard any unopened mussels. To serve, spoon cooking liquid and tomato mixture over mussels.

1 SERVING: Calories 160 (Calories from Fat 20); Fat 2g (Saturated 0g); Cholesterol 70mg; Sodium 340mg; Carbohydrate 9g (Dietary Fiber 0g); Protein 27g

Oyster Casserole

PREP: 15 min; BAKE: 30 min
Makes 4 servings

1 pint shucked select or large oysters, drained
2 tomatoes, chopped
1/2 cup half-and-half
2 cups cracker crumbs (about 20 crackers)
1/2 cup margarine or butter, melted
1/2 teaspoon salt
1/2 teaspoon ground cumin
1/4 teaspoon allspice
1/8 teaspoon ground red pepper
Lemon or lime wedges

1. Heat oven to 375°.

2. Mix oysters and tomatoes; arrange in ungreased rectangular baking dish, 11 × 7 × 1 1/2 inches. Pour 1/4 cup of the half-and-half over mixture. Mix remaining ingredients except lemon wedges; sprinkle over oysters and tomatoes. Pour remaining half-and-half over crumb mixture.

3. Bake uncovered about 30 minutes or until light brown. Garnish with lemon wedges.

1 SERVING: Calories 510 (Calories from Fat 350); Fat 39g (Saturated 10g); Cholesterol 70mg; Sodium 1100mg; Carbohydrate 29g (Dietary Fiber 1g); Protein 12g

Boiled Hard-Shell Crabs

PREP: 10 min; COOK: 1 hr
Makes 4 servings

> 4 quarts water
> 16 live hard-shell blue crabs
> Cocktail sauce, if desired

1. Heat water to boiling in large kettle or canner. Drop 4 crabs at a time into water. Cover and heat to boiling; reduce heat to low. Simmer 10 minutes; drain. Repeat with remaining crabs.

2. Follow the directions below to remove meat. Serve with cocktail sauce.

1 SERVING: Calories 100 (Calories from Fat 20); Fat 2g (Saturated 0g); Cholesterol 105mg; Sodium 290mg; Carbohydrate 0g (Dietary Fiber 0g); Protein 21g

Boiled Lobsters

PREP: 10 min; COOK: 30 min
Makes 2 servings

> 2 to 4 quarts water
> 2 live lobsters (about 1 pound each)
> Margarine or butter, melted, if desired
> Lemon wedges, if desired

1. Fill 6-quart Dutch oven or stockpot one-third full of water. Heat to boiling. Plunge lobsters headfirst into water. Cover and heat to boiling; reduce heat to low. Simmer 10 to 12 minutes or until lobsters turn bright red; drain.

2. Follow the directions below to remove meat. Serve with margarine and lemon wedges.

1 SERVING: Calories 115 (Calories from Fat 10); Fat 1g (Saturated 0g); Cholesterol 85mg; Sodium 450mg; Carbohydrate 2g (Dietary Fiber 0g); Protein 24g

How to Eat Crab

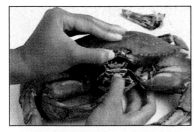

a. Using your thumb, pry off the tail flap, twist off and discard. Turn crab right side up and pry up the top shell. Pull it away from the body and discard.

b. Using a small knife (or your fingers), cut the gray-white gills (called "devil's fingers") from both sides of the crab. Discard gills and internal organs.

c. To remove meat, twist off the crab claws and legs. Use a nutcracker to crack shells at the joints. Remove meat with a small cocktail fork or nut pick. Break the body and remove any remaining meat in the deeper pockets.

How to Eat Lobster

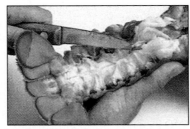

a. Place lobster on its back. Using a kitchen scissors, cut lengthwise down the body up to the tail, cutting to, but not through the back shell.

b. Cut away the membrane on the tail to expose meat. Discard the intestinal vein that runs through the tail and the small sac near the head of the lobster. Serve the green tomalley (liver) and coral roe (only in females) if you like.

c. Twist the large claws away from the body of the lobster. Using a nutcracker, break open the claws. Remove meat from claws, tail and body.

Crab Cakes

PREP: 10 min; CHILL: 1 1/2 hr; COOK: 5 min
Makes 4 servings

These are nice served with hot cooked rice or pasta, Sweet-and-Sour Coleslaw (page 323) and Corn Bread (page 52).

> 1 pound crabmeat, cooked, cartilage
> removed and flaked (2 1/2 to 3 cups)
> 1 1/2 cups soft white bread crumbs
> (without crusts)
> 2 tablespoons margarine or butter, melted
> 1 teaspoon ground mustard (dry)
> 1/2 teaspoon salt
> 1/8 teaspoon pepper
> 2 large egg yolks, beaten
> Vegetable oil

1. Mix all ingredients except oil. Shape mixture into 4 patties, each about 3 1/2 inches in diameter. Cover and refrigerate about 1 1/2 hours or until firm.

2. Heat oil (1 inch) in deep fryer or 10-inch skillet to 375°. Fry patties in oil 4 to 5 minutes, turning once, until golden brown on both sides. Drain on paper towels.

1 SERVING: Calories 465 (Calories from Fat 235); Fat 26g (Saturated 5g); Cholesterol 220mg; Sodium 1000mg; Carbohydrate 30g (Dietary Fiber 1g); Protein 29g

---

LIGHTER CRAB CAKES

For 7 grams of fat and 290 calories per serving, decrease margarine to 1 tablespoon and substitute 1/4 cup fat-free cholesterol-free egg product for the 2 egg yolks. Omit vegetable oil. Spray 10-inch skillet with nonstick cooking spray and heat over medim-high heat. Pan-fry crab cakes about 5 minutes, turning once, until light brown on both sides.

Lobster Newburg

PREP: 10 min; COOK: 15 min
Makes 6 servings

Instead of rice, Lobster Newburg is also delicious served over Fried Polenta (page 210), hot Popovers (page 51) or baked pastry shells.

> 1/4 cup margarine or butter
> 3 tablespoons all-purpose flour
> 1/2 teaspoon salt
> 1/2 teaspoon ground mustard (dry)
> 1/4 teaspoon pepper
> 2 cups milk
> 2 cups cut-up cooked lobster
> 2 tablespoons dry sherry or apple juice
> 6 cups hot cooked rice (page 204)

1. Melt margarine in 3-quart saucepan over medium heat. Stir in flour, salt, mustard and pepper. Cook, stirring constantly, until smooth and bubbly; remove from heat.

2. Stir in milk. Heat to boiling, stirring constantly. Boil and stir 1 minute. Stir in lobster and sherry; heat through. Serve over rice.

1 SERVING: Calories 365 (Calories from Fat 90); Fat 10g (Saturated 3g); Cholesterol 40mg; Sodium 490mg; Carbohydrate 53g (Dietary Fiber 1g); Protein 17g

CRAB NEWBURG: Substitute 2 cups chopped cooked crabmeat or imitation crabmeat.

Curried Scallops

PREP: 30 min; COOK: 5 min
Makes 6 servings

Curry powder is a blend of up to twenty spices. It has a distinctive color and flavor and is often used in Indian cooking.

> 1 tablespoon margarine or butter
> 1 pound sea scallops, cut in half
> 2 tablespoons margarine or butter
> 1/4 cup chopped green onions (3 medium)
> 1 tablespoon all-purpose flour
> 1 tablespoon curry powder
> 1/2 teaspoon salt
> 1/2 cup chicken broth
> 1/2 cup milk
> 1 small tomato, chopped (1/2 cup)
> 3 cups hot cooked rice (page 204)

1. Melt 1 tablespoon margarine in 10-inch skillet over medium-high heat. Cook scallops in margarine 2 to 3 minutes, stirring frequently, until white. Remove scallops from skillet; drain skillet.

2. Melt 2 tablespoons margarine in same skillet over medium heat. Cook onions, flour, curry powder and salt in margarine, stirring constantly, until bubbly; remove from heat.

3. Stir in broth and milk. Heat to boiling, stirring constantly. Boil and stir 1 minute. Stir in tomato and scallops. Cook about 3 minutes, stirring occasionally, until hot. Serve over rice.

1 SERVING: Calories 225 (Calories from Fat 65); Fat 7g (Saturated 2g); Cholesterol 110mg; Sodium 450mg; Carbohydrate 26g (Dietary Fiber 1g); Protein 15g

CURRIED SHRIMP: Substitute 1 pound uncooked peeled deveined medium shrimp, thawed if frozen, for the scallops. Cook shrimp 4 to 5 minutes in step 1 until pink and firm.

Coquilles Saint Jacques

PREP: 45 min; BROIL: 5 min
Makes 6 servings

1 1/2 pounds bay scallops*
1 cup dry white wine (or nonalcoholic) or
    chicken broth
1/4 cup chopped fresh parsley
1/2 teaspoon salt
2 tablespoons margarine or butter
6 ounces mushrooms, sliced (2 cups)
2 shallots or green onions, chopped
3 tablespoons margarine or butter
3 tablespoons all-purpose flour
1/2 cup half-and-half
1/2 cup shredded Swiss cheese (2 ounces)
1 cup soft bread crumbs
2 tablespoons margarine or butter, melted

1. Place scallops, wine, parsley and salt in 3-quart saucepan. Add just enough water to cover scallops. Heat to boiling; reduce heat to low. Simmer uncovered about 6 minutes or until scallops are white.

2. Remove scallops with slotted spoon; reserve liquid. Heat reserved liquid to boiling. Boil until reduced to 1 cup. Strain and reserve.

3. Melt 2 tablespoons margarine in same saucepan over medium heat. Cook mushrooms and shallots in margarine 5 to 6 minutes, stirring occasionally, until mushrooms are tender. Remove from saucepan.

4. Melt 3 tablespoons margarine in same saucepan over medium heat. Stir in flour. Cook, stirring constantly, until smooth and bubbly; remove from heat. Stir in reserved liquid. Cook and stir 1 minute. Stir in half-and-half, scallops, mushroom mixture and 1/4 cup of the cheese; heat through.

5. Toss bread crumbs and 2 tablespoons melted margarine. Lightly grease six 4-inch baking shells or ramekins with margarine and place in jelly roll pan, 15 1/2 × 10 1/2 × 1 inch. Divide scallop mixture among baking shells. Sprinkle with remaining cheese and the bread crumbs.

6. Set oven control to Broil. Broil baking shells with tops 5 inches from heat 3 to 5 minutes or until crumbs are toasted.

2 packages (12 ounces each) frozen scallops, thawed, can be substituted for the fresh scallops.

1 SERVING: Calories 400 (Calories from Fat 190); Fat 21g (Saturated 6g); Cholesterol 55mg; Sodium 700mg; Carbohydrate 22g (Dietary Fiber 1g); Protein 32g

---

LIGHTER COQUILLES SAINT JACQUES
For 12 grams of fat and 330 calories per serving, use nonstick saucepan and decrease margarine to 1 tablespoon each in steps 3 and 5 and 2 tablespoons in step 4. Substitute evaporated skim milk for the half-and-half and use low-fat cheese.

Curried Scallops

Seafood Paella

PREP: 1 1/2 hr; BAKE: 25 min
Makes 6 servings

A Spanish dish made with saffron-flavored rice, paella can include other meats such as chicken, pork and sausage. The dish takes its name from the pan in which it was made, a 14-inch shallow metal pan (traditionally copper) with two handles.

12 mussels in shells
6 medium clams in shells
1/2 pound uncooked fresh or frozen (thawed) medium shrimp in shells
1/4 cup olive or vegetable oil
1/2 pound bay scallops
1/2 pound squid or octopus, cleaned and cut into 1/4-inch rings, if desired
1 medium onion, chopped (1/2 cup)
2 cloves garlic, finely chopped
1 can (16 ounces) whole tomatoes, undrained
2 cups water
1 cup uncooked regular long grain rice
1 teaspoon salt
1/2 teaspoon saffron or ground turmeric
1/4 teaspoon pepper
1/2 cup frozen green peas
1 jar (2 ounces) sliced pimientos, drained
Lemon wedges, if desired

1. Clean mussels and clams as directed for Steamed Mussels, page 196, steps 1 and 2, and Steamed Clams, page 195, step 1. Peel shrimp. Make a shallow cut lengthwise down back of each shrimp; wash out vein (see diagram, page 193).

2. Heat oil in 14-inch metal paella pan or oven-proof Dutch oven over medium heat. Cook shrimp in oil about 2 minutes, stirring occasionally, just until pink and firm; remove with slotted spoon. Cook scallops in oil 1 to 2 minutes, stirring occasionally, until slightly firm; remove with slotted spoon. Cover and refrigerate shrimp and scallops. Cook squid in oil about 2 minutes, stirring occasionally, until rings begin to shrink; remove with slotted spoon.

3. Add more oil to pan if necessary. Cook onion and garlic in oil, stirring occasionally, until onion is tender. Stir in squid and tomatoes, breaking up tomatoes. Heat to boiling; reduce heat to low. Simmer uncovered 20 minutes, stirring occasionally.

4. Stir in shrimp, scallops, water, rice, salt, saffron and pepper. Heat to boiling; reduce heat to low. Simmer uncovered 10 minutes, stirring occasionally.

5. Heat oven to 350°.

6. Arrange mussels, clams and peas on top of rice mixture. Cover loosely with aluminum foil. Bake about 25 minutes in paella pan, 40 minutes in Dutch oven, or until liquid is absorbed. Discard any unopened mussels or clams. Sprinkle paella with pimientos. Garnish with lemon wedges.

1 SERVING: Calories 350 (Calories from Fat 100); Fat 11g (Saturated 2g); Cholesterol 170mg; Sodium 770mg; Carbohydrate 35g (Dietary Fiber 2g); Protein 30g

Scallops with Fettuccine

PREP: 30 min; COOK: 5 min
Makes 4 servings

8 ounces uncooked fettuccine
1 tablespoon vegetable oil
1/4 cup sliced green onions (3 medium)
1 tablespoon finely chopped gingerroot
1 pound bay scallops
2 roma (plum) tomatoes, chopped (1 cup)
1/4 cup chopped fresh or 1 tablespoon dried basil leaves
1/2 cup chicken broth
2 tablespoons cornstarch

1. Cook fettuccine as directed on package.

2. Meanwhile, heat oil in 10-inch skillet over medium heat. Cook onions, gingerroot and scallops in oil 4 to 5 minutes, stirring occasionally, until scallops are white. Stir in tomatoes and basil.

3. Mix broth and cornstarch; *gradually* stir into scallop mixture. Heat to boiling, stirring constantly. Boil and stir about 1 minute or until mixture is slightly thick.

4. Serve scallop mixture with fettuccine.

1 SERVING: Calories 390 (Calories from Fat 70); Fat 8g (Saturated 1g); Cholesterol 85mg; Sodium 420mg; Carbohydrate 48g (Dietary Fiber 3g); Protein 34g

Grains & Legumes

About Grains

Grains have become much more important in our diet, and we are getting more adventurous in experimenting with them. Many of us need some help in learning about new grains—what they look like, how to cook them, and what recipes to use them in. We've gathered all that information right here, to make grains an easy, tasty addition to your meal.

Besides wheat, rice and corn, the most commonly known grains, there are other grains that can bring exciting variety to both tried-and-true and new recipes. Grains offer the benefit of fiber, are low in fat, contain no cholesterol and provide high-quality protein when combined with low-fat dairy products or beans, peas or lentils.

Selecting Grains

Many types of common grains, such as corn, rice and wheat, are widely available in supermarkets, either plain, in seasoned dry mixes and, in some markets, frozen or refrigerated. Look for other grains in the international foods section or health food section of large supermarkets, in food cooperatives and in health food stores. Some grains are sold in bulk form or packaged and found in the refrigerator case.

Grains are available in a variety of forms, from whole kernels to finely ground flours. This chapter features those grains usually cooked in a main dish or used as a side dish. Also see Flour, page 14.

Storing Grains

Uncooked

Most grains can be stored indefinitely, but for optimum quality and flavor, one to two years is the recommended storage time. Whole grains with the bran and hull have a higher fat content and should be refrigerated or frozen to keep them from getting rancid. Store in the original packaging, or transfer to airtight glass or plastic containers and label the contents with storage date. Store in a cool (60° or less), dry location.

Grains

Preceding page: Three-Bean Casserole (page 214)

Cooked

Tightly cover cooked grains and refrigerate up to five days. Freeze in airtight containers up to six months. Long grain rice will become firmer with refrigeration, a natural reversing process called retrogradation. To reheat rice and soften: Add 1 tablespoon water per cup of rice in microwavable container and microwave tightly covered on High 1 to 2 minutes, or add 2 tablespoons water per cup of rice and heat in a covered saucepan over low heat. You can also reheat refrigerated or frozen rice by placing it in a strainer and pouring boiling water over it.

Grains Glossary

White rice:

- **Regular long grain rice** has been milled to remove the hull, germ and most of the bran during milling. About 90% of rice produced in the United States is enriched. It is available in both long and short grains. Long grain is a better all-purpose rice.
- **Parboiled (converted) rice** is steamed under pressure before being milled and polished. This process retains more nutrients but hardens the grain, so it takes longer to cook than regular rice. It also removes excess starch, so the grains remain separate after cooking.
- **Precooked (instant) rice** is commercially cooked, rinsed and dried before packaging, so it's quick and very easy to prepare.
- **Arborio or risotto rice** is shorter, fatter (has larger center core) and has a higher starch content than regular long grain rice. Originally from northern Italy, it is preferred for making risotto, a savory skillet dish made by frequently stirring to release the rice starch while gradually adding hot liquid. The result is a dish that has a creamy texture and is firm to the bite. Arborio rice also is especially good used in paella and jambalaya.
- **Aromatic rices** contain a natural ingredient that is responsible for the nutty or perfumy aroma and taste. The fragrance quality can differ from one year to the next and also intensifies as the rice ages. Origins of popular types or aromatic rices include basmati, which means "queen of fragrance," from India, pecan from Louisiana, popcorn and Texmati from Texas and jasmine from Thailand.

Brown rice is unpolished with only the outer hull removed. It has a slightly firm texture and nutlike flavor, and it will take longer to cook than regular long grain rice. Brown rice has more fiber and nutrients, as the germ and hull have not been removed. Brown rice is also available in precooked (instant) form.

Wild rice is the seed of a grass that grows in marshes. It is dark greenish-brown in color and has a distinctive, nutlike flavor. It is often available in rice mixtures, sometimes combined with white or brown rice.

Other grains:

- **Barley,** one of the first grains ever cultivated, is commercially hulled to soften the outer chaff, which shortens cooking time. Pearl barley, the most common variety, refers to the milling process in which the grain is husked and polished.
- **Bulgur and cracked wheat** are made from whole wheat kernels. When bulgur is made, wheat kernels are parboiled, dried and partially debranned, then cracked into coarse fragments. Cracked wheat is from kernels that are cleaned, then cracked or cut into fine fragments.
- **Cornmeal** is available in degerminated and whole grain forms. *Degerminated* indicates the germ and bran have been removed; it can be stored at room temperature. *Whole grain* (often called stone-ground because of the milling process) refers to cornmeal that contains the germ and the bran, which gives it more flavor, texture and fiber. It can be found in health food stores; store airtight in refrigerator or freezer. Grits is meal that has been coarsely ground from hulled kernels of corn. Also see Polenta, page 210.
- **Kasha,** also called buckwheat groats, is the kernel inside the buckwheat seed. It is roasted for a nutlike flavor, then coarsely ground.
- **Millet** is a small, round, yellow seed that looks similar to whole mustard seed. When cooked, this tiny grain has a chewy texture and a mild flavor that resembles that of brown rice.
- **Quinoa** (keen-wa) is an ancient grain native to South America. Quinoa is higher in protein than most grains and is actually a complete protein. It has a light texture and mild flavor. You can find quinoa in health food stores.
- **Wheat berries** are the unprocessed kernels of wheat. Presoak them to ensure they are tender enough to eat. Wheat berries are slow to cook, but because they contain the entire wheat kernel, they are high in nutritional value. Look for them in health food stores.

Basic Directions for Cooking Rice and Other Grains

1. Use 1 cup uncooked grain, and rinse only if directed to on the package. Be sure to use an extra-fine mesh strainer for tiny grains, such as quinoa.
2. Use a 2-quart saucepan for 1 cup of uncooked grain.
3. For liquid besides water, try broth (chicken, beef, vegetable) or half vegetable or fruit juice. Add salt, if desired, using 1/2 teaspoon per 1 cup of grain.
4. Cook or soak as directed in the following chart. Do not remove lid or stir during cooking.
5. Fluff with fork, lifting grains to release steam.

Note: *Grains lose moisture with age, so more or less liquid than the recipe calls for may be needed. If all the liquid is absorbed but the grain isn't quite tender, add a little more liquid and cook longer. If it is tender but all the liquid hasn't been absorbed, just drain.*

Rice and Other Grains Cooking Chart
(1 cup uncooked)

Type	Cooking Liquid (in cups)	Directions	Approximate Simmer Time (in minutes)	Approximate Yield (in cups)
Rice				
White Rice				
Regular long grain	2	Heat rice and liquid to boiling. Reduce heat to low. Cover and simmer.	15	3
Parboiled (converted)	2 1/2	Heat liquid to boiling. Stir in rice. Reduce heat to low. Cover and simmer. Remove from heat. Let stand covered 5 minutes.	20 to 25	3 to 4
Precooked (instant)	1	Heat liquid to boiling. Stir in rice. Cover and remove from heat. Let stand covered 5 minutes.	0	2
Brown Rice				
Regular long grain	2 3/4	Heat rice and liquid to boiling. Reduce heat to low. Cover and simmer.	45 to 50	4
Precooked (instant)	1 1/4	Heat liquid to boiling. Stir in rice. Reduce heat to low. Cover and simmer.	10	2
Aromatic Rice				
Basmati	1 1/2	Heat rice and liquid to boiling. Reduce heat to low. Cover and simmer.	15 to 20	3
Jasmine	1 3/4		15 to 20	3
Texmati	1 3/4		15 to 20	3
Wild Rice	2 1/2	Heat rice and liquid to boiling. Reduce heat to low. Cover and simmer.	40 to 50	3

continues

Type	Cooking Liquid (in cups)	Directions	Approximate Simmer Time (in minutes)	Approximate Yield (in cups)
Other Grains—Cooking				
Barley				
Quick-cooking	2	Heat liquid to boiling. Stir in barley. Reduce heat to low. Cover and simmer. Let stand covered 5 minutes.	10 to 12	3
Regular	4		45 to 50	4
Millet	2 1/2	Heat millet and liquid to boiling. Reduce heat to low. Cover and simmer.	15 to 20	4
Quinoa	2	Heat quinoa and liquid to boiling. Reduce heat to low. Cover and simmer.	15	3 to 4
Wheat Berries	2 1/2	Heat wheat berries and liquid to boiling. Reduce heat to low. Cover and simmer.	50 to 60	2 3/4 to 3
Other Grains—Soaking				
Bulgur	3	Pour boiling liquid over bulgur or kasha. Cover and soak (do not cook). Drain if needed. Or cook as directed on package.	Soak 30 to 60 minutes	3
Kasha (roasted buckwheat kernels)	2	Pour boiling liquid over bulgur or kasha. Cover and soak (do not cook). Drain if needed. Or cook as directed on package.	Soak 10 to 15 minutes	4

Tips for Cooking Rice

- Rinse rice only if directed to on the package or if the rice is imported.
- Do not stir rice during cooking. Stirring releases more starch and makes rice sticky.
- Add flavor to rice and grains by cooking in equal parts water and broth (beef, chicken or vegetable) or juice (apple, orange, pineapple or tomato).
- For firmer rice, use 2 to 4 tablespoons less liquid and cook a few minutes less. A firmer texture is desired if rice is to be cooked further, such as in a casserole. For softer rice, use 2 to 3 tablespoons more liquid and cook a few minutes longer. Letting rice stand covered ten minutes after cooking also will make rice softer.
- If rice is still wet after cooking, leave it uncovered over low heat a few minutes.
- Fluff rice after cooking with a fork by lifting it upward to release the steam and separate the grains. Stirring with a spoon can cause stickiness.
- After removing cooked rice from the saucepan, fill the saucepan with cold water and allow to soak to make washing easier.
- Rice cookers (electric or nonelectric) are available and becoming more popular for cooking rice. Follow manufacturer's directions.
- It is possible to cook rice in the microwave; however, it does not save any time. Follow microwave manufacturer's directions or the microwave directions on the rice package.

Spanish Rice with Beef

Curried Rice

PREP: 25 min; COOK: 5 min
Makes 4 servings, about 3/4 cup each

Curry powder is a blend of up to twenty spices and often is used in Indian cooking. It loses its pungency quite quickly so should be stored airtight and used within two months.

1 cup uncooked regular long grain rice
2 tablespoons margarine or butter
1 tablespoon finely chopped onion
1/2 to 1 teaspoon curry powder
1/4 teaspoon salt
1/4 teaspoon pepper
1/4 cup slivered almonds, toasted (page 9)
1/4 cup chopped pimiento-stuffed olives or
    ripe olives

1. Cook rice as directed on page 204.

2. Melt margarine in 10-inch skillet over medium heat. Cook onion in margarine about 2 minutes, stirring occasionally, until tender. Stir in curry powder, salt and pepper.

3. Stir onion mixture into hot rice. Sprinkle with almonds and olives.

1 SERVING: Calories 285 (Calories from Fat 125); Fat 14g (Saturated 5g); Cholesterol 0mg; Sodium 420mg; Carbohydrate 42g (Dietary Fiber 1g); Protein 5g

Spanish Rice

PREP: 15 min; COOK: 35 min
Makes 6 servings, about 2/3 cup each

Expand your horizons by using an herbed or other specially flavored tomato sauce.

2 tablespoons vegetable oil
1 cup uncooked regular long grain rice
1 medium onion, chopped (1/2 cup)
2 1/2 cups water
1 1/2 teaspoons salt
3/4 teaspoon chili powder
1/8 teaspoon garlic powder
1 small green bell pepper, chopped (1/2 cup)
1 can (8 ounces) tomato sauce

1. Heat oil in 10-inch skillet over medium heat. Cook rice and onion in oil about 5 minutes, stirring frequently, until rice is golden brown and onion is tender.

2. Stir in remaining ingredients. Heat to boiling; reduce heat to low. Cover and simmer about 30 minutes, stirring occasionally, until rice is tender.

1 SERVING: Calories 180 (Calories from Fat 45); Fat 5g (Saturated 1g); Cholesterol 0mg; Sodium 770mg; Carbohydrate 32g (Dietary Fiber 1g); Protein 3g

SPANISH RICE WITH BEEF: Stir in 1 pound cooked ground beef with the remaining ingredients in step 2.

Pork Fried Rice

PREP: 15 min; COOK: 10 min
Makes 4 servings, about 1 cup each

    1 cup bean sprouts
    1 tablespoon vegetable oil
    3 ounces mushrooms, sliced (1 cup)
    3 cups cold cooked regular long grain rice
        (page 204)
    1 cup cut-up cooked pork
    2 tablespoons sliced green onions
    1 tablespoon vegetable oil
    2 large eggs, slightly beaten
    3 tablespoons soy sauce
    Dash of white pepper

1. Rinse bean sprouts with cold water; drain.

2. Heat 1 tablespoon oil in 10-inch skillet over medium heat; rotate skillet until oil covers bottom. Cook mushrooms in oil about 1 minute, stirring frequently, until coated.

3. Add bean sprouts, rice, pork and onions. Cook over medium heat about 5 minutes, stirring and breaking up rice, until hot.

4. Push rice mixture to side of skillet. Add 1 tablespoon oil to other side of skillet. Cook eggs in oil over medium heat, stirring constantly, until eggs are thickened throughout but still moist. Stir eggs into rice mixture. Stir in soy sauce and white pepper.

1 SERVING: Calories 335 (Calories from Fat 115); Fat 13g (Saturated 3g); Cholesterol 135mg; Sodium 830mg; Carbohydrate 37g (Dietary Fiber 1g); Protein 18g

---

LIGHTER PORK FRIED RICE

For 6 grams of fat and 245 calories per serving, decrease pork to 1/2 cup and finely chop. Use a nonstick skillet and omit the oil in step 4. Substitute 1/2 cup fat-free cholesterol-free egg product for the eggs.

Savory Pilaf

PREP: 10 min; COOK: 20 min; STAND: 5 min
Makes 4 servings, about 3/4 cup each

(photograph on page 268)

    2 tablespoons margarine or butter
    1 small onion, chopped (1/4 cup)
    1 cup uncooked regular long grain rice
    2 cups chicken broth
    1/4 teaspoon salt

1. Melt margarine in 3-quart saucepan over medium heat. Cook onion in margarine about 3 minutes, stirring occasionally, until onion is tender.

2. Stir in rice. Cook 5 minutes, stirring frequently. Stir in broth and salt.

3. Heat to boiling, stirring once or twice; reduce heat to low. Cover and simmer 16 minutes (do not lift cover or stir); remove from heat. Cover and let steam about 5 minutes.

1 SERVING: Calories 300 (Calories from Fat 100); Fat 11g (Saturated 2g); Cholesterol 0mg; Sodium 590mg; Carbohydrate 44g (Dietary Fiber 2g); Protein 8g

BULGUR PILAF: Substitute 1 cup uncooked bulgur for the rice.

INDIAN PILAF: Stir in 1/2 cup diced dried fruit and raisin mixture, 1/4 teaspoon ground allspice, 1/4 teaspoon ground turmeric and 1/4 teaspoon curry powder with the broth and salt in step 2.

MUSHROOM PILAF: Stir in 1 can (4 ounces) mushroom stems and pieces, drained, with the broth and salt in step 2.

Risotto Florentine

PREP: 10 min; COOK: 30 min; STAND: 5 min
Makes 4 servings, about 1 1/3 cups each

The method for cooking this risotto recipe is less traditional, but it's just as tasty. It's also less labor intensive because your constant attention isn't required.

    1 tablespoon margarine or butter
    1 medium onion, chopped (1/2 cup)
    1 clove garlic, crushed
    1 cup uncooked Arborio or other short-grain
        white rice
    3 cups chicken or vegetable broth
    1/2 teaspoon saffron threads or
        1/4 teaspoon ground turmeric
    1 can (15 to 16 ounces) cannellini beans,
        rinsed and drained
    1 package (10 ounces) frozen chopped
        spinach, thawed and squeezed to drain
    1/4 cup grated Parmesan cheese

1. Melt margarine in 10-inch skillet over medium-high heat. Cook onion and garlic in margarine about 2 minutes, stirring occasionally, until onion is just crisp-tender.

2. Add rice; stir to coat with margarine mixture. Stir in broth and saffron. Heat to boiling; stir once thoroughly and reduce heat to low. Cover and simmer 20 to 25 minutes or until rice is almost tender and liquid is absorbed.

3. Stir in remaining ingredients. Cover and let stand 5 minutes.

1 SERVING: Calories 380 (Calories from Fat 55); Fat 6g (Saturated 2g); Cholesterol 5mg; Sodium 970mg; Carbohydrate 69g (Dietary Fiber 7g); Protein 20g

Lemony Seafood Risotto

PREP: 15 min; COOK: 35 min
Makes 4 to 5 servings, about 1 1/3 cups each

The traditional risotto cooking method is used in this recipe, where hot broth is gradually added to the rice mixture and frequent stirring is required.

2 teaspoons olive or vegetable oil
1/4 cup finely chopped shallots (2 large) or green onions (3 medium)
2 cloves garlic, finely chopped
1 cup uncooked Arborio or other short-grain white rice
1/2 cup dry white wine (or nonalcoholic) or chicken broth
2 cans (14 1/2 ounces each) ready-to-serve chicken broth, heated
2 teaspoons olive or vegetable oil
1/2 pound bay scallops
1/2 pound uncooked medium shrimp, peeled and deveined
1 teaspoon grated lemon peel
2 tablespoons chopped fresh parsley

1. Heat 2 teaspoons oil in 12-inch nonstick skillet over medium-high heat. Cook shallots and garlic in oil, stirring frequently, until shallots are crisp-tender; reduce heat to medium.

2. Stir in rice. Cook, stirring frequently, until rice begins to brown. Stir in wine. Cook until liquid is absorbed.

3. Pour 1/2 cup of the broth over rice mixture. Cook uncovered, stirring occasionally, until liquid is absorbed. Continue cooking 15 to 20 minutes, adding broth 1/2 cup at a time and stirring occasionally, until rice is tender and creamy.

4. Meanwhile, heat 2 teaspoons oil in 10-inch skillet over medium heat. Cook scallops and shrimp in oil 4 to 5 minutes, stirring frequently, until shrimp are pink and firm. Remove scallops and shrimp from skillet, using slotted spoon, and *gently* stir into rice mixture with lemon peel. Sprinkle with parsley.

1 SERVING: Calories 340 (Calories from Fat 65); Fat 7g (Saturated 1g); Cholesterol 100mg; Sodium 610mg; Carbohydrate 44g (Dietary Fiber 1g); Protein 26g

Brown Rice and Lentils

PREP: 15 min; COOK: 55 min
Makes 4 servings, about 3/4 cup each

2 tablespoons margarine or butter
1 small onion, chopped (1/4 cup)
1 clove garlic, crushed
1/2 cup dried lentils (4 ounces), sorted and rinsed
1/2 cup uncooked brown rice
1 can (10 1/2 ounces) condensed chicken broth
1/2 broth can water
1/4 teaspoon red pepper sauce
1 medium green bell pepper, coarsely chopped (1 cup)
1/2 cup shredded Havarti cheese with herbs (2 ounces)

1. Melt margarine in 2-quart saucepan over medium heat. Cook onion and garlic in margarine about 3 minutes, stirring occasionally, until onion is tender.

2. Stir in lentils, rice, broth, water and pepper sauce. Heat to boiling; reduce heat to low. Cover and simmer about 50 minutes, adding water if necessary, until rice is tender and liquid is absorbed.

3. Stir in bell pepper. Sprinkle with cheese.

1 SERVING: Calories 290 (Calories from Fat 110); Fat 12g (Saturated 5g); Cholesterol 15mg; Sodium 650mg; Carbohydrate 36g (Dietary Fiber 5g); Protein 15g

---

LIGHTER BROWN RICE AND LENTILS
For 5 grams of fat and 215 calories per serving, decrease margarine to 1 tablespoon and use nonstick saucepan. Omit cheese.

Cranberry-Wild Rice Bake

PREP: 45 min; BAKE: 1 hr 35 min
Makes 8 servings, about 1/2 cup each

Ruby red dried cranberries enhance this robust rice dish that complements pork, turkey or game.

1 cup uncooked wild rice
2 1/2 cups water
1 tablespoon margarine or butter
1 medium onion, chopped (1/2 cup)
3 ounces mushrooms, sliced (1 cup)
2 1/2 cups chicken broth, heated
2 cloves garlic, finely chopped
1/4 teaspoon salt
1 cup dried cranberries

1. Heat oven to 350°. Grease square baking dish, 8 × 8 × 2 inches, with shortening.

2. Place wild rice in wire strainer. Run cold water through rice, lifting rice with fingers to clean thoroughly. Heat rice and water to boiling in 2-quart saucepan, stirring occasionally; reduce heat to low. Cover and simmer 30 minutes; drain.

3. Melt margarine in 10-inch skillet over medium heat. Cook onion and mushrooms in margarine, stirring occasionally, until onion is tender.

4. Mix rice and onion mixture in baking dish. Mix broth, salt and garlic; pour over rice mixture.

5. Cover and bake 1 1/4 hours. Stir in cranberries. Cover and bake 15 to 20 minutes longer or until liquid is absorbed.

1 SERVING: Calories 120 (Calories from Fat 20); Fat 2g (Saturated 0g); Cholesterol 0mg; Sodium 85mg; Carbohydrate 24g (Dietary Fiber 2g); Protein 4g

---

TIMESAVING TIP

Purchase sliced mushrooms, and pick up chopped onion at the salad bar. Use finely chopped garlic from a jar.

Barley-Vegetable Sauté

PREP: 15 min; COOK: 10 min
Makes 4 servings, about 2 cups each

Add sliced tomatoes and crisp breadsticks, and you'll have a delicious meatless meal.

> 2 teaspoons margarine or butter
> 1 large onion, chopped (1 cup)
> 1 medium yellow or red bell pepper, chopped (1 cup)
> 1 clove garlic, crushed
> 4 cups cooked barley (page 205)
> 2 tablespoons chopped fresh or 2 teaspoons dried thyme leaves
> 1/2 teaspoon salt
> 1 package (16 ounces) frozen whole-kernel corn, thawed
> 1 package (10 ounces) frozen lima beans, thawed

1. Melt margarine in 12-inch skillet over medium-high heat. Cook onion, bell pepper and garlic in margarine about 2 minutes, stirring occasionally, until bell pepper is crisp-tender.

2. Stir in remaining ingredients. Cook about 5 minutes, stirring occasionally, until hot.

1 SERVING: Calories 360 (Calories from Fat 25); Fat 3g (Saturated 1g); Cholesterol 0mg; Sodium 410mg; Carbohydrate 84g (Dietary Fiber 15g); Protein 14g

Barley-Vegetable Sauté, Herbed Bread Sticks (page 58)

Cheese Grits

PREP: 20 min; BAKE: 40 min; STAND: 10 min
Makes 8 servings, about 2/3 cup each

A southern favorite at any meal, this dish is especially good served with ham or barbecued ribs.

2 cups milk
2 cups water
1/2 teaspoon salt
1/4 teaspoon pepper
1 cup uncooked white hominy quick grits
1 1/2 cups shredded Cheddar cheese
   (6 ounces)
1/4 cup sliced green onions (3 medium)
2 large eggs, slightly beaten
1 tablespoon margarine or butter
1/4 teaspoon paprika

1. Heat oven to 350°. Grease 1 1/2-quart casserole with shortening.

2. Heat milk, water, salt and pepper to boiling in 2-quart saucepan. *Gradually* add grits, stirring constantly; reduce heat to low. Simmer uncovered about 5 minutes, stirring frequently, until thick. Stir in cheese and onions.

3. Stir 1 cup of the hot mixture into eggs; stir back into remaining hot mixture in saucepan. Pour into casserole. Dot with margarine. Sprinkle with paprika.

4. Bake uncovered 35 to 40 minutes or until set. Let stand 10 minutes.

1 SERVING: Calories 215 (Calories from Fat 100); Fat 11g (Saturated 6g); Cholesterol 80mg; Sodium 330mg; Carbohydrate 19g (Dietary Fiber 0g); Protein 10g

---

LIGHTER CHEESE GRITS

For 6 grams of fat and 180 calories per serving, use skim milk and reduced-fat cheese. Substitute 1 egg plus 2 egg whites for the 2 eggs.

GARLIC-CHEESE GRITS: Stir in 2 cloves garlic, finely chopped, and 1/8 teaspoon red pepper sauce with the onions.

Polenta

PREP: 10 min; COOK: 20 min
Makes 6 servings, about 3/4 cup each

Polenta is a staple of northern Italy and in eastern European countries. It is also known as cornmeal mush and can be served at any meal of the day, either as a side dish or as a base of a main dish, such as polenta with spaghetti sauce.

1 cup yellow cornmeal
3/4 cup water
3 1/4 cups boiling water
1 1/2 teaspoons salt

1. Mix cornmeal and 3/4 cup water in 2-quart saucepan. Stir in 3 1/4 cups boiling water and the salt. Cook, stirring constantly, until mixture thickens and boils; reduce heat to low.

2. Cover and simmer about 10 minutes, stirring occasionally, until very thick; remove from heat. Stir until smooth.

1 SERVING: Calories 180 (Calories from Fat 70); Fat 8g (Saturated 4g); Cholesterol 15mg; Sodium 1000mg; Carbohydrate 19g (Dietary Fiber 1g); Protein 9g

FRIED POLENTA: Grease loaf pan, 9 × 5 × 3 inches, with shortening. After simmering polenta 10 minutes in step 2, spread in loaf pan. Cover and refrigerate at least 12 hours or until firm. Invert pan to unmold. Cut into 1/2-inch slices. Coat slices with flour. Melt 2 tablespoons margarine or butter in 10-inch skillet over low heat. Cook slices in margarine about 5 minutes on each side or until brown. Serve with molasses, jam, maple-flavored syrup, sour cream or spaghetti sauce if desired.

POLENTA WITH CHEESE: Heat oven to 350°. Grease 1 1/2-quart casserole with shortening. Prepare Polenta. Spread one-third of the polenta in casserole. Dot with 1 teaspoon margarine or butter. Sprinkle with 1/3 cup grated Parmesan cheese. Repeat twice. Sprinkle with 1/3 cup shredded Swiss cheese. Bake uncovered 15 to 20 minutes or until hot and bubbly.

TIMESAVING TIP

For Fried Polenta, spread polenta in greased rectangular baking pan 13 × 9 × 2 inches and refrigerate uncovered about 3 hours until firm. Cut into 6 squares. (Diagonally cut squares into triangles before frying, if desired.) Fry as directed.

About Legumes

Legumes, which include beans, peas and lentils, are so-named because they come from leguminous plants (those producing pods with one row of seeds). Legumes are a staple all over the world. Usually found in dried form, many also can be purchased canned or frozen. Their mild flavor makes them perfect partners with spices and herbs.

Beans, especially, are very nutritious. Abundant with soluble fiber, they combine well with grains, especially corn, wheat and rice, to make complete protein. Virtually fat free, they have no cholesterol and are a good source of vitamins. Beans are extremely versatile and can be used in just about every part of a meal.

Intestinal gas can result from eating beans due to the digestive system's inability to digest complex sugars. This is lessened by draining the soaking liquid used to hydrate dried beans or by rinsing and draining canned beans. Additionally, over-the-counter products are available to help minimize this effect.

Selecting Legumes

Many varieties of legumes are available in supermarkets. Check health or ethnic food stores or a food cooperative for the more unusual varieties, which can usually be found in bulk form.

- Quality and freshness are indicated by bright uniform color and smooth, unbroken seed coats.
- Legumes of the same size will result in more even cooking.
- Sort legumes before cooking to remove any damaged pieces or foreign matter.
- 1 cup (8 ounces) dried beans = about 3 cups cooked; 2 cups (1 pound) dried beans = about 6 cups cooked; 1 can (15 to 16 ounces) beans, rinsed and drained = about 1 1/2 to 2 cups beans.

Storing Legumes

Dried Legumes

Most legumes can be stored indefinitely, but for optimum quality and flavor, one to two years is the recommended time. Store in original packaging, or transfer to airtight glass or plastic containers and label contents with storage date. Store in a cool (60° or less), dry location.

Cooked Legumes

- **Refrigerator:** Store cooked legumes covered in the refrigerator for two to three days.
- **Freezer:** Freeze cooked legumes in airtight containers for up to eight months.

Legumes

Legumes Glossary

Adzuki Beans: Small, oval, reddish brown beans with a light, nutty flavor. They originated in China and Japan.

Anasazi Beans: Kidney-shaped white beans with maroon spots that disappear when cooked. The name is Navajo and means "ancient ones." Pinto beans are a good substitute.

Black Beans: Also called turtle beans, black beans are found in the cuisines of South and Central America as well as the Caribbean.

Black-Eyed Peas: Also called cowpeas and black-eyed suzies, black-eyed peas are creamy colored with a small, dark brown to black spot on one side. Native to China, they found their way to Africa and then to the southern United States.

Butter Beans: Large cream-colored lima beans often served as a vegetable side dish or added to soups, main dishes and salads.

Cannellini Beans: White kidney beans originated in South America and are slightly smaller than Great Northern Beans. Adopted by Italy, they are often mixed with pasta.

Fava Beans: Large flat beans with an earthy flavor that appear brown and wrinkled when dried. They are the bean of choice for the Middle Eastern specialty *falafel*.

Garbanzo Beans: Tan, bumpy and round, garbanzo beans need long, slow cooking. Also called chickpeas, they are used in the popular Middle Eastern dip *hummus*. Their firm texture makes them a good addition to soups, stews, casseroles and salads.

Great Northern Beans: Kidney-shaped white beans traditionally used in making baked beans and bean soup. Cannellini beans can be used as a substitute for great northern beans even though they are smaller.

Kidney Beans: Available in dark and light red, they add color and texture to many dishes. A favorite in chili as well as red beans and rice.

Lentils: The familiar small, grayish-green lentil is only one of the many types and colors of lentils used around the world. Also available in white, yellow, red and black, dried lentils do not require soaking, and they cook in a short time.

Lima Beans: The choice of regular and baby sizes make them a wonderful addition to multibean salads, soups and casseroles. (Also see Butter Beans.)

Mung Beans: Called grams, or when hulled, *moong dal,* this sweet-flavored bean is native to India and also popular in China. Americans know its sprouted form as bean sprouts.

Navy Beans: Small white beans so named because they fed many a sailor in the early 1800s. They are also known as pea beans.

Pinto Beans: Two-tone kidney-shaped beans widely used in Central and South American cooking. They turn a uniform pink when cooked and are used for the Mexican staple refried beans.

Soybeans: Soybeans are not widely eaten in the United States as beans. Much of the soybean harvest is processed into oil or tofu (bean curd), often used in meatless dishes.

Split Peas: Used mostly in soups, they are available in green and yellow. Split peas do not require soaking and cook in a shorter time than beans.

Soaking Legumes Before Cooking

All legumes except lentils need to be boiled uncovered for two minutes before cooking to destroy an enzyme that can cause some people to become ill. This boiling time eliminates the need for the traditional, long-soaking method to help rehydrate legumes. Long soaking does, however, allow for more uniform swelling.

Draining the soaking water, instead of cooking in it, reduces intestinal gas-forming sugars without losing large amounts of important nutrients.

If you choose to soak legumes before cooking, use one of the following methods.

- **Long-Soak Method**—Place legumes in large saucepan or bowl in enough cold water to cover. Let stand 8 to 24 hours. Drain and rinse. Boil beans 2 minutes in enough water to cover. Drain water if desired.
- **Quick-Soak Method**—Boil beans 2 minutes in enough water to cover; remove from heat. Cover and let stand 1 hour before cooking. Drain water if desired.

Tips for Cooking Dried Legumes

- Dried legumes double or triple in volume as they cook, so be sure to use a large enough saucepan or casserole.
- Legumes of similar size and with similar cooking times can be interchanged in recipes.
- To prevent beans from foaming during cooking, add one tablespoon margarine or vegetable oil to the cooking water; drain and rinse.
- Simmer, rather than boil beans and stir *gently,* or the skins may burst.
- If the legumes aren't quite tender but all the water is absorbed, add a little more water and cook longer. If tender but all the water hasn't been absorbed, drain if desired.
- Salt and acid tend to toughen beans. Add salt and acidic foods, such as lemon juice, vinegar and tomato-based foods (tomatoes, sauce, paste or juice), only *after* the beans are soft, or the beans may not soften.
- Legumes lose moisture with age, so more water may be needed than a recipe calls for and cooking may take longer. If very old, they may never soften completely.
- High altitude or hard water may increase cooking times.
- Microwaving dried legumes is not recommended because of the long, slow cooking time required and the amount of liquid necessary to hydrate them.
- Using a pressure cooker for cooking dried legumes is not recommended because of the foam created during cooking. The foam can clog the pressure valve and may cause a sudden release of pressure, which could force the lid off without warning.

Basic Directions for Cooking Dried Legumes

1. Sort and rinse legumes. Place 1 cup legumes in 3- to 4-quart saucepan.
2. Add enough cold water (about 3 to 4 cups) to cover legumes.
3. Heat to boiling. Boil uncovered 2 minutes. *Do not boil lentils.*
4. Reduce heat to low. Cover and simmer (do not boil or beans will burst), stirring occasionally, for amount of cooking time in chart below, or until tender.

Dried Legumes Cooking Chart
(1 cup dried legumes)

Type	Approximate Simmer Time	Approximate Yield (In Cups)
Adzuki Beans Lentils	30 to 45 minutes	2 to 3
Mung Beans Split Peas	45 to 60 minutes	2 to 2 1/4
Black-Eyed Peas Butter Beans Cannellini Beans Great Northern Beans Lima Beans Navy Beans Pinto Beans	1 to 1 1/2 hours	2 to 2 1/2
Anasazi Beans Black Beans Fava Beans Kidney Beans	1 to 2 hours	2
Garbanzo Beans	2 to 2 1/2 hours	2
Soy Beans	3 to 4 hours	2

Old-Fashioned Baked Beans

PREP: 20 min; BAKE: 6 1/4 hr
Makes 10 servings, about 1/2 cup each

Serve this favorite along with Creamy Potato Salad (page 321) and Creamy Coleslaw (page 322) the next time you grill burgers, chicken or ribs.

10 cups water
2 cups dried navy beans (1 pound)
1/2 cup packed brown sugar
1/4 cup molasses
1 teaspoon salt
6 slices bacon, crisply cooked and crumbled
1 medium onion, chopped (1/2 cup)
3 cups water

1. Heat oven to 350°.

2. Heat 10 cups water and the beans to boiling in Dutch oven. Boil uncovered 2 minutes. Stir in remaining ingredients except 3 cups water.

3. Cover and bake 4 hours, stirring occasionally.

4. Stir in 3 cups water. Bake uncovered 2 to 2 1/4 hours longer, stirring occasionally, until beans are tender and desired consistency.

1 SERVING: Calories 195 (Calories from Fat 20); Fat 2g (Saturated 1g); Cholesterol 5mg; Sodium 280mg; Carbohydrate 42g (Dietary Fiber 7g); Protein 9g

Easy Skillet Baked Beans

PREP: 15 min; COOK: 25 min
Makes 4 servings, about 1 cup each

Here's a favorite way to jazz up canned beans for a quick dinner. The skillet's large heated surface area helps cook off any extra liquid more quickly.

3 slices bacon, cut into 1-inch pieces
1 medium onion, chopped (1/2 cup)
2 cans (16 ounces each) pork and beans
1/4 cup chili sauce
1 teaspoon mustard

1. Cook bacon and onion in 10-inch skillet over medium heat, stirring occasionally, until bacon is crisp.

2. Stir in remaining ingredients. Heat to boiling; reduce heat to low. Simmer uncovered 15 to 20 minutes, stirring occasionally, until liquid is absorbed.

1 SERVING: Calories 285 (Calories from Fat 55); Fat 6g (Saturated 2g); Cholesterol 20mg; Sodium 1030mg; Carbohydrate 54g (Dietary Fiber 10g); Protein 14g

EASY OVEN BAKED BEANS: Heat oven to 350°. After boiling in step 2, pour beans into ungreased 1 1/2-quart casserole. Bake about 40 minutes.

Pinto Beans

PREP: 15 min; STAND: 1 hr; COOK: 2 hr
Makes 12 servings, about 1/2 cup each

Serve these beans as a side dish or double the amount and serve as a main dish.

4 cups water
2 cups dried pinto or black beans (1 pound)
1 medium onion, chopped (1/2 cup)
1/4 cup vegetable oil
1 teaspoon salt
1 teaspoon cumin seed
2 cloves garlic, crushed
1 slice bacon, cut up

1. Mix water, beans and onion in Dutch oven. Cover and heat to boiling. Boil 2 minutes; remove from heat. Let stand 1 hour.

2. Add just enough water to beans to cover. Stir in remaining ingredients. Heat to boiling; reduce heat to low. Cover and simmer about 2 hours, stirring occasionally and adding water if necessary, until beans are very tender; drain. Beans can be covered and refrigerated up to 10 days.

1 SERVING: Calories 145 (Calories from Fat 45); Fat 5g (Saturated 1g); Cholesterol 0mg; Sodium 190mg; Carbohydrate 24g (Dietary Fiber 6g); Protein 7g

---

LIGHTER PINTO BEANS
For 3 grams of fat and 125 calories per serving, decrease oil to 1 tablespoon.

Three-Bean Casserole

PREP: 20 min; BAKE: 45 min
Makes 8 servings, about 1 1/3 cups each

Popular at potlucks and other gatherings, this dish conveniently stays hot a good while. (photograph on page 201)

1 pound bulk pork sausage
2 medium stalks celery, sliced (1 cup)
1 medium onion, chopped (1/2 cup)
1 large clove garlic, crushed
2 cans (21 ounces each) baked beans in tomato sauce
1 can (15 to 16 ounces) lima beans, drained
1 can (15 to 16 ounces) kidney beans, drained
1 can (8 ounces) tomato sauce
1 tablespoon ground mustard (dry)
2 tablespoons honey
1 tablespoon white vinegar
1/4 teaspoon red pepper sauce

White and Green Beans (page 218), Red Beans and Rice

1. Heat oven to 400°.

2. Cook sausage, celery, onion and garlic in 10-inch skillet over medium heat about 10 minutes, stirring occasionally, until sausage is no longer pink; drain.

3. Mix sausage mixture and remaining ingredients in ungreased 3-quart casserole. Bake uncovered about 45 minutes, stirring once, until hot and bubbly.

1 SERVING: Calories 340 (Calories from Fat 90); Fat 10g (Saturated 3g); Cholesterol 20mg; Sodium 1670mg; Carbohydrate 54g (Dietary Fiber 14g); Protein 22g

Red Beans and Rice

PREP: 25 min; COOK: 1 3/4 hr; STAND: 5 min
Makes 8 servings, about 3/4 cup each

   3 cups water
   1 cup dried kidney beans (8 ounces)
   2 ounces salt pork (with rind), diced, or
      3 slices bacon, cut up
   1 medium onion, chopped (1/2 cup)
   1 medium green bell pepper, chopped
      (1 cup)
   1 cup uncooked regular long grain rice
   1 teaspoon salt

1. Heat water and beans to boiling in 3-quart saucepan. Boil uncovered 2 minutes; reduce heat to low. Cover and simmer 1 to 1 1/4 hours or until tender (do not boil or beans will burst).

2. Drain beans, reserving liquid. Cook salt pork in 10-inch skillet over medium heat, stirring occasionally, until crisp. Stir in onion and bell pepper. Cook, stirring occasionally, until onion is tender.

3. Add enough water to bean liquid, if necessary, to measure 2 cups. Add bean liquid, salt pork mixture, rice and salt to beans in 3-quart saucepan. Heat to boiling, stirring once or twice; reduce heat to low. Cover and simmer 14 minutes (do not lift cover or stir); remove from heat. Fluff with fork. Cover and let steam 5 to 10 minutes.

1 SERVING: Calories 160 (Calories from Fat 35); Fat 4g (Saturated 1g); Cholesterol 5mg; Sodium 520mg; Carbohydrate 29g (Dietary Fiber 4g); Protein 6g

HOPPIN' JOHN: Substitute 1 cup dried black-eyed peas for the kidney beans. Omit bell pepper.

> **TIMESAVING TIP**
> Substitute 1 can (15 to 16 ounces) red kidney beans, drained and liquid reserved, for the dried kidney beans. Omit water and step 1.

Indian Split Peas with Vegetables

Tamale Lentil Casserole

PREP: 50 min; BAKE: 20 min
Makes 6 servings, about 1 1/4 cups each

*This dish will remind you of Mexican tamales, but without
all the work!*

> 1 tablespoon vegetable oil
> 1 large onion, chopped (1 cup)
> 1 medium green bell pepper, chopped
>   (1 cup)
> 2 cloves garlic, finely chopped
> 3 cups water
> 1 1/4 cups dried lentils (10 ounces), sorted
>   and rinsed
> 1 can (14 ounces) tomato sauce
> 1 package (1.25 ounces) taco seasoning mix
> Cornbread Topping (right)

1. Heat oil in 3-quart saucepan over medium-high
heat. Cook onion, bell pepper and garlic in oil, stirring
frequently, until vegetables are tender.

2. Stir in water, lentils, tomato sauce and seasoning
mix; reduce heat to low. Partially cover and simmer 35
to 40 minutes or until lentils are tender.

3. Heat oven to 400°. Grease 2-quart casserole with
shortening.

4. Prepare Cornbread Topping. Spoon lentil mixture into casserole. Spread topping evenly over lentil
mixture. Bake uncovered 15 to 20 minutes until topping is golden brown.

Cornbread Topping

> 1 package (8 1/2 ounces) cornbread muffin
>   mix
> 1 can (8 1/2 ounces) cream-style corn
> 1/2 cup shredded Cheddar cheese (2 ounces)
> 1/4 cup milk
> 1 large egg

Mix all ingredients until moistened.

1 SERVING: Calories 295 (Calories from Fat 70); Fat 8g
(Saturated 3g); Cholesterol 45mg; Sodium 1000mg;
Carbohydrate 48g (Dietary Fiber 2g); Protein 10g

**LIGHTER TAMALE LENTIL
CASSEROLE**

For 4 grams of fat and 250 calories per serving, decrease
oil to 1 teaspoon and use nonstick saucepan. For the
topping, omit cheese and substitute 1/4 cup fat-free
cholesterol-free egg product for the egg.

Indian Split Peas with Vegetables

PREP: 15 min; COOK: 15 min
Makes 4 servings, about 2 cups each

Cooking the spices and chilies in oil develops the flavors more fully in this savory dish. It makes a nice main dish when paired with pita bread and a cucumber and tomato salad.

2 teaspoons vegetable oil
1/2 teaspoon cumin seed or 1/4 teaspoon ground cumin
1/4 teaspoon ground turmeric
2 jalapeño chilies, seeded and chopped
3 cups cauliflowerets (1 pound)
1/4 cup chicken broth or vegetable broth
2 cups cooked yellow split peas (page 213)
2 cups frozen green peas, thawed
1 can (15 ounces) black beans, rinsed and drained

1. Heat oil in 10-inch skillet over medium-high heat. Cook cumin, turmeric and chilies in oil 2 minutes, stirring occasionally.

2. Stir in cauliflowerets and broth. Cover and cook 3 to 4 minutes or until cauliflowerets are tender.

3. Stir in remaining ingredients. Cook about 5 minutes, stirring occasionally, until hot.

1 SERVING: Calories 305 (Calories from Fat 35); Fat 4g (Saturated 1g); Cholesterol 0mg; Sodium 350mg; Carbohydrate 60g (Dietary Fiber 15g); Protein 22g

Spicy Split Peas

PREP: 15 min; COOK: 40 min
Makes 4 servings, about 1/2 cup each

Although split peas are more often used in soup (see Split Pea Soup, page 382), this side dish shows them in a new and tasty light.

3 cups water
3/4 cup dried split peas (6 ounces)
2 tablespoons margarine or butter
1 teaspoon finely chopped gingerroot or 1/4 teaspoon ground ginger
1/2 teaspoon salt
1/2 teaspoon ground turmeric
1/2 teaspoon ground cumin
1 small onion, finely chopped (1/4 cup)

1. Heat water and peas to boiling in 3-quart saucepan. Boil uncovered 2 minutes; reduce heat to low. Cover and simmer about 25 minutes or until peas are tender but not mushy; drain.

2. Melt margarine in 10-inch skillet over medium-high heat. Cook gingerroot, salt, turmeric, cumin and onion in margarine about 3 minutes, stirring occasionally, until onion is tender. Stir in peas until evenly coated.

1 SERVING: Calories 170 (Calories from Fat 55); Fat 6g (Saturated 1g); Cholesterol 0mg; Sodium 340mg; Carbohydrate 24g (Dietary Fiber 4g); Protein 9g

---

LIGHTER SPICY SPLIT PEAS

For 3 grams of fat and 145 calories per serving, decrease margarine to 1 tablespoon and use nonstick skillet.

Southwestern Black-Eyed Peas

PREP: 15 min; COOK: 1 hr
Makes 6 servings, about 1/2 cup each

2 cups water
3/4 cup dried black-eyed peas (6 ounces)
1 tablespoon vegetable oil
1 cup sliced okra
1 small onion, chopped (1/4 cup)
1/2 teaspoon salt
1/4 teaspoon red pepper sauce
2 cloves garlic, crushed
1 tablespoon chopped fresh cilantro
1 small tomato, seeded and chopped (1/2 cup)

1. Heat water and peas to boiling in 2-quart saucepan. Boil uncovered 2 minutes; reduce heat to low. Cover and simmer 30 to 40 minutes, stirring occasionally, until beans are tender (do not boil or peas will burst); drain.

2. Heat oil in same saucepan over medium heat. Cook okra, onion, salt, pepper sauce and garlic in oil about 5 minutes, stirring occasionally, until onion is tender. Stir in cilantro, tomato and beans. Cook, stirring occasionally, until hot.

1 SERVING: Calories 85 (Calories from Fat 25); Fat 3g (Saturated 0g); Cholesterol 0mg; Sodium 180mg; Carbohydrate 16g (Dietary Fiber 6g); Protein 5g

BLACK-EYED PEAS WITH HAM: Cook 1/3 cup chopped fully cooked smoked ham with peas in step 1.

TIMESAVING TIP

Substitute 1 can (15 to 16 ounces) black-eyed peas, rinsed and drained, for the dried black-eyed peas. Omit water and step 1.

Mexican Black Beans

PREP: 10 min; COOK: 1 1/4 hr
Makes 4 servings, about 2/3 cup each

  2 1/4 cups water
  3/4 cup dried black beans (6 ounces)
  1 tablespoon chopped fresh parsley
  1 tablespoon white wine vinegar
  1 teaspoon shredded lime or lemon peel
  1/4 teaspoon red pepper sauce
  2 green onions, thinly sliced
  1 medium red or green bell pepper, chopped
     (1 cup)

1. Heat water and beans to boiling in 2-quart saucepan. Boil uncovered 2 minutes; reduce heat to low. Cover and simmer about 1 hour, stirring occasionally, until beans are tender (do not boil or beans will burst); drain.

2. Stir in remaining ingredients. Cook, stirring occasionally, until hot.

1 SERVING: Calories 115 (Calories from Fat 10); Fat 1g (Saturated 0g); Cholesterol 0mg; Sodium 5mg; Carbohydrate 25g (Dietary Fiber 7g); Protein 8g

> **TIMESAVING TIP**
> Substitute 2 cans (15 ounces each) black beans, rinsed and drained, for the dried black beans. Omit water and step 1.

White and Green Beans

PREP: 15 min; COOK: 20 min
Makes 4 servings, about 3/4 cup each

(photograph on page 215)

  1 pound green beans, cut into 1 to 1 1/2 inch
     pieces
  2 tablespoons margarine or butter, melted
  1 tablespoon lemon juice
  2 teaspoons Dijon mustard
  2 teaspoons honey
  1/2 teaspoon lemon pepper
  1/4 teaspoon salt
  1 can (15 to 16 ounces) great northern or
     navy beans, rinsed and drained

1. Prepare and cook green beans as directed on page 394, using 3-quart saucepan.

2. Stir in remaining ingredients. Cook over medium heat about 5 minutes, stirring occasionally, until hot.

1 SERVING: Calories 190 (Calories from Fat 55); Fat 6g (Saturated 1g); Cholesterol 0mg; Sodium 510mg; Carbohydrate 32g (Dietary Fiber 8g); Protein 10g

> **TIMESAVING TIP**
> Substitute 1 package (16 ounces) frozen cut green beans for the fresh green beans. Cook as directed on package.

Italian White Beans

PREP: 10 min; COOK: 1 hr
Makes 6 servings, about 1/2 cup each

  2 1/2 cups water
  3/4 cup dried great northern beans
     (6 ounces)
  1/2 cup chopped drained oil-packed sun-
     dried tomatoes
  1/4 cup sliced ripe olives
  1 tablespoon chopped fresh or 1 teaspoon
     dried basil leaves
  1 tablespoon olive or vegetable oil
  1 clove garlic, crushed

1. Heat water and beans to boiling in 2-quart saucepan. Boil uncovered 2 minutes; reduce heat to low. Cover and simmer about 45 minutes, stirring occasionally, until beans are tender (do not boil or beans will burst); drain.

2. Stir in remaining ingredients. Cook, stirring occasionally, until hot.

1 SERVING: Calories 115 (Calories from Fat 35); Fat 4g (Saturated 1g); Cholesterol 0mg; Sodium 75mg; Carbohydrate 17g (Dietary Fiber 3g); Protein 6g

> **TIMESAVING TIP**
> Substitute 2 cans (15 to 16 ounces each) great northern beans, rinsed and drained, for the dried great northern beans. Omit water and step 1.

About Meats

We have continued to request more healthful foods, including meats. Thanks to new breeding and feeding techniques, animals are now produced leaner than ever. Meat cuts are being trimmed more closely at the supermarket before purchase, making meats lower in fat, calories and cholesterol than ever before. These changes in meats have required us to change our cooking methods, usually by shortening cooking times, because leaner meats can toughen more quickly than those containing higher amounts of fat.

Standing in front of the meat counter at your local market can be an overwhelming experience. With more than sixty cuts of beef alone to choose from, knowing what you want before you shop is helpful. Although our recipes use the most common names for meat cuts, your supermarket may call them by different names. If you have a question, refer to the identification pictures located in this chapter by meat type, or ask your butcher.

Below you will find the latest in meat information and cooking recommendations. We worked directly with the National Livestock and Meat Board and the Pork Producers Council to give you the most up-to-date information available.

Grades of Meat

Meats bearing a round stamp with the abbreviation for "U.S. Inspected and Passed" guarantees the meat is wholesome and has met federal standards of cleanliness during processing. This stamp is placed only on the primal (wholesale) cuts and could be trimmed before purchase.

The U.S. Department of Agriculture's (USDA) grades of meat quality are found in a shield-shaped stamp, particularly on beef. These grades are USDA Prime, Choice, Select, Good, Standard, Commercial and Utility, in descending order of quality. Most meats sold in supermarkets are Choice. Prime usually is available only in special restaurants. Grades below Select usually are used in combination meats, such as cold cuts and sausage.

Meat Marbling

Marbling in meats refers to the small flecks of fat throughout the lean. The flavor and juiciness of the meat is improved with marbling; however, the higher the amount of marbling, the higher the fat and calories. You may find that the newer lean strains of meats with less marbling cook differently. They may not cook in the same amount of time or produce the same amount of meat juices as the older strains did. Be careful not to overcook meats, as these leaner varieties can toughen easily.

Purchasing Meats

Selecting fresh meat is easy if you follow these guidelines:

- Choose packages that are wrapped, with no sign of leakage.
- Packages should be cold to the touch with no tears or punctures.
- If packages have a sell-by date listed on the label, purchase them on or before the date listed. (Place the packages in plastic bags before putting them in your grocery cart to avoid the meat juices contaminating other foods in your cart that won't be cooked before eating.)
- Do not buy or use any meat that has turned gray in color, has an off odor or is slippery to the touch.

Reading and Using a Meat Label

Labels on prepackaged meats are standardized to give you the same information, no matter what kind of meat you are purchasing. All labels will include the name of the cut, weight, price per pound and total cost. Separated into three parts, the name of the cut tells you the type of meat, where the meat comes from on the carcass and the name of the retail cut. Beef Round Top Round Roast is an example: Beef; Round; Top Round Roast. Knowing what part of the animal the cut is from is a key to determining the cooking method. (See Cooking Meats, page 222.)

Servings Per Pound

You'll want to consider cost per serving when it comes to buying meats. The number of servings per pound varies depending on the type of meat when it's cooked and the amount of bone and fat waste removed. The average serving is 2 1/2 to 3 1/2 ounces of cooked meat. You may want to plan on more meat per serving for heartier appetites. Below is a general guide to use for determining the number of servings you'll get per pound of meat. To figure cost per serving, divide the price per pound of meat by the number of servings per pound:

Type of Meat	Servings per Pound
Boneless cuts (ground, boneless chops, loin, tenderloin)	3 to 4
Bone-in cuts (rib roasts, pot roasts, country-style ribs)	2 to 3
Very bony cuts (back ribs, spareribs, short ribs, shanks)	1 to 1 1/2

Storing and Handling Meats

Storing Meats

These tips will help you keep meats fresh before cooking:

- If meat is wrapped in butcher paper, unwrap it, then rewrap tightly in moisture- and vaporproof materials, such as plastic wrap or aluminum foil, to prevent moisture or air from getting to the meat and causing it to deteriorate faster than it should.
- Store meat immediately in the coldest part of your refrigerator, or freeze as soon as possible. Ground meat deteriorates more quickly than other cuts, so it should be used promptly.
- If the sell-by date listed on the package has expired, cook the meat within two days or freeze it within two days for future use.

Timetable for Storing Meats

Cut	Refrigerator (36° to 40°)	Freezer (0° or colder)
Ground meats	1 to 2 days	3 to 4 months
Meat cuts		
Beef	3 to 4 days	6 to 12 months
Veal	1 to 2 days	6 to 9 months
Pork	2 to 3 days	6 months
Lamb	3 to 5 days	6 to 9 months
Variety meats	1 to 2 days	3 to 4 months
Leftover cooked meats	3 to 4 days	2 to 3 months

Handling Raw Meats

When preparing and cooking meats, following safe handling practices is important (also see Food Safety Know-How, page 419, for more information):

- To avoid possible contamination of other foods, wash all surfaces and utensils that come in contact with raw meat with hot, soapy water before using them for other food preparation. (Cooking meat to the proper temperature kills any bacteria that may be in the meat.)
- Keep hot foods hot (about 140°) and cold foods cold (below 40°). Refrigerate leftovers as soon as possible after cooking to prevent spoilage.
- Cook meat in one step, because bacteria can thrive in meat at partially cooked temperatures. If doing "combination" cooking using a grill with microwave or conventional methods, be sure the grill is hot so the partially cooked meat can be grilled immediately.

Cutting Raw Meats

When cutting or slicing raw meats into cubes, thin slices or strips, place the meat in the freezer until firm but not frozen, 30 minutes to 1 1/2 hours depending on the size of the piece. The partially frozen firm meat will be easier to cut than meat taken directly from the refrigerator.

Thawing Meats

Thaw meats slowly in the refrigerator or quickly in the microwave, following manufacturer's directions. Do not thaw meats on the countertop because room temperature is a perfect environment for bacteria to grow. If the meat was frozen when purchased or frozen immediately after purchase, the thawed meat can be kept in the refrigerator up to the number of days listed in the Timetable for Storing Meats, above. Refer to Storing Meats, left, for directions on refrigerating uncooked meat. If the meat has been refrigerated several days *before* freezing (see Timetable for Storing Meats, page 221), use the thawed meat the same day it is thawed.

Refrigerator Method

Place wrapped meat in a dish or baking pan with sides to prevent leakage on refrigerator shelves during thawing.

Size of Frozen Meat	Thawing Time in Refrigerator
Large roast (4 pounds or larger)	4 to 7 hours per pound
Small roast (under 4 pounds)	3 to 5 hours per pound
Steak or chops (1-inch-thick)	12 to 14 hours total
Ground beef (1 pound)	12 to 24 hours total

Cooking Meats

Tender cuts of meat are muscles that the animal uses infrequently, either due to their location or because the animal is very young. The rib and loin sections are the least exercised and therefore will be the most tender.

Dry cooking methods (without liquid), such as roasting, broiling, panbroiling or panfrying, are generally used for tender meat cuts. Variations of dry methods include grilling, stir-frying and deep-fat frying.

Less-tender cuts of meat are muscles that are used frequently, and they are more flavorful. The shoulder, rump and legs are the most exercised and therefore will be the least tender but most flavorful.

Moist heat methods (with steam or liquid), such as braising or cooking in liquid, are most often used for less-tender cuts. To tenderize and for best flavor development, less-tender meat cuts require long, slow cooking.

Some cuts of meat can be prepared using *either* dry or moist heat methods, depending on their quality, the cooking time and temperature used. One cut of meat is not better than another, as long as the correct method of cooking is used. Recommended cooking methods for meat cuts are featured in the charts within each section by meat category, starting on the following pages: Beef, page 225; Veal, page 242; Pork, page 247; and Lamb, page 263.

Different cooking donenesses are recommended for different types of meat, and in the case of pork, for different cuts. In order to kill any potential microorganisms in the meat, no meat should be cooked to less than medium-rare (veal and pork to no less than medium). You can always cook your meat so it is *more* done than the recommended doneness, but the meat will be more chewy and less juicy. Well doneness is recommended for some pork cuts because, although a little less juicy, the pork is much more flavorful.

Keep in mind that the cooking times are *approximate*. A specific cut of meat purchased on the East Coast may have more or less fat and/or marbling or be somewhat more or less tender than the same cut purchased on the West Coast. Oven or stovetop differences and the type, material and color of the pans used can also affect cooking times.

Using a Meat Thermometer

The best way to determine the doneness of meats is by using a meat thermometer and following temperatures specified in the meat charts. The thermometer should be inserted into the meat surface at a slight angle or through the end of the meat so the tip is in center of thickest part of meat, not touching bone or fat. Some thermometers provide meat temperatures and donenesses. However, if thermometers are older, they may not show the latest doneness recommendations, especially for the leaner meat strains. Two types of thermometers are available:

- A **meat thermometer** (also called a meat and poultry thermometer or roast-yeast thermometer) is designed to be inserted into meat or poultry and left in during cooking.
- An **instant-read thermometer** (also called instant- or rapid-response thermometer) is designed to take an almost immediate temperature reading of the food being cooked (within one minute of insertion). This type of thermometer *is not designed to be left in the oven*. It is great to use for meat being grilled or broiled, when the intense heat makes it difficult to check doneness by cutting into the meat. An instant read thermometer is generally more expensive than a standard meat thermometer.

Determining Meat Doneness

The U.S. Department of Agriculture recommends using a meat thermometer when cooking large cuts of meat, such as roasts, and ground meat mixtures, such as meat loaves. For smaller cuts, you can cut a small slit in the center of boneless cuts or in the center near the bone of bone-in cuts to judge the doneness by the color of the meat. Use the following guide to help you determine the appropriate doneness for the different cuts of meat.

Recommended Meat Doneness

Meat	Thermometer Reading after Cooking	Color of Cooked Meat when Small Cut Is Made
Beef		
Roasts	140° (for medium-rare)*	Does not apply
	155° (for medium)*	Does not apply
Other Beef Cuts	145° (medium-rare)	Very pink in center and slightly brown toward exterior
	160° (medium)	Light pink in center and brown toward exterior
Ground Beef	170° (well)	No longer pink in center and juices run clear
Loaves	160° (medium)	
Patties		
Veal		
Roasts	155° (for medium)*	Does not apply
Other Veal Cuts	160° (medium)	Slightly pink in center
Pork		
Roasts	155° (for medium)*	Does not apply
	165° (for well)*	Does not apply
Other Pork Cuts**	160° (medium)	Slightly pink in center
	170° (well)	No longer pink in center
Ground Pork	170° (well)	No longer pink in center
Ham, fully cooked	135°*	Heated through
Lamb		
Roasts	140° (for medium-rare)*	Does not apply
	155° (for medium)*	Does not apply
Other Lamb Cuts	145° (medium-rare)	Pink in center
	160° (medium)	Light pink in center

Use meat thermometer. Roasts and hams will continue to cook after being removed from oven, so the temperature will rise about 5°. Also see Roasting Beef, page 227; Roasting Veal, page 242; Roasting Pork, page 249; Roasting Ham, page 258; or Roasting Lamb, page 265.

**It is recommended that pork cuts from the leg and shoulder be cooked to well done for best flavor development. Also see Roasting Pork, page 249; Broiling or Grilling Pork, page 253; Panbroiling Pork, page 254.*

Seasoning Meats

You will find that adding seasonings to meat can bring out their best flavor. Meats can be seasoned before, during or after cooking. See Chapter 14, Sauces, Seasonings and Condiments, beginning on page 341, for ways to enhance meat flavors. There's also information in the herb chart (page 350).

Two popular ways to season meats are to use marinades and rubs. A marinade is a highly seasoned liquid used to add unique flavors or, if they contain acidic ingredients, to help tenderize meat. Rubs, which are dry or thick, highly flavorful mixtures of herbs and other seasonings, can also distinctively flavor meats. Rubs are literally rubbed into the surface of the meat.

Besides the recipes in this book, try the excellent prepared marinades, rubs and seasoning mixes available at your supermarket.

What About Seasoning with Salt?

The old rule was to never add salt to any meat until it was cooked because the salt will draw the juices to the surface of the meat, causing the meat to dry out during cooking. Although this is still true for most meat cuts, you *can* break the rule when cooking a roast. Testing has found that rubbing salt into the surface of a roast before cooking enhances the flavor of the roast without overdrying it.

Microwaving Meats

Microwaving is a quick and easy way to cook ground meat, bacon, hot dogs and sausages, especially if you want to keep cleanup to a minimum. Although other meat cuts can be microwaved, achieving tender results is more difficult.

1. Use microwavable dishes.
2. Microwave on High 100%.
3. For most types of meat, stir, rearrange or rotate meat after about half the microwave time.

Timetable for Microwaving Meats
[High (100%)]

Type of Meat	Amount	Time	Doneness

Ground Meat Directions: *Place ground meat in microwavable dish, meatballs or patties on microwavable rack in microwavable dish. Cover with paper towel or waxed paper.*

Type of Meat	Amount	Time	Doneness
Ground			
crumbled	1 pound	5 to 6 minutes, stirring after 3 minutes	Until brown
meatballs (24)	1 pound	6 to 8 minutes, rotating dish after 3 minutes	Until no longer pink in center and juice is clear
patties (3/4 inch thick)	1 pound	6 to 8 minutes, rearranging after 3 minutes	Until no longer pink in center and juice is clear

Bacon Directions: *Place bacon slices on microwavable rack in microwavable dish. Cover with paper towels.*

Type of Meat	Amount	Time	Doneness
Bacon	2 slices	1 minute 30 seconds to 2 minutes	Until crisp
	4 slices	3 to 4 minutes	Until crisp
	6 slices	4 to 6 minutes	Until crisp
	8 slices	6 to 8 minutes	Until crisp

Hot Dog and Sausage Directions: *Place hot dogs or sausages on microwavable plate lined with paper towel. Pierce several times with fork. Cover with paper towel or napkin.*

Type of Meat	Amount	Time	Doneness
Hot Dogs (10 per pound)	1	30 to 45 seconds	Until hot
	2	1 minute to 1 minute 15 seconds	Until hot
	4	1 minute 15 seconds to 1 minute 30 seconds	Until hot
Sausages (cooked) bratwurst, Italian—	2	1 minute 30 seconds to 2 minutes 30 seconds, rearranging after 1 minute	Until hot
6 per pound	4	3 to 4 minutes, rearranging after 2 minutes	Until hot
Sausages (uncooked) bratwurst, Polish—	2	2 minutes to 3 minutes 30 seconds, rearranging after 1 minute	Until no longer pink in center (180° on microwavable meat thermometer)
6 per pound	4	4 to 5 minutes, rearranging after 3 minutes	Until no longer pink in center (180° on microwavable meat thermometer)

Ham Slice Directions: *Place ham slice in microwavable dish. Cover with plastic wrap, folding back one corner to vent.*

Type of Meat	Amount	Time	Doneness
Ham Slice (fully cooked, smoked)	8 to 16 ounces (1/4 to 1/2 inch thick)	3 minutes to 3 minutes 30 seconds, turning over after 1 1/2 minutes	Until hot
	1 1/2 to 2 pounds (1 inch thick)	11 to 12 minutes, turning over after 5 minutes	Until hot

About Beef

Selecting Beef

The color of the lean portions of beef should be bright red. Vacuum-packaged beef and the interior of ground beef have a darker, purplish red color because the meat is not exposed to air. As beef is exposed to air, its color will change to the familiar bright red. Once you purchase beef, use it within the time recommended on page 221.

Ground beef contains meat from beef only (variety meats are not used for ground beef). It comes in varying degrees of leanness, from 70% to 90% or more. Our recipes that call for ground beef are intended for ground beef that is 80% lean.

Cooking Beef

The USDA recommends cooking beef (except for ground beef) to medium-rare or medium doneness for the best flavor and texture as well as to kill any possible microorganisms that may be in the raw beef.

Cooking Ground Beef

Ground beef is handled frequently and touches many surfaces during grinding, which make it easy prey for bacteria. It is, therefore, very important that it be cooked thoroughly. Meat loaves must reach 170° to be safe; other ground beef must be at least medium doneness (160° and no longer pink). Any recipe that uses ground beef that's cooked to under 160° is unsafe.

In general, you don't have to cook regular ground beef with additional fat because the beef contains enough fat that is released during cooking to prevent it from sticking or getting too dry. Leaner ground beef contains less fat, which means it can stick to the pan during cooking. Rather than adding additional fat, which adds calories and fat to your food, use a nonstick skillet to prevent sticking. Lean ground beef loses mostly moisture during cooking, resulting in meat that is drier than cooked regular ground beef. Do not overmix ground beef when making patties, meatballs or loaves since these foods will then be too firm and overly compact in texture.

How to Carve a Standing Rib Roast

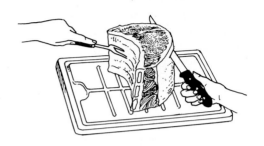

1. Place roast, large side down, on carving board or platter. Remove wedge-shaped slice from large end, if necessary, so roast will stand firmly on this end. Insert meat fork below top rib. Slice from outside of roast toward rib side.

2. After making several slices, cut along inner side of rib bone with tip of knife. As each slice is released slide knife under and lift to plate.

How to Carve a Pot Roast

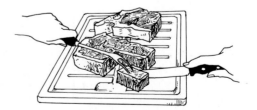

Place roast on carving board or platter. With meat fork in meat to keep the meat from moving, cut between muscles and around bones. Remove one sold section of meat at a time. Turn section so meat grain runs parallel to carving board. Cut meat across grain into 1/4-inch slices.

BEEF

• RETAIL CUTS •
WHERE THEY COME FROM
HOW TO COOK THEM

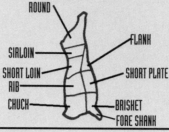

ROUND

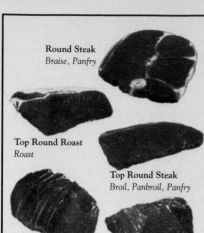

Round Steak
Braise, Panfry

Top Round Roast
Roast

Top Round Steak
Broil, Panbroil, Panfry

Boneless Rump Roast
Roast, Braise

Bottom Round Roast
Braise, Roast

Tip Roast, Cap Off
Roast, Braise

Eye Round Roast
Braise, Roast

Tip Steak
Broil, Panbroil, Panfry

SIRLOIN

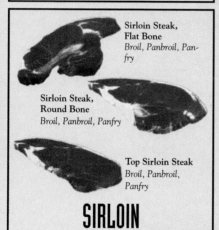

Sirloin Steak, Flat Bone
Broil, Panbroil, Panfry

Sirloin Steak, Round Bone
Broil, Panbroil, Panfry

Top Sirloin Steak
Broil, Panbroil, Panfry

FORE SHANK & BRISKET

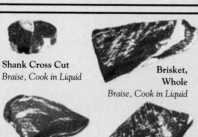

Shank Cross Cut
Braise, Cook in Liquid

Brisket, Whole
Braise, Cook in Liquid

Corned Brisket, Point Half
Braise, Cook in Liquid

Brisket, Flat Half
Braise

CHUCK

Chuck Eye Roast
Braise, Roast

Boneless Top Blade Steak
Braise, Panfry

Arm Pot Roast
Braise

Boneless Shoulder Pot Roast
Braise

Cross Rib Pot Roast
Braise

Mock Tender
Braise

Blade Roast
Braise

Upper Blade Pot Roast
Braise, Roast

Short Ribs
Braise, Cook in Liquid

7-Bone Pot Roast
Braise

Flanken-Style Ribs
Braise, Cook in Liquid

SHORT LOIN

T-Bone Steak
Broil, Panbroil, Panfry

Boneless Top Loin Steak
Broil, Panbroil, Panfry

Tenderloin Roast
Broil, Roast

Porterhouse Steak
Broil, Panbroil, Panfry

Tenderloin Steak
Broil, Panbroil, Panfry

RIB

Rib Roast, Large End
Roast

Rib Roast, Small End
Roast

Rib Steak, Small End
Broil, Panbroil, Panfry

Rib Eye Roast
Roast

Rib Eye Steak
Broil, Panbroil, Panfry

Back Ribs
Braise, Cook in Liquid, Roast

FLANK & SHORT PLATE

Flank Steak
Broil, Braise, Panfry

Flank Steak Rolls
Braise, Broil, Panbroil, Panfry

Skirt Steak
Braise, Broil, Panbroil, Panfry

OTHER CUTS

Ground Beef
Broil, Panfry, Panbroil, Roast (Bake)

Cubed Steak
Panfry, Braise

Beef for Stew
Braise, Cook in Liquid

Cubes for Kabobs
Broil, Braise

This chart approved by
NATIONAL LIVESTOCK & MEAT BOARD

Roasting Beef

Roasting is an easy cooking method, and it's a low-fat way to cook because the fat drips away from the meat during cooking.

1. Select beef roast from those listed in Timetable for Roasting Beef.

2. Place beef, fat side up, on rack in shallow roasting pan. (For easy cleanup, line the roasting pan with aluminum foil before placing beef on rack.) The rack keeps the meat out of the drippings. (With a rib roast, the ribs form a natural rack.) As the fat melts, it bastes the beef, making other basting unnecessary.

3. Season beef with herbs, spices, salt or other seasonings before, during or after cooking, if desired. (Salt roasts *before* cooking to enhance flavor.)

4. Insert meat thermometer into roast surface at a slight angle or through the end of the roast so tip is in center of thickest part of roast and does not touch bone or fat.

5. Do not add water. Do not cover.

6. Roast at oven temperature shown in chart for beef cut being cooked. (It is not necessary to preheat oven.)

7. Roast to temperature listed in chart in column titled "Meat Thermometer Reading (after roasting)" for beef cut chosen and desired degree of doneness. Roast will continue to cook after being removed from oven.

8. Cover roast loosely with tent of aluminum foil and let stand 15 to 20 minutes or until temperature rises to that listed in chart in column titled "Final Meat Thermometer Reading (after standing)." Roast will be easier to carve as juices set up. Avoid covering roast tightly as it creates steam and softens the surface of the beef.

Timetable for Roasting Beef

Beef Cut	Approximate Weight (pounds)	Oven Temperature	Meat Thermometer Reading (*after roasting*)	Final Meat Thermometer Reading (*after standing*)	Approximate Cooking Time (minutes per pound)
Eye Round	2 to 3	325°	140°	145° (medium-rare)	20 to 22
Rib* (small end)	4 to 6	325°	140°	145° (medium-rare)	25 to 30
			155°	160° (medium)	30 to 34
	6 to 8	325°	140°	145° (medium-rare)	23 to 26
			155°	160° (medium)	27 to 32
Rib Eye (small end)	4 to 6	350°	140°	145° (medium-rare)	18 to 20
			155°	160° (medium)	20 to 22
Round Tip (Sirloin Tip) (high quality)	2 1/2 to 4	325°	140°	145° (medium-rare)	30 to 35
			155°	160° (medium)	35 to 40
	4 to 6	325°	140°	145° (medium-rare)	25 to 30
			155°	160° (medium)	30 to 35
	8 to 10	325°	140°	145° (medium-rare)	18 to 22
			155°	160° (medium)	23 to 25
Tenderloin (whole)	4 to 6	425°	140°	145° (medium-rare)	45 to 60 (total time)
(half)	2 to 3	425°	140°	145° (medium-rare)	35 to 45 (total time)
Tri-Tip (bottom sirloin)	1 1/2 to 2	425°	140°	145° (medium-rare)	30 to 40

Ribs that measure 6 to 7 inches from chine bone to tip of rib

Note: *Smaller roasts require more minutes per pound than larger roasts.*

Roast Beef

PREP: 5 min; ROAST: 2 hr
Makes 6 serving

For carving roast beef, a sharp knife with a straight edge or an electric knife works best to cut even slices. Keep beef from moving while cutting by holding it in place with a two-tined meat fork.

Beef roast*
Oven-Browned Potatoes or Yorkshire
   Pudding (below), if desired
Pan Gravy (page 348), if desired

1. Select beef roast from those listed in Timetable for Roasting Beef.

2. Follow steps for Roasting Beef, page 227.

3. Prepare Oven-Browned Potatoes and Pan Gravy, or spoon hot beef drippings over carved beef.

*If serving Yorkshire Pudding, select rib roast or rib eye roast.

1 SERVING (3 ounces): Calories 280 (Calories from Fat 125); Fat 14g (Saturated 5g); Cholesterol 55mg; Sodium 150mg; Carbohydrate 20g (Dietary Fiber 1g); Protein 20g

Oven-Browned Potatoes

About 1 1/2 hours before beef roast is done, prepare and boil 6 medium potatoes as directed on page 400—except make thin crosswise cuts almost through potatoes, if desired, and decrease boiling time to 10 minutes. Place potatoes in beef drippings in pan, turning each potato to coat completely; or brush potatoes with margarine or butter, melted, and place on rack with beef. Continue cooking about 1 1/4 hours, turning potatoes once, until golden brown. Sprinkle with salt and pepper if desired.

Yorkshire Pudding

   1 cup all-purpose flour
   1 cup milk
   1/2 teaspoon salt
   2 large eggs
   Melted shortening, if necessary

Thirty minutes before rib roast or rib eye roast is done, mix all ingredients except shortening with hand beater just until smooth. Heat square pan, 9 × 9 × 2 inches, in oven. Remove beef from oven. Spoon off drippings and add enough melted shortening to drippings, if necessary, to measure 1/2 cup.
Increase oven temperature to 425°. Return beef to oven. Place hot drippings in heated square pan. Pour batter into pan. Bake beef and pudding 20 minutes. Remove beef from oven. Bake pud-ding 15 to 20 minutes longer or until deep golden brown. Cut pudding into squares and serve with beef.

Beef Brisket Barbecue

PREP: 10 min; BAKE 3 hr
Makes 12 servings

   4- to 5-pound well-trimmed fresh beef
      brisket (not corned)
   1 teaspoon salt
   1/2 cup ketchup
   1/4 cup white vinegar
   1 tablespoon Worcestershire sauce
   1 1/2 teaspoons liquid smoke
   1/4 teaspoon pepper
   1 medium onion, finely chopped (1/2 cup)
   1 bay leaf

1. Heat oven to 325°.

2. Rub surface of beef with salt. Place in ungreased rectangular pan, 13 × 9 × 2 inches. Mix remaining ingredients; pour over beef.

3. Cover and bake about 3 hours or until beef is tender.

4. Cut thin diagonal slices across grain at an angle from 2 or 3 "faces" of beef. Spoon any remaining pan juices over sliced beef if desired. Remove bay leaf.

1 SERVING: Calories 245 (Calories from Fat 100); Fat 11g (Saturated 4g); Cholesterol 85mg; Sodium 390mg; Carbohydrate 4g (Dietary Fiber 0g); Protein 33g

---

TIMESAVING TIP
Omit all ingredients except beef brisket. Pour 1 cup purchased barbecue sauce over beef.

How to Carve a Beef Brisket

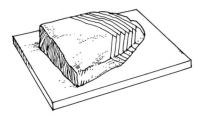

Place beef or corned beef brisket on carving board or platter. Carve across the 2 or 3 "faces" of brisket, as shown, cutting thin slices at right angles, always across the grain. Cut slices in rotations so that the "faces" will remain equal to each other in size.

New England Pot Roast

PREP: 30 min; BAKE: 3 1/2 hr
Makes 8 servings

For an easy meal, serve this savory roast with a hearty multi-grain bread and coleslaw from the deli. (Garlic-Herb Pot Roast photographed on page 219)

> 4-pound beef arm, blade or cross rib pot
>   roast*
> 1 to 2 teaspoons salt
> 1 teaspoon pepper
> 1 jar (8 ounces) prepared horseradish
> 1 cup water
> 8 small potatoes, cut in half
> 8 medium carrots, cut into fourths
> 8 small onions
> Pot Roast Gravy (below)

1. Cook beef in Dutch oven over medium heat until brown on all sides; reduce heat to low.

2. Sprinkle beef with salt and pepper. Spread horseradish over all sides of beef. Add water to Dutch oven. Heat to boiling; reduce heat to low. Cover and simmer 2 1/2 hours.

3. Add potatoes, carrots and onions. Cover and simmer about 1 hour or until beef and vegetables are tender.

4. Remove beef and vegetables to warm platter; keep warm. Prepare Pot Roast Gravy. Serve with beef and vegetables.

Pot Roast Gravy

> Water
> 1/2 cup cold water
> 1/4 cup all-purpose flour

Skim excess fat from broth in Dutch oven. Add enough water to broth to measure 2 cups. Shake 1/2 cup cold water and the flour in tightly covered container; *gradually* stir into broth. Heat to boiling, stirring constantly. Boil and stir 1 minute.

3-pound beef bottom round, rolled rump, tip or chuck eye roast can be substituted; decrease salt to 3/4 teaspoon.

1 SERVING: Calories 365 (Calories from Fat 100); Fat 11g (Saturated 4g); Cholesterol 85mg; Sodium 400mg; Carbohydrate 38g (Dietary Fiber 6g); Protein 35g

BARBECUE POT ROAST: Decrease pepper to 1/2 teaspoon. Omit horseradish and water. Prepare Barbecue Sauce (page 344). After browning beef in step 1, pour Barbecue Sauce over beef. Omit Pot Roast Gravy. Skim fat from sauce after removing beef and vegetables in step 4. Spoon sauce over beef and vegetables.

GARLIC-HERB POT ROAST: Decrease pepper to 1/2 teaspoon. Omit horseradish. After browning beef in step 1, sprinkle with 1 tablespoon chopped fresh or 1 teaspoon dried marjoram leaves, 1 tablespoon chopped fresh or 1 teaspoon dried thyme leaves, 2 teaspoons chopped fresh or 1/2 teaspoon dried oregano leaves and 4 cloves garlic, crushed. Substitute 1 can (10 1/2 ounces) condensed beef broth for the 1 cup water.

> **TIMESAVING TIP**
> Use 1 bag (1 to 1 1/2 pounds) baby-cut carrots instead of the medium carrots.

Corned Beef and Cabbage

PREP: 20 min; COOK: 2 1/4 hr
Makes 6 servings

Corned beef is beef brisket that has been cured in brine to give a distinct flavor. Because salt is added during the curing process, there's no need to add salt while cooking.

> 2-pound well-trimmed beef corned brisket
> 1 small onion, cut into fourths
> 1 clove garlic, crushed
> 1 small head cabbage, cut into 6 wedges

1. Place beef in Dutch oven. Add enough cold water just to cover beef. Add onion and garlic.

2. Heat to boiling; reduce heat to low. Cover and simmer about 2 hours or until beef is tender.

3. Remove beef to warm platter; keep warm. Skim fat from broth.

4. Add cabbage to broth. Heat to boiling; reduce heat to low. Simmer uncovered 15 minutes or until cabbage is tender. Serve cabbage with beef.

1 SERVING: Calories 295 (Calories from Fat 190); Fat 21g (Saturated 7g); Cholesterol 105mg; Sodium 1240mg; Carbohydrate 8g (Dietary Fiber 2g); Protein 21g

NEW ENGLAND BOILED DINNER: Decrease simmer time of beef in step 2 to 1 hour 40 minutes. Skim fat from broth. Add 6 small onions, 6 medium carrots, 3 potatoes, cut in half, and, if desired, 3 turnips, cut into cubes, to broth. Cover and simmer 20 minutes. Remove beef to warm platter; keep warm. Add cabbage to broth. Heat to boiling; reduce heat to low. Simmer uncovered about 15 minutes or until vegetables are tender.

Broiling or Grilling Beef

Broiling and direct-heat grilling are quick, low-fat methods for cooking tender cuts, such as steaks, or ground beef patties. For less tender cuts, marinate beef before cooking. (See Tips for Marinades and Marinating, page 356.) The directions below are for broiling or for grilling over direct heat. Other beef cuts can be cooked over indirect heat. Refer to the instructions that came with your grill or see Grilling Know-How, page 428, for more information.

1. Select beef cut from those listed in Timetable for Broiling or Grilling Beef.

2. Marinate beef if desired. (See Tips for Marinating, page 356.)

3. *To Broil*: Set oven to broil.

To Grill: Heat coals or gas grill (direct heat) to medium heat.

4. Slash outer edge of fat on beef diagonally at 1-inch intervals to prevent curling (do not cut into meat).

5. *To Broil*: Place beef on rack in broiler pan. (For easy cleanup, line the broiler pan with aluminum foil before placing beef on rack.) Place in oven with top of beef the inches from heat listed in chart for beef cut chosen.

To Grill: Place beef on grill the number of inches from heat listed in chart for beef cut chosen.

6. Broil or grill about half the time shown in chart for beef cut or until beef is brown on one side.

7. Turn beef and continue cooking until desired doneness. (To check doneness, cut a small slit in the center of boneless cuts or in the center near the bone of bone-in cuts. Medium-rare is very pink in center and slightly brown toward exterior. Medium is light pink in center and brown toward exterior.) Season each side after cooking if desired.

Timetable for Broiling or Grilling Beef

Beef Cut	Approximate Thickness or Weight	Inches from Heat	Approximate Total Broiling Time (minutes)		Approximate Total Grilling Time (minutes)	
			145° (medium-rare)	160° (medium)	145° (medium-rare)	160° (medium)
Rib and Rib Eye Steaks	3/4 to 1 inch	2 to 4	8	15	7	12
Top Loin Steak (boneless)	3/4 to 1 inch	2 to 4	8	17	7	12
Porterhouse and T-Bone Steaks	1 inch	3 to 4	10	15	10	14
Sirloin Steak (boneless)	3/4 to 1 inch	2 to 4	10	21	12	16
Sirloin Cubes (kabobs)	1 to 1 1/4 inches	3 to 4	9	12	8	11
Tenderloin Steak	1 inch	2 to 3	10	15	11	13
Tri-Tip Roast* (bottom sirloin)	1 1/2 to 2 pounds	4 to 5	25	30	30	35
Chuck Shoulder Steak** (boneless)	1 inch	3 to 4	14	18	14	20
Eye Round Steak	1 inch	2 to 3	9	11	9	12
Top Round Steak**	1 inch	3 to 4	15	18	12	14
Flank Steak**	1 to 1 1/2 pounds	2 to 3	12	14	12	15
Ground Beef Patties	1/2 inch	3 to 4	†	10	†	7 to 9
	3/4 inch	3 to 4	†	13	†	10 to 11

*Cover roast with tent of aluminum foil and let stand 15 to 20 minutes before carving. Temperature will continue to rise about 5° and roast will be easier to carve as juices set up.

**Marinate beef 6 to 8 hours to tenderize.

†USDA recommends cooking ground beef to 160°.

Panbroiling Beef

Panbroiling is a quick, easy and low-fat way to cook thinner steaks and patties.

1. Select beef cut from those listed in Timetable for Panbroiling Beef.
2. Coat heavy skillet with a small amount of vegetable oil, or spray with nonstick cooking spray if beef to be cooked is very lean.
3. Heat skillet over medium-low to medium heat when cooking cuts thicker than 1/2 inch, or heat over medium-high heat for thinner cuts.

4. Place beef in hot skillet. Do not add oil or water. Do not cover.
5. Cook for time shown in chart for beef cut chosen. Remove fat from skillet as it accumulates. Turn beef cuts thicker than 1/2 inch occasionally, thinner cuts once, until brown on both sides and desired doneness. (To check doneness, cut a small slit in the center of boneless cuts or in the center near the bone of bone-in cuts. Medium-rare is very pink in center and slightly brown toward exterior. Medium is light pink in center and brown toward exterior.) Serve immediately.

Timetable for Panbroiling Beef

Beef Cut	Approximate Thickness (inches)	Stovetop Temperature	Approximate Total Cooking Time (minutes) 145° to 160° (medium-rare to medium)
Rib Eye Steak	1/2	Medium-high	3 to 5
Top Loin Steak	1/4	Medium-high	2 to 3
Eye Round Steak	1	Medium	8 to 10
Tenderloin	3/4 to 1	Medium	6 to 9
Round Tip	1/8 to 1/4	Medium-high	1
Sirloin (boneless)	3/4 to 1	Medium-low to Medium	10 to 12
Top Round	1	Medium	13 to 16
Ground Beef Patties	1/2	Medium	7 to 8*

USDA recommends cooking ground beef to 160°.

Herb-Marinated Flank Steak, Au Gratin Potatoes (page 410)

Tenderloins in Pastry

PREP: 30 min; BAKE: 17 min
Makes 4 servings

> 1 tablespoon vegetable oil
> 4 beef tenderloin steaks, 1 inch thick
> (6 ounces each)
> 1/2 package (17 1/4-ounce size) frozen puff
> pastry (1 sheet), thawed
> 1/4 cup Pesto (page 345)

1. Heat oil in 10-inch skillet over medium-high heat. Cook beef in oil about 1 minute on each side or until brown. Drain on paper towels. Cool slightly.

2. Heat oven to 450°. Line shallow roasting pan with aluminum foil.

3. Roll pastry into 12-inch square. Cut pastry into four 6-inch squares.

4. Spread 1 tablespoon of the Pesto over each steak. Place 1 pastry square on top of each steak. *Gently* tuck edges of pastry under steaks. Place pastry sides up on rack in roasting pan.

5. Bake 15 to 17 minutes or until pastry is golden and beef is medium-rare to medium. (Also see Determining Meat Doneness, page 222.)

1 SERVING: Calories 365 (Calories from Fat 225); Fat 25g (Saturated 7g); Cholesterol 85mg; Sodium 140mg; Carbohydrate 2g (Dietary Fiber 0g); Protein 33g

---

> **TIMESAVING TIP**
> Use purchased pesto, found near the refrigerated pastas in your supermarket.

Herb-Marinated Flank Steak

PREP: 10 min; MARINATE: 5 hr; BROIL: 10 min
Makes 6 to 8 servings

Cutting both sides of the steak into a diamond pattern helps to tenderize the beef and give more surface area for the seasonings to cover, adding more flavor. It also keeps the steak from curling while cooking.

> 1 1/2- to 2-pound beef flank or round steak
> 2 tablespoons lemon juice
> 1 1/2 teaspoons chopped fresh or 1/2 teaspoon dried oregano leaves
> 1/2 teaspoon salt
> 1/2 teaspoon celery seed
> 1/2 teaspoon pepper
> 1 clove garlic, finely chopped

1. Make cuts about 1/2 inch apart and 1/4 inch deep in diamond pattern in both sides of beef.

2. Mix remaining ingredients; rub into beef. Place in plastic bag or shallow glass baking dish. Fasten bag securely or cover dish with plastic wrap. Refrigerate at least 5 hours but no longer than 24 hours.

3. Set oven control to Broil.

4. Place beef on rack in broiler pan. (For easy cleanup, line broiler pan with aluminum foil before placing beef on rack.) Broil beef with top 2 to 3 inches from heat about 5 minutes or until brown. Turn; broil about 5 minutes longer for medium-rare to medium. (Also see Determining Meat Doneness, page 222.) Cut beef across grain at slanted angle into thin slices.

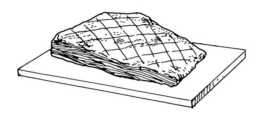

Make cuts about 1/2 inch apart and 1/4 deep in both sides of beef in diamond pattern.

1 SERVING: Calories 170 (Calories from Fat 70); Fat 8g (Saturated 3g); Cholesterol 60mg; Sodium 230mg; Carbohydrate 1g (Dietary Fiber 0g); Protein 23g

Swiss Steak

**PREP: 15 min; COOK: 1 hr 50 min
Makes 6 servings**

Pounding the beef helps to tenderize it by breaking down some of the muscle fibers. If you don't have a meat mallet, the edge of a saucer is a good substitute.

> 3 tablespoons all-purpose flour
> 1 teaspoon ground mustard (dry)
> 1/2 teaspoon salt
> 1 1/2-pound beef boneless round, tip or
>   chuck steak, about 3/4 inch thick
> 2 tablespoons vegetable oil
> 1 can (16 ounces) whole tomatoes,
>   undrained
> 2 cloves garlic, finely chopped
> 1 cup water
> 1 large onion, sliced
> 1 large green bell pepper, sliced

1. Mix flour, mustard and salt. Sprinkle half of the flour mixture over 1 side of beef; pound in with meat mallet. Turn beef and pound in remaining flour mixture. Cut beef into 6 serving pieces.

2. Heat oil in 10-inch skillet over medium heat. Cook beef in oil about 15 minutes, turning once, until brown.

3. Add tomatoes and garlic, breaking up tomatoes. Heat to boiling; reduce heat to low. Cover and simmer about 1 1/4 hours, spooning sauce occasionally over beef, until beef is tender.

4. Add water, onion and bell pepper. Heat to boiling; reduce heat to low. Cover and simmer 5 to 8 minutes or until vegetables are tender.

1 SERVING: Calories 190 (Calories from Fat 70); Fat 8g (Saturated 2g); Cholesterol 55mg; Sodium 340mg; Carbohydrate 10g (Dietary Fiber 2g); Protein 22g

SUN-DRIED TOMATO SWISS STEAK: Omit whole tomatoes. Add 2/3 cup water, 1/2 cup eight-vegetable or tomato juice and 3/4 cup sun-dried tomatoes (not oil-packed) with the garlic in step 3.

Brandied Steak au Poivre

**PREP: 10 min; COOK: 15 min
Makes 4 servings**

Poivre is French for pepper, and these tasty steaks are great with a crisp salad and baked potatoes.

> 1 teaspoon cracked black pepper
> 3/4 teaspoon chopped fresh or 1/4 teaspoon
>   dried basil leaves
> 3/4 teaspoon chopped fresh or 1/4 teaspoon
>   dried rosemary leaves
> 1/8 teaspoon onion powder
> 4 beef cubed steaks (5 ounces each)
> 1 tablespoon margarine or butter
> 2 tablespoons brandy or beef broth
> 1/4 cup beef broth

1. Mix pepper, basil, rosemary and onion powder. Rub pepper mixture into both sides of each steak.

2. Melt margarine in 12-inch skillet over medium heat. Cook beef in margarine 7 to 8 minutes, turning occasionally, until medium-rare to medium. (Also see Determining Meat Doneness, page 222.) Remove beef from skillet; keep warm.

3. Add brandy and broth to skillet. Heat to boiling, stirring to loosen brown bits from bottom of skillet; reduce heat to low. Simmer uncovered 3 to 4 minutes or until slightly thickened. Serve beef with brandy mixture.

1 SERVING: Calories 245 (Calories from Fat 115); Fat 13g (Saturated 5g); Cholesterol 80mg; Sodium 150mg; Carbohydrate 1g (Dietary Fiber 0g); Protein 31g

---

LIGHTER STEAK AU POIVRE

For 10 grams of fat and 220 calories per serving, omit margarine and use nonstick skillet. Spray cold skillet with nonstick cooking spray before cooking beef in step 2.

Fajitas

PREP: 30 min; MARINATE: 8 hr; BROIL: 16 min
Makes 6 servings

> Fajita Marinade (page 357)
> 1 1/2-pound beef boneless top sirloin steak,
>   1 1/2 inches thick
> 12 flour tortillas (10 inches in diameter)
> 2 tablespoons vegetable oil
> 2 large onions, sliced
> 2 medium green or red bell peppers, cut into
>   1/4-inch strips
> 1 jar (8 ounces) picante sauce (1 cup)
> 1 cup shredded Cheddar or Monterey Jack
>   cheese (4 ounces)
> Guacamole (page 18) or 1 1/2 cups prepared
>   guacamole
> 3/4 cup sour cream

1. Prepare Fajita Marinade in ungreased, square glass baking dish, 8 × 8 × 2 inches.

2. Trim excess fat from beef. Pierce beef with fork in several places. Place beef in marinade, turning to coat both sides. Cover and refrigerate at least 8 hours but no longer than 24 hours, turning beef occasionally.

3. Heat oven to 325°.

4. Wrap tortillas in aluminum foil. Heat in oven about 15 minutes or until warm. Remove tortillas from oven; keep wrapped.

5. Set oven control to Broil.

6. Remove beef from marinade; reserve marinade. Place beef on rack in broiler pan. (For easy cleanup, line broiler pan with aluminum foil before placing beef on rack.) Broil beef with top about 3 inches from heat about 8 minutes or until brown. Turn; brush beef with marinade. Broil 7 to 8 minutes longer for medium-rare to medium. (Also see Determining Meat Doneness, page 222.) Discard any remaining marinade.

7. While beef is broiling, heat oil in 10-inch skillet over medium-high heat. Cook onions and bell peppers in oil 6 to 8 minutes, stirring frequently, until crisp-tender. Cut beef across grain into very thin slices.

8. For each fajita, place a few slices of beef, some of the onion mixture, 1 heaping tablespoonful each picante sauce and cheese, about 2 tablespoons Guacamole and 1 tablespoon sour cream in center of tortilla. Fold 1 end of tortilla up about 1 inch over filling; fold right and left sides over folded end, overlapping. Fold remaining end down.

1 SERVING: Calories 690 (Calories from Fat 325); Fat 36g (Saturated 12g); Cholesterol 90mg; Sodium 1110mg; Carbohydrate 64g (Dietary Fiber 7g); Protein 35g

---

LIGHTER FAJITAS

For 22 grams of fat and 565 calories per serving, use reduced-fat tortillas, cheese and sour cream. Omit Guacamole.

Beef Stroganoff

PREP: 20 min; COOK: 30 min
Makes 6 servings, about 1 cup each

To add a fancy touch to this favorite, use a combination of fresh mushrooms, such as chanterelle, enoki, morel, oyster or shiitake.

> 1 1/2 pounds beef tenderloin or boneless top
>   loin steak, about 1/2 inch thick
> 2 tablespoons margarine or butter
> 1 1/2 cups beef broth
> 2 tablespoons ketchup
> 1 teaspoon salt
> 1 small clove garlic, finely chopped
> 3 cups sliced mushrooms (8 ounces)
> 1 medium onion, chopped (1/2 cup)
> 3 tablespoons all-purpose flour
> 1 cup sour cream or plain yogurt
> Hot cooked noodles or rice (page 204),
>   if desired

1. Cut beef across grain into about 1 1/2 × 1/2- inch strips. (Beef is easier to cut if partially frozen, about 1 hour.)

2. Melt margarine in 10-inch skillet over medium-high heat. Cook beef in margarine, stirring occasionally, until brown.

3. Reserve 1/3 cup of the broth. Stir remaining broth, the ketchup, salt and garlic into skillet. Heat to boiling; reduce heat to low. Cover and simmer about 10 minutes or until beef is tender.

4. Stir in mushrooms and onion. Cover and simmer about 5 minutes or until onion is tender.

5. Shake reserved broth and the flour in tightly covered container; *gradually* stir into beef mixture. Heat to boiling, stirring constantly. Boil and stir 1 minute; reduce heat to low.

6. Stir in sour cream; cook until hot. Serve over noodles.

1 SERVING: Calories 300 (Calories from Fat 160); Fat 18g (Saturated 8g); Cholesterol 80mg; Sodium 690mg; Carbohydrate 10g (Dietary Fiber 1g); Protein 25g

---

LIGHTER BEEF STROGANOFF

For 12 grams of fat and 265 calories per serving, decrease margarine to 1 tablespoon and use nonstick skillet. Use reduced-fat sour cream or yogurt.

Thai Beef Stir-Fry

PREP: 30 min; COOK: 20 min
Makes 4 servings, 2 cups each

This stir-fry gets its distinctive Thai flavor from fish sauce. Look for it at an Oriental food store or in the Oriental food section of your supermarket. You can also substitute an equal amount of soy sauce for the fish sauce.

1 pound beef boneless sirloin steak
1/2 cup beef broth
2 tablespoons fish sauce
1 tablespoon cornstarch
1 tablespoon white vinegar
2 teaspoons packed brown sugar
1 tablespoon vegetable oil
2 teaspoons finely chopped gingerroot or
   1/2 teaspoon ground ginger
2 cloves garlic, finely chopped
1 tablespoon vegetable oil
6 medium carrots, thinly sliced (3 cups)
6 green onions, cut into 1/2-inch pieces
1 can (8 ounces) sliced water chestnuts,
   drained
1 tablespoon grated lemon peel
4 cups hot cooked rice (page 204)

1. Trim excess fat from beef. Cut beef with grain into 2-inch strips; cut strips across grain into 1/8-inch slices. (Beef is easier to cut if partially frozen, about 30 minutes.)

2. Mix broth, fish sauce, cornstarch, vinegar and brown sugar.

3. Heat wok or 10-inch skillet over high heat. Add 1 tablespoon oil; rotate wok to coat side. Add beef, gingerroot and garlic; stir-fry about 3 minutes or until beef is brown. Remove beef from wok with slotted spoon.

4. Add 1 tablespoon oil to wok; rotate wok to coat side. Add carrots and onions; stir-fry about 5 minutes or until vegetables are crisp-tender. Stir in beef, water chestnuts and lemon peel; heat to boiling. Stir in broth mixture. Cook and stir about 1 minute or until heated through.

5. Serve beef mixture over rice.

1 SERVING: Calories 475 (Calories from Fat 100); Fat 11g (Saturated 2g); Cholesterol 55mg; Sodium 690mg; Carbohydrate 73g (Dietary Fiber 6g); Protein 27g

---

LIGHTER THAI BEEF STIR-FRY

For 3 grams of fat and 385 calories per serving, decrease beef to 3/4 pound. Omit oil in step 3 and use nonstick wok or skillet. Spray cold skillet with nonstick cooking spray before heating in step 3. Omit oil in step 4; stir-fry vegetables in beef drippings.

Italian Beef Habobs

PREP: 25 min; MARINATE: 1 hr; BROIL: 8 min
Makes 4 servings

3/4 pound beef bone-in sirloin or round
   steak, 1 inch thick
1/4 cup balsamic vinegar
1/4 cup water
1 tablespoon chopped fresh or 1 teaspoon
   dried oregano leaves
2 tablespoons olive or vegetable oil
1 1/2 teaspoons chopped fresh or
   1/2 teaspoon dried marjoram leaves
1 teaspoon sugar
2 cloves garlic, finely chopped
2 small zucchini, cut into 1-inch slices
16 small whole mushrooms
8 cherry tomatoes

1. Trim excess fat and bone from beef. Cut beef into 1-inch pieces.

2. Mix vinegar, water, oregano, oil, marjoram, sugar and garlic in medium glass or plastic bowl. Stir in beef until coated. Cover and refrigerate at least 1 hour but no longer than 12 hours.

3. Set oven control to Broil.

4. Remove beef from marinade; reserve marinade. Thread beef, zucchini and mushrooms alternately on each of eight 10-inch metal skewers, leaving space between each. Brush kabobs with marinade.

5. Place kabobs on rack in broiler pan. (For easy cleanup, line broiler pan with aluminum foil before placing kabobs on rack.) Broil with tops of kabobs about 3 inches from heat 6 to 8 minutes for medium-rare to medium, turning and brushing with marinade after 3 minutes. (Also see Determining Meat Doneness, page 222.) Discard any remaining marinade.

6. Garnish end of each skewer with tomato.

1 SERVING: Calories 175 (Calories from Fat 80); Fat 9g (Saturated 2g); Cholesterol 40mg; Sodium 35mg; Carbohydrate 8g (Dietary Fiber 1g); Protein 17g

---

TIMESAVING TIP

Omit vinegar, water, oregano, oil, marjoram, sugar and garlic. Marinate beef in 2/3 cup purchased Italian dressing in step 2.

Pepper Steak

PREP: 15 min; COOK: 30 min
Makes 6 servings, about 2 cups each

When serving a hot meat mixture over rice, choose long grain rice as the kernels remain separate and fluffy when cooked.

1 1/2 pounds beef top round or sirloin steak,
    3/4 to 1 inch thick
3 tablespoons vegetable oil
1 cup water
1 medium onion, cut into 1/4-inch slices
1 clove garlic, finely chopped
1/2 teaspoon finely chopped gingerroot or
    1/4 teaspoon ground ginger
2 medium green bell peppers, cut into
    3/4-inch-wide strips
1 tablespoon cornstarch
2 teaspoons sugar, if desired
2 tablespoons soy sauce
2 medium tomatoes
6 cups hot cooked rice (page 204)

1. Trim excess fat from beef. Cut beef into 2 × 1/4-inch strips. (Beef is easier to cut if partially frozen, about 1 hour.)

2. Heat oil in 12-inch skillet over medium-high heat. Cook beef in oil about 5 minutes, turning frequently, until brown.

3. Stir in water, onion, garlic and gingerroot. Heat to boiling; reduce heat to low. Cover and simmer 12 to 15 minutes for round steak, 5 to 8 minutes for sirloin steak, adding bell peppers during last 5 minutes of simmering, until beef is tender and peppers are crisp-tender.

4. Mix cornstarch, sugar and soy sauce; stir into beef mixture. Cook, stirring constantly, until mixture thickens and boils. Boil and stir 1 minute.

5. Cut each tomato into 8 wedges and place on beef mixture. Cover and cook over low heat about 3 minutes or just until tomatoes are heated through. Serve with rice.

1 SERVING: Calories 400 (Calories from Fat 100); Fat 11g (Saturated 2g); Cholesterol 55mg; Sodium 390mg; Carbohydrate 52g (Dietary Fiber 2g); Protein 25g

---

LIGHTER PEPPER STEAK

For 6 grams of fat and 355 calories per serving, decrease oil to 1 tablespoon and use nonstick skillet.

Beef with Pea Pods

PREP: 20 min; COOK: 30 min
Makes 8 servings, about 2 cups each

2 pounds beef round steak, 3/4 to 1 inch
    thick
2 tablespoons vegetable oil
1 clove garlic, finely chopped
1/2 teaspoon salt
Dash of pepper
1 can (10 1/2 ounces) condensed beef broth
2 tablespoons cornstarch
1/4 cup water
1 tablespoon soy sauce
1/4 teaspoon finely chopped gingerroot or
    1/8 teaspoon ground ginger
1 package (6 ounces) frozen Chinese pea
    pods, thawed
8 cups hot cooked rice (page 204)

1. Trim excess fat from beef. Cut beef with grain into 2-inch strips; cut strips diagonally across grain into 1/4-inch slices. (Beef is easier to cut if partially frozen, about 1 1/2 hours.)

2. Heat wok or 10-inch skillet over high heat. Add oil; rotate wok to coat side. Add beef and garlic; stir-fry about 3 minutes or until beef is brown. Sprinkle with salt and pepper.

3. Stir in broth. Heat to boiling; reduce heat to low. Simmer uncovered 10 to 15 minutes or until beef is tender. (If liquid evaporates, add small amount of water.)

4. Mix cornstarch, water and soy sauce; stir into beef mixture. Cook, stirring constantly, until mixture thickens and boils. Boil and stir 1 minute. (Sauce will be thin.)

5. Stir in gingerroot and pea pods. Cook about 5 minutes, stirring occasionally, until pea pods are crisp-tender. Serve over rice.

1 SERVING: Calories 365 (Calories from Fat 65); Fat 7g (Saturated 2g); Cholesterol 55mg; Sodium 500mg; Carbohydrate 49g (Dietary Fiber 1g); Protein 27g

---

LIGHTER BEEF WITH PEA PODS

For 4 grams of fat and 335 calories per serving, omit oil and use nonstick skillet or wok. Spray cold skillet or wok with nonstick cooking spray before heating in step 2.

Pepperoni Pizza–Hamburger Pie

PREP: 20 min; BAKE: 30 min
Makes 6 servings

Ring a new change on a family favorite! This pie has the flavors of traditional pizza—but with a ground beef crust!

1 pound lean ground beef
1/3 cup dry bread crumbs
1 large egg
1 1/2 teaspoons chopped fresh or 1/2
    teaspoon dried oregano leaves
1/4 teaspoon salt
1/2 cup sliced mushrooms
1 small green bell pepper
1/3 cup chopped pepperoni (2 ounces)
1/4 cup sliced ripe olives
1 cup spaghetti sauce
1 cup shredded mozzarella cheese (4 ounces)

1. Heat oven to 400°.

2. Mix beef, bread crumbs, egg, oregano and salt; press evenly against bottom and side of ungreased pie plate, 9 × 1 1/4 inches.

3. Sprinkle mushrooms, bell pepper, pepperoni and olives into meat-lined plate. Pour spaghetti sauce over toppings.

4. Bake uncovered 25 minutes or until beef is no longer pink in center and juice is clear; *carefully* drain. Sprinkle with cheese. Bake about 5 minutes longer or until cheese is light brown. Let pie stand 5 minutes before cutting.

1 SERVING: Calories 310 (Calories from Fat 180); Fat 20g (Saturated 8g); Cholesterol 95mg; Sodium 740mg; Carbohydrate 10g (Dietary Fiber 1g); Protein 23g

Stuffed Peppers

PREP: 15 min; COOK: 15 min; BAKE: 1 hr
Makes 6 servings

A great recipe to make when the abundance of bell peppers at the supermarket or farmers' market drives the price down. For variety and color, try orange, yellow or purple bell peppers.

6 large bell peppers (any color)
1 pound lean ground beef
2 tablespoons chopped onion
1 cup cooked rice (page 204)
1 teaspoon salt
1 clove garlic, finely chopped
1 can (15 ounces) tomato sauce
3/4 cup shredded mozzarella cheese
    (3 ounces)

1. Cut thin slice from stem end of each bell pepper. Remove seeds and membranes; rinse peppers. Cook peppers in enough boiling water to cover about 5 minutes; drain.

2. Cook beef and onion in 10-inch skillet over medium heat 8 to 10 minutes, stirring occasionally, until beef is brown; drain. Stir in rice, salt, garlic and 1 cup of the tomato sauce; cook until hot.

3. Heat oven to 350°.

4. Stuff peppers with beef mixture. Stand upright in ungreased square baking dish, 8 × 8 × 2 inches. Pour remaining tomato sauce over peppers.

5. Cover and bake 45 minutes. Uncover and bake about 15 minutes longer or until peppers are tender. Sprinkle with cheese.

1 SERVING: Calories 275 (Calories from Fat 125); Fat 14g (Saturated 6g); Cholesterol 50mg; Sodium 900mg; Carbohydrate 20g (Dietary Fiber 3g); Protein 20g

---

LIGHTER STUFFED PEPPERS

For 11 grams of fat and 250 calories per serving, substitute ground turkey for the ground beef.

Hamburger Stroganoff

PREP: 10 min; COOK: 25 min
Makes 4 servings, about 1 cup each

1 pound lean ground beef
1 medium onion, chopped (1/2 cup)
1 clove garlic, finely chopped
1 can (10 3/4 ounces) condensed cream of
    mushroom soup
1/2 teaspoon salt
1 cup sour cream or plain yogurt
Hot cooked noodles or rice, if desired

1. Cook beef, onion and garlic in 10-inch skillet over medium heat 8 to 10 minutes, stirring occasionally, until beef is brown; drain.

2. Stir in soup and salt. Simmer uncovered 10 minutes.

3. Stir in sour cream; cook until hot. Serve over noodles.

1 SERVING: Calories 430 (Calories from Fat 295); Fat 33g (Saturated 15g); Cholesterol 105mg; Sodium 960mg; Carbohydrate 10g (Dietary Fiber 1g); Protein 24g

---

LIGHTER HAMBURGER STROGANOFF

For 23 grams of fat and 380 calories per serving, use ground turkey and reduced-fat sour cream or yogurt.

Cabbage Rolls

PREP: 20 min; BAKE: 45 min
Makes 4 servings

Cabbage leaves will separate easily if you first remove the core from the head of cabbage and let the cabbage stand in cold water for 10 minutes.

12 cabbage leaves
1 pound lean ground beef
1/2 cup uncooked instant rice
1 can (15 ounces) tomato sauce
1/2 teaspoon salt
1/8 teaspoon pepper
1 medium onion, chopped (1/2 cup)
1 clove garlic, finely chopped
1 can (4 ounces) mushroom stems and
    pieces, undrained
1 teaspoon sugar
1/2 teaspoon lemon juice
1 tablespoon cornstarch
1 tablespoon water

1. Cover cabbage leaves with boiling water. Cover and let stand about 10 minutes or until leaves are limp. Remove leaves; drain.

2. Heat oven to 350°.

3. Mix beef, rice, 1/2 cup of the tomato sauce, the salt, pepper, onion, garlic and mushrooms.

4. Place about 1/3 cup beef mixture at stem end of each leaf. Roll leaf around beef mixture, tucking in sides. Place cabbage rolls, seam sides down, in ungreased square baking dish, 8 × 8 × 2 inches.

5. Mix remaining tomato sauce, the sugar and lemon juice; pour over cabbage rolls.

6. Cover and bake about 45 minutes or until beef mixture is no longer pink in center and juice is clear.

7. Remove cabbage rolls to platter. Pour liquid in baking dish into 1-quart saucepan. Mix cornstarch and water; stir into liquid. Heat to boiling, stirring constantly. Boil and stir 1 minute. Pour sauce over cabbage rolls.

1 SERVING: Calories 390 (Calories from Fat 155); Fat 17g (Saturated 7g); Cholesterol 65mg; Sodium 1090mg; Carbohydrate 37g (Dietary Fiber 4g); Protein 26g

---

LIGHTER CABBAGE ROLLS

For 12 grams of fat and 350 calories per serving, substitute ground turkey for the ground beef.

CORNED BEEF CABBAGE ROLLS: Substitute 1 pound chopped cooked corned beef for the ground beef.

Spinach and Pine Nut Meatloaf, Mashed Potatoes (page 409)

Meat Loaf

PREP: 20 min; BAKE: 1 1/4 hr
Makes 6 servings

For variety, try a mixture of 1/2 pound each ground beef, ground pork and ground turkey.*

1 1/2 pounds lean ground beef
1 cup milk
1 tablespoon Worcestershire sauce
1 teaspoon chopped fresh or 1/4 teaspoon
    dried sage leaves
1/2 teaspoon salt
1/2 teaspoon ground mustard (dry)
1/4 teaspoon pepper
1 clove garlic, finely chopped, or
    1/8 teaspoon garlic powder
1 large egg
3 slices bread, torn into small pieces**
1 small onion, chopped (1/4 cup)
1/2 cup ketchup, chili sauce or barbecue
    sauce

1. Heat oven to 350°.

2. Mix all ingredients except ketchup. Spread mixture in ungreased loaf pan, 8 1/2 × 4 1/2 × 2 1/2 or 9 × 5 × 3 inches, or shape into 9 × 5-inch loaf in ungreased rectangular pan, 13 × 9 × 2 inches. Spread ketchup over top.

3. Insert meat thermometer so tip is in center of loaf. Bake uncovered 1 to 1 1/4 hours until thermometer reads 160°. (Also see Determining Meat Doneness, page 222.)*

4. Let stand 5 minutes; remove from pan.

*Cook to 170° if ground pork is used and 180° if ground turkey is used.

**1/2 cup dry bread crumbs or 3/4 cup quick-cooking oats can be substituted for the 3 slices bread.

1 SERVING: Calories 310 (Calories from Fat 155); Fat 17g (Saturated 6g); Cholesterol 110mg; Sodium 590mg; Carbohydrate 15g (Dietary Fiber 1g); Protein 25g

---

LIGHTER MEAT LOAF
For 14 grams of fat and 285 calories per serving, substitute ground turkey for the ground beef and 1/4 cup fat-free cholesterol-free egg product for the egg. Use skim milk.

INDIVIDUAL MEAT LOAVES: Shape beef mixture into 6 small loaves. Place in ungreased rectangular pan, 13 × 9 × 2 inches. Spoon ketchup over top of each loaf. Bake 45 minutes.

MEXICAN MEAT LOAF: Omit sage. Substitute 2/3 cup milk and 1/3 cup salsa for the 1 cup milk. Stir in 1/2 cup shredded Colby-Monterey Jack cheese (2 ounces) and 1 can (4 ounces) chopped green chilies,

drained, in step 2. Substitute 2/3 cup picante sauce for the ketchup.

SPINACH AND PINE NUT MEAT LOAF: Omit sage and ketchup. Stir in 1 package (10 ounces) frozen chopped spinach, thawed and squeezed to drain, 1/4 cup toasted pine nuts or slivered almonds and 2 teaspoons chopped fresh or 1/2 teaspoon dried basil leaves in step 2.

Skillet Hash

PREP: 10 min; COOK: 15 min
Makes 4 servings, about 1 cup each

2 cups chopped cooked lean beef or corned
    beef
4 small potatoes, cooked and chopped
    (2 cups)
1 medium onion, chopped (1/2 cup)
1 tablespoon chopped fresh parsley
1/2 teaspoon salt
1/8 teaspoon pepper
2 to 3 tablespoons vegetable oil

1. Mix beef, potatoes, onion, parsley, salt and pepper.

2. Heat oil in 10-inch skillet over medium heat. Spread beef mixture evenly in skillet. Cook 10 to 15 minutes, turning frequently, until brown.

1 SERVING: Calories 320 (Calories from Fat 160); Fat 18g (Saturated 5g); Cholesterol 55mg; Sodium 320mg; Carbohydrate 21g (Dietary Fiber 2g); Protein 21g

OVEN HASH: Heat oven to 350°. Grease square baking dish, 8 × 8 × 2 inches, with shortening. Omit oil. Spread beef mixture evenly in baking dish. Bake uncovered about 20 minutes or until hot.

RED FLANNEL SKILLET HASH: Use 1 1/2 cups chopped cooked corned beef and 3 small potatoes, cooked and chopped (1 1/2 cups). Mix in 1 can (16 ounces) diced or shoestring beets, drained.

TIMESAVING TIP
Use 2 cups frozen cubed hash browns, partially thawed, for the potatoes.

Meatballs

PREP: 15 min; BAKE: 25 min
Makes 4 to 5 servings

These versatile meatballs can be stirred into hot Italian Tomato Sauce (page 343), Barbecue Sauce (page 344), Sweet-and-Sour Sauce (page 344) or Peanut Sauce (page 343) and served as a main dish or as appetizers.

1 pound lean ground beef
1/2 cup dry bread crumbs
1/4 cup milk
1/2 teaspoon salt
1/2 teaspoon Worcestershire sauce
1/4 teaspoon pepper
1 small onion, chopped (1/4 cup)
1 large egg

1. Heat oven to 400°.

2. Mix all ingredients. Shape mixture into twenty 1 1/2-inch meatballs. Place in ungreased rectangular pan, 13 × 9 × 2 inches or on a rack in broiler pan.

3. Bake uncovered 20 to 25 minutes or until no longer pink in center and juice is clear.

1 SERVING: Calories 305 (Calories from Fat 160); Fat 18g (Saturated 7g); Cholesterol 120mg; Sodium 460mg; Carbohydrate 12g (Dietary Fiber 1g); Protein 25g

COCKTAIL MEATBALLS: Shape meat mixture into 1-inch meatballs. Bake 15–20 minutes. Makes 3 dozen appetizers.

SKILLET MEATBALLS: Cook meatballs in 10-inch skillet over medium heat about 20 minutes, turning occasionally, until no longer pink in center and juice is clear.

TURKEY OR CHICKEN MEATBALLS: Substitute 1 pound ground turkey or chicken for the ground beef. (If using ground chicken, decrease milk to 2 tablespoons.) To bake, grease rectangular pan with shortening. To panfry, heat 1 tablespoon vegetable oil in 10-inch skillet over medium heat before adding meatballs.

TIMESAVING TIP

Instead of shaping beef mixture into balls, pat mixture into rectangle, 9 × 3 inches, in ungreased rectangular pan, 13 × 9 × 2 inches. Cut into 1 1/2-inch squares; separate slightly. Bake uncovered 25 to 30 minutes.

Mexican Beef and Bean Casserole

PREP: 10 min; COOK: 10 min; BAKE: 50 min
Makes 4 servings, about 1 1/2 cups each

If you like your Mexican food with a little "kick," try using Monterey Jack cheese with jalapeño peppers or one of the shredded pizza cheese mixtures available.

1 pound lean ground beef
2 cans (15 to 16 ounces each) pinto beans, drained
1 can (8 ounces) tomato sauce
1/2 cup mild chunky salsa
1 teaspoon chili powder
1 cup shredded Monterey Jack cheese (4 ounces)

1. Heat oven to 375°.

2. Cook beef in 10-inch skillet over medium heat 8 to 10 minutes, stirring occasionally, until brown; drain.

3. Mix beef, beans, tomato sauce, salsa and chili powder in ungreased 2-quart casserole.

4. Cover and bake 40 to 45 minutes, stirring once or twice, until hot and bubbly. Sprinkle with cheese. Bake uncovered about 5 minutes or until cheese is melted.

1 SERVING: Calories 565 (Calories from Fat 235); Fat 26g (Saturated 12g); Cholesterol 90mg; Sodium 1230mg; Carbohydrate 54g (Dietary Fiber 15g); Protein 44g

---

LIGHTER MEXICAN BEEF AND BEAN CASSEROLE

For 18 grams of fat and 510 calories per serving, substitute ground turkey for the beef and reduced-fat Cheddar cheese for the Monterey Jack cheese.

Beef Enchiladas

Beef Enchiladas

PREP: 15 min; COOK: 20 min; BAKE: 20 min
Makes 4 servings

1 pound lean ground beef
1 medium onion, chopped (1/2 cup)
1/2 cup sour cream
1 cup shredded Cheddar cheese (4 ounces)
2 tablespoons chopped fresh parsley
1/4 teaspoon pepper
1/3 cup chopped green bell pepper
2/3 cup water
1 tablespoon chili powder
1 1/2 teaspoons chopped fresh or 1/2
    teaspoon dried oregano leaves
1/4 teaspoon ground cumin
2 whole green chilies, chopped, if desired
1 clove garlic, finely chopped
1 can (15 ounces) tomato sauce
8 corn tortillas (6 inches in diameter)
Shredded cheese, sour cream and chopped
    onions, if desired

1. Heat oven to 350°.

2. Cook beef in 10-inch skillet over medium heat 8 to 10 minutes, stirring occasionally, until brown; drain. Stir in onion, sour cream, 1 cup cheese, the parsley and pepper. Cover and set aside.

3. Heat bell pepper, water, chili powder, oregano, cumin, chilies, garlic and tomato sauce to boiling, stirring occasionally; reduce heat to low. Simmer uncovered 5 minutes. Pour into ungreased pie plate, 9 × 1 1/4 inches.

4. Dip each tortilla into sauce to coat both sides. Spoon about 1/4 cup beef mixture onto each tortilla; roll tortilla around filling. Place in ungreased rectangular baking dish, 11 × 7 × 1 1/2 inches. Pour remaining sauce over enchiladas.

5. Bake uncovered about 20 minutes or until bubbly. Garnish with shredded cheese, sour cream and chopped onions.

1 SERVING: Calories 560 (Calories from Fat 295); Fat 33g (Saturated 16g); Cholesterol 115mg; Sodium 980mg; Carbohydrate 37g (Dietary Fiber 5g); Protein 34g

---

LIGHTER ENCHILADAS
For 24 grams of fat and 495 calories per serving, use reduced-fat flour tortillas, sour cream and cheese.

CHEESE ENCHILADAS: Substitute 2 cups shredded Monterey Jack cheese (8 ounces) for the beef. Mix with onion, sour cream, 1 cup cheese, the parsley, salt and pepper. Sprinkle 1/4 cup shredded Cheddar cheese (1 ounce) on enchiladas before baking.

About Veal

Selecting Veal

Very young beef is classified as veal. Veal is a mild-flavored meat that's naturally lean and easy to prepare. It should have fine grain and be creamy pink in color. Any fat covering should be milky white. Red-colored meat indicates the veal is older and therefore may have diminished quality, flavor and tenderness.

Cooking Veal

Because veal is lean, all cuts are cooked at low temperatures to prevent them from drying out. Sauces or coatings also help to retain veal's natural juices and enhance its delicate flavor. It is recommended that veal be cooked to 160° (medium). Also see Determining Meat Doneness, page 222.

Roasting Veal

Roasting is an easy cooking method, and it's a low-fat way to cook because the fat drips away from the meat during cooking. Roasting is best used for larger cuts from the loin, sirloin and rib, although a boneless veal shoulder arm, eye round or rump roast also can be roasted successfully .

1. Select veal roast from those listed in Timetable for Roasting Veal.

2. Place veal, fat side up, on rack in shallow roasting pan. (For easy cleanup, line the roasting pan with aluminum foil before placing veal on rack.) The rack keeps the meat out of the drippings. (With a rib roast, the ribs form a natural rack.) As the fat melts, it bastes the veal, making other basting unnecessary.

3. Season veal with herbs, spices, salt or other seasonings before, during or after cooking, if desired. (Salt roasts *before* cooking to enhance flavor.)

4. Insert meat thermometer into roast surface at a slight angle or through the end of the roast so tip is in center of thickest part of roast and does not touch bone or fat.

5. Do not add water. Do not cover.

6. Roast at oven temperature shown in chart for veal cut being cooked. (It is not necessary to preheat oven.)

7. Roast to 155°. Roast will continue to cook after being removed from oven.

8. Cover roast loosely with tent of aluminum foil and let stand 15 to 20 minutes or until temperature rises to 160° (medium). Roast will be easier to carve as juices set up. (Covering roast tightly creates steam and softens the surface of the veal, eliminating its desirable dry, roasted texture.)

Timetable for Roasting Veal
(oven temperature 325°)

Veal Cut	Approximate Weight (pounds)	Approximate Cooking Time (minutes per pound)
Rump (boneless)	2 to 3	33 to 35
Shoulder (boneless)	2 1/2 to 3	31 to 34
Loin (bone in)	3 to 4	34 to 36
(boneless)	2 to 3	18 to 20
Rib	4 to 5	25 to 27
Crown (12 to 14 ribs)	7 1/2 to 9 1/2	19 to 21

Note: *Smaller roasts require more minutes per pound than larger roasts.*

VEAL

• RETAIL CUTS •
WHERE THEY COME FROM
HOW TO COOK THEM

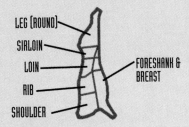

LEG (ROUND)
SIRLOIN
LOIN
RIB
SHOULDER
FORESHANK & BREAST

RIB

Rib Roast
Roast

Boneless Rib Roast
Roast

Crown Roast
Roast

Boneless Rib Chop
Braise, Panfry, Broil

Rib Chop
Braise, Panfry, Broil

Short Ribs
Braise, Cook in Liquid

LEG (ROUND)

Boneless Rump Roast
Braise, Roast

Round Steak
Braise, Panfry

Top Round Steak
Braise, Panfry

Leg Cutlet
Braise, Panfry, Broil

LOIN

Loin Roast
Roast

Boneless Loin Roast
Roast

Loin Chop
Braise, Panfry, Broil

Kidney Chop
Braise, Panfry

Top Loin Chop
Braise, Panfry, Broil

Butterfly Chop
Braise, Panfry, Broil

SIRLOIN

Sirloin Roast
Roast

Boneless Sirloin Roast
Roast

Sirloin Steak
Braise, Panfry, Broil

Top Sirloin Steak
Braise, Panfry, Broil

SHOULDER

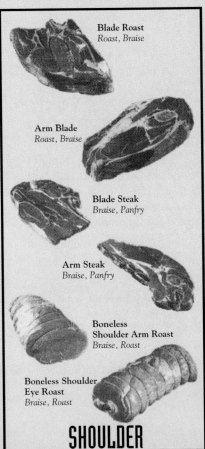

Blade Roast
Roast, Braise

Arm Blade
Roast, Braise

Blade Steak
Braise, Panfry

Arm Steak
Braise, Panfry

Boneless Shoulder Arm Roast
Braise, Roast

Boneless Shoulder Eye Roast
Braise, Roast

FORESHANK & BREAST

Breast
Braise, Roast

Boneless Breast Roast
Braise, Roast

Cross Cut Shank
Braise, Cook in Liquid

Riblet
Braise, Cook in Liquid

Shank
Braise, Cook in Liquid

OTHER CUTS

Veal for Stew
Braise, Cook in Liquid

Ground Veal
Broil, Panfry

Cubes for Kabobs
Braise

Cubed Steak
Braise, Panfry

This chart approved by
NATIONAL LIVESTOCK & MEAT BOARD

Broiling or Grilling Veal

Broiling and direct-heat grilling are quick, low-fat methods for cooking bone-in and boneless veal rib or loin chops or ground veal. Less-tender blade or arm steaks can be broiled if they have been marinated first (see Tips for Marinades and Marinating, page 356). The grilling directions below are for grilling over direct heat. Other veal cuts can be grilled over indirect heat. Refer to the instructions that came with your grill or see Grilling Know-How, page 428, for more information.

1. Select veal cut from those listed in Timetable for Broiling or Grilling Veal.

2. Marinate veal if desired. (See Tips for Marinades and Marinating, page 356).

3. To Broil: Set oven to broil.

To Grill: Heat coals or gas grill (direct heat) to medium heat.

4. To Broil: Place veal on rack in broiler pan. (For easy cleanup, line the broiler pan with aluminum foil before placing veal on rack.) Place in oven with top of veal the inches from heat listed in chart for veal cut chosen.

To Grill: Place veal on grill the inches from heat listed in chart for veal cut chosen.

5. Broil or grill about half the time shown in chart for veal cut chosen or until veal is brown on one side.

Timetable for Broiling or Grilling Veal

Veal Meat Cut	Approximate Thickness	Inches from Heat	Approximate Total Broiling Time (minutes) 160° (medium)	Approximate Total Grilling Time (minutes) 160° (medium)
Loin or Rib Chops	1 inch	4	14 to 16	12 to 14
Arm or Blade Steaks*	3/4 inch	4	14 to 15	16 to 18
Ground Veal Patties	1/2 inch	4	8 to 10	10 to 12

*Marinate at least 6 hours but no longer than 24 hours to tenderize.

Panbroiling Veal

Panbroiling is a quick, easy and low-fat way to cook thinner steaks and patties.

1. Select veal cut from those listed in Timetable for Panbroiling Veal.

2. Coat heavy skillet with a small amount of vegetable oil, or spray with nonstick cooking spray. Or use nonstick skillet.

3. Heat skillet over medium-low to medium heat when cooking cuts 5/8 to 1 inch thick, or heat over medium-high heat for cuts 1/4 to 1/2 inch thick.

4. Place veal in hot skillet. Do not add oil or water. Do not cover.

5. Cook for time shown in chart for veal cut chosen. Remove fat from skillet as it accumulates. Turn veal cuts thicker than 1/2-inch occasionally, thinner cuts once, until brown on both sides and slightly pink in center. (To check doneness, cut a small slit in the center of boneless cuts or in the center near the bone of bone-in cuts.) Serve immediately.

Timetable for Panbroiling Veal

Veal Cut	Approximate thickness (inches)	Stovetop Temperature	Approximate Total Cooking Time (minutes) 160° (medium)
Loin or Rib Chops	3/4 to 1	Medium-low to Medium	10 to 12
Arm or Blade Steaks*	3/4	Medium to Medium-high	13 to 14
Ground Veal Patties	1/2	Medium-low to Medium	6 to 7

*Marinate at least 6 hours but no longer than 24 hours to tenderize.

Veal Scallopini

PRFP· 10 min; COOK. 20 min
Makes 4 servings

1/2 cup all-purpose flour
2 teaspoons garlic salt
1 pound veal for scallopini*
1/4 cup vegetable oil
2 tablespoons margarine or butter
1/4 cup dry white wine (or nonalcoholic) or
    chicken broth
2 tablespoons lemon juice
1/2 lemon, cut into 4 wedges

1. Mix flour and garlic salt. Coat veal with flour mixture.

2. Heat 2 tablespoons of the oil in 10-inch skillet over medium-high heat. Cook half of the veal in oil about 5 minutes, turning once, until brown. Remove veal; keep warm. Repeat with remaining oil and veal. Drain any remaining oil and overly browned particles from skillet.

3. Add margarine, wine and lemon juice to skillet. Heat to boiling, scraping any remaining brown particles from skillet. Boil until liquid is reduced by about half and mixture has thickened slightly. Pour over veal. Serve with lemon wedges.

1 pound veal round steak can be substituted for the veal for scallopini. Cut veal into 8 pieces; flatten between plastic wrap or waxed paper with a meat mallet to 1/4-inch thickness.

1 SERVING: Calories 335 (Calories from Fat 205); Fat 23g (Saturated 5g); Cholesterol 75mg; Sodium 610mg; Carbohydrate 13g (Dietary Fiber 0g); Protein 19g

---

LIGHTER LEMON VEAL
SCALLOPINI

For 14 grams of fat and 255 calories per serving, decrease oil to 2 tablespoons and cook half of the veal at a time in 1 tablespoon oil in nonstick skillet. Decrease margarine to 1 tablespoon.

Braised Veal Shanks

PREP: 40 min; COOK: 2 1/2 hr
Makes 6 servings

This Italian dish, known as osso buco, *consists of veal shanks braised in a flavorful mixture that includes white wine and beef broth. Because this dish typically is served with risotto, try it with our Risotto Florentine, page 207, instead of spaghetti.*

4 pounds veal shanks
1/2 teaspoon salt
1/4 teaspoon pepper
1/4 cup all-purpose flour
2 tablespoons olive or vegetable
1/3 cup dry white wine (or nonalcoholic) or
    apple juice
1 can (10 1/2 ounces) condensed beef broth
1 clove garlic, finely chopped
1 bay leaf
2 tablespoons chopped fresh parsley
1 teaspoon grated lemon peel
6 cups hot cooked spaghetti (page 275)
Grated Romano cheese, if desired

1. Trim excess fat from veal. Cut veal into 2 1/2-inch pieces. Sprinkle veal with salt and pepper; coat with flour.

2. Heat oil in Dutch oven over medium heat. Cook veal in oil about 20 minutes, turning occasionally, until brown on all sides.

3. Stir in wine, broth, garlic and bay leaf. Heat to boiling; reduce heat to low. Cover and simmer 1 1/2 to 2 hours or until veal is tender. Remove veal from Dutch oven. Skim fat from broth. Return veal to broth.

4. Sprinkle veal mixture with parsley and lemon peel. Heat to boiling; reduce heat to low. Cover and simmer 5 minutes. Remove bay leaf. Serve veal and sauce on spaghetti. Sprinkle with cheese.

1 SERVING: Calories 630 (Calories from Fat 170); Fat 19g (Saturated 6g); Cholesterol 260mg; Sodium 660mg; Carbohydrate 45g (Dietary Fiber 1g); Protein 71g

BRAISED BEEF SHANKS: Substitute 4 pounds beef shanks, cut into 2 1/2-inch pieces, for the veal.

Veal Parmigiana

PREP: 1 hr 5 min; COOK: 10 min; BAKE: 25 min
Makes 6 servings

  2 cups Italian Tomato Sauce (page 343)
  1 large egg
  2 tablespoons water
  2/3 cup dry bread crumbs
  1/3 cup grated Parmesan cheese
  1 1/2 pounds veal for scallopini*
  1/4 cup olive or vegetable oil
  2 cups shredded mozzarella cheese
     (8 ounces)

1. Prepare Italian Tomato Sauce.

2. Heat oven to 350°.

3. Mix egg and water. Mix bread crumbs and Parmesan cheese. Dip veal into egg mixture, then coat with bread crumb mixture.

4. Heat oil in 12-inch skillet over medium heat. Cook half of the veal at a time in oil about 5 minutes, turning once, until light brown; drain. Repeat with remaining veal, adding 1 or 2 tablespoons oil if necessary.

5. Place half the veal in ungreased rectangular baking dish, 11 × 7 × 1 1/2 inches, overlapping slices slightly. Spoon half of the sauce over veal. Sprinkle with 1 cup of the mozzarella cheese. Repeat with remaining veal, sauce and cheese.

6. Bake uncovered about 25 minutes or until sauce is bubbly and cheese is light brown.

1 1/2 pounds veal round steak can be substituted for the veal for scallopini. Cut veal into 12 pieces; flatten between plastic wrap or waxed paper with a meat mallet to 1/4-inch thickness.

1 SERVING: Calories 410 (Calories from Fat 225); Fat 25g (Saturated 8g); Cholesterol 130mg; Sodium 950mg; Carbohydrate 15g (Dietary Fiber 1g); Protein 32g

EGGPLANT PARMIGIANA: Substitute 2 small unpeeled eggplants (about 1 pound each) for the veal. Cut each eggplant into 1/4 inch slices.

CHICKEN PARMIGIANA: Substitute 8 boneless, skinless chicken breast halves (about 2 pounds) for the veal. Flatten chicken between plastic wrap or waxed paper with a meat mallet to 1/4-inch thickness.

TIMESAVING TIP
Substitute 2 cups purchased spaghetti sauce for the Italian Tomato Sauce.

Veal Parmigiana

About Pork

Selecting Pork

The lean part of fresh pork should be grayish pink in color and fine-grained in texture. Recent research on today's lean pork and the latest cooking recommendations indicate cooking all pork to at least 160° (medium). For some cuts using specific cooking methods, 170° (well done) is recommended for best flavor development.

Boneless pork cooked to medium, or 160°, will be slightly pink in the center. At 170°, the meat will lose its pink color. Bone-in cuts will have a slightly more intense color near the bone when cooked to 160°, but are perfectly safe to eat. Refer to the cooking charts for specific recommendations.

For ham, the lean should be firm, fine-grained, pink in color and free from excess moisture. The fat covering should be firm and white. You may notice a rainbowlike appearance on the surface of ham. It is called *iridescence* and is caused by the refraction of light on the cut ends of the muscle fibers. The color is not harmful, nor does it affect quality.

The most popular kind of ham is *fully cooked ham.* It's ready to eat without cooking, if you prefer it cold. Or to serve it warm, heat it to 140° (see Roasting Ham, page 258). Hams labeled "cook before eating" are not completely cooked and must be cooked to 160°. If you aren't sure what kind of ham you have purchased, ask your butcher or cook it to 160° to be safe.

Country or *country-style hams* are uniquely flavored and specially processed. They are cured and aged and may be smoked. Country hams are usually saltier than other hams. Follow the package directions for cooking these hams.

Turkey ham is skinless, boneless turkey thigh meat that is cured and smoked to taste like ham made from pork. In some cases, turkey hams have fewer calories and grams of fat per serving than pork hams. Read the label carefully to be sure. Turkey hams are available in large, boneless pieces or as cold cuts. The large pieces, like fully cooked hams, can be eaten cold, or warm by heating to 140°.

How to Carve a Pork Loin Roast

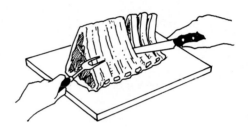

Place roast on carving board or platter; remove backbone from ribs for easy carving. Place roast with rib side toward you. With meat fork inserted in roast to keep the meat from moving, cut slices on each side of rib bones. (Every other slice will contain a bone.)

PORK

• RETAIL CUTS •
WHERE THEY COME FROM
HOW TO COOK THEM

LEG
LOIN
SIDE
ARM SHOULDER
BLADE SHOULDER

LEG/HAM

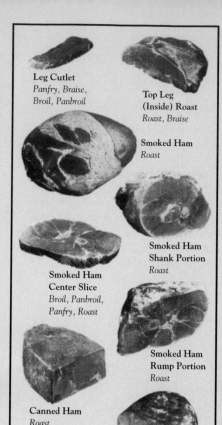

Leg Cutlet
Panfry, Braise, Broil, Panbroil

Top Leg (Inside) Roast
Roast, Braise

Smoked Ham
Roast

Smoked Ham Shank Portion
Roast

Smoked Ham Center Slice
Broil, Panbroil, Panfry, Roast

Smoked Ham Rump Portion
Roast

Canned Ham
Roast

Sliced Ham
Panfry, Panbroil, Braise

Boneless Smoked Ham
Roast

SHOULDER

Blade Roast
Roast, Braise

Blade Steak
Braise, Broil Panbroil, Panfry

Boneless Blade Roast
Roast, Braise

Smoked Shoulder Roll
Roast, Cook in Liquid

Boneless Arm Picnic Roast
Roast, Braise

Smoked Hocks
Braise, Cook in Liquid

Smoked Picnic
Roast, Cook in Liquid

LOIN

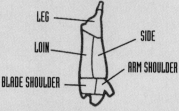

Country-Style Ribs
Roast, Braise, Broil, Cook in Liquid

Center Rib Roast
Roast

Sirloin Cutlet
Braise, Broil, Panbroil, Panfry

Tenderloin
Roast, Braise (Slices: Panfry, Braise)

Back Ribs
Roast, Broil, Braise, Cook in Liquid

Sirloin Roast
Roast

Blade Roast
Roast, Braise

Boneless Blade Roast
Roast, Braise

Top Loin Roast (Double)
Roast

Boneless Sirloin Roast
Roast

Crown Roast
Roast

Smoked Loin Chop
Roast, Broil, Panbroil, Panfry

Center Loin Roast
Roast

Canadian-Style Bacon
Roast, Broil, Panbroil, Panfry

Loin chops (right side)

Blade Chop
Braise, Broil, Panbroil, Panfry

Rib Chop
Broil, Panbroil Panfry, Braise

Top Loin Chop
Broil, Panbroil Panfry, Braise

Loin Chop
Broil, Panbroil Panfry, Braise

Sirloin Chop
Braise

Butterfly Chop
Broil, Panbroil Panfry, Braise

SIDE

Spareribs
Roast, Broil, Cook in Liquid, Braise

Sliced Bacon
Panfry, Broil, Roast (Bake)

This chart approved by
NATIONAL LIVESTOCK & MEAT BOARD

OTHER CUTS

Cubed Steak
Braise, Panbroil, Panfry

Pork Pieces
Braise, Cook in Liquid

Cubes for Kabobs
Broil, Braise

Ground Pork
Broil, Panbroil, Panfry, Roast (Bake)

Sausage Links
Braise, Panfry, Roast

Roasting Pork

Roasting is an easy cooking method, and it's a low-fat way to cook because the fat drips away from the meat while cooking.

1. Select pork roast from those listed in Timetable for Roasting Pork.

2. Place pork, fat side up (if present), on rack in shallow roasting pan. (For easy cleanup, line the roasting pan with aluminum foil before placing pork on rack.) The rack keeps the meat out of the drippings. (With a rib roast, the ribs form a natural rack.) As the fat melts, it bastes the pork, making other basting unnecessary.

3. Season pork with herbs, spices, salt or other seasonings before, during or after cooking, if desired. (Salt roasts *before* cooking to enhance flavor.)

4. Insert meat thermometer into roast surface at a slight angle or through the end of the roast so tip is in center of thickest part of roast and does not touch bone or fat.

5. Do not add water. Do not cover.

6. Roast at oven temperature shown in chart for pork cut being cooked. (It is not necessary to preheat oven.)

7. Roast ribs until tender. For all other cuts, roast to temperature listed in chart in column titled "Meat Thermometer Reading (*after roasting*)" for pork cut chosen. Roast will continue to cook after being removed from oven.

8. Cover roast loosely with tent of aluminum foil and let stand 15 to 20 minutes or until temperature rises to that listed in chart in column titled "Final Meat Thermometer Reading (after standing)." Roast will be easier to carve as juices set up. (Covering roast tightly creates steam and softens the surface of the pork, eliminating its desirable dry, roasted texture.)

Timetable for Roasting Pork
(oven temperature 325°)

Pork Cut	Approximate Weight (pounds)	Meat Thermometer Reading (*after roasting*)	Final Meat Thermometer Reading (*after standing*)	Approximate Cooking Time (minutes per pound)
Loin Center (bone in)	3 to 5	155°	160° (medium)	20 to 25
Blade Loin or Sirloin (boneless, tied)	2 1/2 to 3 1/2	165°	170° (well)	33 to 38
Rib (boneless)	2 to 4	155°	160° (medium)	26 to 31
Top Loin Double (boneless)	3 to 4	155°	160° (medium)	29 to 34
Top Loin (boneless)	2 to 4	155°	160° (medium)	23 to 33
Crown	6 to 10	165°	170° (well)	20 to 25
Blade Boston (boneless)	3 to 4	165°	170° (well)	40 to 45
				Total Cooking Time
Tenderloin*	1/2 to 1	155°	160° (medium)	27 to 29
Back ribs				1 1/2 to 1 3/4 hours
Country-style Ribs	1-inch slices			1 1/2 to 1 3/4 hours
Spareribs				1 1/2 to 1 3/4 hours

*Roast at 425°.

Note: *Smaller roasts require more minutes per pound than larger roasts. All pork should be cooked to 160°; however, 170° is recommended for some cuts for best flavor.*

Pork Crown Roast with Mushroom Stuffing

PREP: 20 min; ROAST: 3 hr 20 min; STAND: 20 min
Makes 12 servings

This special roast may be on hand at your supermarket during the holidays, but call the butcher in advance to be sure. Fancy paper frills are usually provided.

7 1/2- to 8-pound pork crown roast (about
   20 ribs)
2 teaspoons salt
1 teaspoon pepper
Mushroom Stuffing (page 297)

1. Sprinkle pork roast with salt and pepper. Place pork, bone ends up, on rack in shallow roasting pan. Wrap bone ends in aluminum foil to prevent excessive browning. Insert meat thermometer so tip is in thickest part of meat and does not touch bone or rest in fat. Place a small heatproof bowl or crumpled aluminum foil in crown to hold shape of roast evenly. Do not add water. Do not cover.

2. Roast in 325° oven (it is not necessary to preheat oven) 2 1/2 hours to 3 hours 20 minutes or until thermometer reads 165°. (Also see Determining Meat Doneness, page 222.)

3. While pork is roasting, prepare Mushroom Stuffing. One hour before pork is done, remove bowl and fill center of crown with Mushroom Stuffing. Cover stuffing only with aluminum foil during first 30 minutes.

4. Cover roast with tent of aluminum foil and let stand 15 to 20 minutes or until thermometer reads 170°. (Temperature will continue to rise about 5° and roast will be easier to carve as juices set up.)

5. Remove foil wrapping; place paper frills on bone ends. To serve, spoon stuffing into bowl and cut roast between ribs.

1 SERVING: Calories 515 (Calories from Fat 295); Fat 33g (Saturated 10g); Cholesterol 110mg; Sodium 880mg; Carbohydrate 15g (Dietary Fiber 1g); Protein 40g

Saucy Ribs

Saucy Ribs

PREP: 10 min; BAKE: 2 1/4 hr
Makes 6 servings

Prepare any of the following side dishes, or pick them up from a deli, for a sumptuous meal: Creamy Coleslaw (page 322), Baked Beans (page 214), Baked Potatoes (page 400) or Au Gratin Potatoes (page 410).

> 4 1/2 pounds pork loin back ribs, pork spareribs or beef short ribs or 3 pounds pork country-style ribs
> Spicy Barbecue Sauce (below), Mustard Sauce or Sweet-Savory Sauce (right)

1. Heat oven to 325°.

2. Prepare Spicy Barbecue Sauce. Use sauce as directed in chart below.

3. Cut ribs into serving pieces. Place meaty sides up in pan listed in chart.

4. Cook as directed in chart below.

Spicy Barbecue Sauce

> 1/3 cup margarine or butter
> 2 tablespoons white vinegar
> 2 tablespoons water
> 1 teaspoon sugar
> 1/2 teaspoon garlic powder
> 1/2 teaspoon onion powder
> 1/2 teaspoon pepper
> Dash of ground red pepper (cayenne)

Heat all ingredients in 1-quart saucepan over medium heat, stirring frequently, until margarine is melted.

Mustard Sauce

> 1/2 cup molasses
> 1/3 cup Dijon mustard
> 1/3 cup cider vinegar

Mix molasses and mustard. Stir in vinegar.

Sweet-Savory Sauce

> 1 cup chili sauce
> 3/4 cup grape jelly
> 1 tablespoon plus 1 1/2 teaspoons dry red wine or beef broth
> 1 teaspoon Dijon mustard

Heat all ingredients in 1-quart saucepan over medium heat, stirring occasionally, until jelly is melted.

1 SERVING: Calories 615 (Calories from Fat 450); Fat 50g (Saturated 17g); Cholesterol 160mg; Sodium 240mg; Carbohydrate 2g (Dietary Fiber 0g); Protein 39g

> **TIMESAVING TIP**
> Use 2/3 cup of your favorite bottled barbecue sauce instead of preparing the Spicy Barbecue Sauce recipe.

Saucy Ribs Cooking Chart

Kind of Ribs	Pan	Cooking Directions	Serving Tips
Pork loin back ribs	Rack in shallow roasting pan	Bake uncovered 1 1/2 hours; brush with sauce. Bake uncovered about 45 minutes longer, brushing frequently with sauce, until tender.	Heat any remaining sauce to boiling, stirring constantly, boil and stir 1 minute. Serve sauce with ribs.
Pork spareribs	Rack in shallow roasting pan	Bake uncovered 1 hour; brush with sauce. Bake uncovered about 45 minutes longer, brushing frequently with sauce, until tender.	Heat any remaining sauce to boiling, stirring constantly; boil and stir 1 minute. Serve sauce with ribs.
Pork country-style ribs	Rectangular pan, 13 × 9 × 2 inches	Cover and bake about 2 hours or until tender; drain. Pour sauce over ribs. Bake uncovered 30 minutes longer.	Spoon sauce from pan over ribs.
Beef short ribs	Rectangular pan, 13 × 9 × 2 inches	Pour sauce over ribs. Cover and bake about 2 1/2 hours or until tender.	Spoon sauce from pan over ribs.

Apricot-Pistachio Rolled Pork

**PREP: 30 min; MARINATE: 2 1/4 hr; ROAST: 2 1/2 hr;
STAND: 35 min
Makes 12 servings**

*Piercing the pork and allowing it to stand after brushing with
apricot brandy helps to heighten the apricot flavor of the
roast.*

**4-pound pork boneless top loin roast (single
    uncut roast)
1/2 cup chopped dried apricots
1/2 cup chopped pistachio nuts
2 cloves garlic, finely chopped
1/4 teaspoon salt
1/4 teaspoon pepper
1/4 cup apricot brandy or apricot nectar
1/4 cup apricot preserves
Crunchy Topping (below)**

1. To cut pork roast into a large rectangle that can
be filled and rolled, cut lengthwise about 1/2 inch
from top of pork to within 1/2 inch of opposite edge;
open flat. Repeat with other side of pork, cutting from
the inside edge to the outer edge; open flat to form a
rectangle.

2. Sprinkle apricots, pistachios, garlic, salt and pepper over pork to within 1 inch of edges. Beginning
with short side, tightly roll up pork. Secure with
toothpicks or tie with string. Place in glass baking dish.

3. Pierce pork all over with metal skewer. Brush
entire surface with brandy. Let stand 15 minutes.
Brush again with brandy. Cover and refrigerate at least
2 hours but no longer than 24 hours.

4. Place pork, fat side up, on rack in shallow roasting pan. Insert meat thermometer so tip is in center of
thickest part of pork roll. Do not add water. Do not
cover. Roast in 325° oven (it is not necessary to preheat oven) 1 1/2 hours.

5. Prepare Crunchy Topping. Brush preserves over
pork. Sprinkle with topping. Roast 30 to 60 minutes
longer or until meat thermometer reads 155°. (Also see
Determining Meat Doneness, page 222.) Cover pork
with tent of aluminum foil and let stand 15 to 20 minutes or until thermometer reads 160°. (Temperature
will continue to rise about 5°, and roast will be easier
to carve as juices set up.) Cut into slices.

Crunchy Topping

**1 tablespoon margarine or butter
1/4 cup coarsely crushed cracker crumbs
2 tablespoons chopped pistachio nuts
1/4 teaspoon garlic**

Melt margarine in 2-quart saucepan over medium
heat. Stir in remaining ingredients. Cook and stir 1
minute; cool.

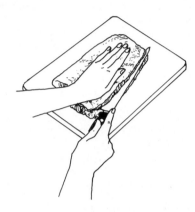

a. Cut lengthwise about 1/2 inch from top of pork to within
1/2 inch of opposite edge; open flat.

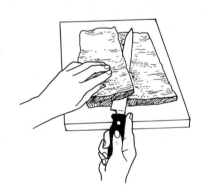

b. Repeat with other side of pork, cutting loose from inside
edge; open flat to form rectangle.

1 SERVING: Calories 260 (Calories from Fat 115); Fat 13g
(Saturated 4g); Cholesterol 65mg; Sodium 140mg;
Carbohydrate 12g (Dietary Fiber 1g); Protein 25g

Broiling or Grilling Pork

Broiling and direct-heat grilling are quick, low-fat methods for chops and other small pieces. Other pork cuts, such as ribs or roasts, can be grilled over indirect heat. Refer to the instructions that came with your grill or see Grilling Know-How, page 428, for more information.

1. Select pork cut from those listed in Timetable for Broiling or Grilling Pork.

2. Marinate pork if desired. (See Tips for Marinades and Marinating, page 356.)

3. *To Broil*: Set oven to Broil.

To Grill: Heat coals or gas grill (direct heat) to medium heat.

4. *To Broil*: Place pork on rack in broiler pan. (For easy cleanup, line the broiler pan with aluminum foil before placing pork on rack.) Place in oven with top of pork the number of inches from heat listed in chart for pork cut chosen.

To Grill: Place pork on grill the inches from heat listed in chart for pork cut chosen.

5. Broil or grill about half the time shown in chart for pork cut chosen or until pork is brown on one side.

6. Turn pork and continue cooking until doneness shown in chart for pork cut chosen.* (To check doneness, cut a small slit in the center of boneless cuts or in the center near the bone of bone-in cuts. Medium pork is slightly pink in center. Well-done pork is no longer pink in center.) Season each side after cooking if desired.

Well-done pork, although a little less juicy, is recommended for some cuts because the pork will be more flavorful.

Timetable for Broiling or Grilling Pork

Pork Cut	Approximate Thickness or Weight	Inches from Heat	Meat Doneness	Approximate Total Broiling Time (minutes)	Approximate Total Grilling Time (minutes)
Loin or Rib Chops (bone in)	3/4 inch	3 to 4	160° (medium)	8 to 11	6 to 8
	1 1/2 inches	3 to 4	160° (medium)	19 to 22	12 to 16
Loin Chop (boneless)	1 inch	3 to 4	160° (medium)	11 to 13	8 to 10
Blade Chop (bone in)	3/4 inch	3 to 4	170° (well)	13 to 15	11 to 13
	1 1/2 inches	3 to 4	170° (well)	26 to 29	19 to 22
Arm Chop (bone in)	3/4 inch	3 to 4	170° (well)	16 to 18	13 to 15
	1 inch	3 to 4	170° (well)	18 to 20	15 to 18
Cubes for Kabobs	1-inch pieces	3 to 4	160° (medium)	9 to 11	10 to 20
Loin or Leg Tenderloin	1-inch pieces	3 to 4	160° (medium)	12 to 14	13 to 21
Ground Pork Patties	1/2 inch thick	3 to 4	170° (well)	7 to 9	7 to 9
Country-Style Ribs	1-inch slices	5	160° (medium)	45 to 60	1 1/2 to 2 hours*
Spareribs		5	160° (medium)	45 to 60	1 1/2 to 2 hours*
Backribs		5	160° (medium)	45 to 55	1 1/2 to 2 hours*

Grill over indirect heat.

Panbroiling Pork

Panbroiling is a quick, easy and low-fat way to cook thinner steaks and patties.

1. Select pork cut from those listed in Timetable for Panbroiling Pork.

2. Coat heavy skillet with a small amount of vegetable oil, or spray with nonstick cooking spray if pork to be cooked is very lean. Or use nonstick skillet.

3. Heat skillet over medium heat.

4. Place pork in hot skillet. Do not add oil or water. Do not cover.

5. Cook for time shown in chart for pork cut chosen. Remove fat from skillet as it accumulates. Turn pork occasionally until brown on both sides and doneness shown in chart for pork cut chosen. (To check doneness, cut a small slit in the center of boneless cuts or in the center near the bone of bone-in cuts. Medium pork is slightly pink in center; well-done pork will not contain any pink.) Serve immediately.

Timetable for Panbroiling Pork
(medium heat)

Pork Cut	Approximate Thickness (inches)	Meat Doneness	Approximate *Total* Cooking Time (minutes)
Loin or Rib Chops	1/2	160° (medium)	7 to 8
(bone in)	1	160° (medium)	12 to 14
Loin Chops	1/2	160° (medium)	7 to 8
(boneless)	1	160° (medium)	10 to 12
Butterflied Chops	1/2	160° (medium)	8 to 9
	1	160° (medium)	12 to 14
Ground Pork Patties	1/2	170° (well)	7 to 9

Pork-Filled Acorn Squash

PREP: 45 min; BAKE: 35 min
Makes 4 servings

2 medium acorn squash (about 1 1/2 pounds each)
3/4 pound ground pork
1/4 cup sliced green onions (3 medium)
1/2 cup dried cranberries or raisins
1/3 cup uncooked rosamarina (orzo) pasta
1 cup beef broth
2 teaspoons chopped fresh or 3/4 teaspoon dried rosemary leaves
1/2 teaspoon salt
1/8 teaspoon pepper

1. Heat oven to 350°.

2. Prepare squash, cutting in half, and cook as directed on page 401; cool slightly.

3. Cook pork and onions in 2-quart saucepan over medium heat, stirring occasionally, until pork is no longer pink; drain.

4. Stir in remaining ingredients. Heat to boiling; reduce heat to low. Cover and simmer about 10 minutes or until pasta is tender and broth is absorbed.

5. If wells in squash halves are shallow, scoop out enough pulp to leave 1/2-inch thickness. (Use pulp for another use.) Place squash, cut sides up, in rectangular baking dish, 13 × 9 × 2 inches.

6. Spoon pork mixture into squash halves. Cover and bake about 35 minutes or until heated through.

1 SERVING: Calories 400 (Calories from Fat 125); Fat 14g (Saturated 5g); Cholesterol 55mg; Sodium 470mg; Carbohydrate 55g (Dietary Fiber 8g); Protein 22g

> **LIGHTER FILLED ACORN SQUASH**
> For 10 grams of fat and 275 calories per serving, substitute ground turkey for the ground pork.

Sweet-and-Sour Pork

PREP: 25 min; COOK: 30 min
Makes 8 servings, about 2 cups each

2 pounds pork boneless top loin
Vegetable oil
1/2 cup all-purpose flour
1/4 cup cornstarch
1/2 cup cold water
1/2 teaspoon salt
1 large egg
1 can (20 ounces) pineapple chunks in syrup,
    drained and syrup reserved
1/2 cup packed brown sugar
1/2 cup white vinegar
1/2 teaspoon salt
2 teaspoons soy sauce
2 medium carrots, cut into thin diagonal
    slices
1 clove garlic, finely chopped
2 tablespoons cornstarch
2 tablespoons cold water
1 medium green bell pepper, cut into
    3/4-inch pieces
8 cups hot cooked rice (page 204)

1. Trim excess fat from pork. Cut pork into 3/4-inch pieces.

2. Heat 1 inch oil in deep fryer or Dutch oven to 360°.

3. Beat flour, 1/4 cup cornstarch, 1/2 cup cold water, 1/2 teaspoon salt and the egg in large bowl with hand beater until smooth. Stir pork into batter until well coated.

4. Add pork pieces, one at a time, to oil. Fry about 20 pieces at a time about 5 minutes, turning 2 or 3 times, until golden brown. Drain on paper towels; keep warm.

5. Add enough water to reserved pineapple syrup to measure 1 cup. Heat syrup mixture, brown sugar, vinegar, 1/2 teaspoon salt, the soy sauce, carrots and garlic to boiling in Dutch oven; reduce heat to low. Cover and simmer about 6 minutes or until carrots are crisp-tender.

6. Mix 2 tablespoons cornstarch and 2 tablespoons cold water; stir into sauce. Add pork, pineapple and bell pepper. Heat to boiling, stirring constantly. Boil and stir 1 minute. Serve with rice.

1 SERVING: Calories 725 (Calories from Fat 315); Fat 35g (Saturated 7g); Cholesterol 80mg; Sodium 410mg; Carbohydrate 81g (Dietary Fiber 3g); Protein 24g

---

LIGHTER SWEET-AND-SOUR PORK
For 7 grams of fat and 435 calories per serving, omit oil, flour, 1/4 cup cornstarch, 1/2 cup cold water, 1/2 teaspoon salt and the egg. Spray nonstick Dutch oven with nonstick cooking spray. Cook half of the uncoated pork at a time in Dutch oven over medium-high heat about 5 minutes, stirring occasionally, until no longer pink in center. Remove from Dutch oven; keep warm. Continue as directed in step 5.

Szechuan Pork

PREP: 15 min; CHILL: 20 min; COOK: 10 min
Makes 6 servings, about 2 cups each

1 pound pork boneless loin or leg
1 tablespoon soy sauce
2 teaspoons cornstarch
1/4 teaspoon crushed red pepper
1 clove garlic, finely chopped
2 tablespoons vegetable oil
3 cups broccoli flowerets
2 small onions, cut into eighths
1 can (8 ounces) whole water chestnuts,
    drained
1/4 cup chicken broth
1/2 cup dry-roasted peanuts
6 cups hot cooked rice (page 204)

1. Trim excess fat from pork. Cut pork into 2 × 1 × 1/8-inch slices. (Pork is easier to cut if partially frozen, about 30 minutes.)

2. Toss pork, soy sauce, cornstarch, red pepper and garlic in glass or plastic bowl. Cover and refrigerate 20 minutes.

3. Heat wok or 12-inch skillet over high heat. Add oil; rotate wok to coat side. Add pork; stir-fry 4 to 5 minutes or until no longer pink. Add broccoli, onions and water chestnuts; stir-fry 2 minutes. Stir in broth; heat to boiling. Stir in peanuts. Serve with rice.

1 SERVING: Calories 650 (Calories from Fat 205); Fat 23g (Saturated 5g); Cholesterol 50mg; Sodium 440mg; Carbohydrate 84g (Dietary Fiber 5g); Protein 32g

SZECHUAN BEEF: Substitute 1 pound beef boneless round or sirloin steak for the pork. Refrigerate 30 minutes in step 1.

TIMESAVING TIP
Use 1 package (16 ounces) frozen broccoli cuts, thawed, instead of the fresh broccoli.

Cheesy Vegetable-Stuffed Pork Chops, Candied Sweet Potatoes (page 410)

Cheesy Vegetable-Stuffed Pork Chops

PREP: 35 min; BAKE: 1 hr
Makes 6 servings

> 6 pork rib chops, 1 1/4 to 1 1/2 inches thick
>   (about 4 pounds)
> 2 tablespoons margarine or butter
> 1 medium stalk celery, chopped (1/2 cup)
> 1 medium onion, chopped (1/2 cup)
> 1 small carrot, shredded (1/2 cup)
> 1 small green bell pepper, chopped (1/2 cup)
> 1 cup shredded sharp Cheddar cheese
>   (4 ounces)
> 1 1/2 teaspoons chopped fresh or
>   1/2 teaspoon dried thyme leaves
> 1/4 teaspoon salt
> 1/8 teaspoon pepper
> 2 tablespoons vegetable oil
> 1/2 teaspoon salt
> 1/4 teaspoon pepper

1. Heat oven to 350°.

2. Make a pocket in each pork chop by cutting into pork toward the bone.

3. Melt margarine in 12-inch skillet over medium heat. Cook celery, onion, carrot and bell pepper in margarine about 5 minutes, stirring occasionally, until vegetables are tender; remove from heat.

4. Stir cheese, thyme, 1/4 teaspoon salt and 1/8 teaspoon pepper into vegetable mixture. Fill pockets in pork with vegetable mixture.

5. Heat oil in same skillet over medium heat. Cook pork in oil about 5 minutes, turning once, until light brown. Sprinkle with 1/2 teaspoon salt and 1/4 teaspoon pepper. Place in ungreased rectangular baking dish, 13 × 9 × 2 inches.

6. Cover tightly and bake 30 minutes. Uncover and bake about 30 minutes longer or until pork is slightly pink in center.

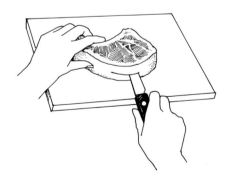

Make a pocket in each chop by cutting into chop toward bone.

1 SERVING: Calories 295 (Calories from Fat 190); Fat 21g (Saturated 8g); Cholesterol 75mg; Sodium 470mg; Carbohydrate 4g (Dietary Fiber 1g); Protein 24g

Pork and Sauerkraut

PREP: 15 min; COOK: 45 min
Makes 6 servings

> 6 whole peppercorns
> 2 whole cloves
> 1 sprig parsley
> 1 bay leaf
> 4 slices bacon, cut into 1-inch pieces
> 1 medium onion, chopped (1/2 cup)
> 1 to 2 tablespoons packed brown sugar
> 1 can (16 ounces) sauerkraut, drained
> 2 medium potatoes, cut into fourths
> 2 medium tart apples, sliced
> 4 smoked pork loin chops, 1/2 inch thick
> 4 hot dogs or smoked sausages, slashed
>   diagonally
> 2 cups chicken broth

1. Tie peppercorns, cloves, parsley and bay leaf in cheesecloth bag or place in tea ball; set aside.

2. Cook bacon and onion in Dutch oven or 12-inch skillet over low heat, stirring occasionally, until bacon is crisp; drain. Stir in brown sugar and sauerkraut. Add potatoes, apples, pork, hot dogs and cheesecloth bag. Pour broth over mixture.

3. Heat to boiling; reduce heat to low. Cover and simmer about 30 minutes or until center of pork is slightly pink and potatoes are tender.

4. Discard cheesecloth bag. Remove sauerkraut, potatoes and apples to large platter with slotted spoon. Arrange pork and hot dogs around edge.

1 SERVING: Calories 290 (Calories from Fat 145); Fat 16g (Saturated 6g); Cholesterol 45mg; Sodium 1770mg; Carbohydrate 22g (Dietary Fiber 4g); Protein 18g

Crunchy Pecan Pork Chops

PREP: 15 min; BROIL: 25 min
Makes 6 servings

> 6 pork rib, loin or shoulder chops, about
>   3/4 inch thick (about 2 pounds)
> 2 tablespoons Dijon mustard
> 2 tablespoons mayonnaise or salad dressing
> 1 tablespoon vegetable oil
> 1/2 cup chopped pecans
> 1/2 teaspoon salt
> 1 slice bread, torn into pieces
> 4 sprigs fresh parsley or 1 tablespoon dried
>   parsley flakes

1. Cut outer edge of fat on pork diagonally at 1-inch intervals to prevent curling (do not cut into meat).

2. Mix mustard, mayonnaise and oil. Place remaining ingredients in blender or food processor. Cover and blend on high speed, using quick on-and-off motions, until pecans are finely chopped.

3. Set oven control to Broil.

4. Spread mustard mixture over pork. Coat evenly with pecan mixture.

5. Place pork on rack in broiler pan. (For easy cleanup, line broiler pan with aluminum foil before placing pork on rack.) Broil pork with tops about 6 inches from heat about 10 minutes or until brown. Turn; broil 10 to 15 minutes longer or until pork is slightly pink in center.

1 SERVING: Calories 280 (Calories from Fat 180); Fat 20g (Saturated 4g); Cholesterol 60mg; Sodium 320mg; Carbohydrate 4g (Dietary Fiber 0g); Protein 21g

CRUNCHY PECAN LAMB CHOPS: Substitute 6 lamb sirloin or shoulder chops for the pork chops. Continue as directed—except broil 8 to 10 minutes after turning for medium or until lamb is desired doneness.

Roasting Ham

Roasting is an easy cooking method, and it's a low-fat way to cook because the fat drips away from the meat while cooking. Also see Glazed Baked Ham, page 260.

1. Select ham from those listed in Timetable for Roasting Ham.

2. Place ham, fat side up, on rack in shallow roasting pan. (For easy cleanup, line the roasting pan with aluminum foil before placing ham on rack.) The rack keeps the meat out of the drippings. (For boneless or canned ham, pour liquid as directed below into pan before placing rack on top.) As the fat melts, it bastes the ham, making other basting unnecessary.

3. Insert meat thermometer into ham surface at a slight angle or through the end of the ham so tip is in center of thickest part of ham and does not touch bone or fat.

4. Preheat the oven only for hams weighing less than 2 pounds. Roast as directed in chart until meat thermometer reads 135°. Ham will continue to cook after being removed from oven. If covering ham with aluminum foil, leave meat thermometer dial exposed.

5. Cover ham with tent of aluminum foil and let stand about 10 minutes or until temperature rises to 140° before carving. The ham will be easier to carve as juices set up.

Timetable for Roasting Ham
(oven temperature 325°)

Fully Cooked Smoked Ham	Approximate Weight (pounds)	Approximate Roasting Time (minutes per pound)
Boneless Ham	1 1/2 to 2	29 to 33
Cook in covered pan with 1/2 cup water.	3 to 4	19 to 23
	6 to 8	16 to 20
	9 to 11	12 to 16
Bone-in Ham	6 to 8	13 to 17
Cook in covered pan with no water.	14 to 16	11 to 14
Canned Ham	1 1/2 to 2	23 to 25
Cook uncovered with can juices.	3	21 to 23
	5	17 to 20

How to Carve a Whole Ham

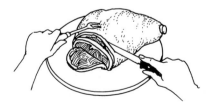

a. Place ham, fat side up and shank to your right, on carving board or platter. (Face shank to your left if you are left-handed.) Cut a few slices from thin side. Turn ham, cut side down, so it rests firmly.

b. Make vertical slices down to the leg bone, then cut horizontally along bone to release slices.

Broiling, Panbroiling and Panfrying Ham

To Broil

1. Select ham cut from those listed in Timetable for Broiling, Panbroiling and Panfrying Ham.

2. Set oven control to Broil.

3. Place ham on rack in broiler pan 4 to 5 inches from heat. (For easy cleanup, line the broiler pan with aluminum foil before placing ham on rack.) Place with top 4 to 5 inches from heat.

4. Broil for time shown in chart, turning once.

To Panbroil

1. Select ham cut from those listed in Timetable for Broiling, Panbroiling and Panfrying Ham.

2. Heat heavy skillet over medium heat.

3. Place ham in hot skillet. Do not add oil or water. Do not cover.

4. Cook for time shown in chart for ham cut chosen, turning ham occasionally, until hot. Remove fat from skillet as it accumulates.

To Panfry

1. Select ham cut from those listed in Timetable for Broiling, Panbroiling and Panfrying Ham.

2. Heat a small amount of oil in heavy skillet over medium heat.

3. Cook ham in oil, turning occasionally, until hot. Do not cover.

Timetable for Broiling, Panbroiling and Panfrying Ham

Fully Cooked Smoked Cut	Approximate Thickness	Total Broiling Time (minutes)	Approximate Total Panbroiling or Panfrying Time (minutes)
Ham Cubes for Kabobs	1-inch pieces	7 to 8	*
Ham Slice	1/4 inch	6 to 7	3 to 4
	1/2 inch	8 to 10	5 to 6

Panbroiling or Panfrying is not recommended for kabobs.

Ham and Apple Skillet

PREP: 15 min; COOK: 15 min
Makes 4 servings, about 1 cup each

The best varieties of apples to use in this zesty ham dish are Jonathan and Rome Beauty. Their deep red color adds flair to the creamy dish.

2 tablespoons margarine or butter
2 medium carrots, thinly sliced (1 cup)
1 large apple, coarsely chopped (1 1/2 cups)
1 small onion, cut into thin wedges
1 cup milk
1 cup apple juice
3 tablespoons all-purpose flour
2 teaspoons ground mustard (dry)
1/4 teaspoon pepper
2 cups cubed fully cooked smoked ham
3 cups hot cooked brown rice (page 204)

1. Melt margarine in 10 inch skillet over medium heat. Cook carrots in margarine 2 minutes, stirring occasionally.

2. Stir in apple and onion. Cook about 5 minutes, stirring occasionally, until apples are slightly soft. Remove, apply mixture from skillet; keep warm.

3. Mix milk, apple juice, flour, mustard and pepper (mixture will look curdled); stir into skillet. Heat to boiling, stirring constantly. Boil and stir about 1 minute or until thickened.

4. Stir apple mixture and ham into sauce. Cook and stir about 1 minute or until heated through. Serve over rice.

1 SERVING: Calories 455 (Calories from Fat 135); Fat 15g (Saturated 5g); Cholesterol 45mg; Sodium 1180mg; Carbohydrate 62g (Dietary Fiber 5g); Protein 23g

Glazed Baked Ham

PREP: 10 min; BAKE: 1 1/2 hr; STAND: 20 min
Makes 12 servings

> Fully cooked smoked ham (page 258)
> Brown Sugar Glaze or Pineapple Glaze
> (below)

1. Select ham from those listed in Timetable for Roasting Ham, page 258, and roast as directed.

2. Remove ham 20 minutes before it is done. Pour drippings from pan. Remove any skin from ham. Cut fat surface of ham lightly in uniform diamond shapes. Insert whole clove in each diamond if desired. Pat or brush on Brown Sugar Glaze or Pineapple Glaze (enough for 4-pound ham).

3. Bake ham about 20 minutes longer or until thermometer reads 135°. (Also see Determining Meat Doneness, page 222.)

4. Cover ham with tent of aluminum foil and let stand 15 to 20 minutes or until thermometer reads 140°. (Temperature will continue to rise about 5°, and ham will be easier to carve as juices set up.)

Brown Sugar Glaze

> 1 cup packed brown sugar
> 1 tablespoon white vinegar
> 1/2 teaspoon ground mustard (dry)

Mix all ingredients.

Pineapple Glaze

> 1 cup packed brown sugar
> 1 tablespoon cornstarch
> 1/4 teaspoon salt
> 1 can (8 1/4 ounces) crushed pineapple in
> syrup, undrained
> 2 tablespoons lemon juice
> 1 tablespoon mustard

Mix brown sugar, cornstarch and salt in 1-quart saucepan. Stir in pineapple, lemon juice and mustard. Cook over medium heat, stirring constantly, until mixture thickens and boils. Boil and stir 1 minute.

1 SERVING: Calories 225 (Calories from Fat 55); Fat 6g (Saturated 2g); Cholesterol 60mg; Sodium 1320mg; Carbohydrate 20g (Dietary Fiber 0g); Protein 23g (**Note:** *Nutrition run calculated on a 6-pound bone-in ham*)

UNGLAZED BAKED HAM: Omit step 2 and Brown Sugar Glaze.

Ham and Scalloped Potatoes

PREP: 20 min; BAKE: 1 hr 40 min
Makes 6 servings

> Scalloped Potatoes (page 409)
> 1 1/2 cups cubed fully cooked smoked ham

1. Heat oven to 350°.

2. Prepare Scalloped Potatoes as directed—except stir ham into sauce before pouring over potatoes.

1 SERVING: Calories 280 (Calories from Fat 115); Fat 13g (Saturated 4g); Cholesterol 30mg; Sodium 1030mg; Carbohydrate 29g (Dietary Fiber 2g); Protein 14g

> ### LIGHTER HAM AND SCALLOPED POTATOES
>
> For 10 grams of fat and 255 calories per serving, use skim milk in Scalloped Potatoes and reduced-fat ham.

Ham Loaf

PREP: 15 min; BAKE: 1 1/2 hr
Makes 8 servings

Either Horseradish Sauce (page 346) or Mustard Sauce (page 347) makes a great accompaniment to this recipe.

> 1 1/2 pounds ground ham
> 1 small onion, finely chopped (1/4 cup)
> 1/2 cup dry bread crumbs
> 1/4 cup finely chopped green bell pepper
> 1/2 cup milk
> 1/2 teaspoon ground mustard (dry)
> 1/4 teaspoon pepper
> 2 large eggs

1. Heat oven to 350°.

2. Mix all ingredients. Spread mixture in ungreased loaf pan, 9 × 5 × 3 or 8 1/2 × 4 1/2 × 2 1/2 inches.

3. Insert meat thermometer so tip is in center of loaf. Bake uncovered about 1 1/2 hours or until thermometer reads 170°.

4. Let stand 5 minutes; remove from pan.

1 SERVING: Calories 360 (Calories from Fat 270); Fat 30g (Saturated 11g); Cholesterol 105mg; Sodium 770mg; Carbohydrate 7g (Dietary Fiber 0g); Protein 16g

> ### LIGHTER HAM LOAF
>
> For 5 grams of fat and 150 calories per serving, use reduced-fat ham and substitute 1/2 cup fat-free cholesterol-free egg product for the eggs.

Bacon, Canadian-Style Bacon, Hot Dogs and Sausages Cooking Chart

Meat Type	To Bake	To Broil (on rack in broiler pan)	To Panfry
Bacon (thinly sliced)	*Heat oven to 400°.* Place separated slices on rack in broiler pan. Bake about 10 minutes (do not turn) or until brown.	*Set oven control to Broil.* Broil separated slices with tops about 3 inches from heat about 2 minutes or until brown. Turn; broil 1 minute longer.	Place separated slices in cold skillet. Cook over low heat 8 to 10 minutes, turning occasionally, until evenly brown.
Canadian-Style Bacon (fully cooked)	*Heat oven to 325°.* Place 2-pound piece of Canadian-style bacon, fat side up, on rack in shallow baking pan. Insert meat thermometer into bacon surface through the end of the bacon so tip is in center of thickest part of bacon and does not touch fat. Bake uncovered 20 to 30 minutes or until thermometer reads 140°.	*Set oven control to Broil.* Broil 1/4-inch slices with tops 2 to 3 inches from heat about 6 minutes, turning once, until heated through.	Place 1/8-inch slices in cold skillet. Cook over low heat 8 to 10 minutes, turning occasionally, until heated through.
Hot Dogs or Cooked Smoked Sausages*†		*Set oven control to Broil.* Broil with tops about 3 inches from heat, turning with tongs, until evenly brown.	Place in cold nonstick skillet. Cook over low heat, turning with tongs, until evenly brown.
Sausage links or patties (uncooked smoked or fresh)**	*Heat oven to 400°.* Arrange in single layer in shallow baking pan. Bake uncovered 20 to 30 minutes, turning sausages to brown evenly, until well done. Spoon off drippings as they accumulate.	*Set oven control to Broil.* Broil with tops 3 to 5 inches from heat, turning with tongs, until well done.	Place in cold skillet with 2 to 4 tablespoons water. Cover tightly and cook over low heat 5 minutes. Uncover and cook, turning occasionally, until evenly brown and no longer pink in the center.

*Hot dogs or cooked smoked sausages need only be heated to serving temperature (140°). Do not pierce with fork.

**Fresh sausage should be cooked until the center is no longer pink but turns gray (180° on meat thermometer).

†For microwave cooking directions, see page 224.

Spicy Mexican Torte

PREP: 30 min; BAKE: 55 min; COOL: 10 min
Makes 8 servings

Chorizo, a coarsely ground pork sausage highly seasoned with garlic, chili powder and other spices, is widely used in Mexican and Spanish cooking.

> 1/2 pound chorizo or spicy Italian sausage links
> 2 medium onions, chopped (1 cup)
> 2 cloves garlic, finely chopped
> 1 can (4 ounces) chopped green chilies, drained
> 8 flour tortillas (10 inches in diameter)*
> 2 cups shredded Monterey Jack cheese (8 ounces)
> 1 can (16 ounces) refried beans
> 1 jar (7 ounces) roasted red bell peppers, drained
> Salsa, sour cream or guacamole, if desired

1. Remove casings from sausage links. Cut sausages into 1/4-inch slices. Cook sausage, onions and garlic in 10-inch skillet over medium heat, stirring occasionally, until sausage is brown; drain. Stir in chilies; set aside.

2. Heat oven to 400°. Grease pie plate, 10 × 1 1/2 inches, with shortening.

3. Place 2 tortillas in pie plate. Spread with half of the sausage mixture; sprinkle with half of the cheese. Place 2 tortillas on cheese; spread with beans. Place 2 tortillas on beans; place peppers on tortillas. Place 2 tortillas on peppers; spread with remaining sausage mixture. Sprinkle with remaining cheese.

4. Cover and bake 40 minutes. Uncover and bake about 15 minutes longer or until cheese is melted and center is hot. Cool 10 minutes before cutting. Serve with salsa.

*16 corn tortillas (6 inches in diameter) can be substituted for the flour tortillas. Overlap 4 tortillas for each layer.

1 SERVING: Calories 425 (Calories from Fat 205); Fat 23g (Saturated 10g); Cholesterol 50mg; Sodium 1120mg; Carbohydrate 39g (Dietary Fiber 5g); Protein 21g

---

LIGHTER SPICY MEXICAN TORTE

For 15 grams of fat and 350 calories per serving, use turkey Italian sausage instead of the chorizo sausage. Use fat-free refried beans.

Italian Sausage on Polenta

PREP: 55 min; COOK: 15 min
Makes 6 servings

For a different look, try using link Italian sausage. Remove the casings by making a lengthwise cut just through the casing of each sausage with a sharp knife. Peel casing off and discard. Cut each link diagonally into 1/2-inch slices.

> 2 cups Italian Tomato Sauce (page 343)
> Polenta or Fried Polenta (page 210)
> 1 pound bulk Italian sausage
> 1 medium green bell pepper, thinly sliced
> 1 medium red bell pepper, thinly sliced
> 1 small onion, thinly sliced
> 1/3 cup grated Parmesan cheese

1. Prepare Polenta; cover and keep warm.

2. Prepare Italian Tomato Sauce.

3. Heat wok or 10-inch skillet over high heat. Add sausage; stir-fry 2 minutes. Add bell peppers and onion; stir-fry about 3 minutes or until sausage is no longer pink and vegetables are crisp-tender; drain.

4. Stir sauce into sausage mixture. Heat over medium heat about 5 minutes, stirring frequently, until hot.

5. Top polenta with sausage mixture. Sprinkle with cheese.

1 SERVING: Calories 450 (Calories from Fat 225); Fat 25g (Saturated 8g); Cholesterol 60mg; Sodium 1680mg; Carbohydrate 38g (Dietary Fiber 3g); Protein 21g

---

TIMESAVING TIP
Use purchased spaghetti sauce instead of Italian Tomato Sauce.

Italian Sausage on Polenta

About Lamb

Selecting Lamb

Lamb is a lean, tender and usually delicately flavored meat. Lamb comes from animals less than one year old. Most lamb, however, is marketed when it is about six to eight months old, so it will be tender and flavorful. Look for lamb that is pinkish red and has a velvety texture. Dark red meat usually indicates the meat is older. Lamb has little marbling and only a thin layer of fat around the outside of the meat. The thin, paperlike covering on the outer fat is called *fell*. Keep the fell on roasts and legs because it helps these cuts keep their shape and juiciness during cooking. Trim the fell from steaks and chops for best appearance and even cooking. For best flavor and juiciness, it is recommended that lamb be cooked to medium-rare (145°) or medium (160°). Also see Determining Meat Doneness, page 222.

How to Carve a Leg of Lamb

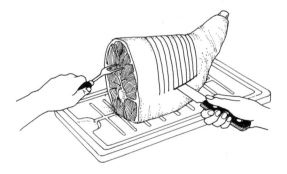

Place leg, shank bone to your right, on carving board or platter. (Place shank bone to your left if you are left-handed.) Cut a few length-wise slices from thin side. Turn leg, cut side down, so it rests firmly. Make vertical slices to the leg bone, then cut horizontally along bone to release slices.

LAMB

• RETAIL CUTS •
WHERE THEY COME FROM
HOW TO COOK THEM

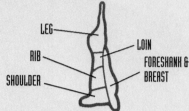

LEG
RIB
SHOULDER
LOIN
FORESHANK & BREAST

LEG

Whole Leg
Roast

Short Cut Leg, Sirloin Off
Roast

Shank Portion Roast
Roast

Center Leg Roast
Roast

Center Slice
Broil, Panbroil, Panfry

American-Style Roast
Roast

Frenched-Style Roast
Roast

Boneless Leg Roast
Roast, Broil if butterflied

Hind Shank
Braise, Cook in Liquid

Sirloin Chop
Broil, Panbroil, Panfry, Braise

Boneless Sirloin Roast
Roast

LOIN

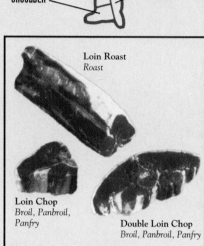

Loin Roast
Roast

Loin Chop
Broil, Panbroil, Panfry

Double Loin Chop
Broil, Panbroil, Panfry

FORESHANK & BREAST

Shank
Braise, Cook in Liquid

Spareribs
Braise, Broil, Roast

Boneless Rolled Breast
Roast, Braise

Riblets
Braise, Cook in Liquid, Broil

RIB

Rib Roast
Roast

Rib Chop
Broil, Panbroil, Panfry, Roast

Frenched Rib Chop
Broil, Panbroil, Panfry

Crown Roast
Roast

SHOULDER

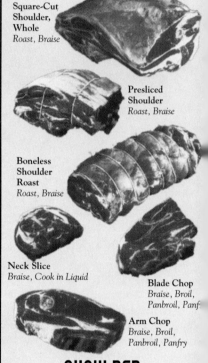

Square-Cut Shoulder, Whole
Roast, Braise

Presliced Shoulder
Roast, Braise

Boneless Shoulder Roast
Roast, Braise

Neck Slice
Braise, Cook in Liquid

Blade Chop
Braise, Broil, Panbroil, Panf

Arm Chop
Braise, Broil, Panbroil, Panfry

OTHER CUTS

Lamb for Stew
Braise, Cook in Liquid

Cubes for Kabobs
Broil, Braise

Ground Lamb
Broil, Panbroil, Roast (Bake)

Roasting Lamb

Roasting is an easy cooking method, and it's a low-fat way to cook because the fat drips away from the meat while cooking.

1. Select lamb roast from those listed in Timetable for Roasting Lamb.

2. Place lamb, fat side up, on rack in shallow roasting pan. (For easy cleanup, line the roasting pan with aluminum foil before placing lamb on rack.) The rack keeps the meat out the drippings. Do not remove the fell (thin, paperlike covering on the outer fat) from roasts and legs; it helps these cuts keep their shape and juiciness during cooking. As the fat melts, it bastes the lamb, making other basting unnecessary.

3. Season lamb with herbs, spices, salt or other seasonings before, during or after cooking, if desired. (Salt roasts *before* cooking to enhance flavor.)

4. Insert meat thermometer into roast surface at a slight angle or through the end of the roast so tip is in center of thickest part of roast and does not touch bone or fat.

5. Do not add water. Do not cover.

6. Roast at 325°. (It is not necessary to preheat oven.)

7. Roast to temperature listed in chart in column titled "Meat Thermometer Reading (after roasting)" for lamb cut chosen and desired degree of doneness. Roast will continue to cook after being removed from oven.

8. Cover roast loosely with tent of aluminum foil and let stand 15 to 20 minutes or until temperature rises to that listed in chart in column titled "Meat Thermometer Reading (after standing)." Roast will be easier to carve as juices set up. (Avoid covering roast tightly as it creates steam and softens the surface of the lamb.)

Timetable for Roasting Lamb
(oven temperature 325°)

Lamb Cut	Approximate Weight (pounds)	Meat Thermometer Reading (*after roasting*)	Meat Thermometer Reading (*after standing*)	Approximate Cooking Time (minutes per pound)
Leg Roast	12	140°	145° (medium-rare)	15 to 20
Whole (bone in)		155°	160° (medium)	20 to 25
	5 to 7	140°	145° (medium-rare)	20 to 25
		155°	160° (medium)	25 to 30
Whole (boneless)	4 to 7	140°	145° (medium-rare)	25 to 30
		155°	160° (medium)	30 to 35
Shank half	3 to 4	140°	145° (medium-rare)	30 to 35
		155°	160° (medium)	40 to 45
Sirloin half	3 to 4	140°	145° (medium-rare)	25 to 30
		155°	160° (medium)	35 to 40
Shoulder Roast	3 1/2 to 5	140°	145° (medium-rare)	30 to 35
boneless		155°	160° (medium)	35 to 40
bone in	3 1/2 to 5	140°	145° (medium-rare)	35 to 40
pre-sliced		155°	160° (medium)	40 to 45

Broiling or Grilling Lamb

Broiling and grilling are quick, low-fat methods for cooking cuts, such as chops, and ground lamb patties. For less tender cuts, marinate lamb before cooking. (See Tips for Marinades and Marinating, page 356). Other lamb cuts can be cooked over indirect heat. Refer to the instructions that came with your grill or see Grilling Know-How, page 428, for more information.

1. Select lamb cut from those listed in Timetable for Broiling or Grilling Lamb.

2. Marinate lamb if desired. (See Tips for Marinades and Marinating, page 356.)

3. *To Broil*: Set oven to Broil.

To Grill: Heat coals or gas grill (direct heat) to medium heat.

4. Slash outer edge of fat on lamb diagonally at 1-inch intervals to prevent curling (do not cut into meat).

5. *To Broil*: Place lamb on rack in broiler pan. (For easy cleanup, line the broiler pan with aluminum foil before placing lamb on rack.) Place in oven with top of lamb the inches from heat listed in chart for lamb cut chosen.

To Grill: Place lamb on grill the inches from heat listed in chart for lamb cut chosen.

6. Broil or grill about half the time shown in chart for lamb cut or until lamb is brown on one side.

7. Turn lamb and continue cooking until desired doneness. (To check doneness, cut a small slit in the center of boneless cuts or in the center near the bone of bone-in cuts. Medium-rare is pink in center. Medium is light pink in center.) Season each side after cooking if desired.

Timetable for Broiling or Grilling Lamb

Lamb Cut	Approximate Thickness or Weight	Inches from Heat	Approximate *Total* Broiling Time (minutes)		Approximate *Total* Grilling Time (minutes)	
			145° (medium-rare)	160° (medium)	145° (medium-rare)	160° (medium)
Shoulder Chop*	3/4 to 1 inch	3 to 4	5 to 9	7 to 11	9 to 12	12 to 14
Loin or Rib Chop	1 inch	3 to 4	5 to 9	7 to 11	7 to 9	9 to 11
	1 1/2 inches	4 to 5	12 to 17	15 to 19	14 to 17	17 to 20
Sirloin Chop	3/4 to 1 inch	3 to 4	10 to 13	12 to 15	15 to 17	17 to 21
Butterflied Leg (sirloin removed, boneless)	4 pounds	5 to 7	40 to 46	47 to 53	33 to 53	40 to 60
Leg Steak	3/4 to 1 inch	3 to 4	11 to 15	14 to 18	15 to 18	17 to 21
Cubes for Kabobs	1- to 1 1/2-inch	4 to 5	6 to 10	8 to 12	7 to 9	9 to 20
Ground Lamb Patties	1/2 inch	3	3 to 6	5 to 8	3 to 5	5 to 7

Marinate at least 6 hours but no longer than 24 hours to tenderize.

Leg of Lamb with Roast Potatoes

**PREP: 20 min; MARINATE: 8 hr; ROAST: 1 3/4 hr;
STAND: 20 min**
Makes 8 servings

*Brushing the lamb and the potatoes with the marinade adds
flavor without additional ingredients.*

> 5- to 7-pound leg of lamb
> 2 cups dry red wine (or nonalcoholic) or beef
>   broth
> 1/4 cup vegetable oil
> 2 tablespoons chopped fresh or 2 teaspoons
>   dried rosemary leaves, crushed
> 1 teaspoon salt
> 1/4 teaspoon pepper
> 2 cloves garlic, crushed
> 16 new red potatoes (about 2 1/4 pounds)

1. Place lamb in large plastic bag or shallow glass
baking dish. Mix remaining ingredients except potatoes; pour over lamb. Fasten bag securely or cover dish
with plastic wrap. Refrigerate at least 8 hours but no
longer than 24 hours, turning lamb occasionally.

2. Heat oven to 425°.

3. Drain lamb; reserve marinade. Place lamb, fat
side up, in shallow roasting pan. Insert meat thermometer so tip is in thickest part of lamb and does not
touch bone or rest in fat. Do not add water. Do not
cover.

4. Prepare potatoes as directed on page 400. Place
potatoes around lamb. Roast lamb and potatoes 45
minutes, brushing lamb occasionally with marinade.

5. Reduce oven temperature to 375°. Stir potatoes
so they don't stick to pan. Roast about 1 hour longer,
brushing lamb and potatoes occasionally with marinade, until thermometer reads 140°. (Also see Determining Meat Doneness, page 222.) Discard any
remaining marinade.

6. Cover roast with tent of aluminum foil and let
stand 15 to 20 minutes or until thermometer reads
145°. (Temperature will continue to rise about 5°, and
roast will be easier to carve as juices set up.)

1 SERVING: Calories 440 (Calories from Fat 180); Fat 20g
(Saturated 6g); Cholesterol 125mg; Sodium 170mg;
Carbohydrate 26g (Dietary Fiber 2g); Protein 41g

Italian Lamb Shanks

PREP: 20 min; MARINATE: 5 hr; COOK: 2 3/4 hr
Makes 4 servings

*If you're in a hurry, use one cup purchased Italian dressing
instead of making your own. Choose a zesty variety if you
like lamb shanks that are highly seasoned.*

> 4 lamb shanks (each about 12 ounces)
> 1 cup Italian Dressing (page 337)
> 1/2 cup grated Parmesan cheese
> 1/4 cup all-purpose flour
> 2 tablespoons chopped fresh or 1 tablespoon
>   dried parsley flakes
> 1/4 teaspoon salt
> 1/4 teaspoon onion powder
> 3 tablespoons vegetable oil
> Grated Parmesan cheese

1. Place lamb in shallow glass baking dish or plastic
dish. Pour Italian Dressing over lamb. Cover and
refrigerate at least 5 hours but no longer than 24 hours,
turning lamb occasionally.

2. Remove lamb from marinade; reserve marinade.
Mix 1/2 cup cheese, the flour, parsley, salt and onion
powder. Coat lamb with cheese mixture, reserving
remaining cheese mixture.

3. Heat oil in 12-inch skillet or Dutch oven over
medium-high heat. Cook lamb in oil, turning occasionally, until brown; reduce heat to low. Sprinkle
remaining cheese mixture over lamb. Stir in marinade.

4. Heat to boiling; reduce heat to low. Cover and
simmer about 2 1/2 hours, turning lamb occasionally,
until tender. Serve with cheese.

1 SERVING: Calories 880 (Calories from Fat 595); Fat 66g
(Saturated 17g); Cholesterol 190mg; Sodium 990mg;
Carbohydrate 13g (Dietary Fiber 0g); Protein 59g

LIGHTER ITALIAN LAMB SHANKS

For 38 grams of fat and 610 calories per serving, use fat-
free Italian dressing and reduced-fat Parmesan cheese
blend. Decrease oil to 2 tablespoons and use nonstick
skillet or Dutch oven.

ITALIAN CHICKEN: Substitute 3- to 3 1/2-pound
cut-up broiler-fryer chicken for the lamb and
decrease simmer time in step 4 to 1 hour.

Shish Kabob, Savory Pilaf (page 207)

Shish Kabobs

PREP: 25 min; MARINATE: 6 hr; BROIL: 15 min
Makes 4 servings

1 pound lamb boneless shoulder
1/4 cup lemon juice
2 tablespoons olive or vegetable oil
2 teaspoons chopped fresh or 1/2 teaspoon
    dried oregano leaves
1 1/2 teaspoons salt
1/4 teaspoon pepper
1 medium green bell pepper, cut into 1-inch
    pieces
1 medium onion, cut into eighths
1 cup cubed eggplant

1. Trim excess fat from lamb. Cut lamb into 1-inch cubes. Mix lemon juice, oil, oregano, salt and pepper in medium glass or plastic bowl. Stir in lamb until coated. Cover and refrigerate at least 6 hours but no longer than 24 hours, stirring occasionally.

2. Set oven control to Broil.

3. Remove lamb from marinade; reserve marinade. Thread lamb on each of four 11-inch metal skewers, leaving space between each piece. Place on rack in broiler pan. (For easy cleanup, line broiler pan with aluminum foil before placing kabobs on rack.) Broil with tops about 3 inches from heat 5 minutes. Turn; brush with marinade. Broil 5 minutes longer.

4. Thread bell pepper, onion and eggplant alternately on each of four 11-inch metal skewers, leaving space between each piece. Place vegetables on rack in broiler pan with lamb. Turn lamb. Brush lamb and vegetables with marinade.

5. Broil kabobs 4 to 5 minutes, turning and brushing twice with marinade, until lamb is light pink in center. Discard any remaining marinade.

1 SERVING: Calories 260 (Calories from Fat 135); Fat 15g (Saturated 4g); Cholesterol 80mg; Sodium 870mg; Carbohydrate 6g (Dietary Fiber 1g); Protein 26g

---

TIMESAVING TIP
Omit lemon juice, oil, salt, oregano and pepper. Marinate lamb in 1/3 cup purchased Italian dressing in step 1.

About Game

Most of the game found in butcher shops, supermarkets and restaurants has been raised commercially on farms. The flavor of this meat is typically more robust than that of beef, veal, pork or lamb. Wild game is leaner, stronger tasting and sometimes tougher than other meats. Marinating these meats will tenderize them and mask some of the unique, gamy flavor without overpowering the flavor of the meat.

Rabbit

Some supermarkets and butcher shops carry rabbit in the freezer case. For other supermarkets and butcher shops, however, you may have to call a few days in advance of when you'll need the rabbit, so it can be ordered for you. Rabbit usually is sold cut up in ready-to-cook parts. If it is frozen, defrost it in the refrigerator, and use within two days.

The lean, mild-flavored meat will darken when marinated and cooked. Typically, rabbit will be 2 1/2 to 3 pounds. It is most flavorful and tender if cooked with moist-heat methods. Smaller rabbits (under 2 pounds) are more tender and therefore can be broiled or roasted. Because the meat is lean, it will dry out quickly when cooked with either of these methods, so be careful not to overcook.

Venison

Venison is a term used for deer, elk or caribou meat. Commercially raised venison, either fresh or frozen and in cuts similar to beef or pork, can be found at butcher shops that carry game. Venison is a very lean meat with a rich, full flavor. It will toughen if overcooked. Steaks and chops can be broiled or grilled. Larger cuts should be braised to bring out their flavor and make them tender. Serve roasts immediately after cooking (do not let stand 15 to 20 minutes like other meat roasts because the small amount of fat in venison congeals quickly and is unpleasant to eat). To tenderize fresh venison, marinate it in the refrigerator overnight. Freezing also helps tenderize venison because it breaks down muscle fibers.

Braised Rabbit Stew

PREP: 20 min; BAKE: 2 1/2 hr
Makes 6 servings, about 1 1/2 cups each

Dunk pieces of a hearty bread, such as oatmeal or nine-grain, into this flavorful stew—you won't want to miss a drop of the rich broth!

> 2 1/2- to 3-pound domestic rabbit, cut up
> 1 teaspoon salt
> 1 teaspoon chopped fresh or 1/2 teaspoon dried rosemary leaves, crushed
> 1/4 teaspoon pepper
> 1/4 cup uncooked quick-cooking tapioca
> 1 bay leaf
> 6 medium carrots, cut into 1-inch pieces
> 1 jar (16 ounces) small whole onions, drained
> 3 cups water
> 3/4 cup dry red wine (or nonalcoholic) or beef broth
> 1/2 teaspoon browning sauce

1. Heat oven to 325°. Melt margarine in Dutch oven in oven.

2. Place rabbit in Dutch oven. Sprinkle with salt, rosemary, pepper and tapioca. Add bay leaf, carrots and onions. Mix water, wine and browning sauce; pour over rabbit and vegetables.

3. Cover and bake about 2 1/2 hours or until rabbit is tender. Remove rabbit meat from bones if desired; stir rabbit meat into broth. Remove bay leaf.

1 SERVING: Calories 320 (Calories from Fat 100); Fat 11g (Saturated 3g); Cholesterol 105mg; Sodium 450mg; Carbohydrate 19g (Dietary Fiber 3g); Protein 39g

Venison Sauerbraten

PREP: 20 min; MARINATE: 24 hr; COOK: 4 hr
Makes 10 to 12 servings

Juniper berries, a classic addition to sauerbraten recipes, have the flavor of pine. If you can't find juniper berries in your supermarket, you can add a dash of gin, if you wish.

3- to 3 1/2-pound venison chuck roast
2 medium onions, sliced
2 bay leaves
12 peppercorns
12 juniper berries, if desired
6 whole cloves
2 teaspoons salt
1 1/2 cups red wine vinegar
1 cup boiling water
2 tablespoons vegetable oil or shortening
12 gingersnap cookies, crushed (3/4 cup)
2 teaspoons sugar
Dumplings (page 51) or hot cooked noodles,
    if desired

1. Place venison in plastic bag or shallow glass baking dish or plastic dish. Add onions, bay leaves, peppercorns, juniper berries, cloves, salt, vinegar and boiling water. Cover and refrigerate at least 24 hours but no longer than 36 hours, turning venison twice a day with tongs.

2. Drain venison; reserve marinade. Heat oil in 10-inch skillet over medium-high heat. Cook venison in oil until brown on all sides. Stir in marinade. Heat to boiling; reduce heat to low. Cover and simmer 3 to 3 1/2 hours or until venison is tender. Remove venison and onions from skillet; keep warm.

3. Strain liquid in skillet. Add enough water to liquid to measure 2 1/2 cups. Return liquid to skillet. Heat to boiling; reduce heat to low. Cover and simmer 10 minutes.

4. Stir crushed cookies and sugar into liquid. Cover and simmer 3 minutes. Serve venison and onions with gingersnap mixture and Dumplings.

1 SERVING: Calories 325 (Calories from Fat 100); Fat 11g (Saturated 3g); Cholesterol 115mg; Sodium 420mg; Carbohydrate 25g (Dietary Fiber 1g); Protein 33g

Liver and Onions

PREP: 10 min; COOK: 15 min
Makes 4 servings

Serve this time-honored recipe with Rosemary-Roasted Red Potatoes, page 410, and Broccoli, page 395.

3 tablespoons margarine or butter
2 medium onions, thinly sliced
3 tablespoons vegetable oil or shortening
1 pound beef, veal or pork liver, 1/2 to
    3/4 inch thick
All-purpose flour
Salt and pepper to taste

1. Melt margarine in 10-inch skillet over medium-high heat. Cook onions in margarine 4 to 6 minutes, stirring frequently, until light brown. Remove onions from skillet; keep warm.

2. Coat liver with flour. Heat oil in same skillet over medium heat. Cook liver in oil 2 to 3 minutes on each side or until brown, returning onions to skillet during last minute of cooking. Sprinkle with salt and pepper.

1 SERVING: Calories 345 (Calories from Fat 205); Fat 23g (Saturated 5g); Cholesterol 325mg; Sodium 690mg; Carbohydrate 14g (Dietary Fiber 1g); Protein 22g

---

LIGHTER LIVER AND ONIONS

For 8 grams of fat and 216 calories per serving, omit margarine and decrease oil to 1 tablespoon. Use nonstick skillet. Spray cold skillet with nonstick cooking spray before cooking onions in step 1.

About Pasta

Pasta is more popular than ever! Versatile pasta includes macaroni, spaghetti and noodles in hundreds of shapes and sizes. From dried to fresh, short to long, curly to ridged and flat to tubular, the tremendous variety available makes for delicious exploration.

Most pasta available for purchase is dried and is made from semolina flour, a flour high in gluten-forming protein, ground from durum wheat. Pasta is made by kneading the dough, then forcing it through dies to create the many different forms and shapes available. Automatic dryers then remove the moisture under controlled conditions.

Macaroni is usually shaped like a hollow tube and may range from large to small, be straight or curved, shaped like shells, corkscrews, or in very tiny pieces for soups.

Spaghetti is long or short rods of pasta.

Noodles are flat, ribbonlike strips cut in narrow, medium and broad widths. American noodles usually contain egg; some Oriental noodles are made with rice flour and without egg.

Many pasta shapes are available in other flavors such as spinach, tomato and whole wheat. Gourmet shops carry specialty flavors such as beet, lemon, herb, chocolate, fruit flavors and squid ink.

Selecting Pasta

Pasta is available in three forms: dried, fresh and frozen. Dried pasta is usually found packaged or in serve-yourself bulk bins. Fresh pasta can be found in the refrigerated section of the supermarket. The most common varieties of frozen pasta are lasagna noodles, egg noodles and filled tortellini and ravioli. Pasta shapes can be substituted for one another, as long as they are similar in size.

- **Dried pasta:** Look for unbroken pieces. Avoid dried pasta with a marblelike surface (many fine lines); this indicates a drying problem, and the pasta may fall apart during cooking.
- **Fresh pasta:** Look for smooth, unbroken pieces with consistent color throughout the shape. Fresh pasta will appear dry but shouldn't be brittle or crumbly. Avoid packages with moisture or liquid, which could indicate molding or mushy pasta.
- **Frozen pasta:** Avoid packages with the pieces frozen together in a solid mass and those containing ice crystals or freezer burn (dry, white spots).

Storing Pasta

Dried

Store in original packaging, or transfer to airtight glass or plastic containers and label contents with starting storage date. Store in a cool, dry place. Most dried pasta can be stored indefinitely, but for optimum quality and flavor, a one- to two-year storage time is recommended.

Fresh

Fresh pasta is perishable and should be stored in the refrigerator. Most fresh pasta packages carry use-by or expiration dates. Store unopened pasta in original packaging. Store opened, unused amounts of pasta tightly covered no longer than three days.

Frozen

Store in the freezer until ready to cook. Store unopened pasta in original packaging and opened, unused amounts in airtight containers to avoid freezer burn. Freeze unopened pasta up to nine months, opened pasta up to three months.

Homemade

Homemade pasta can be stored as for Dried (above) if dried completely; freshly made pasta can be stored tightly covered in the refrigerator up to three days, or freeze airtight up to six months.

Preceding page: Pasta Primavera (page 281),
Garlic Bread (page 66)

Pasta Glossary

A fascinating assortment of sizes and shapes of pasta is on the market. While some shapes are known by more than one name, you can often determine pasta size from the Italian suffix: *-oni* means the pasta is large; *-elle*, *-iti* and *-ina* mean the pasta is small.

Acini de Pepe: Peppercorn-size pieces of cut spaghetti.

Capellini (angel hair): The thinnest of the long spaghettis.

Conchigle: Medium to small shell shapes with or without grooves.

Conchiglioni: Jumbo pasta shells with or without grooves, usually filled and baked.

Couscous ("koos-koos"): The tiniest form of pasta made from granular semolina.

Egg Noodles: Flat or curly short pasta strips usually made with eggs or egg yolks. The widths vary from about 1/8 to 1/2 inch.

Farfalle (bow-ties): Shaped like bow-ties. Miniature bow-ties are known as tripolini.

Fettuccine: Long, flat noodles, usually 1/4 inch wide.

Fusilli: Long or short spring-shaped pasta.

Japanese Curly Noodles: Quick-cooking wavy thin long noodles sold in rectangular "bricks" about 1 inch thick.

Lasagna: Flat noodle about 2 inches wide with either ruffled or straight edges.

Linguine: Long flat thin noodle usually 1/8 inch wide.

Macaroni (elbow): Short, curved, tubular-shaped pasta.

Mafalda (mini-lasagna noodles): Short, flat, narrow noodle with ruffled edges.

Manicotti (Cannelloni): Large, 4-inch hollow pasta tubes that are usually stuffed and baked.

Mostaccioli: Short, diagonal-cut macaroni about 2 inches long, smooth or with grooves.

Novelty Pasta Shapes: Seasonal or other pasta shapes, such as pumpkins, trees, rabbits, hearts, states, cars, quilts, etc., sometimes flavored.

Penne: Narrow straight diagonal-cut macaroni about 1 1/4 inches long, smooth or with grooves.

Radiatore (pasta nuggets): Shaped like ruffled fins of car radiators or air conditioners.

Ramen Noodles: Quick-cooking, deep-fried noodles used dry or cooked.

Ravioli: Square filled pasta (usually stuffed with cheese, meat or spinach).

Rice Noodles: Translucent thin strands made from rice flour and water.

Rigatoni: Short-cut, wide macaroni about 1 inch long with grooves.

Rosamarina (Orzo): Resembles rice but is slightly larger and longer.

Rotelle: Wider version of short-cut corkscrew-shaped pasta.

Rotini: Short-cut corkscrew-shaped pasta. Wider version is called rotelle.

Spaghetti: Long thin solid pasta strands.

Tortellini: Small noodle squares filled then folded diagonally and shaped into rings.

Vermicelli: Long very thin solid strands, thinner than spaghetti but thicker than capellini.

Wagon Wheels: Small round pasta resembling a wheel with spokes.

Ziti: Short-cut, 2-inch straight macaroni with smooth surface.

Japanese Curly Noodles

Lasagna Noodles

Linguine

Rotini

Fettuccine

Capellini

Spaghetti

Rosamarina (orzo)

Fusilli

Rigatoni

Rice Noodles

Manicotti

Farfalle (bow-ties)

Tortellini

Egg Noodles

Wagon Wheels

Penne

Macaroni

Acini de Pepe

Couscous

Novelty Pasta Shapes

Conch

Tips for Cooking Pasta

- Use a large enough pan and plenty of water, and be sure the water is boiling vigorously before adding pasta. Use at least 1 quart water for every 4 ounces of pasta.
- Always cook pasta uncovered at a fast and continuous boil. This allows the pasta to move freely so it cooks more evenly and also helps prevent sticking.
- One ounce of dried pasta will yield approximately 1/2 cup of cooked pasta. This will vary slightly depending on the shape, type and size of pasta.
- Allow 1/2 to 3/4 cup cooked pasta per side dish or appetizer serving. For a main dish, allow 1 to 1 1/2 cups per serving.
- To easily measure 4 ounces of spaghetti or other long pasta such as linguini, make a circle about the size of a quarter with your thumb and index finger and fill it with pasta.
- Salt is optional and not necessary for the proper cooking of pasta. However, it does enhance the flavor. As a guide to adding salt, use 1/2 teaspoon for each 8 ounces of pasta. In place of salt, add a tablespoon of dried herbs or lemon juice to the water for a slightly different flavor.
- Vegetable or olive oil can be added to the water to prevent foaming or boilover, but do so in very small amounts. Use only 1/4 or 1/2 teaspoon for up to 1 pound of pasta because adding larger amounts will cause the pasta to become coated with oil, and sauces will not cling well.
- Prevent sticking by gradually adding pasta to rapidly boiling water and stirring, then stirring occasionally during cooking.
- Follow package directions carefully for cooking times, or refer to the Dried Pasta Cooking Chart on this page. Undercook slightly if the pasta will be used in a recipe with further cooking. Fresh pasta cooks faster than dried pasta.
- Cooked pasta should be tender but firm to the bite (*al dente*). Check for doneness at the minimum recommended cook time to avoid overcooking and mushy texture. Cut several pieces with fork against side of pan and taste; it should be slightly resistant but cut easily, and no raw flour flavor should remain.
- Rinse pasta after draining only when stated in the recipe. For salads, immediately rinse pasta with cold water to stop the cooking and chill it quickly.

Storing and Reheating Cooked Pasta

Using refrigerated or frozen leftover pasta can save precious time during the week when every minute counts to get dinner on the table. To prevent sticking, cooked pasta can be tossed with a small amount of oil before storing. Store in tightly sealed containers or plastic bags in the refrigerator up to five days, or freeze up to two months. To reheat pasta, choose one of the three simple methods below:

- Place pasta in rapidly boiling water for up to 2 minutes. Drain and serve immediately.
- Place pasta in colander and pour boiling water over it until heated through. Drain and serve immediately.
- Place pasta in microwavable dish or container. Cover and microwave on High for 1 to 3 minutes per 2 cups or until heated through. Serve immediately.

Dried Pasta Yields

Uncooked	Cooked	Servings
Macaroni 7 ounces (2 cups)	4 cups	4 to 6
Spaghetti 7 to 8 ounces	4 cups	4 to 6
Noodles, 8 ounces (4 to 5 cups)	4 to 5 cups	4 to 6

Pasta Cooking Guide

Although most pasta packages have cooking directions, many people store their pasta in other containers without directions. This handy reference chart gives *approximate* cooking times for the most popular types and shapes of pasta.

Dried Pasta Cooking Chart

Type	Time (in minutes)	Type	Time (in minutes)
Capellini (angel hair)	5 to 6	Mostaccioli	12 to 14
Conchigle (small or medium shells)	9 to 11	Novelty pasta shapes	8 to 10
Conchiglioni (jumbo shells)	12 to 15	Penne	9 to 13
Couscous	Let stand 5 minutes	Radiatore (pasta nuggets)	9 to 11
		Ramen noodles	5
Egg Noodles, regular	8 to 10	Rice noodles	3
Egg Noodles, extra wide	10 to 12	Rigatoni	12 to 15
Farfalle (bow-ties)	13 to 15	Rosamarina (orzo)	8 to 10
Fettuccine	11 to 13	Rotelle (medium corkscrew)	10 to 12
Fusilli	11 to 13	Rotini (small corkscrew)	8 to 10
Japanese Curly Noodles	4 to 5	Spaghetti	8 to 10
Lasagna Noodles	12 to 15	Tortellini	12 to 15
Linguine	9 to 13	Vermicelli	5 to 7
Macaroni, elbow	8 to 10	Wagon Wheels	10 to 12
Mafalda (mini-lasagna noodles)	8 to 10	Ziti	14 to 15
Manicotti (cannelloni)	10 to 12		

Fresh Purchased Pasta Cooking Chart

Type	Time (in minutes)	Type	Time (in minutes)
Capellini (angel hair)	1 to 2	Linguine	1 to 2
Farfalle (bow-ties)	2 to 3	Ravioli	6 to 8
Fettuccine	1 to 2	Tortellini	8 to 10
Lasagna noodles	2 to 3		

Making Fresh Pasta

Wheat, which is ground into flour, gives pasta its structure and texture. The most common types of flour used to make homemade pasta are semolina flour and all-purpose flour, both of which are interchangeable in scratch pasta recipes.

All-purpose flour is a blend of hard and soft wheat varieties, not durum wheat. It can be used for making all types of baked goods and pasta, too. Pasta dough made with all-purpose flour is smooth, elastic and easy to handle.

Semolina flour is made from durum wheat, a variety high in gluten that makes it great for making pasta, but not for making baked goods. Semolina flour is more coarsely ground than all-purpose flour, is yellowish in color and is more finely ground than cornmeal. Look for it in large supermarkets, Italian markets and gourmet shops. Pasta dough made with semolina flour is slightly drier and stiffer than dough made with other flours because semolina flour absorbs liquid more easily.

Spinach Fettuccine

PREP: 40 min; STAND: 40 min; COOK: 15 min
Makes 8 servings, about 3/4 cup each

Have a pasta-making party and make all three flavors of fettuccine. Then try serving with your three favorite compatible sauces for a memorable feast. (photograph on page 278)

  8 ounces spinach*
  2 large eggs
  1 tablespoon olive or vegetable oil
  1 teaspoon salt
  2 to 2 1/4 cups all-purpose flour**
  4 1/2 quarts water
  1/4 teaspoon salt, if desired

1. Wash spinach; drain. Cover and cook over medium heat with just the water that clings to the leaves 3 to 10 minutes or until tender. Rinse spinach in cold water; drain.

2. Press spinach against side of strainer with back of spoon to remove excess water. Place spinach, eggs, oil and 1 teaspoon salt in blender. Cover and blend on medium speed about 20 seconds or until smooth.

3. Make a well in center of flour in medium bowl. Mix in spinach mixture thoroughly. (If dough is too dry, mix in a few drops water; if dough is too sticky, mix in a small amount of flour.)

4. Gather dough into a ball. Knead on floured surface about 5 minutes or until smooth and elastic. Let stand 10 minutes.

5. Divide dough into 4 equal parts. Roll one part at a time into paper-thin rectangle on generously floured surface (keep remaining dough covered). Loosely fold rectangle lengthwise into thirds. Cut crosswise into 1/4-inch strips. Unfold strips and place in single layer on towels; let stand at least 30 minutes until dry. (If using pasta machine, pass dough through machine until 1/16 inch thick.)

6. Heat 4 1/2 quarts water (salted if desired) to boiling in large pan. Add fettuccine. Cook 3 to 5 minutes or until firm but tender (*al dente*); drain. Begin testing for doneness when fettuccine rise to surface of water.

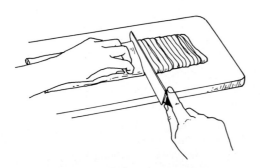

a. Cut folded dough crosswise into 1/4-inch strips.

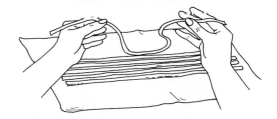

b. Unfold strips and place in single layer on towels; let stand at least 30 minutes until dry.

*1 package (10 ounces) frozen spinach can be substituted for the fresh spinach. Cook as directed on package; drain thoroughly.

**If using self-rising flour, omit the 1 teaspoon salt.

1 SERVING: Calories 145 (Calories from Fat 25); Fat 3g (Saturated 1g); Cholesterol 55mg; Sodium 300mg; Carbohydrate 25g (Dietary Fiber 1g); Protein 5g

BEET FETTUCCINE: Substitute 1 can (8 ounces) whole beets, drained, for the cooked spinach.

CARROT FETTUCCINE: Substitute 1 can (8 1/4 ounces) sliced carrots, drained, for the cooked spinach.

Spaetzle

PREP: 10 min; COOK: 15 min
Makes 6 servings, about 1/2 cup each

German in origin, spaetzle *means "little sparrow." These tiny noodles or dumplings are usually served as a side dish like potatoes or rice and are often served with a sauce or gravy.*

  2 large eggs, beaten
  1/4 cup milk or water
  1 cup all-purpose flour*
  1/4 teaspoon salt
  Dash of pepper
  1 tablespoon margarine or butter

1. Mix eggs, milk, flour, salt and pepper (batter will be thick).

2. Fill Dutch oven half full with water; heat to boiling.

3. Press a few tablespoons batter at a time through colander (preferably one with large holes) into boiling water. Stir once or twice to prevent sticking.

4. Cook about 5 minutes or until spaetzle rise to surface and are tender; drain. Toss with margarine.

*Do not use self-rising flour in this recipe.

1 SERVING: Calories 115 (Calories from Fat 35); Fat 4g (Saturated 1g); Cholesterol 70mg; Sodium 140mg; Carbohydrate 17g (Dietary Fiber 1g); Protein 4g

---

LIGHTER SPAETZLE

For 2 grams of fat and 100 calories per serving, substitute 1/2 cup fat-free cholesterol-free egg product for the eggs.

Homemade Pasta, Spinach Fettucine (page 277), Herb Pasta

Homemade Pasta

PREP: 30 min; STAND: 30 min; COOK: 15 min
Makes 8 servings, about 3/4 cup each

Enjoy this special pasta tossed with Italian Tomato Sauce (page 343) or one of the varieties of Pesto (page 345).

    2 cups all-purpose flour*
    1/2 teaspoon salt
    2 large eggs
    1/4 cup water
    1 tablespoon olive or vegetable oil
    4 1/2 quarts water

1. Mix flour and 1/2 teaspoon salt in medium bowl. Make a well in center of flour mixture. Mix in eggs, 1/4 cup water and the oil thoroughly. (If dough is too dry, mix in a few drops water; if dough is too sticky, mix in a small amount of flour.)

2. Gather dough into a ball. Knead on floured surface about 5 minutes or until smooth and elastic.

3. Divide dough into 4 equal parts. Roll one part at a time into paper-thin rectangle on generously floured surface (keep remaining dough covered). Loosely fold rectangle lengthwise into thirds. Cut crosswise into 1/4-inch strips. Unfold strips and place in single layer on towels; let stand at least 30 minutes until dry. (If

using pasta machine, pass dough through machine until 1/16 inch thick.)

4. Heat 4 1/2 quarts water (salted if desired) to boiling in large pan. Add pasta. Boil uncovered 3 to 5 minutes or until firm but tender (*al dente*); drain. Begin testing for doneness when pasta rises to surface of water.

*If using self-rising flour, omit the 1/2 teaspoon salt.

1 SERVING: Calories 140 (Calories from Fat 25); Fat 3g (Saturated 1g); Cholesterol 55mg; Sodium 150mg; Carbohydrate 24g (Dietary Fiber 1g); Protein 5g

---
LIGHTER HOMEMADE PASTA
For 2 grams of fat and 130 calories per serving, substitute 1/2 cup fat-free cholesterol-free egg product for the eggs.

HERB PASTA: Add 1 tablespoon chopped fresh herb or 1 teaspoon dried herb, crushed, to the flour mixture before adding eggs.

LEMON PASTA: Add 2 to 3 teaspoons finely shredded lemon peel to the flour mixture before adding eggs.

POPPY SEED PASTA: Add 1 tablespoon poppy seed to the flour mixture before adding eggs.

Egg Noodles

PREP: 15 min; STAND: 2 hr; COOK; 15 min
Makes 6 servings, about 3/4 cup each

These noodles are delicious served with a touch of butter and a sprinkle of freshly ground pepper. Or, use in your favorite recipes.

 2 cups all-purpose* or whole wheat flour
 3 large egg yolks
 1 large egg
 1 teaspoon salt
 1/3 to 1/2 cup water
 3 quarts water
 1/4 teaspoon salt, if desired

1. Make a well in center of flour in medium bowl. Mix in egg yolks, egg and 1 teaspoon salt thoroughly. Mix in 1/3 to 1/2 cup water, 1 tablespoon at a time, until dough is stiff but easy to roll.

2. Divide dough into 4 equal parts. Roll one part at a time into paper-thin rectangle on generously floured surface (keep remaining dough covered). Loosely fold rectangle lengthwise into thirds. Cut crosswise into 1/8-inch strips for narrow noodles, 1/4-inch strips for wide noodles. (If using pasta machine, pass dough through machine until 1/16 inch thick.) Unfold strips and place in single layer on towels; let stand about 2 hours or until stiff and dry.

3. Break strips into smaller pieces. Heat 3 quarts water to boiling in large pan. Stir in 1/4 teaspoon salt and the noodles. Boil 5 to 7 minutes or until firm but tender (*al dente*); drain. Begin testing for doneness when noodles rise to surface of water. (To cook half of the noodles, use 2 quarts water.)

*If using self-rising flour, omit the 1 teaspoon salt.

1 SERVING: Calories 190 (Calories from Fat 35); Fat 4g (Saturated 2g); Cholesterol 140 mg; Sodium 400 mg; Carbohydrate 32g (Dietary Fiber 1g); Protein 7g

CORNMEAL NOODLES: Substitute 1/2 cup cornmeal for 1/2 cup of the flour.

Three-Cheese Noodle Bake

PREP: 30 min; BAKE: 20 min
Makes 8 servings, about 3/4 cup each

This also makes a great main dish for four.

 2 tablespoons margarine or butter
 2 tablespoons all-purpose flour
 1/2 teaspoon salt
 1/8 teaspoon pepper
 2 cups milk
 1 cup shredded Fontina or mozzarella cheese
   (4 ounces)
 1 cup shredded Gruyère or Swiss cheese
   (4 ounces)
 1/2 cup grated Parmesan cheese
 6 cups uncooked egg noodles (12 ounces)
 3 tablespoons dry bread crumbs
 1 tablespoon margarine or butter

1. Melt 2 tablespoons margarine in 2-quart saucepan over medium heat. Stir in flour, salt and pepper until blended. Cook, stirring constantly, until smooth and bubbly; remove from heat.

2. *Gradually* stir in milk. Heat to boiling, stirring constantly. Boil and stir 1 minute. Stir in cheeses; keep warm over low heat.

3. Heat oven to 350°.

4. Meanwhile, cook and drain noodles as directed on package.

5. Alternate layers of noodles and cheese mixture, ending with noodles, in ungreased 2-quart casserole.

6. Heat bread crumbs and 1 tablespoon margarine over medium heat, stirring frequently, until crumbs are toasted. Sprinkle over noodles.

7. Bake uncovered about 20 minutes or until hot and bubbly.

1 SERVING: Calories 320 (Calories from Fat 145); Fat 16g (Saturated 8g); Cholesterol 65mg; Sodium 460mg; Carbohydrate 30g (Dietary Fiber 2g); Protein 16g

---

TIMESAVING TIP
Use an 8-ounce package of a shredded cheese blend for the Fontina, Gruyère and Parmesan cheeses.

Noodles Romanoff

PREP: 10 min; COOK: 20 min
Makes 8 servings, about 2/3 cup each

Egg Noodles (page 279) or 4 cups uncooked
  wide noodles (8 ounces)
2 cups sour cream
1/4 cup grated Parmesan cheese
1 tablespoon chopped fresh chives
1/2 teaspoon salt
1/8 teaspoon pepper
1 large clove garlic, crushed
2 tablespoons margarine or butter
1/4 cup grated Parmesan cheese

1. Cook noodles as directed in recipe or on package.

2. While noodles are cooking, mix sour cream, 1/4 cup cheese, the chives, salt, pepper and garlic.

3. Drain noodles. Stir margarine into noodles. Stir in sour cream mixture. Place on warm platter. Sprinkle with 1/4 cup cheese.

1 SERVING: Calories 260 (Calories from Fat 155); Fat 17g (Saturated 9g); Cholesterol 65mg; Sodium 290mg; Carbohydrate 21g (Dietary Fiber 1g); Protein 7g

---

LIGHTER NOODLES ROMANOFF
For 7 grams of fat and 205 calories per serving, use reduced-fat sour cream and reduced-fat Parmesan cheese blend. Decrease margarine to 1 tablespoon.

Curried Vegetables with Ziti

PREP: 15 min; COOK: 20 min
Makes 6 servings, about 1 1/3 cups each

This tasty dish brings basic Pasta Primavera to new heights with the addition of curry powder, gingerroot, soy sauce and raisins. (photograph on page 307)

3 cups uncooked ziti pasta (8 ounces)
1 tablespoon olive or vegetable oil
1 medium onion, cut into thin strips
1 clove garlic, finely chopped
2 teaspoons curry powder
1 teaspoon grated gingerroot
3/4 cup water
3/4 cup apple juice
1 tablespoon soy sauce
1 medium carrot, cut into 1/2-inch slices
1 tablespoon cornstarch
2 cups cauliflowerets
1 cup frozen green peas, rinsed to separate
1/2 cup raisins
1 medium zucchini, cut into 1/2-inch slices
1 small red or green bell pepper, cut into
  thin strips

1. Cook pasta as directed on package.

2. While pasta is cooking, heat oil in Dutch oven over medium-high heat. Cook onion, garlic, curry powder and gingerroot in oil, stirring frequently, until onion is crisp-tender.

3. Stir in water, 1/2 cup of the apple juice, the soy sauce and carrot. Heat to boiling; reduce heat to low. Cover and simmer 10 minutes.

4. Mix cornstarch and remaining 1/4 cup apple juice. Stir cornstarch mixture and remaining ingredients into carrot mixture. Cover and simmer 3 to 5 minutes, stirring occasionally, until zucchini is tender.

5. Drain ziti. Serve vegetable mixture over ziti or toss.

1 SERVING: Calories 260 (Calories from Fat 25); Fat 3g (Saturated 1g); Cholesterol 0mg; Sodium 210mg; Carbohydrate 54g (Dietary Fiber 4g); Protein 8g

Fettuccine Alfredo

PREP: 10 min; COOK: 15 min
Makes 6 servings, about 3/4 cup each

A rich northern Italian dish named after the restaurant where it was created, it can be served as a side dish as well as a main dish. Note that freshly grated Parmesan cheese will result in a thinner sauce than when canned grated cheese is used.

8 ounces uncooked fettuccine
Alfredo Sauce (below)
Chopped fresh parsley

1. Cook fettuccine as directed on package.

2. While fettuccine is cooking, prepare Alfredo Sauce.

3. Drain fettuccine. Pour sauce over fettuccine; toss until fettuccine is well coated. Sprinkle with parsley.

Alfredo Sauce

1/2 cup margarine or butter
1/2 cup whipping (heavy) cream
3/4 cup grated Parmesan cheese
1/2 teaspoon salt
Dash of pepper

Heat margarine and whipping cream in 2-quart saucepan over low heat, stirring constantly, until margarine is melted. Stir in cheese, salt and pepper.

1 SERVING: Calories 365 (Calories from Fat 235); Fat 26g (Saturated 9g); Cholesterol 65mg; Sodium 560mg; Carbohydrate 26g (Dietary Fiber 2g); Protein 9g

---

LIGHTER FETTUCCINE ALFREDO
For 15 grams of fat and 275 calories per serving, decrease margarine to 1/3 cup. Substitute evaporated milk for the whipping cream and use reduced-fat Parmesan cheese blend.

Spaghetti with White Clam Sauce

PREP: 10 min; COOK: 15 min
Makes 4 servings, about 1 1/4 cups each

For a change, omit the parsley, and add chopped fresh basil.

1 package (7 ounces) spaghetti
1/4 cup margarine or butter
2 cloves garlic, finely chopped
2 tablespoons chopped fresh parsley
2 cans (6 1/2 ounces each) minced clams, undrained
Chopped fresh parsley
1/2 cup grated Parmesan cheese

1. Cook spaghetti as directed on package.

2. While spaghetti is cooking, melt margarine in 1 1/2-quart saucepan over medium heat. Cook garlic in margarine about 3 minutes, stirring occasionally, until light golden. Stir in 2 tablespoons parsley and the clams. Heat to boiling; reduce heat to low. Simmer uncovered 3 to 5 minutes.

3. Drain spaghetti. Pour sauce over spaghetti; toss. Sprinkle with parsley and cheese.

1 SERVING: Calories 400 (Calories from Fat 145); Fat 16g (Saturated 5g); Cholesterol 35mg; Sodium 370mg; Carbohydrate 43g (Dietary Fiber 1g); Protein 22g

Turkey Tetrazzini

PREP: 25 min; BAKE: 40 min
Makes 6 servings, about 1 cup each

In a hurry? Omit steps 3 and 4. Mix one can each (10 3/4 ounces) condensed cream of mushroom soup and condensed cream of chicken soup, 3/4 cup milk and 2 tablespoons dry white wine or chicken broth in casserole. Stir in spaghetti, turkey, olives and almonds and sprinkle with cheese before baking.

1 package (7 ounces) spaghetti
2 cups chicken or turkey broth
2 cups half-and-half or milk
1/2 cup all-purpose or quick-mixing flour
1/4 cup margarine or butter
1/2 teaspoon salt
1/4 teaspoon pepper
2 cups cut-up cooked turkey or chicken
1 cup sliced ripe olives
1/2 cup slivered almonds
1 cup shredded Cheddar cheese (4 ounces)

1. Cook and drain spaghetti as directed on package. Rinse with cold water, drain.

2. Heat oven to 350°.

3. Mix broth, half-and-half, flour, margarine, salt and pepper in 3-quart saucepan. Heat to boiling over medium heat, stirring constantly. Boil and stir 1 minute.

4. Stir in spaghetti, turkey, olives and almonds. Spread in ungreased 2-quart casserole. Sprinkle with cheese.

5. Bake uncovered 25 to 30 minutes or until hot and bubbly.

1 SERVING: Calories 590 (Calories from Fat 315); Fat 35g (Saturated 13g); Cholesterol 90mg; Sodium 910mg; Carbohydrate 42g (Dietary Fiber 3g); Protein 30g

---

LIGHTER TURKEY TETRAZZINI

For 14 grams of fat and 430 calories per serving, substitute evaporated skimmed milk for the half-and-half and 1/2 cup reduced-fat Cheddar cheese for the regular cheese. Decrease olives to 1/2 cup, margarine to 2 tablespoons and almonds to 1/4 cup.

Pasta Primavera

PREP: 15 min; COOK: 20 min
Makes 4 servings, about 1 3/4 cups each

(photograph on page 271)

8 ounces uncooked fettuccine or linguine
1 tablespoon olive or vegetable oil
1 cup broccoli flowerets
1 cup cauliflowerets
2 medium carrots, thinly sliced (1 cup)
1 cup frozen green peas, rinsed to separate
1 small onion, chopped (1/4 cup)
Alfredo Sauce (page 280)
1 tablespoon grated Parmesan cheese

1. Cook fettuccine as directed on package.

2. While fettuccine is cooking, heat oil in 12-inch skillet over medium-high heat. Cook broccoli, cauliflowerets, carrots, peas and onion in oil 6 to 8 minutes, stirring frequently, until vegetables are crisp-tender.

3. Prepare Alfredo Sauce. Stir sauce into vegetable mixture. Drain fettuccine. Stir fettuccine into sauce mixture; heat through. Sprinkle with cheese.

1 SERVING: Calories 635 (Calories from Fat 390); Fat 43g (Saturated 15g); Cholesterol 95mg; Sodium 910mg; Carbohydrate 50g (Dietary Fiber 6g); Protein 18g

---

TIMESAVING TIP

Substitute 1 container (10 ounces) refrigerated Alfredo sauce for the Alfredo Sauce recipe and pick up all the vegetables from the salad bar at your supermarket.

Linguini with Red Clam Sauce

Linguine with Red Clam Sauce

PREP: 40 min; COOK: 35 min; STAND: 30 min
Makes 6 servings, about 1 1/2 cups each

> Homemade Pasta (page 278) or
>   6 cups hot cooked linguine or
>   penne pasta
> Red Clam Sauce (below)
> 4 quarts water
> Chopped fresh parsley

1. Prepare dough for Homemade Pasta—except roll and cut into 1/8-inch strips for linguine.

2. Prepare Red Clam Sauce.

3. While clam sauce is cooking, heat water (salted if desired) to boiling in large pan. Add linguine. Boil uncovered 2 to 4 minutes, stirring occasionally, until firm but tender (*al dente*). Begin testing for doneness when linguine rise to surface of water.

4. Drain linguine. Toss linguine and sauce. Sprinkle with parsley.

Red Clam Sauce

> 1 pint shucked fresh small clams, drained and
>   liquid reserved*
> 1/4 cup olive or vegetable oil
> 3 cloves garlic, finely chopped
> 1 can (28 ounces) whole Italian-style
>   tomatoes, drained and chopped
> 1 small red chili, seeded and finely chopped
> 1 tablespoon chopped fresh parsley
> 1 teaspoon salt

Chop clams; reserve. Heat oil in 3-quart saucepan over medium-high heat. Cook garlic in oil, stirring frequently, until golden. Stir in tomatoes and chili. Cook 3 minutes, stirring frequently. Stir in clam liquid. Heat to boiling; reduce heat to low. Simmer uncovered 10 minutes. Stir in clams, parsley and salt. Cover and simmer about 15 minutes, stirring occasionally, until clams are tender.

* 2 cans (6 1/2 ounces each) minced clams, undrained, can be substituted for the fresh clams. Decrease simmering time to 5 minutes.

1 SERVING: Calories 290 (Calories from Fat 90); Fat 10g (Saturated 1g); Cholesterol 5mg; Sodium 580mg; Carbohydrate 44g (Dietary Fiber 3g); Protein 9g

Seafood Lasagna

PREP: 30 min; BAKE: 40 min; STAND: 10 min
Makes 12 servings

1/2 cup margarine or butter
2 cloves garlic, crushed
1/2 cup all-purpose flour
2 cups milk
2 cups chicken broth
2 cups shredded mozzarella cheese
    (8 ounces)
1/2 cup sliced green onions (5 medium)
1 teaspoon dried basil leaves
1/4 teaspoon pepper
9 uncooked lasagna noodles (about
    8 ounces)
1 cup small curd creamed cottage cheese
1 can (7 1/2 ounces) crabmeat, drained and
    cartilage removed
1 can (4 to 4 1/2 ounces) tiny shrimp,
    drained
1/2 cup grated Parmesan cheese

1. Melt margarine in 3-quart saucepan over low heat. Stir in garlic and flour. Cook, stirring constantly, until mixture is smooth and bubbly; remove from heat. Stir in milk and broth. Heat to boiling, stirring constantly. Boil and stir 1 minute.

2. Stir in mozzarella cheese, onions, basil and pepper. Cook over low heat, stirring constantly, until cheese is melted.

3. Heat oven to 350°.

4. Spread one-fourth of the cheese sauce (about 1 1/2 cups) in ungreased rectangular baking dish, 13 × 9 × 2 inches. Top with 3 uncooked noodles, overlapping if necessary. Spread cottage cheese over noodles; spread with one-fourth of the cheese sauce. Top with 3 noodles, the crabmeat and shrimp; spread with one-fourth of the cheese sauce. Top with remaining noodles and cheese sauce. Sprinkle with Parmesan cheese.

5. Bake uncovered 35 to 40 minutes or until noodles are firm but tender (*al dente*). Let stand 15 minutes before cutting.

1 SERVING: Calories 290 (Calories from Fat 125); Fat 14g (Saturated 5g); Cholesterol 45mg; Sodium 540mg; Carbohydrate 23g (Dietary Fiber 1g); Protein 19g

---

LIGHTER SEAFOOD LASAGNA

For 7 grams of fat and 230 calories per serving, decrease margarine to 1/4 cup and increase flour to 2/3 cup. Use skim milk, reduced-fat mozzarella cheese, fat-free cottage cheese and reduced-fat Parmesan cheese blend.

Chunky Vegetable Lasagna

PREP: 35 min; BAKE: 40 min; STAND: 10 min
Makes 8 servings

This recipe works best with cooked rather than uncooked lasagna noodles, and pesto sauce adds distinctive flavor.

12 uncooked lasagna noodles (about
    12 ounces)
3 cups frozen broccoli flowerets, thawed
3 large carrots, coarsely shredded (2 cups)
1 can (14 1/2 ounces) diced tomatoes,
    drained
1 medium red bell pepper, cut into thin strips
1 medium green bell pepper, cut into thin
    strips
3/4 cup Pesto (page 345) or prepared pesto
1/4 teaspoon salt
1 container (15 ounces) ricotta cheese
1/2 cup grated Parmesan cheese
1/4 cup chopped fresh parsley
1 large egg
3 tablespoons margarine or butter
1 clove garlic, finely chopped
3 tablespoons all-purpose flour
2 cups milk
2 cups shredded mozzarella cheese
    (8 ounces)

1. Cook and drain noodles as directed on package.

2. Mix broccoli, carrots, tomatoes, bell peppers, Pesto and salt.

3. Mix ricotta cheese, Parmesan cheese, parsley and egg.

4. Melt margarine in 2-quart saucepan over medium heat. Cook garlic in margarine about 2 minutes, stirring frequently, until garlic is tender. Stir in flour. Cook over medium heat, stirring constantly, until mixture is smooth and bubbly; remove from heat. Stir in milk. Heat to boiling, stirring constantly. Boil and stir 1 minute.

5. Heat oven to 350°.

6. Place 3 noodles in ungreased rectangular pan, 13 × 9 × 2 inches. Spread half of the cheese mixture over noodles. Top with 3 noodles; spread with half of the vegetable mixture. Sprinkle with 1 cup of the mozzarella cheese. Top with 3 noodles; spread with remaining cheese mixture. Top with 3 noodles; spread with remaining vegetable mixture. Pour sauce evenly over the top. Sprinkle with remaining 1 cup mozzarella cheese.

7. Bake uncovered 35 to 40 minutes or until hot in center. Let stand 10 minutes before cutting.

1 SERVING: Calories 550 (Calories from Fat 290); Fat 32g (Saturated 11g); Cholesterol 70mg; Sodium 640mg; Carbohydrate 42g (Dietary Fiber 4g); Protein 27g

Italian Sausage Lasagna

PREP: 1 hr 10 min; BAKE: 45 min; STAND: 15 min
Makes 8 servings

This is a great recipe to make ahead. Cover the unbaked lasagna with aluminum foil and refrigerate no longer than twenty-four hours or freeze no longer than two months. Bake covered, 45 minutes; uncover and bake refrigerated lasagna 15 to 20 minutes longer or frozen lasagna 35 to 45 minutes longer until hot and bubbly.

- 1 pound bulk Italian sausage
- 1 medium onion, chopped (1/2 cup)
- 1 clove garlic, crushed
- 3 tablespoons chopped fresh parsley
- 1 tablespoon chopped fresh or 1 teaspoon dried basil leaves
- 1 teaspoon sugar
- 1 can (16 ounces) whole tomatoes, undrained
- 1 can (15 ounces) tomato sauce
- 12 uncooked lasagna noodles (about 12 ounces)
- 1 container (15 ounces) ricotta cheese or small curd creamed cottage cheese (2 cups)
- 1/4 cup grated Parmesan cheese
- 1 tablespoon chopped fresh or 1 1/2 teaspoons dried oregano leaves
- 2 cups shredded mozzarella cheese (8 ounces)
- 1/4 cup grated Parmesan cheese

1. Cook sausage, onion and garlic in 10-inch skillet over medium heat, stirring occasionally until no longer pink; drain.

2. Stir in 2 tablespoons of the parsley, the basil, sugar, tomatoes and tomato sauce, breaking up tomatoes. Heat to boiling, stirring occasionally; reduce heat to low. Simmer uncovered about 45 minutes or until slightly thickened.

3. Heat oven to 350°. Cook and drain noodles as directed on package.

4. Mix ricotta cheese, 1/4 cup Parmesan cheese, remaining 1 tablespoon parsley and the oregano.

5. Spread 1 cup of the sauce mixture in ungreased rectangular baking dish, 13 × 9 × 2 inches. Top with 4 noodles. Spread 1 cup of the cheese mixture over noodles; spread with 1 cup of the sauce mixture. Sprinkle with 2/3 cup of the mozzarella cheese. Repeat with 4 noodles, the re-maining cheese mixture, 1 cup of the sauce mixture and 2/3 cup of the mozzarella cheese. Top with remaining noodles and sauce mixture. Sprinkle with remaining mozzarella cheese and 1/4 cup Parmesan cheese.

6. Cover and bake 30 minutes. Uncover and bake about 15 minutes longer or until hot and bubbly. Let stand 15 minutes before cutting.

1 SERVING: Calories 500 (Calories from Fat 235); Fat 26g (Saturated 12g); Cholesterol 80mg; Sodium 1250mg; Carbohydrate 36g (Dietary Fiber 2g); Protein 33g

---

LIGHTER ITALIAN SAUSAGE LASAGNA
For 14 grams of fat and 400 calories per serving, use reduced-fat sausage, reduced-fat ricotta cheese and reduced-fat mozzarella cheese.

EASY ITALIAN SAUSAGE LASAGNA: Substitute 5 cups (40 ounces) regular sauce with meat for the first 8 ingredients (do not use thick or extra thick varieties).

GROUND BEEF LASAGNA: Substitute 1 pound ground beef for the Italian sausage.

Skillet Lasagna

PREP: 10 min; COOK: 15 min
Makes 8 servings, about 1 cup each

If you have broken regular lasagna noodles, this is a good way to use them up.

- 1 pound ground beef
- 1 medium onion, chopped (1/2 cup)
- 1 medium green bell pepper, chopped (1 cup)
- 3 cups uncooked mafalda (mini-lasagna noodles) pasta (6 ounces)
- 2 1/2 cups water
- 1/2 teaspoon Italian seasoning
- 1 jar (30 ounces) spaghetti or marinara sauce
- 1 jar (4.5 ounces) sliced mushrooms, drained

1. Cook beef, onion and bell pepper in 12-inch skillet or Dutch oven over medium-high heat about 6 minutes, stirring occasionally, until beef is brown; drain.

2. Stir in remaining ingredients. Heat to boiling, stirring occasionally; reduce heat to low. Simmer uncovered 10 to 12 minutes or until pasta is tender.

1 SERVING: Calories 280 (Calories from Fat 115); Fat 13g (Saturated 4g); Cholesterol 30mg; Sodium 810mg; Carbohydrate 29g (Dietary Fiber 3g); Protein 15g

SKILLET PIZZA LASAGNA: Substitute 2 cans (15 ounces each) pizza sauce for the spaghetti sauce and add 1/2 cup diced pepperoni.

Spaghetti and Meatballs

PREP: 1 hr 10 min; COOK: 30 min
Makes 6 servings, about 1 3/4 cups each

Italian Tomato Sauce (page 343)
Meatballs (page 240)
4 cups hot cooked spaghetti (page 276)
Grated Parmesan cheese, if desired

1. Prepare Italian Tomato Sauce.

2. Prepare Meatballs; drain.

3. Stir meatballs into sauce. Cover and simmer 30 minutes, stirring occasionally. Serve over spaghetti. Serve with cheese.

1 SERVING: Calories 450 (Calories from Fat 170); Fat 19g (Saturated 6g); Cholesterol 80mg; Sodium 1260mg; Carbohydrate 50g (Dietary Fiber 5g); Protein 25g

SPAGHETTI AND BEEF SAUCE: Omit Meatballs. Cook 1 pound lean ground beef, 1 large onion, chopped (1 cup), and 2 cloves garlic, crushed, in 10-inch skillet over medium heat, stirring occasionally, until beef is brown; drain. Stir beef mixture into sauce. Simmer as directed in step 3.

TIMESAVING TIP

Substitute 1 jar (26 ounces) spaghetti sauce for the Italian Tomato Sauce and 1 1/2 pounds cooked meatballs for the Meatballs.

Manicotti

PREP: 40 min; BAKE: 1 1/2 hr
Makes 7 servings

This is a convenient recipe to make ahead—it will definitely come in handy! Cover and refrigerate manicotti up to 24 hours. Or wrap airtight, label and freeze up to 1 month. Refrigerated manicotti takes about 10 minutes longer to bake. Unwrap frozen manicotti; cover and bake about 2 hours.

Red Sauce (right)
2 packages (10 ounces each) frozen chopped
    spinach, thawed
2 cups small curd creamed cottage cheese
1/3 cup grated Parmesan cheese
1/4 teaspoon ground nutmeg
1/4 teaspoon pepper
14 uncooked manicotti shells
2 tablespoons grated Parmesan cheese

1. Prepare Red Sauce.

2. Squeeze spinach to drain, spread on paper towels and pat dry. Mix spinach, cottage cheese, 1/3 cup Parmesan cheese, the nutmeg and pepper.

3. Heat oven to 350°.

4. Spread about one-third of the sauce in ungreased rectangular baking dish, 13 × 9 × 2 inches. Fill uncooked manicotti shells with spinach mixture. Place shells in sauce in dish. Pour remaining sauce evenly over shells, covering shells completely. Sprinkle with 2 tablespoons Parmesan cheese.

5. Cover and bake about 1 1/2 hours or until shells are tender.

Red Sauce

1 pound ground beef
1 large onion, chopped (1 cup)
2 large cloves garlic, crushed
1 can (28 ounces) whole tomatoes,
    undrained
1 can (8 ounces) mushroom stems and
    pieces, drained
1/4 cup chopped fresh parsley
1 teaspoon salt
1 tablespoon chopped fresh or 1 teaspoon
    dried basil leaves

Cook beef, onion and garlic in 10-inch skillet over medium heat about 10 minutes, stirring occasionally, until beef is brown; drain. Stir in tomatoes, mushrooms, parsley, salt and basil, breaking up tomatoes. Heat to boiling; reduce heat to low. Cover and simmer 10 minutes.

1 SERVING: Calories 385 (Calories from Fat 135); Fat 15g (Saturated 7g); Cholesterol 50mg; Sodium 1010mg; Carbohydrate 38g (Dietary Fiber 5g); Protein 29g

---

TIMESAVING TIP

You can substitute 1 jar (about 30 ounces) spaghetti sauce for the tomatoes, mushrooms, parsley, salt and basil. Stir sauce into beef and heat as directed in step 2.

Curry Pork Sausage Couscous

PREP: 10 min; COOK: 15 min
Makes 4 servings, about 1 1/3 cups each

Ground pork or mild bulk Italian sausage also could be used in this dish.

    1 1/2 cups uncooked couscous
    1/2 pound bulk pork sausage
    1 large onion, chopped (1 cup)
    1/2 cup pistachio nuts, coarsely chopped
    1 teaspoon curry powder
    1 teaspoon salt
    2 cloves garlic, finely chopped
    2 tablespoons chopped fresh parsley

1. Prepare couscous as directed on package.

2. While couscous is standing, cook sausage, onion, nuts, curry powder, salt and garlic in 10-inch skillet over medium heat, stirring occasionally, until sausage is no longer pink; drain.

3. Stir in couscous and parsley. Cook over medium heat about 5 minutes, stirring occasionally, until mixture is hot.

1 SERVING: Calories 345 (Calories from Fat 145); Fat 16g (Saturated 4g); Cholesterol 20mg; Sodium 1190mg; Carbohydrate 40g (Dietary Fiber 4g); Protein 14g

Orzo with Creamy Chicken

PREP: 15 min; COOK: 15 min
Makes 4 servings, about 1 cup each

    1 1/3 cups uncooked rosamarina (orzo) pasta
       (8 ounces)
    2 tablespoons margarine or butter
    3/4 pound skinless boneless chicken breast
       halves, cut into 1-inch pieces
    3 cups sliced mushrooms (8 ounces)
    1/4 cup sliced green onions (3 medium)
    2 cloves garlic, finely chopped
    2 tablespoons all-purpose flour
    2 teaspoons chopped fresh or 1/2 teaspoon
       dried thyme leaves
    1/8 teaspoon pepper
    1 cup milk
    1/2 cup grated Parmesan cheese

1. Cook pasta as directed on package.

2. While pasta is cooking, melt margarine in 3-quart saucepan over medium heat. Cook chicken, mushrooms, onions and garlic in margarine about 5 minutes, stirring occasionally, until chicken is no longer pink in center.

3. Stir in flour, thyme and pepper. Cook over medium heat, stirring constantly, until mixture is smooth and bubbly; remove from heat. *Gradually* stir in milk. Heat to boiling, stirring constantly. Boil and stir 1 minute. Stir in cheese until melted.

4. Drain orzo. Pour chicken mixture over orzo; toss if desired.

1 SERVING: Calories 475 (Calories from Fat 125); Fat 14g (Saturated 5g); Cholesterol 60mg; Sodium 330mg; Carbohydrate 55g (Dietary Fiber 2g); Protein 34g

---

TIMESAVING TIP

Purchase chicken already cut into 1-inch pieces and fresh mushrooms already sliced.

Far East Pasta

PREP: 15 min; COOK: 15 min
Makes 4 servings, about 1 1/2 cups each

This is a fun combination of Oriental flavors and Italian—or even Japanese—noodles!

    4 cups uncooked fusilli pasta (12 ounces) or
       Japanese curly noodles
    3/4 cup mayonnaise or salad dressing
    1 tablespoon sesame oil
    1 tablespoon soy sauce
    1/4 to 1/2 teaspoon crushed red pepper
    3/4 pound cooked peeled deveined medium
       shrimp, thawed if frozen
    4 ounces Chinese pea pods, cut lengthwise
       into thin strips (1 cup)
    1 medium carrot, cut into julienne strips
       (1/2 cup)
    1/2 cup diagonally sliced green onions
       (5 medium)
    Sesame seed, toasted (page 9), if desired

1. Cook pasta as directed on package.

2. While fusilli is cooking, mix mayonnaise, oil, soy sauce and red pepper in serving bowl. Drain pasta. Stir pasta into mayonnaise mixture.

3. Add shrimp, pea pods, carrot and onions; toss. Sprinkle with sesame seed.

1 SERVING: Calories 750 (Calories from Fat 350); Fat 39g (Saturated 6g); Cholesterol 190mg; Sodium 690mg; Carbohydrate 72g (Dietary Fiber 3g); Protein 31g

---

LIGHTER FAR EAST PASTA

For 6 grams of fat and 480 calories per serving, substitute fat-free mayonnaise for the regular mayonnaise.

Macaroni and Cheese

PREP: 25 min; BAKE: 25 min
Makes 6 servings, about 3/4 cup each

Add extra pep to this favorite recipe by using pizza-flavored or jalapeño pepper cheese.

> 2 cups uncooked elbow macaroni (7 ounces)
> 1/4 cup margarine or butter
> 1/4 cup all-purpose flour
> 1/2 teaspoon salt
> 1/4 teaspoon pepper
> 1/4 teaspoon ground mustard (dry)
> 1/4 teaspoon Worcestershire sauce
> 2 cups milk
> 2 cups shredded or cubed sharp Cheddar cheese (8 ounces)

1. Heat oven to 350°.

2. Cook macaroni as directed on package.

3. While macaroni is cooking, melt margarine in 3-quart saucepan over low heat. Stir in flour, salt, pepper, mustard and Worcestershire sauce. Cook over low heat, stirring constantly, until mixture is smooth and bubbly; remove from heat. Stir in milk. Heat to boiling, stirring constantly. Boil and stir 1 minute. Stir in cheese. Cook, stirring occasionally, until cheese is melted.

4. Drain macaroni. *Gently* stir macaroni into cheese sauce. Pour into ungreased 2-quart casserole. Bake uncovered 20 to 25 minutes or until bubbly.

1 SERVING: Calories 445(Calories from Fat 205); Fat 23g (Saturated 11g); Cholesterol 45mg; Sodium 540mg; Carbohydrate 42g (Dietary Fiber 1g); Protein 18g

---

LIGHTER MACARONI AND CHEESE

For 10 grams of fat and 325 calories per serving, decrease margarine to 2 tablespoons. Use skim milk and 1 1/2 cups (6 ounces) reduced-fat cheese.

Chili Macaroni

PREP: 20 min; COOK: 25 min
Makes 8 servings, about 1 cup each

A great way to use 2 cups of leftover cooked macaroni or other pasta of similar size.

> 1 cup uncooked elbow macaroni
>   (3 1/2 ounces)
> 1 pound ground beef
> 1 medium onion, chopped (1/2 cup)
> 1 small green bell pepper, chopped (1/2 cup)
> 2 cloves garlic, finely chopped
> 1 can (15 to 16 ounces) kidney beans, drained
> 1 can (14 ounces) diced tomatoes, undrained*
> 1 can (11 ounces) whole kernel corn, drained
> 1 can (8 ounces) tomato sauce
> 1 can (6 ounces) tomato paste
> 1 tablespoon chili powder
> 1 teaspoon ground cumin
> 1 cup shredded Cheddar cheese (4 ounces)

1. Cook macaroni as directed on package.

2. While macaroni is cooking, cook beef, onion, bell pepper and garlic in Dutch oven over medium-high heat, stirring occasionally, until beef is brown; drain.

3. Drain macaroni. Stir macaroni and remaining ingredients except cheese into beef mixture. Heat to boiling, stirring occasionally; reduce heat to low. Simmer uncovered about 20 minutes, stirring occasionally, until hot. Sprinkle with cheese.

*1 can (16 ounces) whole tomatoes, cut up and undrained can be substituted for the diced tomatoes.

1 SERVING: Calories 325 (Calories from Fat 125); Fat 14g (Saturated 6g); Cholesterol 45mg; Sodium 820mg; Carbohydrate 35g (Dietary Fiber 6g); Protein 21g

---

LIGHTER CHILI MACARONI

For 10 grams of fat and 300 calories per serving, substitute ground turkey for the ground beef and use reduced-fat cheese.

SOUTHWESTERN CHILI MACARONI: Substitute 4 ounces similar size pasta for the elbow macaroni, 1 can (4 ounces) chopped green chilies for the bell pepper, 1 can (15 ounces) black beans, rinsed and drained, for the kidney beans and shredded Monterey Jack cheese for the Cheddar cheese.

Tuna-Stuffed Shells

Tuna-Stuffed Shells

PREP: 30 min; COOK: 15 min
Makes 4 servings

These jumbo shells can be served either cold or warm. To serve warm: Place shells on a microwavable platter. Cover with plastic wrap, venting one edge. Microwave on High 2 to 3 minutes or until warm. Serve with the vinaigrette, heated if desired.

> 16 uncooked jumbo pasta shells
> (conchiglioni)
> Tomato-Basil Vinaigrette (right)
> 1/3 cup mayonnaise or salad dressing
> 2 tablespoons chopped fresh or 2 teaspoons
> dried basil leaves
> 1/4 teaspoon salt
> 2 cans (6 1/8 ounces each) solid white tuna
> in water, drained and flaked
> 1 large carrot, shredded (1 cup)
> 1 small zucchini, shredded (1 cup)
> 1 small onion, chopped (1/4 cup)
> Lettuce leaves

1. Cook pasta shells as directed on package.

2. While pasta is cooking, prepare Tomato-Basil Vinaigrette.

3. Mix mayonnaise, basil and salt in medium bowl. Stir in tuna, carrot, zucchini and onion until evenly mixed. Drain pasta. Rinse with cold water; drain. Fill each pasta shell with 1 rounded tablespoon tuna mixture.

4. Line serving platter with lettuce leaves. Arrange shells on lettuce. Serve with Tomato-Basil Vinaigrette.

Tomato-Basil Vinaigrette

> 2 large tomatoes, seeded and chopped
> (2 cups)
> 2 tablespoons chopped onion
> 2 tablespoons chopped fresh or 2 teaspoons
> dried basil leaves
> 2 tablespoons olive or vegetable oil
> 1 tablespoon red wine vinegar
> 1/8 teaspoon salt
> 1/8 teaspoon pepper

Mix all ingredients.

1 SERVING: Calories 445 (Calories from Fat 205); Fat 23g (Saturated 3g); Cholesterol 35mg; Sodium 610mg; Carbohydrate 36g (Dietary Fiber 3g); Protein 27g

About Poultry

Poultry is a popular choice for the dinner table these days—and it's no wonder! Parts, including boneless, skinless breast halves, are conveniently packaged for quick-to-fix meals. Poultry is economical, its mild flavor combines well with many different flavors, and it is relatively low in fat, which makes it a favorite for healthful eating! Chicken is approaching beef in popularity, and new turkey products are appearing everywhere in the meat section of supermarkets.

Purchasing Poultry

Selecting fresh, wholesome poultry is easy when you follow these guidelines:

Label and Package

- Check the sell-by date on the label (product dating is not a federal requirement, so it may or may not appear on the label). This date indicates the last day the product should be sold, but the product still will be fresh and wholesome if prepared and eaten within two days after this date.
- Packages should be cold.
- Package trays and bags should have very little or no liquid in the bottom. (A lot of liquid may be an indication that the chicken has been sitting for a long time and is not fresh.)
- Avoid torn and leaking packages.
- Frozen poultry should be firm to the touch and free of freezer burn (dry, white areas on the edges of the chicken) and packaging tears.

Appearance and Odor

- Check for a fresh odor (off odors, like that of bad poultry, usually can be detected through the plastic). If any unusual odors are detected, the product is not fresh.
- Select whole birds and cut-up pieces that are plump and meaty with smooth, moist-looking skin. Boneless, skinless products should be plump and moist.
- The color of chicken skin does not indicate quality. Skin color ranges from yellow to white, depending on the breed of chicken and what it was fed. Turkey, however, should have cream-colored skin.
- The cut ends of the poultry bones should be pink to red in color—if they are gray, the poultry is not very fresh.
- Avoid poultry that has traces of feathers. (This may indicate care was not taken to clean the poultry carefully, and there may be other parts of the chicken that need to be removed before cooking, such as organs.)

Preceding page: Turkey Tenderloins with Caramelized Onions (page 309)

Storing Poultry

Refrigerating

Uncooked Poultry: Store poultry packaged on trays or whole poultry packaged in plastic bags in their original wrapping in the coldest part of refrigerator (40° or below). Rinse poultry wrapped in meat-market paper with cold water, pat dry with paper towels and repackage in heavy-duty plastic bags, several layers of plastic wrap or food storage containers with tight-fitting lids. (If using plastic wrap, place poultry in a dish or baking pan with sides to prevent leakage on refrigerator shelves during storage.) Refrigerate no longer than two days.

Cooked Poultry: Cover cooked poultry or wrap it tightly and refrigerate within two hours after cooking. Store in refrigerator no longer than two days. Store chicken or turkey, giblets, stuffing and gravy in separate containers because they cannot be stored for the same lengths of time. Thoroughly reheat leftovers (to 165°). Cover leftovers when reheating to retain moisture and ensure thorough heating in the center. Heat leftover gravies and sauces to a rolling boil, and boil 1 minute before serving.

Freezing

Uncooked Poultry: Wrap tightly in moisture- and vapor-resistant freezer wrap, heavy plastic freezer bags or heavy-duty aluminum foil. Store giblets separately because they cannot be stored for the same length of time as the chicken meat. Press as much air as possible out of the package before sealing it, to prevent the formation of ice crystals or freezer burn. Mark the package with the date and contents, and freeze. Cut-up chicken or turkey can be frozen up to nine months; whole chicken or turkey can be frozen up to twelve months.

Cooked Poultry: Store chicken or turkey, giblets, stuffing and gravy in separate containers. Wrap poultry tightly in moisture- and vapor-resistant freezer wrap, heavy-duty plastic freezer bags or heavy-duty aluminum foil. Press as much air as possible out of the package before sealing it, to prevent the formation of ice crystals and freezer burn. Mark the package with the date and contents, and freeze. Freeze for no longer than one month.

Thawing Poultry

Thaw frozen uncooked poultry slowly in the refrigerator, in cold water or quickly in the microwave following manufacturer's directions. Do not thaw poultry on the countertop because room temperature is a perfect environment in which bacteria can grow. If the poultry was frozen when purchased or frozen immediately after purchase, the thawed poultry can be kept in the refrigerator up to two days. Refer to Storing Poultry, page 290, for directions on refrigerating uncooked poultry. If the poultry had been refrigerated two days *before* freezing, use the thawed poultry the same day it is thawed.

Refrigerator Method

To thaw in the refrigerator, place poultry in original wrap in a dish or baking pan with sides to prevent leakage on refrigerator shelves during thawing, or place on the bottom shelf, for the time specified below:

Poultry Thawing Chart

Poultry Cut	Approximate Weight (pounds)	Thawing Time in Refrigerator
Whole Chicken	3 to 4	24 hours
Whole Turkey	8 to 12	1 to 2 days
	12 to 16	2 to 3 days
	16 to 20	3 to 4 days
	20 to 24	4 to 5 days
Chicken or Turkey, cut-up pieces	Up to 4	3 to 9 hours

Cold Water Method

Uncooked whole poultry or poultry parts also can be safely thawed in cold water. Leave poultry in its original wrap (free from tears or holes) or place in a sealable, heavy-duty plastic bag. Place in cold water. Allow 30 minutes per pound for thawing, and change the water often.

Cooked Poultry

Thaw frozen cooked poultry slowly in the refrigerator. Do not thaw poultry on the countertop because room temperature is a perfect environment in which bacteria can grow. Allow approximately 3 to 9 hours for 1 pound cubed, chopped or shredded pieces and up to 24 hours for whole pieces (bone in or boneless). You also may thaw cooked poultry in the microwave following manufacturer's directions.

Cooking Poultry

Always cook poultry to well done to eliminate any possible bacteria that may be present in the raw poultry. Once you have started cooking poultry, do not stop and then continue cooking at some later time, because partial cooking may encourage bacterial growth before cooking is complete. You will find cooking methods for poultry featured in charts, starting on the following pages: Roasting Poultry, page 293, Broiling or Grilling Poultry, page 294, and Microwaving Poultry, page 295. Keep in mind that the cooking times are *approximate,* so be sure to check doneness, as indicated in the steps that accompany each chart. Cooking times will be affected by types of ovens, actual oven temperatures and the shape and tenderness of the poultry.

The U.S. Department of Agriculture recommends using a meat thermometer when cooking whole poultry. You can read about the different types of thermometers available in Using a Meat Thermometer, page 222. If you don't have a meat thermometer, however, there are other ways to check for doneness.

Cooked Poultry Yields

Use the following guidelines for determining how much *uncooked* chicken or turkey is needed for a recipe that calls for chopped, cubed or shredded *cooked* chicken or turkey. For extra convenience, you can use frozen cooked cubed chicken, canned chunk chicken or cooked chicken and turkey from the deli department for recipes calling for cooked chicken or turkey.

Cooked Poultry Yields Chart

Poultry Type	Weight of Uncooked Poultry (pounds)	Approximate Yield of Chopped, Cubed or Shredded Cooked Poultry
Chicken		
Broiler-fryer, whole	3 to 3 1/2	2 1/2 to 3 cups
Whole breast, bone in	1 1/2	2 cups
Boneless, skinless breast halves	1 1/2	3 cups
Legs (thighs and drumsticks)	1 1/2	1 3/4 cups
Turkey		
Whole turkey	6 to 8	7 to 10 cups
Whole breast, bone in	1 1/2	2 1/2 cups
Tenderloins	1 1/2	3 cups

How to Cut Up a Whole Chicken

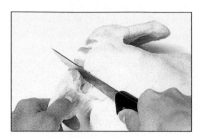

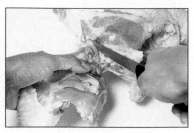

1. Place chicken, breast down, on cutting board. Remove wing from body by cutting into wing joint with a sharp knife, rolling knife to let the blade follow through at the curve of the joint as shown. Repeat with remaining wing.

2. Cut off each leg by cutting skin between the thigh and body of the chicken; continue cutting through the meat between the tail and hip joint, cutting as closely as possible to the backbone. Bend leg back until hip joint pops out as shown.

3. Continue cutting around bone and pulling leg from body until meat is separated from the bone as shown. Cut through remaining skin. Repeat on other side.

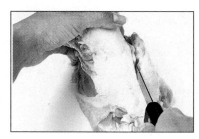

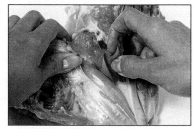

4. Separate thigh and drumstick by cutting about 1/8 inch from the fat line toward the drumstick side as shown. (A thin, white fat line runs crosswise at joint between drumstick and thigh.) Repeat with remaining leg.

5. Separate back from breast by holding body, neck end down, and cutting downward along each side of backbone through the rib joints.

6. Placing breast with skin side down, cut just through the white cartilage at the V of the neck. Then bend breast halves back to pop out the keel bone; remove keel bone. Using kitchen scissors or knife, cut breast into halves through wishbone.

Cutting Poultry into Pieces

Partially frozen raw poultry is easier to cut or slice than poultry taken directly from the refrigerator. Place chicken in the freezer until firm but not frozen, 30 minutes to 1 1/2 hours depending on the size of the piece, before cutting into cubes, thin slices or strips.

Seasoning Poultry

Chicken can be seasoned before, during or after cooking. See chapter 14, "Sauces, Seasonings and Condiments," beginning on page 341, for ways to enhance the flavor of poultry. One popular way to season poultry is by using a marinade. Marinades are highly seasoned liquids used to add unique flavors to poultry. They usually contain one or more liquids, such as fruit or vegetable juices, wine, water or oil, combined with seasonings and herbs. Besides the recipes in this book, try the excellent prepared marinades, rubs and seasoning mixes available at your supermarket.

Roasting Poultry

1. Remove giblets if present (gizzard, heart and neck). Rinse cavity. Rub cavity of bird lightly with salt if desired. Do not salt cavity if bird is to be stuffed.

2. If stuffing poultry, stuff just before roasting—not ahead of time. (See Rice Stuffing, page 298, and Bread Stuffing, page 297.) Fill wishbone area with stuffing first. Fasten neck skin to back with skewer. Fold wings across back with tips touching. Fill body cavity lightly. (Do not pack—stuffing will expand while cooking.) Tuck drumsticks under band of skin at tail, or tie or skewer to tail.

3. Place bird, breast side up, on rack in shallow roasting pan. (For easy cleanup, line the roasting pan with aluminum foil before placing poultry on rack in roasting pan.) Brush with melted margarine or butter. Do not add water. Do not cover. Place meat thermometer in thickest part of thigh muscle, so thermometer does not touch bone. Follow Timetable (right) for approximate roasting time. For turkey, place a tent of aluminum foil loosely over turkey when it begins to turn golden. When two-thirds done, cut band or remove skewer holding legs.

4. Roast until thermometer reads 180° for whole poultry (170° for whole turkey breast) and juice is no longer pink when center of thigh is cut. For whole poultry, the drumstick should move easily when lifted or twisted. When poultry is done, remove from oven and let stand about 15 minutes for easiest carving.

Timetable for Roasting Poultry

Ready to Cook Weight (pounds)	Oven Temperature	Approximate Roasting Time* (hours)
Whole Chicken (stuffed)		
3 to 3 1/2	325°	2 to 2 1/2
Whole Chicken (not stuffed)		
3 to 3 1/2	375°	1 3/4 to 2
Duck		
3 1/2 to 4	350°	2
5 to 5 1/2	350°	3
Goose		
7 to 9	350°	2 1/2 to 3
9 to 11	350°	3 to 3 1/2
11 to 13	350°	3 1/2 to 4
Pheasant		
2 to 3	350°	1 1/4 to 1 1/2
Rock Cornish Hen		
1 to 1 1/2	350°	1 to 1 1/4
Whole Turkey (stuffed)		
6 to 8	325°	3 to 3 1/2
8 to 12	325°	3 1/2 to 4 1/2
12 to 16	325°	4 to 5
16 to 20	325°	4 1/2 to 5 1/2
20 to 24	325°	5 to 6 1/2
Whole Turkey (not stuffed)		
6 to 8	325°	2 1/4 to 3 1/4
8 to 12	325°	3 to 4
12 to 16	325°	3 1/2 to 4 1/2
16 to 20	325°	4 to 5
20 to 24	325°	4 1/2 to 5 1/2
Turkey Breast (bone in)		
2 to 4	325°	1 1/2 to 2
3 to 5	325°	1 1/2 to 2 1/2
5 to 7	325°	2 to 2 1/2

Times given are for unstuffed birds unless noted. Stuffed birds, other than turkey, require 15 to 30 minutes longer. Begin checking turkey doneness about one hour before end of recommended roasting time. For prestuffed turkeys, follow package directions very carefully—do not use this timetable.

Broiling or Grilling Poultry

Broiling and grilling are quick, low-fat methods for cooking poultry. Whole chicken and turkey can be grilled using the indirect method. Follow the guidelines that came with your grill, or see Grilling Know-How, page 428.

1. Marinate poultry if desired. (See Tips for Marinades and Marinating, page 356.)

2. *To Broil*: Brush rack of broiler pan with vegetable oil, or spray with nonstick cooking spray. Set oven to Broil.

***To Grill*:** Brush grill rack with vegetable oil, or spray with nonstick cooking spray. Heat coals or gas grill (direct heat) to medium heat.

3. *To Broil:* Place poultry on rack in broiler pan.

(For easy cleanup, line broiler pan with aluminum foil before placing poultry on rack.) For whole chicken, turkey or Rock Cornish hen, insert meat thermometer in thickest part of inside thigh muscle, not touching bone.

***To Grill*:** Place poultry on grill 4 to 6 inches from heat. For even cooking, place meatier poultry pieces in center of grill rack, smaller pieces on the edges. For whole chicken, turkey or Rock Cornish hen, insert meat thermometer in thickest part of inside thigh muscle, not touching bone.

4. Broil or grill as directed below in Timetable for Broiling or Grilling Poultry, turning frequently with tongs and, if desired, brushing with barbecue or other sauce during the last 15 to 20 minutes.

Timetable for Broiling or Grilling Poultry

Poultry Type	Approximate Weight (pounds)	Approximate Broiling Time	Approximate Grilling Time (minutes)	Doneness
Chicken				
Cut-up chicken pieces	3 to 3 1/2	Skin sides down 30 minutes; turn. Broil 15 to 25 minutes longer (7 to 9 inches from heat).	35 to 40 (dark meat may take longer to cook)	Cook until juice of chicken is no longer pink when centers of thickest pieces are cut.
Breast halves (bone in)	1	25 to 35 minutes (7 to 9 inches from heat)	20 to 25	Cook until juice of chicken is no longer pink when centers of thickest pieces are cut.
Breast halves (boneless)	1	15 to 20 minutes, turning once (4 to 6 inches from heat)	15 to 20	Cook until juice of chicken is no longer pink when centers of thickest pieces are cut.
Wings	3 to 3 1/2	10 minutes, turning once (5 to 7 inches from heat)	12 to 18	Cook until juice of chicken is no longer pink when centers of thickest pieces are cut.
Ground turkey or chicken patties (1/2 inch thick)	1	6 minutes on each side (3 inches from heat)	15 to 20	Cook until no longer pink.
Turkey				
Tenderloins	1 to 1 1/2	8 to 12 minutes on each side (6 inches from heat)	20 to 30	Cook until juice of turkey is no longer pink when centers of thickest pieces are cut.
Breast slices	1 to 1 1/2	7 minutes, turning once (4 inches from heat)	8 to 10	Cook until turkey is no longer pink in center.
Rock Cornish Hens*	2 to 3 (two hens)	30 to 40 minutes (4 to 6 inches from heat)	30 to 40	Cook until meat thermometer reads 180° and juice of hen is no longer pink when center of thigh is cut.

Cut hens in half before broiling or grilling, for best results.

Microwaving Poultry

1. Marinate poultry if desired. (See Tips for Marinades and Marinating, page 356.)

2. Arrange poultry pieces, skin sides up and thickest parts to outside edge, in a microwavable dish large enough to hold the pieces in a single layer.

3. Cover with plastic wrap, folding back one corner to vent. Microwave on High as directed below in Timetable for Microwaving Poultry.

Note: *Use a microwave meat thermometer designed to remain in the microwave during cooking, or use an instant-read thermometer after removing poultry from microwave.*

Timetable for Microwaving Poultry

Poultry Type	Approximate Weight (pounds)	Approximate Grilling Time (minutes)	Doneness
Chicken			
Broiler-fryer (cut up)	3 to 3 1/2	15 to 20 minutes, rotating dish 1/2 turn after 10 minutes	Cook until juice of chicken is no longer pink when centers of thickest pieces are cut.
Breast halves (bone in)	1	8 to 10 minutes, rotating dish 1/2 turn after 4 minutes	Cook until juice of chicken is no longer pink when centers of thickest pieces are cut.
Breast halves (boneless)	1	8 to 10 minutes, rotating dish 1/2 turn after 4 minutes	Cook until juice of chicken is no longer pink when centers of thickest pieces are cut.
Wings	3 to 3 1/2	12 to 15 minutes, rotating dish 1/2 turn after 6 minutes	Cook until juice of chicken is no longer pink when centers of thickest pieces are cut.
Legs or thighs	2	16 to 19 minutes, rotating dish 1/2 turn after 10 minutes	Cook until juice of chicken is no longer pink when centers of thickest pieces are cut.
Ground turkey or chicken	1	6 to 8 minutes, stirring after 4 minutes	Cook until no longer pink.
Ground chicken or turkey patties (1/2 inch thick)	1	6 to 8 minutes, turning patties over after 4 minutes	Cook until no longer pink.
Turkey			
Tenderloins	1 to 1 1/2	About 10 minutes, rotating dish 1/2 turn after 4 minutes	Cook until juice of turkey is no longer pink when centers of thickest pieces are cut.
Breast slices	1 to 1 1/2	3 to 5 minutes, rotating dish 1/2 turn after 2 minutes	Cook until turkey is no longer pink in center.
Rock Cornish Hens	2 to 3 (two hens)	15 to 20 minutes, turning after 10 minutes	Cook until meat thermometer reads 180° and juice of hen is no longer pink when center of thigh is cut.

About Chicken

Selecting Chicken

The variety of chicken available in the refrigerator case of the supermarket can make choosing the right chicken confusing. Use the information below to help you purchase just what you want.

When choosing chicken, keep in mind that the bigger the bird, the more meat there is in proportion to the bone. Allow about 3/4 pound (bone in) per serving.

- **Broiler-fryer:** This all-purpose chicken weighs from 3 to 3 1/2 pounds.
- **Cut-up Pieces:** Cut-up broiler-fryers and boneless chicken parts, such as breasts and thighs, will cost more per pound but offer greater convenience than cutting up your own broiler-fryer.
- **Roaster:** This chicken is a little older and larger than the broiler-fryer. It weighs 4 to 6 pounds and is so named because the older, somewhat less tender meat tastes great when roasted (that is, cooked slowly) to make it flavorful and tender.
- **Stewing**: This chicken (also referred to as *hen*) weighs 4 1/2 to 6 pounds and provides a generous amount of meat. It is a mature, less tender bird and is best cooked by simmering or using in stews and soups.
- **Rock Cornish Hen:** This small, young, specially bred chicken (also referred to as *game hen*) weighs 1 to 1 1/2 pounds and has all white meat. Allow one-half to one small hen per person. Most supermarkets carry these hens in the freezer case.

Substituting Chicken Parts

You can use your favorite chicken parts in any recipe that calls for a 3- to 3 1/2-pound cut-up broiler-fryer chicken. Substitute 2 to 2 1/2 pounds bone-in breasts, thighs, drumsticks or wings. The cooking time may be longer if the parts are thicker and meatier than the parts called for in the recipe. Remember, although breasts, thighs and drumsticks may cost more per pound than a whole bird, they have a higher yield of edible meat. If a recipe calls for 2 whole chicken breasts (about 1 1/2 pounds), you can use 1 pound boneless, skinless chicken breast halves.

How to Carve a Whole Cooked Chicken or Turkey

For best results and for safety when carving a whole chicken or turkey, use a sharp carving knife. While carving, keep the chicken or turkey from moving by holding it in place with a meat fork (long-handled with two tines). Carve on a stable cutting surface, such as a plastic cutting board or platter. Carving is easier if the bird is allowed to stand for 15 to 20 minutes after roasting. This resting period allows the juices to settle and the meat to become more firm, resulting in smoother, more uniform slices.

1. Place bird, breast up and with its legs to carver's right if right-handed or to the left if left-handed. Remove ties or skewers.

2. While gently pulling leg and thigh away from body, cut through joint between leg and body. Separate drumstick and thigh by cutting down through connecting joint. *Special note for turkey:* Remove and separate drumstick and thigh as directed above. Serve drumstick and thighs whole, or carve them. Remove meat from drumstick by slicing at an angle. Slice thigh by cutting even slices parallel to the bone.

3. Make a deep horizontal cut into breast just above wing. Insert fork in top of breast as shown and, starting halfway up breast, carve thin slices down to the horizontal cut, working upward. Repeat steps 1 through 3 on other side of bird.

Tips for Stuffing

- Traditionally, white bread is used for stuffing, but with today's appetite for new flavor combinations, you may wish to try breads such as whole grain, sourdough, rye, herb or corn bread.
- Day-old or stale bread works the best for stuffing because it is easier to cut into cubes and doesn't get as soft or compact during baking as fresh bread does.
- Allow 1/2 cup stuffing per pound of poultry when determining the amount needed for stuffing the cavity.
- Always stuff poultry just before cooking, to prevent any bacteria in the poultry from contaminating the stuffing.
- Always stuff poultry cavities loosely to allow stuffing to expand and cook thoroughly. **The center of the stuffing inside the poultry should reach 165°.**
- Spoon any extra stuffing into a greased casserole. Cover with lid or aluminum foil and refrigerate until about 30 minutes before the poultry is done. Bake covered in the same oven with the poultry about 45 minutes or until hot. (Continue to bake the stuffing while you let the poultry stand 15 minutes before carving.)
- Always remove stuffing from the cavities of cooked poultry promptly after cooking. *Do not refrigerate leftover poultry with the stuffing still inside.* If stuffing is left in the warm poultry, bacteria could grow, making the stuffing unsafe to eat. Store leftovers in separate shallow containers (less than 2 inches deep) to cool them quickly and avoid bacteria growth.

Bread Stuffing

PREP: 15 min; COOK: 5 min
Makes 10 servings, about 1/2 cup each

> 3/4 cup margarine or butter
> 2 large celery stalks (with leaves), chopped
> (1 1/2 cups)
> 3/4 cup finely chopped onion
> 9 cups soft bread cubes
> 1 1/2 teaspoons chopped fresh or
> 1/2 teaspoon dried thyme leaves
> 1 teaspoon salt
> 1/2 teaspoon ground sage
> 1/4 teaspoon pepper

1. Melt margarine in Dutch oven over medium-high heat. Cook celery and onion in margarine, stirring occasionally, until tender; remove from heat.

2. Toss celery mixture and remaining ingredients.

1 SERVING: Calories 220 (Calories from Fat 135); Fat 15g (Saturated 3g); Cholesterol 0mg; Sodium 570mg; Carbohydrate 19g (Dietary Fiber 1g); Protein 3g

---

LIGHTER BREAD STUFFING

For 6 grams of fat and 140 calories per serving, decrease margarine 1/4 cup. Heat margarine and 1/2 cup chicken broth to boiling in Dutch oven over medium-high heat. Cook celery and onion in broth mixture.

APPLE-RAISIN STUFFING: Increase salt to 1 1/2 teaspoons. Add 3 cups finely chopped apples and 3/4 cup raisins with the remaining ingredients. Makes 15 servings, 1/2 cup each.

CORN BREAD STUFFING: Substitute corn bread cubes for the soft bread cubes.

GIBLET STUFFING: Simmer heart, gizzard and neck from chicken or turkey in water seasoned with salt and pepper 1 to 2 hours or until tender. Add liver during the last 15 minutes of cooking. Drain giblets. Chop and add with the remaining ingredients. Makes 12 servings, 1/2 cup each.

MUSHROOM STUFFING: Cook 2 cups sliced mushrooms (6 ounces) with the celery and onion. Makes 10 servings, 1/2 cup each.

OYSTER STUFFING: Add 2 cans (8 ounces each) oysters, drained and chopped, or 2 cups shucked oysters, drained and chopped, with the remaining ingredients. Makes 12 servings, 1/2 cup each.

SAUSAGE STUFFING: Omit salt. Cook 1 pound bulk pork sausage in 10-inch skillet over medium heat, stirring occasionally, until no longer pink; drain, reserving drippings. Substitute drippings for part of the margarine. Add cooked sausage with the remaining ingredients. Makes 12 servings, 1/2 cup each.

Chicken Fingers, Creamy Coleslaw (page 322)

Rice Stuffing

PREP: 20 min; COOK: 5 min
Makes 8 servings, about 1/2 cup each

Mix and match any cooked rice varieties, or substitute soft-ened bulgur or kasha, cooked barley, cooked quinoa or cooked wheat berries for part or all of the cooked rice.

> 2 tablespoons margarine or butter
> 1 medium stalk celery, chopped (1/2 cup)
> 1 small onion, chopped (1/4 cup)
> 1/2 teaspoon salt
> 1/8 teaspoon pepper
> 2 cups cooked rice (page 204)
> 1/2 cup chopped walnuts
> 1/3 cup raisins
> 1/4 teaspoon paprika
> 4 slices bacon, crisply cooked and crumbled

1. Melt margarine in 10-inch skillet over medium-high heat. Cook celery, onion, salt and pepper in margarine, stirring occasionally, until vegetables are tender; remove from heat.

2. Toss celery mixture and remaining ingredients.

1 SERVING: Calories 165 (Calories from Fat 80); Fat 9g (Saturated 2g); Cholesterol 5mg; Sodium 220mg; Carbohydrate 19g (Dietary Fiber 1g); Protein 3g

FRUITED BROWN RICE STUFFING: Use brown rice. Omit raisins and paprika. Add 1/3 cup cut-up

prunes and 1/3 cup cut-up dried apricots with the remaining ingredients.

WILD RICE STUFFING: Substitute 1 cup cooked wild rice (page 204) for 1 cup of the cooked rice. Substitute pecans for the walnuts. Omit raisins and paprika.

TIMESAVING TIP

When making rice for a meal, make more than you will need. Freeze the extra rice in 2-cup amounts in airtight containers up to 6 months. To use, thaw overnight in the refrigerator, or place in microwavable container with 1 tablespoon water per cup of rice and microwave uncovered on High for 2 to 3 minutes.

Oven-Fried Chicken

PREP: 10 min; BAKE: 1 hr
Makes 6 servings

> 1/4 cup margarine or butter
> 1/2 cup all-purpose flour
> 1 teaspoon paprika
> 1/2 teaspoon salt
> 1/4 teaspoon pepper
> 3- to 3 1/2-pound cut-up broiler-fryer chicken

1. Heat oven to 425°. Melt margarine in rectangular pan, 13 × 9 × 2 inches, in oven.

2. Mix flour, paprika, salt and pepper. Coat chicken with flour mixture. Place chicken, skin sides down, in pan.

3. Bake uncovered 30 minutes. Turn chicken; bake about 30 minutes longer or until juice is no longer pink when centers of thickest pieces are cut.

1 SERVING: Calories 311 (Calories from Fat 170); Fat 19g (Saturated 5g); Cholesterol 85mg; Sodium 340mg; Carbohydrate 8g (Dietary Fiber 1g); Protein 28g

LIGHTER OVEN-FRIED CHICKEN
For 10 grams of fat and 230 calories per serving, remove skin from chicken before cooking. Do not melt margarine in pan. Spray pan with nonstick cooking spray. Decrease margarine to 2 tablespoons and drizzle over chicken after turning in step 3.

CHICKEN FINGERS: Substitute 1 1/2 pounds boneless, skinless chicken breast halves, cut crosswise into 1 1/2-inch strips. Decrease margarine to 2 tablespoons. After coating chicken with flour mixture in step 2, toss with melted margarine in pan. Bake uncovered 15 minutes. Turn strips; bake 10 to 15 minutes longer or until no longer pink in center.

CRUNCHY OVEN-FRIED CHICKEN: Substitute 1 cup cornflake crumbs for the 1/2 cup flour. Dip chicken into 1/4 cup margarine, butter or spread, melted, before coating with crumb mixture.

Spicy Jamaican Chicken and Potatoes

PREP: 15 min; BAKE: 1 1/4 hr; STAND: 15 min
Makes 6 servings

This tantalizing roast chicken borrows its flavor from traditional Jamaican seasoning. Serve it with a refreshing fruit salad to mellow the fiery flavor.

Jamaican Jerk Seasoning (page 356)
3 to 3 1/2-pound broiler-fryer chicken
2 tablespoons vegetable oil
3 medium potatoes, cut lengthwise into
    fourths

1. Prepare Jamaican Jerk Seasoning.

2. Heat oven to 375°. Line roasting pan with aluminum foil.

3. Place chicken, breast side up, on rack in roasting pan. Brush 1 tablespoon of the oil over chicken. Rub 2 tablespoons of the seasoning mix into chicken skin. Insert meat thermometer in chicken so tip is in thickest part of inside thigh muscle and does not touch bone.

4. Brush remaining 1 tablespoon oil over potatoes. Sprinkle with remaining seasoning mix. Place potatoes on rack around chicken.

5. Roast uncovered 1 to 1 1/4 hours or until potatoes are tender, thermometer reads 180° and juice of chicken is no longer pink when center of thigh is cut. Let chicken stand about 15 minutes for easiest carving.

1 SERVING: Calories 310 (Calories from Fat 145); Fat 16g (Saturated 4g); Cholesterol 85mg; Sodium 80mg; Carbohydrate 15g (Dietary Fiber 1g); Protein 28g

LIGHTER JAMAICAN CHICKEN AND POTATOES
For 13 grams of fat and 285 calories per serving, omit the 1 tablespoon oil for chicken; rub the seasoning mix directly into chicken skin. Decrease the 1 tablespoon oil for potatoes to 2 teaspoons.

Skillet-Fried Chicken

PREP: 10 min; COOK: 45 min
Makes 6 servings

1/2 cup all-purpose flour
1 teaspoon paprika
1/2 teaspoon salt
1/4 teaspoon pepper
3- to 3 1/2-pound cut-up broiler-fryer chicken
Vegetable oil

1. Mix flour, paprika, salt and pepper. Coat chicken with flour mixture.

2. Heat oil (1/4 inch) in 12-inch skillet over medium-high heat. Cook chicken in oil about 10 minutes or until light brown on all sides; reduce heat to low.

3. Cover tightly and simmer about 35 minutes, turning once or twice, until juice of chicken is no longer pink when centers of thickest pieces are cut. (If skillet cannot be covered tightly, add 1 to 2 tablespoons water. Remove cover during last 5 minutes of cooking to crisp chicken.)

1 SERVING: Calories 370 (Calories from Fat 225); Fat 25g (Saturated 5g); Cholesterol 85mg; Sodium 250mg; Carbohydrate 8g (Dietary Fiber 0g); Protein 28g

LIGHTER SKILLET-FRIED CHICKEN
For 10 grams of fat and 230 calories per serving, remove skin from chicken before cooking. Use 2 tablespoons oil and nonstick skillet in step 2.

BUTTERMILK FRIED CHICKEN: Increase flour to 1 cup, paprika to 2 teaspoons and salt to 1 teaspoon. Dip chicken into 1 cup buttermilk before coating with flour mixture.

Oven-Barbecued Chicken

PREP: 10 min; BAKE: 1 hr
Makes 6 servings

(photograph on page 417)

3- to 3 1/2-pound cut-up broiler-fryer chicken
3/4 cup chili sauce
2 tablespoons honey
2 tablespoons soy sauce
1 teaspoon ground mustard (dry)
1/2 teaspoon prepared horseradish
1/2 teaspoon red pepper sauce

1. Heat oven to 375°.

2. Place chicken, skin sides up, in ungreased rectangular pan, $13 \times 9 \times 2$ inches. Mix remaining ingredients; pour over chicken.

3. Cover and bake 30 minutes. Spoon sauce over chicken. Bake uncovered about 30 minutes longer or until juice of chicken is no longer pink when centers of thickest pieces are cut.

1 SERVING: Calories 275 (Calories from Fat 110); Fat 12g (Saturated 3g); Cholesterol 85mg; Sodium 780mg; Carbohydrate 15g (Dietary Fiber 0g); Protein 27g

> **TIMESAVING TIP**
> Omit all ingredients except chicken. Pour 1 cup purchased barbecue sauce over chicken in step 2.

Lemon-Basil Chicken

Prep: 15 min Roast: 1 1/2 hr Stand: 15 min
Makes 6 servings

(photograph on cover)

3- to 3 1/2-pound broiler-fryer chicken
1 lemon
2 tablespoons margarine or butter, melted
1 clove garlic, finely chopped
1 clove garlic, thinly sliced
1/4 cup chopped fresh or 2 teaspoons dried
    basil leaves

1. Heat oven to 375°.

2. Fold wings of chicken across back with tips touching. Tie or skewer drumsticks to tail.

3. Grate 2 teaspoons lemon peel from lemon. Mix lemon peel, margarine and chopped garlic; set aside.

4. Cut lemon in half. Rub chicken with juice from half of the lemon. Place sliced garlic, half of the basil and remaining lemon half in cavity of chicken.

5. Place chicken, breast side up, on rack in shallow roasting pan. Brush margarine mixture on chicken. Sprinkle evenly with remaining basil, then press basil into chicken. Insert meat thermometer in chicken so

tip is in thickest part of inside thigh muscle and does not touch bone.

6. Roast uncovered about 1 1/2 hours, brushing 2 or 3 times with pan drippings, until thermometer reads 180° and juice is no longer pink when center of thigh is cut. Let stand about 15 minutes for easiest carving.

1 Serving: Calories 290 (Calories from Fat 170); Fat 19g (Saturated 5g); Cholesterol 85mg; Sodium 160mg; Carbohydrate 1g; (Dietary Fiber 0g); Protein 27g.

LEMON-BASIL CHICKEN WITH VEGETABLES: After chicken has roasted 30 minutes, arrange around chicken 6 small red potatoes, cut in half, and 1 medium onion, cut into eighths. Brush vegetables with pan drippings and roast uncovered 30 minutes. Add 2 small zucchini, cut crosswise, then lengthwise into eighths; 2 small yellow squash, cut into 1/2-inch slices; and 1 large red bell pepper, cut into 1-inch chunks. Brush vegetables with pan drippings. Roast uncovered about 30 minutes longer or until chicken is done (see step 6) and squash and bell pepper are crisp-tender.

TARRAGON CHICKEN: Omit lemon, garlic and basil. Mix margarine, chopped garlic, 1 tablespoon chopped fresh or 1 teaspoon dried tarragon leaves, 3/4 teaspoon lemon pepper and 1/2 teaspoon onion powder. Brush on chicken in step 5 (omit steps 3 and 4).

> **TIMESAVING TIP**
> Omit margarine, chopped and sliced garlic and basil. Mix the 2 teaspoons lemon peel and 1/4 cup pesto. Substitute pesto for the margarine mixture in step 3. Place lemon half in cavity as directed in step 4.

Chicken Paprikash

PREP: 15 min; COOK: 1 hr
Makes 6 servings

2 tablespoons vegetable oil
3- to 3 1/2-pound cut-up broiler-fryer chicken
2 medium onions, chopped (1 cup)
1 clove garlic, finely chopped
1/2 cup chicken broth
2 tablespoons paprika
1 teaspoon salt
1/4 teaspoon pepper
1 medium tomato, chopped (3/4 cup)
1 green bell pepper, cut into 1/2-inch strips
1 cup sour cream

1. Heat oil in 12-inch skillet over medium heat. Cook chicken in oil about 15 minutes or until brown on all sides; remove chicken from skillet.

2. Cook onions and garlic in oil in skillet over medium heat about 3 minutes, stirring occasionally, until onions are crisp-tender; drain oil from skillet.

3. Stir broth, paprika, salt, pepper and tomato into onion mixture in skillet; loosen brown particles from bottom of skillet. Return chicken to skillet. Heat to boiling; reduce heat to low. Cover and simmer 20 minutes.

4. Stir in bell pepper. Cover and simmer 10 to 15 minutes longer or until juice of chicken is no longer pink when centers of thickest pieces are cut. Remove chicken from skillet; keep warm.

5. Skim fat from liquid in skillet. Stir sour cream into liquid in skillet. Heat over medium heat just until hot. Serve with chicken.

1 SERVING: Calories 360 (Calories from Fat 215); Fat 24g (Saturated 9g); Cholesterol 110mg; Sodium 510mg; Carbohydrate 8g (Dietary Fiber 1g); Protein 29g

---

LIGHTER CHICKEN PAPRIKASH

For 14 grams of fat and 265 calories per serving, omit oil and use nonstick skillet sprayed with nonstick cooking spray. Remove skin from chicken before cooking. Use reduced-fat sour cream.

Chicken Cacciatore

PREP: 20 min; COOK: 1 hr
Makes 6 servings

Slash time from the preparation of this dish by substituting 2 cups prepared spaghetti sauce for the whole tomatoes, tomato sauce, oregano, basil and salt.

3- to 3 1/2-pound cut-up broiler-fryer chicken
1/2 cup all-purpose flour
1/4 cup vegetable oil
1 medium green bell pepper
2 medium onions
2 cloves garlic, crushed
1 can (16 ounces) whole tomatoes, drained
1 can (8 ounces) tomato sauce
1 cup sliced mushrooms (3 ounces)*
1 1/2 teaspoons chopped fresh or
　　1/2 teaspoon dried oregano leaves
1 teaspoon chopped fresh or 1/4 teaspoon
　　dried basil leaves
1/2 teaspoon salt
Grated Parmesan cheese

1. Coat chicken with flour.

2. Heat oil in 12-inch skillet over medium-high heat. Cook chicken in oil 15 to 20 minutes or until brown on all sides; drain.

3. Cut bell pepper and onions crosswise in half; cut each half into fourths. Stir bell pepper, onions and remaining ingredients except cheese into chicken in skillet, breaking up tomatoes. Heat to boiling; reduce heat. Cover and simmer 30 to 40 minutes or until juice

of chicken is no longer pink when centers of thickest pieces are cut. Serve with cheese.

*1 can (4 ounces) sliced mushrooms, drained, can be substituted for the fresh mushrooms.

1 SERVING: Calories 330 (Calories from Fat 145); Fat 16g (Saturated 4g); Cholesterol 75mg; Sodium 730mg; Carbohydrate 19g (Dietary Fiber 3g); Protein 30g

---

LIGHTER CHICKEN CACCIATORE

For 12 grams of fat and 290 calories per serving, remove skin from chicken before cooking. Decrease oil to 2 tablespoons and use nonstick skillet.

Stir-Fried Sweet-and-Sour Chicken

PREP: 20 min; COOK: 10 min
Makes 5 servings, about 1 cup each

1 can (15 1/4 ounces) pineapple chunks in
　　juice, drained and 1/3 cup juice reserved
1 tablespoon cornstarch
3 tablespoons white vinegar
1 tablespoon honey
1 tablespoon vegetable oil
1 pound boneless, skinless chicken breast
　　halves, cut into 3/4-inch pieces
1 tablespoon vegetable oil
1 medium green bell pepper, cut into
　　3/4-inch pieces
1 medium onion, sliced
2 medium carrots, coarsely shredded
　　(1 1/4 cups)

1. Mix reserved 1/3 cup pineapple juice, the cornstarch, vinegar and honey.

2. Heat wok or 12-inch skillet over high heat. Add 1 tablespoon oil; rotate wok to coat side. Add chicken; stir-fry about 4 minutes or until no longer pink in center. Remove chicken from wok; keep warm.

3. Add 1 tablespoon oil to wok; rotate wok to coat side. Add bell pepper and onion; stir-fry 1 minute.

4. Add cornstarch mixture and carrots to wok. Cook and stir about 1 minute until sauce thickens.

5. Stir in pineapple and chicken; cook until hot.

1 SERVING: Calories 240 (Calories from Fat 70); Fat 8g (Saturated 2g); Cholesterol 50mg; Sodium 60mg; Carbohydrate 25g (Dietary Fiber 3g); Protein 20g

---

TIMESAVING TIP

Omit pineapple juice, cornstarch, vinegar and honey. Omit steps 1 and 4. Add 1/2 cup purchased sweet-and-sour sauce and the carrots in step 5.

Stuffed Chicken Breasts

Stuffed Chicken Breasts

PREP: 20 min; BAKE: 55 min
Makes 4 servings

Stuffing chicken breasts is a beautiful way to dress up chicken. Not only do the stuffings add color, they are delicious as well!

> **4 chicken breast halves (about 1 1/4 pounds)**
> **Apple-Hazelnut Stuffing, Pesto-Couscous**
>   **Stuffing or Smoked Gouda-Spinach**
>   **Stuffing (right)**
> **1/2 teaspoon salt**
> **1/4 teaspoon pepper**
> **2 teaspoons margarine or butter**

1. Heat oven to 375°. Grease square pan, $9 \times 9 \times 2$ inches, with shortening.

2. Remove bones from chicken breasts. Do not remove skin.

3. Loosen skin from chicken breasts (see illustration, page 303).

4. Prepare desired stuffing.

5. Spread one-fourth of the stuffing evenly between meat and skin of each chicken breast. Smooth skin over breasts, tucking under loose areas. Place chicken, skin sides up, in pan. Sprinkle with salt and pepper. Drizzle with margarine.

6. Bake uncovered 45 to 55 minutes or until juice of chicken is no longer pink when centers of thickest pieces are cut.

Apple-Hazelnut Stuffing

> **1/4 cup chopped hazelnuts**
> **1 medium apple, chopped (1 cup)**
> **1 package (3 ounces) cream cheese, softened**

Mix all ingredients.

Pesto-Couscous Stuffing

> **1/2 cup chicken broth**
> **1/3 cup uncooked couscous**
> **1/4 cup pesto**

Heat broth to boiling in 1-quart saucepan. Stir in couscous; remove from heat. Cover and let stand 5 minutes. Fluff couscous with fork. Stir in pesto.

Smoked Gouda-Spinach Stuffing

> **1/2 cup shredded smoked Gouda or Swiss**
>   **cheese (2 ounces)**
> **1/4 teaspoon ground nutmeg**
> **1 package (10 ounces) frozen chopped**
>   **spinach, thawed and squeezed to drain**

Mix all ingredients.

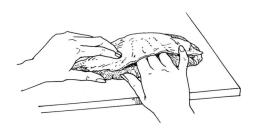

a. Insert fingers between skin and flesh; gently separate in center but leave skin attached at ends.

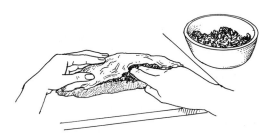

b. Push stuffing between skin and meat evenly with fingers.

1 SERVING: Calories 355 (Calories from Fat 205); Fat 23g (Saturated 8g); Cholesterol 100mg; Sodium 420mg; Carbohydrate 7g (Dietary Fiber 1g); Protein 31g

Oven Chicken Kiev

PREP: 20 min; FREEZE: 30 min; BAKE: 35 min
Makes 6 servings

> 1/4 cup margarine or butter
> 1 tablespoon chopped fresh chives or parsley
> 1 clove garlic, finely chopped
> 6 skinless, boneless chicken breast halves
>   (about 1 1/2 pounds)
> 3 cups cornflakes, crushed (1 1/2 cups)
> 2 tablespoons chopped fresh parsley
> 1/2 teaspoon paprika
> 1/4 cup buttermilk or milk

1. Mix margarine, chives and garlic. Shape mixture into rectangle, 3 × 2 inches. Cover and freeze about 30 minutes or until firm.

2. Heat oven to 425°. Grease square pan, 9 × 9 × 2 inches, with shortening.

3. Flatten each chicken breast half to 1/4-inch thickness between plastic wrap or waxed paper.

4. Cut margarine mixture crosswise into 6 pieces. Place 1 piece on center of each chicken breast half. Fold long sides of chicken over margarine. Fold ends up and secure with toothpick.

5. Mix cornflakes, parsley and paprika. Dip chicken into buttermilk, then coat evenly with corn-flake mixture. Place chicken, seam sides down, in pan.

6. Bake uncovered about 35 minutes or until juice of chicken is no longer pink when centers of thickest pieces are cut. Remove toothpicks.

1 SERVING: Calories 265 (Calories from Fat 100); Fat 11g (Saturated 3g); Cholesterol 70mg; Sodium 300mg; Carbohydrate 13g (Dietary Fiber 0g); Protein 28g

OVEN CHICKEN CORDON BLEU: Omit margarine, chives, garlic and step 1. For step 4, place 1 thin slice fully cooked smoked ham and 1 thin slice Swiss cheese on each piece of chicken. Roll up carefully, beginning at narrow end; secure with toothpick.

Cashew Chicken

PREP: 20 min; COOK: 10 min
Makes 4 servings, about 1 cup each

> 1/3 cup chicken broth
> 1 tablespoon cornstarch
> 3 tablespoons soy sauce
> 1/2 teaspoon ground ginger
> 1/2 teaspoon red pepper sauce
> 2 tablespoons vegetable oil
> 1 pound boneless, skinless chicken breast
>   halves, cut crosswise into 1/2-inch strips
> 1 large green bell pepper, cut into 3/4-inch
>   pieces
> 1 medium onion, sliced
> 1 can (8 ounces) sliced water chestnuts,
>   drained
> 2/3 cup dry-roasted cashews
> 2 green onions, sliced

1. Mix broth, cornstarch, soy sauce, ginger and pepper sauce.

2. Heat wok or 12-inch skillet over high heat. Add 1 tablespoon of the oil; rotate wok to coat side. Add chicken; stir-fry about 4 minutes or until no longer pink in center. Remove chicken from wok; keep warm.

3. Add remaining 1 tablespoon oil to wok; rotate wok to coat side. Add bell pepper, onion and water chestnuts; stir-fry 2 minutes.

4. Add cornstarch mixture to wok. Cook and stir about 1 minute or until sauce thickens. Stir in chicken and cashews. Garnish with green onions.

1 SERVING: Calories 375 (Calories from Fat 190); Fat 21g (Saturated 4g); Cholesterol 60mg; Sodium 1050mg; Carbohydrate 20g (Dietary Fiber 3g); Protein 30g

---

LIGHTER CASHEW CHICKEN

For 12 grams of fat and 275 calories per serving, decrease oil to 1 tablespoon. (Use half of the oil in step 2 and remaining half in step 3.) Decrease cashews to 1/3 cup.

Chicken Curry

PREP: 1 hr 20 min; COOK: 40 min
Makes 8 servings, about 1 1/2 cups each

Serve various toppings with your curry and let folks help themselves. Try chopped peanuts, chopped green onions, chopped cilantro, shredded coconut and mandarin orange sections.

2 tablespoons vegetable oil
2 1/2 pounds chicken breast halves or thighs
1/2 teaspoon salt
1 medium onion, chopped (1/2 cup)
2 tablespoons water
1 cup sour cream
2 teaspoons curry powder
1/8 teaspoon ground ginger
1/8 teaspoon ground cumin
1/2 cup Papaya-Apricot Chutney (page 359)
   or prepared chutney
6 cups hot cooked rice (page 204)

1. Heat oil in 12-inch skillet or Dutch oven over medium heat. Cook chicken in oil about 15 minutes, turning occasionally, until brown on all sides. Drain fat from skillet.

2. Sprinkle chicken with salt. Add onion and water to chicken in skillet. Heat to boiling; reduce heat. Cover and simmer about 20 minutes or until juice of chicken is no longer pink when centers of thickest pieces are cut.

3. Remove chicken from skillet; keep warm. Pour liquid from skillet into bowl; skim off fat.

4. Return 1/4 cup liquid to skillet (discard remaining liquid). Stir in sour cream, curry powder, ginger and cumin. Heat, stirring constantly, just until hot.

5. Pour sauce over chicken. Serve chicken with Papaya-Apricot Chutney and rice.

1 SERVING: Calories 440 (Calories from Fat 155); Fat 17g (Saturated 7g); Cholesterol 80mg; Sodium 210mg; Carbohydrate 47g (Dietary Fiber 1g); Protein 26g

---

LIGHTER CHICKEN CURRY

For 5 grams of fat and 355 calories per serving, remove skin from chicken before cooking. Omit oil; spray cold skillet with nonstick cooking spray. Use reduced-fat sour cream.

LAMB CURRY: Substitute 2 1/2 pounds lamb shoulder chops for the chicken. Increase cooking time in step 2 to 45 to 60 minutes or until lamb is tender.

Spicy Peanut Chicken

Spicy Peanut Chicken

PREP: 20 min; COOK: 5 min
Makes 4 servings, about 1 cup each

Fresh gingerroot can be covered tightly and frozen for up to four months. Grate it straight from the freezer as needed if you don't use it very often.

1/4 cup chicken broth
1 tablespoon cornstarch
1 tablespoon sugar
2 tablespoons soy sauce
1 tablespoon white vinegar
1/4 teaspoon ground red pepper (cayenne)
1 tablespoon vegetable oil
1 pound boneless, skinless chicken thighs, cut into 3/4-inch pieces
1 clove garlic, finely chopped
1 teaspoon grated gingerroot
1 medium red bell pepper, cut into 3/4-inch pieces
1/3 cup dry-roasted peanuts
2 green onions, sliced

1. Mix broth, cornstarch, sugar, soy sauce, vinegar and red pepper.

2. Heat wok or 12-inch skillet over high heat. Add oil; rotate wok to coat side. Add chicken, garlic and gingerroot; stir-fry about 3 minutes or until chicken is no longer pink in center.

3. Add bell pepper to wok; stir-fry 1 minute.

4. Add cornstarch mixture to wok. Cook and stir about 1 minute or until sauce thickens. Stir in peanuts. Garnish with onions.

1 SERVING: Calories 305 (Calories from Fat 155); Fat 17g (Saturated 4g); Cholesterol 75mg; Sodium 690mg; Carbohydrate 11g (Dietary Fiber 1g); Protein 28g

---

LIGHTER SPICY PEANUT CHICKEN
For 10 grams of fat and 225 calories per serving, omit oil and spray wok with nonstick cooking spray before heating. Decrease peanuts to 2 tablespoons; sprinkle peanuts over finished dish instead of stirring in.

Chicken à la King

PREP: 20 min; COOK: 10 min
Makes 6 servings, about 1 1/2 cups each

If you use the canned mushrooms, add the mushroom liquid with the milk in step 2 for a little extra flavor.

1/2 cup margarine or butter
1 small green bell pepper, chopped (1/2 cup)
1 cup sliced mushrooms (3 ounces)*
1/2 cup all-purpose flour
1/2 teaspoon salt
1/4 teaspoon pepper
1 1/2 cups milk
1 1/4 cups chicken broth
2 cups cut-up cooked chicken or turkey
1 jar (2 ounces) diced pimientos, drained
3 cups hot cooked rice or 12 toasted bread triangles

1. Melt margarine in 3-quart saucepan over medium-high heat. Cook bell pepper and mushrooms in margarine, stirring occasionally, until bell pepper is crisp-tender.

2. Stir in flour, salt and pepper. Cook over medium heat, stirring constantly, until bubbly; remove from heat. Stir in milk and broth. Heat to boiling, stirring constantly. Boil and stir 1 minute. Stir in chicken and pimientos; cook until hot. Serve over rice.

*1 can (4 ounces) mushroom stems and pieces, drained, can be substituted for the fresh mushrooms.

1 SERVING: Calories 395 (Calories from Fat 180); Fat 20g (Saturated 5g); Cholesterol 45mg; Sodium 590mg; Carbohydrate 35g (Dietary Fiber 1g); Protein 20g

TUNA À LA KING: Substitute 1 can (12 1/2 ounces) tuna, drained, for the chicken.

Chicken Pot Pie

PREP: 40 min; BAKE: 35 min
Makes 6 servings, about 1 cup each

   1 package (10 ounces) frozen peas and
     carrots
   1/3 cup margarine or butter
   1/3 cup all-purpose flour
   1/3 cup chopped onion
   1/2 teaspoon salt
   1/4 teaspoon pepper
   1 3/4 cups chicken broth
   2/3 cup milk
   2 1/2 to 3 cups cut-up cooked chicken
     or turkey
   Pastry for 9-Inch Two-Crust Pie (page 93)

1. Rinse frozen peas and carrots in cold water to separate; drain.

2. Melt margarine in 2-quart saucepan over medium heat. Stir in flour, onion, salt and pepper. Cook, stirring constantly, until mixture is bubbly; remove from heat. Stir in broth and milk. Heat to boiling, stirring constantly. Boil and stir 1 minute. Stir in chicken and peas and carrots; remove from heat.

3. Heat oven to 425°.

4. Prepare pastry. Roll two-thirds of the pastry into 13-inch square. Ease into ungreased square pan, 9 × 9 × 2 inches. Pour chicken mixture into pastry-lined pan.

5. Roll remaining pastry into 11-inch square. Cut out designs with 1-inch cookie cutter. Place square over chicken mixture. Arrange cutouts on pastry. Turn edges of pastry under and flute. (See page 96 for fluting directions.)

6. Bake about 35 minutes or until golden brown.

1 SERVING: Calories 640 (Calories from Fat 380); Fat 42g (Saturated 11g); Cholesterol 50mg; Sodium 970mg; Carbohydrate 44g (Dietary Fiber 4g); Protein 26g

---

LIGHTER CHICKEN POT PIE

For 24 grams of fat and 410 calories per serving, decrease margarine to 3 tablespoons and use skim milk. Grease square pan, 9 × 9 × 2 inches, with shortening. Pour chicken mixture into greased pan (not pastry-lined). Substitute Pastry for 9-inch One-Crust Pie (page 93) for the Pastry for 9-inch Two-Crust Pie; use pastry for top crust in step 5.

TUNA POT PIE: Substitute 1 can (12 1/2 ounces) tuna, drained, for the chicken.

Chicken-Rice Casserole

PREP: 20 min; BAKE: 45 min
Makes 6 servings, about 1 cup each

For a crunchy topping, don't mix the almonds in with the other ingredients. Instead, sprinkle the almonds over the casserole 10 minutes before it's done baking.

   1/4 cup margarine or butter
   1/3 cup all-purpose flour
   3/4 teaspoon salt
   1/8 teaspoon pepper
   1 1/2 cups milk
   1 cup chicken broth
   2 cups cut-up cooked chicken
   1 1/2 cups cooked white rice
   3 ounces mushrooms, sliced (about 1 cup)*
   1/3 cup chopped green bell pepper
   1/4 cup slivered almonds
   2 tablespoons chopped pimientos

1. Heat oven to 350°.

2. Melt margarine in 2-quart saucepan over medium heat. Stir in flour, salt and pepper. Cook, stirring constantly, until bubbly; remove from heat. Stir in milk and broth. Heat to boiling, stirring constantly. Boil and stir 1 minute. Stir in remaining ingredients.

3. Pour into ungreased 2-quart casserole or square baking dish, 8 × 8 × 2 inches. Bake uncovered 40 to 45 minutes or until bubbly. Garnish with parsley sprig if desired.

*1 can (4 ounces) mushroom stems and pieces, drained, can be substituted for the fresh mushrooms.

1 SERVING: Calories 300 (Calories from Fat 135); Fat 15g (Saturated 4g); Cholesterol 45mg; Sodium 550mg; Carbohydrate 22g (Dietary Fiber 1g); Protein 19g

TUNA-RICE CASSEROLE: Substitute 1 can (12 1/2 ounces) tuna, drained, for the chicken.

TURKEY-WILD RICE CASSEROLE: Substitute 2 cups cut-up cooked turkey for the chicken, and wild rice for the white rice.

Honey-Poppy Seed Cornish Hens, Curried Vegetables with Ziti (page 280)

Honey-Poppy Seed Cornish Hens

PREP: 15 min; BAKE: 1 hr 10 min
Makes 4 servings

Cutting the hens in half is easy and quick when you use poultry or kitchen scissors.

   2 Rock Cornish hens (24 ounces each)
   1/2 teaspoon salt
   1/2 teaspoon pepper
   1/3 cup honey
   1 tablespoon poppy seed
   1 1/2 teaspoons ground mustard (dry)
   3/4 teaspoon ground ginger

1. Heat oven to 350°. Spray rack of shallow roasting pan with nonstick cooking spray.

2. Cut each hen in half along backbone and breastbone from tail to neck with kitchen scissors. Place skin sides down on rack in roasting pan. Sprinkle with salt and pepper. Mix remaining ingredients; brush over both sides of hens. Insert meat thermometer so tip is in thickest part of inside thigh muscle and does not touch bone.

3. Roast uncovered 1 hour to 1 hour 10 minutes, turning once, until thermometer reads 180° and juice of hens is no longer pink when center of thigh is cut.

1 SERVING: Calories 440 (Calories from Fat 170); Fat 19g (Saturated 5g); Cholesterol 130mg; Sodium 380mg; Carbohydrate 24g (Dietary Fiber 0g); Protein 43g

About Turkey

Turkey isn't just for Thanksgiving anymore! With today's variety of convenient turkey cuts and turkey products, you can eat turkey for any meal.

Whole ready-to-cook turkeys can range in size from 4 to 24 pounds. Whether you buy them fresh or frozen, the quality will be the same. Whole frozen turkeys can be stored in your freezer at 0° for up to one year. Fresh whole turkeys should be used within one to two days after purchasing. Allow about 1 pound of turkey (bone in) per serving.

Fresh turkey breasts, wings, drumsticks, boneless breasts, breast slices, tenderloins and ground turkey are popular turkey selections available in many supermarkets. Also available are turkey deli products, such as turkey sausage, salami, pastrami and hot dogs. Also see About Poultry, page 290; Roasting Poultry, page 293; Broiling or Grilling Poultry, page 294; Microwaving Poultry, page 295; and How to Carve a Whole Cooked Chicken or Turkey, page 296.

Turkey with Asparagus

PREP: 15 min; COOK: 10 min
Makes 4 servings, about 1 1/4 cups each

1/4 cup chicken broth or water
1 tablespoon lemon juice
2 teaspoons cornstarch
1 teaspoon soy sauce
1/2 teaspoon salt
3/4 pound asparagus
1 tablespoon vegetable oil
1 pound 1/2-inch-thick slices cooked turkey*
1 clove garlic, finely chopped
1 tablespoon vegetable oil
1 jar (2 ounces) sliced pimientos

1. Mix broth, lemon juice, cornstarch, soy sauce and salt.

2. Prepare asparagus as directed on page 394; cut into 1-inch pieces.

3. Heat wok or 12-inch skillet over high heat. Add 1 tablespoon oil; rotate wok to coat side. Add turkey and garlic; stir-fry about 3 minutes or until turkey is no longer pink in center. Remove turkey from wok; keep warm.

4. Add 1 tablespoon oil to wok; rotate wok to coat side. Add asparagus; stir-fry about 2 minutes or until crisp-tender.

5. Add pimientos and cornstarch mixture to wok. Cook and stir about 1 minute or until sauce thickens. Stir in turkey.

1 pound cooked boneless, skinless chicken breast, cut crosswise into 1/2-inch strips, can be substituted for the turkey slices.

1 SERVING: Calories 270 (Calories from Fat 110); Fat 12g (Saturated 2g); Cholesterol 85mg; Sodium 490mg; Carbohydrate 5g (Dietary Fiber 1g); Protein 36g

---

TIMESAVING TIP
1 package (10 ounces) frozen cut asparagus, thawed, can be substituted for the fresh asparagus.

Turkey with Creamy Salsa

PREP: 15 min; COOK: 10 min
Makes 4 servings, about 1 cup each

You can vary the spiciness of the sauce by using mild, medium or hot salsa.

2 tablespoons margarine or butter
1 pound turkey breast slices
1/4 teaspoon salt
1/4 teaspoon pepper
1/2 cup salsa
2 teaspoons soy sauce
2 teaspoons lime juice
1 clove garlic, finely chopped
1/2 cup sour cream
2 green onions, sliced

1. Melt 1 tablespoon of the margarine in 12-inch skillet over medium-high heat. Sprinkle both sides of turkey with salt and pepper. Cook half of the turkey in margarine about 3 minutes, turning once, until no longer pink in center. Remove turkey from skillet; keep warm. Repeat with remaining margarine and turkey.

2. Stir salsa, soy sauce, lime juice and garlic into skillet. Heat to boiling, stirring constantly; remove from heat. Stir in sour cream. Pour sauce over turkey. Garnish with onions.

1 SERVING: Calories 300 (Calories from Fat 145); Fat 16g (Saturated 6g); Cholesterol 105mg; Sodium 670mg; Carbohydrate 4g (Dietary Fiber 1g); Protein 36g

Turkey Tenderloins with Caramelized Onions

PREP: 20 min; COOK: 1 hr 10 min
Makes 6 servings

(photograph on page 289)

> 1 teaspoon vegetable oil
> 2 turkey breast tenderloins (about 1 1/2 pounds)
> 3/4 teaspoon salt
> 1/4 teaspoon pepper
> 1/3 cup dry white wine or chicken broth
> 2 tablespoons margarine, butter or spread
> 4 large onions, thinly sliced (4 cups)
> 1 tablespoon packed brown sugar
> 1/2 teaspoon chopped fresh or 1/4 teaspoon dried thyme leaves
> 1/4 teaspoon pepper

1. Heat oil in 12-inch skillet over medium-high heat. Sprinkle both sides of turkey with salt and 1/4 teaspoon pepper. Cook turkey in oil about 5 minutes, turning once, until brown on both sides.

2. Pour wine into skillet; reduce heat to low. Cover and simmer 30 to 40 minutes or until juice of turkey is no longer pink when centers of thickest pieces are cut. Remove turkey from skillet; keep warm.

3. Melt margarine in skillet over medium-high heat. Cook onions in margarine 5 minutes, stirring frequently; reduce heat to medium. Stir in brown sugar, thyme and 1/4 teaspoon pepper. Cook 15 to 20 minutes, stirring occasionally, until onions are golden brown.

4. Slice turkey. Serve turkey with onions.

1 SERVING: Calories 210 (Calories from Fat 70); Fat 8g (Saturated 2g); Cholesterol 65mg; Sodium 380mg; Carbohydrate 9g (Dietary Fiber 1g); Protein 27g

TIMESAVING TIP
Omit wine. Use 1 pound turkey breast slices. Cook as directed in step 1—except increase cooking time to 10 to 12 minutes, turning once, until turkey is no longer pink in center. Omit step 2.

Lemon-Roasted Turkey Breast with Couscous Stuffing

PREP: 35 min; BAKE: 1 1/2 hr; STAND: 15 min
Makes 8 servings

Couscous is a tiny pasta made from semolina wheat and has a granular texture similar to rice. Easy to prepare, couscous is versatile because it lends itself so well to other flavors.

> 2- to 2 1/2-pound bone-in turkey breast half
> 2 teaspoons olive or vegetable oil
> 1/2 teaspoon grated lemon peel
> 1 teaspoon lemon juice
> 1/4 teaspoon salt
> 1/8 teaspoon pepper
> 1 clove garlic, finely chopped
> Couscous Stuffing (below)

1. Heat oven to 350°.

2. Place turkey breast, skin side up, to one side in ungreased roasting pan, $13 \times 9 \times 2$ inches. Mix oil, lemon peel, lemon juice, salt, pepper and garlic; brush over turkey. Insert meat thermometer so tip is in thickest part of turkey breast and does not touch bone.

3. Prepare Couscous Stuffing. Spoon stuffing into other side of roasting pan, shaping into a mound, about $9 \times 5 \times 2$ inches. Cover pan tightly with aluminum foil.

4. Bake 45 minutes. Fold foil back from turkey breast, leaving foil over stuffing.

5. Bake 30 to 45 minutes longer or until thermometer reads 170° and juice of turkey is no longer pink when center is cut. Let stand 15 minutes for easiest carving. Slice turkey breast. Serve with stuffing.

Couscous Stuffing

> 1 1/2 cups boiling water
> 1 cup uncooked couscous
> 1/2 cup raisins
> 1/4 cup slivered almonds
> 1/3 cup chicken broth
> 2 tablespoons chopped fresh parsley
> 1 medium carrot, shredded

Pour boiling water over couscous in medium bowl. Cover and let stand about 5 minutes or until water is absorbed. Add remaining ingredients; toss.

1 SERVING: Calories 305 (Calories from Fat 100); Fat 11g (Saturated 3g); Cholesterol 65mg; Sodium 160mg; Carbohydrate 27g (Dietary Fiber 2g); Protein 27g

Turkey Meatballs in Tangy Cranberry Sauce

PREP: 20 min; COOK: 25 min
Makes 4 servings, 5 meatballs each

Meatballs (page 239), made with ground beef, also can be used for this zesty recipe.

> Turkey or Chicken Meatballs (page 240)
> 1 can (8 ounces) whole berry cranberry sauce
> 1 can (8 ounces) tomato sauce
> 2 tablespoons prepared horseradish
> 1 tablespoon Worcestershire sauce
> 1 tablespoon lemon juice

1. Mix ingredients for Turkey or Chicken Meatballs. Shape mixture into twenty 1 1/2-inch meatballs.

2. Cook meatballs in 10-inch skillet over medium-high heat about 10 minutes, turning occasionally, until brown.

3. Stir remaining ingredients into skillet with meatballs. Heat to boiling; reduce heat to low. Simmer uncovered about 10 minutes, stirring occasionally, until meatballs are no longer pink in center.

1 SERVING: Calories 385 (Calories from Fat 125); Fat 14g (Saturated 4g); Cholesterol 130mg; Sodium 880mg; Carbohydrate 40g (Dietary Fiber 2g); Protein 27g

---

TIMESAVING TIP
Cook meatballs in advance, then freeze. Or purchase frozen meatballs. (Frozen meatballs are best when used within one month.) Add frozen meatballs to sauce and simmer 15 to 20 minutes or until heated through.

Turkey Divan

PREP: 35 min; BROIL: 5 min
Makes 6 servings

Don't wait until you have Thanksgiving leftovers to make this recipe! Purchase 6 large slices of turkey (sliced about 1/4 inch thick) from the deli if you don't have leftover cooked turkey.

> 1 1/2 pounds broccoli*
> 1/4 cup margarine or butter
> 1/4 cup all-purpose flour
> 1/8 teaspoon ground nutmeg
> 1 1/2 cups chicken broth
> 1/2 cup grated Parmesan cheese
> 2 tablespoons dry white wine or chicken broth
> 1/2 cup whipping (heavy) cream
> 6 large slices cooked turkey breast, 1/4 inch thick (3/4 pound)
> 1/2 cup grated Parmesan cheese

1. Prepare and cook broccoli as directed for spears on page 395.

2. Melt margarine in 1-quart saucepan over medium heat. Stir in flour and nutmeg. Cook, stirring constantly, until smooth and bubbly; remove from heat. Stir in broth. Heat to boiling, stirring constantly. Boil and stir 1 minute; remove from heat. Stir in 1/2 cup cheese and the wine.

3. Beat whipping cream in chilled small bowl on high speed until stiff. Fold cheese sauce into whipped cream.

4. Place hot broccoli in ungreased rectangular baking dish, 11 × 7 × 1 1/2 inches. Top with turkey. Pour cheese sauce over turkey. Sprinkle with 1/2 cup cheese.

5. Set oven control to Broil.

6. Broil with top 3 to 5 inches from heat, about 3 minutes, or until cheese is bubbly and light brown.

*2 packages (10 ounces each) frozen broccoli spears, cooked and drained, can be substituted for the fresh broccoli.

1 SERVING: Calories 325 (Calories from Fat 190); Fat 21g (Saturated 9g); Cholesterol 75mg; Sodium 600mg; Carbohydrate 9g (Dietary Fiber 2g); Protein 27g

---

LIGHTER TURKEY DIVAN
For 14 grams of fat and 270 calories per serving, substitute 1/2 cup evaporated skimmed milk for the whipping cream (do not beat in step 3); stir into cheese sauce. Decrease Parmesan cheese in step 4 to 1/4 cup.

CHICKEN DIVAN: Substitute 3/4 pound sliced cooked chicken for the turkey.

Duckling with Orange Sauce

Duckling with Orange Sauce

**PREP: 20 min; ROAST: 2 1/2 hr; COOK: 5 min;
STAND: 15 min
Makes 4 servings**

Piercing the skin of the duckling releases much of the unwanted fat. Using a fork, pierce the skin all over, especially at the breast, but do not pierce the flesh.

4- to 5-pound duckling
2 teaspoons grated orange peel
1/2 cup orange juice
1/4 cup currant jelly
1 tablespoon lemon juice
1/8 teaspoon ground mustard (dry)
1/8 teaspoon salt
1 tablespoon cold water
1 1/2 teaspoons cornstarch
1 orange, peeled and sectioned
1 tablespoon orange-flavored liqueur, if
   desired

1. Heat oven to 350°.

2. Fasten neck skin of duckling to back with skewer. Fold wings across back with tips touching. Place duckling, breast side up, on rack in shallow roasting pan. Pierce skin all over with fork. Loosely tie legs to the tail with string, if desired, to better hold even shape during cooking. Insert meat thermometer so tip is in thickest part of inside thigh muscle and does not touch bone.

3. Roast uncovered about 2 1/2 hours or until thermometer reads 180° and juice is no longer pink when center of thigh is cut. Place tent of aluminum foil loosely over breast during last hour to prevent excessive browning. Place duckling on heated platter. Let stand 15 minutes for easier carving.

4. Heat orange peel, orange juice, jelly, lemon juice, mustard and salt to boiling in 1-quart saucepan. Mix water and cornstarch; stir into sauce. Cook over medium heat, stirring constantly, until mixture thickens and boils. Boil and stir 1 minute.

5. Stir in orange sections and liqueur. Brush duckling with some of the orange sauce. Serve with remaining sauce.

1 SERVING: Calories 665 (Calories from Fat 450); Fat 50g (Saturated 17g); Cholesterol 150mg; Sodium 180mg; Carbohydrate 21g (Dietary Fiber 1g); Protein 34g

About Salads

The word *salad* is derived from the word *salt*, since all salads were once only edible herbs and plant leaves seasoned with salt. The definition of a salad has expanded significantly to include an array of greens, vegetables, fruits, pastas, meats and cheeses, and other foods, served with any one of a variety of moist dressings. Salads can be served as an appetizer, an accompaniment, a main dish and even dessert!

- **Appetizer** salads are usually light and tangy to stimulate the appetite for the main meal to follow. An easy favorite is mixed greens with a simple vinaigrette dressing, to which vegetables or fruits are sometimes added for flavor and texture. Marinated vegetable salads are often served as appetizers and also featured in salad bars.
- **Accompaniment salads** are usually a heartier combination of greens, vegetables, cooked pasta or rice, gelatin and fruits. Dressings range from light vinaigrettes to heavier creamy types.
- **Dessert salads** are usually a combination of fruits with nuts or cheese added. A sweet light dressing or one based on whipping cream or sour cream is usually added.
- **Main-dish salads** are a cold version of a hot main-dish mixture and are served in larger amounts than the other salads. They include adequate amounts of protein such as cooked meat, poultry, seafood, eggs, cheese and beans, along with the other ingredients in accompaniment salads.

Storing and Handling Salad Greens

- Store greens in the refrigerator until needed. You can keep them in the original wrap, or place in a plastic bag. Store in the crisper section of your refrigerator. Wash them when ready to use.
- Be sure to wash greens thoroughly in several changes of cold water, then shake off excess moisture. For greens that may be sandy, such as

spinach, separate the leaves with your fingers to remove all grit. Toss in a cloth towel, gently blot dry or use a salad spinner to remove excess moisture. Refrigerate unused washed greens in a sealed plastic bag or bowl with an airtight lid.
- Romaine and iceberg lettuce will keep up to one week. Most other greens will wilt within a few days of purchasing.
- If you plan to use iceberg lettuce within a day or two, remove the core before washing by striking the core end against a flat surface, then twisting and lifting out core. Hold the head, cored end up, under running cold water to separate and clean leaves. Turn right side up and drain thoroughly. Refrigerate in a sealed plastic bag or bowl with an airtight lid.

Selecting Salad Greens

Choosing salad greens is the first step in creating a tossed salad or main-dish salad. Greens also can be mixed with fruit or vegetables to add color and texture, and they can be used to line a plate or bowl for serving a fruit, vegetable or main-dish salad. Knowing the different types of greens available helps when selecting greens and allows you more variety when preparing salads. Some greens tend to have a "bite" or be bitter—taste greens before adding to salads, as they may taste better cooked and served as a vegetable. See Salad Greens Glossary, page 315. Be sure to purchase fresh crisp greens. Avoid limp or bruised greens and those with rust spots.

Salad Greens Glossary

Arugula (or rocket) has small, slender, dark green leaves similar to radish leaves with a slightly bitter peppery mustard flavor. Choose smaller leaves for a less distinctive flavor.

Belgian endive (or French) has closed, narrow, pale leaves with a distinct bitter flavor.

Bibb lettuce has tender, pliable leaves similar to Boston. Bibb is smaller than Boston but has the same delicate, mild flavor.

Boston lettuce (or butterhead) has small rounded heads of soft, buttery leaves with a delicate flavor.

Cabbage comes in a variety of types and is commonly available. Green and red cabbage are the most familiar. Look for compact heads. Savoy cabbage has crinkled leaves, and napa (or Chinese) cabbage has long, crisp leaves

Curly endive has frilly narrow leaves with a slightly bitter taste.

Escarole, also part of the endive family, is a less frilly, broad-leafed endive with dark green leaves.

Greens (beet, dandelion, mustard) all have a strong biting flavor. They are milder in flavor and tender when young and can be added to tossed salads. However, older greens are too bitter for salads and should be cooked for best flavor.

Iceberg lettuce (or crisphead) has a bland, mild flavor, making it the most popular green. Look for solid, compact heads with tight leaves that range from medium green outer leaves to pale green inside.

Leaf lettuce, either red or green, has tender leaves that don't form heads. These leafy bunches have a mild, bland flavor.

Mixed salad greens, prepackaged, are already cleaned and ready to use and available in the produce section of your supermarket. The package can include one kind of green or a mixture of several varieties adding more color, flavor and texture.

Radicchio, another member of the endive family, resembles a small, loose-leaf cabbage with smooth, tender leaves. The Rosso variety has rose-colored leaves with white veins, and Castelfranco, which is both blander and sweeter, has leaves sprinkled with bright colors.

Romaine (or cos) has narrow, elongated dark leaves with a crisp texture. This is the favored green for the traditional Caesar salad.

Sorrel (or sourgrass) looks similar to spinach, but the leaves are smaller. Sorrel has a sharp, lemony flavor.

Spinach has smooth, tapered, dark green leaves, sometimes with crumpling at the edges.

Watercress has large, dark green leaves with a strong peppery flavor.

Tips for Tossed Salads

- Use a variety of greens for a complementary medley of textures, flavors and colors. And remember, fresh herbs can perk up even the simplest combinations.
- Mix dark greens with light, crisp greens with tender, and straight greens with curly. Team pale iceberg lettuce with dark green spinach, romaine with curly endive. Red leaf lettuce provides both color and delicate flavor. Red cabbage and radicchio add color and texture, too.
- The drier the leaves, the better the dressing will hold. Blot any leftover moisture that may be in the crevices. Greens keep better and look fresher if torn into bite-size pieces rather than cut. If you do use a knife, shred or slice greens just before serving. Otherwise, the cut edges will appear darker and limp.
- Pour dressing over greens just before serving, using only enough to coat the leaves lightly, then toss. Or serve the salad with dressing on the side so that each person can add the desired amount.
- Salads can be served either family style from a large bowl or portioned out on individual plates or bowls. Any remaining dressed tossed salad can be refrigerated but the greens will become limp.

Curly Endive

Romaine

Cabbage

Turnip Greens

Escarole

Iceberg Lettuce

Boston Lettuce

Spinach

Leaf Lettuce

Belgian Endive

Radicchio

Mustard Greens

Watercress

Mixed Salad Greens

Arugula

Tossed Salad Chart
Makes 4 to 6 servings

- Toss all ingredients in a large salad bowl, and top with your favorite dressing.
- For a heartier main-dish salad, add 1/2 to 1 cup cooked cut-up meat, poultry, seafood, eggs, cheese or canned beans (rinsed and drained) per person.

Greens	Vegetable Additions	Fruit Additions	Garnish with
Choose one or more to total 5 cups	**Choose one or more to total 1 cup**	**Choose one or more to total 1 cup**	**Choose one or more to total 1/3 cup**
Arugula	Alfalfa sprouts	Apples—unpeeled, sliced or chopped	Bacon—cooked and crumbled
Bibb lettuce	Asparagus—1-inch pieces	Apricots—pitted and quartered	Capers
Boston lettuce	Beans—cut, French-cut or Italian	Avocado—sliced or cut into chunks	Cheese—crumbled, grated or shredded
Endive	Beets—raw and shredded or cooked and diced	Bananas—sliced	Chili peppers—sliced or chopped
Escarole	Bell peppers—cut into strips or chopped; roast if desired	Berries	Chutney
Iceberg lettuce	Broccoli flowerets or prepackaged broccoli slaw	Cherries—pitted	Coconut—shredded, toasted if desired
Leaf lettuce	Cabbage, shredded or prepackaged coleslaw mix	Dried fruit—apricots, cherries, cranberries, dated, figs, mixed, raisins	Corn relish
Mixed salad greens—prepackaged	Carrots—chopped, shredded, sliced, or julienne strips	Grapes—seedless, whole or cut in half	Crackers, miniature
Radicchio	Cauliflowerets	Grapefruit—sections	Croutons
Romaine	Corn-on-the-cob—miniature, pickled	Kiwifruit—sliced	Eggs—hard-cooked and chopped or sliced
Sorrel	Cucumbers—sliced or chopped	Melons—cut into chunks or balls	Flowers—edible
Spinach	Green peas	Nectarines—sliced or chopped	French-fried onions—canned
Watercress	Jicama—diced or julienne strips	Oranges—sections, sliced, or cut into chunks	Fresh herbs—chopped
	Mushrooms—whole or sliced	Papaya—sliced or cut into chunks	Granola
	Onions—sliced or chopped	Peaches—sliced or chopped	Guacamole
	Radishes—sliced	Pineapple—cut into chunks	Nuts—whole or chopped, toasted if desired
	Tomatoes—sliced, chopped or wedges	Pomegranate seeds	Olives—whole or sliced
	Vegetables—marinated		Pickles
	Zucchini—sliced, chopped or shredded		Salsa
			Sour cream
			Sunflower seeds
			Trail mix
			Yogurt

Mandarin Salad

PREP: 20 min
Makes 6 servings, about 1 1/3 cups each

1/4 cup sliced almonds
1 tablespoon plus 1 teaspoon sugar
Sweet-Sour Dressing (below)
1/2 small head lettuce, torn into bite-size
   pieces (3 cups)
1/2 bunch romaine, torn into bite-size pieces
   (3 cups)
2 medium stalks celery, chopped (1 cup)
2 tablespoons thinly sliced green onions
1 can (11 ounces) mandarin orange
   segments, drained

1. Cook almonds and sugar in 1-quart saucepan over low heat, stirring constantly, until sugar is melted and almonds are coated; cool and break apart.

2. Prepare Sweet-Sour Dressing.

3. Toss almonds, dressing and remaining ingredients.

Sweet-Sour Dressing

1/4 cup vegetable oil
2 tablespoons sugar
2 tablespoons white vinegar
1 tablespoon chopped fresh parsley
1/2 teaspoon salt
Dash of pepper
Dash of red pepper sauce

Shake all ingredients in tightly covered container. Refrigerate until serving.

1 SERVING: Calories 165 (Calories from Fat 100); Fat 11g (Saturated 2g); Cholesterol 0mg; Sodium 200mg; Carbohydrate 16g (Dietary Fiber 1g); Protein 1g

---

TIMESAVING TIP

Up to 2 days before serving, place lettuce, romaine, celery and onions in large heavy plastic bag, and prepare the Sweet-Sour Dressing. Prepare the almonds and store covered at room temperature. When ready to serve, add almonds, dressing and orange segments to plastic bag. Close bag tightly and shake until salad greens are well coated with dressing.

Caesar Salad

PREP: 15 min
Makes 6 servings, about 1 3/4 cups each

(photograph on page 313)

1 clove garlic, cut in half
8 anchovy fillets, cut up*
1/3 cup olive or vegetable oil
3 tablespoons lemon juice
1 teaspoon Worcestershire sauce
1/4 teaspoon salt
1/4 teaspoon ground mustard (dry)
Freshly ground pepper
1 large or 2 small bunches romaine, torn into
   bite-size pieces (10 cups)
1 cup garlic-flavored croutons
1/3 cup grated Parmesan cheese

1. Rub large wooden salad bowl with cut clove of garlic. Allow a few small pieces of garlic to remain in bowl if desired.

2. Mix anchovies, oil, lemon juice, Worcestershire sauce, salt, mustard and pepper in salad bowl.

3. Add romaine; toss until coated. Sprinkle with croutons and cheese; toss.

*2 teaspoons anchovy paste can be substituted for the anchovy fillets.

1 SERVING: Calories 170 (Calories from Fat 125); Fat 14g (Saturated 3g); Cholesterol 10mg; Sodium 420mg; Carbohydrate 7g (Dietary Fiber 1g); Protein 5g

---

LIGHTER CAESAR SALAD

For 9 grams of fat and 120 calories per serving, decrease oil to 3 tablespoons, increase lemon juice to 1/4 cup and add 2 tablespoons water to anchovy mixture. Decrease cheese to 3 tablespoons.

CHICKEN CAESAR SALAD: Broil or grill 6 boneless, skinless chicken breast halves (page 294); slice diagonally and arrange on salads. Serve chicken warm or chilled.

SHRIMP CAESAR SALAD: Arrange 1 pound cooked, peeled and deveined large shrimp on salads. Serve shrimp warm or chilled.

Greek Salad

PREP: 20 min
Makes 8 servings, about 1 3/4 cups each

Tangy feta cheese is Greek in origin and is traditionally made from sheep or goat milk. It is sometimes referred to as "pickled" cheese because it's cured and stored in its own salty whey brine.

> Lemon Dressing (below)
> 7 ounces spinach, torn into bite-size pieces
>   (5 cups)
> 1 head Boston lettuce, torn into bite-size
>   pieces (4 cups)
> 1/2 cup crumbled feta cheese, crumbled
>   (3 ounces)
> 1/4 cup sliced green onions (3 medium)
> 24 pitted ripe olives
> 3 medium tomatoes, cut into wedges
> 1 medium cucumber, sliced

1. Prepare Lemon Dressing.

2. Toss dressing and remaining ingredients.

Lemon Dressing

> 1/4 cup vegetable oil
> 2 tablespoons lemon juice
> 1/2 teaspoon sugar
> 1 1/2 teaspoons Dijon mustard
> 1/4 teaspoon salt
> 1/8 teaspoon pepper

Shake all ingredients in tightly covered container.

1 SERVING: Calories 130 (Calories from Fat 100); Fat 11g (Saturated 3g); Cholesterol 10mg; Sodium 320mg; Carbohydrate 7g (Dietary Fiber 2g); Protein 3g

Bacon-Spinach Salad

PREP: 15 min; COOK: 10 min
Makes 4 servings, about 1 1/2 cups each

(photograph on page 417)

> 4 slices bacon, diced
> 1/4 cup white vinegar
> 8 ounces spinach or 2 bunches leaf lettuce,
>   coarsely shredded (6 cups)
> 1/3 cup chopped green onions (4 medium)
> 2 teaspoons sugar
> 1/4 teaspoon salt
> 1/8 teaspoon pepper

1. Cook bacon in 12-inch skillet over low heat, stirring occasionally, until crisp. Stir in vinegar. Heat through; remove from heat.

2. Add spinach and onions to bacon mixture. Sprinkle with sugar, salt and pepper. Toss 1 to 2 minutes or until spinach is wilted.

1 SERVING: Calories 60 (Calories from Fat 25); Fat 3g (Saturated 1g); Cholesterol 5mg; Sodium 270mg; Carbohydrate 6g (Dietary Fiber 1g); Protein 3g

---

TIMESAVING TIP
Use the packaged already cleaned spinach found in the salad section of the produce department.

Seven-Layer Salad

PREP: 25 min; CHILL: 2 hr
Makes 6 servings, about 1 1/4 cups each

> 6 cups bite-size pieces mixed salad greens
> 2 medium stalks celery, thinly sliced (1 cup)
> 1 cup thinly sliced radishes
> 1/2 cup sliced green onions (5 medium)
> 12 slices bacon, crisply cooked and crumbled
> 1 package (10 ounces) frozen green peas,
>   thawed
> 1 1/2 cups mayonnaise or salad dressing
> 1/2 cup grated Parmesan cheese or shredded
>   Cheddar cheese (2 ounces)

1. Place salad greens in large glass bowl. Layer celery, radishes, onions, bacon and peas on salad greens.

2. Spread mayonnaise over peas, covering top completely and sealing to edge of bowl. Sprinkle with cheese. Cover and refrigerate at least 2 hours to blend flavors but no longer than 12 hours. Toss before serving if desired. Cover and refrigerate any remaining salad.

1 SERVING: Calories 550 (Calories from Fat 480); Fat 53g (Saturated 10g); Cholesterol 50mg; Sodium 720mg; Carbohydrate 11g (Dietary Fiber 3g); Protein 10g

---

LIGHTER SEVEN-LAYER SALAD
For 11 grams of fat and 185 calories per serving, substitute 1/2 cup reduced-fat mayonnaise and 1 cup plain fat-free yogurt for the 1 1/2 cups mayonnaise. Decrease bacon to 6 slices and cheese to 1/4 cup.

Strawberry-Jicama Toss

Roquefort and Toasted Walnut Salad

PREP: 20 min
Makes 6 servings, about 1 1/3 cups each

True Roquefort cheese is made from sheep's milk and aged in caverns near the village of Roquefort, France. Distinctive in taste and texture, the name Roquefort is protected by law from imitators, and unless true Roquefort cheese is used in products, the name cannot be used.

> 2/3 cup coarsely chopped walnuts
> Toasted Walnut Dressing (right)
> 1 head radicchio, torn into bite-size pieces
>   (4 cups)
> 1 head Bibb lettuce, torn into bite-size pieces
>   (4 cups)
> 1/2 cup crumbled Roquefort or blue cheese
>   (2 ounces)
> 1/2 cup 1/2-inch pieces fresh chives
> 1/3 cup coarsely chopped walnuts, toasted
>   (page 9)

1. Toast walnuts as directed on page 9; cool. Reserve 1/3 cup walnuts.

2. Prepare Toasted Walnut Dressing using remaining toasted walnuts.

3. Toss reserved walnuts, dressing and remaining ingredients.

Toasted Walnut Dressing

> 1/3 cup olive or vegetable oil
> 1/3 cup coarsely chopped toasted walnuts
> 2 tablespoons lemon juice
> 1 clove garlic
> 1/8 teaspoon salt
> Dash of pepper

Place all ingredients in blender or food processor. Cover and blend on high speed about 1 minute or until smooth.

1 SERVING: Calories 235 (Calories from Fat 200); Fat 22g (Saturated 4g); Cholesterol 10mg; Sodium 210mg; Carbohydrate 5g (Dietary Fiber 1g); Protein 5g

---

LIGHTER ROQUEFORT AND TOASTED WALNUT SALAD

For 13 grams of fat and 140 calories per serving, decrease cheese to 1/4 cup and walnuts in salad to 1/4 cup. In dressing, decrease oil to 3 tablespoons and walnuts to 2 tablespoons. Increase lemon juice to 3 tablespoons and add 1 tablespoon water.

Strawberry-Jicama Toss

PREP: 15 min
Makes 4 servings, about 1 3/4 cups each

Arrange the strawberries, alfalfa sprouts, jicama and kiwifruit in rows on a bed of salad greens on individual salad plates. Or, for a more dramatic presentation, use a deep platter.

> Poppy Seed Dressing (below)
> 6 cups bite-size pieces mixed salad greens
> 1/2 pint strawberries (1 cup), sliced
> 1 cup alfalfa sprouts
> 3/4 cup 1 × 1/4-inch pieces jicama
> 2 kiwifruit, peeled, cut in half lengthwise and sliced

1. Prepare Poppy Seed Dressing.

2. Toss dressing and remaining ingredients.

Poppy Seed Dressing

> 2 tablespoons vegetable oil
> 2 tablespoons honey
> 2 tablespoons orange juice
> 1 tablespoon seasoned rice vinegar
> 1 teaspoon poppy seed
> 2 teaspoons Dijon mustard

Shake all ingredients in tightly covered container.

1 SERVING: Calories 170 (Calories from Fat 70); Fat 8g (Saturated 1g); Cholesterol 0mg; Sodium 100mg; Carbohydrate 24g (Dietary Fiber 4g); Protein 4g

Creamy Potato Salad

PREP: 45 min; CHILL: 4 hr
Makes 10 servings, about 3/4 cup each

> 6 medium boiling potatoes (2 pounds)
> 1 1/2 cups mayonnaise or salad dressing
> 1 tablespoon white vinegar
> 1 tablespoon mustard
> 1 teaspoon salt
> 1/4 teaspoon pepper
> 2 medium stalks celery, chopped (1 cup)
> 1 medium onion, chopped (1/2 cup)
> 4 hard-cooked eggs, chopped

1. Prepare and cook potatoes as directed on page 400; cool slightly. Cut potatoes into cubes.

2. Mix mayonnaise, vinegar, mustard, salt and pepper in large glass or plastic bowl. Add potatoes, celery and onion; toss. Stir in eggs. Cover and refrigerate at least 4 hours to blend flavors and chill. Cover and refrigerate any remaining salad.

1 SERVING: Calories 340 (Calories from Fat 250); Fat 28g (Saturated 5g); Cholesterol 105mg; Sodium 460mg; Carbohydrate 19g (Dietary Fiber 1g); Protein 4g

---

> **LIGHTER CREAMY POTATO SALAD**
> For 1 gram of fat and 110 calories per serving, substitute 1/2 cup fat-free mayonnaise and 1 cup plain fat-free yogurt for the 1 1/2 cups mayonnaise. Decrease eggs to 2.

Hot German Potato Salad

PREP: 25 min; COOK: 20 min
Makes 6 servings, about 2/3 cup each

Studded with bacon and a sweet-sour dressing, this versatile salad can be served hot, cold or at room temperature.

> 4 medium boiling potatoes (1 1/2 pounds)
> 3 slices bacon, cut into 1-inch pieces
> 1 medium onion, chopped (1/2 cup)
> 1 tablespoon all-purpose flour
> 1 tablespoon sugar
> 1/2 teaspoon salt
> 1/4 teaspoon celery seed
> Dash of pepper
> 1/2 cup water
> 1/4 cup white vinegar

1. Prepare and cook potatoes as directed on page 400; cool slightly. Cut potatoes into 1/4-inch slices.

2. Cook bacon in 10-inch skillet until crisp. Remove bacon from skillet and reserve. Cook onion in bacon fat in skillet over medium heat, stirring occasionally, until tender. Stir in flour, sugar, salt, celery seed and pepper. Cook over low heat, stirring constantly, until mixture is bubbly; remove from heat.

3. Stir in water and vinegar. Heat to boiling, stirring constantly. Boil and stir 1 minute; remove from heat.

4. Stir in potatoes and bacon. Heat, stirring gently to coat potato slices, until hot and bubbly.

1 SERVING: Calories 125 (Calories from Fat 20); Fat 2g (Saturated 1g); Cholesterol 5mg; Sodium 230mg; Carbohydrate 26g (Dietary Fiber 2g); Protein 3g

Dilled New Potato Salad, Sweet-and-Sour Coleslaw

Dilled New Potato Salad

PREP: 35 min; CHILL: 2 hr
Makes 8 servings, about 3/4 cup each

    2 pounds new red potatoes (14 to 16)
    3/4 cup Italian Dressing (page 337) or
        prepared Italian dressing
    1 tablespoon chopped fresh or 1 teaspoon
        dried dill weed
    1/2 teaspoon salt
    1/4 cup chopped green onions
    3 hard-cooked eggs, chopped

1. Prepare and cook potatoes as directed on page 400; cool slightly. Cut potatoes into 1/4-inch slices.

2. Mix dressing, dill weed and salt in large glass or plastic bowl. Add potatoes and onion; toss. Stir in eggs. Cover and refrigerate at least 2 hours to blend flavors, stirring occasionally. Cover and refrigerate any remaining salad.

1 SERVING: Calories 230 (Calories from Fat 115); Fat 13g (Saturated 2g); Cholesterol 80mg; Sodium 340mg; Carbohydrate 26g (Dietary Fiber 2g); Protein 4g

---

**LIGHTER DILLED NEW
POTATO SALAD**

For 2 grams of fat and 115 calories per serving, use low-fat Italian dressing and substitute 1 medium cucumber, chopped, for the eggs.

Creamy Coleslaw

PREP: 15 min; CHILL: 1 hr
Makes 8 servings, about 2/3 cup each

(photograph on page 298)

    1/2 cup sour cream
    1/4 cup mayonnaise or salad dressing
    1 tablespoon sugar
    2 teaspoons lemon juice
    2 teaspoons Dijon mustard
    1/2 teaspoon celery seed
    1/4 teaspoon pepper
    1/2 medium head cabbage, finely shredded
        or chopped (4 cups)
    1 small carrot, shredded (1/2 cup)
    1 small onion, chopped (1/4 cup)

1. Mix all ingredients except cabbage, carrot and onion in large glass or plastic bowl. Add remaining ingredients; toss until evenly coated.

2. Cover and refrigerate at least 1 hour to blend flavors. Cover and refrigerate any remaining salad.

1 SERVING: Calories 110 (Calories from Fat 80); Fat 9g (Saturated 3g); Cholesterol 15mg; Sodium 75mg; Carbohydrate 7g (Dietary Fiber 1g); Protein 1g

---

LIGHTER CREAMY COLESLAW
For 1 gram of fat and 55 calories per serving, use reduced-fat sour cream and fat-free mayonnaise.

Carrot-Raisin Salad

PREP: 10 min
Makes 5 servings, about 1/2 cup each

Tailor this salad to your tastes—if you like, leave out the celery or substitute chopped apple or crushed drained pineapple. For a spicy flavor add a touch of nutmeg or cinnamon.

3 large carrots, shredded (2 1/2 cups)
1 medium stalk celery, sliced (1/2 cup)
1/2 cup raisins
1/2 cup mayonnaise or salad dressing
1 teaspoon lemon juice
Salad greens, if desired

Mix all ingredients except salad greens. Serve on salad greens. Cover and refrigerate any remaining salad.

1 SERVING: Calories 235 (Calories from Fat 160); Fat 18g (Saturated 3g); Cholesterol 15mg; Sodium 150mg; Carbohydrate 19g (Dietary Fiber 2g); Protein 1g

---

LIGHTER CARROT-RAISIN SALAD

For 0 grams of fat and 90 calories per serving, substitute 1/4 cup fat-free mayonnaise and 1/4 cup plain or lemon fat-free yogurt for the 1/2 cup mayonnaise. Add 1 teaspoon sugar.

Cucumber Salad

PREP: 10 min; CHILL: 3 hr
Makes 6 servings, about 1/2 cup each

For a scalloped look, run fork tines down the length of each peeled or unpeeled cucumber before slicing. (photograph on page 333)

2 medium cucumbers, thinly sliced
1/3 cup cider vinegar
1/3 cup water
2 tablespoons sugar
1/2 teaspoon salt
1/8 teaspoon pepper
Chopped fresh dill weed or parsley, if desired

1. Place cucumbers in small glass or plastic bowl. Shake remaining ingredients except dill weed in tightly covered container. Pour over cucumbers. Cover and refrigerate at least 3 hours to blend flavors.

2. Drain salad. Sprinkle with dill weed.

1 SERVING: Calories 30 (Calories from Fat 0); Fat 0g (Saturated 0g); Cholesterol 0mg; Sodium 180mg; Carbohydrate 7g (Dietary Fiber 0g); Protein 0g

CREAMY CUCUMBER SALAD: After draining salad, stir in 3/4 cup sour cream or plain yogurt. (If desired, omit vinegar and water; stir in the sour cream.) Cover and refrigerate any remaining salad.

Sweet-and-Sour Coleslaw

PREP: 15 min; CHILL: 3 hr
Makes 8 servings, about 3/4 cup each

1/2 medium head cabbage, finely shredded
   (4 cups)
1 large carrot, finely shredded (1 cup)
1 large green bell pepper, chopped
   (1 1/2 cups)
1/4 cup thinly sliced green onions
   (3 medium)
1/2 cup sugar
1/2 cup white wine vinegar
1/4 cup vegetable oil
1 teaspoon ground mustard (dry)
1/2 teaspoon celery seed
1/2 teaspoon salt

1. Place cabbage, carrot, bell pepper and onions in large bowl.

2. Shake remaining ingredients in tightly covered container. Pour over vegetables and stir. Cover and refrigerate at least 3 hours, stirring several times, until chilled. Serve with slotted spoon.

1 SERVING: Calories 130 (Calories from Fat 55); Fat 7g (Saturated 1g); Cholesterol 0mg; Sodium 150mg; Carbohydrate 19g (Dietary Fiber 2g); Protein 1g

---

TIMESAVING TIP

Use 6 1/2 cups packaged coleslaw mix and omit the cabbage, carrot and bell pepper.

Three-Bean Salad

PREP: 20 min; CHILL: 3 hr
Makes 6 servings, about 3/4 cups each

Looking for a new twist to this favorite? Try substituting garbanzo, cannellini or black beans for the kidney beans, and stir in 1/2 cup roasted red bell peppers, coarsely chopped.

> 1 cup Italian Dressing (page 337)
> 1 can (15 to 16 ounces) cut green beans, drained
> 1 can (15 to 16 ounces) wax beans, drained
> 1 can (15 to 16 ounces) kidney beans, rinsed and drained
> 1/4 cup chopped green onions (3 medium)
> 1/4 cup chopped fresh parsley
> 1 tablespoon sugar
> 2 cloves garlic, crushed

1. Prepare Italian dressing.

2. Mix beans, onions and parsley in medium bowl.

3. Mix dressing, sugar and garlic. Pour over salad and toss. Cover and refrigerate at least 3 hours to blend flavors, stirring occasionally.

4. Spoon bean mixture into bowl, using slotted spoon, just before serving.

1 SERVING: Calories 165 (Calories from Fat 90); Fat 10g (Saturated 1g); Cholesterol 0mg; Sodium 700mg; Carbohydrate 21g (Dietary Fiber 7g); Protein 5g

---

TIMESAVING TIP
Substitute 1 cup prepared Italian dressing for the dressing recipe.

Marinated Roasted Peppers

PREP: 15 min; CHILL: 4 hr
Makes 8 servings, about 1/2 cup each

Besides serving these delicious peppers as a salad, try adding them to sandwiches, tossed salads or eating them on toasted French bread spread with cream cheese.

> 6 large bell peppers (any color)
> 1/4 cup olive or vegetable oil
> 2 tablespoons chopped fresh parsley
> 2 tablespoons lemon juice
> 2 tablespoons lime juice
> 1 teaspoon chopped fresh or 1/4 teaspoon dried oregano leaves
> 1 teaspoon chopped fresh or 1/4 teaspoon dried basil leaves
> 1/2 teaspoon chopped fresh or 1/8 teaspoon dried sage leaves
> 1/2 teaspoon salt
> 1/8 teaspoon pepper
> 2 large cloves garlic, finely chopped

1. Set oven control to Broil. Place bell peppers on rack in broiler pan. Broil with tops about 5 inches from heat, turning occasionally, until skin is blistered and evenly browned. Place peppers in plastic bag and close tightly. Let stand 20 minutes.

2. Remove skin, stems, seeds and membranes from peppers. Cut peppers into 1/4-inch strips. Place in glass or plastic bowl.

3. Shake remaining ingredients in tightly covered container. Pour over peppers. Cover and refrigerate at least 4 hours to blend flavors, stirring occasionally.

1 SERVING: Calories 85 (Calories from Fat 65); Fat 7g (Saturated 1g); Cholesterol 0mg; Sodium 140mg; Carbohydrate 6g (Dietary Fiber 1g); Protein 1g

Roasted Vegetables with Pesto

PREP: 30 min
Makes 8 servings, about 3/4 cup each

This salad is also delicious when marinated in the refrigerator at least 2 hours and served cold.

> 1/4 cup Pesto (page 345) or prepared pesto
> 1 small eggplant (1 pound), cut lengthwise in half
> 2 medium zucchini, cut lengthwise in half
> 1 medium red bell pepper, seeded and cut in half
> 1 medium green bell pepper, seeded and cut in half
> 4 teaspoons vegetable oil

1. Prepare Pesto.

2. Set oven control to Broil. Place eggplant, zucchini and bell peppers, cut sides down, on rack in broiler pan. Brush with some of the oil.

3. Broil with tops 4 to 6 inches from heat about 5 minutes or until skins begin to blister. Turn vegetables; brush with remaining oil. Broil 4 to 6 minutes longer or until vegetables are light brown. Cool slightly.

4. Cut vegetables into bite-size pieces. Toss with Pesto. Serve warm.

1 SERVING: Calories 90 (Calories from Fat 65); Fat 7g (Saturated 2g); Cholesterol 2mg; Sodium 30mg; Carbohydrate 7g (Dietary Fiber 2g); Protein 2g

---

LIGHTER VEGETABLE SALAD WITH PESTO
For 3 grams of fat and 45 calories per serving, omit vegetable oil. Spray vegetables with nonstick cooking spray before broiling. Decrease Pesto to 2 tablespoons.

Garlic-Basil Tomatoes with Mozzarella, Roasted Vegetables with Pesto

Garlic-Basil Tomatoes

PREP: 10 min; CHILL: 3 hr
Makes 8 servings

The fresh mozzarella cheese called for in the variation is a soft white cheese with a mild, delicate flavor, and does have a different taste from regular mozzarella. It can be found in Italian markets, cheese shops and some supermarkets.

> 4 medium tomatoes, cut into 1/4-inch slices
> 1/4 cup olive or vegetable oil
> 1 tablespoon chopped fresh or 1 teaspoon
>   dried basil leaves
> 2 tablespoons red wine vinegar
> 1/8 teaspoon salt
> 3 drops red pepper sauce
> 2 large cloves garlic, finely chopped
> Salad greens if desired

1. Place tomatoes in glass or plastic dish.

2. Shake remaining ingredients in tightly covered container. Pour over tomatoes. Cover and refrigerate at least 3 hours to blend flavors, turning occasionally. Serve on salad greens.

1 SERVING: Calories 75 (Calories from Fat 65); Fat 7g (Saturated 1g); Cholesterol 0mg; Sodium 40mg; Carbohydrate 3g (Dietary Fiber 0g); Protein 0g

---

LIGHTER GARLIC-BASIL TOMATOES

For 4 grams of fat and 50 calories per serving, decrease the oil to 2 tablespoons and add 1 tablespoon water.

GARLIC-BASIL TOMATOES WITH MOZZARELLA: Layer 8 ounces fresh mozzarella cheese, sliced, alternately with the tomatoes. Increase the oil and vinegar by 1 tablespoon each.

Apples and Their Uses

Have you ever wondered which varieties of apples are best for different uses? The chart below features many popular apple varieties and can help answer that question. Whether you harvest apples from the orchard or buy them in the farmers' market or produce section at the supermarket, this guide will help you pick the right apple for cooking or eating.

Apple Varieties and Characteristics

Variety	Flavor	Texture	Eating & Salads	General Baking & Cooking	Pies
Beacon	Sweet	Mealy		X	
Braeburn	Slightly tart	Crisp	X	X	X
Cortland	Slightly tart	Crisp	X		X
Empire	Slightly tart	Crisp	X		X
Fireside	Slightly sweet	Slightly crisp	X		
Fuji	Sweet	Crisp	X	X	
Gala	Slightly sweet	Slightly crisp	X	X	X
Golden Delicious	Tart	Mealy	X	X	X
Granny Smith	Tart	Crisp	X	X	X
Greening	Tart	Crisp		X	X
Haralson	Tart	Crisp	X	X	X
Honey Gold	Sweet	Slightly crisp	X		X
Jon-A-Mac	Slightly sweet	Mealy	X		
Jonathan	Slightly tart	Mealy	X		X
McIntosh	Slightly tart	Mealy	X		
Newtown Pippin	Slightly tart	Crisp	X	X	X
Paula Red	Slightly tart	Slightly crisp	X		X
Prairie Spy	Slightly sweet	Crisp	X	X	X
Red Delicious	Sweet	Slightly crisp	X		
Regent	Sweet	Crisp	X		X
Rome Beauty	Slightly tart	Slightly crisp		X	X
San Rose	Slightly sweet	Crisp	X	X	X
Spartan	Slightly tart	Mealy	X		X
Wealthy	Slightly tart	Mealy		X	
Winesap	Slightly tart	Crisp	X		
York Imperial	Slightly tart	Slightly crisp	X	X	X

Waldorf Salad

PREP: 10 min
Makes 4 servings, about 3/4 cup each

If desired, stir in two tablespoons dried cherries or cranberries.

- 1/2 cup mayonnaise or salad dressing
- 1 tablespoon lemon juice
- 1 tablespoon milk
- 2 medium unpeeled red eating apples, coarsely chopped (2 cups)
- 2 medium stalks celery, chopped (1 cup)
- 1/3 cup coarsely chopped nuts
- Salad greens, if desired

1. Mix mayonnaise, lemon juice and milk in medium bowl.

2. Stir in apples, celery and nuts. Serve on salad greens. Cover and refrigerate any remaining salad.

1 SERVING: Calories 315 (Calories from Fat 260); Fat 29g (Saturated 4g); Cholesterol 15mg; Sodium 180mg; Carbohydrate 14g (Dietary Fiber 2g); Protein 1g

> **LIGHTER WALDORF SALAD**
>
> For 3 grams of fat and 90 calories per serving, substitute 1/4 cup fat-free mayonnaise and 1/4 cup plain fat-free yogurt for the 1/2 cup mayonnaise. Decrease nuts to 2 tablespoons.

Fresh Fruit Medley

PREP: 20 min
Makes 6 servings, about 1 cup each

- Creamy Dressing (below) or 1/2 cup Honey-Poppy Seed Dressing (page 338)
- 2 apricots or nectarines, sliced
- 1 orange, sliced
- 1 medium pineapple, peeled, cored and cut into 1-inch pieces
- 1 small bunch seedless grapes, cut in half (2 cups)

1. Prepare Creamy Dressing.

2. Toss dressing and remaining ingredients. Cover and refrigerate until ready to serve. Cover and refrigerate any remaining salad.

Creamy Dressing

- 1/2 cup whipping (heavy) cream
- 1 tablespoon powdered sugar
- 1/2 teaspoon grated lemon peel

Beat whipping cream and powdered sugar in chilled small bowl with electric mixer on high speed until soft peaks form.

1 SERVING: Calories 160 (Calories from Fat 65); Fat 7g (Saturated 4g); Cholesterol 20mg; Sodium 10mg; Carbohydrate 25g (Dietary Fiber 2g); Protein 1g

> **LIGHTER FRESH FRUIT MEDLEY**
>
> For 2 grams of fat and 120 calories per serving, substitute 1 cup frozen (thawed) reduced-fat whipped topping for the Creamy Dressing; stir in 1/2 teaspoon grated lemon peel. Stir the whipped topping until creamy before measuring and serve immediately.

Twenty-Four-Hour Fruit Salad

PREP: 30 min; CHILL: 12 hr
Makes 8 servings, about 1 cup each

- Whipped Cream Dressing (below)
- 1 can (16 1/2 ounces) pitted light or dark sweet cherries, drained
- 2 cans (15 1/4 ounces each) pineapple chunks in juice, drained and 2 tablespoons juice reserved
- 3 oranges, cut into small chunks*
- 1 cup miniature marshmallows

1. Prepare Whipped Cream Dressing.

2. *Gently* toss dressing and remaining ingredients in large glass or plastic bowl. Cover and refrigerate at least 12 hours to blend flavors but no longer than 24 hours. Cover and refrigerate any remaining salad.

*2 cans (11 ounces each) mandarin orange segments, drained, can be substituted for the oranges.

Whipped Cream Dressing

- 2 large eggs, beaten
- 2 tablespoons sugar
- 2 tablespoons white vinegar or lemon juice
- 2 tablespoons reserved pineapple juice
- 1 tablespoon margarine or butter
- Dash of salt
- 3/4 cup whipping (heavy) cream

Heat all ingredients except whipping cream just to boiling in 1-quart saucepan over medium heat, stirring constantly; cool. Beat whipping cream in chilled medium bowl with electric mixer on high speed until stiff. Fold in egg mixture.

1 SERVING: Calories 235 (Calories from Fat 90); Fat 10g (Saturated 5g); Cholesterol 80mg; Sodium 80mg; Carbohydrate 36g (Dietary Fiber 3g); Protein 3g

> **LIGHTER TWENTY-FOUR-HOUR SALAD**
>
> For 3 grams of fat and 165 calories per serving, omit Whipped Cream Dressing. For dressing, reserve 1/4 cup pineapple juice; fold juice into 2 cups frozen (thawed) reduced-fat whipped topping.

Orange-Avocado Salad

Orange-Avocado Salad

PREP: 20 min
Makes 6 servings, about 1 cup each

When an avocado is cut and exposed to air, it discolors quickly. You can add avocados to the salad at the last minute or brush with lemon or lime juice to minimize the discoloration.

    Orange Dressing (below)
    3 oranges, sliced
    2 avocados, sliced
    6 thin slices red onion, separated into rings
    Salad greens

1. Prepare Orange Dressing.

2. Arrange oranges, avocados and onion on salad greens on 6 salad plates. Serve with dressing.

Orange Dressing

    1/3 cup vegetable oil
    1 teaspoon grated orange peel
    1/4 cup orange juice
    2 tablespoons sugar
    2 tablespoons lemon juice
    1/2 teaspoon ground mustard (dry)
    1/4 teaspoon salt

Shake all ingredients in tightly covered container.

1 SERVING: Calories 255 (Calories from Fat 190); Fat 21g (Saturated 3g); Cholesterol 0mg; Sodium 95mg; Carbohydrate 19g (Dietary Fiber 4g); Protein 2g

---

LIGHTER ORANGE-AVOCADO SALAD
For 2 grams of fat and 145 calories per serving, decrease the oil in the dressing to 2 tablespoons and the avocado to 1. Cut the oranges and avocado into chunks and mix with the onion and dressing.

Tips for Gelatin Salads

There are two types of gelatin: flavored (with sugar or artificial sweetener, coloring and flavors added) and unflavored (clear and plain). Flavored gelatin is a family favorite and is easiest to work with. Unflavored gelatin is very versatile as it can be used to gel or thicken any flavor of mixture.

- Gelatin must be completely dissolved in hot liquid for it to gel. Keep these basic differences in mind:
  Flavored gelatin—add boiling liquid (water, fruit juice). Because the gelatin is premixed with sugar, it does not need to be softened before dissolving.
  Unflavored gelatin—sprinkle on cold liquid and allow to stand 1 to 2 minutes to soften. Stir in boiling liquid, or heat over low heat until gelatin is dissolved.
- If adding solids such as small fruit or vegetable pieces, chill the gelatin mixture first until it is the consistency of unbeaten egg whites (from 20 to 40 minutes). If the mixture becomes too thick, heat over hot water (or microwave on High 5 to 10 seconds at a time) until it reaches the desired consistency. Up to 1 1/2 cups of solids can be added for each 4-serving size of gelatin. Large pieces of fruit or vegetables may cause breakage when the mixture is unmolded but can be used in mixtures served from bowl.
- If adding whipped cream or sour cream, chill the gelatin mixture until it mounds when dropped from a spoon (from 30 to 40 minutes).
- *Do not use fresh or frozen pineapple (or pineapple juice), papaya or kiwifruit in gelatin mixtures.* They contain an enzyme that breaks down the gelatin so it will not set. Use these fruits only if they are canned or cooked.
- Chilling time varies with the quantity of the mixture and the container used (metal will chill faster than glass). A recipe for 4 servings usually takes about 3 hours of refrigeration to chill to the "firm" stage; larger recipes need to be refrigerated 4 to 6 hours or overnight.
- To unmold a salad, quickly dip the mold in warm (not hot) water up to the line of the gelatin. Loosen edge of salad with the tip of a knife. Tip the mold slightly to allow air into the mold and break the vacuum. Rotate the mold so all sides are loose. Place a plate, upside down, on top of mold. Holding both the mold and plate tightly, invert and shake gently. Carefully remove the mold. Repeat if necessary. Wetting the plate before unmolding a salad will allow you to easily center the salad on the plate after unmolding.
- Gelatin mixtures keep at least 24 hours, and most will keep up to 3 days. If acid such as lemon juice or vinegar has been added or there is too much sugar, the mixture will be softer and may leak liquid.

Ribbon Mold

PREP: 30 min; CHILL: 4 hr
Makes 9 servings, about 3/4 cup each

Be sure each layer is not completely firm before adding the next layer, or the layers may separate when unmolded.

> 1 cup boiling water
> 1 package (4-serving size) raspberry-flavored gelatin
> 1 package (10 ounces) frozen raspberries
> 1 cup boiling water
> 1 package (4-serving size) orange-flavored gelatin
> 1 package (8 ounces) cream cheese, softened
> 1 can (11 ounces) mandarin orange segments, undrained
> 1 cup boiling water
> 1 package (4-serving size) lime-flavored gelatin
> 1 can (8 1/4 ounces) crushed pineapple in juice, undrained

1. For raspberry layer, pour boiling water on raspberry-flavored gelatin in medium bowl; stir until gelatin is dissolved. Stir in frozen raspberries. Refrigerate uncovered 20 to 40 minutes, until the consistency of unbeaten egg whites; pour into 8-cup mold or square pan, 9 × 9 × 2-inches. Refrigerate about 30 minutes or until almost firm.

2. For orange layer, pour boiling water on orange-flavored gelatin in large bowl; stir until gelatin is dissolved; stir gradually into cream cheese. Refrigerate uncovered 30 to 40 minutes until mixture mounds when dropped from a spoon. Mix in orange segments (with syrup); pour evenly on raspberry layer. Refrigerate about 30 minutes or until almost firm.

3. For lime layer, pour boiling water on lime-flavored gelatin in large bowl; stir until gelatin is dissolved. Stir in pineapple (with juice). Refrigerate uncovered 30 to 40 minutes until mixture mounds when dropped from a spoon. Pour evenly on orange layer. Cover and refrigerate about 6 hours or until firm; unmold or cut into pieces.

1 SERVING: Calories 260 (Calories from Fat 80); Fat 9g (Saturated 6g); Cholesterol 30mg; Sodium 150mg; Carbohydrate 42g (Dietary Fiber 1g); Protein 4g

Carrot-Pineapple Salad

PREP: 45 min; CHILL: 3 hr
Makes 6 servings, about 1/2 cup each

This salad can also be poured into an 8-inch square baking dish, then served in squares.

> 1 cup boiling water
> 1 package (4-serving size) orange-flavored
>   gelatin
> 1/2 cup cold water
> 1/8 teaspoon salt
> 1 can (8 1/4 ounces) crushed pineapple in
>   syrup, undrained
> 1 cup shredded carrot (1 medium)
> Salad greens, if desired

1. Pour boiling water on gelatin in medium glass or plastic bowl; stir until gelatin is dissolved.

2. Stir in cold water, salt and pineapple. Refrigerate 20 to 40 minutes until the consistency of unbeaten egg whites.

3. Stir in carrot. Pour into 3-cup mold or 6 individual molds. Refrigerate about 3 hours or until firm; unmold. Garnish with salad greens.

1 SERVING: Calories 75 (Calories from Fat 0); Fat 0g (Saturated 0g); Cholesterol 0mg; Sodium 85mg; Carbohydrate 19g (Dietary Fiber 1g); Protein 1g

White Bean Salad

PREP: 15 min; CHILL: 1 hr
Makes 8 servings, about 1/2 cup each

Make this salad heartier by adding four cups cut-up smoked chicken or turkey and doubling the dressing.

> 1/4 cup chopped fresh parsley
> 1/4 cup olive or vegetable oil
> 3 tablespoons lemon juice
> 1/2 teaspoon pepper
> 1/4 teaspoon salt
> 1/4 cup sliced green onions (3 medium)
> 1 small red bell pepper, chopped (1/2 cup)
> 2 cans (15 to 16 ounces each) great northern
>   beans, rinsed and drained
> 1/2 cup chopped walnuts
> Salad greens, if desired

1. Shake parsley, oil, lemon juice, pepper and salt in tightly covered container.

2. Toss parsley mixture with onions, bell pepper and beans in medium glass or plastic bowl. Cover and refrigerate at least 1 hour to blend flavors.

3. Stir in walnuts. Serve on salad greens.

1 SERVING: Calories 240 (Calories from Fat 110); Fat 12g (Saturated 1g); Cholesterol 0mg; Sodium 310mg; Carbohydrate 28g (Dietary Fiber 6g); Protein 11g

Tortellini-Broccoli Salad

PREP: 20 min; CHILL: 1 hr
Makes 4 servings, about 3/4 cup each

Balsamic vinegar originated in Italy—it gets its dark color and distinctive flavor from aging in wooden barrels. (photograph on page 187)

> 1 package (7 ounces) cheese-filled tricolor
>   tortellini
> Balsamic Vinaigrette (below)
> 1 medium carrot, sliced (1/2 cup)
> 2 cups broccoli flowerets
> 2 green onions, sliced

1. Cook and drain tortellini as directed on package. Rinse with cold water; drain.

2. Prepare Balsamic Vinaigrette.

3. Mix carrot, broccoli, onions and vinaigrette in large bowl. Add pasta and toss until evenly coated. Cover and refrigerate at least 1 hour to blend flavors.

Balsamic Vinaigrette

> 1/4 cup balsamic or cider vinegar
> 2 tablespoons olive or vegetable oil
> 1 tablespoon chopped fresh or 1 teaspoon
>   dried basil leaves
> 1/4 teaspoon paprika
> 1/8 teaspoon salt
> 1 clove garlic, crushed

Shake all ingredients in tightly covered container.

1 SERVING: Calories 180 (Calories from Fat 90); Fat 10g (Saturated 2g); Cholesterol 45mg; Sodium 300mg; Carbohydrate 17g (Dietary Fiber 2g); Protein 8g

---

TIMESAVING TIP
Buy the carrot, broccoli and onions from the salad bar and use 1/3 cup purchased balsamic vinaigrette dressing.

Artichoke-Rice Salad

Artichoke-Rice Salad

PREP: 20 min; CHILL: 3 hr
Makes 8 servings, about 3/4 cup each

> 1 cup uncooked regular long grain rice
> Lemon-Garlic Vinaigrette (below)
> 1/4 cup chopped green onions (3 medium)
> 1/4 cup chopped fresh parsley
> 1 small red bell pepper, chopped (1/2 cup)
> 1 can (14 ounces) artichoke hearts, drained
>   and cut into fourths

1. Cook rice as directed on package.

2. Prepare Lemon-Garlic Vinaigrette.

3. Mix rice and remaining ingredients in medium bowl. Toss with vinaigrette. Cover and refrigerate at least 3 hours until chilled.

Lemon-Garlic Vinaigrette

> 1/4 cup vegetable oil
> 1 tablespoon grated lemon peel
> 3 tablespoons lemon juice
> 1/2 teaspoon salt
> 1/4 teaspoon pepper
> 1 clove garlic, finely chopped

Mix all ingredients.

1 SERVING: Calories 165 (Calories from Fat 65); Fat 7g (Saturated 1g); Cholesterol 0mg; Sodium 170mg; Carbohydrate 24g (Dietary Fiber 2g); Protein 3g

Tabbouleh

PREP: 35 min; CHILL: 1 hr
Makes 6 servings, about 3/4 cup each

This Middle-Eastern salad is especially tasty when served with soft pita wedges or Baked Pita Chips (page 29).

> 3/4 cup uncooked bulgur
> 1 1/2 cups chopped fresh parsley
> 3 medium tomatoes, chopped (2 1/4 cups)
> 1/3 cup thinly sliced green onions
>   (4 medium)
> 2 tablespoons chopped fresh or 2 teaspoons
>   crushed dried mint leaves
> 1/4 cup olive or vegetable oil
> 1/4 cup lemon juice
> 3/4 teaspoon salt
> 1/4 teaspoon pepper
> Whole ripe olives, if desired

1. Cover bulgur with cold water. Let stand 30 minutes; drain. Press out as much water as possible.

2. Place bulgur, parsley, tomatoes, onions and mint in medium glass or plastic bowl.

3. Shake remaining ingredients except olives in tightly covered container. Pour over cracked wheat mixture and toss. Cover and refrigerate at least 1 hour to blend flavors. Garnish with olives.

1 SERVING: Calories 155 (Calories from Fat 90); Fat 10g (Saturated 1g); Cholesterol 0mg; Sodium 280mg; Carbohydrate 16g (Dietary Fiber 3g); Protein 3g

Tuna-Pasta Salad

PREP: 20 min; CHILL: 1 hr
Makes 4 servings, about 2 cups each

Fresh basil, zucchini and a Dijon-flavored vinaigrette put a new twist on macaroni salad.

    Dijon Vinaigrette (below)
    1 package (7 ounces) medium pasta shells
    1/3 cup chopped fresh or 1 tablespoon dried
        basil leaves
    1/4 cup chopped green onions (3 medium)
    1 medium zucchini, sliced (2 cups)
    1 medium tomato, chopped (3/4 cup)
    1 can (12 1/2 ounces) chunk tuna in water,
        drained and drained
    1 can (4 ounces) sliced ripe olives, drained

1. Prepare Dijon Vinaigrette.

2. Cook and drain pasta as directed on package. Rinse with cold water; drain.

3. Mix pasta and remaining ingredients in medium bowl. Toss with vinaigrette. Cover and refrigerate at least 1 hour to blend flavors.

Dijon Vinaigrette

    1/3 cup vegetable oil
    3 tablespoons red wine vinegar
    1 tablespoon Dijon mustard

Shake all ingredients in tightly covered container.

1 SERVING: Calories 485 (Calories from Fat 205); Fat 23g (Saturated 3g); Cholesterol 25mg; Sodium 310mg; Carbohydrate 45g (Dietary Fiber 3g); Protein 28g

CREAMY TUNA-PASTA SALAD: Beat 1/2 cup mayonnaise or salad dressing into Dijon Vinaigrette with wire whisk. Cover and refrigerate any remaining salad.

CHICKEN-PASTA SALAD: Substitute 2 cups cut-up cooked chicken or turkey for the tuna.

SHRIMP-PASTA SALAD: Substitute 2 cups cooked, peeled and deveined medium shrimp (1/2 pound), thawed if frozen, or 2 cans (about 4 to 4 1/2 ounces each) tiny shrimp, rinsed and drained, for the tuna.

Chinese Chicken Salad

PREP: 35 min
Makes 4 servings, about 2 cups each

You'll find many of these ingredients in the Oriental section of your supermarket.

    Vegetable oil
    2 ounces cellophane noodles (bean threads)
    2 cups shredded cooked chicken
    1/2 small head iceberg lettuce, shredded
        (3 cups)
    1 small carrot, shredded (1/2 cup)
    1/2 cup canned shoestring potatoes
    1 tablespoon sesame seed, toasted (page 9)
    1/3 cup mayonnaise or salad dressing
    1 tablespoon sugar
    2 tablespoons white wine vinegar
    2 tablespoons hoisin sauce
    1 tablespoon sesame oil
    1 teaspoon soy sauce
    1 tablespoon chopped green onion

1. Heat vegetable oil (1 inch) in wok or 3-quart saucepan to 425°. Fry one-fourth of the noodles at a time in oil about 5 seconds, turning once, until puffed; drain on paper towels.

2. Place half of the noodles, the chicken, lettuce, carrot and shoestring potatoes in large bowl. Sprinkle with sesame seed.

3. Mix remaining ingredients except onion. Pour over chicken mixture. Top with remaining noodles and the onion. Toss before serving. Cover and refrigerate any remaining salad.

1 SERVING: Calories 480 (Calories from Fat 305); Fat 34g (Saturated 6g); Cholesterol 70mg; Sodium 520mg; Carbohydrate 21g (Dietary Fiber 2g); Protein 24g

Salad Niçoise

PREP: 20 min; CHILL: 1 hr
Makes 4 servings, about 2 cups each

This salad is also delicious with a half-pound cut-up cooked chicken or turkey instead of the tuna and roasted red pepper strips substituted for the anchovies.

    1 package (10 ounces) frozen French-style
        green beans
    3/4 cup Classic French Dressing (page 337)
    1 head Bibb lettuce, torn into bite-size pieces
        (4 cups)
    2 medium tomatoes, cut into sixths
    2 hard-cooked eggs, cut into fourths
    1 can (6 1/8 ounces) tuna in water, drained
        and flaked
    2 tablespoons sliced ripe olives, drained
    Chopped fresh parsley
    6 anchovy fillets, if desired

1. Cook and drain beans as directed on package. Refrigerate at least 1 hour until chilled.

2. Prepare Classic French Dressing.

3. Place lettuce in deep platter or salad bowl. Arrange beans, tomatoes and eggs around edge of lettuce. Mound tuna in center; sprinkle with olives. Sprinkle parsley over salad. Garnish with anchovies.

Salmon-Stuffed Tomatoes, Cucumber Salad (page 323), Foccacia (page 57)

Serve with dressing. Cover and refrigerate any remaining salad.

1 SERVING: Calories 325 (Calories from Fat 205); Fat 23g (Saturated 6g); Cholesterol 145mg; Sodium 750mg; Carbohydrate 16g (Dietary Fiber 3g); Protein 16g

---

TIMESAVING TIP

Substitute 3/4 cup purchased vinaigrette dressing for the Classic French Dressing and 4 cups packaged mixed salad greens for the lettuce. Purchase hard-cooked eggs.

Salmon-Stuffed Tomatoes

PREP: 20 min
Makes 4 servings

Rosamarina, or orzo, is a small, oval-shaped pasta that looks like rice. It can be used in many recipes that call for rice.

  1 cup uncooked rosamarina (orzo)*
  4 large tomatoes
  1/2 cup ranch or creamy dill dressing
  1 medium cucumber, peeled, seeded and
      chopped (1 cup)
  1 can (14 3/4 ounces) salmon, drained and
      skin removed

1. Cook and drain pasta as directed on package. Rinse with cold water; drain.

2. Cut stem ends from tomatoes. Remove pulp, leaving 1/2-inch wall. Chop tomato pulp; drain. Cut thin slice from bottom of each tomato to prevent tipping.

3. Mix pasta, chopped tomato and remaining ingredients. Spoon 1/2 cup pasta mixture into each tomato. Serve with remaining pasta mixture. Or, cut tomato in half or into fourths and divide pasta mixture evenly between shells.

3 cups cooked cold rice can be substituted for the cooked rosamarina.

1 SERVING: Calories 400 (Calories from Fat 160); Fat 18g (Saturated 3g); Cholesterol 60mg; Sodium 770mg; Carbohydrate 37g (Dietary Fiber 2g); Protein 25g

---

LIGHTER SALMON-STUFFED TOMATOES

For 7 grams of fat and 305 calories per serving, use fat-free ranch dressing.

CHICKEN-STUFFED TOMATOES: Substitute 2 cups cut-up cooked chicken or turkey for the salmon.

TUNA-STUFFED TOMATOES: Substitute 1 can (12 1/2 ounces) tuna, rinsed and drained, for the salmon.

Taco Salads

PREP: 1 hr 15 min
Makes 8 servings, about 2 cups each

This salad is even easier when you use purchased tortilla salad bowls and Thousand Island dressing. Look in both the refrigerated and the international foods sections of your supermarket for the salad bowls.

Tortilla Shells (below)
3/4 cup Thousand Island Dressing (page 340)
1 pound ground beef
2/3 cup water
1 tablespoon chili powder
1/2 teaspoon salt
1/4 teaspoon garlic powder
1/4 teaspoon ground red pepper (cayenne)
1 can (15 to 16 ounces) kidney beans, drained (reserve can)
1 medium head lettuce, torn into bite-size pieces (10 cups)
1 cup shredded Cheddar cheese (4 ounces)
2/3 cup sliced ripe olives
2 medium tomatoes, coarsely chopped (1 1/2 cups)
1 medium onion, chopped (1/2 cup)
1 medium avocado, thinly sliced
Sour cream

1. Prepare Tortilla Shells and Thousand Island Dressing.

2. Cook beef in 10-inch skillet over medium heat, stirring occasionally, until brown; drain. Stir in water, chili powder, salt, garlic powder, red pepper and beans. Heat to boiling; reduce heat. Simmer uncovered 15 minutes, stirring occasionally. Cool 10 minutes.

3. Mix lettuce, cheese, olives, tomatoes and onion in large bowl. Toss with Thousand Island Dressing. Add beef mixture and toss. Divide among Tortilla Shells. Garnish with avocado and sour cream. Serve immediately. Cover and refrigerate any remaining salad.

Tortilla Shells

Reserved empty kidney bean can
Vegetable oil
8 flour tortillas (10 inches in diameter)

Remove label and both ends of kidney bean can. Wash can and dry thoroughly. Heat oil (1 1/2 inches) in 3-quart saucepan to 375°. (Diameter of saucepan should be at least 9 inches.) Place 1 tortilla on top of saucepan. Hold can with long-handled tongs and place can on center of tortilla. Push tortilla into oil by gently pushing can down. Fry tortilla about 5 seconds or until set; remove can with tongs. Fry tortilla 1 to 2 minutes longer, turning tortilla in oil, until crisp and golden brown. Carefully remove tortilla from oil and drain excess oil from inside. Turn tortilla shell upside down; cool. Repeat with remaining tortillas.

1 SERVING: Calories 595 (Calories from Fat 360); Fat 40g (Saturated 14g); Cholesterol 70mg; Sodium 900mg; Carbohydrate 42g (Dietary Fiber 6g); Protein 23g

---

LIGHTER TACO SALADS

For 16 grams of fat and 310 calories per serving, omit Tortilla Shells. Prepare Baked Tortilla Chips (page 29). Substitute ground turkey for the ground beef. Use reduced-fat Cheddar cheese, Thousand Island Dressing and sour cream. Omit avocado. Serve the salad on chips.

Chef's Salad

PREP: 25 min
Makes 5 servings, about 3 cups each

1/4 cup Classic French Dressing (page 337)*
1/2 cup julienne strips cooked meat (beef, pork or smoked ham)
1/2 cup julienne strips cooked chicken or turkey
1/2 cup julienne strips Swiss cheese
1/2 cup chopped green onions (5 medium)
1 medium head lettuce, torn into bite-size pieces (10 cups)
1 small bunch romaine, torn into bite-size pieces (6 cups)
1 medium stalk celery, sliced (1/2 cup)
1/2 cup mayonnaise or salad dressing
2 hard-cooked eggs, sliced
2 medium tomatoes, cut into wedges

1. Prepare Classic French Dressing.

2. Reserve a few strips of meat, chicken and cheese. Mix remaining meat, chicken and cheese, the onions, lettuce, romaine and celery in large bowl.

3. Mix mayonnaise and Classic French Dressing. Pour over lettuce mixture and toss. Top with reserved meat, chicken and cheese strips, the eggs and tomatoes. Cover and refrigerate any remaining salad.

1/4 cup purchased vinaigrette dressing can be substituted for the Classic French Dressing.

1 SERVING: Calories 385 (Calories from Fat 280); Fat 31g (Saturated 8g); Cholesterol 140mg; Sodium 400mg; Carbohydrate 11g (Dietary Fiber 2g); Protein 17g

---

LIGHTER CHEF'S SALAD

For 11 grams of fat and 215 calories per serving, use reduced-fat cheese and fat-free mayonnaise. Decrease eggs to 1.

Spicy Beef Salad

PREP: 55 min; CHILL: 1 hr
Makes 6 servings, about 1 1/2 cups each

1 pound beef flank steak or boneless
 sirloin steak
2 tablespoons dry sherry or apple juice
2 tablespoons olive or vegetable oil
1 tablespoon soy sauce
2 teaspoons sugar
1/2 cup thinly sliced green onions
 (5 medium)
2 medium tomatoes, cut into bite-size pieces
4 cups sliced mushrooms (10 ounces)
1 small head lettuce, shredded (6 cups)
Ginger Dressing (right)

1. Trim fat from beef. Cut beef with grain into 2-inch strips. Cut strips across grain into 1/8-inch slices. (Beef is easier to cut if partially frozen, about 1 1/2 hours.) Toss beef, sherry, oil, soy sauce and sugar in glass or plastic bowl. Cover and refrigerate 30 minutes.

2. Heat 10-inch skillet over medium-high heat until 1 or 2 drops of water bubble and skitter when sprinkled on surface. Add half of the beef; stir-fry about 3 minutes or until beef is no longer pink. Remove beef from skillet; drain. Repeat with remaining beef.

3. Toss beef and onions in large bowl. Layer tomatoes, mushrooms and lettuce on beef. Cover and refrigerate at least 1 hour until chilled but no longer than 10 hours.

4. Prepare Ginger Dressing. Pour over salad and toss until well coated.

Ginger Dressing

1/4 cup rice wine vinegar or white wine
 vinegar
2 tablespoons soy sauce
1 teaspoon finely chopped fresh gingerroot
1 teaspoon sesame oil
1/8 teaspoon ground red pepper (cayenne)
1 clove garlic, finely chopped

Shake all ingredients in tightly covered container.

1 SERVING: Calories 205 (Calories from Fat 100); Fat 11g (Saturated 3g); Cholesterol 40mg; Sodium 560mg; Carbohydrate 9g (Dietary Fiber 1g); Protein 18g

---

LIGHTER SPICY BEEF SALAD
For 6 grams of fat and 160 calories per serving, omit olive oil and use a nonstick skillet.

SPICY PORK SALAD: Substitute pork tenderloin for the flank steak.

Taco Salads

Caribbean Turkey Salad

PREP: 25 min; BROIL: 20 min
Makes 6 servings

Spicy Dressing (below)
8 ounces curly Chinese noodles or linguine
1/4 cup soy sauce
3 tablespoons honey
1 tablespoon chopped gingerroot or
   1 teaspoon ground ginger
1 clove garlic, finely chopped
1 1/2 pounds turkey breast tenderloins,
   about 1/2 inch thick
2 papayas, peeled and sliced*
1 small red bell pepper, sliced
1 small red onion, thinly sliced
1/4 cup chopped fresh cilantro or parsley

1. Prepare Spicy Dressing.

2. Cook and drain noodles as directed on package. Rinse with cold water; drain.

3. Set oven control to Broil. Mix soy sauce, honey, ginger and garlic.

4. Place turkey on rack in broiler pan; brush with soy sauce mixture. Broil with tops 4 to 6 inches from heat 15 to 20 minutes, turning once and brushing with soy sauce mixture, until juice of turkey is no longer pink when centers of thickest pieces are cut. Discard any remaining soy sauce mixture.

5. Cut turkey into thin diagonal slices. Arrange noodles, papayas, bell pepper and onion on 6 serving plates. Top with turkey. Sprinkle with cilantro. Serve with dressing.

3 medium nectarines or peaches can be substituted for the papayas.

Spicy Dressing

1/4 cup vegetable oil
3 tablespoons lime juice
2 tablespoons honey
1/4 teaspoon crushed red pepper
1/4 teaspoon ground allspice

Shake all ingredients in tightly covered container.

1 SERVING: Calories 415 (Calories from Fat 115); Fat 13g (Saturated 2g); Cholesterol 65mg; Sodium 750mg; Carbohydrate 48g (Dietary Fiber 3g); Protein 29g

---

TIMESAVING TIP
You can omit the soy sauce, honey, ginger and garlic and use 1/4 cup prepared teriyaki sauce to brush on the turkey in step 4.

Cobb Salad

PREP: 1 hr 10 min
Makes 4 servings, about 3 cups each

For an impressive presentation, arrange salad on a large, deep platter.

Lemon Vinaigrette (below)
1 small head lettuce, finely shredded (6 cups)
2 cups cut-up cooked chicken
3 hard-cooked eggs, chopped
2 medium tomatoes, chopped (1 1/2 cups)
1 ripe avocado, chopped
1/4 cup crumbled blue cheese (1 ounce)
4 slices bacon, crisply cooked and crumbled

1. Prepare Lemon Vinaigrette.

2. Divide lettuce among 4 salad plates or shallow bowls. Arrange remaining ingredients in rows on lettuce. Serve with vinaigrette.

Lemon Vinaigrette

1/2 cup vegetable oil
1/4 cup lemon juice
1 tablespoon red wine vinegar
2 teaspoons sugar
1/2 teaspoon salt
1/2 teaspoon ground mustard (dry)
1/2 teaspoon Worcestershire sauce
1/4 teaspoon pepper
1 clove garlic, finely chopped

Shake all ingredients in tightly covered container. Refrigerate at least 1 hour to blend flavors.

1 SERVING: Calories 590 (Calories from Fat 430); Fat 48g (Saturated 10g); Cholesterol 230mg; Sodium 610mg; Carbohydrate 12g (Dietary Fiber 3g); Protein 31g

---

TIMESAVING TIP
Substitute 3/4 cup purchased vinaigrette dressing for the Lemon Vinaigrette.

About Salad Dressings

Salad dressings are sauces most often served cold, used to top or toss with any type of salad. There are a variety of excellent bottled dressings, mayonnaises and packaged mixes available, and the selection keeps growing. Most can be divided into the following general categories:

French (vinaigrette) dressing is the classic oil-and-vinegar combination, usually three parts oil to one part acid (vinegar or lemon juice), and added seasonings. Many people only think of the commercial bottled red French dressing, which usually contains tomato paste or puree and has vegetable gums or pectin added to keep it mixed. With the wide selection of bottled prepared vinaigrettes, more elaborate ingredients have been added, such as Dijon mustard, sun-dried tomatoes, fruit and various combinations of herbs and spices.

Vinaigrette dressings form a temporary emulsion, and it's best to shake the ingredients in a tightly covered container for best mixing. The dressing will separate on standing, so shake it well before serving. Use on simple to elaborate tossed salads as well as those including meats, pasta, vegetables and fruits. Vinaigrettes are also used to marinate food before cooking foods or as a cold marinade.

Mayonnaise is an emulsion of oil and raw egg yolks or whole eggs with acid and seasonings. Because the preparation of foods using raw eggs is not recommended for food safety reasons, we suggest you purchase prepared mayonnaise as it is pasteurized and safe. Many dressings use mayonnaise as a base.

Cooked salad dressing is based on a thickened white sauce with added eggs, acid, seasonings and a small amount of sugar. It is especially good when used with meat, potato, pasta and vegetable salads.

Creamy salad dressings can be made with whipped cream, sour cream, cream cheese, yogurt or buttermilk as the base. They are often sweetened and used with fruit; unsweetened, they are used in meat, potato, pasta and vegetable salads.

Italian Dressing

PREP: 10 min
Makes about 1 1/4 cups dressing

1 cup olive or vegetable oil
1/4 cup white vinegar
2 tablespoons finely chopped onion
1 teaspoon sugar
1 teaspoon ground mustard (dry)
1 tablespoon chopped fresh or 1 teaspoon
   dried basil leaves
1/2 teaspoon salt
1/2 teaspoon dried oregano leaves
1/4 teaspoon pepper
2 cloves garlic, crushed

Shake all ingredients in tightly covered container. Shake before serving.

1 TABLESPOON: Calories 105 (Calories from Fat 100); Fat 11g (Saturated 2g); Cholesterol 0mg; Sodium 55mg; Carbohydrate 1g (Dietary Fiber 0g); Protein 0g

---

LIGHTER ITALIAN DRESSING
For 5 grams of fat and 50 calories per serving, substitute 1/2 cup apple juice for 1/2 cup of the oil.

CREAMY ITALIAN DRESSING: Beat 1/2 cup Italian Dressing and 1/2 cup mayonnaise or salad dressing with hand beater until smooth. Cover and refrigerate any remaining dressing.

Classic French Dressing

PREP: 5 min
Makes about 1 1/2 cups dressing

This nicely dresses fresh leaf lettuce or any combination of mixed greens.

1 cup olive or vegetable oil
1/4 cup white vinegar
1/4 cup lemon juice
1/2 teaspoon salt
1/2 teaspoon ground mustard (dry)
1/2 teaspoon paprika

Shake all ingredients in tightly covered container. Shake before serving.

1 TABLESPOON: Calories 80 (Calories from Fat 80); Fat 9g (Saturated 1g); Cholesterol 0mg; Sodium 45mg; Carbohydrate 0g (Dietary Fiber 0g); Protein 0g

CLASSIC RED FRENCH DRESSING: Mix 1/2 cup Classic French Dressing and 1/2 cup ketchup.

Honey-Dijon Dressing

PREP: 5 min
Makes about 1 cup dressing

You'll also like this easy dressing on a pasta salad made with cooked ham or pork.

1/2 cup vegetable oil
1/3 cup honey
1/4 cup lemon juice
1 tablespoon Dijon mustard

Shake all ingredients in tightly covered container. Shake before serving.

1 TABLESPOON: Calories 85 (Calories from Fat 65); Fat 7g (Saturated 1g); Cholesterol 0mg; Sodium 15mg; Carbohydrate 6g (Dietary Fiber 0g); Protein 0g

HONEY-POPPY SEED DRESSING: Omit mustard. Add 1 tablespoon poppy seed.

Lime-Cilantro Dressing

PREP: 10 min
Makes about 1 cup dressing

This zesty dressing combines the Southwest favorites: cilantro and cumin.

1/2 cup olive or vegetable oil
1/3 cup lime juice or white vinegar
3 tablespoons chopped fresh cilantro
1 1/2 teaspoons ground cumin
1 teaspoon salt
1/8 teaspoon pepper
3 cloves garlic, finely chopped

Shake all ingredients in tightly covered container. Shake before serving.

1 TABLESPOON: Calories 65 (Calories from Fat 65); Fat 7g (Saturated 1g); Cholesterol 0mg; Sodium 135mg; Carbohydrate 1g (Dietary Fiber 0g); Protein 0g

Fresh Herb Vinaigrette

PREP: 10 min
Makes about 1 cup dressing

1/2 cup olive or vegetable oil
1/2 cup white vinegar
1 tablespoon finely chopped green onion
1 tablespoon chopped fresh parsley
1 tablespoon chopped fresh herb (basil, marjoram, oregano, rosemary, tarragon or thyme)

Shake all ingredients in tightly covered container. Shake before serving.

1 TABLESPOON: Calories 65 (Calories from Fat 65); Fat 7g (Saturated 1g); Cholesterol 0mg; Sodium 0mg; Carbohydrate 0g (Dietary Fiber 0g); Protein 0g

> ### LIGHTER FRESH HERB VINAIGRETTE
> For 0 grams of fat and 5 calories per serving, substitute apple juice for the olive oil and decrease vinegar to 1/3 cup.

NUTTY FRESH HERB VINAIGRETTE: Substitute walnut, hazelnut or almond oil for the olive oil.

SUN-DRIED TOMATO FRESH HERB VINAI-GRETTE: Mix in 1/4 cup sun-dried tomatoes (not oil-packed), soaked as directed on package and chopped.

Oriental Dressing

PREP: 5 min
Makes about 1 cup dressing

1/3 cup rice wine vinegar or white vinegar
1/4 cup vegetable oil
3 tablespoons soy sauce
1 tablespoon sesame seed, toasted, if desired (page 9)
2 tablespoons dry sherry or apple juice
1 teaspoon grated gingerroot or 1/4 teaspoon ground ginger
2 drops dark sesame oil, if desired

Shake all ingredients in tightly covered container. Shake before serving.

1 TABLESPOON: Calories 40 (Calories from Fat 35); Fat 4g (Saturated 1g); Cholesterol 0mg; Sodium 190mg; Carbohydrate 1g (Dietary Fiber 0g); Protein 0g

> ### TIMESAVING TIP
> Toasting really brings out sesame flavor, so toast a whole 2-ounce package or jar of sesame seed (about 1/2 cup), then keep it in the freezer to use when needed.

Italian Dressing (page 337), Sun-Dried Tomato Fresh Herb Vinaigrette, Lime-Cilantro Dressing, Buttermilk Parmesan Dressing, Blue Cheese Dressing

Buttermilk Dressing

PREP: 5 min; CHILL: 2 hr
Makes about 1 1/4 cups dressing

> 3/4 cup mayonnaise or salad dressing
> 1/2 cup buttermilk
> 1 teaspoon parsley flakes
> 1/2 teaspoon instant minced onion
> 1/2 teaspoon salt
> Dash of freshly ground pepper
> 1 clove garlic, crushed

Mix all ingredients. Cover and refrigerate at least 2 hours to blend flavors. Cover and refrigerate any remaining dressing.

1 TABLESPOON: Calories 65 (Calories from Fat 65); Fat 7g (Saturated 1g); Cholesterol 5mg; Sodium 105mg; Carbohydrate 1g (Dietary Fiber 0g); Protein 0g

---

LIGHTER BUTTERMILK DRESSING
For 3 grams of fat and 30 calories per serving, use reduced-fat mayonnaise and fat-free buttermilk.

BUTTERMILK PARMESAN DRESSING: Add 1/3 cup grated Parmesan cheese and 1/2 teaspoon paprika.

Blue Cheese Dressing

PREP: 10 min; CHILL: 3 hr
Makes about 1 2/3 cups dressing

> 3/4 cup crumbled blue cheese (3 ounces)
> 1 package (3 ounces) cream cheese, softened
> 1/2 cup mayonnaise or salad dressing
> 1/3 cup half-and-half

1. Reserve 1/3 cup of the blue cheese. Beat remaining blue cheese and the cream cheese in small bowl with electric mixer on low speed until blended.

2. Add mayonnaise and half-and-half. Beat on medium speed until creamy. Stir in reserved blue cheese. Cover and refrigerate at least 3 hours to blend flavors. Cover and refrigerate any remaining dressing.

1 TABLESPOON: Calories 60 (Calories from Fat 55); Fat 6g (Saturated 2g); Cholesterol 10mg; Sodium 80mg; Carbohydrate 0g (Dietary Fiber 0g); Protein 1g

---

LIGHTER BLUE CHEESE DRESSING
For 3 grams of fat and 35 calories per serving, decrease the blue cheese to 1/2 cup. Substitute 1/2 package (8-ounce size) reduced-fat cream cheese (Neufchâtel) for the regular cream cheese and 1/4 cup skim milk for the half-and-half. Use reduced-fat mayonnaise.

Green Goddess Dressing

PREP: 15 min
Makes about 2 cups dressing

You can also use this dressing as a sauce for hot or cold seafood or poultry.

1 cup mayonnaise or salad dressing
1/2 cup sour cream
1/3 cup finely chopped fresh parsley
3 tablespoons finely chopped fresh chives
3 tablespoons anchovy paste or finely
    chopped anchovy fillets
3 tablespoons tarragon or wine vinegar
1 tablespoon lemon juice
1/8 teaspoon freshly ground pepper

Mix all ingredients. Cover and refrigerate any remaining dressing.

1 TABLESPOON: Calories 60 (Calories from Fat 55); Fat 6g (Saturated 1g); Cholesterol 10mg; Sodium 95mg; Carbohydrate 0g (Dietary Fiber 0g); Protein 1g

> #### LIGHTER GREEN GODDESS DRESSING
> For 3 grams of fat and 35 calories per serving, use reduced-fat mayonnaise and reduced-fat sour cream.

Thousand Island Dressing

PREP: 15 min
Makes about 1 cup dressing

1 cup mayonnaise or salad dressing
1 tablespoon chopped fresh parsley
2 tablespoons chopped pimiento-stuffed
    olives or sweet pickle relish
2 tablespoons chili sauce or ketchup
1 teaspoon finely chopped onion
1/2 teaspoon paprika
1 hard-cooked egg, finely chopped

Mix all ingredients. Cover and refrigerate any remaining dressing.

1 TABLESPOON: Calories 105 (Calories from Fat 100); Fat 11g (Saturated 2g); Cholesterol 20mg; Sodium 130mg; Carbohydrate 1g (Dietary Fiber 0g); Protein 1g

> #### LIGHTER THOUSAND ISLAND DRESSING
> For 5 grams of fat and 55 calories per serving, use reduced-fat mayonnaise and substitute 2 hard-cooked egg whites for the hard-cooked egg.

RUSSIAN DRESSING: Omit parsley, olives and egg. Increase chili sauce to 1/4 cup. Add 1 teaspoon prepared horseradish.

Creamy Low-Cal Dressing

PREP: 10 min
Makes about 2 cups dressing

This dressing also makes a great dip with fresh vegetables.

1/2 cup skim milk
2 tablespoons lemon juice
1 tablespoon vegetable oil
1 1/2 cups low-fat cottage cheese
    (12 ounces)
1 small onion, chopped (1/4 cup)
2 cloves garlic, crushed
1/2 teaspoon salt
1/4 teaspoon pepper
1/4 teaspoon paprika

1. Place all ingredients in blender or food processor in order listed.

2. Cover and blend on medium speed about 1 minute, or process, until smooth. Cover and refrigerate any remaining dressing.

1 TABLESPOON: Calories 20 (Calories from Fat 10); Fat 1g (Saturated 0g); Cholesterol 0mg; Sodium 80mg; Carbohydrate 1g (Dietary Fiber 0g); Protein 2g

Cooked Salad Dressing

PREP: 15 min; CHILL: 2 hr
Makes about 2 cups dressing

Homemade salad dressing is delicious! Use it in your favorite potato and pasta salads for extra flavor.

1/4 cup all-purpose flour
2 tablespoons sugar
1 teaspoon ground mustard (dry)
1/2 teaspoon salt
1 1/2 cups milk
2 egg yolks, slightly beaten
1/3 cup white vinegar
1 tablespoon margarine or butter

1. Mix flour, sugar, mustard and salt in 2-quart saucepan. Gradually stir in milk. Heat to boiling over medium heat, stirring constantly. Boil and stir 1 minute.

2. Gradually stir at least half of the hot mixture into egg yolks; stir back into hot mixture in saucepan. Boil and stir 1 minute; remove from heat.

3. Stir in vinegar and margarine. Cover and refrigerate at least 2 hours until chilled. Cover and refrigerate any remaining salad dressing.

1 TABLESPOON: Calories 20 (Calories from Fat 10); Fat 1g (Saturated 0g); Cholesterol 15mg; Sodium 45mg; Carbohydrate 2g (Dietary Fiber 0g); Protein 1g

Sauces, Seasonings & Condiments

About Sauces

Sauces make the dish, whether it's a simple butter sauce, a savory barbecue sauce or an extra-special bordelaise sauce. They make plain dishes sing, and add rich flavor to more complex dishes. Want a dessert sauce? See pages 159-160. Here are some great ways to use sauces:

Mix with foods: Barbecue Sauce (page 344) with cocktail meatballs, or White Sauce (page 347) used as a base for casseroles.

Top foods: Hollandaise Sauce (page 347) over asparagus, or Pesto (page 345) over grilled chicken breasts.

Serve on the side: Prune-Almond Sauce (page 344) with pork, or Applesauce-Horseradish Sauce (page 346) with beef.

Pool or drizzle on the plate before adding the food, as served in restaurants and seen in magazines and cookbooks: Winter Tomato Sauce (page 343) under broiled fish fillets, or Peanut Sauce (page 343) under steamed shrimp.

Mixing Sauces

- When making sauces, a wire whisk is one of the best mixing tools you can use to prevent lumps.
- The most common thickener for a savory sauce is called a *roux.* A roux is made of fat and flour. Some of the most popular sauces are made in this manner, such as White Sauce, Velouté Sauce and Brown Sauce. For proper thickening, it's important to stir the cooking fat-flour mixture and allow it to bubble before adding the liquid. This evenly distributes the flour and allows the roux to cook fully and absorb the liquid, while any raw flour taste is eliminated and the sauce thickens properly. Flour-thickened sauces are opaque.
- When flour is used to thicken foods such as stews, stir it into a small amount of *cold* liquid to avoid clumping, before adding to the hot mixture. If flour is added directly to hot liquid, it will immediately begin cooking and form lumps.
- Another way to thicken sauces is with cornstarch. Cornstarch is usually stirred into a small amount of cold liquid to avoid lumping before being added to a hot mixture. Cornstarch-thickened sauces are clear in appearance rather than opaque. For this reason, cornstarch is often preferred when thickening fruit sauces.
- Other ways to thicken sauces are with egg yolks (as in Hollandaise Sauce) or by reduction (usually a stock, broth or wine mixture). Sauces thickened with egg yolks or eggs must be cooked thoroughly at low temperatures to be safe.
- A reduction sauce is made by rapidly boiling a liquid until the volume is reduced by evaporation, which intensifies the flavor and thickens

the consistency. This happens more quickly if a pan with a large surface area, such as a 10-inch skillet, is used rather than a 1- or 2-quart saucepan.

Storing and Reheating Sauces

- Refrigerate leftover sauces immediately in covered containers for up to one week. For food safety reasons, avoid keeping sauces made with egg or cream for more than two days.
- To keep sauces longer than one week, freeze in small amounts in covered containers. However, sauces containing sour cream or eggs, or those thickened with cornstarch or flour, may separate.
- Use a saucepan large enough for the amount of sauce being reheated, but not too large or there will be excessive evaporation.
- Stir sauces frequently during reheating.
- Heat sauces without added thickening (such as barbecue sauce) to boiling over medium heat before serving. Sauces thickened with flour or cornstarch (such as white sauce) can be reheated over low to medium heat. Sauces thickened with eggs (such as Hollandaise Sauce) should be reheated over low heat to avoid separating.
- If sauces stick to the pan during reheating, you may need to reduce the heat, stir more frequently, add a little liquid or use a combination of these tips.
- Sauces can be reheated in the microwave using similar power settings to the ones used on the stovetop. Heatproof glass measuring cups in various sizes make great containers. Stir at least once during heating and then before serving.

Preceding page: Red Onion Salsa (page 359), Cranberry-Orange Relish (page 358), Mexican Seasoning Mix (page 355)

Italian Tomato Sauce

PREP: 15 min; COOK: 50 min
Makes about 4 cups sauce

> 2 tablespoons olive or vegetable oil
> 1 large onion, chopped (1 cup)
> 1 medium green bell pepper, chopped
>   (1/2 cup)
> 2 large cloves garlic, finely chopped
> 2 cans (16 ounces each) whole tomatoes,
>   undrained
> 2 cans (8 ounces each) tomato sauce
> 2 tablespoons chopped fresh or 2 teaspoons
>   dried basil leaves
> 1 tablespoon chopped fresh or 1 teaspoon
>   dried oregano leaves
> 1/2 teaspoon salt
> 1/2 teaspoon fennel seed
> 1/4 teaspoon pepper

1. Heat oil in 3-quart saucepan over medium heat. Cook onion, bell pepper and garlic in oil about 2 minutes, stirring occasionally.

2. Stir in remaining ingredients, breaking up tomatoes. Heat to boiling; reduce heat to low. Cover and simmer 45 minutes. Serving suggestions: meat loaf, meatballs, hot cooked pasta.

1 TABLESPOON: Calories 5 (Calories from Fat 0); Fat 0g (Saturated 0g); Cholesterol 0mg; Sodium 85mg; Carbohydrate 1g (Dietary Fiber 0g); Protein 0g

---

TIMESAVING TIP
Substitute 1 jar (32 ounces) marinara sauce or spaghetti sauce for the recipe and heat in 2-quart saucepan over medium heat about 5 minutes or until hot, stirring occasionally.

Winter Tomato Sauce

PREP: 5 min; CHILL: 1 hr
Makes about 1 2/3 cups sauce

This sauce is best made in winter when fresh tomatoes are often flavorless. It's good served as a condiment with fish or as a dip for vegetables. It's also appetizing spread on cocktail bread and broiled.

> 1 cup unsweetened applesauce
> 1 tablespoon chopped fresh or 1 teaspoon
>   dried basil leaves
> 1 tablespoon cider vinegar
> 1 1/2 teaspoons olive or vegetable oil
> 1 can (6 ounces) tomato paste
> 1 clove garlic, finely chopped

1. Mix all ingredients.

2. Cover and refrigerate at least 1 hour to blend flavors. Serving suggestions: poultry, fish, pasta, vegetables.

1 TABLESPOON: Calories 10 (Calories from Fat 0); Fat 0g (Saturated 0g); Cholesterol 0mg; Sodium 50mg; Carbohydrate 2g (Dietary Fiber 0g); Protein 0g

Teriyaki Sauce

PREP: 5 min
Makes about 2/3 cup sauce

If you like, try spicy ketchup to heat up the sauce.

> 1/4 cup vegetable oil
> 1/4 cup soy sauce
> 2 tablespoons ketchup
> 1 tablespoon white vinegar
> 1/4 teaspoon pepper
> 2 cloves garlic, crushed

Mix all ingredients. Serving suggestions: pork, chicken, shrimp, fish, vegetables.

1 TABLESPOON: Calories 55 (Calories from Fat 45); Fat 5g (Saturated 1g); Cholesterol 0mg; Sodium 450mg; Carbohydrate 2g (Dietary Fiber 0g); Protein 0g

Peanut Sauce

PREP: 10 min; COOK: 10 min
Makes about 1 3/4 cups sauce

> 1 cup salted peanuts
> 1 cup flaked coconut
> 1 1/2 cups milk
> 3/4 teaspoon curry powder
> 1/8 teaspoon ground red pepper (cayenne)

1. Place 1/2 cup of the peanuts in blender or food processor. Cover and blend on medium speed until peanuts are coarsely chopped. Remove from blender; set aside.

2. Place remaining 1/2 cup peanuts and remaining ingredients in blender or food processor. Cover and blend on high speed until almost smooth.

3. Place blended mixture and chopped peanuts in 1-quart saucepan. Heat to boiling; reduce heat to low. Simmer uncovered 5 minutes, stirring occasionally. Serving suggestions: chicken, shrimp, pork or beef.

1 TABLESPOON: Calories 55 (Calories from Fat 35); Fat 4g (Saturated 1g); Cholesterol 0mg; Sodium 35mg; Carbohydrate 3g (Dietary Fiber 0g); Protein 2g

Barbecue Sauce

PREP: 10 min; COOK: 10 min
Makes about 2 cups sauce

1 cup ketchup
1/4 cup margarine or butter
1/3 cup water
1 tablespoon paprika
1 teaspoon packed brown sugar
1/4 teaspoon pepper
1 medium onion, finely chopped (1/2 cup)
2 tablespoons lemon juice
1 tablespoon Worcestershire sauce

1. Heat all ingredients except lemon juice and Worcestershire sauce to boiling in 1 1/2-quart saucepan over medium heat.

2. Stir in lemon juice and Worcestershire sauce. Heat until hot. Serving suggestions: ribs, burgers, sliced cooked meat, chicken.

1 TABLESPOON: Calories 20 (Calories from Fat 10); Fat 1g (Saturated 0g); Cholesterol 0mg; Sodium 110mg; Carbohydrate 3g (Dietary Fiber 0g); Protein 0g

---

TIMESAVING TIP

To microwave, decrease water to 1/4 cup. Mix all ingredients except lemon juice and Worcestershire sauce in 4-cup microwavable measure. Cover loosely and microwave on High (100%) 4 to 6 minutes, stirring every 2 minutes, until boiling. Stir in lemon juice and Worcestershire sauce. Cover loosely and microwave on High 1 to 2 minutes longer or until boiling.

Sweet-and-Sour Sauce

PREP: 15 min; COOK: 20 min
Makes about 2 1/2 cups sauce

Turn this sauce into a main dish by adding two cups cut-up cooked pork or chicken and serving it over rice.

1/2 cup sugar
1/2 cup chicken broth or water
1/3 cup white vinegar
1 teaspoon vegetable oil
1 teaspoon soy sauce
1/4 teaspoon salt
1 clove garlic, crushed
2 tablespoons cornstarch
2 tablespoons cold water
1 medium tomato, cut into thin wedges
1 small green bell pepper, cut into 1-inch pieces
1 can (8 ounces) pineapple chunks in syrup, drained

1. Heat sugar, broth, vinegar, oil, soy sauce, salt and garlic to boiling in 2-quart saucepan over medium-high heat, stirring occasionally.

2. Mix cornstarch and water. Stir into sugar mixture. Cook and stir about 10 seconds or until thickened.

3. Stir in tomato, bell pepper and pineapple. Heat to boiling. Serving suggestions: pork, ham or poultry.

1 TABLESPOON: Calories 15 (Calories from Fat 0); Fat 0g (Saturated 0g); Cholesterol 0mg; Sodium 30mg; Carbohydrate 4g (Dietary Fiber 0g); Protein 0g

Prune-Almond Sauce

PREP: 30 min
Makes about 2 cups sauce

A nice accompaniment for pork or ham and equally delicious as a bread spread or pastry filling.

1 1/2 cups apple juice
1/2 package (16-ounce size) pitted prunes
   (2 cups)
2 tablespoons apple brandy, brandy or water
1 teaspoon grated lemon peel
1/2 cup slivered almonds

1. Heat apple juice and prunes to boiling in 2-quart saucepan; reduce heat to low. Cover and simmer about 20 minutes or until prunes are soft.

2. Drain prunes, reserving 1/2 cup liquid. Place prunes, reserved liquid, the brandy and lemon peel in blender or food processor. Cover and blend on high speed until smooth. Remove from blender. Stir in almonds. Store tightly covered in refrigerator up to 4 weeks. Serving suggestions: pork, ham, chicken or as a spread on bread.

1 TABLESPOON: Calories 55 (Calories from Fat 10); Fat 1g (Saturated 0g); Cholesterol 0mg; Sodium 0mg; Carbohydrate 11g (Dietary Fiber 1g); Protein 1g

PRUNE SAUCE: Omit apple brandy, lemon peel and almonds. Makes 1 1/2 cups sauce.

TIMESAVING TIP

To microwave, decrease apple juice to 3/4 cup. Place apple juice and prunes in 1 1/2-quart microwavable casserole. Cover tightly and microwave on High 6 to 8 minutes, stirring after 4 minutes, until prunes are tender. Continue as directed in step 2.

Pesto, Cilantro Pesto, Sun-Dried Tomato Pesto

Pesto

PREP: 10 min
Makes about 1 1/3 cups sauce

This is four recipes in one, and all are equally as good! Keep pesto on hand to toss with pasta, spread on sandwiches, mix into salads or to top hot meats or vegetables.

> 2 cups firmly packed fresh basil leaves
> 3/4 cup grated Parmesan cheese
> 3/4 cup olive or vegetable oil
> 3 cloves garlic
> 1/4 cup pine nuts

Place all ingredients in blender or food processor. Cover and blend on medium speed about 3 minutes, stopping occasionally to scrape sides, until smooth. Toss with hot cooked pasta, if desired.

1 TABLESPOON: Calories 90 (Calories from Fat 80); Fat 9g (Saturated 2g); Cholesterol 2mg; Sodium 55mg; Carbohydrate 1g (Dietary Fiber 0g); Protein 1g

CILANTRO PESTO: Substitute 1 1/2 cups firmly packed fresh cilantro and 1/2 cup firmly packed fresh parsley for the fresh basil.

SPINACH WINTER PESTO: Substitute 2 cups firmly packed fresh spinach and 1/2 cup firmly packed fresh or 1/4 cup dried basil leaves for the fresh basil.

SUN-DRIED TOMATO PESTO: Use food processor. Omit the basil. Decrease oil to 1/3 cup and add 1/2 cup oil-packed sun-dried tomatoes (undrained).

Yogurt-Mint Sauce

PREP: 10 min; CHILL: 1 hr
Makes about 1 cup sauce

> 3/4 cup plain yogurt
> 1 tablespoon finely chopped fresh or
>   1 teaspoon dried mint leaves
> 1 tablespoon mayonnaise or salad dressing
> 1 teaspoon grated orange peel
> 1 clove garlic, finely chopped

1. Mix all ingredients.

2. Cover and refrigerate at least 1 hour to blend flavors. Refrigerate any remaining sauce. Serve with couscous or Gyros Sandwiches (page 385).

1 TABLESPOON: Calories 15 (Calories from Fat 10); Fat 1g (Saturated 0g); Cholesterol 0mg; Sodium 15mg; Carbohydrate 1g (Dietary Fiber 0g); Protein 1g

---

LIGHTER YOGURT-MINT SAUCE
For 0 grams of fat and 10 calories per tablespoon, use plain fat-free yogurt and reduced-fat mayonnaise.

Applesauce

PREP: 5 min; COOK: 20 min
Makes 6 servings, about 1/2 cup each

4 medium cooking apples, peeled and each
    cut into fourths (1 1/3 pounds)
1/2 cup water
1/4 cup packed brown sugar or 3 to
    4 tablespoons granulated sugar
1/4 teaspoon ground cinnamon
1/8 teaspoon ground nutmeg

1. Heat apples and water to boiling in 2-quart saucepan over medium heat, stirring occasionally; reduce heat to low. Simmer uncovered 5 to 10 minutes, stirring occasionally to break up apples, until tender.

2. Stir in remaining ingredients. Heat to boiling. Boil and stir 1 minute.

1 SERVING: Calories 85 (Calories from Fat 0); Fat 0g (Saturated 0g); Cholesterol 0mg; Sodium 5mg; Carbohydrate 22g (Dietary Fiber 1g); Protein 0g

---

TIMESAVING TIP

To microwave, decrease water to 1/4 cup. Place all ingredients in 2-quart microwavable casserole. Cover tightly and microwave on High 10 to 12 minutes, stirring and breaking up apples every 3 minutes, until apples are tender.

Applesauce-Horseradish Sauce

PREP: 10 min; CHILL: 1 hr
Makes about 1 cup sauce

This sauce also makes a great sandwich spread.

1/2 cup unsweetened applesauce
1/4 cup sour cream
3 tablespoons grated horseradish or
    prepared horseradish
1 tablespoon white wine vinegar or
    white vinegar
1 teaspoon mustard
1/4 teaspoon white pepper

1. Mix all ingredients.

2. Cover and refrigerate at least 1 hour until chilled. Refrigerate any remaining sauce. Serving suggestions: beef, pork or ham.

1 TABLESPOON: Calories 15 (Calories from Fat 10); Fat 1g (Saturated 1g); Cholesterol 2mg; Sodium 10mg; Carbohydrate 1g (Dietary Fiber 0g); Protein 0g

WHIPPED HORSERADISH SAUCE: Substitute 1/2 cup whipping (heavy) cream, whipped, for the applesauce. Makes 1 1/4 cups sauce.

Cranberry Sauce

PREP: 10 min; COOK: 20 min; CHILL: 3 hr
Makes 16 servings, about 1/4 cup each

Be sure to cook the cranberries until they pop, to release the natural pectin, which thickens the sauce. This is a classic at Thanksgiving, but it's welcome any time, served with pork, turkey or chicken.

4 cups fresh or frozen cranberries (1 pound)
2 cups water
2 cups sugar
1 tablespoon grated orange peel, if desired

1. Wash cranberries; remove any stems or blemished berries.

2. Heat sugar and water in 3-quart saucepan over medium heat to boiling, stirring occasionally. Boil 5 minutes.

3. Stir in cranberries. Heat to boiling and boil about 5 minutes longer or until cranberries pop. Cover and refrigerate about 3 hours or until chilled.

1 SERVING: Calories 110 (Calories from Fat 0); Fat 0g (Saturated 0g); Cholesterol 0mg; Sodium 0mg; Carbohydrate 29g (Dietary Fiber 1g); Protein 0g

Herbed Butter Sauce

PREP: 5 min; COOK: 5 min
Makes about 1/2 cup sauce

A perennial pleaser, it deliciously suits everyone's taste and is so easy to make.

1/2 cup stick butter*
2 tablespoons chopped fresh or 1 teaspoon
    dried herb leaves (basil, chives, oregano,
    savory, tarragon or thyme)
2 teaspoons lemon juice

1. Melt butter in heavy 1-quart saucepan or 8-inch skillet over medium heat.

2. Stir in lemon juice and herb leaves. Serve over vegetables or with fish, seafood or meat.

*We do not recommend using margarine or vegetable oil spreads.

1 TABLESPOON: Calories 110 (Calories from Fat 110); Fat 12g (Saturated 7g); Cholesterol 30mg; Sodium 75mg; Carbohydrate 0g (Dietary Fiber 0g); Protein 0g

CLARIFIED BUTTER: Omit herb leaves, lemon juice and salt. Skim off any foam from top of melted butter. Pour off clear (clarified) butter, and discard the milky residue. Clarified butter can withstand higher cooking temperatures than regular butter but does not have as rich a flavor. Serve with fish or seafood.

Rhubarb Sauce

Prep: 10 min Cook: 15 min
Makes 6 servings, about 1/2 cup each

Rhubarb varies in sweetness, so add sugar to taste.

1/2 to 3/4 cup sugar
1/2 cup water
1 pound rhubarb, cut into 1-inch pieces
   (4 cups)
Ground cinnamon, if desired

1. Heat sugar and water to boiling in 2-quart saucepan, stirring occasionally. Stir in rhubarb; reduce heat to low. Simmer uncovered about 10 minutes, stirring occasionally, until rhubarb is tender and slightly transparent.

2. Stir in cinnamon. Serve sauce warm or chilled.

1 SERVING: Calories 75 (Calories from Fat 0); Fat 0g (Saturated 0g); Cholesterol 0mg; Sodium 0mg; Carbohydrate 19g (Dietary Fiber 1g); Protein 1g

STRAWBERRY-RHUBARB SAUCE: Substitute 1 cup strawberries, cut in half, for 1 cup of the rhubarb. After simmering rhubarb, stir in strawberries; heat just to boiling.

Hollandaise Sauce

PREP: 10 min; COOK: 5 min
Makes about 3/4 cup sauce

If this delicate sauce curdles, add about one tablespoon boiling water and beat vigorously with wire whisk or hand beater until it's smooth. (photograph on page 359)

3 large egg yolks
1 tablespoon lemon juice
1/2 cup firm stick butter*

1. Stir egg yolks and lemon juice vigorously in 1 1/2-quart saucepan. Add 1/4 cup of the butter. Heat over *very low heat,* stirring constantly with wire whisk, until butter is melted.

2. Add remaining butter. Continue stirring vigorously until butter is melted and sauce is thickened. (Be sure butter melts slowly so eggs have time to cook and thicken sauce without curdling.) Serve over cooked vegetables, eggs or broiled meats. Cover and refrigerate any remaining sauce. To serve refrigerated sauce, stir in small amount of water when reheating over very low heat.

*We do not recommend using margarine or vegetable oil spreads.

1 TABLESPOON. Calories 85 (Calories from Fat 80); Fat 9g (Saturated 5g); Cholesterol 75mg; Sodium 55mg; Carbohydrate 0g (Dietary Fiber 0g); Protein 1g

BÉARNAISE SAUCE: Stir in 1 tablespoon dry white wine with the lemon juice. After sauce thickens, stir in 1 tablespoon finely chopped onion, 1 1/2 teaspoons chopped fresh or 1/2 teaspoon dried tarragon leaves and 1 1/2 teaspoons chopped fresh or 1/4 teaspoon dried chervil leaves. Serve with fish or meat.

White Sauce

PREP: 5 min; COOK: 5 min
Makes about 1 cup sauce

2 tablespoons margarine or butter
2 tablespoons all-purpose flour
1/4 teaspoon salt
1/8 teaspoon pepper
1 cup milk

1. Melt margarine in 1 1/2-quart saucepan over low heat. Stir in flour, salt and pepper. Cook over medium heat, stirring constantly, until mixture is smooth and bubbly; remove from heat.

2. *Gradually* stir in milk. Heat to boiling, stirring constantly. Boil and stir 1 minute. Serve with vegetables, or use as a sauce in casseroles.

1 TABLESPOON: Calories 25 (Calories from Fat 20); Fat 2g (Saturated 1g); Cholesterol 0mg; Sodium 60mg; Carbohydrate 2g (Dietary Fiber 0g); Protein 0g

CHEESE SAUCE: Stir in 1/4 teaspoon ground mustard (dry) with the flour. After boiling and stirring sauce 1 minute, stir in 1/2 cup shredded Cheddar cheese (2 ounces) until melted. Serve with eggs or vegetables or over toast for Welsh Rabbit. Makes 1 1/3 cups sauce.

CURRY SAUCE: Stir in 1/2 teaspoon curry powder with the flour. Serve with chicken, lamb or shrimp.

DILL SAUCE: Stir in 1 teaspoon chopped fresh or 1/2 teaspoon dried dill weed and dash of ground nutmeg with the flour. Serve with fish.

MUSTARD SAUCE: Decrease margarine to 1 tablespoon and flour to 1 tablespoon. After boiling and stirring sauce 1 minute, stir in 3 tablespoons mustard and 1 tablespoon prepared horseradish. Serve with beef, veal, ham or vegetables.

THICK WHITE SAUCE: Increase margarine to 1/4 cup and flour to 1/4 cup.

THIN WHITE SAUCE: Decrease margarine to 1 tablespoon and flour to 1 tablespoon.

TIMESAVING TIP

To microwave, place margarine in 4-cup microwavable measure. Microwave uncovered on High 15 to 30 seconds or until melted. Stir in flour, salt, pepper and milk. Microwave uncovered 2 to 3 minutes, stirring every minute with wire whisk or fork, until thickened.

Pan Gravy

PREP: 5 min; COOK: 5 min
Makes about 1 cup gravy

This recipe can easily be doubled if you like to use lots of gravy, or are serving more than four or six people.

> 2 tablespoons meat drippings (fat and juices)
> 2 tablespoons all-purpose flour
> 1 cup liquid* (meat juices, broth, water)
> Browning sauce, if desired
> Salt and pepper to taste

1. Place meat on warm platter; keep warm while preparing gravy. Pour drippings from cooking pan into bowl, leaving brown particles in pan. Return 2 tablespoons drippings to pan. (Measure accurately because too little fat makes gravy lumpy.)

2. Stir flour into drippings in pan. (Measure accurately so gravy is not greasy.) Cook over low heat, stirring constantly, until mixture is smooth and bubbly; remove from heat.

3. *Gradually* stir in liquid. Heat to boiling, stirring constantly. Boil and stir 1 minute. Stir in a few drops browning sauce. Sprinkle with salt and pepper. Serving suggestions: roasted meat, mashed potatoes, stuffing.

*Vegetable cooking water, consommé or tomato or vegetable juice can be substituted for part of the liquid.

1 TABLESPOON: Calories 15 (Calories from Fat 10); Fat 1g (Saturated 0g); Cholesterol 2mg; Sodium 170mg; Carbohydrate 1g (Dietary Fiber 0g); Protein 0g

CREAMY GRAVY: Substitute milk for half of the liquid. Serve with turkey, chicken, pork or veal.

GIBLET GRAVY: Cook gizzard, heart and neck of fowl in 4 cups salted water 1 to 2 hours or until tender. Add liver the last 30 minutes. Remove meat from neck and finely chop with giblets. Substitute broth from giblets for the liquid. Stir giblets into gravy. Heat until hot.

MUSHROOM GRAVY: Before stirring in flour, cook 3 cups sliced mushrooms (8 ounces) in 2 tablespoons drippings in pan, stirring occasionally, until light brown. Stir 1/2 teaspoon Worcestershire sauce into gravy. Serve with beef, veal or chicken.

THIN GRAVY: Decrease drippings to 1 tablespoon and flour to 1 tablespoon.

Velouté Sauce

PREP: 5 min; COOK: 5 min
Makes about 1 cup sauce

This classic sauce is a white sauce with a light broth or stock base.

> 2 tablespoons margarine or butter
> 2 tablespoons all-purpose flour
> 1 cup chicken broth
> 1/4 teaspoon salt
> 1/8 teaspoon pepper
> 1/8 teaspoon ground nutmeg

1. Melt margarine in 1 1/2-quart saucepan over low heat. Stir in flour. Cook over low heat, stirring constantly, until mixture is smooth and bubbly; remove from heat.

2. *Gradually* stir in broth. Heat to boiling, stirring constantly. Boil and stir 1 minute. Stir in salt, pepper and nutmeg. Serving suggestions: chicken, fish, broccoli and carrots.

1 TABLESPOON: Calories 20 (Calories from Fat 20); Fat 2g (Saturated 0g); Cholesterol 0mg; Sodium 100mg; Carbohydrate 1g (Dietary Fiber 0g); Protein 0g

MORNAY SAUCE: Substitute 1/2 cup half-and-half for 1/2 cup of the chicken broth. After boiling and stirring 1 minute, stir in 1/8 teaspoon ground red pepper (cayenne) and 1/2 cup grated Parmesan or shredded Swiss cheese with the salt; stir until cheese is melted. Serve with meat, fish, eggs or vegetables.

Raisin Sauce, Dark Pumpernickel Bread (page 60)

Brown Sauce

PREP: 5 min; COOK: 10 min
Makes about 1 cup sauce

This basic recipe is also the base for the many sauces listed at right.

>   2 tablespoons margarine or butter
>   1 thin slice onion
>   2 tablespoons all-purpose flour
>   1 cup beef broth
>   1/4 teaspoon salt
>   1/8 teaspoon pepper

1. Melt margarine in 1 1/2-quart saucepan over low heat. Cook onion in margarine, stirring occasionally, until onion is brown; discard onion.

2. Stir flour into margarine. Cook over low heat, stirring constantly, until flour is deep brown; remove from heat.

3. *Gradually* stir in broth. Heat to boiling, stirring constantly. Boil and stir 1 minute. Stir in salt and pepper. Serving suggestions: beef, veal, or pork.

1 TABLESPOON: Calories 15 (Calories from Fat 10); Fat 1g (Saturated 0g); Cholesterol 0mg; Sodium 90mg; Carbohydrate 1g (Dietary Fiber 0g); Protein 0g

BORDELAISE SAUCE: Decrease broth to 1/2 cup and add 1/2 cup dry red wine. Stir in 1/2 teaspoon chopped fresh parsley, 1/2 teaspoon finely chopped onion, 1/2 teaspoon crushed 1 bay leaf and 3/4 teaspoon chopped fresh or 1/4 teaspoon dried thyme leaves with the broth. Remove bay leaf before serving. Serve with steaks, pork chops or hamburgers.

MUSHROOM-WINE SAUCE: Substitute 1/3 cup red or white wine for 1/3 cup of the beef broth. Sauté 1 cup sliced mushrooms or 1 jar (4 1/2 ounces) sliced mushrooms, drained, until brown after removing the onion slice. Stir mushrooms and a few drops Worcestershire sauce into sauce. Serve with fish, chicken or meat.

RAISIN SAUCE: Substitute 1/2 cup apple cider for 1/2 cup of the beef broth. Stir in 1/4 cup raisins with the broth. Serve with ham, pork, beef or poultry.

Herbs Chart

Herbs are the aromatic leaves of plants grown in temperate regions. Some herbs (such as cilantro, oregano, rosemary, tarragon and thyme) have a dominant flavor and can be used by themselves or in combination with milder ones. Milder herbs (such as basil, dill weed, chervil, chives, marjoram and mint) can be blended into wonderful flavor combinations or used on their own for a delicate flavor.

Use small amounts of herbs, then taste before adding more, as too much of any herb can overwhelm the food or become bitter. Start by adding 1 teaspoon of fresh herbs or 1/4 teaspoon of dried herbs for every 4 servings.

For dried herbs, measure then crush the herbs in the palm of your hand to help release more flavor before adding to foods.

Fresh homegrown herbs have more flavor than fresh store-bought herbs. To use fresh herbs instead of dried, use three to four times more fresh herbs than dried. Chop fresh herbs with a knife or snip with a kitchen scissors.

Herb and Form	Flavor	Use
Basil (leaves, ground)	Sweet, with clovelike pungent tang	Eggs, meats, pesto, salads, soups, stews, tomato dishes
Bay leaves (leaves, ground)	Pungent, aromatic	Meats, pickling, sauces, soups, stews, vegetables
Chervil (leaves)	More aromatic than parsley, slight anise flavor	Eggs, fish, salads, sauces, soups, stuffings
Chives (freeze-dried)	Onionlike	Appetizers, cream soups, eggs, garnish, salads
Cilantro (leaves; also called Chinese parsley)	Distinctively aromatic, parsleylike	Chinese, Italian and Mexican dishes, garnish, pasta salads, pesto
Dill weed (whole, dried)	Pungent, tangy	Breads, cheese, fish, salads, sauces, vegetables
Marjoram (leaves, ground)	Aromatic, with slightly bitter overtone	Cottage cheese, fish, lamb, poultry, sausages, soups, stews, stuffings, vegetables
Mint (leaves, flakes)	Strong, sweet with cool aftertaste	Beverages, desserts, fish, lamb, sauces, soups
Oregano (leaves, ground)	Strong, aromatic with pleasantly bitter undertone	Cheese, eggs, fish, Italian dishes, meats, sauces, soups, vegetables
Parsley (leaves)	Slightly peppery	Garnish, herb mixtures, sauces, soups, stews
Rosemary (leaves)	Fresh, sweet flavor	Casseroles, fish, lamb, salads, seafood, soups, vegetables
Sage (leaves, rubbed, ground)	Aromatic, slightly bitter	Fish, meats, poultry, salads, sausages, soups, stuffings
Savory (leaves, ground)	Aromatic, slightly pungent	Poultry, meats, salads, sauces, soups, stuffings, vegetables
Tarragon (leaves)	Piquant, aniselike	Eggs, meats, pickling, poultry, salads, sauces, tomatoes
Thyme (leaves, ground)	Aromatic, pungent	Chowders, fish, meats, poultry, stews, stuffings, tomatoes

Cilantro

Chives

Basil

Rosemary

Mint

Sage

Oregano

Chervil

Marjoram

Savory

Dill Weed

Bay Leaves

Thyme

Parsley (curly)

Tarragon

Spices and Seeds Chart

Spices consist of the seeds, buds, fruit or flower parts, bark or roots of aromatic plants from tropical regions. A mortar and pestle, spice grinder or small electric coffee grinder works well for crushing and blending.

Form	Flavor	Use
Allspice (whole, ground; a spice, not a blend)	Pungent, sweet	Cakes, cookies, fruits, jerk seasoning, pickling, pies, poaching fish, spinach, stews
Cinnamon (stick, ground)	Aromatic, pungent, sweet	Cakes, cappuccino, cookies, fruit desserts, maple syrup, pies, pickling, puddings, hot drinks
Cloves (whole, ground)	Aromatic, strong, pungent, sweet	Baked beans, desserts, fruits, gravies, meats, pickling, sausages, stews, syrups, tea, vegetables
Garlic (minced, powdered)	Pungent aroma and taste	Fish, meats, salads, sauces, soups, vegetables
Ginger (whole, cracked bits, ground)	Pungent, spicy	Baked goods, fish, fruits, meats, sauces, sausages, soups, tea, vegetables
Nutmeg (whole, ground; mace is the covering and can be used the same way)	Fragrant, sweet with spicy undertone	Beverages, cakes, cookies, fruit desserts, parsnips, puddings, sauces, sweet potatoes, winter squash
Paprika (ground; from dried sweet red peppers)	Slightly bitter, ranges from sweet to hot	Casseroles, eggs, fish, garnish, meats, salads, soups, vegetables
Pepper, black and white (whole, ground, cracked)	Pungent and peppery	Meats, savory foods
Pepper, red (cayenne) (ground)	Very hot, peppery	Barbecue and savory sauces, chili, corn bread, eggs, fish, guacamole, meats, vegetables
Saffron (strands, powdered)	Distinctive, softly bitter	Poultry, rice, rolls, sauces, seafood, Spanish dishes
Turmeric (ground)	Aromatic, slightly bitter	Curry powder, eggs, food color, pickling, rice

Seeds add texture and flavor to foods. Seeds can be made more fragrant by toasting in a dry skillet.

Anise seed (whole)	Licoricelike	Baked goods, candy, sweetened warm milk
Caraway seed (whole)	Intense, aromatic	Cabbage, meats, pickling, bread, sauerkraut, soups, stews
Cardamom (whole pod, seeds, ground)	Pungent with slight menthol flavor	Coffee, curry, custard, fruits, Scandinavian breads, sausages
Celery seed (whole, ground)	Concentrated celery flavor, slightly bitter	Meats, pickling, salads, sauces, soups, stuffings, tomato juice-based drinks
Coriander (whole, ground)	Mildly fragrant, similar to lemon peel and sage	Curry powder, marinades, Mexican and Spanish dishes, pastries, pickling, sausages, seafood
Cumin (whole, ground)	Pungent, savory, slightly bitter	Cheese, chili, chili powder, curry powder, pickling, pork, sauerkraut
Dill seed (whole, ground)	Tangy, like caraway	Fish, meats, pickling, processed meats, soups
Fennel seed (whole, ground)	Aromatic, sweet, anise-like (resembles licorice)	Breads, eggs, fish, Italian dishes, sauces, sausages, soups, sweet pickles
Mustard seed (whole, ground)	Hot, pungent with dry aftertaste	Casseroles, Chinese dishes, meats, pickling, relishes, salads, vegetables
Poppy seed (whole)	Nutty flavor, crunchy	Baked goods, noodles, salad dressings, vegetables
Sesame seed (whole)	Nutty, slightly sweet	Breads, dips, salad dressings, poultry, seafood

Seasonings Chart

Seasonings include a wide array of dry flavor blends that can include spices, herbs, and salt. They can also include wet flavor blends in the form of red pepper sauce, Worcestershire sauce, marinades and other ingredients. Whether purchased already mixed or blended at home, they are a shortcut for adding lots of flavor to food.

Seasonings and Form	Flavor	Use
Apple Pie Spice (ground blend of cinnamon, cloves, nutmeg or mace, allspice and ginger)	Sweet and spicy	Chutneys, fruit pies, fruit sauces, pastries
Chili powder (ground blend of chili peppers, cumin, powder, oregano, cloves, allspice or other spices)	Spicy and hot	Cocktail sauce, cottage cheese, eggs, Mexican dishes, soups, stews coriander, garlic, onion
Crab Boil (blend of whole spices such as whole peppercorns, bay leaves, crushed red peppers, mustard seed, gingerroot)	Savory and aromatic	Add to water when boiling seafood
Curry powder (ground blend of as many as 20 spices—ginger, turmeric, fenugreek, vegetables seed, cloves, cinnamon, cumin seed, black pepper and red pepper are typical)	Pungent, mild (Indian) to hot (Madras)	Appetizers, chicken and shrimp salads, eggs, fish, fruit compotes, meats, sauces, split pea soup
Fines Herbs (blend of herbs such as parsley, chives and tarragon)	Delicate	Dips, eggs, fish, French dishes, poultry, salad dressings, salads, sauces, veal, vegetables
Five-Spice Powder (varied blend of five spices—star anise, cinnamon and cloves are usually used)	Slightly sweet and pungent	Chinese and other Oriental dishes, marinades, meats, poultry, sauces
Grill Seasoning (varied blends for different kinds of meat, poultry and fish)	Mild to spicy	Fish and seafood, meats, poultry, vegetables
Herb Seasoning (varied blends of mild dried herb leaves such as marjoram, oregano, basil and chervil)	Mild and savory	Casseroles, meat loaves, salad dressings, salads, vegetables
Italian Seasoning (oregano, basil, red pepper, rosemary, garlic powder)	Savory and pungent	Italian dishes, pasta, pizza
Poultry Seasoning (ground blend of sage, thyme, marjoram, savory, sometimes rosemary and other spices)	Savory and musty	Meat loaves, poultry and other meat stuffings
Pumpkin Pie Spice (ground blend of cinnamon, nutmeg, cloves and ginger)	Sweet and aromatic	Cookies and bars, pumpkin pie, winter squash

About Seasonings

Adding seasonings to foods is often a mystery to many cooks. Herbs, spices, seasonings and seeds are nature's gifts to cooks because their flavors and fragrances enhance foods and add significant flavor.

Seasonings and seasoning mixes (dry seasonings) and marinades (wet seasonings) are a great way to add delicious and unique flavors to your favorite meats and vegetables. You can create your own seasoning mixes and marinades with a few on-hand ingredients or sample the excellent selection of highly flavored seasonings, seasoning mixes, marinades and other seasoning items available at your supermarket.

Seasonings can also be used as "rubs." This means food such as poultry, meat or vegetables is moistened with vegetable oil or other liquid, then the seasoning or mix is rubbed into the food for more flavor than when just sprinkled on.

The charts in this chapter are a general guide to selecting the herbs, spices, seasonings and aromatic seeds that are compatible with a variety of foods. Experimenting with spices and herbs is exciting—explore and enjoy!

Storing Seasonings

Store most fresh herbs with stems wrapped in a damp paper towel in plastic bags in the refrigerator. To keep herbs such as parsley and cilantro freshest, place stems in about 2 inches of water in a jar and cover with a plastic bag, securing the bag to the jar with a rubber band.

Store ground spices, dried herbs and seeds in airtight containers away from light, especially if they are packed in clear jars. Keep spices away from all heat sources, but locate them closest to where food is prepared, for greatest efficiency. Store marinades in the refrigerator after opening.

❖

Tips for Seasoning Mixes

- Seasoning mixes or rubs are highly concentrated blends of dried herbs and spices that flavor the outside of the food as it cooks.
- Store seasoning mixes tightly covered in a cool, dry place up to six months.
- To apply a seasoning mix or rub to meat and vegetables, moisten the food with vegetable oil or other liquid first. Sprinkle with the seasoning mix, and rub it into the surface of the food using your hands. Wear plastic gloves to avoid food odors on your hands if desired.
- The food can be cooked immediately using your favorite cooking method. Or it can be covered and refrigerated at least 1 hour but no longer than 24 hours before cooking, for a more intense flavor.

Mexican Seasoning Mix

PREP: 5 min
Makes 16 servings, about 1/2 cup mix

This mixture will liven up meats and can be sprinkled on potato wedges before baking, too. (photograph on page 341)

   1/4 cup ground dried red chilies or chili
      powder
   3 tablespoon dried oregano leaves
   1 tablespoon ground cumin
   2 teaspoons ground coriander
   1/2 teaspoon salt

Mix all ingredients in storage container with tight-fitting lid. Store in cool, dry location for up to 6 months. Stir before each use.

TO USE AS A RUB: Brush 1 pound boneless meat (chicken, pork, beef) with 1 tablespoon vegetable oil. Rub with 2 tablespoons seasoning mix.

TO USE AS A MARINADE: Mix 2 tablespoon seasoning mix, 1/4 cup dry white wine or chicken broth, 1/4 cup lime juice and 1 tablespoon vegetable oil.

1 SERVING (2 teaspoons): Calories 10 (Calories from Fat 0); Fat 0g (Saturated 0g); Cholesterol 0mg; Sodium 85mg; Carbohydrate 2g (Dietary Fiber 0g); Protein 0g

Garlic-Pepper Rub

PREP: 5 min
Makes 8 servings, about 2 tablespoons rub

If you're a real pepper fan, increase the amount to suit your taste. You'll notice a mouth-watering aroma during roasting, when you use this rub.

> **1 to 2 tablespoons teriyaki sauce or liquid smoke seasoning**
> **1 teaspoon garlic powder**
> **2 teaspoons cracked black pepper**

1. Brush or rub 4- to 5-pound bone-in beef, pork or lamb roast with teriyaki sauce. Sprinkle evenly with garlic powder and rub into meat. Sprinkle with pepper and press into meat. Cover and refrigerate at least 1 hour but no longer than 24 hours.

2. Roast meat as desired (see Timetable for Roasting specific meat).

1 SERVING: Calories 5 (Calories from Fat 0); Fat 0g (Saturated 0g); Cholesterol 0mg; Sodium 85mg; Carbohydrate 1g (Dietary Fiber 0g); Protein 0g

Jamaican Jerk Seasoning

PREP: 5 min
Makes 6 servings, about 3 tablespoons seasoning

The tradition of "jerking" meat is unique to Jamaica. Originally, the hot spicy seasonings were applied to wild boar to make it more edible. It's also great on other foods.

> **1 tablespoon instant minced onion**
> **2 teaspoons dried thyme leaves**
> **1 teaspoon ground allspice**
> **1 teaspoon ground pepper**
> **1/2 teaspoon ground cinnamon**
> **1/4 teaspoon ground red pepper (cayenne)**
> **1/2 teaspoon salt**

Mix all ingredients in storage container with tight-fitting lid. Store in cool, dry location for up to 6 months. Stir before each use.

TO USE AS A RUB: Brush 3- to 3 1/2-pound cut-up broiler fryer chicken or 1 1/2 pounds boneless meat (chicken, pork, beef) with 1 tablespoon vegetable oil. Rub with seasoning mix.

TO USE AS A MARINADE: Mix seasoning mix, 1/2 cup dry red wine or chicken broth, 1 tablespoon olive oil and 1 clove garlic, finely chopped.

1 SERVING (2 teaspoons): Calories 10 (Calories from Fat 0); Fat 0g (Saturated 0g); Cholesterol 0mg; Sodium 270mg; Carbohydrate 2g (Dietary Fiber 0g); Protein 0g

Tips for Marinades and Marinating

- Marinating is soaking food in a seasoned liquid (marinade) to give flavor or to tenderize less tender cuts of meat such as round steak.
- For mixing and marinating, use nonmetal containers such as glass or plastic or heavy plastic bags that will not react with the acid (i.e., vinegar, wine or lemon juice) in the marinade. Avoid using aluminum containers, which react with acid, or using earthenware containers, because they are more porous and fired at lower temperatures and the marinade may seep into the container.
- Allow about 1/4 to 1/2 cup marinade for each 1 to 2 pounds of meat, poultry, fish or vegetables.
- Marinate food covered in the refrigerator, turning occasionally. Do not marinate foods at room temperature. The flavor of the marinade will penetrate about 1/4 inch into the food.
- To add flavor, marinate 15 minutes to 2 hours or longer. To help tenderize food, marinate longer, up to 24 hours. The texture of meats can become mushy if marinated longer than 24 hours.
- *Never* serve cooked meat on the same unwashed platter on which raw marinated meat was carried to the oven or grill, to avoid bacteria contamination.
- Marinades drained from raw meat, poultry and fish that you plan to serve as a sauce must be cooked in a saucepan immediately to avoid bacteria contamination. Heat the marinade to a rolling boil and boil 1 minute, stirring constantly, before serving.

Garlic Marinade

PREP: 10 min; COOK: 5 min
Makes about 3/4 cup marinade

This marinade also works well as a dressing for tossed salads or hearty pasta salads.

1/4 cup vegetable oil
4 cloves garlic, finely chopped
1 tablespoon chopped fresh or 1 teaspoon
   dried rosemary leaves, crushed
1/2 teaspoon ground mustard (dry)
2 teaspoons soy sauce
1/4 cup red or white wine vinegar
1/4 cup dry sherry or apple juice

1. Heat oil in 10-inch skillet over medium-high heat. Cook garlic in oil, stirring frequently, until golden. Stir in rosemary, mustard and soy sauce; remove from heat. Stir in vinegar and sherry; cool.

2. Place 1 to 1 1/2 pounds boneless or 3 to 4 pounds bone-in beef, pork or lamb in shallow glass or plastic dish. Pour marinade over meat. Cover and refrigerate up to 24 hours.

3. Remove meat from marinade; reserve marinade. Cook meat as desired, brushing occasionally with marinade.

4. Remaining marinade must be boiled to serve as a sauce. Heat marinade to boiling, stirring constantly; boil and stir 1 minute.

1 TABLESPOON: Calories 50 (Calories from Fat 45); Fat 5g (Saturated 1g); Cholesterol 0mg; Sodium 60mg; Carbohydrate 1g (Dietary Fiber 0g); Protein 0g

Lemon-Herb Marinade

PREP: 10 min
Makes about 2/3 cup marinade

1/3 cup vegetable oil
1/4 cup lemon juice
1 tablespoon chopped fresh or 1 teaspoon
   dried basil leaves
2 teaspoons chopped fresh or 1/2 teaspoon
   dried thyme leaves
1/4 teaspoon salt
1/4 teaspoon pepper
2 cloves garlic, finely chopped

1. Mix all ingredients in shallow glass or plastic dish. Add about 1 pound boneless chicken, about 3 1/2 pounds bone-in chicken or about 1 pound seafood; turn to coat with marinade. Cover and refrigerate up to 24 hours.

2. Remove meat from marinade; reserve marinade. Cook meat as desired, brushing occasionally with marinade.

3. Remaining marinade must be boiled to serve as a sauce. Heat marinade to boiling, stirring constantly; boil and stir 1 minute.

1 TABLESPOON: Calories 65 (Calories from Fat 65); Fat 7g (Saturated 1g); Cholesterol 0mg; Sodium 55mg; Carbohydrate 1g (Dietary Fiber 0g); Protein 0g

> **TIMESAVING TIP**
> Use dried herbs and already-chopped garlic from a jar.

Fajita Marinade

PREP: 5 min
Makes about 1/2 cup marinade

Meats marinated in this mixture and then cooked are also good in salads or sandwiches. To make Fajitas, see page 234.

1/4 cup vegetable oil
1/4 cup red wine vinegar
1 teaspoon sugar
1 teaspoon dried oregano leaves
1 teaspoon chili powder
1/2 teaspoon garlic powder
1/2 teaspoon salt
1/4 teaspoon pepper

1. Mix all ingredients in shallow glass or plastic dish. Add about 1 pound boneless or about 2 to 3 pounds bone-in beef, pork or chicken; turn to coat with marinade. Cover and refrigerate up to 24 hours.

2. Remove meat from marinade; reserve marinade. Cook meat as desired, brushing occasionally with marinade.

3. Remaining marinade must be boiled to serve as a sauce. Heat marinade to boiling, stirring constantly; boil and stir 1 minute.

1 TABLESPOON: Calories 65 (Calories from Fat 65); Fat 7g (Saturated 1g); Cholesterol 0mg; Sodium 140mg; Carbohydrate 1g (Dietary Fiber 0g); Protein 0g

> **TIMESAVING TIP**
> When measuring the oil and vinegar, use a glass measuring cup, adding the oil to the 1/4 cup line, then add the vinegar to the oil up to the 1/2 cup line.

About Condiments

If you're looking for ways to add zest to your food, try using condiments. Condiments are accompaniments to food that are added by each person at the dining table, so everyone gets just what he or she likes. Condiments include small amounts of savory, piquant, spicy, sweet or salty foods such as flavorful salsas, feisty relishes, sweet chutneys and even seasoning mixtures.

Salsa, ketchup and mustard are three of the most popular condiments. Others include steak sauce, chutneys, red pepper sauce, jams, jellies, butters and spreads.

Condiments can be made ahead and, depending on the ingredients, are most often served from the refrigerator or at room temperature. Your supermarket is a mecca for a bountiful collection of high-flavored already-prepared condiments. Besides the condiments section, look for them in the refrigerator and freezer sections as well as the aisle where international foods are located.

Corn Relish

PREP: 15 min; COOK: 5 min; CHILL: 4 hr
Makes about 2 cups relish

>   4 ears fresh corn
>   1/2 cup water
>   2 tablespoons chopped green bell pepper
>   1 tablespoon finely chopped onion
>   1 jar (2 ounces) diced pimientos, drained
>   1/2 cup sugar
>   1/2 cup cider or white vinegar
>   1/2 teaspoon celery seed
>   1/4 teaspoon salt
>   1/4 teaspoon mustard seed
>   1/4 teaspoon red pepper sauce

1. Prepare corn as directed (page 397). Cut enough kernels from corn to measure 2 cups. Heat water to boiling in 1 1/2-quart saucepan. Add corn. Heat to boiling; reduce heat to medium. Cover and cook 9 to 10 minutes or until corn is tender; drain.

2. Mix corn, bell pepper, onion and pimientos in medium heatproof glass or plastic bowl.

3. Heat remaining ingredients to boiling in 1-quart saucepan, stirring occasionally. Boil 2 minutes. Pour over corn mixture. Cover and refrigerate at least 4 hours to blend flavors but no longer than 5 days. Serving suggestions: poultry, pork, beef.

1 TABLESPOON: Calories 25 (Calories from Fat 0); Fat 0g (Saturated 0g); Cholesterol 0mg; Sodium 20mg; Carbohydrate 6g (Dietary Fiber 0g); Protein 0g

BLACK BEAN-CORN RELISH: Stir in 1 can (15 ounces) black beans, rinsed and drained. Makes 3 1/2 cups relish.

> **TIMESAVING TIP**
> Substitute 1 can (16 ounces) whole kernel corn, drained, or 2 cups frozen whole kernel corn, thawed, for the cooked fresh corn.

Cranberry-Orange Relish

PREP: 10 min; CHILL: 24 hr
Makes about 2 1/2 cups relish

A food grinder can be used to chop the cranberries and oranges. Using a fine blade will give a velvety texture, while a coarse blade will give a rougher texture. (photograph on page 341)

>   1 cup sugar
>   1 tablespoon finely chopped crystallized
>   ginger, if desired
>   1 package (12 ounces) fresh or frozen
>   cranberries (3 cups)
>   1 unpeeled orange, cut into 1-inch pieces

1. Place sugar and ginger in medium bowl.

2. Place half of the cranberries and orange pieces at a time in food processor. Cover and process with short on-and-off motions about 15 seconds or until evenly chopped. Stir into sugar. Cover and refrigerate at least 24 hours to blend flavors but no longer than 1 week. Serving suggestions: pork, ham or poultry.

1 TABLESPOON: Calories 25 (Calories from Fat 0); Fat 0g (Saturated 0g); Cholesterol 0mg; Sodium 0mg; Carbohydrate 6g (Dietary Fiber 0g); Protein 0g

Tomato Salsa

PREP: 20 min
Makes about 3 1/2 cups salsa

(photograph on page 341)

    3 large tomatoes, seeded and chopped
        (3 cups)
    1 small green bell pepper, chopped (1/2 cup)
    3 cloves garlic, finely chopped
    1/2 cup sliced green onions (5 medium)
    2 tablespoons chopped fresh cilantro
    1 tablespoon finely chopped jalapeño chilies
    2 to 3 tablespoons lime juice
    1/2 teaspoon salt

Mix all ingredients in glass or plastic bowl. Cover and refrigerate until serving. Serving suggestions: tortilla chips, crackers, vegetables, fish, chicken.

1 TABLESPOON: Calories 5 (Calories from Fat 0); Fat 0g (Saturated 0g); Cholesterol 0mg; Sodium 20mg; Carbohydrate 1g (Dietary Fiber 0g); Protein 0g

PINEAPPLE SALSA: Substitute 3 cups chopped fresh pineapple for the tomatoes. Omit garlic. Add 3/4 teaspoon ground cumin.

RED ONION SALSA: Substitute 1 1/2 cups finely chopped red onion (2 medium) for 2 of the tomatoes. Add 1 tablespoon olive or vegetable oil and 1/4 teaspoon ground red pepper (cayenne).

Pear-Apricot Chutney

PREP: 25 min; COOK: 35 min; COOL: 1 hr
Makes about 4 half-pints chutney

This is nice as a bread spread, served with cheese or mixed with sour cream or yogurt and used as a topping for fruit or pound cake.

    5 cups coarsely chopped peeled pears
        (2 pounds)
    3 cups sugar
    1/2 cup chopped dried apricots
    1 teaspoon grated lemon peel
    3 tablespoons lemon juice
    1 teaspoon finely chopped gingerroot or
        1/2 teaspoon ground ginger

   1. Mix all ingredients in 3-quart saucepan. Heat to boiling over medium heat, stirring frequently. Boil 25 to 30 minutes, stirring occasionally, until mixture thickens.

   2. *Immediately* pour into hot, sterilized jars, leaving 1/4-inch headspace. Wipe rims of jars; seal. Cool on rack 1 hour. Store in refrigerator up to 2 months.

1 TABLESPOON: Calories 50 (Calories from Fat 0); Fat 0g (Saturated 0g); Cholesterol 0mg; Sodium 0mg; Carbohydrate 12g (Dietary Fiber 0g); Protein 0g

PAPAYA-APRICOT CHUTNEY: Substitute 2 ripe medium papayas (1 pound each) for the pears. Peel papayas; cut in half and scoop out seeds. Chop papaya.

Hollandaise Sauce (page 347), Black Bean–Corn Relish

Savory Butters

PREP: 5 min
Makes about 1/4 cup butter

Top grilled or broiled beef or fish steaks, pork chops or chicken breasts with these easy butters, or toss with hot pasta, rice or vegetables. And of course, they are also great as a spread for bread.

Beat 1/4 cup *stick* margarine or butter*,
softened, and one of the following:
Garlic: 1/2 teaspoon paprika, 1/8 teaspoon
pepper and 2 cloves garlic, crushed
Herb: 1 to 2 tablespoons chopped fresh or
1 to 2 teaspoons dried herb leaves (basil,
chives, oregano, savory, tarragon or
thyme), 1 teaspoon lemon juice and
1/4 teaspoon salt
Mustard: 1 tablespoon chopped fresh
parsley, 2 tablespoons mustard and
1/4 teaspoon salt
Sesame: 1 tablespoon toasted sesame seed,
1 teaspoon Worcestershire sauce and
1/2 teaspoon garlic salt

We do not recommend using vegetable oil spreads (see page 13).

1 TABLESPOON (average for all flavors): Calories 105
(Calories from Fat 100); Fat 11g (Saturated 2g);
Cholesterol 0mg; Sodium 135mg; Carbohydrate 1g
(Dietary Fiber 0g); Protein 0g

Sweet Butters

PREP: 5 min
Makes about 1/2 cup butter

You'll especially enjoy the aroma of these butters when they're served on warm breads, rolls and biscuits.

Beat 1/2 cup *stick* margarine or butter*,
softened, and one of the following:
Almond: 1 tablespoon finely chopped
almonds and 1/2 teaspoon almond
extract
Date: 1/4 cup finely chopped dates
Orange: 1 teaspoon grated orange peel and
1 tablespoon orange juice
Raspberry: 1/2 cup raspberries, crushed, and
1 tablespoon sugar, or 1/4 cup raspberry
jam

We do not recommend using vegetable oil spreads (see page 13).

1 TABLESPOON (average for all flavors): Calories 110
(Calories from Fat 110); Fat 12g (Saturated 2g); Cholesterol 0mg;
Sodium 135mg; Carbohydrate 0g (Dietary Fiber 0g); Protein 0g

Mixed Berry Jam

PREP: 25 min; STAND: 24 hr
Makes about 5 half-pints jam

If fresh berries aren't readily available, frozen berries, thawed and drained, are a good substitute.

1 cup crushed strawberries (1 pint
whole berries)
1 cup crushed raspberries (1 pint
whole berries)
4 cups sugar
1/2 teaspoon grated lemon peel
1 tablespoon lemon juice
1 pouch (3 ounces) liquid fruit pectin

1. Mix berries and sugar in large glass or plastic bowl. Let stand at room temperature about 10 minutes, stirring occasionally, until sugar is dissolved.

2. Mix in lemon peel, lemon juice and pectin. Stir 3 to 5 minutes or until slightly thickened.

3. Spoon mixture into freezer containers, leaving 1/2-inch headspace. Seal *immediately.* Let stand at room temperature until set, about 24 hours. Refrigerate up to 3 weeks, or freeze up to 1 year (thaw in refrigerator or at room temperature before serving). Use as a spread or in desserts.

1 TABLESPOON: Calories 45 (Calories from Fat 0); Fat 0g
(Saturated 0g); Cholesterol 0mg; Sodium 0mg;
Carbohydrate 11g (Dietary Fiber 0g); Protein 0g

Rosy Grape Jelly

PREP: 1 1/4 hr; COOK: 5 min; COOL: 1 hr
Makes about 5 half-pints jelly

2 cups cranberry juice cocktail
3/4 cup grape juice
1 package (1 3/4 ounces) powdered fruit
pectin
3 1/4 cups sugar

1. Mix cranberry juice cocktail, grape juice and pectin in 3-quart saucepan until smooth. Heat to boiling over high heat, stirring constantly.

2. Stir in sugar, all at once. Heat to boiling, stirring constantly. Boil and stir 1 minute; remove from heat.

3. *Quickly* skim off foam. *Immediately* pour into hot, sterilized jars, leaving 1/2-inch headspace. Cool uncovered on rack 1 hour. Wipe rims of jars; seal. Let stand at room temperature until set, about 24 hours. Refrigerate up to 3 weeks, or freeze up to 6 months (thaw in refrigerator or at room temperature before serving). Use as a spread or in desserts.

1 TABLESPOON: Calories 35 (Calories from Fat 0); Fat 0g
(Saturated 0g); Cholesterol 0mg; Sodium 0mg; Carbohydrate 9g
(Dietary Fiber 0g); Protein 0g

Spirited Pumpkin Butter, Mixed Berry Jam on Waffles (page 51)

Spirited Apple Butter

PREP: 20 min; COOK: 3 hr
Makes about 5 half-pints butter

Even though this thick mixture contains no butter, its name comes from the fact that it spreads like butter.

- 1 can (12 ounces) frozen apple juice
    concentrate
- 1/2 cup sweet red wine or apple cider
- 4 pounds cooking apples, peeled, cored and
    cut into fourths (about 3 quarts)
- 3/4 cup packed brown sugar
- 1 cup apple brandy or apple cider
- 1 teaspoon ground cinnamon
- 1 teaspoon ground ginger
- 1/4 teaspoon ground cloves

1. Heat apple juice concentrate, wine and apples to boiling in Dutch oven; reduce heat to low. Simmer uncovered about 1 hour, stirring occasionally, until apples are very soft. Mash with potato masher if necessary, to remove all lumps.

2. Stir in remaining ingredients. Heat to boiling; reduce heat to low. Simmer uncovered about 2 hours, stirring occasionally, until no liquid separates from pulp.

3. *Immediately* pour into hot, sterilized jars, leaving 1/4-inch headspace. Wipe rims of jars; seal. Cool on rack 1 hour. Store in refrigerator up to 2 months. Use as a bread spread or in desserts.

1 TABLESPOON: Calories 30 (Calories from Fat 0); Fat 0g (Saturated 0g); Cholesterol 0mg; Sodium 2mg; Carbohydrate 8g (Dietary Fiber 0g); Protein 0g

SPIRITED PUMPKIN BUTTER: Omit wine. Substitute 3 cans (16 ounces each) pumpkin for the apples. Increase brown sugar to 1 cup and cinnamon to 1 1/2 teaspoons. Heat all ingredients to boiling in Dutch oven, stirring frequently; reduce heat to low. Simmer uncovered about 1 hour, stirring frequently. Continue as directed in step 3. Makes about 6 half-pints butter.

TIMESAVING TIP

Use a crank-type apple peeler to quickly peel the apples. Or, leave them unpeeled and just quarter and core, then put them through a mesh strainer or food mill to quickly remove the cooked peelings.

Lemon Curd

PREP: 15 min; COOK: 10 min
Makes about 2 cups curd

1 cup sugar
1 tablespoon finely shredded lemon peel
1 cup lemon juice (5 large lemons)
3 tablespoons firm *stick* margarine or butter*,
    cut up
3 large eggs, slightly beaten

1. Mix sugar, lemon peel and lemon juice in heavy
1 1/2-quart saucepan with wire whisk.

2. Stir in margarine and eggs. Cook over medium
heat about 8 minutes, stirring constantly, until mixture
thickens and coats back of spoon (do not boil).

3. *Immediately* pour into 1-pint container or two 1-
cup containers. Cover and store in refrigerator up to 2
months. Use as a spread or dessert filling or topping.

We do not recommend using vegetable oil spreads (see page 13).

1 TABLESPOON: Calories 50 (Calories from Fat 20); Fat 2g
(Saturated 0g); Cholesterol 20mg; Sodium 20mg;
Carbohydrate 7g (Dietary Fiber 0g); Protein 1g

KEY LIME CURD: Substitute lime peel for the lemon
peel and Key lime juice for the lemon juice.

TIMESAVING TIP

Use 1 lemon for the shredded lemon peel and part of
the juice, and add frozen (thawed) or bottled lemon
juice to make 1 cup.

Nut-Flavored Oil

PREP: 10 min; STAND: 10 days
Makes about 2 cups oil

*If you like, use other kinds of nuts, or try a mixture of two or
more kinds.*

1 cup walnuts, almonds or hazelnuts
2 cups vegetable oil

1. Place nuts and 1/2 cup of the oil in blender or
food processor. Cover and blend until nuts are finely
chopped.

2. Place nut mixture and remaining oil in glass jar
or bottle. Cover tightly and let stand in cool, dry place
10 days.

3. Strain oil. Cover and store in refrigerator up to 3
months. Use in salad dressings, sauces and marinades.

1 TABLESPOON: Calories 125 (Calories from Fat 125); Fat
14g (Saturated 2g); Cholesterol 0mg; Sodium 0mg;
Carbohydrate 0g (Dietary Fiber 0g); Protein 0g

Herb Vinegar

PREP: 10 min; STAND: 10 days
Makes about 2 cups vinegar

*Flavored vinegars can add a more distinctive taste to your
favorite recipes. And making them yourself not only gives
satisfaction, but it's usually less costly than buying them.*

2 cups white wine or white vinegar
1/2 cup firmly packed herb leaves (basil,
    chives, dill weed, mint, oregano, rosemary
    or tarragon)

1. Shake vinegar and herb in tightly covered glass
jar or bottle. Let stand in cool, dry place 10 days.

2. Strain vinegar. Place 1 sprig of fresh herb in jar to
identify if desired. Cover and store at room temperature up to 6 months. Use in salad dressings, sauces and
marinades.

1 TABLESPOON: Calories 5 (Calories from Fat 0); Fat 0g
(Saturated 0g); Cholesterol 0mg; Sodium 0mg; Carbohydrate 1g
(Dietary Fiber 0g); Protein 0g

BERRY VINEGAR: Substitute 2 cups berries, crushed,
for the herb.

GARLIC VINEGAR: Substitute 6 cloves garlic, cut in
half, for the herb.

GINGER VINEGAR: Substitute 1/2 cup chopped
peeled gingerroot for the herb.

LEMON VINEGAR: Substitute peel from 2 lemons
for the herb.

Stews, Soups & Sandwiches

About Stews and Soups

Soups and stews have many traits in common—but they do have some differences. Stews are usually hearty combinations of meat, poultry or fish, with vegetables and seasonings. Some are vegetable only, such as our Garden Vegetable Stew. Made on top of the stove or in the oven, the pieces of meat and vegetables in a stew are generally larger than in soup, and the mixture is usually thickened before serving. On the other hand, soup is much more variable. It can be served hot or cold, as a first course or main course. Ranging from clear to creamy, quick cooking or slow simmered, soup plays many roles.

Tips for Stews and Soups

- Be sure to use the size of pan specified. Using a pan that is too small can cause spillovers or cause the mixture to heat too slowly, possibly overcooking some vegetables or meats.
- To save time, buy fresh or frozen cut-up or chopped vegetables from the produce section, frozen food section or salad bar of your supermarket. If chopping your own vegetables, use a sharp chef's knife or your food processor. A blender or food processor makes quick work of blending or pureeing cream soups.
- Don't cheat on cooking time—simmering stews and soups over low heat helps to extract the maximum flavor from the ingredients.
- When thickening stews and soups with a flour mixture, prevent lumps by mixing the flour thoroughly in cold liquid before adding it to the boiling mixture. To achieve the proper consistency and to prevent a starchy flavor, heat the thickened liquid to boiling, and boil for the time specified in the recipe.
- When cooking soups containing dairy products, be sure to heat them slowly, and do not allow them to come to a boil because the ingredients may separate.
- Chill stew, soup or broth several hours or overnight in the refrigerator. The fat will rise to the surface and solidify. Skim off the fat and discard.
- Puree one or more of the vegetables used in the soup or stew by placing the cooked vegetable in a blender or food processor container with a little of the stew or soup liquid. Cover and puree until smooth. Add it back to the soup or stew to thicken it, rather than using a fat and flour mixture to thicken it. Or stir mashed potato mix (dry) into the hot soup or stew to thicken it.

Storing and Reheating Stews and Soups

In most cases, stews and soups are great when made ahead and reheated, as the flavor frequently improves with age. Most stews and soups can be covered and refrigerated up to three days. Those made with fish or shellfish should be stored no longer than one day.

Stews thickened with flour or cornstarch may break down and separate after freezing. To prepare these kinds of stews for freezing, save the thickening step until it's reheated. Soups and broths freeze very well. You can double a soup recipe and freeze half of it in freezer containers, leaving 1/4- to 1/2-inch headspace for the soup to expand when frozen. Broths, like soups, can be stored in freezer containers, or they can be frozen in ice-cube trays. The broth cubes can then be transferred to a heavy plastic freezer bag and used as needed. Soups and broths can be kept frozen two to three months.

Some soups may have flavor and textural changes when frozen. Certain ingredients such as green bell peppers may intensify during freezing, and onion gradually loses its flavor. Adjust the seasoning to taste after reheating soups. Freezing makes potatoes grainy and soft; to avoid this, leave the potatoes out of the soup until it's time to reheat, then add cooked potatoes. Dense soups tend to get thicker during storage. Add a little broth, milk or half-and-half while reheating, until you reach the desired consistency.

Thaw soups in the refrigerator and use fully thawed soups immediately. Heat broth-based soups over medium heat, stirring occasionally, until hot. These soups also can be microwaved to reheat; they heat quickly and evenly without separating. Thick purees or soups containing milk, cream, eggs or cheese need to be reheated using low heat, stirring frequently, and not allowed to boil, or the ingredients may separate. If microwaving, use lower power setting.

Preceding page: Easy Cioppino (page 370)

Harvest Beef Stew

PREP: 35 min; BAKE: 4 hr
Makes 8 servings, about 1 1/2 cups each

Tapioca's not just for pudding! It also makes a great thickener in recipes such as this savory stew. It doesn't require stirring and can withstand long periods of cooking without breaking down.

2 pounds beef stew meat, cut into 1-inch cubes
4 medium carrots, cut into 1-inch pieces
2 medium onions, cut into eighths
4 cloves garlic, finely chopped
2 cans (16 ounces each) whole tomatoes, undrained
1/3 cup uncooked quick-cooking tapioca
1 tablespoon chopped fresh or 1 teaspoon dried basil leaves
1 tablespoon cumin seed
1 teaspoon salt
2 ears corn, cut into fourths*, or 1 package (10 ounces) frozen whole kernel corn
8 small new potatoes (1 pound), cut in half
2 small zucchini, thinly sliced

1. Heat oven to 325°.

2. Mix all ingredients except corn, potatoes and zucchini in Dutch oven, breaking up tomatoes. Cover and bake 2 1/2 hours, stirring 2 or 3 times during the first 1 1/2 hours.

3. Stir in corn and potatoes. Cover and bake 1 to 1 1/2 hours longer or until beef and vegetables are tender.

4. Stir in zucchini. Cover and let stand 10 minutes.

*4 ears frozen corn, thawed and cut in half, can be substituted for the fresh corn.

1 SERVING: Calories 405 (Calories from Fat 200); Fat 22g (Saturated 9g); Cholesterol 70mg; Sodium 520mg; Carbohydrate 34g (Dietary Fiber 5g); Protein 23g

Hungarian Goulash

PREP: 30 min; COOK: 1 hr 40 min
Makes 6 servings, about 1 cup each

1 tablespoon vegetable oil or bacon fat
1 1/2 pounds beef boneless chuck, tip or round roast or pork boneless shoulder, cut into 3/4-inch cubes
1 cup beef broth
3 tablespoons paprika
1 1/2 teaspoons salt
1/2 teaspoon caraway seed
1/4 teaspoon pepper
3 large onions, chopped (3 cups)
2 cloves garlic, chopped
1 can (8 ounces) whole tomatoes, undrained
1/4 cup cold water
2 tablespoons all-purpose flour
6 cups hot cooked noodles

1. Heat oil in Dutch oven or 12-inch skillet over medium heat. Cook beef in oil about 15 minutes, stirring occasionally, until beef is brown; drain.

2. Stir in remaining ingredients except water, flour and noodles, breaking up tomatoes. Heat to boiling; reduce heat to low. Cover and simmer about 1 1/4 hours, stirring occasionally, until beef is tender.

3. Shake water and flour in tightly covered container; *gradually* stir into beef mixture. Heat to boiling, stirring constantly. Boil and stir 1 minute. Serve over noodles.

1 SERVING: Calories 540 (Calories from Fat 235); Fat 26g (Saturated 9g); Cholesterol 120mg; Sodium 770mg; Carbohydrate 52g (Dietary Fiber 5g); Protein 29g

---

LIGHTER HUNGARIAN GOULASH
For 10 grams of fat and 380 calories per serving, omit vegetable oil. Spray Dutch oven with nonstick cooking spray before heating. Reduce beef to 1 pound. Use noodles made without egg yolks.

Beef Stew, Easy Garlic Cheese Biscuits (page 47)

Beef Stew

PREP: 25 min; COOK: 3 hr 40 min
Makes 6 servings, about 1 1/2 cups each

1 tablespoon vegetable oil or shortening
1 pound beef boneless chuck, tip or round
   roast, cut into 1-inch cubes
3 cups hot water
1/2 teaspoon salt
1/8 teaspoon pepper
2 medium carrots, cut into 1-inch pieces
   (1 cup)
1 large potato, cut into 1 1/2-inch pieces
   (1 1/4 cups)
1 medium turnip, cut into 1-inch pieces
   (1 cup)
1 medium green bell pepper, cut into 1-inch
   pieces (1 cup)
1 medium stalk celery, cut into 1-inch pieces
   (1/2 cup)
1 small onion, chopped (1/4 cup)
1/2 teaspoon browning sauce, if desired
1 teaspoon salt
1 bay leaf
Dumplings (page 51), if desired
1/2 cup cold water
2 tablespoons all-purpose flour

1. Heat oil in 12-inch skillet or Dutch oven. Cook beef in oil about 15 minutes, stirring occasionally, until beef is brown. Add hot water, 1/2 teaspoon salt and the pepper. Heat to boiling; reduce heat to low. Cover and simmer 2 to 2 1/2 hours or until beef is almost tender.

2. Stir in remaining ingredients except Dumplings, cold water and flour. Cover and simmer about 30 minutes or until vegetables are tender. Remove bay leaf.

3. Prepare Dumplings.

4. Shake cold water and flour in tightly covered container; *gradually* stir into beef mixture. Heat to boiling, stirring constantly. Boil and stir 1 minute; reduce heat to low.

5. Drop dumpling dough by 10 to 12 spoonfuls onto hot stew (do not drop directly into liquid). Cook uncovered 10 minutes. Cover and cook 10 minutes longer.

1 SERVING: Calories 250 (Calories from Fat 145); Fat 16g (Saturated 6g); Cholesterol 45mg; Sodium 590mg; Carbohydrate 14g (Dietary Fiber 2g); Protein 14g

CHICKEN STEW: Substitute 1 1/2- to 2-pounds stewing chicken, cut up, for the beef.

Beef Burgundy Stew

PREP: 1 hr; COOK: 2 hr
Makes 8 servings, about 1 cup each

This favorite stew can be easily made into a casserole by stirring in four cups of hot cooked noodles before serving.

2 tablespoons margarine or butter
5 medium onions, sliced
6 cups sliced mushrooms (1 pound)
3 pounds beef stew meat, cut into
   1-inch cubes
2 cloves garlic, finely chopped
2 teaspoons salt
1 teaspoon chopped fresh or 1/2 teaspoon
   dried marjoram leaves
1 teaspoon chopped fresh or 1/2 teaspoon
   dried thyme leaves
1/4 teaspoon pepper
3 cups beef broth
3 tablespoons all-purpose flour
3 1/2 cups red Burgundy
Crusty French bread (page 58), if desired

1. Melt margarine in Dutch oven or 3-quart saucepan over medium heat. Cook onions and mushrooms in margarine about 10 minutes, stirring occasionally, until onions are tender. Remove vegetables from Dutch oven; drain and reserve.

2. Cook beef and garlic in Dutch oven over medium heat, stirring occasionally, until beef is brown; drain. Sprinkle with salt, marjoram, thyme and pepper.

3. Mix broth and flour; pour over beef. Heat to boiling, stirring constantly. Boil and stir 1 minute.

4. Stir in Burgundy. Cover and simmer 1 1/2 to 2 hours, stirring in onions and mushrooms 5 minutes before end of simmer time. Serve in bowls with bread for dipping into sauce.

1 SERVING: Calories 550 (Calories from Fat 315); Fat 35g (Saturated 14g); Cholesterol 100mg; Sodium 890mg; Carbohydrate 13g (Dietary Fiber 2g); Protein 33g

Chicken and Dumplings

PREP: 20 min; COOK: 2 3/4 hr
Makes 4 to 6 servings

3- to 3 1/2-pound stewing chicken, cut up
4 celery stalk tops
1 medium carrot, sliced (1/2 cup)
1 small onion, sliced
2 sprigs parsley, chopped
1 teaspoon salt
1/8 teaspoon pepper
5 cups water
2 1/2 cups Bisquick® Original baking mix
2/3 cup milk

1. Remove any excess fat from chicken. Place chicken, giblets (except liver), neck, celery, carrot, onion, parsley, salt, pepper and water in Dutch oven. Cover and heat to boiling; reduce heat to low. Cook over low heat about 2 hours or until juice of chicken is no longer pink when centers of thickest pieces are cut.

2. Remove chicken and vegetables from Dutch oven. Skim 1/2 cup fat from broth; reserve. Remove broth; reserve 4 cups.

3. Heat reserved fat in Dutch oven over low heat. Stir in 1/2 cup of the baking mix. Cook, stirring constantly, until mixture is smooth and bubbly; remove from heat.

4. Stir in reserved broth. Heat to boiling, stirring constantly. Boil and stir 1 minute. Return chicken and vegetables to Dutch oven; heat until hot.

5. Mix remaining 2 cups baking mix and the milk until soft dough forms. Drop dough by spoonfuls onto hot chicken mixture (do not drop directly into liquid). Cook uncovered over low heat 10 minutes. Cover and cook 10 minutes longer.

1 SERVING: Calories 645 (Calories from Fat 260); Fat 29g (Saturated 8g); Cholesterol 130mg; Sodium 1750mg; Carbohydrate 51g (Dietary Fiber 2g); Protein 47g

---

TIMESAVING TIP

Omit stewing chicken, salt and water. Place celery, carrot, onion, parsley, pepper and 4 cups chicken broth in Dutch oven. Cover and heat to boiling; reduce heat. Simmer until vegetables are soft, about 15 minutes. Remove vegetables from broth; reserve vegetables and broth. Substitute 1/2 cup margarine spread or butter for the 1/2 cup fat. Add 3 cups of cut-up cooked chicken with the vegetables as directed in step 4.

White Chili

Shrimp Gumbo

PREP: 20 min; COOK: 1 hr 10 min
Makes 6 servings, about 1 1/2 cups each

Often used in Creole cooking, okra has a mild, asparagus-like flavor. During cooking it develops a slippery texture and thickens any liquid in which it is cooked. Avoid cooking gumbo in an aluminum or iron pan, to prevent the okra from discoloring.

1/4 cup margarine or butter
2 medium onions, sliced
1 medium green bell pepper, cut into thin
    strips
2 cloves garlic, crushed
2 tablespoons all-purpose flour
3 cups beef broth
1/2 teaspoon red pepper sauce
1/4 teaspoon salt
1/4 teaspoon pepper
1 bay leaf
1 package (10 ounces) frozen cut okra,
    thawed
1 can (16 ounces) whole tomatoes,
    undrained
1 can (6 ounces) tomato paste
1 1/2 pounds medium uncooked shrimp
    in shells
3 cups hot cooked rice (page 204)
1/4 cup chopped fresh parsley

1. Melt margarine in Dutch oven over medium heat. Cook onions, bell pepper and garlic in margarine 5 minutes, stirring occasionally. Stir in flour. Cook over medium heat, stirring constantly, until bubbly; remove from heat.

2. Stir in remaining ingredients except shrimp, rice and parsley, breaking up tomatoes. Heat to boiling; reduce heat to low. Simmer uncovered 45 minutes, stirring occasionally.

3. Peel shrimp. (If shrimp are frozen, do not thaw; peel in cold water.) Make a shallow cut lengthwise down back of each shrimp; wash out vein. See diagram, page 193.

4. Stir shrimp into soup. Cover and simmer about 5 minutes or until shrimp are pink and firm. Remove bay leaf. Serve soup over rice. Sprinkle with parsley.

*1 pound frozen uncooked peeled and deveined medium shrimp, thawed, can be substituted for the 1 1/2 pounds shrimp in shells.

1 SERVING: Calories 305 (Calories from Fat 80); Fat 9g (Saturated 2g); Cholesterol 105mg; Sodium 970mg; Carbohydrate 41g (Dietary Fiber 5g); Protein 20g

CHICKEN GUMBO: Substitute 4 cups 1/2-inch pieces cut-up cooked chicken for the 1 1/2 pounds shrimp in shells.

White Chili

PREP: 20 min; COOK: 1 hr 10 min
Makes 6 servings, about 1 1/2 cups each

1/4 cup margarine or butter
1 large onion, chopped (1 cup)
1 clove garlic, finely chopped
4 cups 1/2-inch cubes cooked chicken or
 turkey
3 cups chicken broth
2 tablespoons chopped fresh cilantro
1 tablespoon dried basil leaves
2 teaspoons ground red chilies or chili
 powder
1/4 teaspoon ground cloves
2 cans (15 to 16 ounces each) great northern
 beans, undrained
1 medium tomato, chopped (3/4 cup)
Blue or yellow corn tortilla chips

1. Melt margarine in Dutch oven over medium heat. Cook onion and garlic in margarine, stirring occasionally, until onion is tender.

2. Stir in remaining ingredients except tomato and tortilla chips. Heat to boiling; reduce heat to low. Cover and simmer 1 hour, stirring occasionally.

3. Serve with tomato and tortilla chips.

1 SERVING: Calories 500 (Calories from Fat 160); Fat 18g (Saturated 4g); Cholesterol 80mg; Sodium 1020mg; Carbohydrate 49g (Dietary Fiber 9g); Protein 45g

---

TIMESAVING TIP

To microwave, place onion, garlic and margarine in 4-quart casserole. Cover tightly and microwave on High 2 minutes; stir. Cover and microwave until celery is tender, about 3 minutes longer. Stir in remaining ingredients except tomato and tortilla chips. Microwave covered 10 minutes longer, stirring occasionally.

Chili con Carne

PREP: 25 min; COOK: 1 hr 25 min
Makes 4 servings, about 1 1/2 cups each

1 pound ground beef
1 large onion, chopped (1 cup)
2 cloves garlic, crushed
1 tablespoon chili powder
1/2 teaspoon salt
1 teaspoon ground cumin
1 teaspoon dried oregano leaves
1 teaspoon cocoa
1/2 teaspoon red pepper sauce
1 can (16 ounces) whole tomatoes,
 undrained
1 can (15 to 16 ounces) red kidney beans,
 undrained

1. Cook beef, onion and garlic in 3-quart saucepan, stirring occasionally, until beef is brown; drain.

2. Stir in remaining ingredients except beans, breaking up tomatoes. Heat to boiling; reduce heat to low. Cover and simmer 1 hour, stirring occasionally.

3. Stir in beans. Heat to boiling; reduce heat to low. Simmer uncovered about 20 minutes, stirring occasionally, until desired thickness.

1 SERVING: Calories 340 (Calories from Fat 155); Fat 17g (Saturated 7g); Cholesterol 65mg; Sodium 890mg; Carbohydrate 27g (Dietary Fiber 9g); Protein 29g

CINCINNATI-STYLE CHILI: For each serving, spoon about 3/4 cup beef mixture over 1 cup hot cooked spaghetti. Sprinkle each serving with 1/4 cup shredded Cheddar cheese and 2 tablespoons chopped onion. Top with sour cream if desired.

QUICK CHILI CON CARNE: Increase chili powder to 2 tablespoons. Omit cumin, oregano, cocoa and pepper sauce.

Everyday Cassoulet

PREP: 20 min; BAKE: 1 hr
Makes 8 servings, about 1 cup each

Cassoulet is a French bean and meat stew.

1 pound Polish or smoked sausage,
 diagonally cut into 1-inch pieces
1 can (15 to 16 ounces) great northern
 beans, rinsed and drained
1 can (15 to 16 ounces) kidney beans, rinsed
 and drained
1 can (15 ounces) black beans, rinsed and
 drained
1 can (15 ounces) tomato sauce
3 medium carrots, thinly sliced (1 1/2 cups)
2 small onions, thinly sliced and separated
 into rings
2 cloves garlic, finely chopped
1/2 cup dry red wine or beef broth
2 tablespoons packed brown sugar
2 tablespoons chopped fresh or
 1 1/2 teaspoons dried thyme leaves

1. Heat oven to 375°.

2. Mix all ingredients in ungreased 3-quart casserole. Cover and bake 50 to 60 minutes or until mixture is hot and bubbly and carrots are tender.

1 SERVING: Calories 370 (Calories from Fat 155); Fat 17g (Saturated 6g); Cholesterol 40mg; Sodium 1210mg; Carbohydrate 44g (Dietary Fiber 10g); Protein 20g

---

LIGHTER EVERDAY CASSOULET

For 7 grams of fat and 295 calories per serving, use low-fat smoked sausage.

Oyster Stew

PREP: 10 min; COOK: 10 min
Makes 4 servings, about 1 cup each

1/4 cup margarine or butter
1 pint shucked oysters, undrained
2 cups milk
1/2 cup half-and-half
1/2 teaspoon salt
Dash of pepper

1. Melt margarine in 1 1/2-quart saucepan over low heat. Stir in oysters. Cook, stirring occasionally, just until edges curl.

2. Heat milk and half-and-half in 2-quart saucepan over medium-low heat until hot. Stir in salt, pepper and oyster mixture; heat until hot.

1 SERVING: Calories 280 (Calories from Fat 180); Fat 20g (Saturated 7g); Cholesterol 80mg; Sodium 710mg; Carbohydrate 12g (Dietary Fiber 0g); Protein 13g

---

TIMESAVING TIP

To microwave, place margarine in 2-quart microwavable casserole. Microwave uncovered on High 30 to 60 seconds or until melted. Stir in oysters. Microwave uncovered 4 minutes, stirring after 2 minutes. Stir in remaining ingredients. Microwave uncovered 3 to 6 minutes longer or until hot.

Easy Cioppino

PREP: 25 min; COOK: 45 min
Makes 6 servings, about 1 1/3 cups each

Cioppino, a San Francisco specialty fish stew usually prepared from whatever fish and shellfish are caught the day it's made. When readily available, a mixture of clams and mussels can be used. (photograph on page 363)

2 tablespoons margarine or butter
1 medium onion, chopped (1/2 cup)
1 medium green bell pepper, chopped
   (1 cup)
2 cloves garlic, finely chopped
1 can (14 1/2 ounces) Italian-style stewed
   tomatoes, undrained
1 cup dry red wine (or nonalcoholic) or beef
   broth
1 cup spicy eight-vegetable juice
1 bottle (8 ounces) clam juice
1 teaspoon salt
1 pound halibut or haddock steaks, cut into
   bite-size pieces
12 clams or mussels, cleaned (page 195)
1 pound uncooked peeled deveined medium
   raw shrimp with tails on, thawed if frozen

1. Melt margarine in Dutch oven over medium-high heat. Cook onion, bell pepper and garlic in margarine about 5 minutes, stirring occasionally, until soft.

2. Stir in tomatoes, wine, vegetable juice, clam juice and salt. Heat to boiling; reduce heat to low. Cover and simmer 15 minutes.

3. Stir in fish and clams. Heat to boiling; reduce heat to low. Cover and simmer 5 minutes.

4. Add shrimp. Heat to boiling; reduce heat to low. Cover and simmer 5 minutes or until fish flakes easily with fork and shrimp are pink and firm. Discard any unopened clams.

1 SERVING: Calories 230 (Calories from Fat 55); Fat 6g (Saturated 1g); Cholesterol 155mg; Sodium 860mg; Carbohydrate 9g (Dietary Fiber 1g); Protein 30g

---

Garden Vegetable Stew

PREP: 25 min; COOK: 45 min
Makes 6 servings, about 1 3/4 cups each

2 tablespoons margarine or butter
1 1/2 medium onions, chopped (3/4 cup)
2 medium carrots, thinly sliced (1 cup)
3 1/2 cups Vegetable Broth* (page 372)
2/3 cup uncooked brown rice or regular long
   grain rice
1 cup fresh or frozen whole kernel corn
1/2 medium zucchini, thinly sliced (1 cup)
1/2 medium yellow summer squash, thinly
   sliced (1 cup)
1 tablespoon chopped fresh or 1 teaspoon
   dried basil leaves
1 teaspoon chopped fresh or 1/4 teaspoon
   dried thyme leaves
1/4 teaspoon pepper
4 new potatoes, cut into fourths
1 large red bell pepper, cut into 2 × 1/2-inch
   strips
1 can (15 to 16 ounces) garbanzo beans,
   rinsed and drained

1. Melt margarine in Dutch oven over medium heat. Cook onions and carrots in margarine, stirring occasionally, until onions are tender.

2. Stir in Vegetable Broth and rice. Heat to boiling; reduce heat to low. Cover and simmer 20 minutes.

3. Stir in remaining ingredients. Cover and simmer 10 to 15 minutes or until vegetables are tender.

2 cans (14 1/2 ounces each) ready-to-serve chicken broth can be substituted for the Vegetable Broth.

1 SERVING: Calories 325 (Calories from Fat 65); Fat 7g (Saturated 1g); Cholesterol 0mg; Sodium 650mg; Carbohydrate 60g (Dietary Fiber 8g); Protein 13g

TIMESAVING TIP

Substitute 3 cups loose-pack frozen mixed vegetables for the zucchini, yellow squash and bell pepper.

Quick Jambalaya

PREP: 15 min; COOK: 15 min
Makes 4 servings, about 1 1/2 cups each

If your 10-inch skillet isn't deep, use a 12-inch skillet.

1 package (8 ounces) brown-and-serve
    sausage links
1 1/2 cups uncooked instant rice
1 1/2 cups chicken broth
1 teaspoon chopped fresh or 1/4 teaspoon
    dried thyme leaves
1/4 teaspoon chili powder
1/8 teaspoon ground red pepper (cayenne)

1 small green bell pepper, chopped (1/2 cup)
1 small onion, chopped (1/4 cup)
1 can (14 1/2 ounces) stewed tomatoes,
    undrained
1 package (10 ounces) frozen quick-cooking
    cleaned shrimp

1. Cut sausages into 1-inch diagonal slices. Cook in deep 10-inch skillet as directed on package; drain.

2. Stir remaining ingredients into sausage. Heat to boiling, stirring occasionally; reduce heat to low. Simmer uncovered 10 minutes, stirring occasionally.

1 SERVING: Calories 560 (Calories from Fat 205); Fat 23g (Saturated 8g); Cholesterol 140mg; Sodium 1030mg; Carbohydrate 64g (Dietary Fiber 3g); Protein 27g

LIGHTER QUICK JAMBALAYA

For 2 grams of fat and 335 calories per serving, omit the sausage links.

Tips for Broths

- Wash vegetables, and cut into large pieces; there's no need to peel or trim them first.
- You control the amount of salt and spices in broths that are homemade. Follow the recipes, then adjust seasonings to taste if desired.
- Make a quick soup by adding leftover cooked vegetables, meats and/or pasta to broth.
- Leftover sauces and strongly flavored vegetable cooking liquid can be frozen and used as part of the water in recipes that use broth.
- If you don't have time to make your own broth, try one of these quick alternatives:
  Ready-to-serve broth: 1 can (14 1/2 ounces) chicken, beef or vegetable broth = about 1 3/4 cups broth
  Condensed broth: 1 can (10 1/2 ounces) condensed chicken or beef broth diluted with 1 soup can water = 2 2/3 cups broth
  Bouillon: 1 chicken, beef or vegetable bouillon cube or 1 teaspoon instant bouillon granules prepared mixed with 1 cup water = 1 cup broth
  Broth or Stock Base: Follow directions on container; directions are different for each brand.

Fish Broth

PREP: 20 min; COOK: 40 min
Makes about 6 cups broth

1 1/2 pounds fish bones and trimmings
4 cups cold water
2 cups dry white wine or clam juice
1 tablespoon lemon juice
1 teaspoon salt
1/2 teaspoon ground thyme or 2 teaspoons
    chopped fresh thyme leaves
1 large celery stalk, chopped
1 small onion, sliced
3 mushrooms, chopped
3 sprigs parsley
1 bay leaf

1. Rinse fish bones and trimmings with cold water; drain. Mix bones, trimmings, 4 cups cold water and remaining ingredients in Dutch oven or stockpot; heat to boiling. Skim foam from broth; reduce heat to low. Cover and simmer 30 minutes.

2. Strain broth through cheesecloth-lined sieve; discard skin, bones, vegetables and seasonings. Use immediately, or cover and refrigerate up to 24 hours or freeze for future use.

1 CUP: Calories 55 (Calories from Fat 0); Fat 0g (Saturated 0g); Cholesterol 0mg; Sodium 360mg; Carbohydrate 1g (Dietary Fiber 0g); Protein 0g

Vegetable Broth

PREP: 20 min; COOK: 1 hr 10 min
Makes about 8 cups broth

6 cups coarsely chopped mild vegetables
(bell peppers, carrots, celery, leeks,
mushroom stems, potatoes, spinach,
zucchini)
1 medium onion, coarsely chopped (1/2 cup)
1/2 cup parsley sprigs
8 cups cold water
2 tablespoons chopped fresh or 2 teaspoons
dried basil leaves
2 tablespoons chopped fresh or 2 teaspoons
dried thyme leaves
1 teaspoon salt
1/4 teaspoon cracked black pepper
4 cloves garlic, chopped
2 bay leaves

1. Heat all ingredients to boiling in Dutch oven or
stockpot; reduce heat to low. Cover and simmer 1
hour, stirring occasionally.

2. Cool slightly. Strain broth and use immediately,
or cover and refrigerate up to 24 hours or freeze for
future use. Stir before measuring.

Note: *Some strong vegetables, such as broccoli, cabbage, cauliflower, turnips and rutabagas, may be used sparingly with mild vegetables. When using strong vegetables, tilt the lid on the pan to allow
the strong odors to escape.*

1 CUP: Calories 5 (Calories from Fat 0); Fat 0g (Saturated 0g);
Cholesterol 0mg; Sodium 270mg; Carbohydrate 2g (Dietary
Fiber 0g); Protein 0g

> **TIMESAVING TIP**
> Start with already cut-up vegetables from the produce
> or salad bar section of your supermarket. Or use up
> those leftover vegetables from a relish tray or frozen
> loose-pack vegetables.

Chicken and Broth

PREP: 25 min; COOK: 1 hr
Makes about 6 cups

*Leaving the skin on the chicken for this recipe gives the broth
a great flavor. After the chicken is cooked and cooled, the
skin slips off easily and can be discarded.*

3- to 3 1/2-pound cut-up broiler-fryer
chicken*
4 1/2 cups cold water
1 teaspoon salt
1/2 teaspoon pepper
1 medium stalk celery with leaves, cut up
1 carrot, cut up
1 small onion, cut up
1 sprig parsley

1. Remove any excess fat from chicken. Place
chicken, giblets (except liver) and neck in Dutch oven or
stockpot. Add remaining ingredients; heat to boiling.
Skim foam from broth; reduce heat to low. Cover and
simmer about 45 minutes or until juice of chicken is no
longer pink when centers of thickest pieces are cut.

2. Remove chicken from broth. Cool chicken
about 10 minutes or just until cool enough to handle.
Strain broth through cheesecloth-lined sieve; discard
vegetables.

3. Remove skin and bones from chicken. Cut
chicken into 1/2-inch pieces. Skim fat from broth. Use
immediately, or cover and refrigerate broth and
chicken in separate containers up to 24 hours or freeze
for future use.

**3 to 3 1/2 pounds chicken necks, backs and giblets (except liver)
can be used to make broth.*

1 CUP: Calories 135 (Calories from Fat 45); Fat 5g
(Saturated 2g); Cholesterol 60mg; Sodium 440mg;
Carbohydrate 0g (Dietary Fiber 0g); Protein 23g

Beef and Broth

PREP: 30 min; COOK: 3 1/4 hr
Makes about 7 cups

*Keep Beef and Broth on hand for quick, homemade soups
any time. Stir bite-size pieces of fresh or frozen vegetables
and uncooked pasta into the simmering broth. Simmer until
the pasta and vegetables are tender, 12 to 15 minutes. Add
the beef and heat through.*

2 pounds beef shank cross-cuts or soup
bones
6 cups cold water
1 teaspoon salt
1/4 teaspoon dried thyme leaves
1 medium carrot, cut up
1 medium stalk celery with leaves, cut up
1 small onion, cut up
5 peppercorns
3 whole cloves
3 sprigs parsley
1 bay leaf

1. Remove marrow from center of bones. Heat
marrow in Dutch oven over low heat until melted, or
heat 2 tablespoons vegetable oil until hot. Cook beef
shanks over medium heat until brown on both sides.

2. Add water; heat to boiling. Skim foam from
broth. Stir in remaining ingredients; heat to boiling.
Skim foam from broth; reduce heat to low. Cover and
simmer 3 hours.

3. Remove beef from broth. Cool beef about 10
minutes or just until cool enough to handle. Strain
broth through cheesecloth-lined sieve; discard vegetables and seasonings.

4. Remove beef from bones. Cut beef into 1/2-inch pieces. Skim fat from broth. Use immediately, or cover and refrigerate broth and beef in separate containers up to 24 hours or freeze for future use.

1 CUP: Calories 160 (Calories from Fat 80); Fat 9g (Saturated 3g); Cholesterol 50mg; Sodium 400mg; Carbohydrate 1g (Dietary Fiber 0g); Protein 19g

Vegetable-Beef Soup

PREP: 50 min; COOK: 4 hr
Makes 7 servings, about 1 1/2 cups each

Beef and Broth (page 372)
1 ear corn
2 medium potatoes, cubed (2 cups)
2 medium tomatoes, chopped (1 1/2 cups)
1 medium carrot, thinly sliced (1/2 cup)
1 medium stalk celery, sliced (1/2 cup)
1 medium onion, chopped (1/2 cup)
1 cup 1-inch pieces green beans
1 cup shelled green peas
1/4 teaspoon pepper

1. Prepare Beef and Broth. Add enough water to broth to measure 5 cups. Return strained beef and broth to Dutch oven.

2. Cut kernels from corn. Stir corn and remaining ingredients into broth. Heat to boiling; reduce heat to low. Cover and simmer about 30 minutes or until vegetables are tender.

1 CUP: Calories 235 (Calories from Fat 80); Fat 9g (Saturated 4g); Cholesterol 50mg; Sodium 440mg; Carbohydrate 19g (Dietary Fiber 3g); Protein 22g

BARLEY-VEGETABLE-BEEF SOUP: Omit potatoes. Stir 2/3 cup uncooked barley and 1/2 teaspoon salt into Beef and Broth in step 1. Heat to boiling; reduce heat to low. Cover and simmer 30 minutes. Stir in remaining ingredients. Cover and simmer about 30 minutes or until barley and vegetables are tender.

TIMESAVING TIP

Substitute 4 cups prepared beef broth and 3 cups cut-up cooked beef for the Beef and Broth, and 1 cup each frozen whole kernel corn, cut green beans and green peas for the 1 ear corn, 1-inch pieces green beans and shelled green peas. Add potatoes, tomatoes, carrot, celery, onion and pepper to beef broth. Heat to boiling; reduce heat to low. Simmer uncovered 15 minutes. Stir in frozen vegetables. Heat to boiling; reduce heat to low. Cover and simmer about 15 minutes or until vegetables are tender.

Steak Soup with Winter Vegetables

PREP: 20 min; COOK: 1 hr
Makes 4 servings, about 1 1/2 cups each

Brussels sprouts have a flavor similar to cabbage. Look for unblemished, bright green sprouts with compact leaves.

1 pound beef boneless sirloin steak, 1 inch thick
2 cans (14 1/2 ounces each) ready-to-serve beef broth
1/4 teaspoon pepper
1 cup Brussels sprouts, cut lengthwise in half
1 cup sliced shiitake or fresh mushrooms
1 teaspoon chopped fresh or 1/2 teaspoon dried marjoram leaves
1 teaspoon chopped fresh or 1/2 teaspoon dried thyme leaves
2 medium carrots, cut into 1/2-inch pieces
1 large sweet potato, cubed (1 cup)
1 clove garlic, finely chopped

1. Trim excess fat from beef. Cut beef into 1-inch pieces. Cook beef in 3-quart saucepan over medium-high heat about 10 minutes, stirring several times, until brown.

2. Stir in broth and pepper; reduce heat to low. Simmer uncovered 20 to 30 minutes or until beef is tender.

3. Stir in remaining ingredients. Heat to boiling; reduce heat to low. Cover and simmer about 15 minutes or until vegetables are tender.

1 SERVING: Calories 305 (Calories from Fat 115); Fat 13g (Saturated 5g); Cholesterol 65mg; Sodium 620mg; Carbohydrate 21g (Dietary Fiber 4g); Protein 30g

Chicken Noodle Soup, Cream of Mushroom Soup (page 377)

Chicken Noodle Soup

PREP: 1 hr 25 min; COOK: 30 min
Makes 6 servings, about 1 cup each

Everyone loves this soup! If you like, vary the soup by using different sized noodles. Adjust cooking time according to package directions.

> Chicken and Broth (page 372)
> 2 medium carrots, sliced (1 cup)
> 2 medium stalks celery, sliced (1 cup)
> 1 small onion, chopped (1/4 cup)
> 1 tablespoon chicken bouillon granules
> 1 cup uncooked medium noodles (2 ounces)
> Chopped fresh parsley, if desired

1. Prepare Chicken and Broth. Reserve cut-up chicken. Add enough water to broth to measure 5 cups.

2. Heat broth, carrots, celery, onion and bouillon granules to boiling in Dutch oven; reduce heat to low. Cover and simmer about 15 minutes or until carrots are tender.

3. Stir in noodles and chicken. Heat to boiling; reduce heat to low. Simmer uncovered 7 to 10 minutes or until noodles are tender. Sprinkle with parsley.

1 CUP: Calories 161 (Calories from Fat 45); Fat 5g (Saturated 1g); Cholesterol 50mg; Sodium 1340mg; Carbohydrate 11g (Dietary Fiber 2g); Protein 20g

CHICKEN RICE SOUP: Substitute 1/2 cup uncooked regular long grain rice for the uncooked noodles. Stir in rice with the vegetables. Cover and simmer about 15 minutes or until rice is tender. Stir in chicken; heat until chicken is hot.

> **TIMESAVING TIP**
> Substitute 3 cups purchased chicken broth and 3 cups cut-up cooked chicken or turkey for the Chicken and Broth.

Gazpacho

PREP: 20 min; CHILL: 1 hr
Makes 8 servings, about 1/2 cup each

Usually served chilled, refreshing Gazpacho was originally a gypsy soup from eastern Europe.

> 1 can (28 ounces) whole tomatoes, undrained
> 1 medium green bell pepper, finely chopped (1 cup)
> 1 cup finely chopped cucumbers
> 1 cup croutons
> 1 medium onion, chopped (1/2 cup)
> 2 tablespoons dry white wine or chicken broth

2 tablespoons olive or vegetable oil
1 tablespoon ground cumin
1 tablespoon white vinegar
1/2 teaspoon salt
1/4 teaspoon pepper

1. Place tomatoes, 1/2 cup of the bell pepper, 1/2 cup of the cucumbers, 1/2 cup of the croutons, 1/4 cup of the onion and the remaining ingredients in blender or food processor. Cover and blend on medium speed until smooth.

2. Cover and refrigerate at least 1 hour. Serve remaining vegetables and croutons as accompaniments.

1 SERVING: Calories 75 (Calories from Fat 35); Fat 4g (Saturated 1g); Cholesterol 0mg; Sodium 330mg; Carbohydrate 10g (Dietary Fiber 2g); Protein 2g

Cream of Broccoli Soup

PREP: 35 min; COOK: 10 min
Makes 8 servings, about 1 cup each

1 1/2 pounds broccoli
2 cups water
1 large stalk celery, chopped (3/4 cup)
1 medium onion, chopped (1/2 cup)
2 tablespoons margarine or butter
2 tablespoons all-purpose flour
2 1/2 cups chicken broth
1/2 teaspoon salt
1/8 teaspoon pepper
Dash of ground nutmeg
1/2 cup whipping (heavy) cream
Shredded cheese, if desired

1. Prepare broccoli as directed on page 395. Remove flowerets from broccoli; set aside. Cut stalks into 1-inch pieces.

2. Heat water to boiling in 3-quart saucepan. Add broccoli flowerets and stalk pieces, celery and onion. Cover and heat to boiling. Boil about 10 minutes or until broccoli is tender (do not drain).

3. *Carefully* place broccoli mixture in blender. Cover and blend on medium speed until smooth.

4. Melt margarine in 3-quart saucepan over medium heat. Stir in flour. Cook, stirring constantly, until mixture is smooth and bubbly; remove from heat.

5. Stir broth into flour mixture. Heat to boiling, stirring constantly. Boil and stir 1 minute.

6. Stir in broccoli mixture, salt, pepper and nutmeg. Heat just to boiling. Stir in whipping cream. Heat just until hot (do not boil). Serve with cheese.

1 CUP: Calories 105 (Calories from Fat 70); Fat 8g (Saturated 4g); Cholesterol 15mg; Sodium 440mg; Carbohydrate 6g (Dietary Fiber 2g); Protein 4g

CREAM OF CAULIFLOWER SOUP: Substitute 1 head cauliflower (about 2 pounds), separated into flowerets, for the broccoli. Add 1 tablespoon lemon juice with the onion in step 2.

> **TIMESAVING TIP**
> Substitute 3 packages (10 ounces each) frozen chopped broccoli for the fresh broccoli.

Cream of Chicken Soup

PREP: 1 hr 25 min; COOK: 25 min
Makes 6 servings, about 1 cup each

Chicken and Broth (page 372)
1 medium onion, chopped (1/2 cup)
1 medium stalk celery, thinly sliced (1/2 cup)
1 1/2 teaspoons chopped fresh or
    1/2 teaspoon dried basil leaves
1 1/2 teaspoons chopped fresh or
    1/2 teaspoon dried thyme leaves
3 tablespoons all-purpose flour
3/4 cup half-and-half
1/4 cup shredded carrot
Freshly ground pepper or Parmesan cheese

1. Prepare Chicken and Broth. Reserve cut-up chicken. Heat broth, onion, celery, basil and thyme to boiling in 3-quart saucepan; reduce heat to low. Cover and simmer 15 minutes.

2. Stir flour into half-and-half until smooth; stir into soup. Heat to boiling, stirring constantly. Boil and stir 1 minute.

3. Stir in chicken and carrot; cook until hot. Sprinkle with pepper.

1 SERVING: Calories 205 (Calories from Fat 80); Fat 9g (Saturated 4g); Cholesterol 70mg; Sodium 460mg; Carbohydrate 7g (Dietary Fiber 1g); Protein 25g

> **TIMESAVING TIP**
> Substitute 3 cups purchased chicken broth and 3 cups cut-up cooked chicken for the Chicken and Broth.

Borscht

PREP: 25 min; COOK: 3 hr 50 min
Makes 6 servings, about 1 1/4 cups each

3/4 pound beef boneless chuck, tip or round,
    cut into 1/2-inch cubes
1 smoked pork hock
4 cups water
1 can (10 1/2 ounces) condensed beef broth
1 teaspoon salt
1/4 teaspoon pepper
4 medium beets, cooked
1 large onion, sliced
2 cloves garlic, chopped
2 medium potatoes, cubed (2 cups)
3 cups shredded cabbage
2 teaspoons dill seed or 1 sprig dill weed
1 tablespoon pickling spice
1/4 cup red wine vinegar
3/4 cup sour cream
Chopped fresh dill weed, if desired

1. Heat beef, pork, water, broth, salt and pepper to boiling in Dutch oven; reduce heat to low. Cover and simmer 1 to 1 1/2 hours or until beef is tender.

2. Shred beets, or cut into 1/4-inch strips. Remove pork from soup. Cool pork slightly. Remove pork from bone; cut pork into bite-size pieces.

3. Stir pork, beets, onion, garlic, potatoes and cab-bage into soup. Tie dill seed and pickling spice in cheesecloth bag, or place in tea ball, and add to soup. Cover and simmer 2 hours.

4. Stir in vinegar. Simmer uncovered 10 minutes. Remove spice bag. Serve sour cream with soup. Sprinkle with dill weed.

1 SERVING: Calories 270 (Calories from Fat 145); Fat 16g (Saturated 7g); Cholesterol 50mg; Sodium 780mg; Carbohydrate 20g (Dietary Fiber 3g); Protein 14g

---

TIMESAVING TIP

Substitute 2 cups canned beets (about one 16-ounce can) for the cooked beets and use packaged shredded cabbage (about 3/4 pound).

Borscht, Challah Braid (page 59)

Cheddar Cheese Soup

PREP: 15 min; COOK: 10 min
Makes 4 servings, about 1 cup each

> 2 tablespoons margarine or butter
> 1 small onion, chopped (1/4 cup)
> 1 medium stalk celery, thinly sliced (1/2 cup)
> 2 tablespoons all-purpose flour
> 1/4 teaspoon pepper
> 1/4 teaspoon ground mustard (dry)
> 1 cup milk
> 1 can (10 1/2 ounces) condensed chicken
>   broth
> 2 cups shredded Cheddar cheese (8 ounces)
> Paprika, if desired

1. Melt margarine in 2-quart saucepan over medium heat. Cook onion and celery in margarine about 2 minutes, stirring occasionally, until tender.

2. Stir in flour, pepper and mustard. Stir in milk and broth. Heat to boiling over medium heat, stirring constantly. Boil and stir 1 minute.

3. Stir in cheese. Heat over low heat, stirring occasionally, just until cheese is melted. Sprinkle with paprika.

1 SERVING: Calories 355 (Calories from Fat 245); Fat 27g (Saturated 14g); Cholesterol 65mg; Sodium 940mg; Carbohydrate 9g (Dietary Fiber 1g); Protein 20g

BEER-CHEESE SOUP: Substitute 1 1/2 cups beer (or nonalcoholic) for the chicken broth.

Cream of Mushroom Soup

PREP: 15 min; COOK: 15 min
Makes 4 servings, about 1 cup each

(photograph on page 374)

> 1 pound mushrooms
> 1/4 cup margarine or butter
> 3 tablespoons all-purpose flour
> 1/2 teaspoon salt
> 1 cup whipping (heavy) cream
> 1 can (14 1/2 ounces) ready-to-serve chicken
>   broth
> 1 tablespoon dry sherry, if desired
> Freshly ground pepper

1. Slice enough mushrooms to measure 1 cup. Chop remaining mushrooms.

2. Melt margarine in 3-quart saucepan over medium heat. Cook all the mushrooms in margarine about 10 minutes, stirring occasionally, until mushrooms are golden brown. Sprinkle with flour and salt. Cook, stirring constantly, until thickened.

3. *Gradually* stir in whipping cream and broth; heat until hot. Stir in sherry. Sprinkle with pepper.

1 SERVING: Calories 345 (Calories from Fat 280); Fat 31g (Saturated 15g); Cholesterol 65mg; Sodium 750mg; Carbohydrate 12g (Dietary Fiber 1g); Protein 6g

---

LIGHTER CREAM OF MUSHROOM SOUP

For 7 grams of fat and 165 calories per serving, decrease margarine to 2 tablespoons and substitute 1 cup evaporated skimmed milk for the whipping cream.

Vichyssoise

PREP: 15 min; COOK: 25 min; CHILL: 5 hr
Makes 4 servings, about 1 1/4 cups each

This cold soup is named for the French town of Vichy.

> 1 tablespoon margarine or butter
> 1 medium onion, chopped (1/2 cup)
> 2 medium potatoes, peeled and coarsely
>   chopped (2 cups)
> 1 medium stalk celery, chopped (1/2 cup)
> 1 can (14 1/2 ounces) ready-to-serve chicken
>   broth
> 1 1/2 cups milk
> 1 cup half-and-half
> 1/4 teaspoon salt
> 1/4 teaspoon ground nutmeg
> 1/8 teaspoon pepper
> Chopped fresh chives or ground nutmeg,
>   if desired

1. Melt margarine in 2-quart saucepan over medium heat. Cook onion in margarine about 2 minutes, stirring occasionally, until crisp-tender.

2. Stir in potatoes, celery and broth. Heat to boiling; reduce heat to low. Cover and simmer about 15 minutes or until vegetables are tender.

3. *Carefully* place undrained potato mixture in blender or food processor. Cover and blend on low speed until uniform consistency. Pour into large bowl.

4. Stir in remaining ingredients except chives and nutmeg. Cover and refrigerate soup about 5 hours or until thoroughly chilled. Garnish with chives.

1 SERVING: Calories 225 (Calories from Fat 110); Fat 12g (Saturated 6g); Cholesterol 30mg; Sodium 580mg; Carbohydrate 23g (Dietary Fiber 2g); Protein 8g

---

TIMESAVING TIP

To microwave, place margarine and onion in 2-quart microwavable casserole. Cover tightly and microwave on High 2 minutes. Stir in potatoes, celery and broth. Cover tightly and microwave 8 to 10 minutes or until boiling; stir. Cover tightly and microwave 7 to 9 minutes or until vegetables are tender. Continue as directed in step 3.

Cheesy Golden Onion Soup

Golden Onion Soup

PREP: 20 min; COOK: 2 hr 50 min
Makes 6 servings, about 1 cup each

Parmesan Croutons (right)
1/4 cup margarine or butter
1 tablespoon packed brown sugar
1 teaspoon Worcestershire sauce
2 large onions (3/4 pound each), cut into
    fourths and sliced
2 cans (10 1/2 ounces each) condensed beef
    broth
2 soup cans water

1. Prepare Parmesan Croutons; reserve.

2. Reduce oven temperature to 325°.

3. Melt margarine in ovenproof Dutch oven over medium heat. Stir in brown sugar and Worcestershire sauce. Toss onions in margarine mixture.

4. Bake uncovered about 2 1/2 hours, stirring every hour, until onions are deep golden brown. Stir in broth and water. Heat to boiling. Serve with Parmesan Croutons.

Parmesan Croutons

1/4 cup margarine or butter
3 slices bread, cut into 1-inch cubes
Grated Parmesan cheese

Heat oven to 400°. Melt margarine in rectangular pan, $13 \times 9 \times 2$ inches, in oven. Toss bread cubes in margarine until evenly coated. Sprinkle with cheese. Bake uncovered 10 to 15 minutes, stirring occasionally, until golden brown and crisp.

1 CUP: Calories 230 (Calories from Fat 145); Fat 16g (Saturated 4g); Cholesterol 2mg; Sodium 830mg; Carbohydrate 15g (Dietary Fiber 1g); Protein 7g

CHEESY GOLDEN ONION SOUP: Spoon soup into ovenproof bowls. Top with croutons. Sprinkle each serving with 1/4 cup shredded mozzarella cheese. Place bowls in shallow baking pan. Broil with tops 4 to 5 inches from heat about 2 minutes, until cheese is melted and light brown.

> **TIMESAVING TIP**
> Substitute 3 cups cracked pepper and Parmesan croutons, found near the salad dressings at your supermarket, for the Parmesan Croutons.

Hearty Tomato Soup

PREP: 15 min; COOK: 10 min
Makes 8 servings, about 1 cup each

Would you like to enjoy two soups in one bowl? It's easy! Prepare Cream of Broccoli Soup (page 375) and Hearty Tomato Soup. Simultaneously pour soups from two cups into bowl for a colorful combination.

2 tablespoons margarine or butter
1 medium onion, finely chopped (1/2 cup)
1 clove garlic, finely chopped
1/2 teaspoon paprika
1 1/2 teaspoons chopped fresh or 1/2 teaspoon dried basil leaves
2 packages (3 ounces each) cream cheese, softened
1 1/4 cups milk
2 cans (10 3/4 ounces each) condensed tomato soup
2 cans (16 ounces each) whole tomatoes, undrained

1. Melt margarine in 3-quart saucepan over medium heat. Cook onion and garlic in margarine about 2 minutes, stirring occasionally, until onion is tender; remove from heat.

2. Stir in paprika, basil and cream cheese. *Gradually* stir in milk and soup. Beat with hand beater until smooth.

3. Stir in tomatoes, breaking them up. Heat over medium heat, stirring frequently, until hot.

1 CUP: Calories 195 (Calories from Fat 110); Fat 12g (Saturated 2g); Cholesterol 25mg; Sodium 830mg; Carbohydrate 19g (Dietary Fiber 2g); Protein 5g

Wild Rice Soup

PREP: 20 min; COOK: 25 min
Makes 5 servings, about 1 cup each

2 tablespoons margarine or butter
2 medium stalks celery, sliced (1 cup)
1 medium carrot, coarsely shredded (1 cup)
1 medium onion, chopped (1/2 cup)
1 small green bell pepper, chopped (1/2 cup)
3 tablespoons all-purpose flour
1/4 teaspoon pepper
1 1/2 cups cooked wild rice (page 204)
1 cup water
1 can (10 1/2 ounces) condensed chicken broth
1 cup half-and-half
1/3 cup slivered almonds, toasted (page 9)
1/4 cup chopped fresh parsley

1. Melt margarine in 3-quart saucepan over medium-high heat. Cook celery, carrot, onion and bell pepper in margarine about 4 minutes, stirring occasionally, until tender.

2. Stir in flour and pepper. Stir in wild rice, water and broth. Heat to boiling; reduce heat to low. Cover and simmer 15 minutes, stirring occasionally.

3. Stir in half-and-half, almonds and parsley. Heat just until hot (do not boil).

1 CUP: Calories 255 (Calories from Fat 135); Fat 15g (Saturated 5g); Cholesterol 20mg; Sodium 480mg; Carbohydrate 23g (Dietary Fiber 2g); Protein 9g

---

LIGHTER WILD RICE SOUP

For 5 grams of fat and 185 calories per serving, spray saucepan with nonstick cooking spray before heating. Omit margarine. Substitute 1 cup evaporated skimmed milk for the half-and-half.

New England Clam Chowder

PREP: 10 min; COOK: 25 min
Makes 4 servings, about 1 cup each

The same cut of meat as bacon, salt pork is cured with salt, not smoked like bacon. Tightly wrapped, salt pork will keep in the refrigerator up to six weeks. It does not freeze well because of its salt content.

1/4 cup cut-up bacon or lean salt pork
1 medium onion, chopped (1/2 cup)
2 cans (6 1/2 ounces each) minced or whole clams*
1 medium potato, finely chopped (1 cup)
1/2 teaspoon salt
Dash of pepper
2 cups milk

1. Cook bacon and onion in 2-quart saucepan over medium heat, stirring occasionally, until bacon is crisp and onion is tender.

2. Drain clams, reserving liquor. Add enough water, if necessary, to clam liquor to measure 1 cup.

3. Stir clams, clam liquor, potato, salt and pepper into bacon and onion. Heat to boiling; reduce heat to low. Cover and simmer about 15 minutes or until potato is tender.

4. Stir in milk. Heat, stirring occasionally, just until hot (do not boil).

*1 pint shucked fresh clams with liquor can be substituted for the canned clams. Chop clams and stir in with the potato in step 3.

1 CUP: Calories 190 (Calories from Fat 55); Fat 6g (Saturated 2g); Cholesterol 40mg; Sodium 460mg; Carbohydrate 18g (Dietary Fiber 1g); Protein 17g

Manhattan Clam Chowder

PREP: 15 min; COOK: 20 min
Makes 4 servings, about 1 1/2 cups each

The classic New England Clam Chowder, from colonial days, called for cream and clams. Later, the recipe was altered to use tomatoes in place of the cream—and Manhattan Clam Chowder was born.

> 1/4 cup finely chopped bacon or salt pork
> 1 small onion, finely chopped (1/4 cup)
> 1 pint shucked fresh clams with liquor*
> 2 medium potatoes, finely chopped (2 cups)
> 1/3 cup chopped celery
> 1 cup water
> 2 teaspoons chopped fresh parsley
> 1 teaspoon chopped fresh or 1/4 teaspoon
>   dried thyme leaves
> 1/2 teaspoon salt
> 1/8 teaspoon pepper
> 1 can (16 ounces) whole tomatoes,
>   undrained

1. Cook bacon and onion in Dutch oven over medium heat, stirring occasionally, until bacon is crisp and onion is tender.

2. Stir in clams and clam liquor, potatoes, celery and water. Heat to boiling; reduce heat to low. Cover and simmer about 10 minutes or until potatoes are tender.

3. Stir in remaining ingredients, breaking up tomatoes. Heat to boiling, stirring occasionally.

*2 cans (6 1/2 ounces each) minced clams, undrained, can be substituted for fresh clams. Stir in clams with remaining ingredients in step 3.

1 SERVING: Calories 130 (Calories from Fat 25); Fat 3g (Saturated 1g); Cholesterol 10mg; Sodium 550mg; Carbohydrate 23g (Dietary Fiber 3g); Protein 6g

Vegetable-Corn Chowder

PREP: 15 min; COOK: 20 min
Makes 8 servings, about 1 1/3 cups each

(photograph on page 389)

> 1 tablespoon margarine or butter
> 1 medium green bell pepper, coarsely
>   chopped (1 cup)
> 1 medium red bell pepper, coarsely chopped
>   (1 cup)
> 3/4 cup sliced green onions (7 medium)
> 3 cups water
> 3/4 pound new potatoes, cut into chunks
>   (2 1/2 cups)
> 1 tablespoon chopped fresh or 1 teaspoon
>   dried thyme leaves
> 1/2 teaspoon salt
> 1 cup half-and-half
> 1/8 teaspoon pepper
> 2 cans (15 ounces each) cream-style corn

1. Melt margarine in Dutch oven over medium heat. Cook bell peppers and onions in margarine 3 minutes, stirring occasionally.

2. Stir in water, potatoes, thyme and salt. Heat to boiling; reduce heat to low. Cover and simmer about 10 minutes or until potatoes are tender.

3. Stir in remaining ingredients; cook until hot (do not boil).

1 SERVING: Calories 205 (Calories from Fat 55); Fat 6g (Saturated 3g); Cholesterol 10mg; Sodium 510mg; Carbohydrate 39g (Dietary Fiber 4g); Protein 5g

---

LIGHTER VEGETABLE-CORN CHOWDER

For 1 gram of fat and 195 calories per serving, omit margarine. Spray Dutch oven with nonstick cooking spray before heating. Substitute 1 cup evaporated skimmed milk for the half-and-half.

SANTA FE DIRTY CORN CHOWDER: Substitute 2 red Anaheim chilies, chopped, for the red bell pepper. Omit thyme. Stir in 1 teaspoon ground cumin and 1/8 teaspoon crushed red pepper with the potatoes. Stir in 1 can (15 ounces) black beans, rinsed and drained, with the corn. Garnish with shredded Monterey Jack cheese and chopped fresh cilantro if desired.

Hamburger Minestrone

PREP: 20 min; COOK: 25 min
Makes 6 servings, about 1 1/2 cups each

1 pound ground beef
1 medium onion, chopped (1/2 cup)
1 clove garlic, crushed
1 cup shredded cabbage
1/2 cup uncooked elbow macaroni or broken
    spaghetti
1 1/4 cups water
2 teaspoons beef bouillon granules
1 teaspoon Italian seasoning
2 medium stalks celery, thinly sliced (1 cup)
1 small zucchini, sliced (1 cup)
1 can (28 ounces) whole tomatoes,
    undrained
1 can (8 ounces) kidney beans, undrained
1 can (8 ounces) whole kernel corn,
    undrained
Grated Parmesan cheese

1. Cook beef, onion and garlic in Dutch oven over medium heat, stirring occasionally, until beef is brown; drain.

2. Stir in remaining ingredients except cheese, breaking up tomatoes. Heat to boiling; reduce heat to low. Cover and simmer about 15 minutes, stirring occasionally, until macaroni is tender. Serve with cheese.

1 SERVING: Calories 295 (Calories from Fat 115); Fat 13g (Saturated 5g); Cholesterol 45mg; Sodium 950mg; Carbohydrate 29g (Dietary Fiber 5g); Protein 21g

---

LIGHTER HAMBURGER MINESTRONE
For 10 grams of fat and 280 calories per serving, substitute ground turkey for the ground beef and spray the Dutch oven with nonstick cooking spray.

Senate Bean Soup

PREP: 20 min; STAND: 1 hr; COOK: 3 1/4 hr
Makes 12 servings, about 1 cup each

This hearty soup, served every day in the cafeteria of the U.S. Senate, goes very nicely with hunks of full-flavored breads such as multi-grain, sourdough or focaccia. (photograph on page 382)

2 cups dried navy beans (1 pound)
12 cups water
1 ham bone, 2 pounds ham shanks or
    2 pounds smoked pork hocks
2 1/2 cups mashed cooked potatoes
2 teaspoons salt
1/4 teaspoon pepper
1 large onion, chopped (1 cup)
2 medium stalks celery, chopped (1 cup)
1 clove garlic, finely chopped

1. Heat beans and water to boiling in Dutch oven. Boil uncovered 2 minutes; remove from heat. Cover and let stand 1 hour.

2. Add ham bone. Heat to boiling; reduce heat to low. Cover and simmer about 2 hours or until beans are tender.

3. Stir in remaining ingredients. Cover and simmer 1 hour.

4. Remove ham bone; remove ham from bone. Trim excess fat from ham; cut ham into 1/2-inch pieces. Stir ham into soup.

1 CUP: Calories 170 (Calories from Fat 35); Fat 4g (Saturated 1g); Cholesterol 5mg; Sodium 490mg; Carbohydrate 32g (Dietary Fiber 7g); Protein 9g

SOUTHWESTERN BEAN SOUP: Add 1 can (4 ounces) chopped green chilies, 1 tablespoon chili powder and 1 teaspoon ground cumin in step 3. Top with salsa if desired.

Cuban Black Bean Soup

PREP: 20 min; COOK: 2 1/4 hr
Makes 8 servings, about 1 1/2 cups each

2 tablespoons vegetable oil
1 large onion, chopped (1 cup)
3 cloves garlic, finely chopped
2 2/3 cups dried black beans (1 pound)
1 cup finely chopped fully cooked smoked
    ham
3 cups beef broth
3 cups water
1/4 cup dark rum or apple cider
1 1/2 teaspoons ground cumin
1 1/2 teaspoons dried oregano leaves
1 medium green bell pepper, chopped
    (1 cup)
1 large tomato, chopped (1 cup)
Chopped hard-cooked eggs
Chopped onions

1. Heat oil in Dutch oven over medium heat. Cook 1 cup onion and the garlic in oil, stirring occasionally, until onion is tender.

2. Stir in remaining ingredients except eggs and onions; heat to boiling. Boil 2 minutes; reduce heat to low. Cover and simmer about 2 hours or until beans are tender.

3. Serve soup with eggs and onion.

1 SERVING: Calories 280 (Calories from Fat 70); Fat 8g (Saturated 2g); Cholesterol 90mg; Sodium 530mg; Carbohydrate 41g (Dietary Fiber 10g); Protein 21g

---

LIGHTER CUBAN BLACK BEAN SOUP
For 4 grams of fat and 215 calories per serving, omit ham and eggs.

Split Pea Soup, Senate Bean Soup (page 381), Four-Grain Batter Bread (page 64)

Split Pea Soup

PREP: 20 min; STAND: 1 hr; COOK: 2 1/2 hr
Makes 8 servings, about 1 1/2 cups each

To prepare the split peas for cooking, pick over the dried split peas and discard any grit or discolored peas. Place the split peas in a bowl and cover them with water. After a minute or two, remove any skins or split peas that float to the top. Finally rinse the split peas in a colander.

2 1/4 cups dried split peas (1 pound)
8 cups water
1 large onion, chopped (1 cup)
2 medium stalks celery, finely chopped
    (1 cup)
1/4 teaspoon pepper
1 ham bone, 2 pounds ham shanks or
    2 pounds smoked pork hocks
3 medium carrots, cut into 1/4-inch slices

1. Heat peas and water to boiling in Dutch oven. Boil uncovered 2 minutes; remove from heat. Cover and let stand 1 hour.

2. Stir in onion, celery and pepper. Add ham bone. Heat to boiling; reduce heat to low. Cover and simmer about 1 1/2 hours or until peas are tender.

3. Remove ham bone; remove ham from bone. Trim excess fat from ham; cut ham into 1/2-inch pieces.

4. Stir ham and carrots into soup. Heat to boiling; reduce heat to low. Cover and simmer about 30 minutes or until carrots are tender and soup is desired consistency.

1 SERVING: Calories 250 (Calories from Fat 45); Fat 5g (Saturated 2g); Cholesterol 15mg; Sodium 220mg; Carbohydrate 40g (Dietary Fiber 6g); Protein 17g

About Sandwiches

The definition of a sandwich depends on who you ask, but one thing's for certain: It's not restricted to "a filling between two pieces of bread." Almost every cuisine has its own version of a sandwich, from filled Mexican tortillas to Middle Eastern pitas to Italian calzones and Chinese pork buns, and the list goes on. The versatile sandwich can be served cold, hot, grilled, baked, fried, layered, stacked, rolled, open-face, with knife and fork, cut in half or quartered. It can be eaten as a quick snack, with soup or salad or alone for a light meal. Hearty sandwiches, such as calzones, can serve as your whole meal.

Tips for Sandwiches

- Breads with firm textures work the best for making sandwiches. Their sturdiness helps to hold the fillings without collapsing. When choosing breads, look beyond the typical white or wheat variety.
- Spread margarine or other spreads to the edges of the bread on the sides that will touch the filling. This will seal the bread and prevent moisture from making it soggy.
- Filling amounts vary according to individual likes and dislikes. Some like hearty, thick fillings, and others prefer them lighter and thinner.
- For saucy sandwich fillings, you may want to toast the bread before assembling the sandwich. Toasting keeps saucy fillings from soaking in too quickly.
- Hold together mixed fillings (such as those with chopped eggs, cut-up pieces of meat or vegetables) with mayonnaise or salad dressing, cream cheese, barbecue sauce or other sandwich spreads. Season these fillings with a little mustard, herbs, salt or pepper, if you like.
- When choosing a sandwich to serve with a soup or salad, keep the following in mind: color and texture—choose one plain, the other colorful; flavor—choose one with high flavor, the other mild.
- Sandwiches can be frozen up to 1 month if you follow a few guidelines: Avoid adding mayonnaise, sour cream, hard-cooked eggs, tomatoes or lettuce to sandwiches that will be frozen—those items don't freeze well. Add them just before serving. Wrap sandwiches individually in moisture- and vaporproof wrap. Sandwiches will thaw at room temperature in about three hours—the perfect amount of time for taking to school or the office for lunch. If sandwiches will not be eaten in three hours, keep them refrigerated or on ice to avoid food safety problems.

Hamburgers

PREP: 10 min; BROIL: 15 min
Makes 4 sandwiches

Tired of the same-old, same-old? Try brushing patties with a spunky topping, such as taco sauce, chili sauce, honey mustard, Worcestershire sauce or your favorite salad dressing before and after cooking.

    1 pound ground beef, pork or turkey
    3 tablespoons finely chopped onion, if
       desired
    3 tablespoons water
    1/2 teaspoon salt
    1/4 teaspoon pepper
    4 slices (1 ounce each) cheese, if desired
    4 hamburger buns, split and toasted

1. Set oven control to Broil.

2. Mix all ingredients except cheese and buns. Shape mixture into 4 patties, each about 3/4 inch thick. Place patties on rack in broiler pan.

3. Broil with tops about 3 inches from heat 5 to 7 minutes on each side for medium, turning once, until no longer pink in center and juice is clear. About 1 minute before hamburgers are done, top with cheese. Broil until cheese is melted. Serve on buns.

1 SANDWICH: Calories 340 (Calories from Fat 160); Fat 18g (Saturated 7g); Cholesterol 65mg; Sodium 560mg; Carbohydrate 22g (Dietary Fiber 1g); Protein 24g

TO GRILL: Grill patties about 4 inches from medium coals 7 to 8 minutes on each side for medium, turning once, until no longer pink in center and juice is clear. Brush barbecue sauce on patties before and after turning, if desired.

TO PANFRY: Cook patties in 10-inch skillet over medium heat about 10 minutes for medium, turning occasionally, until no longer pink in center and juice is clear.

Sloppy Joes

PREP: 10 min; COOK: 20 min
Makes 6 sandwiches

> 1 pound ground beef
> 1 medium onion, chopped (1/2 cup)
> 1/3 cup chopped celery
> 1/3 cup chopped green bell pepper
> 1/3 cup ketchup
> 1/4 cup water
> 1 tablespoon Worcestershire sauce
> 1/2 teaspoon salt
> 1/8 teaspoon red pepper sauce
> 6 hamburger buns, split and toasted

1. Cook beef and onion in 10-inch skillet over medium heat, stirring occasionally, until beef is brown; drain.

2. Stir in remaining ingredients except buns. Cover and cook over low heat 10 to 15 minutes or just until vegetables are tender.

3. Fill buns with beef mixture.

1 SANDWICH: Calories 295 (Calories from Fat 115); Fat 13g (Saturated 5g); Cholesterol 45mg; Sodium 640mg; Carbohydrate 28g (Dietary Fiber 2g); Protein 18g

---
LIGHTER SLOPPY JOES

For 10 grams of fat and 270 calories per serving, substitute ground turkey for the ground beef and spray skillet with nonstick cooking spray.

Reuben Sandwiches

PREP: 20 min; COOK: 20 min
Makes 6 sandwiches

> 1/3 cup mayonnaise or salad dressing
> 1 tablespoon chili sauce
> 12 slices rye bread
> 6 slices (1 ounce each) Swiss cheese
> 3/4 pound thinly sliced cooked corned beef
> 1 can (16 ounces) sauerkraut, drained
> 1/4 cup margarine or butter, softened

1. Mix mayonnaise and chili sauce. Spread over 6 slices bread. Place cheese, corned beef and sauerkraut on mayonnaise mixture. Top with remaining bread slices. Spread 1 teaspoon margarine over each top slice of bread.

2. Place sandwiches, margarine sides down, in skillet. Spread margarine over top slices of bread. Cook uncovered over low heat about 10 minutes or until bottoms are golden brown. Turn and cook about 8 minutes or until bottoms are golden brown and cheese is melted.

1 SANDWICH: Calories 595 (Calories from Fat 405); Fat 45g (Saturated 14g); Cholesterol 90mg; Sodium 1770mg; Carbohydrate 30g (Dietary Fiber 5g); Protein 23g

---
LIGHTER REUBEN SANDWICHES

For 11 grams of fat and 295 calories per serving, use fat-free mayonnaise or salad dressing and substitute thinly sliced turkey or chicken for the corned beef. Omit margarine; spray skillet with nonstick cooking spray before heating.

Barbecued Roast Beef Sandwiches

PREP: 25 min; COOK: 5 min
Makes 6 sandwiches

> Zesty Barbecue Sauce (below)
> 1 pound thinly sliced cooked roast beef, cut
>   into 1-inch strips (3 cups)
> 6 hamburger buns, split

1. Prepare Zesty Barbecue Sauce.

2. Stir beef into sauce. Cover and simmer about 5 minutes or until beef is hot.

3. Fill buns with beef mixture.

Zesty Barbecue Sauce

> 1/2 cup ketchup
> 1/4 cup white vinegar
> 2 tablespoons chopped onion
> 1 tablespoon Worcestershire sauce
> 2 teaspoons packed brown sugar
> 1/4 teaspoon ground mustard (dry)
> 1 clove garlic, crushed

Heat all ingredients to boiling in 1-quart saucepan over medium heat, stirring constantly; reduce heat to low. Simmer uncovered 15 minutes, stirring occasionally.

1 SANDWICH: Calories 340 (Calories from Fat 125); Fat 14g (Saturated 5g); Cholesterol 60mg; Sodium 550mg; Carbohydrate 30g (Dietary Fiber 1g); Protein 24g

---
TIMESAVING TIP

Substitute 1 cup prepared barbecue sauce for the Zesty Barbecue Sauce and 3 packages (2 1/2 ounces each) sliced smoked chicken, ham, turkey, beef or pastrami, cut into 1-inch strips, for the beef.

Gyros

PREP: 25 min; COOK: 15 min
Makes 4 sandwiches

For a Mediterranean meal, serve this flavorful sandwich with Greek Salad (page 319).

4 pita breads (6 inches in diameter)
1/2 cup plain yogurt
1 tablespoon chopped fresh or 1 teaspoon dried mint leaves
1 teaspoon sugar
1 small cucumber, seeded and chopped (3/4 cup)
1 pound ground lamb or beef
2 tablespoons water
1 tablespoon lemon juice
1/2 teaspoon salt
1/2 teaspoon ground cumin
1/2 teaspoon dried oregano leaves
1/4 teaspoon pepper
2 cloves garlic, crushed
1 small onion, chopped (1/4 cup)
2 tablespoons vegetable oil
2 cups shredded lettuce
1 medium tomato, chopped (3/4 cup)

1. Split each pita bread halfway around edge with knife; separate to form pocket.

2. Mix yogurt, mint and sugar in small bowl. Stir in cucumber.

3. Mix lamb, water, lemon juice, salt, cumin, oregano, pepper, garlic and onion. Shape mixture into 4 thin patties.

4. Heat oil in 10-inch skillet over medium heat. Cook patties in oil 10 to 12 minutes, turning frequently, until no longer pink in center. Place cooked patty in each pita pocket. Top with yogurt mixture, lettuce and tomato.

1 SANDWICH: Calories 475 (Calories from Fat 215); Fat 24g (Saturated 8g); Cholesterol 75mg; Sodium 670mg; Carbohydrate 42g (Dietary Fiber 3g); Protein 26g

---

TIMESAVING TIP

To microwave, omit oil. Arrange patties on microwavable rack in microwavable dish. Cover loosely with microwavable paper towel and microwave on High 7 to 9 minutes, rotating dish 1/2 turn after 3 minutes, until no longer pink in center. Let stand covered 3 minutes.

Gyros

Italian Sausage Calzone

PREP: 30 min; BAKE: 20 min; COOL: 5 min
Makes 4 servings

> 1/2 pound bulk Italian sausage
> 1 small onion, chopped (1/4 cup)
> 1/3 cup pizza sauce
> 1 can (2 ounces) mushroom stems and
>   pieces, drained
> 2 cups Bisquick Original baking mix
> 1/3 cup hot water
> 1 tablespoon vegetable oil
> 1 cup shredded mozzarella cheese (4 ounces)
> 1/4 cup grated Parmesan cheese
> 1 large egg white

1. Heat oven to 450°.

2. Cook sausage in 10-inch skillet over medium heat, stirring occasionally, until no longer pink; drain. Stir in onion, pizza sauce and mushrooms; remove from heat.

3. Mix baking mix, water and oil until dough forms. Roll dough into 12-inch circle on cloth-covered surface dusted with baking mix. Place dough on ungreased cookie sheet.

4. Top half of the dough circle with mozzarella cheese, sausage mixture and Parmesan cheese to within 1 inch of edge. Fold dough over filling; pinch edges or press with fork to seal securely. Brush with egg white.

5. Bake 15 to 20 minutes or until golden brown. Cool 5 minutes. Cut into wedges.

1 SERVING: Calories 570 (Calories from Fat 305); Fat 34g (Saturated 12g); Cholesterol 65mg; Sodium 1760mg; Carbohydrate 41g (Dietary Fiber 1g); Protein 26g

Calzone

PREP: 45 min; PROOF: 40 min; BAKE: 25 min
Makes 6 servings

> Pizza Dough (right)
> 2 cups shredded mozzarella cheese
>   (8 ounces)
> 1/4 pound salami, cut into thin strips
> 1/2 cup ricotta cheese
> 1/4 cup chopped fresh basil leaves
> 2 roma (plum) tomatoes, chopped
> Freshly ground pepper
> 1 large egg, slightly beaten

1. Prepare Pizza Dough.

2. Heat oven to 375°. Grease 2 cookie sheets.

3. Punch down dough; divide into 6 equal parts. Roll each part into 7-inch circle on lightly floured surface with floured rolling pin.

4. Top half of each dough circle with mozzarella cheese, salami, ricotta cheese, basil and tomatoes to within 1 inch of edge. Sprinkle with pepper. *Carefully* fold dough over filling; pinch edges or press with fork to seal securely.

5. Place calzones on cookie sheets. Brush with egg. Bake about 25 minutes or until golden brown.

Pizza Dough

> 1 package regular or quick active dry yeast
> 1 cup warm water (105° to 115°)
> 1 teaspoon sugar
> 1 teaspoon salt
> 1 tablespoon vegetable oil
> 2 1/4 to 2 1/2 cups all-purpose* or bread
>   flour

1. Dissolve yeast in warm water in large bowl. Stir in sugar, salt, oil and 1 cup of the flour. Beat until smooth. Stir in enough remaining flour to make dough easy to handle.

2. Turn dough onto lightly floured surface. Knead about 5 minutes or until smooth and elastic. Place in greased bowl; turn greased side up. Cover and let rise in warm place 30 to 40 minutes or until almost double.

* If using self-rising flour, omit salt.

1 SERVING: Calories 390 (Calories from Fat 145); Fat 16g (Saturated 7g); Cholesterol 75mg; Sodium 800mg; Carbohydrate 41g (Dietary Fiber 2g); Protein 22g

---

LIGHTER CALZONE

For 6 grams of fat and 320 calories per serving, use reduced-fat mozzarella cheese, substitute cooked chicken for the salami and use fat-free ricotta cheese.

Beef Burritos

PREP: 30 min
Makes 8 servings

> 2 cups shredded cooked beef
> 1 cup refried beans
> 8 flour tortillas (10 inches in diameter),
>   warmed as directed on package
> 2 cups shredded lettuce
> 2 medium tomatoes, chopped (1 1/2 cups)
> 1 cup shredded Cheddar cheese (4 ounces)

1. Heat beef and refried beans separately.

2. Place about 1/4 cup of the beef on center of each tortilla. Spoon about 2 tablespoons beans onto beef. Top with 1/4 cup of the lettuce, 3 tablespoons tomatoes and 2 tablespoons cheese.

3. Fold one end of tortilla up about 1 inch over filling; fold right and left sides over folded end, overlapping. Fold remaining end down.

1 SERVING: Calories 340 (Calories from Fat 145); Fat 16g (Saturated 7g); Cholesterol 45mg; Sodium 390mg; Carbohydrate 33g (Dietary Fiber 3g); Protein 19g

---

LIGHTER BEEF BURRITOS

For 11 grams of fat and 300 calories per serving, substitute 1 cup fat-free refried beans for the Refried Beans and use reduced-fat Cheddar cheese.

Chimichangas

PREP: 30 min; COOK: 35 min
Makes 8 sandwiches

1 pound ground beef
1 small onion, finely chopped (1/4 cup)
1 clove garlic, finely chopped
1/4 cup slivered almonds
1/4 cup raisins
1 tablespoon red wine vinegar
1 teaspoon ground red chilies or chili powder
1/2 teaspoon salt
1/4 teaspoon ground cinnamon
1/8 teaspoon ground cloves
1 medium tomato, chopped (3/4 cup)
1 can (4 ounces) chopped green chilies
8 flour tortillas (10 inches in diameter),
    warmed as directed on package
1 large egg, beaten
Vegetable oil
Salsa, if desired

1. Cook beef, onion and garlic in 10-inch skillet over medium heat, stirring occasionally, until beef is brown; drain.

2. Stir in remaining ingredients except tortillas, egg, oil and salsa. Heat to boiling; reduce heat to low. Simmer uncovered 20 minutes, stirring occasionally.

3. Spoon about 1/2 cup beef mixture onto center of each tortilla. Fold one end of tortilla up about 1 inch over beef mixture; fold right and left sides over folded end, overlapping. Fold remaining end down. Brush edges with egg to seal.

4. Heat oven to 300°. Heat oil (about 1 inch) to 365° in 10-inch skillet.

5. Fry 2 or 3 chimichangas at a time in oil 3 to 4 minutes, turning once, until golden brown. Keep warm in oven.

6. Serve chimichangas with salsa.

a. Fold one end of tortilla up about 1 inch over beef mixture.

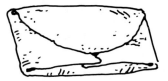

b. Fold right and left sides over folded end, overlapping.

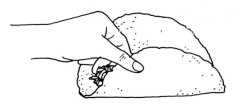

c. Fold remaining end down.

1 SANDWICH: Calories 380 (Calories from Fat 200); Fat 22g (Saturated 5g); Cholesterol 60mg; Sodium 500mg; Carbohydrate 31g (Dietary Fiber 2g); Protein 16g

---

LIGHTER CHIMICHANGAS

For 17 grams of fat and 335 calories per serving, omit vegetable oil and steps 4 and 5. Heat oven to 500°. Brush chimichangas with 2 tablespoons margarine, butter or spread, softened. Place seam sides down in ungreased jelly roll pan, 15 1/2 × 10 1/2 × 1 inch. Bake 8 to 10 minutes or until tortillas begin to brown and filling is hot.

Chicken Tacos

PREP: 15 min; COOK: 10 min
Makes 5 servings

Mexico's enchanting taco dishes have rapidly gained popularity across the country. This quick, colorful dish is just the ticket for casual entertaining. Fresh pineapple would make a refreshing dessert for this easy meal.

1 small avocado
Lemon juice
1/2 teaspoon salt
2 tablespoons vegetable oil
2 cups chopped cooked chicken
1 can (4 ounces) chopped green chilies, drained
1 small onion, sliced
3/4 teaspoon salt
10 taco shells
2 cups shredded Monterey Jack cheese (8 ounces)
1/3 cup sliced pimiento-stuffed olives
1 cup shredded lettuce
Taco sauce and sour cream, if desired

1. Cut avocado in half; cut halves into slices. Sprinkle with lemon juice and 1/2 teaspoon salt.

2. Heat oil in 10-inch skillet over medium heat. Cook chicken, chilies, onion and 3/4 teaspoon salt in oil, stirring occasionally, until chicken is hot.

3. Heat taco shells as directed on package. Spoon about 1/4 cup chicken mixture into each shell. Top with cheese, olives, lettuce and avocado. Serve with taco sauce and sour cream.

1 SERVING: Calories 515 (Calories from Fat 315); Fat 35g (Saturated 13g); Cholesterol 90mg; Sodium 1830mg; Carbohydrate 24g (Dietary Fiber 4g); Protein 30g

Club Sandwiches

PREP: 25 min
Makes 4 sandwiches

Mayonnaise or salad dressing
12 slices bread, toasted, if desired
4 lettuce leaves
12 slices tomatoes (2 medium)
12 slices bacon, crisply cooked
3/4 pound sliced cooked turkey or chicken
4 lettuce leaves

1. Spread mayonnaise over toast.

2. Place lettuce leaf, 3 slices tomato and 3 slices bacon on each of 4 slices toast. Top with another toast slice, mayonnaise side up. Arrange turkey on toast. Top with lettuce leaves. Top with third toast slice, mayonnaise side down.

3. Secure with toothpicks. Cut sandwiches diagonally into 4 triangles.

1 SANDWICH: Calories 515 (Calories from Fat 205); Fat 23g (Saturated 6g); Cholesterol 45mg; Sodium 590mg; Carbohydrate 14g (Dietary Fiber 2g); Protein 14g

---

LIGHTER CLUB SANDWICHES
For 12 grams of fat and 440 calories per serving, use fat-free mayonnaise, light bread, reduced-fat bacon and low-fat turkey. Decrease the bacon amount to 8 slices.

SHRIMP CLUB SANDWICHES: Substitute 2 cans (4 to 4 1/2 ounces each) medium shrimp, rinsed and drained, for the turkey and 1 large avocado, thinly sliced, for the lettuce leaves.

Chicken Salad Sandwiches

PREP: 15 min
Makes 4 sandwiches

1 1/2 cups chopped cooked chicken or turkey
1/2 cup mayonnaise or salad dressing
1/4 teaspoon salt
1/4 teaspoon pepper
1 medium stalk celery, chopped (1/2 cup)
1 small onion, chopped (1/4 cup)
8 slices bread

1. Mix all ingredients except bread.

2. Spread chicken mixture on each of 4 slices bread. Top with remaining bread.

1 SANDWICH: Calories 425 (Calories from Fat 245); Fat 27g (Saturated 5g); Cholesterol 60mg; Sodium 610mg; Carbohydrate 27g (Dietary Fiber 1g); Protein 20g

---

LIGHTER CHICKEN SALAD SANDWICHES
For 5 grams of fat and 255 calories per serving, use fat-free mayonnaise.

EGG SALAD SANDWICHES: Substitute 6 hard-cooked eggs, chopped, for the chicken.

HAM SALAD SANDWICHES: Substitute 1 1/2 cups chopped fully cooked smoked ham for the chicken. Omit salt and pepper. Stir in 1 teaspoon mustard.

TUNA SALAD SANDWICHES: Substitute 1 can (9 1/4 ounces) tuna in water, drained, for the chicken. Stir in 1 teaspoon lemon juice.

Vegetable Corn Chowder (page 380), Pesto-Parmesan Grilled Cheese

American Grilled Cheese

PREP: 10 min; COOK: 15 min
Makes 4 sandwiches

A dynamite dunker! Cut these sandwiches into sticks and dunk them into steaming bowlfuls of Chili con Carne (page 369), Cream of Broccoli Soup (page 375), Wild Rice Soup (page 379) or Cuban Black Bean Soup (page 381).

> **12 slices process American cheese**
> **8 slices white or whole wheat bread**
> **Margarine or butter, softened**

1. Place 3 slices cheese on each of 4 slices bread. Top with remaining bread slices. Spread margarine over top slices of bread.

2. Place sandwiches, margarine sides down, in skillet. Spread margarine over top slices of bread. Cook uncovered over medium heat about 5 minutes or until bottoms are golden brown. Turn and cook 2 to 3 minutes or until bottoms are golden brown and cheese is melted.

1 SANDWICH: Calories 435 (Calories from Fat 260); Fat 29g (Saturated 15g); Cholesterol 60mg; Sodium 1270mg; Carbohydrate 26g (Dietary Fiber 1g); Protein 18g

SUPER GRILLED CHEESE: Use 8 ounces Monterey Jack, Muenster, provolone or mozzarella cheese, thinly sliced. Place half of the cheese on 4 slices bread. Top with 1 small onion, chopped (1/4 cup), 8 slices bacon, crisply cooked, 1 medium tomato, thinly sliced, and 1 avocado, thinly sliced, then remaining cheese and bread. Spread margarine over top slices of bread. Continue as directed in step 2.

PESTO-PARMESAN GRILLED CHEESE: Spread each bread slice lightly with prepared pesto before adding cheese in step 1. Sprinkle margarine-topped slices with Parmesan cheese before grilling.

Denver Pocket Sandwiches

PREP: 20 min; COOK: 5 min
Makes 6 sandwiches

Bulk up these tasty sandwiches with just a few extra calories and no extra fat, for a super-hearty meal. Line the pita breads with salad greens, alfalfa sprouts, tomato slices, shredded carrot, pea pods or sliced mushrooms before filling with the egg mixture.

> 2 tablespoons margarine or butter
> 1 medium onion, chopped (1/2 cup)
> 1 small green bell pepper, chopped (1/2 cup)
> 6 large eggs
> 1/2 cup chopped fully cooked smoked ham
>   or 1 can (5 ounces) chunk ham
> 1 jar (2 ounces) diced pimientos, drained
> 1/4 teaspoon salt
> 1/8 teaspoon pepper
> 3 pita breads (6 inches in diameter), cut in
>   half to form pockets

1. Melt margarine in 10-inch skillet over medium heat. Cook onion and bell pepper in margarine, stirring occasionally, until onion is tender.

2. Beat eggs slightly in medium bowl. Stir in ham, pimientos, salt and pepper.

3. Pour egg mixture into skillet. Cook over low heat, *gently* lifting cooked portions with spatula so that thin uncooked portion can flow to bottom. Avoid constant stirring. Cook 3 to 5 minutes or until eggs are thickened throughout but still moist.

4. Divide egg mixture among pita breads.

1 SANDWICH: Calories 215 (Calories from Fat 90); Fat 10g (Saturated 3g); Cholesterol 220mg; Sodium 540mg; Carbohydrate 20g (Dietary Fiber 1g); Protein 12g

---

LIGHTER DENVER POCKET
SANDWICHES

For 3 grams of fat and 145 calories, decrease margarine to 1 tablespoon and use nonstick skillet. Substitute 1 1/2 cups fat-free cholesterol-free egg substitute for the 6 eggs.

Muffuletta

PREP: 20 min
Makes 6 servings

The Central Grocery in New Orleans created this mammoth sandwich. Its pungent Olive Salad sets it apart from a hero or a Submarine Sandwich.

> Olive Salad (below)
> 1 large round or oval unsliced loaf Italian or
>   sourdough bread (8 to 10 inches in
>   diameter)
> 1/2 pound thinly sliced Italian salami
> 6 ounces thinly sliced provolone cheese
> 1/4 pound thinly sliced fully cooked smoked
>   ham

1. Prepare Olive Salad.

2. Cut bread horizontally in half. Remove 1/2-inch layer of soft bread from inside of each half to within 1/2 inch of edge.

3. Drain Olive Salad; reserve marinade. Brush marinade over cut sides of bread. Layer salami, half of the Olive Salad, the cheese, ham and remaining Olive Salad on bottom half of bread. Cover with top half of bread.

Olive Salad

> 1 anchovy fillet, mashed
> 1 large clove garlic, crushed
> 1/3 cup olive or vegetable oil
> 1/2 cup chopped pimiento-stuffed olives
> 1/2 cup chopped Greek or ripe olives
> 1/2 cup chopped mixed pickled vegetables
> 2 tablespoons chopped fresh parsley
> 1 1/2 teaspoons chopped fresh or 1/2
>   teaspoon dried oregano leaves, crushed
> 1/8 teaspoon pepper

Stir anchovy and garlic into oil in small glass or plastic bowl until well blended. Stir in remaining ingredients. Cover and refrigerate at least 8 hours, stirring occasionally.

1 SANDWICH: Calories (Calories from Fat 295); Fat 33g (Saturated 12g); Cholesterol 65mg; Sodium 1960mg; Carbohydrate 43g (Dietary Fiber 3g); Protein 27g

Vegetables

About Vegetables

Today's supermarkets, grocery stores and farmers' markets sell a wide variety of fresh, frozen and canned vegetables. With just a few exceptions, you can enjoy your favorite vegetables all year long. Don't forget to check the international section of your supermarket or the specialty section of the produce department for the latest offerings—there are often some pleasant surprises.

Selecting and Cooking

- **For fresh vegetables**, look for the specific vegetable in the Fresh Vegetable Cooking Chart (page 394) for selection, preparation and cooking guidelines. Cooking times will vary depending on the ripeness, age, size, amount of moisture and storage location of the vegetables.

  Salting cooking water can cause some vegetables to dehydrate and become firm. So salt the cooking water (1/4 teaspoon salt per cup of water) only if desired. Use about 1 cup of water for each pound of vegetables.

  Baby (or miniature) vegetables, such as beans, beets, broccoli, carrots, corn, eggplant, potatoes and squash, are now more commonly available. These are either harvested early in their growing stages or are genetically bred to be true miniatures. Baby vegetables are more tender and delicately flavored than the regular-size vegetables and can be eaten raw or cooked like their regular-size counterparts. They also are generally more expensive. To avoid overcooking, *check for doneness several minutes before the minimum cooking time* due to their size and tenderness. Baby vegetables are often sautéed in a small amount of margarine or butter to enhance their delicate flavor.

- **For frozen vegetables,** cook according to package directions. Frozen vegetables will cook in less time than fresh vegetables because the process of blanching and freezing tenderizes them somewhat. They are available in many interesting combinations, with or without sauces or additions such as pasta. Some even have directions for adding meat or poultry to make a main dish. Choose unopened packages that are not in a solid block. If they are in a solid block they may have been thawed and refrozen.

- **For commercially canned vegetables,** heat, undrained, until hot. Drain before serving. Choose cans without dents.

- **For home-canned vegetables,** do not use the vegetables if the jar is not sealed properly. As a safety precaution, boil all low-acid home-canned foods for at least 10 minutes before serving.

Storing Vegetables

Storing vegetables properly will help them stay fresh until you are ready to prepare and serve them. Use vegetables as soon as possible for best results. Storage times given are for optimum freshness.

- *Refrigerator crisper or in a plastic bag in refrigerator.* Place vegetables in plastic bags if refrigerator crisper is not kept 2/3 full. *1 to 2 days*: asparagus, beet greens, broccoli, Brussels sprouts, chard, collard greens, green peas, green onions, fresh lima beans, mushrooms, mustard greens, spinach and turnip greens. *3 to 5 days*: cauliflower, celery, cucumber, green beans, okra, bell peppers and summer squash. *1 or 2 weeks*: beets, cabbage, carrots, parsnips, radishes and turnips.

- *Refrigerate uncovered. 1 or 2 days*: Sweet corn in husks and ripe tomatoes. Keep *unripe* tomatoes at room temperature until they ripen, but away from direct sunlight, which promotes mushiness.

- *Cool (between 45° and 60°), dark, dry, well-ventilated place. 7 weeks*: garlic, onions, potatoes and uncut winter squash with hard rinds. Store onions and potatoes separately to reduce spoiling. Potatoes stored at warmer temperatures should be used within 1 week to prevent sprouting or shriveling. A greenish tinge on potatoes is caused by long exposure to light and should be removed before cooking. Refrigerating can cause some varieties of potatoes to become sweeter and turn dark when cooked.

Preceding page: Mixed Roasted Vegetables (page 413)

Vegetable Doneness

While most vegetables can be eaten raw, cooking vegetables to the proper doneness can mean the difference between an inviting, tasty dish or one with vegetables that are overcooked (too soft) or undercooked (too raw and hard to eat with a fork). When cooking vegetables, be sure to check them at the minimum cooking time, then add additional time if necessary until the desired doneness. Microwave vegetables until *almost* tender or crisp-tender because they will continue to cook while standing.

Vegetables such as potatoes, eggplants, peas and greens should be cooked until tender. Other vegetables, such as asparagus, broccoli, beans, carrots, mushrooms and bell peppers, should be cooked until crisp-tender. Cooking certain vegetables until crisp-tender not only keeps the color of the vegetable bright but also retains more vitamins and minerals than if cooked for a longer time.

❖

Cooking Fresh Vegetables

The Fresh Vegetable Cooking Chart that follows gives you basic information about what to look for when shopping for vegetables, how to prepare vegetables and a choice of several cooking methods. The sizes of cut vegetable pieces are indicated where important, because cooking times will be different. Before using the chart, read the general cooking directions for each cooking method.

Conventional Directions

Bake:

1. Oven need not be preheated.
2. Place vegetables in baking pan (vegetables in skin, such as potatoes, may be placed directly on oven rack).
3. Bake for amount of time in chart.

Boil:

1. Heat 1 inch water (salted, if desired) to boiling in saucepan, unless directed otherwise. Add vegetables.
2. Heat to boiling; reduce heat to low.
3. Boil gently (simmer) for amount of time in chart.
4. Drain.

Sauté:

1. Heat margarine, butter, spread or olive or vegetable oil in 10-inch skillet over medium-high heat.
2. Cook uncovered, stirring frequently, for amount of time in chart.

Steam:

1. Place steamer basket in 1/2 inch water in saucepan or skillet (water should not touch bottom of basket). Place vegetables in steamer basket.
2. Cover tightly and heat to boiling; reduce heat to low.
3. Steam for amount of time in chart.

Microwave Directions

1. Use microwavable casserole (1 1/2 or 2 quart, or other size if given), unless directed otherwise.
2. Add amount of water (salted, if desired) if given. Add vegetables.
3. Cover with lid, or cover with plastic wrap, folding back 2-inch edge to vent.
4. Microwave on High for amount of time in chart. Stir, rearrange or turn over vegetables once or twice during cooking.
5. Vegetables will continue to cook a short time after microwaving. For crisp-tender vegetables, let stand covered 1 to 2 minutes. For tender vegetables, let stand covered 3 to 5 minutes.
6. Drain.

Fresh Vegetable Cooking Chart

Vegetable with Amounts for 4 Servings	To Prepare	Conventional Directions	Microwave Directions
Artichokes, Globe 4 medium Choose plump compact globes that are heavy in relation to their size, with fresh, green inner leaves.	Remove discolored leaves; trim stem even with base. Cut 1 inch off top and discard. Snip off points of the remaining leaves with scissors. Rinse with cold water. To prevent discoloration, dip into cold water mixed with small amount of lemon juice (1 tablespoon lemon juice per 1 quart water). To fill and bake, remove center leaves and the choke before cooking. (Choke is the fuzzy growth covering artichoke heart.)	**Boil:** Use 6 quarts water, 2 tablespoons lemon juice and 1 clove garlic, cut into fourths. Boil uncovered 30 to 40 minutes, rotating occasionally, until leaves pull out easily and bottom is tender when pierced with knife. **Steam:** 20 to 25 minutes or until bottom is tender when pierced with knife.	Use 3-quart casserole. Add 1 cup water, 1 teaspoon lemon juice and 1 small clove garlic. Microwave 14 to 20 minutes or until leaves pull out easily.
Asparagus 1 1/2 pounds Choose smooth, round, tender, medium-size green spears with closed tips.	Break off tough ends as far down as stalks snap easily. Wash asparagus; remove scales if sandy or tough. (If necessary, remove sand particles with a vegetable brush.) For spears, tie whole stalks in bundles with string, or hold together with band of aluminum foil. Or cut stalks into 1-inch pieces.	**Boil:** *Spears*—Place stalks upright in deep, narrow pan. Boil uncovered 5 minutes; cover and boil 7 to 10 minutes or until crisp-tender. *Pieces*—Add lower stalk pieces; boil uncovered 6 minutes. Add tips; cover and boil 5 to 8 minutes or until crisp-tender. **Steam:** 6 to 8 minutes or until crisp-tender.	*Spears*—Use square dish, 8 × 8 × 2 inches. Add 1/4 cup water. Microwave 6 to 9 minutes or until crisp-tender. *Pieces*—Add 1/4 cup water. Microwave 6 to 9 minutes or until crisp-tender.
Beans, Green, Purple Wax and Yellow Wax 1 pound Choose bright, smooth, crisp pods. Just-picked beans will feel pliable and velvety.	Wash beans; remove ends. Leave beans whole or cut into 1-inch pieces.	**Boil:** Boil uncovered 5 minutes. Cover and boil 5 to 10 minutes longer or until crisp-tender. **Steam:** 10 to 12 minutes or until crisp-tender.	*Pieces*—Add 1/2 cup water. Microwave 9 to 12 minutes or until crisp-tender.
Beans, Lima 3 pounds (unshelled) Choose broad, thick, shiny pods that are plump with large seeds.	Wash beans. Shell just before cooking. To shell beans, remove thin outer edge of pod with sharp knife or scissors. Slip out beans.	**Boil:** Boil uncovered 5 minutes. Cover and boil 15 to 20 minutes longer or until tender.	Use 1-quart casserole. Add 1/2 cup water. Microwave 16 to 18 minutes, stirring every 6 minutes, until tender.

Fresh Vegetable Cooking Chart (continued)

Vegetable with Amounts for 4 Servings	To Prepare	Conventional Directions	Microwave Directions
Beets 5 medium (1 1/4 pounds) Choose firm, round, smooth, deep red beets with fresh unwilted tops.	Cut off all but 1 inch of beet tops. Wash beets; leave whole with root ends attached.	**Boil:** Use 6 cups water, 1 tablespoon white vinegar (to preserve color) and salt (if desired). Boil 40 to 50 minutes or until tender. **Steam:** 45 to 50 minutes or until tender. Add boiling water during steaming if necessary.	Add 1/2 cup water. Microwave 18 to 25 minutes, stirring every 5 minutes, until tender.
Bok Choy 1 1/2 pounds Choose firm, white stalks with shiny, dark leaves.	Wash bok choy; cut off leaves. Cut stems into 1/4-inch slices; cut leaves into 1/2-inch strips.	**Boil:** Add bok choy stems. Cover and heat to boiling; reduce heat to low. Boil 5 minutes. Add bok choy leaves. Cover and boil 2 to 3 minutes or until stems are crisp-tender. **Steam:** Add bok choy stems; steam 5 minutes. Add bok choy leaves; steam 2 to 3 minutes or until stems are crisp-tender.	Use 3-quart casserole. Add bok choy stems and 2 tablespoons water. Microwave 4 minutes. Stir in bok choy leaves. Microwave 3 to 4 minutes or until stems are crisp-tender.
Broccoli 1 1/2 pounds Choose firm, compact dark green clusters; avoid thick, tough stems.	Trim off large leaves; remove tough ends of lower stems. Wash broccoli; peel if desired. For spears, cut lengthwise into 1/2-inch-wide stalks. For pieces, cut lengthwise into 1/2-inch-wide stalks, then cut cross-wise into 1-inch pieces.	**Boil:** 10 to 12 minutes or until stems are crisp-tender. **Steam:** 10 to 11 minutes or until stems are crisp-tender.	*Spears*—Use square dish, 8 × 8 × 2 inches. Arrange broccoli with flowerets in center. Add 1 cup water. Microwave 9 to 11 minutes or until stems are crisp-tender. *Pieces*—Add 1 cup water. Microwave 9 to 11 minutes or until stems are crisp-tender.
Brussels Sprouts 1 pound Choose unblemished, bright green sprouts with compact leaves.	Remove any discolored leaves; cut off stem ends. Wash sprouts; cut large sprouts in half.	**Boil:** 8 to 10 minutes or until tender. **Steam:** 20 to 25 minutes or until tender.	Add 1/4 cup water. Microwave 8 to 11 minutes or until tender.
Cabbage, Celery and Napa (Chinese) 1 pound (1 medium head) Choose crisp, green heads with no signs of browning. The leaves can be firm or leafy.	Remove root ends. Wash cabbage; shred.	**Boil:** 4 to 5 minutes or until crisp-tender. **Steam:** 4 to 5 minutes or until tender.	Add 1/4 cup water. Microwave 4 to 7 minutes or until crisp-tender.

Fresh Vegetable Cooking Chart [continued]

Vegetable with Amounts for 4 Servings	To Prepare	Conventional Directions	Microwave Directions
Cabbage, Red and Green 1 pound (1 small head) Choose firm heads that are heavy in relation to their size. Outer leaves should have good color and be free of blemishes.	Remove outside leaves. Wash cabbage; cut into 4 wedges. Trim core to within 1/4 inch of leaves, or shred cabbage and discard core.	**Boil:** *Wedges*—Add cabbage (and 2 tablespoons white vinegar or lemon juice for red cabbage). Boil 10 to 17 minutes, turning wedges once, until crisp-tender. *Shredded*—Add cabbage (and 2 tablespoons white vinegar or lemon juice for red cabbage). Boil 5 to 8 minutes or until crisp-tender. **Steam:** Wedges—18 to 24 minutes or until crisp-tender. *Shredded*—5 to 7 minutes or until crisp-tender.	*Wedges*—Arrange cabbage wedges with core ends to outside edge. Add 1/2 cup water. Microwave 10 to 14 minutes or until crisp-tender. *Shredded*—Add 1/4 cup water. Microwave 8 to 10 minutes or until crisp-tender.
Carrots 1 pound (6 to 7 medium) Choose firm, nicely shaped carrots with good color.	Peel carrots thinly and remove ends. Leave carrots whole, shred, cut lengthwise into julienne strips or cut crosswise into 1/4-inch slices.	**Boil:** *Whole*—25 minutes. *Julienne strips*—18 to 20 minutes. *Slices*—12 to 15 minutes. *Shredded*—5 minutes or until tender. **Steam:** *Whole*—12 to 15 minutes. *Slices*—9 to 11 minutes or until tender.	*Julienne—strips or slices*—Add 1/4 cup water. Microwave 6 to 8 minutes or until tender.
Cauliflower 2 pounds (1 medium head) Choose clean, nonspreading flower clusters (the white portion) and green "jacket" leaves.	Remove outer leaves and stalk; cut off any discoloration. Wash cauliflower. Leave whole, cutting cone-shaped center from core, or separate into flowerets.	**Boil:** *Whole*—20 to 25 minutes. *Flowerets*—10 to 12 minutes or until tender. **Steam:** *Whole*—18 to 22 minutes. *Flowerets*—6 to 8 minutes or until tender.	*Whole*—Add 1/4 cup water. Microwave 12 to 14 minutes or until tender. *Flowerets*—Add 1/4 cup water. Microwave 12 to 14 minutes or until tender.
Celery 1 medium bunch (1 1/4 pounds) Choose crisp, unblemished stalks with fresh leaves.	Remove leaves and trim off root ends. Remove any coarse strings. Wash celery; cut stalks into 1-inch pieces.	**Boil:** 15 to 20 minutes or until crisp-tender. **Steam:** 18 to 20 minutes or until crisp-tender.	Add 2 tablespoons water. Microwave 7 to 11 minutes or until crisp-tender.

Fresh Vegetable Cooking Chart (continued)

Vegetable with Amounts for 4 Servings	To Prepare	Conventional Directions	Microwave Directions
Corn 4 ears Choose bright green, tight-fitting husks, fresh-looking silk, plump but not too large kernels.	Refrigerate unhusked corn until ready to use. (Corn is best when eaten as soon after picking as possible.) Husk ears and remove silk just before cooking.	**Boil:** Place ears in enough unsalted cold water to cover (salt toughens corn). Add 1 tablespoon sugar and 1 tablespoon lemon juice to each gallon of water, if desired. Heat to boiling. Boil uncovered 2 minutes; remove from heat. Let stand uncovered 10 minutes before serving. **Steam:** 6 to 9 minutes or until tender.	Use square dish, $8 \times 8 \times 2$ inches. Add 1/4 cup water. Microwave 9 to 14 minutes or until tender.
Cucumbers 2 medium (1 pound) Choose firm, dark green cucumbers.	Wash cucumbers; peel if desired. Cut into 1/2-inch slices or 1/2-inch pieces.	**Steam:** About 5 minutes or until crisp-tender.	Do not add water. Microwave 4 to 5 minutes or until crisp-tender.
Eggplant 1 1/2 pounds (1 medium) Choose smooth, glossy, taut-skinned eggplant that is free from blemishes and rust spots. Caps and stems should be intact and free of mold.	Just before cooking, wash eggplant; peel if desired. Cut into 1/2-inch cubes or 1/4-inch slices.	**Boil:** 5 to 8 minutes or until tender. **Sauté:** Melt 3 to 4 tablespoons margarine, butter or spread in 10-inch skillet over medium-high heat. Sauté eggplant in margarine 5 to 10 minutes or until tender. **Steam:** 5 to 7 minutes or until tender.	*Cubes*—Add 2 tablespoons water. Microwave 8 to 10 minutes or until tender. *Slices*—Arrange slices, overlapping, in a circle around edge of pie plate, $9 \times 1 \ 1/4$ inches. Add 2 tablespoons water. Microwave 5 to 7 minutes or until tender.
Fennel 1 pound (3 to 4 medium) Choose compact, unblemished smooth whitish-green bulbs with fresh tops.	Remove feathery tops* and tough or discolored outer ribs; trim base. Cut in fourths lengthwise. *Slice to use as a seasoning.	**Boil:** 8 to 11 minutes or until tender. **Steam:** 12 to 15 minutes or until tender.	Add 1/4 cup water. Microwave 6 to 10 minutes or until crisp-tender.
Greens: Beet, Chicory, Collards, Escarole, Kale, Mustard, Spinach, Swiss Chard, Turnip 1 pound Choose tender, young, unblemished leaves with bright green color.	Remove root ends and imperfect leaves. Wash several times in water, lifting out each time; drain.	**Boil:** Cover and cook with just the water that clings to leaves until tender: *beet tops*—5 to 15 minutes; *chicory, escarole, mustard and Swiss chard*—15 to 20 minutes; *collards*—10 to 15 minutes; *kale and turnip*—15 to 25 minutes; *spinach*—3 to 10 minutes.	*Beet tops, chicory, escarole or spinach:* Use 3-quart casserole. Add greens with just the water that clings to the leaves. Microwave 8 to 10 minutes or until tender.

Fresh Vegetable Cooking Chart (continued)

Vegetable with Amounts for 4 Servings	To Prepare	Conventional Directions	Microwave Directions
Jerusalem Artichokes 4 medium (1 pound) Choose smooth, firm, light-colored tubers with the fewest "knobs." Tubers should be free of blotches, green-tinged areas and sprouts.	Scrub artichokes; peel thinly if desired. Leave whole or cut into 1/4-inch slices or 1/2-inch cubes. To prevent discoloration, toss with cold water mixed with small amount of lemon juice (1 tablespoon lemon juice per 1 quart water).	**Boil:** *Whole*—20 to 25 minutes. *Slices or cubes*—7 to 9 minutes or until crisp-tender. **Steam:** 15 to 20 minutes or until crisp-tender.	Add 1/4 cup water. Microwave 6 to 7 minutes or until crisp-tender.
Kohlrabi 1 pound (4 medium) Choose firm, purple-tinged white bulbs with no soft spots or yellowing leaf tips. Those under 3 inches in diameter are most tender.	Cut off root ends and tops. Wash; peel thinly. Leave whole or cut into 1/2-inch pieces.	**Boil:** *Whole*—25 to 30 minutes. *Pieces*—15 to 20 minutes or until tender. **Steam:** 15 to 20 minutes or until tender.	*Pieces*—Add 1/4 cup water. Microwave 10 to 12 minutes or until tender.
Leeks 2 pounds (6 medium) Choose white bulbs with pliable, crisp, green tops. Bulbs less than 1 1/2 inches in diameter are the most tender.	Remove green tops to within 2 inches of white part (reserve greens for soup or stew). Peel outside layer of bulbs. Wash leeks several times in cold water; drain. Cut large leeks lengthwise into fourths.	**Boil:** 12 to 15 minutes or until tender. **Steam:** 13 to 15 minutes or until tender.	Use square dish, 8 × 8 × 2 inches. Add 1/4 cup water. Microwave 6 to 7 minutes or until tender.
Mushrooms 1 pound Choose creamy white to light brown caps, closed around the stems; if slightly open, gills should be light pink or tan.	Rinse mushrooms and trim off stem ends. Do not peel. Leave whole or cut into 1/4-inch slices.	**Sauté:** *Whole or slices*—Melt 1/4 cup margarine, butter or spread in 10-inch skillet over medium-high heat. Sauté mushrooms in margarine 6 to 8 minutes or until tender. **Steam:** 6 to 8 minutes or until tender.	*Slices*—Do not add water. Microwave 5 to 6 minutes or until tender.
Okra 1 pound Choose tender, unblemished, bright green pods, less than 4 inches long.	Wash okra; remove ends. Leave whole or cut into 1/2-inch slices.	**Boil:** About 10 minutes or until tender. **Steam:** 6 to 8 minutes or until tender.	*Whole*—Add 1/4 cup water. Microwave 5 to 7 minutes or until tender.

Fresh Vegetable Cooking Chart (continued)

Vegetable with Amounts for 4 Servings	To Prepare	Conventional Directions	Microwave Directions
Onions, Green 3 bunches Choose crisp green tops; 2 to 3 inches of white root.	Wash onions; remove any loose layers of skin. Leave about 3 inches of green tops.	**Boil:** 8 to 10 minutes or just until tender. **Steam:** 8 to 10 minutes or just until tender.	Add 2 tablespoons water. Microwave 1 to 2 minutes or just until tender.
Onions, White, Yellow or Red 1 1/2 pounds (8 to 10 small) Choose firm, well-shaped onions with unblemished, papery skins and no sign of sprouting.	Peel onions in cold water to prevent eyes from watering. See cooking directions for piece size.	**Bake:** Place large onions in ungreased baking dish. Pour water into dish until 1/4 inch deep. Cover and bake in 350° oven 40 to 50 minutes or until tender. **Boil:** *Small*—15 to 20 minutes. *Large*—30 to 35 minutes or until tender. **Sauté:** Cut onions into 1/4-inch slices. Melt 3 to 4 tablespoons margarine, butter, spread, olive oil or vegetable oil in 10-inch skillet over medium-high heat. Sauté onions in margarine 6 to 9 minutes or until tender. **Steam:** 15 to 20 minutes or until tender.	Add 1/4 cup water. Microwave 6 to 11 minutes or until tender.
Parsnips 1 1/2 pounds (6 to 8 medium) Choose firm, nicely shaped, unblemished parsnips that are not too wide.	Scrape or peel. Leave whole or cut into halves or fourths or 1/4-inch slices or strips.	**Boil:** *Whole or halves*—15 to 20 minutes. *Slices or strips*—7 to 9 minutes or until tender. **Steam:** *Whole*—20 to 25 minutes. *Slices or strips*—8 to 10 minutes or until tender.	*Slices or strips*—Use 1-quart casserole. Add 1/4 cup water. Microwave 8 to 10 minutes or until tender.
Pea Pods, Chinese 1 pound Choose flat, crisp and evenly green pods with a velvety feel.	Wash pods; remove tips and strings.	**Boil:** Boil uncovered 2 to 3 minutes, stirring occasionally, until crisp-tender. **Steam:** 5 to 7 minutes or until crisp-tender.	Use 1-quart casserole. Add 1/4 cup water. Microwave 6 to 7 minutes or until crisp-tender.
Peas, Green 2 pounds Choose plump, tender, bright green pods.	Wash and shell peas just before cooking.	**Boil:** Boil uncovered 5 minutes. Cover and boil 3 to 7 minutes longer or until tender. If desired, add 1/2 teaspoon sugar and a few pea pods or a lettuce leaf to boiling water for added flavor. **Steam:** 10 to 12 minutes or until tender.	Use 1-quart casserole. Add 1/4 cup water. Microwave 9 to 11 minutes or until tender.

Fresh Vegetable Cooking Chart (continued)

Vegetable with Amounts for 4 Servings	To Prepare	Conventional Directions	Microwave Directions
Peppers, Bell 2 medium (1/2 pound) Choose well-shaped, shiny, bright-colored unblemished peppers with firm sides.	Wash peppers; remove stems, seeds and membranes. Leave whole to stuff and bake, or cut into thin slices or rings.	**Sauté:** *Slices or rings*—Melt 1 to 2 tablespoons margarine, butter or spread in 10-inch skillet over medium-high heat. Sauté peppers in margarine 3 to 5 minutes or until crisp-tender. **Steam:** 8 to 10 minutes or until crisp-tender.	Do not add water. Microwave 4 to 5 minutes or until crisp-tender.
Potatoes, New 1 1/2 pounds new potatoes (10 to 12) Choose nicely shaped, smooth, firm potatoes with unblemished skins of similar size.	Wash potatoes; peel narrow strip around centers if desired.	**Boil:** 20 to 25 minutes or until tender. **Steam:** 18 to 22 minutes or until tender.	Pierce potatoes to allow steam to escape. Arrange with larger potatoes to outside edge. Add 1/4 cup water. Microwave 10 to 12 minutes or until tender.
Potatoes, Sweet and Yams 4 medium (1 1/2 pounds) Choose nicely shaped, smooth, firm potatoes with even-colored skins. See Varieties of Potatoes, page 406. Choose potatoes of similar size.	Scrub potatoes but do not peel. *To bake*—Pierce potatoes to allow steam to escape. *To boil or steam*—Leave whole or cut into large pieces.	**Bake:** Pierce potatoes to allow steam to escape. Bake in 375° oven about 45 minutes, in 350° oven about 1 hour, in 325° oven about 1 1/4 hours or until tender. **Boil:** 30 to 35 minutes or until tender. **Steam:** Steam 25 to 30 minutes or until tender.	Pierce potatoes to allow steam to escape. Arrange about 1 inch apart in circle on paper towel. Microwave uncovered 8 to 10 minutes or until tender.
Potatoes, White and Red 6 medium (2 pounds) Choose nicely shaped, smooth, firm potatoes with unblemished skins, free from discoloration. See page 406).	*To bake*—Choose potatoes of similar size. Scrub potatoes but do not peel, and, if desired, rub with shortening for softer skins. Pierce potatoes to allow steam to escape. *To boil or steam*—Scrub potatoes. Leave skins on whenever possible, or peel thinly and remove eyes. Leave whole or cut into large pieces.	**Bake:** Bake in 375° oven 1 to 1 1/4 hours, in 350° oven 1 1/4 to 1 1/2 hours, in 325° oven about 1 1/2 hours or until tender. **Boil:** Whole 30 to 35 minutes, pieces 20 to 25 minutes or until tender. **Steam:** 30 to 35 minutes or until tender.	*Whole*—Pierce potatoes to allow steam to escape. Arrange about 1 inch apart in circle on paper towel. Microwave uncovered 12 to 14 minutes or until tender. *Pieces*—Add 1/2 cup water. Microwave 10 to 12 minutes or until tender; drain.
Rutabagas 1 1/2 pounds (2 medium) Choose rutabagas that are heavy, well shaped (round or elongated) and smooth.	Wash rutabagas; peel thinly. Cut into 1/2-inch cubes or 2-inch pieces.	**Boil:** *Cubes*—20 to 25 minutes. *Pieces*—30 to 40 minutes or until tender. **Steam:** 25 to 28 minutes or until tender.	*Cubes*—Add 1/2 cup water. Microwave 15 to 18 minutes or until tender.

Fresh Vegetable Cooking Chart (continued)

Vegetable with Amounts for 4 Servings	To Prepare	Conventional Directions	Microwave Directions
Squash, Summer (Chayote, Crookneck, Pattypan, Straight-neck, Yellow Zucchini) 1 1/2 pounds Choose squash that are heavy in relation to size, with smooth and glossy skin. Small squash are more tender.	Wash squash; remove stem and blossom ends but do not peel. Cut small squash in half. Cut large squash into 1/2-inch slices or cubes.	**Boil:** *Slices*—5 to 10 minutes. *Cubes*—3 to 6 minutes or until tender. **Steam:** 5 to 7 minutes or until tender.	Add 1/4 cup water. Microwave 8 to 10 minutes (pattypan 9 to 13 minutes) or until almost tender.
Squash, Winter (Acorn, Buttercup, Butternut, Spaghetti) and Pumpkin 2 pounds Choose squash that are heavy in relation to size, with good yellow-orange color and hard, tough rinds with no soft spots.	Wash squash. *To bake*—Cut each squash lengthwise in half; remove seeds and fibers. *To boil*—Peel squash if desired. Cut into 1-inch slices or cubes.	**Bake:** Place squash halves, cut sides up, in ungreased rectangular baking dish, $13 \times 9 \times 2$ inches. Sprinkle cut sides with salt and pepper. Dot with margarine, butter or spread. Pour water into dish until 1/4 inch deep. Cover and bake in 400° oven 30 to 40 minutes, in 350° oven about 40 minutes, in 325° oven about 45 minutes or until tender. **Boil:** *Slices or cubes*—15 to 20 minutes or until tender. **Steam:** *Slices*—12 to 15 minutes. *Cubes*—7 to 10 minutes or until tender.	*Acorn, Buttercup, Butternut*—Pierce whole squash with knife in several places to allow steam to escape. Place on paper towel. Microwave 4 to 6 minutes or until squash is hot and rind is firm but easy to cut; cool slightly. Carefully cut in half; remove seeds. Arrange halves, cut sides down, on 10-inch plate. Cover and microwave 5 to 8 minutes or until squash is tender when pierced knife. *Spaghetti*—Pierce whole squash in several places to allow steam to escape. Place on paper towel. Microwave uncovered 18 to 23 minutes, turning squash over after 8 minutes, until tender. Let stand uncovered 10 minutes. Cut in half; remove seeds and fibers.
Tomatoes 4 medium (1 1/3 pounds) Choose nicely ripened, well-shaped tomatoes. Fully ripe tomatoes should be slightly soft but not mushy, and have a rich red color.	Wash tomatoes. *To sauté*—Cut into 8 wedges or slice 1/2-inch thick. Peel tomatoes before cutting if desired. To remove skin easily, dip tomato into boiling water 30 seconds, then into cold water. Or scrape surface of tomato with blade of knife to loosen; peel.	**Sauté:** Melt 3 to 4 tablespoons margarine, butter, spread, olive oil or vegetable oil in 10-inch skillet over medium-high heat. Sauté tomatoes in margarine about 3 to 4 minutes or until hot.	*Wedges*—Do not add water. Microwave 7 to 9 minutes, gently stirring after 4 minutes, until hot. *Slices*—Do not add water. Microwave 5 to 7 minutes, gently stirring after 3 minutes, until hot.
Turnips 1 pound (4 medium) Choose turnips that are smooth, round and firm, with fresh tops.	Cut off tops. Wash turnips; peel thinly. Leave whole or cut into 1/2-inch pieces.	**Boil:** *Whole*—25 to 30 minutes. *Pieces*—15 to 20 minutes or until tender. **Steam:** 15 to 20 minutes or until tender.	*Pieces*—Add 1/4 cup water. Microwave 12 to 14 minutes or until tender.

Grilling Fresh Vegetables

Grilling is a favorite cooking method that gives a distinctive and delicious flavor to vegetables as well as to meats.

1. Follow directions for preparation in the Fresh Vegetable Cooking Chart (page 394).
2. Heat coals or gas grill (direct heat) to medium heat.
3. Grill vegetables 4 to 5 inches from heat.
4. Brush occasionally with melted margarine or butter, olive or vegetable oil, or your favorite bottled or homemade salad dressing, to prevent them from drying out.
5. Use the chart below as an easy guide for *approximate* grilling times; types of grills and weather conditions vary and will affect the time.

Fresh Vegetable Grilling Chart

Time	Vegetable
10 minutes	Carrots, small whole, partially cooked*
	Cherry tomatoes, whole
	Mushrooms, whole
	Onions, cut into 1/2-inch slices
	Potatoes, cut into 1-inch wedges, partially cooked*
15 minutes	Bell peppers, cut into 1-inch strips
	Eggplant, cut into 1/4-inch slices
	Green beans, whole
	Pattypan squash, whole
	Zucchini, cut into 3/4-inch pieces
20 minutes	Asparagus spears, whole
	Broccoli spears, cut lengthwise in half
	Cauliflowerets, cut lengthwise in half
	Corn on the cob, husked and wrapped in aluminum foil

Before grilling, cook in boiling water 5 to 10 minutes or just until crisp-tender.

Favorite Green Bean Casserole

PREP: 20 min; BAKE: 40 min
Makes 6 servings, about 3/4 cup each

> 2 packages (16 ounces each) frozen cut green beans
> 1 can (10 3/4 ounces) condensed cream of celery, cream of chicken or cream of mushroom soup
> 1/2 cup milk
> 1 jar (2 ounces) diced pimientos, drained
> 1/8 teaspoon pepper
> 1 can (2.8 ounces) French fried onions

1. Heat oven to 350°.

2. Cook green beans as directed on package for the minimum amount of time; drain.

3. Mix soup, milk, pimientos and pepper in 2-quart casserole or square baking dish, $8 \times 8 \times 2$ inches. Stir in beans. Sprinkle with onions.

4. Bake uncovered 30 to 40 minutes or until hot in center.

1 SERVING: Calories 155 (Calories from Fat 90); Fat 10g (Saturated 3g); Cholesterol 5mg; Sodium 500mg; Carbohydrate 17g (Dietary Fiber 5g); Protein 4g

---

TIMESAVING TIP

Substitute 2 cans (16 ounces each) cut green beans, drained, for the frozen green beans, but do not cook. To microwave, use microwavable casserole. Decrease milk to 1/4 cup. Stir beans into soup mixture. Cover and microwave on High 5 minutes; stir. Sprinkle with onions. Microwave uncovered 3 to 5 minutes or until hot.

Stir-Fried Broccoli with Mustard Glaze

PREP: 15 min; COOK: 5 min
Makes 4 servings, about 3/4 cup each

Try this easy recipe using other mustards such as stone ground, Dijon, jalapeño, sweet-hot or even raspberry mustard—whatever you like!

> 1 tablespoon margarine or butter, melted
> 1 tablespoon packed brown sugar
> 1 tablespoon stone-ground mustard
> 1 tablespoon vegetable oil
> 4 cups broccoli flowerets (1 pound)
> 3 tablespoons water
> 1 tablespoon water

Stir-Fried Broccoli with Mustard Glaze

1. Mix margarine, brown sugar and mustard; set aside.

2. Heat oil in 10-inch skillet or wok over medium-high heat. Add broccoli; stir-fry 1 minute. Add 3 table-spoons water. Cover and cook about 3 minutes or until broccoli is crisp-tender.

3. Add margarine mixture and 1 tablespoon water; toss until broccoli is coated.

1 SERVING: Calories 105 (Calories from Fat 65); Fat 7g (Saturated 1g); Cholesterol 0mg; Sodium 110mg; Carbohydrate 10g (Dietary Fiber 3g); Protein 3g

Sweet-Sour Red Cabbage

PREP: 20 min; COOK: 10 min
Makes 6 servings, about 2/3 cup each

Cabbage can be shredded using the largest holes of a shred-der or a knife. Cut the cabbage into quarters through the core and shred the leaves only.

    1 medium head red cabbage (1 1/2 pounds)
    4 slices bacon, diced
    1/4 cup packed brown sugar
    2 tablespoons all-purpose flour
    1/2 cup water

    1/4 cup white vinegar
    1/4 teaspoon salt
    1/8 teaspoon pepper
    1 small onion, sliced

1. Shred cabbage and cook as directed (page 396).

2. Cook bacon in 10-inch skillet over medium heat, stirring occasionally, until crisp. Remove bacon with slotted spoon and reserve 1 tablespoon fat in skillet. Drain bacon on paper towels.

3. Stir brown sugar and flour into bacon fat in skil-let. Stir in water, vinegar, salt, pepper and onion. Cook over medium heat about 5 minutes, stirring fre-quently, until mixture thickens.

4. Stir bacon and sauce mixture into hot cabbage; cook until hot.

1 SERVING: Calories 105 (Calories from Fat 25); Fat 3g (Saturated 1g); Cholesterol 5mg; Sodium 190mg; Carbohydrate 20g (Dietary Fiber 3g); Protein 3g

---

TIMESAVING TIP
Substitute 1 package (16 ounces) coleslaw mix for the red cabbage.

Glazed Carrots

PREP: 30 min; COOK: 10 min
Makes 6 servings

1 1/2 pounds carrots
1/3 cup packed brown sugar
2 tablespoons margarine or butter
1/2 teaspoon salt
1/2 teaspoon grated orange peel

1. Prepare carrots, cutting into julienne strips, and cook as directed (page 396).

2. Cook remaining ingredients in 12-inch skillet over medium heat, stirring constantly, until bubbly.

3. Stir in carrots. Cook over low heat about 5 minutes, stirring occasionally, until carrots are glazed and hot.

1 SERVING: Calories 115 (Calories from Fat 35); Fat 4g (Saturated 1g); Cholesterol 0mg; Sodium 260mg; Carbohydrate 22g (Dietary Fiber 3g); Protein 1g

> **TIMESAVING TIP**
> Substitute 1 1/2 packages (16-ounce size) baby-cut carrots or frozen sliced carrots, cooked as directed on package, for the regular carrots.

Harvard Beets

PREP: 1 hr; COOK: 5 min
Makes 4 servings, about 1/2 cup each

Make the flavor sparkle by substituting orange juice for the water and stirring 1 teaspoon grated orange peel in with the sugar.

5 medium beets (1 1/4 pounds)
1 tablespoon cornstarch
1 tablespoon sugar
1/2 teaspoon salt
Dash of pepper
2/3 cup water
1/4 cup white vinegar

1. Prepare and cook beets as directed (page 395). Cut into slices.

2. Mix cornstarch, sugar, salt and pepper in 2-quart saucepan. *Gradually* stir in water and vinegar. Cook, stirring constantly, until mixture thickens and boils. Boil and stir 1 minute.

3. Stir in beets; cook until hot.

1 SERVING: Calories 65 (Calories from Fat 0); Fat 0g (Saturated 0g); Cholesterol 0mg; Sodium 340mg; Carbohydrate 16g (Dietary Fiber 2g); Protein 2g

> **TIMESAVING TIP**
> Substitute 1 can (16 ounces) sliced beets, drained and liquid reserved for the cooked fresh beets. Add enough water to reserved liquid to measure 2/3 cup. Substitute beet liquid for the water.

Scalloped Corn

PREP: 25 min; BAKE: 35 min
Makes 4 servings, about 3/4 cup each

4 ears corn
2 tablespoons margarine or butter
1 small onion, chopped (1/4 cup)
1/4 cup chopped green bell pepper
2 tablespoons all-purpose flour
1/2 teaspoon salt
1/2 teaspoon paprika
1/4 teaspoon ground mustard (dry)
Dash of pepper
3/4 cup milk
1 large egg, slightly beaten
1/3 cup fine dry cracker crumbs
1 tablespoon margarine or butter, melted

1. Prepare and cook corn as directed (page 397). Cut enough kernels from ears to measure 2 cups.

2. Heat oven to 350°.

3. Melt 2 tablespoons margarine in 1-quart saucepan over medium heat. Cook onion and bell pepper in margarine about 2 minutes, stirring occasionally, until onion is tender; remove from heat.

4. Stir in flour, salt, paprika, mustard and pepper. Cook, stirring constantly, until mixture is bubbly; remove from heat.

5. *Gradually* stir in milk. Heat to boiling, stirring constantly. Boil and stir 1 minute. Stir in corn and egg. Pour into ungreased 1-quart casserole.

6. Mix cracker crumbs and 1 tablespoon melted margarine. Sprinkle over corn mixture. Bake uncovered 30 to 35 minutes or until bubbly.

1 SERVING: Calories 255 (Calories from Fat 115); Fat 13g (Saturated 3g); Cholesterol 55mg; Sodium 480mg; Carbohydrate 31g (Dietary Fiber 3g); Protein 7g

CHILI SCALLOPED CORN: Omit paprika and mustard. Add 1/2 teaspoon chili powder and 1/2 teaspoon ground cumin with the flour. Stir in 1 can (4 ounces) chopped green chilies, drained, with the egg.

> **TIMESAVING TIP**
> Substitute 1 package (10 ounces) frozen whole kernel corn, cooked and drained, or 1 can (16 ounces) whole kernel corn, drained, for the cooked fresh corn.

Mushrooms

Regular White

Shiitake

Enoki

Morel

Oyster

Portobello (whole & sliced)

Wood Ear

Wood Ear (dried)

Large White (stuffing)

Crimini

Porcini (dried)

Spicy Corn

PREP: 10 min; BAKE: 25 min
Makes 4 servings

So flavorful and yet so easy! (photograph on page 417)

> 4 ear corn
> 2 tablespoons margarine or butter
> 1 tablespoon taco seasoning mix or lemon
>   pepper
> 2 tablespoons water

1. Heat oven to 400°.

2. Husk ears and remove silk.

3. Mix margarine and taco seasoning mix. Spread over corn. Place each ear on double thickness heavy-duty aluminum foil. Sprinkle ears with water. Wrap securely in foil and twist ends. Place ears on oven rack.

4. Bake 15 to 25 minutes, turning once, until tender.

1 SERVING: Calories 150 (Calories from Fat 65); Fat 7g (Saturated 2g); Cholesterol 0mg; Sodium 200mg; Carbohydrate 21g (Dietary Fiber 2g); Protein 3g

---

TIMESAVING TIP

To microwave, place each ear on double thickness of waxed paper or kitchen parchment paper. Omit water. Wrap securely and twist ends. Place on paper towel and microwave on High (100%) 9 to 12 minutes, rearranging after 55 minutes.

Sautéed Mushrooms

PREP: 15 min; COOK: 5 min
Makes 4 servings

Using a hard-cooked egg slicer, available at grocery stores and other stores, is an easy way to slice fresh mushrooms.

> 1 pound mushrooms
> 2 tablespoons margarine or butter
> 2 tablespoons olive or vegetable oil
> 2 cloves garlic, finely chopped
> 2 tablespoons lemon juice
> 1/2 teaspoon salt
> 1/4 teaspoon pepper
> Chopped fresh parsley, if desired

1. Prepare sliced mushrooms as directed (page 398).

2. Heat margarine, oil and garlic in 10-inch skillet over medium-high heat. Stir in mushrooms, lemon juice, salt and pepper.

3. Cook about 5 minutes, stirring frequently, until mushrooms are light brown. Stir in parsley.

1 SERVING: Calories 145 (Calories from Fat 115); Fat 13g (Saturated 2g); Cholesterol 0mg; Sodium 340mg; Carbohydrate 13g (Dietary Fiber 1g); Protein 2g

---

LIGHTER SAUTÉED MUSHROOMS

For 7 grams of fat and 90 calories, use a nonstick skillet and decrease margarine and oil to 1 tablespoon each.

Ratatouille

PREP: 20 min; COOK: 15 min
Makes 6 servings, about 1 cup each

Leftover Ratatouille? Place in a blender or food processor and blend until smooth. Serve the cold spread as an appetizer on crackers or slices of French bread.

1 medium eggplant (1 1/2 pounds)
2 small zucchini (1/2 pound)
1 medium green bell pepper, chopped
   (1 cup)
1 medium onion, finely chopped (1/2 cup)
2 medium tomatoes, cut into fourths
1/4 cup vegetable oil
1 1/2 teaspoons salt
1/4 teaspoon pepper
2 cloves garlic, finely chopped

1. Prepare cubed eggplant as directed (page 397). Prepare sliced zucchini as directed (page 401).

2. Cook eggplant, zucchini and remaining ingredients in 12-inch skillet over medium heat 10 to 15 minutes, stirring occasionally, until zucchini is tender.

1 SERVING: Calories 135 (Calories from Fat 90); Fat 10g (Saturated 2g); Cholesterol 0mg; Sodium 540mg; Carbohydrate 12g (Dietary Fiber 3g); Protein 2g

Potatoes

Although there are hundreds of varieties of potatoes, they can be classified into four basic categories:

- **Russet potatoes** (also known as Idaho or Burbank)—long, slightly rounded with rough brown skin and many eyes. Low in moisture and high in starch. Best for baking and French fries.
- **Long white potatoes**—long, slightly rounded with thin, pale brown skin and tiny shallow eyes. Best for baking, boiling and roasting.
- **Round white or "boiling" potatoes**—freckled brown skin and waxy flesh because they contain less starch and more moisture than russets or long whites. Best for mashed potatoes, boiling, roasting, frying and salads.
- **Round red potatoes**—reddish-brown coat with same characteristics and uses as round whites.

New potatoes are thin-skinned small young potatoes of any variety that are waxy in texture because there has not been enough time for them to convert their sugar to starch. They are best for salads, roasting and boiling.

Unusual potato varieties include purple potatoes, Finnish Yukon Gold or yellow butter potatoes, finger potatoes and about 1-inch-diameter baby potatoes.

Potatoes

Okra Skillet

PREP: 15 min; COOK. 25 min
Makes 4 servings

If you prefer not to use salt pork, substitute 2 tablespoons margarine or butter, and stir in 1/2 teaspoon salt with the pepper.

> 3/4 pound okra
> 2 to 3 ears corn
> 1/4 cup finely cut-up lean salt pork (about
> 1/4 pound)
> 1 medium onion, chopped (1/2 cup)
> 4 medium tomatoes, cut into eighths
> Dash of pepper

1. Prepare okra as directed (page 398). Cut into enough slices to measure 2 cups.

2. Prepare corn as directed (page 397). Cut enough kernels from ears to measure 1 cup.

3. Cook pork and onion in 10-inch skillet over medium heat, stirring occasionally, until pork is golden brown. Stir in okra. Cook over medium-high heat 3 minutes, stirring constantly.

4. Stir in tomatoes and corn; reduce heat to low. Cover and simmer 10 to 15 minutes or until corn is tender. Stir in pepper.

1 SERVING: Calories 230 (Calories from Fat 135); Fat 15g (Saturated 5g); Cholesterol 15mg; Sodium 260mg; Carbohydrate 24g (Dietary Fiber 6g); Protein 6g

---

TIMESAVING TIP

Substitute 1 package (10 ounces) frozen whole okra for the fresh okra. Rinse with cold water to separate; cut crosswise into slices. And, substitute 1 package (10 ounces) frozen whole kernel corn, thawed and drained, can be substituted for the fresh corn.

Twice-Baked Potatoes

PREP: 1 hr 25 min; BAKE: 20 min
Makes 8 servings

These potatoes can be refrigerated before baking; increase baking time to 30 minutes. Or wrap airtight and freeze; bake uncovered about 40 minutes.

> 4 large baking potatoes (8 to 10 ounces
> each)
> 1/4 to 1/2 cup milk
> 1/4 cup margarine or butter, softened
> 1/4 teaspoon salt
> Dash of pepper
> 1 cup shredded Cheddar cheese (4 ounces)
> 1 tablespoon chopped fresh chives

1. Prepare and cook whole potatoes as directed (page 400).

2. Cut potatoes lengthwise in half; scoop out inside, leaving a thin shell. Mash potato in medium bowl until no lumps remain. Add milk in small amounts, beating after each addition (amount of milk needed to make potatoes smooth and fluffy depends on kind of potatoes used).

3. Add margarine, salt and pepper; beat vigorously until potato is light and fluffy. Stir in cheese and chives. Fill potato shells with mashed potato. Place on ungreased cookie sheet.

4. Heat oven to 400°.

5. Bake about 20 minutes or until hot.

1 SERVING: Calories 180 (Calories from Fat 100); Fat 11g (Saturated 4g); Cholesterol 15mg; Sodium 230mg; Carbohydrate 16g (Dietary Fiber 1g); Protein 5g

---

TIMESAVING TIP

To microwave, arrange filled potatoes in circle on 10-inch microwavable plate. Cover with waxed paper and microwave on High 8 to 10 minutes, rotating plate 1/2 turn after 5 minutes, until hot.

Potato Pancakes

Potato Pancakes

PREP: 15 min; COOK: 20 min
Makes 16 pancakes

Potato pancakes can also be served as a dessert—omit the onions, and serve with applesauce or other fruit sauce.

> 4 medium boiling potatoes (1 1/2 pounds)
> 4 large eggs, beaten
> 1 small onion, finely chopped (1/4 cup), if desired
> 1/4 cup all-purpose flour
> 1 teaspoon salt
> 1/4 cup margarine, butter or bacon fat (do not use spread or tub products)

1. Prepare potatoes as directed (page 400); peel. Shred enough potatoes to measure 4 cups. Rinse well; drain and pat dry.

2. Mix potatoes, eggs, onion, flour and salt. Melt 2 tablespoons of the margarine in 12-inch skillet over medium heat. Pour about 1/4 cup batter into skillet for each pancake. Flatten each with spatula into pancake about 4 inches in diameter.

3. Cook pancakes about 2 minutes on each side or until golden brown. Keep them warm while cooking remaining pancakes. Repeat with remaining batter. (Add remaining margarine as needed to prevent sticking.)

1 PANCAKE: Calories 75 (Calories from Fat 35); Fat 4g (Saturated 1g); Cholesterol 55mg; Sodium 180mg; Carbohydrate 8g (Dietary Fiber 0g); Protein 2g

Hash Brown Potatoes

PREP: 15 min; COOK: 30 min
Makes 4 servings

For more color, substitute 2 cups shredded carrots for 2 cups of the shredded potatoes. (photograph on page 168)

> 4 medium boiling potatoes (1 1/2 pounds)
> 2 tablespoons finely chopped onion
> 1/4 teaspoon salt
> 1/8 teaspoon pepper
> 1/4 cup margarine or butter

1. Prepare potatoes as directed (page 400); peel if desired. Shred enough potatoes to measure 4 cups. Rinse well; drain and pat dry.

2. Mix potatoes, onion, salt and pepper. Melt margarine in 10-inch skillet over medium heat. Pack potato mixture firmly in skillet, leaving 1/2-inch space around edge.

3. Cook over medium-low heat about 15 minutes or until bottom is brown. Cut potato mixture into fourths; turn over. Add 1 tablespoon margarine if necessary. Cook about 12 minutes longer or until bottom is brown.

1 SERVING: Calories 210 (Calories from Fat 110); Fat 12g (Saturated 2g); Cholesterol 0mg; Sodium 270mg; Carbohydrate 25g (Dietary Fiber 2g); Protein 2g

Note: *Potato mixture can be kept in one piece if desired. Place large plate over skillet and invert potatoes onto plate. Slide potatoes back into skillet.*

Mashed Potatoes

PREP: 10 min; COOK: 25 min
Makes 4 to 6 servings

Use a hand-held potato masher or electric mixer for the fluffi-est potatoes. (photograph on page 238)

    6 medium boiling potatoes (1 1/2 pounds)
    1/3 to 1/2 cup milk
    1/4 cup margarine or butter, softened
    1/2 teaspoon salt
    Dash of pepper

1. Prepare and cook potato pieces as directed (page 400). Shake pan with potatoes over low heat to dry.

2. Mash potatoes in medium bowl until no lumps remain. Add milk in small amounts, beating after each addition (amount of milk needed to make potatoes smooth and fluffy depends on kind of potatoes used).

3. Add margarine, salt and pepper. Beat vigorously until potatoes are light and fluffy. If desired, dot with margarine or sprinkle with paprika, chopped fresh parsley, watercress or chives.

1 SERVING: Calories 270 (Calories from Fat 110); Fat 12g (Saturated 3g); Cholesterol 2mg; Sodium 420mg; Carbohydrate 38g (Dietary Fiber 2g); Protein 4g

---
LIGHTER MASHED POTATOES
For 6 grams of fat and 215 calories per serving, use skim milk and reduce the margarine to 2 tablespoons.

GARLIC MASHED POTATOES: Cook 6 cloves garlic, peeled, with the potatoes.

Fried Potatoes

PREP: 15 min; COOK: 30 min
Makes 4 servings

    6 medium boiling potatoes (2 pounds)
    2 tablespoons shortening or vegetable oil
    1 large onion, thinly sliced, if desired
    1 1/2 teaspoons salt
    Pepper
    2 tablespoons margarine or butter

1. Prepare potatoes as directed (page 400). Cut into enough thin slices to measure about 4 cups.

2. Melt shortening in 10-inch skillet over medium heat. Layer one-third each of the potatoes and onion in skillet; sprinkle with 1/2 teaspoon of the salt and dash of pepper. Repeat layers twice. Dot with margarine.

3. Cover and cook over medium heat 20 minutes. Uncover and cook, turning once, until potatoes are brown.

1 SERVING: Calories 230 (Calories from Fat 110); Fat 12g (Saturated 3g); Cholesterol 0mg; Sodium 870mg; Carbohydrate 30g (Dietary Fiber 2g); Protein 3g

---
TIMESAVING TIP
Slice potatoes ahead of cooking time. Place them in a bowl of cold water to prevent them from darkening; cover and refrigerate. Drain and pat dry with paper towels before cooking, otherwise the water will make the hot fat spatter.

Scalloped Potatoes

PREP: 20 min; BAKE: 1 hr 40 min; STAND: 5 min
Makes 6 servings

This dish can be made with either peeled or unpeeled potatoes.

    6 medium boiling or baking potatoes
        (2 pounds)
    3 tablespoons margarine or butter
    1 small onion, finely chopped (1/4 cup)
    3 tablespoons all-purpose flour
    1 teaspoon salt
    1/4 teaspoon pepper
    2 1/2 cups milk
    1 tablespoon margarine or butter

1. Heat oven to 350°. Grease bottom and side of 2-quart casserole with shortening.

2. Prepare potatoes as directed (page 400). Cut into enough thin slices to measure about 4 cups.

3. Melt 3 tablespoons margarine in 2-quart saucepan over medium heat. Cook onion in margarine about 2 minutes, stirring occasionally, until tender. Stir in flour, salt and pepper. Cook, stirring constantly, until smooth and bubbly; remove from heat.

4. Stir in milk. Heat to boiling, stirring constantly. Boil and stir 1 minute.

5. Spread potatoes in casserole. Pour sauce over potatoes. Dot with 1 tablespoon margarine.

6. Cover and bake 30 minutes. Uncover and bake 1 hour to 1 hour 10 minutes longer or until potatoes are tender. Let stand 5 to 10 minutes before serving.

1 SERVING: Calories 240 (Calories from Fat 90); Fat 10g (Saturated 3g); Cholesterol 10mg; Sodium 500mg; Carbohydrate 33g (Dietary Fiber 2g); Protein 6g

Au Gratin Potatoes

PREP: 25 min; BAKE: 1 hr 20 min
Makes 6 servings

Want to try something a bit different? Make the variation with sun-dried tomatoes, which adds bursts of deep tomato flavor. Sun-dried tomatoes can be easily cut by using kitchen scissors. (photograph on page 232)

> 6 medium boiling or baking potatoes
>   (2 pounds)
> 1/4 cup margarine or butter
> 1 medium onion, chopped (1/2 cup)
> 1 tablespoon all-purpose flour
> 1 teaspoon salt
> 1/4 teaspoon pepper
> 2 cups milk
> 2 cups shredded natural sharp Cheddar
>   cheese (8 ounces)
> 1/4 cup fine dry bread crumbs
> Paprika

1. Heat oven to 375°.

2. Prepare potatoes as directed (page 400). Cut into 1/8-inch slices to measure about 4 cups.

3. Melt margarine in 2-quart saucepan over medium heat. Cook onion in margarine about 2 minutes, stirring occasionally, until tender. Stir in flour, salt and pepper. Cook, stirring constantly, until bubbly; remove from heat.

4. Stir in milk and 1 1/2 cups of the cheese. Heat to boiling, stirring constantly. Boil and stir 1 minute.

5. Spread potatoes in ungreased 1 1/2-quart casserole. Pour cheese sauce over potatoes.

6. Bake uncovered 1 hour. Mix remaining cheese and the bread crumbs; sprinkle over potatoes. Sprinkle with paprika. Bake uncovered 15 to 20 minutes longer or until top is brown and bubbly.

1 SERVING: Calories 390 (Calories from Fat 200); Fat 22g (Saturated 11g); Cholesterol 45mg; Sodium 770mg; Carbohydrate 35g (Dietary Fiber 2g); Protein 15g

SUN-DRIED TOMATO AU GRATIN POTATOES: Increase milk to 2 1/2 cups. Mix 1 package (3 ounces) sun-dried tomatoes (not oil-packed), cut up, with the potatoes.

> **TIMESAVING TIP**
> Use frozen chopped onions and purchase already shredded cheese.

Rosemary-Roasted Red Potatoes

PREP: 15 min; BAKE: 1 1/4 hr
Makes 6 servings

> 2 1/4 pounds new red potatoes (16 to 18)
> 3 tablespoons olive or vegetable oil
> 1/4 cup finely chopped green onions
>   (3 medium)
> 2 tablespoons chopped fresh or 2 teaspoons
>   crushed dried rosemary leaves

1. Prepare potatoes as directed (page 400).

2. Heat oven to 350°. Grease rectangular pan, 13 × 9 × 2 inches, with shortening.

3. Place potatoes in pan. Drizzle with oil; stir to coat. Sprinkle with onions and rosemary; stir.

4. Bake uncovered about 1 1/4 hours, stirring occasionally, until skins are crispy and potatoes are tender.

1 SERVING: Calories 200 (Calories from Fat 65); Fat 7g (Saturated 1g); Cholesterol 0mg; Sodium 10mg; Carbohydrate 34g (Dietary Fiber 3g); Protein 3g

> **TIMESAVING TIP**
> Use a foil pan or line the pan with heavy-duty aluminum foil. Omit the shortening and spray with nonstick cooking spray.

Candied Sweet Potatoes

PREP: 45 min; COOK: 5 min
Makes 6 servings

(photograph on page 256)

> 6 medium sweet potatoes or yams (2 pounds)*
> 1/3 cup packed brown sugar
> 3 tablespoons margarine or butter
> 3 tablespoons water
> 1/2 teaspoon salt

1. Prepare and cook sweet potatoes as directed (page 400). Slip off skins. Cut into 1/2-inch slices or chunks.

2. Heat remaining ingredients in 10-inch skillet over medium heat, stirring constantly, until smooth and bubbly. Add sweet potatoes. *Gently* stir until glazed and hot.

*1 can (23 ounces) sweet potatoes or yams, drained and cut into 1/2-inch slices, can be substituted for the fresh sweet potatoes.

1 SERVING: Calories 185 (Calories from Fat 55); Fat 6g (Saturated 1g); Cholesterol 0mg; Sodium 260mg; Carbohydrate 34g (Dietary Fiber 2g); Protein 1g

Squash

Hubbard · Banana · Buttercup · Butternut · Delicata · Spaghetti · Sweet Dumpling · Golden Nugget · Straightneck · Chayote · Green Zucchini · Yellow Zucchini · Pattypan · Squash Blossoms · Turban · Acorn (green) · Baby Green Zucchini

---

> **LIGHTER CANDIED SWEET POTATOES**
> For 2 grams of fat and 150 calories, use a nonstick skillet and decrease margarine to 1 tablespoon.

ORANGE SWEET POTATOES: Substitute orange juice for the water. Add 1 tablespoon grated orange peel.

PINEAPPLE SWEET POTATOES: Omit water. Add 1 can (8 1/4 ounces) crushed pineapple in syrup, undrained.

Glazed Acorn Squash

PREP: 10 min; BAKE: 1 hr
Makes 4 servings

> 2 acorn squash (1 to 1 1/2 pounds each)
> 4 tablespoons maple-flavored syrup
> 4 tablespoons whipping (heavy) cream or
>   margarine or butter

1. Heat oven to 350°.

2. Cut each squash lengthwise in half; remove seeds and fibers. Place squash, cut sides up, in ungreased pan. Spoon 1 tablespoon syrup and 1 tablespoon whipping cream into each half.

3. Bake uncovered about 1 hour or until tender.

1 SERVING: Calories 160 (Calories from Fat 55); Fat 6g (Saturated 3g); Cholesterol 15mg; Sodium 10mg; Carbohydrate 29g (Dietary Fiber 5g); Protein 2g

> **LIGHTER GLAZED ACORN SQUASH**
> For 1 gram of fat and 130 calories per serving, omit whipping cream.

APPLE-STUFFED ACORN SQUASH: Bake squash 30 minutes. Mix 1 large tart red apple, diced, 2 tablespoons chopped nuts, 2 tablespoons packed brown sugar and 1 tablespoon margarine or butter, melted. Spoon apple mixture into squash halves. Bake about 30 minutes longer or until tender.

Spaghetti Squash with Tomatoes

PREP: 15 min; BAKE: 1 hr; COOK: 10 min
Makes 6 servings, about 2/3 cup each

Spaghetti squash can be served in the spaghetti shell. If you cut it crosswise, you'll get the longest squash strands, but cutting the squash lengthwise is the easiest way to serve from the shell. The choice is yours.

1 spaghetti squash (about 1 1/2 pounds)
1 medium onion, chopped (about 1/2 cup)
1 small green pepper, chopped (about
  1/2 cup)
1 large clove garlic, finely chopped
2 tablespoons olive or vegetable oil
4 medium tomatoes, chopped (about 4 cups)
1/2 teaspoon salt
1/4 teaspoon dried oregano leaves
1/4 teaspoon dried basil leaves
1/4 teaspoon fennel seed
1/8 teaspoon pepper
2 tablespoons margarine or butter
1/4 cup grated Parmesan cheese

1. Prepare and cook squash whole as directed on page 401.

2. Cook onion, green pepper and garlic in oil in 3-quart saucepan over medium heat about 5 minutes, stirring occasionally, until onion is tender, Stir in tomatoes, salt, oregano, basil, fennel and pepper. Simmer uncovered, stirring occasionally, 5 minutes.

3. Cut squash in half; remove seeds and fibrous strings. Remove squash strands with two forks; toss with margarine and cheese. Spoon tomato mixture over squash.

1 SERVING: Calories 145 (Calories from Fat 90); Fat 10g (Saturated 2g); Cholesterol 2mg; Sodium 290mg; Carbohydrate 15g (Dietary Fiber 4g); Protein 3g

Spaghetti Squash with Tomatoes

Wilted Spinach

PREP: 20 min; COOK: 10 min
Makes 4 servings, about 1/2 cup each

Lime juice adds refreshing tang to this dish—you can also use lemon juice.

>   1 pound spinach
>   2 tablespoons olive or vegetable oil
>   1 medium onion, chopped (1/2 cup)
>   1 slice bacon, cut up
>   1 clove garlic, finely chopped
>   1/2 teaspoon salt
>   1/4 teaspoon pepper
>   1/4 teaspoon ground nutmeg
>   2 tablespoons lime juice

1. Prepare spinach as directed (page 397).

2. Heat oil in Dutch oven over medium heat. Cook onion, bacon and garlic in oil, stirring occasionally, until bacon is crisp; reduce heat to low.

3. Stir in salt, pepper and nutmeg. *Gradually* add spinach. Toss just until spinach is wilted. Drizzle with lime juice.

1 SERVING: Calories 100 (Calories from Fat 70); Fat 8g (Saturated 1g); Cholesterol 1mg; Sodium 360mg; Carbohydrate 6g (Dietary Fiber 2g); Protein 3g

Spinach Soufflé

PREP: 25 min; BAKE: 35 min
Makes 4 to 6 servings

Soufflés stay fluffy and are easiest to serve when two forks or a fork and spoon are used to divide the servings.

>   3 tablespoons all-purpose flour
>   1/2 teaspoon dried dill weed
>   1/4 teaspoon salt
>   1/4 teaspoon pepper
>   1 cup milk
>   1 cup shredded Cheddar cheese (4 ounces)
>   1 package (9 ounces) frozen chopped
>   spinach, thawed and squeezed to drain
>   5 large eggs, separated

1. Heat oven to 350°. Grease bottom and side of 2-quart casserole with shortening.

2. Mix flour, dill weed, salt, pepper and milk in 2-quart saucepan. Cook over medium-high heat, stirring constantly, until thickened. Stir in cheese and spinach; remove from heat.

3. Beat egg yolks in large bowl with wire whisk. *Gradually* stir in spinach mixture. Beat egg whites in large bowl with electric mixer on high speed until stiff. *Gently* fold egg whites into egg yolk mixture.

4. Spoon spinach mixture into casserole. Bake uncovered 30 to 35 minutes or until golden brown and puffed.

1 SERVING: Calories 270 (Calories from Fat 155); Fat 17g (Saturated 9g); Cholesterol 300mg; Sodium 460mg; Carbohydrate 11g (Dietary Fiber 1g); Protein 19g

CORN SOUFFLÉ: Omit dill weed. Substitute Monterey Jack cheese with jalapeño peppers for the Cheddar cheese and 1 1/2 cups frozen whole kernel corn, thawed, for the spinach.

Mixed Roasted Vegetables

PREP: 25 min; BAKE: 45 min
Makes 8 servings, about 1 cup each

This also makes a tasty meatless main dish; just toss roasted vegetables with 8 ounces of cooked pasta. (photograph on page 391)

>   1 medium eggplant (1 1/2 pounds), cut into
>   1 1/2-inch chunks
>   1 medium green bell pepper, cut into 1-inch
>   pieces
>   1 medium red bell pepper, cut into 1-inch
>   pieces
>   1 medium onion, cut into 8 wedges and
>   separated
>   2 medium zucchini, cut into 1-inch pieces
>   1/2 pound whole mushrooms
>   1/3 cup chopped fresh or 2 tablespoons
>   dried basil leaves
>   3 tablespoons olive or vegetable oil
>   2 tablespoons red wine vinegar
>   1 teaspoon dried oregano leaves
>   1/2 teaspoon salt
>   1/4 teaspoon pepper
>   1 medium tomato, seeded and cut into
>   2-inch pieces
>   Grated Parmesan cheese, if desired

1. Heat oven to 350°.

2. Place eggplant, bell peppers, onion, zucchini and mushrooms in 3-quart casserole. Sprinkle evenly with basil.

3. Mix oil, vinegar, oregano, salt and pepper. Drizzle evenly over vegetables.

4. Bake uncovered 30 minutes. Add tomatoes; toss to coat. Bake uncovered about 15 minutes longer or until vegetables are tender. Serve with cheese.

1 SERVING: Calories 95 (Calories from Fat 55); Fat 6g (Saturated 1g); Cholesterol 0mg; Sodium 140mg; Carbohydrate 11g (Dietary Fiber 3g); Protein 2g

Broiled Parmesan Tomatoes

PREP: 10 min; BAKE: 8 min; BROIL: 4 min
Makes 4 servings

>   2 firm medium tomatoes
>   2 tablespoons mayonnaise or salad dressing
>   1 tablespoon grated Parmesan cheese
>   1 teaspoon chopped fresh or 1/4 teaspoon
>   dried basil leaves
>   1 teaspoon Dijon mustard
>   1 tablespoon grated Parmesan cheese

1. Heat oven to 350°.

2. Core tomatoes. Cut crosswise into 3/4-inch slices. Place in single layer on rack in broiler pan.

3. Mix mayonnaise, 1 tablespoon cheese, the basil and mustard. Spread about 1 teaspoon mixture over each tomato slice. Sprinkle 1 tablespoon cheese over tomatoes. Bake about 8 minutes or until hot.

4. Set oven control to Broil. Broil tomatoes with tops 6 inches from heat 2 to 4 minutes or until topping is golden and bubbly.

1 SERVING: Calories 70 (Calories from Fat 55); Fat 6g (Saturated 1g); Cholesterol 5mg; Sodium 90mg; Carbohydrate 3g (Dietary Fiber 0g); Protein 1g

Stewed Tomatoes

PREP: 15 min; COOK: 15 min
Makes 4 servings, 3/4 cup each

>   3 large ripe tomatoes (1 1/2 pounds)
>   1 medium onion, finely chopped (1/2 cup)
>   2 tablespoons finely chopped green bell
>   pepper
>   1 tablespoon sugar
>   1/2 teaspoon salt
>   1/8 teaspoon pepper
>   2 slices bread, toasted and cut into 1/2-inch
>   cubes

1. Peel tomatoes as directed (page 401). Cut tomatoes into small pieces.

2. Mix tomatoes and remaining ingredients except bread cubes in 2 1/2-quart saucepan. Cover and heat to boiling; reduce heat to low. Simmer uncovered about 10 minutes or until tomatoes are soft.

3. Stir in bread cubes.

1 SERVING: Calories 80 (Calories from Fat 10); Fat 1g (Saturated 0g); Cholesterol 0mg; Sodium 350mg; Carbohydrate 18g (Dietary Fiber 2g); Protein 2g

---

TIMESAVING TIP
Substitute 1 can (28 ounces) peeled whole tomatoes, undrained, for the fresh tomatoes. Break up tomatoes in saucepan in step 2.

Root Vegetable Medley

PREP: 20 min; COOK: 10 min
Makes 6 servings, about 2/3 cup each

For a different look and taste, substitute melted butter for the mayonnaise.

>   3 medium carrots, cut into julienne strips
>   (2 cups)
>   3 medium parsnips, cut into julienne strips
>   (2 cups)
>   1 small rutabaga, cut into julienne strips
>   (2 cups)
>   2 small turnips, cut into julienne strips
>   (2 cups)
>   1/4 cup mayonnaise or salad dressing
>   1/2 teaspoon dried thyme leaves
>   1/2 teaspoon salt
>   1/4 teaspoon pepper

1. Heat 1 inch water (salted, if desired) to boiling in Dutch oven. Add carrots, parsnips, rutabaga and turnips. Cover and heat to boiling; reduce heat. Cook 2 to 3 minutes or until vegetables are tender; drain.

2. Mix remaining ingredients; pour over vegetables. *Gently* toss until coated.

1 SERVING: Calories 140 (Calories from Fat 70); Fat 8g (Saturated 1g); Cholesterol 5mg; Sodium 260mg; Carbohydrate 19g (Dietary Fiber 4g); Protein 2g

Rutabaga Casserole

PREP: 35 min; BAKE: 50 min
Makes 6 servings, about 3/4 cup each

>   2 medium rutabagas* (about 2 pounds)
>   2 eggs, beaten
>   1/4 cup dry bread crumbs
>   1/4 cup half-and-half
>   2 teaspoons sugar or corn syrup
>   1 teaspoon salt
>   1/4 teaspoon ground nutmeg
>   2 tablespoons margarine or butter

1. Prepare and cook rutabagas as directed, page 400.

2. Heat oven to 350°. Grease 1 1/2-quart casserole.

3. Drain rutabagas, reserving 1/4 cup cooking liquid. Mash rutabagas with reserved liquid. Stir remaining ingredients except margarine into rutabagas. Pour into casserole; dot with margarine.

4. Bake 45 to 50 minutes until top is light brown.

*6 medium turnips (about 2 pounds) can be substituted for the rutabagas.

1 SERVING: Calories 140 (Calories from Fat 65); Fat 7g (Saturated 2g); Cholesterol 75mg; Sodium 490mg; Carbohydrate 16g (Dietary Fiber 1g); Protein 4g

Special Helps

Menu Planning Know-How

Not only have our lifestyles changed, but there are also so many new food opportunities available, all of which make menu planning not a scientific chore, but an adventure to explore! Our busy work schedules and activities often call for sharing food shopping and preparation responsibilities among everyone in the household. And, the variety of fresh produce and international foods and flavors available at our doorstep helps to make eating fun! Entertaining has become more casual—often it's potluck or spur-of-the-moment.

There are hundreds of recipes in this book that can be put together for quick everyday meals, leisurely weekend dinners, special occasion feasts or casual nibbling at just about any type of get-together. You can also combine the recipes with convenience foods from your supermarket and local deli to help you get food on the table quickly, and deliciously. Use the menu planning tips that follow to help make planning your meals, parties and get-togethers easy and well-balanced.

- Some people plan weekly menus on paper while others like to keep track in their heads. Do what suits your lifestyle. Check to see what foods you have on hand and use them in the menus you are planning.

- No longer do you need to plan meals based on three items on the plate. And, you may choose to have two meals plus snacks rather than the more traditional three meals a day, or to eat a heavier meal at noon rather than in the evening. Try a special family night and feature a meatless, ethnic or other type of dinner with a theme.

- Plan the main course first. It could be meat-based, such as Herb-Marinated Flank Steak, page 232; a mixture of meat, vegetables and starch, such as Chicken Rice Casserole, page 306; or meatless, such as Pasta Primavera, page 281. Think about what food you want to highlight, then plan the other foods to complement it.

- Make sure that flavors are compatible and don't compete. A strongly flavored main dish needs a milder-flavored accompaniment for balance; a subtle main dish works well with a boldly flavored side dish.

- Choose food combinations with interesting visual and sensual contrasts. Select foods with variety in flavors, textures, colors, shapes and temperatures. For example, serve spicy with bland; soft with crisp; white or brown with red, yellow or green; tiny pieces with big chunks; and, hot dishes with cold.

  If you're serving meat loaf with mashed potatoes, then round out the meal by adding more flavor, color and texture with a crunchy colorful green salad that includes a variety of raw vegetables topped with a tangy dressing. A light dessert such as frozen yogurt, a baked apple or crisp cookie nicely rounds out this meal. If you want a very hearty meal—such as a dinner after skiing or other strenuous exercise, try adding another vegetable and some bread.

- Use seasonings, sauces, condiments, salsas, relishes and marinades to add pizzazz to easy-to-make, plain foods, such as broiled chicken, cooked pasta or steamed vegetables. See chapter 14 or check the shelf-stable and refrigerated sections of your supermarket for new ideas. There are new flavors combinations and flavors available almost every day.

- Use the Food Guide Pyramid (page 418) as a guide for the recommended number of servings from each food group in order to maintain a balanced and healthful diet. Plan your meals for an entire day, including at least the minimum recommended number of servings from each food group.

Aim for meals with less than 30% of their total calories from fat, and get plenty of complex carbohydrates and fiber (the bottom half of the pyramid). Give emphasis to grain foods such as whole grain breads and cereals, and lots of different vegetables and fruits. Eat moderate amounts of low-fat dairy foods, and lean meats and only a few fats and sweets each day.

To control fat, saturated fat and cholesterol, select more plant foods, such as cereals, rice, pasta and beans. Use meat, poultry and fish in smaller amounts rather than as the main feature, while increasing the vegetables, rice or pasta in the meal. Try the lighter variations for recipes in this book, and use fats and oils sparingly in all your cooking.

Menu: Oven Barbecue Chicken (page 300), Spicy Corn (page 405), Pepper Cheese Twists (page 66), Bacon-Spinach Salad (page 319), Baked Apples (page 139)

Nutrition Glossary

Have you been confused by the terms used by nutrition and health experts? Consult this reference list for explanations of some key words.

Carbohydrate: Key human energy source. Includes simple sugars and complex carbohydrates (starches).

Cholesterol: Fatlike substance found in animal foods that is essential for hormones to function properly. Our bodies also make cholesterol.

Dietary fiber: Often described as the components of plant foods that are not broken down or absorbed by the human digestive tract. Fiber is technically a complex carbohydrate.

Fat: Provides more than twice the amount of energy supplied by an equal quantity of carbohydrate or protein. Also provides essential nutrients and insulates and protects body organs.

    Saturated: Primarily found in animal foods, this type of fat is solid at room temperature. Diets high in saturated fats have been linked to higher levels of blood cholesterol.

    Unsaturated: Found most commonly in plant foods, this type of fat is usually liquid at room temperature. Unsaturated fats may be monounsaturated or polyunsaturated.

Food Guide Pyramid: A nutrition educational guide from the U.S. Department of Health and Human Services and U.S. Department of Agriculture. Used to teach people about foods and the recommended number of servings required from each food group in order to maintain a balanced and healthy diet. See diagram on page 448.

Minerals: Elements other than carbon, hydrogen, oxygen and nitrogen that are nutritionally essential in very small amounts. Minerals are inorganic elements, such as calcium and iron, found in food and water.

Nutrients: Substances necessary for life. Build, repair and maintain body cells. Nutrients include protein, carbohydrate, fat, water, vitamins and minerals.

Protein: Vital for life. Provides energy and structural support of body cells. Is important for growth. Made from amino-acid building blocks.

Vitamins: Substances found in small amounts in many foods; essential for controlling body processes. Vitamins, unlike minerals, are organic compounds that contain carbon. Vitamins include vitamin A, B vitamins (such as thiamin, niacin, riboflavin) and vitamin C, among others.

How Much Is a Serving from the Food Pyramid?

Breads, Cereal, Rice and Pasta Group: 1 slice bread; a small roll or muffin; 1/2 of a bun, bagel or English muffin; 1 to 1 1/2 ounces ready-to- eat cereal; 1/2 cup cooked cereal, rice or pasta; 3 or 4 small or 2 large crackers; 2 breadsticks (4 × 1/2 inch); 3 cups popcorn; 2 medium cookies.

Fruit Group: 1 medium fresh fruit or 1/2 grapefruit; 1 medium wedge melon; 3/4 cup fruit juice; 1/2 cup berries; 1/2 cup cooked or canned fruit; 1/4 cup dried fruit.

Vegetable Group: 1/2 cup chopped raw, cooked or canned vegetables; 3/4 cup vegetable juice; 1 cup raw leafy vegetables; 1 medium potato.

Meat, Poultry, Fish, Dry Beans, Eggs and Nuts Group: 2 to 3 ounces cooked lean meat, poultry or fish (3 ounces is about the size of an average hamburger or medium chicken breast half); 4 ounces tofu. Count the following as 1 ounce of meat: 1 egg (maximum of 3 weekly); 3 egg whites; 2 tablespoons peanut butter or whole nuts or seeds; 1/2 cup cooked dried beans.

Milk, Yogurt and Cheese Group: 1 cup milk, yogurt or pudding; 1 1/2 ounces cheese; 1 1/2 cups ice cream, ice milk or frozen yogurt; 2 cups cottage cheese.

Fats, Oils and Sweets Group: Use sparingly.

Food Guide Pyramid
A Guide to Daily Food Choices

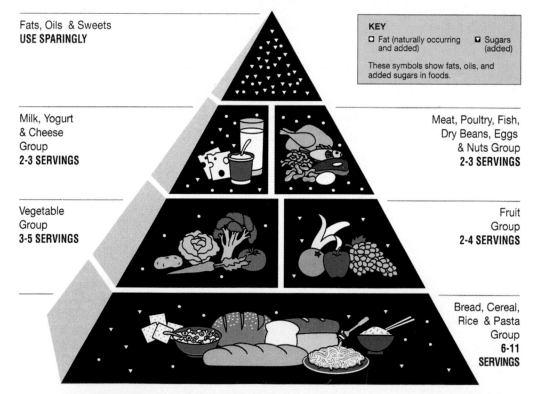

Source: U.S. Department of Agriculture, U.S. Department of Health and Human Services

Food Safety Know-How

America's food supply is one of the safest in the world, with farmers, food manufacturers, supermarkets and restaurants required to follow strict rules and regulations while preparing and selling food. However, these requirements end when the food goes into your shopping cart, leaves the store and reaches your kitchen.

Why worry about food safety? Because most of the "bad food" reported illnesses are due to bacterial contamination. Nearly all these cases can be linked to improper food handling, in both our homes and restaurants, which means they could have been avoided.

Microorganisms are always with us—on people and animals, in the air and water and on raw food. Some bacteria are useful, such as the bacteria that cause fermentation in cheese and beer. Other bacteria can cause foods to spoil, and even others can cause food poisoning. The major difference between food-spoiling and food-poisoning bacteria is the temperatures at which they can survive and grow. Bacteria that causes food to spoil can grow at refrigerator temperatures (below 40°F). They make the food look or smell bad, an obvious clue to throw it out.

Most bacteria that cause food poisoning don't grow at refrigerator temperatures. The best temperature for these microorganisms to reproduce and cause illness is around 100°. But, the actual temperature varies with the organism and may range from 40° to 130°. These are pathogens, the type of bacteria that if consumed may lead to illness, disease or even death. To prevent these bacteria from becoming harmful, they must be stopped from multiplying. Pathogenic bacteria are among the most important organisms to control because of the illness they cause in humans. The majority of them are invisible attackers—they can't be seen, smelled or tasted.

When contaminated food is eaten, people most often get sick within four to 48 hours and it's not always easy to tell if the problem is the flu or the result of food poisoning. Judgment is needed to determine if and when medical care is needed. If symptoms are severe such as vomiting, diarrhea, fever or cramps, or the victim is very young, elderly, pregnant or already ill, call a doctor or go to the hospital immediately.

The majority of food-poisoning bacteria can be controlled by proper cleaning, cooking and refrigeration. Constantly follow these three rules when preparing food:

1. Keep everything in the kitchen clean.
2. Keep hot foods *hot*.
3. Keep cold foods *cold*.

For questions about safe food handling and foodborne illness, contact:

- Your local health department
- Extension home economists, listed in the phone book
- USDA's Meat and Poultry Hotline, 800-535-4555 (weekdays, 10 A.M. to 4 P.M. eastern time)
- Centers for Disease Control and Prevention, Foodborne Illness Line, 404-332-4597 (24-hour recorded information)

Keeping the Kitchen Clean

- Keep countertops, appliances, utensils and dishes sanitary by cleaning with soap and water or the antibacterial cleaners now available.

- Clean refrigerator surfaces regularly with hot soapy water.

- Wash hands thoroughly with soap and water, for at least 20 seconds before handling food. This is about the time it takes to recite or sing the alphabet. If you stop to do something else, wash your hands again—especially after blowing your nose, using the bathroom, changing diapers or touching pets.

- If you sneeze or cough while preparing food, turn your face away and cover your mouth and nose with a tissue; wash your hands afterwards.

- If you have any kind of skin cut or infection on your hands, cover it with a bandage or wear protective plastic or rubber gloves.

- Do not use wooden cutting boards for raw meat, poultry or fish. Hard plastic cutting boards are less porous and are safer for meats. They are easily cleaned or can be washed in a dishwasher. If possible use a separate cutting board for preparing raw meats and another for nonmeat foods. Wash your hands and all utensils and surfaces with hot soapy water after contact with raw meat.

- Carefully wash cutting boards with a mixture of 2 teaspoons chlorine bleach and 1 teaspoon white vinegar to 1 gallon of water.

- Do not chop fresh vegetables or salad ingredients on a cutting board that was used for raw meat, poultry or fish without first cleaning it properly.

- Be careful not to transfer bacteria from raw meat to cooked meat. Do not, for example, carry raw hamburgers to the grill on a platter, then serve the cooked meat on the same unwashed platter.

- Wash the meat keeper and crisper drawer of your refrigerator often, and keep containers for storing refrigerated food very clean.

- Use disposable paper towels when working with or cleaning up after raw foods.

- Keep pets out of the kitchen. Be sure to wash hands after playing with pets before handling food. Teach children to do this, too.

- Wash kitchen linen often because bacteria can "loiter" in towels and cloths used over and over. Throw out dirty dish sponges or ones that have mildewed.

Keeping Food Hot

- Don't allow hot foods to remain at room temperature for more than two hours, including time for preparation; bacteria thrive at room temperature or in lukewarm food. A standard rule, recommended by the U.S. Department of Agriculture, is to keep hot foods hot (above 140°).

- Do not partially cook or heat perishable foods then set aside or refrigerate to finish cooking later. The food may not reach a temperature high enough to destroy bacteria.

- Roast meat or poultry at 325°F or above. Lower temperatures used when cooking meats can encourage bacterial growth before cooking is complete.

- Cook meat and poultry thoroughly, following the "doneness" temperatures and times throughout this book. Use a meat thermometer to assure proper doneness.

- Once food has been cooked, keep it hot until serving, or refrigerate it as soon as possible.

- Thoroughly reheat leftovers until steaming hot (165°), stirring often. Covering retains moisture and assures thorough heating in the center. Bring soups, sauces and gravies to a rolling boil for 1 minute before serving. Do not taste leftover food that looks or smells strange to see if it's "OK." If in doubt, throw it out!

Keeping Food Cold

- Don't allow cold foods to remain at room temperature for more than two hours, including time for preparation; bacteria thrive at room temperature. A standard rule, recommended by the U.S. Department of Agriculture, is to keep cold foods cold (below 40°).

- The most perishable foods are those that contain eggs, milk (custard-based foods, cream pies), seafood (seafood salads), meat and poultry. When you shop, pick up your meat and poultry selections last. Place them in plastic bags to prevent meat juices from dripping on other foods in your cart.

- Take perishable foods straight home and refrigerate immediately. Or if the time from the store to home is longer than 30 minutes, bring an iced cooler. Short stops during hot weather can cause perishable groceries in a hot car to reach unsafe temperatures.

- Buy "keep refrigerated" foods only if they are in a refrigerated case and are cold to the touch. Follow "keep refrigerated," "safe handling" and "use by" labels on packaged products.

- Allow space between foods in the refrigerator and freezer for air to circulate and faster chilling. Divide large amounts of foods to be refrigerated or frozen into shallow containers for faster chilling.

- Purchase a refrigerator thermometer and check to make sure your refrigerator is cooling at 35° to 40°, and a freezer thermometer to check to make sure your freezer is maintaining 0° or lower temperature.

- Buy frozen foods only if frozen solid without excessive ice crystals, an indicator food may have thawed and been refrozen.

- When cleaning the refrigerator or freezer, pack perishables in iced coolers.

- Never leave foods at room temperature to thaw. Thaw foods only in the refrigerator or in the microwave. If foods are thawed in the microwave, finish cooking immediately.

Keeping Food Safe to Eat

Canned Foods: Do not buy or use food in leaking, bulging or dented cans or in jars with cracks or loose or bulging lids. If you are in doubt about a can of food, don't taste it! Return it to your grocer, and report it to your local health authority.

Eggs: Refrigerator storage for uncooked "do-ahead" recipes using raw eggs should not exceed 24 hours before cooking. Do not eat cookie dough or cake batter containing raw eggs.

Foods that contain cooked eggs (such as cheesecakes, cream fillings, custards, quiches and potato salads) must be served hot or cold (depending on the recipe), and leftovers must be refrigerated immediately after serving. Also see Safe Handling and Storage of Eggs (page 162).

Recipes that call for raw eggs in the finished product to give a unique texture, such as for frostings, mousses or traditional Caesar salad, should not be prepared using eggs from the shell. Throw away or update the recipe. The only raw eggs that can be used in this type of recipe are pasteurized egg products, such as egg products or substitutes found in the dairy case or freezer section in your supermarket, or reconstituted dried eggs or egg whites.

Fruits and Vegetables: Wash with cold running water, using a scrub brush if necessary.

Ground Meat: Cook thoroughly—it's handled often in preparation, so bacteria can get mixed into it. Make sure ground beef is at least medium doneness, 160°, brownish pink in the center, before you serve it. Don't eat raw ground meat—it's not safe! Meat loaves should reach at least 170° in the center, particularly if they contain pork.

Ham: Know what kind of ham you're buying; most are fully cooked and can be heated to 140°, but a small number need to be cooked. Check the label. If you have any doubts, cook it to a temperature of 165°.

Luncheon Meats, Hot Dogs: Refrigerate; use within one week. If the liquid that forms around hot dogs is cloudy, discard them.

Marinades: Place foods to be marinated in a heavy plastic bag or nonmetal utensil. Always refrigerate when marinating; do not leave marinating foods at room temperature. Discard leftover marinades or sauces that have had contact with raw meat or heat to a rolling boil and boil 1 minute before serving.

Milk: Fresh milk products are highly perishable; refrigerate them as soon after purchase as possible. Store unopened evaporated milk and nonfat dry milk in a cool area up to several months. Refrigerate unopened dry whole milk, which contains fat; use within a few weeks. Do not drink unpasteurized milk or milk products.

Poultry: Cook all poultry products as long as the directions state. Stuff poultry just before you're ready to cook it. This will keep any bacteria in the raw poultry from tainting the starchy dressing. Stuff poultry loosely to allow it to be thoroughly cooked. The center of the stuffing should reach 165°. Place cooked poultry, stuffing and giblets in separate containers and refrigerate as soon as possible within two hours; use within a few days or freeze.

Keeping Food Safe at Buffets

- Serve food at buffets in small dishes, replacing with new dishes frequently from stove or refrigerator. Keep the temperature of hot foods above 140°. Do not mix fresh food with the food that has been out for serving.

- Food can be kept hot in an electric skillet, chafing dish or on a hot tray. Don't depend on warming units with candles; the temperature is not hot enough to keep foods safe.

- Refrigerate salads made with seafood, poultry or meat; chill both the food and the dish before serving.

- Place containers of cold foods over crushed ice at a temperature below 40°.

Keeping Food Safe Away from Home

- Pack lunches in an insulated cooler with a freeze-pack or frozen juice-box or small plastic bottle of frozen water. Do not place in sunlight. Refrigerate perishable foods if carried in an uninsulated lunch bag.

- Wash vacuum bottles and rinse with boiling water after each use. Be sure hot foods are boiling when poured into vacuum bottles.

- Wash fruits and vegetables before packing.

- Chill picnic food before packing in an iced cooler. Do not use a cooler to chill room temperature foods. If possible, use one cooler for beverages and one for perishable foods.

- Tightly wrap raw meat, poultry and fish or use a separate cooler to avoid dripping onto other foods. Take a bottle filled with soapy water for washing hands and surfaces after handling raw meat, or use moistened towelettes.

- Check salad bars and buffets for a clean, sanitary appearance of serving containers and utensils. Make sure cold foods are cold and hot foods are steaming.

Note: *For a free copy of the brochure "A Quick Consumer Guide to Safe Food Handling," write to Publications, Room 1165-S, USDA, Washington, D.C. 20250.*

Table Settings and Entertaining

Setting the Table

For many people, setting the table was one of their first big responsibilities in childhood. And setting the table correctly was usually rewarded in some special way! These basic guidelines for individual table settings can serve as a welcome reminder or as a teaching guide.

Sample table setting

- Be sure to allow plenty of room for people to be seated at the table.

- Place the flatware 1 inch from the table edge, arranging the pieces used first the farthest from the plate, so a diner can use the flatware from the outside in. The forks are set to the left of the plate, and the knife (with the blade toward the plate), then the spoons, to the right. A seafood fork usually is placed to the right of the spoons.

- If a butter plate is used, place it above the forks. Place the butter knife in a horizontal or a vertical position on the rim or toward the plate edge.

- For salad served *with* the main course, place the salad plate to the left of the forks and the salad fork at either side of the dinner fork.

- Arrange glasses above the knife. The water glass is usually at the tip of the knife, with beverage and/or wine glasses to the right.

- If coffee or tea is served at the table, place the cup slightly above and to the right of the spoons.

- Place the napkin either in the center of the dinner plate, to the left of the forks or in another creative position at each place setting.

- Dessert flatware can be set with the other flatware or be brought to the table with the dessert. To leave it on the table throughout the meal, place it across the top of the dinner plate or next to the other flatware closest to the plate.

- Before dessert, clear the table of all serving dishes, plates, salt and pepper shakers and flatware that won't be used for dessert.

Serving Buffet Style

Buffet service is a convenient way to serve small or large groups and works well for both casual or formal occasions. It's also an easy way of serving because guests serve themselves.

There are basically three types of buffet service:

True Buffet: Guests select food, beverage and flatware from the buffet table, then move to another room and sit wherever they are comfortable. It's important to serve foods that do not need to be cut with a knife, as most often plates will be balanced on one's lap. Serve rolls or bread already buttered, and provide small tables on which beverages may be placed.

Seated Buffet: Only the food is placed on the buffet table. Guests serve themselves and then find places at a table set with glasses, flatware and napkins. This buffet need not be limited to "fork food," since guests are not balancing plates on their laps.

Semi-Buffet: Guests can serve themselves from the buffet table and then be seated at a set table. The host or hostess then may serve each guest any accompaniments, such as sauce or gravy, at the table. Or the host or hostess may fill each guest's plate from the buffet table, then serve the plates to the seated guests. Table-carved roasts and poultry are often served this way.

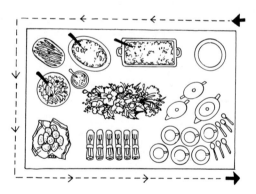

Sample buffet

- The buffet can be set up wherever it is most convenient—on the dining room table, a sideboard, a picnic table, two card tables placed together, a kitchen counter or a desk.

- The key to success is to create a buffet table setting so the traffic flows smoothly and easily. The serving line should begin and end at a logical point to avoid congestion and confusion.

- Place the buffet table in the center of the room so guests can help themselves from all sides of the table, or push it against a wall to save space while having it accessible from three sides. For large groups, place the table in the center of the room, but have identical serving lines on each side to make service faster.

- Place the food in order so guests can serve themselves without backtracking. Plates first, main course and vegetables next, then salad, condiments, bread and, if it is a true buffet, flatware and napkins last. Placing flatware and napkins at the end of the line allows guests to serve themselves with their hands free.

- While guests finish the main course, the host clears the buffet table and arranges the dessert, dessert plates and flatware on the buffet table or on a side table.

Entertaining Tips

Entertaining guests at home can be enjoyable and relaxing. Planning and preparing as much as possible ahead of time will let you enjoy the event, whether you've invited one guest or one hundred.

- Entertaining does not require an occasion, but it can be fun to plan an event with a theme. The beginning of football, an anniversary, experimenting with new recipes, a pumpkin-carving party all are good reasons to entertain.

- Decide on the number of guests and whom you will invite. Think about combinations of personalities—really interesting parties often include people with varied backgrounds. Spend time introducing them to one another. For a large group, try providing name tags with added information, such as guests' most interesting hobbies.

- Invite guests early so they can schedule busy calendars. Use ten days to two weeks in advance for casual events, and use at least two to three weeks for more formal events. Although a formal event calls for a written invitation, the telephone is appropriate for informal get-togethers. Be specific with your invitation regarding time, food and dress.

- Have the house clean a few days ahead, so you can focus on food and decorations.

- Plan enough food and beverages so you won't run out. Be sure to have nonalcoholic beverages available.

- Select a variety of foods, but don't wear yourself out trying to outdo your favorite restaurant! Prepare a limited number of foods, based on your skills and equipment. Pick up the rest from the deli or ask guests to contribute. See Menu Planning Know-How, page 416.

- Plan foods suitable to the weather, seasonal availability, guests' preferences or diet needs, and the serving style you plan to use.

- Plan foods that can be prepared ahead as much as possible so you spend less time in the kitchen while guests are there.

- Planning a large get-together where food is served can be a little tricky if you're not used to serving a crowd. The charts Fruit and Vegetable Yields (below) and Amounts of Food for a Crowd (page 424) will help you figure out how much food you will need. Be sure to keep in mind the appetites and eating habits of your guests when figuring the number of servings. Also consider the time of day, weather conditions and the types and amounts of foods served. Plan on one drink per hour per guest, or, if it's very warm, plan on two.

Fruit and Vegetable Yields

Fruits	Approximate Yield
Cantaloupe, 4-pound	36 chunks
Grapes, 1 pound seedless	12 to 15 clusters
Honeydew, 2-pound	36 chunks
Pineapple, 3- to 4-pound	40 chunks
Strawberries, 1-pound large	20 to 25 berries

Vegetables	Approximate Yield
Asparagus, 1 pound	30 to 45 spears
Bell pepper, 1 large	24 strips, 3 1/2 × 1/2"
Broccoli or cauliflower, 2 pounds	32 flowerets, 1 1/4"
Carrots, 1 pound	65 sticks, 3 × 1/2"
Celery, 4 medium stalks	33 sticks, 4 × 1/2"
Cucumbers, 2 large	45 sticks, 4 × 3/4"
Mushrooms, 1 pound	20 medium
Pea pods, 4 ounces	30 pea pods
Zucchini, 3 medium	35 slices, 1/2"

Salad Greens	Bite-Size Pieces
Boston lettuce, 1/2-pound head	6 cups
Iceberg lettuce, 1 1/2-pound head	12 cups
Leaf lettuce, 1-pound bunch	8 cups
Romaine, 1 1/2-pound bunch	12 cups
Spinach, 3/4-pound bunch	8 cups

Amounts of Food for a Crowd

Food Item	Serving Size	12 Servings	24 Servings	48 Servings
Meat, Poultry and Shellfish (bone-in, unshelled)	3/4 pound	9 pounds	18 pounds	36 pounds
Meat, Poultry and Fish (boneless)	1/4 pound	3 pounds	6 pounds	12 pounds
Chicken Salad, Side Dish	1/2 cup	1 1/2 quarts	3 quarts	1 1/2 gallons
Main Dish	1 cup	3 quarts	1 1/2 gallons	3 gallons
Potato Salad, Baked Beans or Coleslaw	1/2 cup	1 1/2 quarts	3 quarts	1 1/2 gallons
Meat Cold Cuts	2 1/2 ounces	2 pounds	4 pounds	8 pounds
Cheese Slices	1 ounce	1 pound	2 pounds	4 pounds
Rolls	1 1/2 rolls	2 dozen	3 dozen	6 dozen
Crackers	4 crackers	8 ounces	1 pound	2 pounds
Tossed Salad	1 1/2 cups	4 1/2 quarts	9 quarts	4 1/2 gallons
Salad Dressing	2 tablespoons	1 1/2 cups	3 cups	1 1/2 quarts
Dip	2 tablespoons	1 1/2 cups	3 cups	6 cups
Chips	1 ounce	12 ounces	1 1/2 pounds	3 pounds
Fruit or Vegetable Dippers	4 pieces	4 dozen	8 dozen	16 dozen
Cakes, 13 × 9″, 12-cup Ring or 9″ Layer	1/16 cake	1 cake	2 cakes	3 cakes
Cookies	2	2 dozen	4 dozen	8 dozen
Ice Cream	1/2 cup	2 quarts	1 gallon	2 gallons
Coffee, Brewed	3/4 cup	9 cups water	18 cups water	36 cups water
Ground Coffee		1 1/2 cups	3 cups	5 cups
Tea, Brewed	3/4 cup	9 cups water	18 cups water	36 cups water
Loose Tea		1/4 cup	1/2 cup	1 cup
Tea Bags		12 bags	24 bags	48 bags
Iced Tea	1 cup	3 quarts	1 1/2 gallons	3 gallons
Punch	1/2 cup	1 1/2 quarts	3 quarts	1 1/2 gallons
Mineral Water	8 ounces	3 quarts	6 quarts	12 quarts
Ice	4 ounces	3 pounds	6 pounds	12 pounds

Refrigerator and Freezer Food Storage

Below are some pointers and a time chart to help you keep foods safely stored. We recommend you purchase a refrigerator/freezer thermometer and check it often to make sure the correct temperatures are being maintained.

Refrigerator

- Keep the refrigerator temperature at 40° or slightly lower. Adjust the temperature to a colder setting when large amounts of room-temperature or warm foods are added. Readjust the temperature to the normal setting after about 8 hours.

- Cover foods or close original containers tightly before refrigerating, to prevent drying out or the transfer of odors. Store produce and strong-flavored foods in tightly covered containers or plastic bags.

- Remove foods from the refrigerator just before you are ready to use them.

Freezer

- Keep the freezer temperature at 0° or lower.
- Wrap food in moistureproof, vaporproof containers and materials.
- Label and date all packages and containers.
- Remove as much air from packages as possible to prevent freezer burn.
- Keep purchased frozen foods in the original packages.
- Use longest-stored foods first.
- Always thaw frozen meats, poultry and seafood in refrigerator, never at room temperature. Allow about 5 hours for each pound. Or thaw foods in your microwave following manufacturer's directions, then cook immediately.
- Use the times given in the chart for freezing foods, to maintain best flavor and texture. Frozen foods kept slightly longer still are safe to eat.

Special Directions for Refrigerated or Frozen Foods

Baked Products: Cool completely before wrapping in airtight packaging for freezing. Allow frostings to set or freeze uncovered *before* packaging.

Breads: Refrigerate only during hot, humid weather. Loosen wrap on frozen bread and thaw at room temperature 2 to 3 hours.

Cakes: Refrigerate cakes with custard or whipped cream filling or frosting; do not freeze, as these toppings can separate. Loosen wrap on frozen unfrosted cakes and thaw at room temperature 2 to 3 hours. Loosen wrap on frozen frosted cakes and thaw overnight in refrigerator.

Cheesecakes: Thaw wrapped in refrigerator 4 to 6 hours.

Cookies: Freeze delicate or frosted and decorated cookies in single layers separated by waxed paper. Thaw covered in container at room temperature 1 to 2 hours. Crisp-textured cookies should be removed from container to thaw.

Pies: *Frozen unbaked fruit pies:* Unwrap and carefully cut slits in top crust. Bake at 425° for 15 minutes. Reduce oven temperature to 375° and bake 30 to 45 minutes longer or until crust is golden brown and juice begins to bubble through slits.
   Frozen baked fruit, pecan and pumpkin pies: Unwrap and thaw at room temperature until completely thawed. Or unwrap and thaw at room temperature 1 hour, then heat in 375° oven for 35 to 40 minutes or until warm. Unwrap and thaw baked pumpkin pies in refrigerator.

Dairy Products: Check packages for the freshness date, and refrigerate in original containers. Refrigeration time is for *opened* products.

   Cream Cheese and Hard Cheese: If hard cheese is moldy, trim 1/2 inch from affected area and replace wrap each time. Thaw frozen cheeses in refrigerator, use only in baked goods due to texture changes.

   Ice Cream, Sorbet, Frozen Yogurt: Freeze in original container. Cover surface directly with aluminum foil or plastic wrap, to reduce ice crystals. For best quality, do not thaw and refreeze.

   Whipped Cream: Freeze in small mounds on waxed paper until firm, then place in airtight container. Let stand about 15 minutes at room temperature to thaw.

Eggs: To refrigerate yolks only, cover with cold water and refrigerate tightly covered. To freeze yolks and whites, add 1/8 teaspoon salt or 1/2 teaspoon sugar for every 4 yolks or yolks and whites of 2 whole eggs and freeze tightly covered.

Meat Products: Check packages for the freshness date. Refrigerate or freeze meat in original packages, because repeated handling can introduce bacteria to meat and poultry. To freeze, overwrap with heavy-duty aluminum foil or freezer wrap or place in freezer bags.

Cold Food Storage Chart

Foods	Refrigerator (34° to 40°)	Freezer (0° or below)
Baked Products		
Breads—coffee cakes, muffins, quick breads and yeast breads	5 to 7 days	2 to 3 months
Cakes—unfrosted and frosted	3 to 5 days	Unfrosted—3 to 4 months Frosted—2 to 3 months
Cheesecakes—baked	3 to 5 days	4 to 5 months
Cookies—baked	Only if stated in recipe	Unfrosted—no longer than 12 months Frosted—no longer than 3 months
Pies—unbaked or baked fruit pies, baked pecan and baked pumpkin pies	Baked pumpkin pies, 3 to 5 days. Store fresh fruit or baked fruit pies and baked pecan pies loosely covered at room temperature no longer than 3 days.	Unbaked fruit pies—2 to 3 months Baked fruit pies—3 to 4 months
Pie shells—unbaked or baked	Store in freezer.	Unbaked shells—no longer than 2 months Baked shells—no longer than 4 months
Dairy Products		
Cheese		
Cottage and ricotta	1 to 10 days	Not recommended
Cream	No longer than 2 weeks	No longer than 2 months
Hard	3 to 4 weeks	6 to 8 weeks
Ice Cream, Sorbet and Frozen Yogurt	Freeze only.	2 to 4 months
Milk Products		
Buttermilk	No longer than 1 week	Not recommended
Cream, half-and-half and whipping	No longer than 5 days	Not recommended
Cream, whipped	1 or 2 days	No longer than 3 months
Regular milk–whole, 2%, 1% and skim	No longer than 5 days	No longer than 1 month
Sour Cream	No longer than 1 week	Not recommended
Yogurt	No longer than 3 weeks	No longer than 1 month
Eggs		
Raw		
Whole in shell	3 weeks	Not recommended
Yolks, whites	2 to 4 days Cover yolks with cold water.	No longer than 12 months; see Eggs, page 162.
Cooked		
Whole in shell	1 week	Not recommended
Yolks, whites	1 week	Not recommended.

Foods	Refrigerator (34° to 40°)	Freezer (0° or below)
Fats and Oils		
Butter	No longer than 2 weeks	No longer than 2 months
Margarine and Spread	No longer than 1 month	No longer than 2 months
Mayonnaise and Salad Dressing	No longer than 6 months	Not recommended
Meats		
Meats—Uncooked		
Chops	3 to 5 days	4 to 6 months
Ground	1 to 2 days	3 to 4 months
Roasts and Steaks	3 to 5 days	6 to 12 months
Meats—Cooked	3 to 4 days	2 to 3 months
Meats—Processed		
Cold cuts	Opened—3 to 5 days Unopened—2 weeks	Not recommended
Cured bacon	5 to 7 days	No longer than 1 month
Hot dogs	Opened—1 week Unopened—2 weeks	1 to 2 months 1 to 2 months
Ham		
• Canned, unopened	6 to 9 months	Not recommended
• Whole or half, fully cooked	5 to 7 days	1 to 2 months
• Slices, fully cooked	3 to 4 days	1 to 2 months
Poultry		
Poultry—Uncooked		
Whole (including game birds, ducks and geese)	1 to 2 days	No longer than 12 months
Cut up	1 to 2 days	No longer than 9 months
Giblets	1 to 2 days	No longer than 3 months
Poultry—Cooked	3 to 4 days	4 months
Seafood		
Fin Fish		
Uncooked fatty fish (mackerel, salmon, trout, tuna, etc.)	1 to 2 days	2 to 3 months
Uncooked lean fish (cod, flounder, grouper, halibut, orange roughy, red snapper, scrod, etc.)	1 to 2 days	4 to 6 months
Cooked and breaded fish	Store in freezer.	2 to 3 months
Shellfish		
Uncooked	1 to 2 days	3 to 4 months
Cooked	3 to 4 days	1 to 2 months

Grilling Know-How

Grilled foods are now enjoyed all year long! Besides following the manufacturer's directions for use, care and cleaning of your grill, use the tips that follow to grill foods to perfection. Look for the grilling directions in the Meats, Poultry, Fish and Seafood and Vegetables chapters. A charcoal grill was used for developing the directions.

Heating the Grill

- For charcoal grills, follow manufacturer's directions of lighting coals at least 30 minutes before cooking begins to ensure proper temperature is reached. Most coals take between 30 and 45 minutes to reach proper temperature.

- When are the coals ready? In the daylight, the coals should be completely covered with light gray ash. After dark, the coals will glow red.

- For gas grills, follow manufacturer's directions or heat 5 to 10 minutes before cooking.

Direct Heat: In this method, food is cooked directly over the heat.

Indirect Heat: This is the preferred method for longer-cooking foods, such as whole poultry and whole turkey breasts. In this method, food is cooked away from the heat. When using coals, arrange them around the edge of the firebox, and place a drip pan under the grilling area. If using a dual-burner gas grill, heat only one side, and place food under the burner that is not lit. For single-burner gas grills, place food in a foil tray or on several layers of aluminum foil and use **low** heat.

Cooking

- Grease or oil the rack before lighting coals or turning gas on.

- Place the grill rack 4 to 6 inches above the coals or gas burners.

- For even cooking, place thicker foods in the center of the grill rack and smaller pieces on the edges and turn pieces frequently.

- To retain meat juices, turn with tongs instead of piercing with a fork.

- To prevent overbrowning or burning of meats, brush sauces on during the last 15 to 20 minutes of cooking, especially sauces that contain tomato or sugar.

Food Safety for Grilling

- **Never** serve cooked meats on the same unwashed platter on which raw meat was carried to the grill. Do not carry raw hamburgers to the grill on a platter, then serve cooked meat on the same unwashed platter.

- Use a long-handled brush for adding sauces or marinades to meat before or during grilling. Once the meat is cooked, do not use the same brush to add additional sauce, to prevent transferring any bacteria from the uncooked meat to the cooked meat. Wash the brush in hot, soapy water, and dry thoroughly. To save time, have a second, clean brush available.

- Heat marinades and sauces left over from contact with raw meat to boiling, and boil 1 minute before serving.

Tips for Grilling

- The type of grill, outdoor temperature and wind can affect cooking times. Check the food and fire often for best results.

- Whether using a gas, electric or charcoal grill, keeping the heat as even as possible throughout the grilling period is important.

- If you're not getting a sizzle, the fire may be too cool. Regulate the heat by spreading the coals or raking them together, opening or closing the vents or adjusting the control on a gas or electric grill. Raising or lowering the cooking grill or covering it also will help control the heat.

- To enhance flavors, use wood chips to add a smoky taste to grilled foods. Soak hickory, mesquite, green hardwood or fruitwood chips in water for 30 minutes; drain and toss on the hot coals.

- For a different flavor and aroma when grilling, sprinkle the hot coals with soaked and drained dried herbs, fresh herbs or garlic cloves.

- Using long-handled barbecue tools allows for a safe distance between you and the intense heat of the grill.

Combination Cooking

To speed cooking or quickly cook foods partially without the risk of overbrowning, combine the talents of your grill with those of your microwave. A general rule of thumb: Microwave foods for only half of their total microwave time if they are to finish cooking on the grill. Plan preparation time so that foods can go directly from the microwave to the grill. Do not let partially cooked foods stand for any length of time. Have coals ready by the time foods are to be removed from the microwave so the food can immediately be placed on the grill.

Microwave Know-How

What would we do without our microwaves? Not only do they save us time by cooking foods quickly, they also save on dishwashing chores because food can be cooked on serving plates and leftovers heated in their storage containers. Follow your microwave manufacturer's use and care guide for safety precautions and information about microwavable utensils. Whether you use your microwave for reheating, cooking or using the quick how-to tips that follow, keep these basics in mind:

Density of Food: Porous foods (breads, cakes) cook quickly; dense foods (roasts, potatoes) need longer cooking.

Moisture, Sugar, Fat in Food: Microwaves are particularly attracted to these ingredients, so foods including these ingredients cook or heat quickly.

Shape of Food: Round or doughnut-shaped foods or foods in round or ring-shaped containers cook most evenly. Foods with irregular shapes need more attention during cooking.

Size of Food Pieces: Small pieces of food cook faster than large pieces, so keep pieces uniform in size to prevent uneven cooking.

Standing Time: Allows foods to finish cooking or distributes heat more evenly.

Temperature of Food: The colder the food, the longer the cooking time. Testing for this book was done with foods taken from their normal storage areas, whether freezer, refrigerator or cupboard shelf.

Volume of Food: As the amount of the food increases, so must the cooking time.

Microwave Techniques

Common techniques that speed heating, ensure more even cooking and make some food appear more attractive when microwaved include:

- *Adding color* to uncooked food by coating with crumbs or brushing on a sauce or glaze before microwaving.

- *Arranging* foods in a circle, with thickest parts to the outside for most even cooking.

- *Covering* with a lid or plastic wrap, leaving a corner or 2-inch edge of wrap turned back , to vent steam for faster cooking. Use waxed paper or microwavable paper towel to prevent spattering.

- *Elevating* the food on a dish turned upside down to better cook the bottom center of very moist foods in some microwaves.

- *Checking food at minimum time* is important to avoid overcooking. Add additional time if necessary.

- *Rotating* a dish a 1/2 or 1/4 turn to help food cook more evenly if cannot be stirred and the microwave does not have a turntable.

- *Stirring* food from the outer edge to the center helps even out and speed cooking.

- *Turning* some foods over after part of the cooking time can help even out cooking.

Microwave Testing for This Book

The microwave directions in this book were tested using countertop microwaves with 600 to 700 watts. If your microwave has a rating of less than 600 watts or more than 700 watts, cooking time must be lengthened or shortened accordingly.

Helpful Microwave How-To's

The following tips provide quick, practical helps for preparing food. We have referred to many of these tips in recipes. Foods are grouped alphabetically. **Use microwavable utensils only.**

Food, Utensil and Tips	Power Level	Amount	Time
Bacon, thin sliced (*cooking*) Plate lined with paper towels; cover with paper towel.	High (100%)	1 slice 4 slices	45 seconds to 2 minutes 3 to 4 minutes 4 to 6 minutes 6 to 8 minutes
Brown sugar, hard (*softening*) Paper box or bowl	High (100%)	Up to 2 cups	Check every 30 seconds.
Caramels (*melting*) 4-cup glass measure, uncovered	High (100%)	1 package (14 ounces) caramels mixed with 2 tablespoons water	3 to 4 minutes, stirring every 45 seconds
Chocolate , baking (*melting*) Paper wrapper or bowl	Medium (50%)	1 or 2 ounces	3 or 4 minutes, stirring after 2 minutes
Chocolate Chips (*melting*) Bowl or glass measuring cup, uncovered. Chips will not change shape.	Medium (50%)	1/2 to 1 cup	3 to 4 minutes
Coconut (*toasting*) Shallow bowl or pie plate, uncovered Stir every 30 seconds.	High (100%)	1/4 to 1/2 cup 1 to 1 1/2 minutes	1 cup 2 to 2 1/2 minutes
Cream Cheese (*softening*) Remove foil wrapper. Place on waxed paper or plate, uncovered.	Medium (50%)	3-ounce package 30 to 45 seconds	8-ounce package 1 to 1 1/2 minutes
Dried Fruit (*softening*) 2-cup measure; cover tightly.	High (100%)	1 cup raisins or apricot halves sprinkled with 1 teaspoon water	45 seconds to 1 minute; let stand a few minutes.
Fruit, refrigerated (*warming*) Place on floor of microwave.	High (100%)	1 medium	15 seconds
Honey (*crystallized*) Jar with lid removed, uncovered	High (100%)	8-ounce jar	30 seconds to 2 minutes, stirring every 30 seconds

Food, Utensil and Tips	Power Level	Amount	Time
Ice Cream (*softening*) Original container; remove any foil.	Low (10%)	1/2 gallon	1 1/2 minutes, rotating 1/2 turn after 1 minute
Margarine or Butter (*melting*) Remove foil wrapper. Measuring cup or small bowl, uncovered.	High (100%)	1 to 2 tablespoons 3 to 4 tablespoons 1/3 to 1/2 cup 2/3 to 1 cup	15 to 30 seconds 30 to 45 seconds 45 to 60 seconds 1 to 1 1/2 minutes
Margarine or Butter (*softening*) Remove foil wrapper. Measuring cup or small bowl, uncovered.	Medium-low (30%)	1 to 3 tablespoons 1/4 to 1 cup	15 to 30 seconds 30 to 45 seconds
Muffins or rolls (*reheating*) Plate or napkin-lined basket; uncovered	Medium (50%)	1 2 3 4	15 to 30 seconds 25 to 40 seconds 35 to 60 seconds 45 seconds to 1 1/4 minutes
Nuts, chopped (*toasting*) Shallow bowl or pie plate. Stir every 30 seconds until light brown. Mix nuts with 1 teaspoon melted margarine or butter.	High (100%)	1/4 cup 1/2 cup 1 to 1 1/2 cups	1 1/2 to 2 minutes 2 1/2 to 3 minutes 3 to 4 minutes
Snacks (*crisping popcorn, pretzels, corn chips or potato chips*) Napkin-lined basket, uncovered	High (100%)	2 cups 4 cups	30 to 60 seconds 1 to 2 minutes
Syrup (*heating*) Measuring cup or pitcher, uncovered. Stir before serving.	High (100%)	1/2 cup	45 to 60 seconds
Vegetables or Fruits, frozen (*thawing*) Remove outer wrap from box; pierce box or bag with fork. Place on paper towel. Turn over after half the time; drain.	Medium-low (30%)	9- to 12-ounce package	6 to 10 minutes 8 to 12 minutes
Water (*boiling*) Glass measuring cup	High (100%)	1 cup	2 to 3 minutes

Cooking at Higher Altitudes

People who live at elevations of 3,500 feet or higher face some unique cooking challenges. Air pressure is lower, so water has a lower boiling point and liquid evaporates faster. Because certain foods and methods of preparation are affected by the pressure at higher elevations, recipes for both conventional and microwave cooking must be adjusted for optimum performance. Unfortunately, trial and error often is the only way to make improvements, as no set of rules applies to all recipes. Try the following guidelines:

- Foods that require boiling, such as vegetables or cooked eggs, take longer to cook.

- Foods cooked in a microwave oven often require additional water and longer cook times; however, changes vary according to the type and amount of food, the initial water content of the food and the elevation.

- Meats cooked in boiling liquid or steam take longer to cook, sometimes 50% to 100% longer. Large meat cuts, such as roasts and turkeys, cooked in the oven also need more time. Record the time required as a future guide.

- Most baked goods (leavened with baking powder or baking soda, not yeast) will be improved by one or more of the following adjustments: increased temperature (25°), increased liquid, decreased leavening, decreased sugar and/or a larger pan size. For very rich recipes, such as pound cakes, decreasing the fat will improve results. Quick breads and cookies usually require the fewest adjustments.

- Yeast bread dough rises more rapidly at high altitudes and can overrise easily. Allow dough to rise for a shorter time. Flour dries out more quickly too, so use the minimum amount called for or use 1/4 to 1/2 cup less than the total amount.

- Many mixes that require adjustment for high altitudes have specific directions right on the package. Be sure to look for them.

- Boiled candy and cooked frostings (sugar mixtures) become concentrated more rapidly because of the faster evaporation of water. Watch cooking closely to prevent scorching. Reduce recipe temperature by 2° for every 1,000 feet of elevation. Or use the cold water test for candy (page 128).

- Deep-fried foods are often overbrowned but undercooked at higher elevations. To ensure that the outside and inside of food are done at the same time, reduce temperature of the oil by 3° for every 1,000 feet of elevation and increase frying time if necessary.

If you are new to high-altitude cooking, call your local U. S. Department of Agriculture (USDA) Extension Service office, listed in the phone book under county government, for help with any questions you may have. Recipes are also available from Colorado State University, Fort Collins, Colorado 80521. Local libraries and bookstores also are sources of high-altitude cookbooks.

Home Canning

Canning foods can be an economical way to preserve food at home. Not only is canning a way to keep favorite foods, but many people enjoy the reward of canning and preserving foods from their garden or local farmers' market. Sharing these foods as gifts also gives extra pleasure.

Because organisms that cause food spoilage, such as molds, yeast and bacteria, are always present in the air, water and soil, following proper canning procedures is extremely important to ensure that canned goods are processed safely. Foods must be processed for a long enough time at high enough temperatures to destroy any spoilage organism. *Clostridium botulinum* is the bacterium that can remain present in canned foods if they are not properly processed. This bacteria can be destroyed only if food is processed at the correct temperature and for the correct time in a pressure canner.

The canning method is determined by the acidity of the food. The pressure canner method is recommended by the United States Department of Agriculture (USDA) for nonacid foods such as meat, poultry, seafood and vegetables. The water canner method is recommended for all acid foods: fruits, tomatoes with added acid such as lemon juice or vinegar, jams, jellies and pickled vegetables. *The open kettle method of canning is not recommended.*

If *clostridium botulinum* survive and grow inside a sealed jar of food, they can produce a poisonous toxin. When consumed, even in small amounts, this toxin may be fatal. If you are unsure about the safety of certain home-canned foods, boiling food 10 minutes at altitudes below 1,000 feet will destroy these toxins. Add 1 additional minute per 1,000 feet of additional elevation.

For additional canning information, procedures and recipes, refer to the USDA consumer publication "Complete Guide to Home Canning." This publication is available through the Consumer Information Center, Pueblo, Colorado 81009, 719-948-4000. Or contact the local USDA Extension Service office listed in the phone book under county government.

Index

Numbers in *italics* refer to photos and illustrations.

Blue type indicates a lighter version is available.

January 1995 #100

Betty Crocker

NEW **Soup, Stew & Chili**

CHAMPIONSHIP **5** PRIZEWINNING RECIPES CHILIES

WOW!
NEW FLAVORS
Pizza Soup, p. 25
Pumpkin-Chicken Stew, p. 37
Chunky Salsa Chili, p. 66

$2.95 U.S. $3.50 Canada

HURRY!
SPECIAL
OFFER

TWELVE
ISSUES FOR
$14.95!
SAVE 58%

THIS SPECIAL SUBSCRIPTION OFFER MEANS YOU PAY ONLY $1.25 PER ISSUE!

You'll receive 12 monthly issues of Betty Crocker Creative Recipes — over 1,000 recipes a year — delivered to your home. Order today and *save $20.00* off the regular news-stand price with this subscription offer.

These 96-page recipe magazines are filled with delicious recipes, beautiful photography, plus complete nutrition information for every recipe.

SEE REVERSE SIDE FOR ORDERING INFORMATION →